Civilizing Capitalism

Civilizing Capitalism

The National

Consumers' League,

Women's Activism,

and Labor Standards

in the New Deal Era

Landon R. Y. Storrs

The University of

North Carolina Press

Chapel Hill & London

Designed by April Leidig-Higgins
Set in Carter & Cone Galliard
by Keystone Typesetting, Inc.
Manufactured in the United States
of America

*Publication of this work was aided by
a generous grant from the Z. Smith
Reynolds Foundation.*

The paper in this book meets the
guidelines for permanence and
durability of the Committee on
Production Guidelines for Book
Longevity of the Council on
Library Resources.

Material in Chapters 3 and 4
appeared in different form in
Landon R. Y. Storrs, "Gender and
the Development of the Regula-
tory State: The Controversy over
Restricting Women's Night Work
in the Depression-Era South,"
Journal of Policy History 10, no. 2
(1998): 179–206, © 1998 by The
Pennsylvania State University;
reproduced by permission of The
Pennsylvania State University Press,
and "An Independent Voice for
Unorganized Workers: The
National Consumers' League
Speaks to the Blue Eagle," *Labor's
Heritage* 6, no. 3 (1995): 21–39,
reprinted with permission.

04 03 02 01 00   5 4 3 2 1

Library of Congress Cataloging-in-Publication Data
Storrs, Landon R. Y.
Civilizing capitalism: the National Consumers'
League, women's activism, and labor standards
in the New Deal era / Landon R. Y. Storrs.
p. cm. — (Gender & American culture)
Includes bibliographical references and index.
ISBN 0-8078-2527-1 (cloth: alk. paper).
ISBN 0-8078-4838-7 (paper: alk. paper)
1. National Consumers' League — History.
2. National Consumers' League — Biography.
3. Women social reformers — United States —
Biography. 4. Working-women's clubs — United
States — History. 5. Women — Employment —
United States — History. 6. Children — Employment — United States — History. 7. Industrial
welfare — United States — History. 8. Labor
movement — United States — History. 9. New Deal,
1933–1939. 10. Labor laws and legislation — United
States — History. I. Title. II. Series.
HD6067.2.U6S76 2000   331.4′25 — dc21
99-32197 CIP

For Landon T. Storrs and David K. Storrs

contents

illustrations

acknowledgments

I am indebted to numerous people and institutions for their assistance on this project. For financial support over the years, I thank the Mellon Fellowships in the Humanities program, the University of Wisconsin Graduate School, the Polly Rousmaniere Gordon Fund, and the University of Houston Research Initiation Grant, Limited-Grant-in-Aid, and publication subvention programs.

The story told in these pages required research on widely scattered local developments as well as national ones. The resourcefulness of many archivists around the country was indispensable to completing this research. I thank in particular the staff at the State Historical Society of Wisconsin, the Schlesinger Library at Radcliffe College, the Labor-Management Documentation Center at Cornell University, and the Library of Congress, as well as Tab Lewis and Fred Romanski at the National Archives. Archivists who offered valuable assistance from afar include Kathleen Nutter at the Smith College Library, Betsy Pittman at the Virginia Commonwealth University Library, Claire McCann at the University of Kentucky Library, and Kathie Johnson at the University of Louisville Library. I also thank the interlibrary loan staff at the University of Houston. During the difficult process of locating suitable illustrations, several people came through in a pinch, including Mary Ternes at the District of Columbia Public Library, the staff of the Prints and Photographs Room at the Library of Congress, and, above all, my mother, Landon T. Storrs, who was an extraordinarily quick study as my East Coast research surrogate.

Several fortuitous coincidences enriched the experience of researching this book. After I decided to study the history of women-only labor laws in the 1930s, I learned that the lead organization backing such laws was headed in those years by my mother's great-aunt, Lucy Randolph Mason. A central figure in this study, Mason died before I was born, and surviving relatives know very little about her. My kinship to Mason did not yield any research advantages, but it improved my work by making me strive for high standards of scholarly detachment. In a second coincidence, a suggestion from my paternal grandmother Frances R. Storrs led me to her cousin's college roommate, Asho Ingersoll Craine, who generously shared her memories of working for the Consumers' League in the 1930s. Finally, Tom Dublin and Kitty Sklar helped me locate and interpret materials on Tom's aunt Mary Dublin, who led the league in the late 1930s. Thanks also are due to Mary's brother Thomas Davidson Dublin, who kindly permitted me to examine letters from Mary to her parents and then donated those letters to the Schlesinger Library, and to Taylor Burke Jr., who shared a small collection of Lucy Mason's papers.

Astute criticism from many people improved this project over the course of its long journey from idea to book. The diverse approaches of the members of my dissertation committee at the University of Wisconsin — Linda Gordon, John Cooper, Carl Kaestle, Ann Orloff, and Jonathan Zeitlin — forced me to examine the topic from many angles. The now-scattered members of my dissertator group were more helpful than they know. The same is true of numerous conference session commentators and copanelists over the years, all of whom I thank here, along with the Houston Area Southern Historians. Scholars who offered constructive comments on portions of the manuscript include Jacquelyn Dowd Hall, Sarah Fishman-Boyd, Ellis Hawley, William Leuchtenburg, Ken Lipartito, Nancy Mac-Lean, Cathy Patterson, and Beth Rose. I am especially grateful to those who read the entire manuscript at one stage or another: Eileen Boris, Nancy Cott, Colin Gordon, Ty Priest, and Kitty Sklar. Two readers for the University of North Carolina Press, Susan Ware and an anonymous reader, made shrewd suggestions and asked difficult questions that greatly strengthened the book. I also thank Kate Torrey, Paula Wald, and Mary Reid of the University of North Carolina Press for their expert guidance and assistance.

My largest debt is to Linda Gordon, who challenged me to think harder and write better from the moment this study was conceived in one of her seminars at the University of Wisconsin. In the early stages, she helped me see what was significant about my findings, and later on, she encouraged me to have confidence in my interpretations even when they differed from her own. As a scholar, teacher, citizen, and friend, she offers an inspiring model.

It is hard to find words to thank my family for the moral and material support they offered during the many years that this study consumed a large part of my life. They learned when to ask how the book was coming and when not to ask. When they did have questions, they asked good ones that helped me recast the manuscript for a wider audience. Finally, my deepest appreciation goes to Ty Priest, who undertook the delicate task of commenting on early drafts, and whose intelligence and patience improved the final result immeasurably.

abbreviations

The following abbreviations are used throughout the book.

AALL   American Association for Labor Legislation

AAOAS   American Association for Old Age Security

ACWA   Amalgamated Clothing Workers of America

AFL   American Federation of Labor

AWP   Atlanta Woman's Party

CAB   Consumers' Advisory Board,
National Recovery Administration

CIO   Congress of Industrial Organizations

CP   Communist Party

CTI   Cotton Textile Institute

DLS   Division of Labor Standards, U.S. Department of Labor

DOL   U.S. Department of Labor

EEOC   Equal Employment Opportunity Commission

ERA   Equal Rights Amendment

FBI   Federal Bureau of Investigation

FDR   Franklin Delano Roosevelt

FLSA   Fair Labor Standards Act of 1938

FWC   Federation of Women's Clubs

GFWC   General Federation of Women's Clubs

HUAC   House Un-American Activities Committee

ILGWU	International Ladies' Garment Workers' Union
JCNR	Joint Committee for National Recovery
KCL	Kentucky Consumers' League
LAB	Labor Advisory Board, National Recovery Administration
LWS	League of Women Shoppers
LWV	League of Women Voters
NAACP	National Association for the Advancement of Colored People
NCJW	National Council of Jewish Women
NCL	National Consumers' League
NCLC	National Child Labor Committee
NLRA	National Labor Relations Act (Wagner Act)
NLRB	National Labor Relations Board
NLSC	National Labor Standards Committee
NRA	National Recovery Administration
NRPB	National Resources Planning Board
NWP	National Woman's Party
SPC	Southern Policy Committee
TWOC	Textile Workers Organizing Committee
UOPWA	United Office and Professional Workers of America
VCL	Virginia Consumers' League
WTUL	Women's Trade Union League
YWCA	Young Women's Christian Association

Civilizing Capitalism

introduction

The sweatshop is back. In the United States and in foreign factories producing goods for American companies, there are workers who face the
wage slavery and hazardous conditions that horrified reformers a century
ago. Labor exploitation never disappeared, nor was it ever confined to
"sweating," a specific practice usually associated with subcontracting in the
garment industries. But reforms initiated in the turn-of-the-century period
known as the Progressive Era and consolidated during the New Deal of the
1930s curbed the most egregious abuses of employees in American manufacturing for many decades. In the 1980s and 1990s, however, the weakening of the labor movement, budget cuts for regulatory agencies, and free
trade policies blind to labor practices combined to permit a resurgence of
the sweatshop and to spread its features to other kinds of workplaces.[1]

Fresh evidence of these developments surfaces regularly. In August 1995
a U.S. Department of Labor raid in southern California found seventy-two
undocumented Thai workers, most of them women, who literally had been
enslaved for as long as seven years. Kept behind barbed-wire fences under
the eye of armed guards, they worked eighteen-hour days making clothes
for major American manufacturers and retailers. In 1996 labor activists
embarrassed television personality Kathie Lee Gifford by exposing human
rights violations in the production of her Wal-Mart clothing line in Hon-
duras and New York. American consumers expressed growing concern for
the people who made their favorite clothes and sneakers. Basketball hero
Michael Jordan was pressed to justify the endorsement of Nike shoes that
earned him more in one year than Nike paid to its entire Indonesian workforce. Editorials and cartoons appeared at the expense of image-conscious
corporations. (A typical cartoon, showing people crowded onto the embassy roof in Saigon with a helicopter overhead, read "Of course we want
to leave. . . . We all work for Nike.") On college campuses around the nation, students staged sit-ins to demand that products bearing their school's
name be made under humane conditions.[2]

This publicity stimulated various approaches to cleaning up labor abuses
in global clothing production. In 1995 Secretary of Labor Robert Reich

created a "white list" of companies with fair labor practices, an attempt to embarrass excluded companies. In 1997 a presidential task force proposed a voluntary international code of conduct for the apparel industries. This initiative, known as the Apparel Industry Partnership (AIP), produced an agreement in late 1998 that authorized employers who honor the AIP code to advertise their goods with a "No Sweat" label. It remains to be seen whether the AIP code will yield meaningful change, or whether it will be reduced to a public relations maneuver that merely obscures exploitation.[3]

This book is about an organization that links these current labor reform campaigns to those of a century ago. In the 1890s affluent women who were appalled by working women's reports of conditions in department stores founded the National Consumers' League (NCL). In the 1990s the NCL was a lead organization on President Clinton's antisweatshop task force.[4] For many of the intervening decades, the NCL was at the heart of the nation's evolving reform tradition. This book tells the story of the National Consumers' League during the turbulent, experimental era of the New Deal. The league's history offers a lens through which to examine shifting intellectual currents and tactics in American social justice activism. Led by women and supported by both women and men, the Consumers' League attracted leading representatives of progressive, social democratic, and liberal thought. Yet remarkably little has been published on the league, least of all for the period after the 1920s, when it experienced a resurgence of influence and energy.[5]

The women of the NCL pioneered the tactic of using consumer pressure on employers to raise labor standards. Turn-of-the-century league activists promoted "white lists" of fair employers, soon widening their focus from retailers to include manufacturing and other occupations. As the movement for "ethical consumption" spread, league branches sprang up in cities across the country.[6] Before long, however, the NCL recognized that the strategy of using public pressure to elicit voluntary compliance by employers had serious limitations. The reformers concluded that employers would have to be coerced, rather than persuaded, into fair labor practices.

The NCL proceeded to coordinate a drive that by the early 1920s had built a substantial body of state labor legislation. The league is perhaps best known for its role in the 1908 *Muller v. Oregon* decision, in which the Supreme Court upheld a state maximum hours law for women just a few years after a similar law affecting men was found unconstitutional. The brief that the league prepared for lawyer Louis Brandeis made legal as well as labor history, because it argued from sociological data rather than from court precedent alone. The NCL drafted the nation's first minimum wage law, enacted in Massachusetts in 1912, and it spread the minimum wage movement to a dozen other states within a few years. The NCL's leader from 1899 to 1932, the feminist and socialist Florence Kelley, anchored a coalition that won the creation of federal labor agencies dedicated to women and children. Other achievements at the national level included minimum labor standards for goods produced under government contract during World War I and the Sheppard-Towner Maternity and Infancy Act of 1921. The league also spearheaded the opposition to the Equal Rights Amendment (ERA), beginning in the 1920s and continuing for many years. Sponsored by the National Woman's Party from 1923 on, the ERA would have invalidated women-only labor laws.

Consumers' League women wanted to improve working conditions for all workers, but it was the low labor standards of women and the employment of children that outraged them most of all. Then as now, the most severely exploited workers were likely to be young or female, or both. Employers, unions, and family members treated female workers differently from male ones, and the combination of these discriminations and pressures often made women especially vulnerable to abuses in the workplace. Female wages typically were a fraction of male wages; women's unpaid domestic obligations on top of long paid hours of work left them less time for leisure and rest than men, on average; and it was not uncommon for supervisors to demand more subservience from female workers, not to mention sexual favors. Dire need, combined with lack of union support and employer expectations of submissiveness, undercut wage-earning women's ability to protest these injustices.[7]

Meanwhile, in response to nineteenth-century proscriptions on women's participation in public affairs, female reformers had carved out a niche by arguing that they, as women, had special sensibilities for protecting the vulnerable.[8] This thinking resonated well into the twentieth century. In 1922, in the first flush of enthusiasm after women's enfranchisement, future NCL leader Lucy Mason claimed that "the instinct of women is for the conservation of life." Furthermore, Mason believed that women "have come into power and are directly able to shape legislation at a time when there is critical need of mitigating the pressure of 'the Iron Man' upon countless numbers of individuals." She meant that women would harness the forces of the machine age — which her metaphor cast as masculine — and channel them toward serving the many rather than the few. Significantly, Mason did not limit women reformers' agenda to women and children. The NCL program began with raising labor standards for women and prohibiting child labor, but it by no means ended there. Mason and many other league women believed their feminine perspective entitled them to authority over social policies affecting all members of society. It was up to women to "make business serve the community."[9] For many decades, the Consumers' League attracted remarkable women who dedicated themselves to "civilizing" capitalism.

The 1930s were exhilarating years for NCL activists, all the more so because they came after a decade of political and legal setbacks. The Great Depression gave new urgency to the question of the government's authority to regulate hours and wages. Those who could find jobs saw their wages slashed. In some occupations, the workday lengthened; in others, workers were "stretched out," or pressed to speed up the production process. Individual and collective efforts by workers to resist these changes were risky because the pool of replacement workers was deep. Also, manufacturers were increasingly willing to relocate toward cheaper labor. Even the threat to relocate could force concessions from workers, so the availability of low-cost labor in one place dragged down labor standards nationally.

The Great Depression intensified what then was a fairly new problem of industry migration toward the low-cost labor of the U.S. South. The NCL's search for solutions to this problem is a major theme of this book, and one that resonates with contemporary dilemmas. Long before Ross Perot warned in 1992 that the North American Free Trade Agreement would produce "a giant sucking sound" as jobs were pulled across the U.S. national border, and long before the revelations of abuse in Asian factories and Caribbean Basin *maquilas*, NCL activists and allied forces tried to staunch the flow of jobs across state borders by raising labor standards in the southern states. This drive to crack the South's separate market of low-cost labor was one of the NCL's most important initiatives in the 1930s.

In addition to analyzing the changing strategies and priorities of a group of extraordinary individuals, this book reconstructs the history of a specific public policy. In the 1930s wage-hour regulation was transformed from a state-level policy that affected women alone to a national policy extending to men and women alike. The NCL played a critical and hitherto unappreciated role in this transition. The league's tale offers a prime example of how attention to women, and to gender, enriches political and labor history.[10]

Labor standards policy has fallen through the cracks between political, labor, and welfare state history. Recent studies of the New Deal discuss wage-hour policy only in passing. This is partly because the Fair Labor Standards Act of 1938 does not fit neatly into prevailing schematics for the trajectory of the New Deal.[11] Mirroring the priorities of many labor leaders in the first third of the century, labor historians of the 1930s generally focus on union organizing and collective bargaining policy.[12] Meanwhile, the rich new literature on gender and New Deal welfare policy has concentrated on the Social Security Act of 1935 and its antecedents.[13]

Government regulation of labor standards forms a more important component of the American welfare state than the relatively thin scholarship on it might suggest. Labor standards law includes a myriad of regulations affecting workplace safety and sanitation, child labor, industrial homework, maximum hours, night work, and minimum wages. The emergence of these laws in the Progressive Era was tremendously significant, not only for their direct impact on workers, but also for their potent assault on the idea that government intervention in "private" relations between employer and employee was illegitimate. During the Great Depression the NCL stressed that minimum wage laws would promote economic recovery and reinvigorate American democracy by raising the purchasing power of the working class. As league thinkers noted, uniform labor standards could discourage industry migration and facilitate union organizing. More recently, opposing groups have debated whether raising the minimum wage increases unemployment (by making U.S. workers less competitive with lower-wage workers abroad) or reduces it (by making minimum wage work more attractive to welfare recipients). After the abolition in 1996 of the Aid to Families with Dependent Children program, the exemption of "workfare" recipients from the minimum wage triggered a significant protest movement. Thus today, as in the 1930s, wage-hour laws, collective bargaining policy, and public assistance programs are interdependent.[14] But labor standards policy has received less attention from historians than these others.

Scholars who take regulation of hours and wages as their central concern generally have focused on the period before 1923, the year of an important Supreme Court ruling against a women's minimum wage law.[15] One early explanation for the emergence of labor standards regulation suggested that these laws were a natural outgrowth of the process of "modernization." This analysis was rejected by New Left historians who argued that this regulation was one aspect of a far-sighted capitalist program to co-opt worker self-organization and radicalism with ameliorative measures.[16] New Left interpretations improved on earlier ones by demonstrating that social policy was a product of struggle, but, as feminist scholars soon pointed out, they all failed to explain why most early protective labor legislation applied to women but not to men.

The earliest feminist interpretations argued that sex-based labor laws reinforced women's secondary status in the workforce and their economic dependence on men. These scholars assumed that male politicians, employers, and trade unions were the leading advocates of sex-based policy.[17] The discovery of middle- and upper-class women's "state-building" activism in the Progressive Era superseded this view. Historians now recognize that female reformers were the chief architects of protective labor legislation for women, but their assessments of these reformers and their legacy diverge sharply. Kathryn Kish Sklar argues that, due to certain distinctive features of American politics, "gendered policies acted as a surrogate for class policies." That is, organized women accomplished through sex-based policies what in other countries was achieved by labor parties through class-based policies.[18] Others describe advocates of women's labor laws as "maternalists" whose priority was protecting "motherhood." Theda Skocpol celebrates maternalism as a positive force that succeeded in winning necessary reforms where party politics (men's politics) had failed.[19] Some have taken a dimmer view, arguing that maternalism was largely to blame for women's inequality in the welfare state. In the latter analysis, white women reformers sought to shore up an eroding sexual division of labor by imposing a race- and class-biased ideology of domesticity upon working women. These scholars charge the so-called maternalists with defining women's citizenship rights and obligations in terms of motherhood, creating a dichotomy between motherhood and wage work that forestalled generous day care and maternity leave policies, and delaying the extension of labor standards protection to men.[20]

The truncation of the literature on women's labor laws at 1923 is partially responsible for this bewildering range of interpretations. This periodization has obscured the NCL's work to raise labor standards in the South and to win national, male-inclusive regulation. Following the trajectory of NCL activism through the early 1940s yields a fresh assessment of the legacy of sex-based labor laws and a new picture of this reform engine. First, despite some real limitations, the league's sex-based strategy succeeded as an "entering wedge" for broadening governmental obligations to all workers. To give the most obvious example, in 1941 the Supreme Court upheld the sex-neutral Fair Labor Standards Act of 1938, which the NCL was instrumental in passing. Second, "maternalism"—whether used in the critical or celebratory sense—does not adequately capture the essence of the NCL program. Consumers' League activists might be considered maternalists in the sense that they used arguments about women's distinctive values to claim authority over public policy. But they were not maternalists in the way the term is often used, meaning bent on protecting an idealized vision of motherhood. Labeling the league "maternalist" misses the complexity of its social analysis and political program, in addition to obscuring its feminism.[21] The New Deal era casts the commitment of NCL leaders to a federal system of labor standards regulation—and, more broadly, to a social democratic state—into high relief. Furthermore, these years saw the league build on its older ideas about the interconnectedness of all workers to conclude that racial inequality was the linchpin of the South's separate political economy, and that the unreformed South was blocking the path to American social democracy.

In the process of examining women's activism and the development of wage-hour policy in the 1930s, this study seeks to correct an overemphasis in the New Deal literature on government actors. Historians of the Progressive Era have done a better job of reconstructing the "tissue of connections" between government agencies and voluntary organizations than historians of the New Deal. Even the scholars most sensitive to these connections assume that in the early 1930s government officials replaced civic organizations as key instigators of state development.[22] In fact, women's voluntary associations shaped social policy not just in the absence of the state — by creating model programs, or by acting as a bridge between eras of reform — but also in concert with the state.[23] Without the NCL's work during the 1930s, the New Deal record on labor standards would have been quite different.

This discovery that the Consumers' League, hitherto associated chiefly with the Progressive Era, flourished again in the 1930s refines our understanding of the shifting contours of white women's politics. Historians still debate the fate of the "first wave" women's movement after the Nineteenth Amendment was ratified in 1920. The early view that enfranchisement killed white women's separate, autonomous reform networks has given way to an emphasis on persistence, but scholars disagree on when and why this female political culture ultimately withered. The NCL story suggests that we have underestimated the longevity of progressive women's networks. Their demise — never absolute — was the result of many factors, but the impacts of World War II and the early Cold War were profound, thwarting hopes that had been sustained since the suffrage victory and disrupting transmission between the first and second waves of organized feminism.[24]

Chapter 1 discusses the NCL's formation and traces institutional changes and continuities between the Progressive Era and the New Deal period. In the 1930s the NCL had a smaller grassroots constituency than in earlier years, but the league attracted some new blood and new league branches formed in several states. In Washington the NCL enjoyed better connections than ever before. The league had friends in the White House, and the Depression created opportunities for league members who were experts in labor and welfare-related fields. The NCL called for raising "mass purchasing power" and for reforming the South, and these goals brought it into harmony with New Deal impulses. A composite sketch of the league's core leadership in the 1930s illustrates that the women who led the NCL were on the radical edge of the reform spectrum. They were feminists and social democrats who supported union rights and opposed race discrimination. This portrait offers a corrective to the widespread tendency to flatten out differences in political ideology among non-wage-earning white women. NCL leaders called for wider government control over production, to curb what they saw as the antisocial excesses of capitalism and to provide a more equitable distribution of resources. They intersected with intellectual circles that scholars have labeled left-liberal, regulatory, or social Keynesian, to distinguish them from the more conservative fiscal Keynesians who triumphed after World War II.[25] In emphasizing how this program would benefit women workers in particular, the league represented a distinctive, feminist voice.

League gender ideology was not backward-looking or coercive, contrary to recent findings about white women reformers in general.[26] Chapter 2 explicates the feminist component of the league's promotion of women-only labor laws and, after examining the constitutional and political obstacles to government regulation of men's hours and wages, reinterprets the famous controversy among women's organizations over the Equal Rights Amendment. The conflict between the National Consumers' League and the National Woman's Party in the 1930s reflected not so much differing ideas about gender as differing attitudes toward the state and toward the relationship of feminism to other social justice causes.

The remaining chapters are loosely chronological, alternating in focus between the state and national levels, as dictated by political and judicial developments that affected league priorities. Chapter 3 shows how the sex-based strategy became intertwined with another league state-building strategy, its campaign to raise labor standards in the South. Early on, NCL leaders grasped that the South might hold the key to the development of labor and social policy nationwide. Through a case study of the 1931 conflict over women's working hours in Georgia, this chapter observes the Consumers' League in action on the eve of the New Deal, encountering distinctively southern obstacles to its goal of uniform national labor standards. This southern case study also vividly demonstrates the liabilities of the alternative feminist strategy promoted by the National Woman's Party. The alliances made by the Woman's Party to defeat sex-based labor laws discredited the organization and its program in the eyes of those whose vision of social transformation through feminism incorporated a commitment to labor rights and black civil rights.

The election of Franklin Delano Roosevelt to the White House transformed the political landscape, swelling the hopes of the National Consumers' League and others who favored democratic state planning and regulation of the economy. Chapter 4 examines the complex relationship of the NCL to the National Recovery Administration (NRA), a temporary agency (1933–35) whose industry codes included minimum wage and maximum hours standards as part of the agency's mandate for ending the Depression. Initially, league members were delighted to win federal endorsement of their program. The league's national and local efforts on behalf of the NRA illustrate how effective a civic organization could be, operating in the penumbra between "public" and "private," in prompting and legitimizing new government initiatives. Ultimately, however, the league was unable to offset the domination of NRA policy by employers, and the content and administration of the labor provisions of the codes deeply disappointed the NCL. The NRA experience convinced the NCL that federal labor standards would not be fully effective without supplemental state-level regulation, and without real guarantees of collective bargaining rights.

Even before FDR took office, the NCL revived the drive for state maximum hours and minimum wage laws that had stalled during the 1920s. As a result, the early New Deal saw a burst of new state labor laws. Few of these were in the South, however. When the Supreme Court declared the NRA unconstitutional in 1935, the Consumers' League intensified its push for state labor laws in the South. Chapter 5 analyzes NCL general secretary Lucy Mason's ideas and strategies for breaking southern resistance to labor reform, at a moment when she was emboldened by the rise of the labor movement and the resurgence of the Left. Through case studies of league campaigns in three southern states, Chapter 6 highlights how interactions of gender, race, and class in southern politics inhibited state development in the region. Although most white southerners rejected Lucy Mason's message, those who responded to it were middle-class women. Across the region, small groups of white women formed allegiances to a national female reform network, rejecting states' rights arguments and instigating pro–New Deal insurgencies in their states. These women deserve credit for the wage and hour laws that did pass in the South, notably in Virginia, Kentucky, and North Carolina. However, these were modest victories. The slow progress at the state level in the South renewed momentum for a national policy.

In 1937 Lucy Mason left the Consumers' League to spend the rest of her years working in the South for the Congress of Industrial Organizations (CIO). Her successor, a young economist named Mary Dublin, orchestrated a prodigious lobbying effort on behalf of the Fair Labor Standards Act (FLSA) of 1938. Chapter 7 analyzes the mixed results of league efforts to win the strongest possible FLSA and to influence its implementation.

Almost as soon as it passed, the FLSA came under ferocious fire from conservatives, who simultaneously stepped up their opposition to the National Labor Relations Act of 1935 and to hours and wage laws in the states. The league's resistance to this tide of reaction, the subject of Chapter 8, highlights its faith in an administrative state and shows how that faith was a gendered one. League leaders believed that "public" or "consumer" participation in the implementation of labor standards and labor relations policy would increase women's access to and benefits from the state. However, challenging employer power and men's control over the state at the same time proved to be a formidable task.

Chapter 9 illustrates that some changes of the 1930s were good for the league's program but problematic for the league itself. New labor groups and government agencies encroached on the NCL's role as the lead strategist on labor standards policy. Also, winning federal wage-hour policy that regulated men as well as women had a mixed impact on the Consumers' League. The Fair Labor Standards Act attracted male experts to the field who challenged the league's authority. Furthermore, the enactment of national policy undercut the program of the league's branches in the states. For league women, this marginalization was an ironic effect of changes they themselves wholeheartedly supported. The NCL might have weathered these changes better had they not been immediately followed by World War II and the Cold War, which strengthened antilabor forces and further delegitimized women's participation in the making of labor policy. The NCL survived. But the 1940s and 1950s furthered institutional changes that began during the New Deal. Once a decentralized, nonpartisan organization aligned chiefly with women's associations, the Consumers' League emerged from this period as a Washington-centered group whose strongest working ties were with labor unions and liberal Democrats.

A word is in order as to the boundaries of this study. I have not attempted an assessment of all the Consumers' League branches, many of which merit their own histories.[27] I explore the league's engagement in each phase of regulation, which means in drafting, lobbying, enforcement, and court defense of the various types of laws. However, I do not fully review the constitutional test cases involving the league because others have done this skillfully.[28] This study concentrates on the history of maximum hours and minimum wage laws, the league's chief priorities in the 1930s, and also, to a lesser extent, on night work and industrial homework regulation. Laws affecting child labor and adult working conditions (ventilation, safety guards) are not treated here; in general, those were more germane to an earlier period. Lastly, in this book about the politics of workplace regulation, workers themselves are part of the story but not its central actors. This is not to imply that wage earners did not shape the policies that affected them. In the 1930s NCL leaders themselves believed that working-class organization was the best means to improved labor standards. However, most workers were not organized. League activists thought their program would offer immediate relief to the unorganized and also make it easier for them to form unions. This study explores the successes and disappointments of a middle-class effort to strengthen the working class by raising the labor standards of some of its most exploited members.

Investigate, Agitate, Legislate

*The National
Consumers'
League*

Florence Kelley's father reportedly told her, "My generation has created industry, and your generation must humanize it."[1] Years later, Paul Kellogg, editor of the eminent reform journal *Survey*, saw this division of labor in gendered terms rather than generational ones. Looking back on the career of Florence Kelley, who had been the heart of the National Consumers' League for over thirty years, Kellogg said that Kelley personified "the quickening of women's concern for the humanizing of industry" during an era of convulsive change.[2] Paul Kellogg's perspective was shared by several generations of women reformers, including a cohort that would help carve out the New Deal. In choosing Kelley's successor, Consumers' League officials never considered hiring a man. "We need a woman's approach," said Molly Dewson, explaining that male candidates' interest in workers seemed purely academic.[3] Veteran feminists who themselves had broken into arenas previously considered male territory, Kelley and Dewson nonetheless believed that women and men had distinct perspectives, reflecting different experiences and assigned roles. In their eyes, women valued selflessness and cooperation more highly than men, whose socialization emphasized competition and self-promotion. The thousands of people who joined the NCL—most of them women—seemed to agree that women had a particular aptitude and responsibility for the task of civilizing capitalism.

Armed with this belief, the reformers of the National Consumers' League accomplished extraordinary things. From the 1890s on, the league was the guiding force in a movement to improve the working conditions, hours, and wages of workers, beginning with women in department stores, factories, laundries, and other workplaces. NCL activists became the preeminent experts in the field of labor standards, savvy about the legislative, administrative, and judicial aspects of policy making. Motivated by what they thought of as feminine values, these reformers also were strategic thinkers with a coherent, far-sighted program.[4] NCL leaders sought immediate protections for women workers, but they wanted more than piecemeal, ameliorative reforms. They understood their program as one aspect of a broader social justice movement to redistribute economic and political power to workers, particularly to the worst-off groups of workers. The NCL's ideas and methods are best introduced through an overview of the league's early history, strategies for ethical consumption, organizational structure, leadership, and reform networks. Examination of these factors illuminates key changes and continuities in the league from the Progressive Era through the 1930s. These factors also explain how it was that throughout this period, the league wielded an influence far beyond its numbers.

League Origins and Early Leadership

The Consumers' League emerged in response to an initiative by workers. In 1888 a New York shirtmaker and organizer named Leonora O'Reilly invited some of the city's prominent women to a meeting of the New York Working Women's Society, at which they heard an appeal for assistance from their "toiling and down-trodden sisters." The group decided to appoint a committee to assist the Working Women's Society by "making a list which shall keep shoppers informed of such shops as deal justly with their employees, and so bring public opinion and public action to bear in favor of just employers, and also in favor of such employers as desire to be just, but are prevented by the stress of competition, from following their own sense of duty."[5]

In response to this prodding from wage-earning women, the Consumers' League of New York took shape in early 1891, headed by Josephine Shaw Lowell, blue-blooded leader of the "scientific charity" movement. Other branches formed in Massachusetts, Pennsylvania, and Illinois, and in 1899 they united as the National Consumers' League. Adopting the motto

"Investigate, agitate, legislate," the movement spread rapidly. Within five years the NCL included sixty-four branches in twenty states. Most branches were in the industrialized states of the Northeast and Midwest. Only two leagues were in the South, in Louisville, Kentucky, and New Orleans. Membership peaked in 1916, when the NCL claimed 15,000 members in forty-three states.[6]

The NCL's growth was part of a veritable explosion of organized reform activity by women in the Progressive Era. Many members of the first generations of college-educated women found outlets for their talents in the suffrage, settlement house, and women's club movements. Justifying their increased public activism in terms consistent with the existing sexual division of labor, these women staked out their responsibility for "social housekeeping," extending woman's ideal sphere from the family to the community.[7] Settlement and social work fostered an interest in improving the living and labor standards of the urban poor. Local reform activities led some of these women, along with a few men, to reject the political views that were dominant within their social class. Dismayed by the casualties inflicted by the "invisible hand" of the market, they advocated using state power to subordinate private interests to the welfare of the entire community.[8] Many of these activists joined the National Consumers' League. One of the most prominent and admired of these highly educated, public-spirited women was Florence Kelley, who presided over the Consumers' League and a whole network of interlocking reform groups from the 1890s to 1932.

Kelley's stature among her contemporaries is illustrated by the claim of U.S. Supreme Court Justice Felix Frankfurter that she "had probably the largest single share in shaping the social history of the United States during the first thirty years of this century," particularly in "securing legislation for the removal of the most glaring abuses of our hectic industrialization following the Civil War."[9] Like another reform giant of the Progressive Era, Jane Addams, Kelley hailed from an elite Protestant political family of abolitionist sentiments. Her father, William "Pig-Iron" Kelley, was a Republican U.S. congressman from Pennsylvania for three decades after 1860. Although Florence disagreed with her father's protectionist ideas about trade, she took great pride in his early support of woman suffrage. Her mother's aunt was the Philadelphia Quaker Sarah Pugh, an abolitionist who led a movement to boycott slave-made goods. Florence Kelley admired Pugh's efforts, and the Consumers' League may have been a direct descendant of the abolitionist effort to promote ethical consumption.[10]

After graduating from Cornell in 1882, Kelley studied law and government at the University of Zurich (most American graduate schools refused to admit women). There she became an ardent socialist, married a Russian medical student, and had three children. In 1891 she left her abusive husband in New York and moved to Hull House, the new Chicago settlement house. Kelley soon established herself as an expert on tenement labor, and in 1893 the reform governor John Altgeld of Illinois made her the first woman to head a state labor department. Kelley also earned a degree from Northwestern Law School, acquiring the legal expertise that became a hallmark of her reform strategy. In 1898 Kelley moved from Hull House to its New York counterpart, the Henry Street Settlement, which provided her with a supportive community during her succeeding decades as the driving force of the NCL.[11]

Kelley's work in Illinois as chief factory inspector foreshadowed the NCL operating mode. After meeting with Chicago trade unionists, she persuaded the state government to fund her survey of industrial working conditions in Chicago. She then helped draft and pass a remedial law (the 1893 eight-hour day for women and children) and managed to get herself appointed to enforce it. Her aggressive enforcement pressed many Chicago employers to institute the eight-hour day. John Commons, the renowned University of Wisconsin labor economist, observed that Kelley's work "was a revelation of what a factory inspection department should be and do." Kelley's stringent administration stimulated the formation of the Illinois Association of Manufacturers, which succeeded in having the women's and minors' hours law found unconstitutional in 1895.[12] This was just the beginning of Kelley's long battle with the courts. As the NCL's general secretary from 1899 on, Kelley masterminded the movement that by 1917 produced maximum hours laws for women in most states and minimum wage laws for women in a dozen states.[13]

Florence Kelley viewed her work for labor laws as consistent with the philosophy of evolutionary socialism. In 1887 she wrote an article urging the emerging phalanx of college-educated women to reject "bourgeois philanthropy" because it was palliative activity to return to workers a fraction of the wealth they had created without changing the arrangements creating poverty and its ills. She called on her generation of college women to undertake more fundamental reforms, understanding that "any radical measures directed against this profit-plunder are measures directly against the class that lives by it; and to that class we belong by birth, and especially by education."[14] Although hours and minimum wage laws do not now seem like "radical measures" directed against "profit-plunder," their turn-of-the-century opponents certainly believed they were. Labor legislation was thought to be reform "along socialist lines" because it sought to limit the appropriation of surplus value from workers by employers and to

This 1914 photograph of past and present women factory inspectors includes Florence Kelley, chief state factory inspector of Illinois from 1893 to 1897 (third from left). (National Consumers' League Collection, LC)

strengthen trade unions. Kelley believed that the very process of fighting for labor laws educated and mobilized the middle class to resist "the brutalizing of us all by Capitalism."[15] Kelley joined the Socialist Party of her friend Eugene V. Debs, and she stirred students in frequent addresses to the Intercollegiate Socialist Society and its successor, the League for Industrial Democracy.[16]

The extent to which the NCL membership sympathized with Kelley's socialist views is unclear. Before World War I the boundary between socialists and progressives was relatively fluid and permeable. In 1912 "respectable" people helped the Socialist Party win 6 percent of the popular presidential vote, an impressive showing given the strong competition that year from another challenger to the two-party system, the Progressive Party. One unscientific sampling of the league's female membership in 1914 found that among those few who identified with a political party, most were Progressives or Socialists.[17] Although some NCL members thus shared Kelley's political views, before the war other members may have been unaware of them. By the 1920s most NCL members must have known that Kelley was a socialist because her opponents publicly attacked her as one. The prewar climate of political tolerance evaporated after the Russian Revolution and a wave of official crackdowns on radicals. Red-baiting by "patriotic" groups taxed Kelley's patience and energies. In 1926 the child labor amendment (of which Kelley was a leading backer) was attacked in the U.S. Senate as "part of the Engels-Kelley program . . . derived straight from the fundamental Communist manifesto of 1848." Although Kelley never renounced socialism, later in life she carefully downplayed its importance to her thinking.[18]

The intense loyalty that Kelley inspired in several generations of league members suggests that they endorsed her objectives and methods, whether or not they fully embraced her socialist analysis. In the 1920s Kelley's radical associations probably reduced the pool of people willing to support the league. However, those who joined or stayed with the NCL into the 1920s and 1930s were hardy, independent-minded types.[19] The general secretaries who led the league in the 1930s worked comfortably with members of the resurgent Left, through left-led unions and through various Popular Front coalitions of progressives and radicals, and several league branches maintained friendly relations with socialist groups. In the 1930s NCL thinkers perceived fascism, not socialism or communism, as the chief threat confronting Americans.

During and after Kelley's years, many of the league's most active leaders were influenced by European and American social democratic thought. Characteristics of the social democratic perspective included a desire to "extend the democratic principle of equality from the civil and political spheres to the entire society and the economy," and a belief that progress toward the ideal of socialism would come through gradual, constitutional reform rather than through revolution. Where strict Marxists opposed reform measures that might hinder the development of revolutionary class consciousness, social democrats argued that civilizing capitalism through redistributive policies was a step in the evolutionary process from liberal democracy to social democracy.[20] By emphasizing the interdependence of classes and evolutionary change, social democrats appealed to middle-class reformers who sought a constructive role in social change. A related feature of social democratic theory was the important role it accorded to consumers as arbiters of the interests of the community, or "the general welfare." Because consumers often were construed as female, this vision had special resonance for progressive women.

"Right Goods, Rightly Made": The Changing Methods of Ethical Consumption

At the turn of the century many women who might not have responded to social democratic philosophy were inspired by the NCL's call for ethical consumption. This phrase touched a nerve among women eager to play a meaningful role in a society that increasingly equated worth with wage-earning, while defining wage-earning by women as a deviation from the ideal. In the interwar decades the league continued to think of consumers as female, even as its own arguments for raising "mass" purchasing power began to alter the consumer's image. By the end of the 1920s the shrinking of the NCL constituency had combined with the arrival of the Great Depression to undermine the effectiveness of economic strategies of ethical consumption. However, the league belief in consumers' political power and legitimacy gained a wider following in the 1930s among New Deal intellectuals. Ethical consumption became a strategy that could be deployed effectively even by small numbers of league members, acting as expert representatives of the consumers' interest.

The league's early program offered moral regeneration and economic empowerment to the non-wage-earning woman, whom social critics from Charlotte Perkins Gilman to Thorstein Veblen were condemning as an economic parasite and fueler of "conspicuous consumption."[21] NCL propaganda invoked images of the frivolous or bargain-hunting woman shopper as negative reference points. Through joining in the league's work, non-wage-earning women could avoid the label of idleness. According to Josephine Shaw Lowell, head of the Consumers' League of New York, "The responsibility for some of the worst evils from which producers suffer rests with the consumers, who seek the cheapest markets regardless of how cheapness is brought about. It is, therefore, the duty of consumers to find out under what conditions the articles they purchase are produced and distributed, and to insist that these conditions shall be wholesome and consistent with a respectable existence on the part of the workers."[22]

In its early years the NCL defined consumers as women. Josephine Shaw Lowell portrayed the league's work as part of a historical continuum in women's activism, invoking women's patriotic refusal to buy British goods in the revolutionary era and female abolitionists' boycotts of slave-made goods. At the same time, Lowell observed that the task of identifying "right goods, rightly made" had grown more complicated under "the conditions of so called 'free labor.'" The work of non-wage-earning women, then, was the increasingly challenging work of reform through informed, responsible consumption. This activity held potential for cross-class cooperation among women. In the early decades of the twentieth century, working-class groups began to wield their purchasing power as a reform tool. The NCL welcomed and encouraged this development. Nonetheless, its prime constituency remained middle-class women with the time and expertise to ascertain "right goods, rightly made."[23]

League thinkers drew on economic theories that value was a function of demand rather than of labor. Because consumer demand determined the nature of production, organized consumers could demand goods made and sold under right conditions. To women, this vision of the rational, powerful consumer was an appealing alternative to the image of a passive consumer subject to the dictates of supply. The rational consumer could tackle social problems through individual and collective action. She could change buying habits (shopping early during busy holiday periods, for example, and buying only approved goods), join consumer cooperatives, investigate working conditions, and lobby for improved labor laws. The Consumers' League example influenced many of the first economists to emphasize the power of the consumer, so the league and the new economic thinking shaped each other.[24]

The league's earliest tactics, the "white list" and "white label," tried to extract voluntary concessions from employers. The white list was a roster of employers—at first primarily upscale department stores—ascertained by the league to adhere to the "standard of a fair house." The league published this list in newspapers, calling it a white list to emphasize that it was not a blacklist, or boycott, which had been found illegal under conspiracy laws. NCL leaders eventually decided the white list was impractical because so few stores met its modest standards.[25] The Consumers' League white label, a tactic borrowed from unions, ran into similar difficulties. The first white label had been affixed to cigar boxes by San Francisco cigar makers in 1874 to identify the product of white labor, as opposed to the labor of Asians receiving substandard wages. The industries to which the Consumers' League label was applied employed few native-born whites, however, and in any case the league label distinguished between types of employers, not types of employees.[26] The NCL started its drive in the muslin underwear industry, eventually granting sixty-nine factories its white label, but the league could not keep up the inspections required to maintain use of the label. Although not successful in changing employer practices, the league lists and labels were nonetheless effective devices for recruiting middle-class women and educating them on labor issues and the workings of state government.[27]

During the 1930s the NCL increasingly urged consumers to wield their power politically rather than through economic action. In the face of a nationwide catastrophe of the scale of the Great Depression, it seemed unrealistic to expect "that consumers themselves, in any considerable numbers, [could] combat the abrupt fall of wages by refusing to purchase sweated goods."[28] There still were opportunities to deploy purchasing-oriented strategies. The labor movement was gaining strength, and the

NCL urged members not to buy products of companies that refused to negotiate with unions.[29] However, more often the league asked members to fulfill their responsibilities as consumers by backing league state-building activities. One 1935 league flyer, "Dining Out," featured a dialogue between a young woman and a young man discussing whether to eat at a certain restaurant. The woman pricks the man's conscience by telling him what she has learned from "Jean Adams" about the exploitation of waitresses. "Jean says the best way to help is by joining the League," she tells him. "There isn't much we can do by ourselves." The two agree to join. Twenty years earlier, they might also have ended up investigating the restaurant or telling friends not to eat there. Not incidentally, this flyer implied that women were more sensitive to injustice than men and had a responsibility to educate the men around them. The methods had changed, but women were still the NCL's targeted constituency for the project of ethical consumption.[30]

When it seemed unfeasible for consumers to use their economic power directly, the league's social democratic thinking legitimized the political authority of consumers based on their alleged disinterestedness. Beatrice Webb, the English Fabian socialist, had argued that consumers were better protectors of the "general welfare" than capital or labor alone, because both employers and workers organized to advance their own interests rather than the public interest.[31] In the interwar United States, some who sought to empower consumers assumed that women embodied the consumer's aptitude for representing the whole community. When the Massachusetts labor commissioner argued in 1933 that consumers should be represented on labor standards enforcement boards, he meant non-wage-earning women: "When I say consumer . . . I think very frankly of the representation of women, because there are more women than men . . . who, by the very fact that they are not directly connected with the processes of industry, are more capable of exercising this social viewpoint." Similarly, New Deal economist Rexford Tugwell noted that "housewives" were the largest group of pure consumers, whereas most people were both producers and consumers.[32] League activists never claimed that non-wage-earning women had no class interests, but they did imply that these women would be more likely than the men of their class to work for the greater good. According to one NCL official, the league proceeded from "the conviction that consumers have a far-reaching responsibility to use their buying power and their power as citizens to advance the general welfare of the community."[33]

In the interwar years, newly influential ideas that underconsumption was a cause of economic depression led to an emphasis on "mass purchasing power" that challenged the exclusive association of consumption with women. The Depression enhanced the authority of a circle of experts, trade unionists, businessmen, and politicians who argued that organizing the wage-earning majority as workers *and* as consumers was necessary to challenge corporate power and secure the high wages and low prices essential to a healthy mass-consumption economy. The NCL itself was an important forum for the development of the most redistributive versions of under-consumptionist thought. Its large annual conferences aired the views of such leading consumer-oriented thinkers as Paul Douglas, Sidney Hillman, Caroline Ware, and Leon Henderson. In its support of minimum wage laws, unionization, and other measures, the NCL favored government intervention to stimulate consumption. The league assumed such policies would redistribute income toward low-paid workers. League officer Josephine Goldmark argued in 1933 that the abysmally low wages of at least half the population were disastrous for everyone, not just "the employed class." The growth of advertising indicated business awareness of the importance of expanding markets even in boom times, and the Depression now underscored the "crucial importance of purchasing power." Broadly based consumption was in the interest of a healthy economy as well as fairness.[34]

Reflecting the shifting ideas about the role of the consumer, the league sent mixed messages about the consumer's identity. In 1925 the league's official history, *The First Quarter Century*, promoted a vision of the consumer as male or female of any class: "Responsibility for working conditions in this country rests upon each man and woman who makes purchases. Every person who buys anything, from a bun to a yacht, is a consumer."[35] In testifying for higher minimum wages in 1933, Lucy Mason would assert the right of southern black men to be consumers. Although the NCL sought to increase lower-class consumption, league fund-raising and publicity materials continued to focus on middle-class women as agents of the consumers' conscience, and the general public continued to identify consumption as a female activity. The NCL received many inquiries such as this one from a Missouri woman concerned about sweatshops: "As a consumer I want to know if something can't be done about it. Is there any way women can be aroused to the situation?" The category of consumer was no longer imagined as exclusively female (or exclusively affluent), but it certainly included women, more clearly so than the categories of worker or employer. Consumerist activism and policies continued to hold particular appeal for women.[36]

Increasingly, league members acted as the consumers' conscience by administering labor standards laws. Florence Kelley in Illinois in the 1890s was just the first of many league activists who won positions enforcing the laws they had drafted. NCL members Clara Beyer (who in the 1930s would run the new U.S. Division of Labor Standards) and Elizabeth Brandeis (daughter of Louis Brandeis, and soon to be an economist at the University of Wisconsin) staffed the Washington, D.C., minimum wage board from about 1918 to 1923. League members won appointment to various kinds of labor boards as representatives of the consumer or the public. For league activists, the idea that consumers represented the good of the community, not a special interest, was shored up by a belief that women were less partisan and self-interested than men. Assumptions about the disinterestedness of consumers and women were mutually reinforcing, and together they produced a strong commitment on the part of the Consumers' League and its network to see women in charge of labor standards laws. In the years when labor laws chiefly affected women and minors, the league succeeded in creating a female-dominated labor standards bureaucracy in certain state and federal agencies. This was a step toward the vision of a feminist administrative state that gave voice to both consumers and workers, and to women in the process.

In sum, one reason for the league's rapid growth and substantial influence in the Progressive Era was the appeal of its call for ethical consumption to a broad audience of organized middle-class white women. In the 1930s the identification between consumption and non-wage-earning women persisted but was less clear-cut. Also, after suffrage, the memberships of most women's organizations contracted, shrinking the league's prime constituency. However, in the 1930s newly influential ideas about the importance of consumption to national economic health gave the league's analysis fresh salience. The NCL continued to promote ethical consumption, but now through political methods more than economic ones, and more often as a strategy executed by small numbers of women experts rather than by large numbers of women shoppers.

NCL Organizational Structure and Finances

The NCL never had much money or millions of members. But visionary, dedicated officers and effective organization at national and local levels enabled the league to make an enormous impact. During the 1930s the league's budget and membership shrank, continuing a trend already under way in the 1920s. On the other hand, the Depression era gave birth to new league committees and branches in over half a dozen states, and the national membership decline was partially offset by the recruitment of new members.

The heart of the NCL was always its general secretary. The league's successes — and its unusually progressive positions on labor and race issues — stemmed in large part from the extraordinary women it attracted to that office. During the New Deal, Lucy Randolph Mason of Virginia faced the formidable challenge of filling Florence Kelley's shoes. NCL leaders had for some time wanted to press the group's agenda in the South, and in the fifty-year-old Mason, they chose someone with a long record of work for the rights of women, workers, and African Americans. Lucy Mason developed a sophisticated analysis of the causes of social injustice, becoming, in the words of one contemporary, "the nearest thing to a Beatrice Webb the South has produced."[37] In her youth, Mason drew inspiration from Walter Rauschenbusch, the American preacher of the social gospel who was, like Beatrice Webb, a foremost proponent of social democracy. Mason led the league for five years before departing to work for the CIO.[38] Succeeding Mason was Mary Dublin, an economist trained at the London School of Economics and Columbia. Dublin pressed the league agenda from 1938 through early 1941, when the New Deal's legislative momentum was waning. Only twenty-eight years old when she became head of the league, Dublin was too young to have shared the experience of most league activists in woman suffragism and the peak of the settlement movement. However, she did share their commitment to expanding state programs on behalf of the working class, working women in particular. Her NCL years came early in a long career of agitating for higher minimum wages, union rights, federally funded child care, and national health insurance. In the 1960s Dublin would head the U.S. Women's Bureau under Lyndon Johnson, and in the 1970s she chaired the D.C. Committee on the Status of Women.[39]

Working closely with the general secretary to define league priorities and tactics was the NCL board. The board's composition varied over time, but a regular core of board members provided continuity (see Appendix 1). From 1932 to 1942, nine people, six of whom were women, were on the board for at least nine years. These nine represented about half the total board but well over half of the board's active members.[40] Lawyer Nicholas Kelley, Florence's son, chaired the board until 1937, when he was succeeded by Columbia economist Paul Brissenden. For practical reasons, most board members were based in New York City. The board met at least monthly, in the 1930s usually over dinner at the Woman's City Club with about a dozen regulars in attendance. Reflecting its affluent membership, the board did not meet in the summers (when many members joined the fashionable exodus from the hot city).[41]

Beyond the board, a substantial roster of officers augmented the league's expertise, contacts, and credibility (see Appendix 1). Council members and vice presidents tended to be old friends of the league, often former league activists whose other commitments or geographic location no longer permitted them to attend regular meetings. The league cultivated ties with universities around the country through its honorary vice presidents. These were prominent sociologists, economists, social workers, and lawyers, often challengers of orthodoxy in their disciplines. Florence Kelley observed that as honorary vice presidents, professors had been "of incalculable value in silencing criticism" and in facilitating the league's recruitment of college students.[42]

Until the late 1930s the league sought to increase its visibility by having famous men as its presidents. Rarely more than figureheads, these included Unitarian minister John Graham Brooks (1899–1915), Cleveland mayor and secretary of war Newton D. Baker (1915–23), John R. Commons (1923–34), and John G. Winant (1934–38). John Commons fathered the Wisconsin School of labor economics during the Progressive Era as well as the American Association for Labor Legislation. John Winant, liberal Republican governor of New Hampshire, headed a textile labor relations board under the National Recovery Administration and then was the first chairman of the Social Security Board. In 1938 Josephine Roche became the league's first female president. She had made labor relations history in the 1920s by inviting the United Mine Workers to unionize her Colorado coal-mining company, Rocky Mountain Fuel. From 1934 to 1937 she served as assistant secretary of the treasury. Roche and her successor, Alice Hamilton, a pioneer in industrial medicine and Harvard's first female professor, took more active roles as league president than the men had. Apparently NCL women no longer believed they needed the legitimizing presence of a well-known man.[43]

Long-term commitment to the NCL on the part of its officers helped make up for the league's chronic financial insecurity. Many NCL activists devoted decades to the league, most of them on an unpaid basis. Full-time staff received modest salaries and paid their own expenses while traveling on league business.[44] A few wealthy members regularly contributed several hundred dollars, but the league was funded primarily by small annual dues and contributions of $2 to $10 per year, plus dues from branches at ten cents per member. On principle, the NCL kept its membership open to people of limited means. Even when the league faced a budget crisis during the Great Depression, its leaders did not raise the minimum dues, which at $2 per year were low relative to dues for other voluntary associations.[45]

The league had more acute financial pains in the 1930s than ever before. Its membership contracted, and its annual budget dropped to below

$30,000 and then below $20,000.[46] The Depression made it harder for small donors to pay league dues, and reduced stock dividends made the league's rich backers less generous. Applications for support from foundations such as the Twentieth Century Fund were unsuccessful. Turnover in the office of the general secretary and the perception that New Deal legislation was taking care of labor exploitation also took their toll on membership levels. The NCL managed to find a few hundred new members in most years during the 1930s. Still, the number of paid memberships in the national organization declined from about 3,200 in 1931 to about 1,700 in 1940. (This was a dramatic change from 15,000 members back in 1916.) During and after World War II the decline in national and branch memberships continued. The postwar decades would find the league searching for new constituencies and funding sources.[47]

Branch leagues were vital to the NCL's lobbying effectiveness as well as to its financial health. The league's federated structure was a factor in its rapid growth and in giving it the influence that came from being organized at both national and local levels. The NCL could boast a distinctive combination of elite expertise with grassroots activism. Its fostering of local chapters and recruitment of ordinary citizens made it better at lobbying than its closest equivalent, the predominantly male American Association for Labor Legislation (AALL). The AALL never had more than a handful of branches, and those had faded away by 1916. In that year the Consumers' League had sixty-four branches. By 1932 the NCL was down to a dozen branches, but that number would rise to eighteen by the end of the decade. Many of these branches had hundreds of members and dozens of active officers.[48]

Local branches did not form out of thin air. In the Progressive Era many emerged shortly after a visit from Florence Kelley, who spent as much as half of her time traveling.[49] Lucy Mason undertook extended tours of the South in the 1930s, trying to start league branches. Once established, locals remained in close contact with the national office through detailed correspondence. The general secretary visited the locals often, addressing annual luncheons and helping out at critical political junctures. At NCL annual conferences, activists from around the country pooled ideas, data, and tactics. These meetings fostered the development of capable, confident leaders and helped each group to be more effective at the local level. They also created a nationwide reform alliance that could be mobilized readily on a variety of issues. This network took on special importance where it penetrated states traditionally hostile to national forces, most clearly in the South. Even where no branch formed, the league network could be a lifeline to isolated activists, such as Effie Dupuis of North Dakota. After her first labor standards conference, Dupuis wrote, "It was a great pleasure to meet all of the splendid women. . . . I feel a little homesick and lonesome out here so far away from all such contacts."[50]

Having local branches with their own officers and activities (rather than scattered individuals tied only to national headquarters) was not only an effective way of building membership, it was well suited to the issue of labor standards regulation. Legislative progress in one state often depended on circumstances in competing states, because employers could jeopardize a bill by claiming that their rivals in more lax states would put them out of business. Thus coordination between state leagues was invaluable. The existence of strong organizations at both state and national levels also generated political advantages for the league. The national could exert outside influence on a state politician (for example, bringing Roosevelt administration pressure to bear on an antilabor governor). In turn, branch members could initiate letter-writing campaigns and local editorial support to put pressure on their state's federal representatives.

Harmony between the national and branch leagues was not always perfect. League branches enjoyed substantial autonomy and developed their own programs and local networks. The national board periodically rededicated itself to providing better service to the branches. New general secretaries were told that their first priority was "building up branch leagues." This cultivation of the branches reflected the league's philosophy that local civic involvement improved the content and administration of public policy. Even as the Depression deepened the league's conviction that uniform national standards and an expansion of federal authority were necessary, the NCL retained its commitment to complementary state-level legislation. Its leaders asserted that joint federal-state action would stimulate democracy as well as the economy. When the New Deal focused attention on Washington, some officers grumbled that the league was neglecting its traditional program in the states.[51] Notwithstanding such tensions, however, the league's federated structure was a crucial source of strength.

League Activists in the 1930s:
A Demographic and Ideological Profile

Data on the NCL's full membership is not available, but a portrait of the league's warmest supporters may be derived by examining fifty people who in the 1930s were at the policy-making core of the national league or were key individuals in state branches (see Appendix 2 for a summary of biographical data).[52] A collective profile of this group reveals educational and occupational experiences and personal circumstances that were conducive to a set of unusually progressive attitudes. These included a positive view of women's wage-earning and public office-holding, a commitment to labor rights and to a redistributive, administrative state, and a growing interest in civil rights for racial minorities. This profile also reveals the league's ties with the Democratic Party, an alliance that the league did not wear comfortably, but which it sustained in the hope that the New Deal might give birth to a social democratic state. The usual characterization of the NCL as white and middle-class holds true, but it obscures significant nuances. Not all white middle-class women held the same political views.

Gender, Education, Marital Status, and Class

The Consumers' League was always female-dominated. As one male board member later put it, "There are some men, but it is really a women's movement, a very powerful and effective movement."[53] The NCL general secretaries were female, as were most branch executives. In 1917 eighteen of the NCL's twenty officers were women, as were 240 of the 269 branch officers. From 1932 to 1942 men comprised almost half of the NCL board, but among those who regularly attended board meetings, women significantly outnumbered men. Women also tended to stay on the board longer.[54] In the 1930s, when the linkage between women and consumers was slipping, and when it at last seemed possible for the league's program to be extended to male as well as female workers, the NCL downplayed its public image as a women's organization. Probably concerned that the credibility of a women's group on the subject of male workers would be subject to challenge, the national league and some branches attempted to recruit men.[55] However, the league continued to participate in the Women's Joint Congressional Committee, a Washington lobbying coalition, and it continued to make women workers its highest priority.

Most league activists were educated, urban, white women, but beneath those commonalities lay a range of backgrounds. A surprisingly high number had midwestern origins, and a few southerners and westerners were part of the league backbone. Most league activists had college degrees, and over half had undertaken some graduate study. Roughly a quarter of the women were full-time volunteers who lived on inheritances or on husbands' incomes. The rest supported themselves, or at least supplemented their incomes, with their own earnings. Employed league women most commonly were paid reformers or social scientists. Several women worked in government or politics, and a few were artists, lawyers, or other professionals. The sprinkling of men among the league's core included lawyers, labor economists, and a few trade unionists and clergymen. Among the women, almost half never married. Among those who did marry, a third had no children. By contrast, all the men whose marital status can be determined were married and had several children.[56]

Uniting many female league activists was firsthand familiarity with female wage-earning, gained through reform work, academic study, or, in a few cases, personal experience. Most of these women had had some association with the settlement house movement or YWCA industrial clubs. A striking number of them—including younger women as well as those of Florence Kelley's generation—had degrees in economics, statistics, sociology, and social work. As notable as the high number of NCL women who attended elite women's colleges is the number who received advanced training at places like Columbia and the University of Chicago. At the turn of the century, women had led the development of applied social research. Generally excluded from university positions, these pioneers built their own institutions and churned out quantitative studies of social problems. In the 1930s the association between women, statistics, and reform was beginning to yield to a new linkage of men, statistics (now "hard" science), and "objectivity," but this was a gradual shift.[57] Many league women engaged in social scientific research that gave them extensive knowledge of female poverty and wage work.

Most of the league's key women were single or widowed during their years of activism. A significant minority are known to have lived in long-term partnerships with other women. These relationships created personal and professional support systems without the loss of autonomy that heterosexual marriage and childbearing often implied for women.[58] Lucy Mason suggested the pressures on women to choose between career and family when she recommended Anna Settle of the Kentucky league for a job by emphasizing that Settle was a widow and childless.[59] The league periodically lost women activists to "the pressure of home duties," as when the Michigan committee's leader resigned to care for an ailing husband, or when the Tennessee committee's executive married and moved away.[60] Husbands also could bring ideological pressure to bear: a New Hampshire correspondent asked Lucy Mason to come "wake up" some wives whose husbands were "making them more conservative."[61] In the 1930s, although the proportion of unmarried and widowed women in the league's core remained high, several younger members combined activism and marriage, seemingly more optimistic about the possibility of preserving their independence in marriage.[62]

The high proportion of women without male breadwinners had mixed implications for the perspective of the league's leadership. On one hand, in a period when most women could not earn enough to support themselves, remaining single was something of a class privilege, most available to the very educated or independently wealthy. On the other hand, lack of financial support from husbands attuned some league women to the difficulties of women wage earners. Recent studies of women's social welfare activism argue that a class double standard limited the vision of white reformers. Studies of the mothers' pension movement conclude that well-meaning but backward-looking elite women drafted policies that ultimately promoted the family wage, or women's economic dependence on a male breadwinner. Scholars have found irony in the fact that these women themselves enjoyed the independence of an "alternative gender system." In this view, even as they eschewed marriage and built careers themselves, these reformers prescribed the family wage for working-class women.[63] This assessment does not ring true for the Consumers' League leadership in the 1930s. In that decade few league activists, whether single or married themselves, believed that full-time domesticity was a likely option for working-class women. Perhaps the Depression dramatized this point. Also at work was a modest diversification in the class composition of the NCL leadership.

By the 1930s the league's traditional core of independently wealthy and highly educated professional women had been supplemented by the arrival of some less affluent people. To be sure, rich women remained prominent among NCL leaders. Myrta Jones Cannon, an old friend of Florence Kelley's and the daughter of an Ohio judge, late in life married one of the nation's leading bankers. Florina Lasker made large donations to the NCL as well as to the American Civil Liberties Union and the New York School of Social Work. Most of the league's wealthy women were very progressive, but board member Florence Canfield Whitney, the daughter of a self-made California oil baron, quit the NCL after she developed reservations about the New Deal. Whatever their politics, these rich women were outnumbered by geographically mobile professionals like Elizabeth Magee and Margaret Wiesman, the paid executives of the Cleveland and Massachusetts branches, respectively.[64] There also emerged a few leaders from working-class backgrounds. Elizabeth Nord, an organizer for the United Textile Workers, joined the board of the Rhode Island league in 1934 and remained an active officer for many years. A dynamic figure in the New York branch was Mabel Leslie, a veteran organizer of electrical workers and telephone operators. John Edelman and later James Carey, union leaders in female-employing industries, were labor voices on the national board.[65]

Finally, a few of the NCL's most influential leaders in the 1930s were women who enjoyed middle-class status, but who had held working-class occupations during earlier periods of hardship. After Lucy Mason's parents decided they could not afford to send her to college (although her brothers all went), Mason contributed to the family budget by working as a legal stenographer in Richmond, Virginia.[66] Clara Beyer was the daughter of Danish immigrants who ran a chicken ranch in California. After an accident killed her father, the nine children were split up, and Beyer put herself through high school and college by working as a domestic servant.[67] Another example is Elinore Morehouse Herrick, who headed the New York league and remained an NCL adviser after she became a regional director of the National Labor Relations Board. After dropping out of college, marrying, and having children, Herrick found herself divorced with two young sons to support. She took a series of factory jobs, earning piecework wages in shoe blacking, paper box making, and rayon mill work. It was firsthand experience that shaped her interest in labor economics (she earned her B.S. at thirty-five) and the problems of wage-earning women.[68] This sort of background was hardly typical for NCL members, but people like Mason, Beyer, and Herrick were central enough in the NCL leadership to shape its perspective. These women believed that for women of any class, dependence on male wages was a precarious strategy.

Ethnicity and Race

Across the years, most NCL activists were native-born whites. However, in the 1930s, at least, they displayed less conviction of their own cultural superiority than historians have found to be the case for white reformers in earlier years. This may reflect the Depression decade's diminished concern with assimilating immigrants and rural migrants, as well as the views of league members.[69] Most NCL members were Protestants, but at least a dozen Jewish women and men were part of the league's core leadership in the 1930s. Jewish women were more likely to be active in labor-related causes than others, reflecting a greater tolerance for women's public activism and a more sanguine attitude toward female employment among Jews, as well as a European socialist tradition. Their participation may well have reinforced the positive view of women's wage-earning that distinguished the Consumers' League from some other women's organizations. In general, Catholics were less supportive of labor regulation than other groups. The NCL worked hard to recruit Catholic members, but their numbers remained small.[70]

The league did not attract many African Americans, if any. Black women organized on many issues of concern to their communities, but labor standards legislation was not high on their list.[71] The call for ethical consumption first was directed at affluent department store patrons in northeastern and western cities, few of whom would have been African American. Also, the NCL's early emphasis on "white" labels may have alienated black reformers through the association with trade unions, which notoriously discriminated against black workers. Most important, the league's initial focus on department store clerks and factory workers limited its relevance to black women, who were excluded by white prejudice from these occupations. Through World War II, most minority women workers were employed in domestic service or agriculture.[72] Well into the postwar period, domestic and agricultural labor were deemed beyond the scope of wage-hour regulation. Agricultural employers, who possessed enormous political clout, nurtured an image of agricultural production as wholesome, all-American, and nonindustrial. As for domestic service, idealized images of domesticity helped forestall recognition of the home as a workplace, to the detriment of paid and unpaid household workers alike. These images reinforced political and legal barriers to regulation. There also were practical obstacles to enforcing regulations in individual homes and for migratory field workers.[73] Because domestic servants and farm laborers generally worked longer hours for lower pay than most other workers, the people who arguably most needed labor standards regulation were not covered by it.

It has been argued that this outcome reflected the racism of labor reformers. They allegedly worried about the negative effects of long hours and low wages on white women and their families but were indifferent to employer exploitation of minority women. Female reformers were particularly vulnerable to the charge of hypocrisy where domestic servants were concerned. As Jessie Daniel Ames of Atlanta told a league audience, "It has weakened our position before legislators when we exclude domestic service, because they say that we [women] are trying to regulate other people's employees and not our own." African American women, too, suspected that white women reformers' dependence on servants prevented them from working wholeheartedly on behalf of laws for domestic workers. Bills protecting domestic servants did receive less support from mainstream white women's groups than bills affecting "factory girls" and "shop girls" (who were white). In the case of the NCL, however, it was an incrementalist, legalistic orientation, more than racist self-interest, that delayed its inclusion of domestic workers in most bills until the mid-1930s.[74]

Initially the Consumers' League was indeed myopic where wage-earning women of racial minorities were concerned. It focused on urban workers in the Northeast at a time when most African Americans (and increasing numbers of Mexican Americans) lived in the rural South and Southwest. Although the league's early program ignored minority women, some of its leaders were in the vanguard of racial liberalism. True to her abolitionist heritage, Kelley was a friend of W. E. B. Du Bois and a founding member of the National Association for the Advancement of Colored People (NAACP). During the final stages of the woman suffrage campaign, Kelley roundly criticized the National Woman's Party for accommodating white supremacist southern women by "welsh[ing] on the Negro question." But Kelley's racial egalitarianism had its limits. In 1920 she threatened to resign from the NAACP if it did not distance itself from a Du Bois article asserting the "social equality" of the races, which was often (in white minds, at least) a euphemism for interracial marriage.[75]

By the 1930s changing circumstances had pushed the league into an appreciation of the ways in which racial inequality facilitated labor exploitation. These factors included black migration northward, growing competition between northern and southern manufacturers, and the impact of the Depression in pitting groups of low-paid workers against each other. The NCL increasingly heard the voices of black activists: representatives of the Commission on Interracial Cooperation, the NAACP, and the Urban League attended its conferences and joined its state labor standards committees. NCL leaders came into contact with black radicals in forums such as the National Recovery Administration hearings. Furthermore, the league's southern drive made it impossible to ignore race. Under the leadership of Lucy Mason, the NCL and several of its branches would pursue a program that was as antiracist as any white organization offered at the time. Mason's successor Mary Dublin would focus less on the South, but, influenced by the race egalitarianism of the Popular Front era and appalled by Nazi racial views, she too would link labor and race justice. The league battled against race discrimination in occupations that were within the scope of its bills. As new things began to seem possible during the New Deal, the NCL called for including domestic and agricultural workers in labor laws and social security programs, but with little success.[76]

Political Parties and Philosophies

The political affiliations and ideologies of league activists reflected subtly gendered ideas about partisan politics and the state. At first glance, the attitude of NCL women activists in the 1930s toward political parties seems contradictory. On the one hand, some league women had strong ties to the Democratic Party; on the other hand, many of them still thought of party politics as a men's game, and a dirty one at that. League activists reconciled this tension by viewing themselves as building a social democratic state, not playing partisan politics.

In the presuffrage era, many league women thought of themselves as nonpartisan. Virtually all of them had been active suffragists, and one potent argument of the woman suffrage movement had been that women deserved the vote because they were above the self-promotion and corruption of party politics.[77] After 1920 the National American Woman Suffrage Association, the largest suffrage organization, became the League of Women Voters (LWV), which sustained a nonpartisan, educate-them-on-the-issues approach. In the 1920s and 1930s many former suffragists did pursue opportunities within political parties, but the idea lingered that women worked for the greater good while men worked for themselves. In 1934 one league veteran warned against getting into "dirty state politics, which unfortunately, even though we dabble in, we can't control; we are just not slimy enough."[78] League activists implied that women supported individuals who were on the right side of specific public issues, whereas men sought to advance their own careers through blind party loyalty. They also felt a need to translate their values into a language that male politicians could understand. "Do put over with your men leaders that the very best way to carry a close state is by giving a good administration," Molly Dewson told New Jersey congresswoman Mary Norton, urging her to select a labor commissioner based on qualifications rather than party service.[79]

League women came from a political culture that held that women were, or ought to be, less selfish than men. This belief had the power to shape reality, for a time producing some female politicians and bureaucrats who were more self-effacing and issue-oriented than their male counterparts. Molly Dewson opposed the choice of Emma Guffey Miller for a position with the Democratic Party Women's Division because Miller would "reduce the women from active workers for the New Deal to a bunch of schemers for personal advancement in which none of our type are interested." In describing her own role in an important cabinet appointment, Clara Beyer admitted that she had been "a conniver . . . but not for myself." These women did not see themselves as engaging in turf wars or playing politics, even as they created patronage networks of their own in government agencies and political parties. They saw their own motives as more altruistic than those of the "old boys' network." There often was a grain of truth to this assumption. NCL women did not seek or promote others for positions unless they had top credentials for the post. Most NCL members' expertise grew out of an intense commitment to social justice. However, as increasing numbers of women entered party politics and government, it would become clear that men had no monopoly on cronyism and self-promotion.[80]

The league forged ties to the Democratic Party in New York in the 1920s, where league leaders such as Frances Perkins and Molly Dewson played key roles in the political fortunes of Governor Al Smith and his successor, Franklin Roosevelt. In New York, Smith and Roosevelt backed the league agenda and other policies that foreshadowed the New Deal. Dewson and Perkins were close to Eleanor Roosevelt, herself an officer of the New York

Frances Perkins and Franklin D. Roosevelt (1943). (Corbis/Bettmann-UPI)

league. After FDR won the presidential election in 1932, he appointed Frances Perkins as secretary of labor, making her the first woman cabinet member. Dewson became head of the Women's Division of the Democratic Party, which she turned into a potent educational and campaign force for Roosevelt. Several other league women were Democratic Party workers.[81] A few league activists were Republicans, but general secretary Mary Dublin was less than straightforward when she told a House committee in 1939 that the league was "absolutely nonpolitical. We have I think as many Republican as Democratic members."[82]

Many league activists who voted for Franklin Roosevelt hoped to push him leftward on the political spectrum. The Democratic umbrella covered a range of views in the 1930s. The league's Elinore Herrick was in 1936 the campaign manager for the fledgling American Labor Party, which New York labor leaders founded in order to give socialists a comfortable vehicle for voting for Roosevelt.[83] Some NCL leaders called their vision "industrial democracy."[84] Several league officers participated in left-liberal coalitions that had some Communist members, such as the League of Women Shoppers and the Southern Conference for Human Welfare. A number of league women were prominent in planning-oriented groups such as the

Taylor Society (which had moved leftward in the 1920s), the Social Policy Committee, the National Policy Committee, and later the National Resources Planning Board (NRPB).[85] Whatever they called themselves, NCL leaders broadly favored government measures to tame the selfish excesses — competitive or monopolistic — of employers under capitalism.

In Florence Kelley's view, the Depression was the result of "our past planless conduct of industry."[86] During and after the 1930s, NCL thinkers argued that government economic planning was needed to stabilize production and employment. They expected that labor and consumer participation would make this a democratic, "bottom-up" form of planning. In the 1930s the league took a newly aggressive stance in promoting labor's right to organize. Some league members also advocated state control of the power, transportation, and communication industries, and of consumer necessities such as milk. In addition to high national labor standards, the NCL favored broad social insurance policies and permanent public works and housing programs. Many of these policies were understood to be of particular importance to women.[87] A few league leaders were more tentative in their support for social democracy, including the aforementioned Florence Whitney, as well as Nicholas Kelley, who reportedly supported the Fair Labor Standards Act but was "less intensely committed to our wider range of issues." These members frustrated the rest of the league's activist core.[88] Many NCL leaders eventually would be disappointed with the results of the New Deal, but in the early 1930s they enthusiastically supported FDR as their best hope for a social democratic state, in which they assumed labor and consumer representatives (prominently including women) would wield real power.

Reform Networks

The National Consumers' League's ambiguous status as a women's organization, but not only a women's organization, positioned it to draw support from an extensive network of mainstream women's institutions, in addition to the circle of legal experts and social scientists of both sexes interested in labor legislation. By the 1930s the major women's organizations were more cautious than before, and they gave league bills less support. However, labor movement allies gained strength, and league activists inside and outside of government enjoyed new influence.

The NCL cooperated in pursuit of common objectives with the National Child Labor Committee (NCLC), the American Association for Labor Legislation (AALL), and, after 1927, the American Association for Old Age Security (AAOAS). The memberships and officers of these groups overlapped significantly. In the Progressive Era, Florence Kelley was the key link among these groups and served as mentor to many of their leaders. Men headed the NCLC, whose southern contingent sometimes curbed the group's program, particularly with regard to national measures.[89] The AALL, founded in 1906, was run by John B. Andrews and Irene Osgood Andrews, two former students of John Commons. Its fields were social insurance and workplace health and safety. With the exception of Irene Andrews, after the early years the AALL's most active leaders were academic men.[90]

The overlap among reform organizations created the potential for rivalry as well as for cooperation. However, the male-led groups were less interested in wage-hour regulation and were content to let the NCL be the uncontested expert in that niche. Early on, the fields of working conditions, wages, and hours for women, on one hand, and child labor, on the other, were "formally declared to be the province of the National Consumers' League and NCLC, respectively."[91] Although the NCL once worked extensively on child labor with the NCLC, in the 1930s the league concentrated on adult labor standards, reasoning that the economic crisis provided new opportunities on that more controversial front.[92]

Liberal lawyers also were part of the NCL's wider community of policy intellectuals. NCL leaders enlisted the services of some of the nation's most prominent lawyers, many of them from Harvard Law School. These included Louis Brandeis, Roscoe Pound, Felix Frankfurter, and later Benjamin Cohen and Dean Acheson. The older members of this group led the charge against legal formalism in the Progressive Era, and most were associated with the "constitutional revolution" of the New Deal. The legal experts upon whom the NCL relied did not always comprehend or share the league's feminist vision, but their talents were indispensable to the league's drafting and litigating victories.[93]

In the Progressive Era the designation of wage and hour legislation as "for women and children" not only freed the NCL from challenges to its leadership by male-dominated reform groups, it strengthened the league's appeal to a potentially enormous audience of organized white middle-class women. The call for ethical consumption was even more persuasive when it could be expressed in terms that imagined a cross-class sisterhood. Women's groups such as the General Federation of Women's Clubs (GFWC), the National Congress of Mothers, the Women's Christian Temperance Union, and the Young Women's Christian Association (YWCA) could mobilize major campaigns. These organizations commanded huge memberships and, even without the vote, significant political influence.[94] Most of these groups did not endorse the wider political goals of the Consumers'

League. They generally supported minimum wage laws less enthusiastically than child labor laws, and in hostile climates such as the South, they sometimes would not commit even on child labor bills. NCL activists tried to galvanize the large women's organizations through speaking tours and by founding "committees on industry" within the larger groups. Imperfect as it was, this cooperation between the NCL and broad-based women's groups underlay the success of many legislative drives.[95]

In the 1930s mainstream women's organizations would provide less support for league bills than they had earlier, because they had less muscle and less nerve. In the triumphant afterglow of the Nineteenth Amendment's ratification, a coalition of white women's groups had won significant victories, notably the passage of the 1921 Sheppard-Towner Maternity and Infancy Act. Florence Kelley acknowledged the powerful ties among women's organizations when she commented that they had "more interlocking Directorates than business." However, external and internal pressures soon began to weaken organized women's political voice. Employer-backed "patriotic" groups charged supporters of women's labor laws with "un-Americanism." In 1923 antipacifist army officials created and circulated the infamous "Spider-Web Chart," a diagram that purportedly linked the major women's organizations to Moscow; it cited Kelley's remark about interlocking directorates as proof of conspiracy by a pink sisterhood.[96] Antifeminists, alarmed by signs of female voting power such as the prohibition amendment and the Sheppard-Towner Act, assailed the very idea of a "woman bloc" in politics. They accused women's groups of fostering antagonistic separatism between the sexes, even in the same breath as they charged them with trying to erase sex distinctions. On top of these reactions against female voting, broad economic and cultural changes were challenging the rationale for and appeal of separate women's institutions. A growing proportion of women entered the paid workforce, and new norms of heterosocial leisure made gender-segregated institutions seem old-fashioned, even "unnatural." Finally, internal divisions weakened the women's lobby after the unifying goal of enfranchisement was won. In the late 1920s Congress's refusal to renew the Sheppard-Towner Act signaled the declining influence of the female reform coalition. As a result of all these changes, many women's organizations shrank during the 1920s. They also grew more wary of drawing fire.[97]

Although the biggest women's groups backed away from labor and welfare measures, a mostly female labor standards network survived, to flourish again in the New Deal years. The NCL remained the focal point for this group, with crucial support from the Women's Trade Union League (WTUL) and from women in government labor agencies.[98] The WTUL, founded in 1903 by settlement house residents, female trade unionists, and wealthy supporters, had much in common with the Consumers' League. Each group believed that women wage earners needed both trade unions and wage-hour legislation, which they asserted were complementary rather than competing tactics. The WTUL specialized in organizing women workers, and the NCL took the lead on legislative campaigns. In some places, separating the activities of the two groups is difficult for the interwar years.[99] The WTUL enjoyed major organizing successes in the 1910s and a few small but important ones in the 1930s. By the 1930s, however, it faced even greater budget and recruiting difficulties than the NCL. Women's clubs were less likely to support the WTUL than the NCL, and it had strongholds only in New York and Chicago, whereas the Consumers' League had more than a dozen reasonably healthy branches. Franklin Roosevelt's administration brought new opportunities to the WTUL, most notably to its leader Rose Schneiderman, who was appointed to the Labor Advisory Board of the National Recovery Administration in 1933. But the legal and administrative expertise of the Consumers' League positioned it especially well for the battles of the New Deal. When the NCL joined forces with workers in the 1930s, they were as likely to be CIO members as WTUL members.[100]

Increasingly important to the NCL network in the 1930s were women in government labor departments. The Consumers' League had a long record of successfully lobbying for new agencies and then having its members appointed to them. This was true of many state labor departments, beginning with Florence Kelley's factory inspection work in Illinois and extending to departments or departmental divisions in dozens of states. At the federal level, agitation by the league and allied groups had yielded the Children's Bureau in 1912, the Women's Bureau in 1920, and the Division of Labor Standards in 1934, all within the Department of Labor. NCL members were a strong presence in all these divisions. (Of course, FDR's appointment of Frances Perkins as secretary of labor also enhanced the NCL's influence in that department.)[101] League members moved easily between government and league work, especially during the 1930s. The fact that some league activists wore many hats required a certain discretion and could also be a source of amusement, as when women who were old friends addressed each other on official letterhead with mock formality.[102] However, league leaders consciously preserved the organization's autonomy from the government. Even as some members enjoyed increased opportunities in government during the early New Deal, NCL activists reminded one another that their allies would not be in office forever, and that it was essential for the league to remain an independent watchdog over labor standards policy.[103] In the long run, the development of state and federal labor standards bureaucracies would have mixed implications for the National Consumers' League. The process of building these agencies increased the league's importance during the 1930s, but eventually the labor departments changed the scope of NCL activities in ways that would diminish the organization's vitality.

During the New Deal, the Consumers' League would decisively shape state and national labor standards policy, just as it had in earlier decades. However, in the 1930s different arguments, methods, and allies would come to the fore. The NCL was a smaller, poorer organization by the 1930s. More than ever it depended on the energy of small clusters of brilliant individuals in cities around the nation. Ethical consumption would become a political strategy that could be effected by small numbers of league members acting as representatives of the consumer, rather than a tool for mobilizing masses of women shoppers. Underconsumptionist arguments would bolster the league's call for a stronger redistributive, regulatory state. A core of league activists would build on Florence Kelley's vision, broadening their focus to include the South and black civil rights. Heartened by the growth of organized labor and the Left, the league would back the Democratic Party, hoping it would be midwife to a social democratic state. The NCL's support from ordinary middle-class women contracted after the First World War, but the New Deal would provide new opportunities for progressive experts and trade unionists, including many women; these groups became increasingly important allies for the NCL. Lastly, the league would retain a feminist commitment to wage-earning women and to women's voice in policy making, but it would have difficulty articulating its feminism publicly. To understand why, it is necessary to examine the history of the sex-based strategy and the league's conflict with the National Woman's Party.

chapter 2

Toward Feminist
Social Democracy

The Entering
Wedge Strategy

For several decades after the First World War, one of the most vociferous foes of the Consumers' League was another women's organization. In the early 1920s opposition to the principle of women-only labor laws crystallized in the National Woman's Party (NWP). Formerly a suffrage group, the Woman's Party decided that an equal rights amendment to the Constitution was its next priority. Because an ERA would have invalidated women-only labor legislation, virtually every member of the NCL and its network opposed the amendment through the New Deal years and beyond. By the end of the 1930s both sides would be incredulous that the battle boiled on. Each accused the other of opposition out of pure habit. One participant characterized the controversy as "a perennial headache consuming time, energy, paper . . . and much language."[1] Many scholars might sympathize with her assessment. But this protracted conflict was not just an "irrelevant wrangle," dragged out by personal rivalries or ossified thinking. Nor was it about whether women and men were ultimately alike or essentially different.[2] Because this bitter postsuffrage split among women's organizations affected the fortunes of labor regulation and of feminism for many decades, a fresh look at it is in order.

In creating the sex-based strategy, and defending it from the Woman's Party, the Consumers' League sought to use the fact that women workers experienced greater exploitation than men as the basis for legislation that would be an "entering wedge" for broadening governmental jurisdiction over the welfare of all workers. Although the league was concerned about all workers, its program had a feminist component. The NCL documented and tried to change the fact that most women wage earners worked for lower wages, and often for longer hours, than men. According to the NCL, raising women's wages and shortening their hours would give women a measure of economic security and lighten the "double burden" of paid and unpaid labor. These changes would expand women's collective and individual opportunities, making it easier for them to organize into unions, for example, or to seek higher education. Apparently agreeing with the league's analysis, most wage-earning women who publicly expressed an opinion on the matter favored hours laws and minimum wage laws, whether they applied to all workers or to women alone.

The Woman's Party assessed the effects of sex-based labor laws very differently. Furthermore, in its attack on the Consumers' League strategy, it used the language of liberal individualism and forged alliances with opponents of a regulatory state. Along with conservative employers, these opponents included a handful of antistatist working women. In linking "feminism" with the defense of laissez-faire capitalism, the Woman's Party not only hindered the development of labor regulations, it weakened the position of feminists within liberal and left movements.[3]

Early Sex-Based Legislation

The sex-based strategy for winning government regulation of labor standards had its roots in the textile factories of nineteenth-century Massachusetts. After defeating a bill to limit the hours of all workers to ten per day, the Massachusetts legislature in 1874 passed a ten-hour bill that covered only women and minors. The impetus for a shorter working day had come from workers themselves, originally without reference to sex. Workers argued that the long days that had been tolerable on farms and in preindustrial workplaces were too taxing in factories. Skilled workers negotiated for shorter hours through trade unions, and by the 1890s groups such as builders, cigar makers, and machinists worked fifty-hour weeks. By contrast, the work week in the textile, laundry, and garment industries, which all employed large numbers of women, averaged between sixty and sixty-five hours. Workers in these less organized industries sought legislative protection. Massachusetts textile workers promoted the women-only bill in 1874 on the understanding that it would in practice shorten men's hours as well, because of the interdependence of men's and women's mill work. As in England, sex-based legislation was intended to reduce all workers' hours.[4]

Expansion of maximum hours legislation to men in nonhazardous occupations proved difficult. In 1898 the U.S. Supreme Court upheld a Utah eight-hour law for miners. However, in the *Lochner v. New York* decision in 1905, the Court struck down a ten-hour law for (male) bakers. The Court's majority found that the hours statute interfered with the bakers' right to contract freely, or "liberty of contract." The wording of the *Lochner* ruling did provide an opening to Florence Kelley's band of reformers by inviting proof of a connection between the general welfare and hours worked. Having gone for "the whole loaf" — protection of men and women workers — and lost, labor standards reformers decided to go for half a loaf. They won in 1908, when the Supreme Court unanimously sustained Oregon's ten-hour law for women in *Muller v. Oregon*.[5] This ruling was the cornerstone for the edifice of women-only labor laws that the Consumers' League and its allies constructed over the next thirty years.

Two aspects of the political and legal climate shaped the sex-based strategy of labor reform with which the Consumers' League was so closely identified in 1908 and thereafter. One was the indifference of American labor leaders to organizing women and to legislative methods of raising labor standards. The other was the clash in the legal arena between advocates of "legal formalism" and the architects of a new "sociological jurisprudence."

Organized Labor and Labor Legislation

At the turn of the century, American labor leaders were more skeptical of state regulation than their counterparts in other industrial countries. Speaking for skilled, predominantly native-born white men, American Federation of Labor (AFL) leader Samuel Gompers opposed government intervention in employer-labor relations, arguing that collective bargaining, not legislation, was the best way to raise labor standards. This "voluntarism" reflected suspicion that government-set standards would undercut better ones established through collective bargaining and also would undermine union recruiting efforts. Although there was some divergence of opinion among AFL unions and between the national and state leadership on whether to support hours laws for men, Gompers's stance prevailed.[6] However, the AFL did support hours laws for women. This position reflected working men's self-interested assumption that women were in the workforce only temporarily and hence were not organizable. In this view, legislation for women was an acceptable substitute that relieved unions of the expense of organizing women.[7]

Strongly committed to the principle of organizing women, NCL leaders did not accept male labor leaders' claim that women did not make good union members. They did believe that interrelated characteristics of the female workforce — including youth, low skill levels, and high turnover — meant that women were concentrated in hard-to-organize occupations. However, the league blamed women's low level of organization more on union leaders than on women. "Legislation is women's only hope of shorter hours as men control the unions and give scant attention to organizing women," observed one league activist in 1931.[8]

The AFL was even less enthusiastic about minimum wage regulation than it was about hours laws. Again, its opposition was stronger to bills that included men. Insisting that any legislated minimum would in effect become the maximum wage, labor leaders opposed wage laws for all workers on principle. In practice they rarely bothered to oppose women-only minimum wage bills. Although Florence Kelley initially had hoped to regulate the wages of all "sweated" workers, along the lines of Britain's 1909 legislation, she settled for the sex-based approach that was proving successful for hours regulation. Noting that English and Australian trade unionists were less suspicious of wage regulation, Kelley grumbled that wage-earning women in the United States should not have to wait "alone in the whole industrial world" while "slow and reactionary" American labor leaders caught up.[9] Molly Dewson expressed much the same view in 1934, when she explained wryly that the NCL's objective was "the prevention of the exploitation of the labor of women and children. We should have included men if they had not preferred to fight their own battles through the Federation of Labor."[10] Organized labor's lack of support for labor standards laws deprived the league of its most likely ally in the political battle with employers and in the legal battle in the courts. Not until the late 1930s would some powerful labor leaders become a force on behalf of wage and hour legislation that included men.

Labor Regulation and the Constitution

The NCL's advocacy of protective labor legislation placed it on the cutting edge of the Progressive Era challenge to legal formalism, as embodied in the "liberty of contract" doctrine. In the *Muller v. Oregon* case (1908), the NCL orchestrated the preparation of the successful brief that became a landmark of legal history. Florence Kelley and NCL research director Josephine Goldmark persuaded Goldmark's brother-in-law, the prominent Boston lawyer Louis Brandeis, to appear as counsel for the Oregon Industrial

Commission. Working at a phenomenal pace, Goldmark amassed over one hundred pages of evidence on the effects of long hours. The Goldmark-Brandeis partnership won a series of court cases in the years before Brandeis was appointed to the Supreme Court in 1916.[11]

The Brandeis brief, which could as well have been called the "Consumers' League brief," was the weapon of those who sought to broaden the basis of judicial decisions to include sociological data — practical knowledge gleaned in "the world's experience" — as well as legal precedent and theory. More than hours and wage regulation was at stake. The question was whether judges were "objective discoverers of the law," where law was a static body apart from politics, or whether judges were creators of law, where law responded to social needs as expressed by the will of the people. Under debate as well, therefore, was the proper balance of power between legislatures and the judiciary. This wider significance helps explain why the NCL attracted some of the great legal minds of its time.[12]

Because the Court had found regulation of men's hours unconstitutional in *Lochner v. New York* (1905), the league developed a range of arguments to suggest that women, even more than men, needed state protection. In the *Muller* brief, Josephine Goldmark asserted that long hours injured the health of all workers, but women's more than men's. She emphasized social, as well as biological, differences between the sexes. In addition to noting women's "special physical organization" (childbearing capacity) and lesser physical strength than men, she claimed that women's lesser bargaining power with employers (due to their exclusion from unions) made them especially vulnerable to exploitation. Further, Goldmark offered evidence that women suffered graver effects than men from long hours because women's unpaid domestic labor left them less time to sleep and relax than men. But Justice Brewer's opinion emphasized biological differences between the sexes, not the differences that flowed from social inequality: "That woman's physical structure and the performance of maternal functions place her at a disadvantage in the struggle for subsistence is obvious. . . . [C]ontinuance for a long time on her feet at work, repeating this from day to day, tends to injurious effects upon the body, and as healthy mothers are essential to vigorous offspring, the physical well-being of woman becomes an object of public interest and care in order to preserve the strength and vigor of the race."[13] Although the Court heard (or agreed with) only part of the NCL's message, the league considered the ruling a triumph because it set a precedent on which to build. Between 1908 and 1917 nineteen states passed their first women's hours laws, and twenty other states improved existing laws.

The league viewed maximum hours laws as just one piece of a whole system of labor regulations. The spread of hours laws gave new urgency to minimum wage laws, because reducing hours could cut workers' incomes. On the heels of the *Muller* decision, Florence Kelley and a handful of others started the American minimum wage movement. The first victory came in 1912 in Massachusetts, aided by a dramatic textile strike in Lawrence in which immigrant women were prominent. By 1917 twelve states had passed minimum wage laws for women. That year, a minimum wage test case orchestrated by the Consumers' League, *Stettler v. O'Hara,* ended inconclusively with a 4-4 Supreme Court decision. Unluckily for the minimum wage movement, league counsel Louis Brandeis, who in 1914 had argued the case for the Oregon Industrial Commission, was appointed to the Supreme Court in 1916 and therefore could not vote on the case. The Oregon court had sustained the law, so the tie vote by the U.S. Supreme Court let the law stand. However, no opinion was issued and no precedent was set. Had a full court sustained a women's minimum wage law before World War I, constitutional history and New Deal history might look quite different.[14]

In the years surrounding the war, the NCL tried to establish the constitutionality of new kinds of labor regulations, including sex-neutral hours laws and national child labor laws. In *Bunting v. Oregon* (1917), the NCL defended a ten-hour law for men using arguments based on *men's* physiological weakness. The NCL believed that all workers needed state protection from excessive hours and below-subsistence wages. However, the court's ruling only weakly affirmed regulation of men's hours.[15] In 1918 and 1922 the Supreme Court struck down two successive federal prohibitions on child labor. The NCL and the National Child Labor Committee had won each national child labor law over virulent opposition, particularly from southern textile mills. The judge who initiated the process that killed both child labor laws was from North Carolina, whose politicians fought the legislation most bitterly of all. These battles in the courts convinced NCL leaders that judges were not immune to political pressures and other biases.[16]

The Woman's Party Joins the Struggle between Legal Philosophies

Florence Kelley's opinion that judges were swayed by considerations other than objective legal principles was confirmed by *Adkins v. Children's Hospital*, which in 1923 overturned the Washington, D.C., minimum wage law for women. Seeking a more solid legal foundation for minimum wage regulation than *Stettler*, the NCL had succeeded in 1918 in having its model bill passed in the District of Columbia. The District's minimum wage board became a model of effective enforcement, with Consumers' League members Clara Mortenson Beyer and Elizabeth Brandeis as its chief staff.[17] The resulting test case again pitted the NCL and other advocates of sociological jurisprudence against defenders of the "liberty of contract" doctrine. This time, conservative lawyers were joined by a new voice, the National Woman's Party.

The Consumers' League brief for *Adkins*, written by Molly Dewson, argued that social factors, more than biological ones, put women at a disadvantage in the paid labor force. Dewson first tried to establish a connection between minimum wages and the "general welfare," amassing mountains of data that described a cycle of low wages, poor health, and a "descending spiral into the regions of destitution," all of which imposed costs on the community. To explain why the need for a minimum wage was gender-specific, the NCL brief argued that because women earned much less than men, often while supporting dependents, women's low wages particularly affected the general welfare. Because inequality of bargaining power had proven to be a successful justification for state interference with "liberty of contract," the league again argued that women had less leverage with employers than men because a smaller proportion of women enjoyed union protection. The brief urged that the state intervene to offset women's lesser bargaining power and to assure that women's pay reflected the value of their work.[18]

Not swayed by these feminist arguments in favor of women's labor laws, the National Woman's Party held that no circumstances justified different legal treatment of the sexes. In its emphasis on women's individual rights, the NWP view fit well with the reasoning of legal experts opposed to all labor regulation. The Woman's Party had not before been associated with a conservative political outlook. It was best known for its confrontational style during the latter years of the woman suffrage campaign, as exemplified by its picketing of the White House in 1917. During the First World War it attracted many socialists and pacifists who resented the National American Woman Suffrage Association's support of the war. At that point, Florence Kelley and other Consumers' League members belonged to the NWP. However, after 1920 the practices and program of the Woman's Party changed in ways that alienated many of its left-leaning activists. Faced with a large debt from the suffrage campaign, party leaders raised dues and curried the favor of its wealthiest supporters. In 1921 Beulah Amidon, an NWP organizer who became a Consumers' League mainstay, already feared that the party was becoming "a conservative, property-holding, upper-crust group" with whom she was "out of sympathy."[19] Now a small but dedicated group with a flair for publicity, the NWP decided to make an equal rights amendment its highest priority.

Because the ERA threatened sex-based labor laws, Florence Kelley and the Consumers' League became the foremost critics of the Woman's Party. Kelley argued that ending legal sex discrimination through one "blanket" measure was impossible and even dangerous to women. In her view, the courts' "perverted applications" of the Fourteenth Amendment illustrated the unpredictable effects of attempts to "put social and political equality into the Constitution." (Kelley referred to the courts' use of the Fourteenth Amendment to protect corporations more than its intended beneficiaries, former slaves.) Far better for women to use their newly acquired ballots to support "specific bills for specific ills" such as sex-discriminatory property laws or citizenship requirements.[20] NWP leader Alice Paul disagreed. At first Paul hoped to reconcile an equal rights amendment with women's labor laws, but she soon was persuaded that women-only labor laws hurt women. She drafted an amendment that would certainly, not just incidentally, eliminate sex-based labor laws.[21] Not one to hold her fire, Kelley responded by doing her best to discredit the ERA with progressive politicians and feminists. For decades the NCL, WTUL, Socialist Party, and other advocates of stronger public control over production opposed the ERA. They did not want to jeopardize women's labor laws in exchange for the uncertain rewards of an ERA.[22]

In *Adkins* in 1923, the Woman's Party equal rights drive served the purposes of lawyers and judges committed to repelling the NCL's attack on the "freedom of contract" doctrine. The NCL defense team, Molly Dewson and Felix Frankfurter, won an early victory in the case, but it was reversed after some highly irregular maneuvering on the part of the lawyer bringing suit, Challen Ellis. Ellis, who harbored a personal and philosophical animosity to Frankfurter, opposed the very principle of minimum wage. However, his argument, which quoted from NWP materials, implied that it was the woman-only aspect that constituted the chief objection to the law.[23] In the majority opinion for the final 5-3 decision against the law, Supreme Court Justice Sutherland argued that women no longer needed special protection, because they had the vote. At the same time, the opinion was hostile to all minimum wage legislation (for men or women), denying a connection between high wages and the general welfare. Before he joined the Supreme Court, Sutherland had advised Alice Paul on the drafting of an ERA. Ellis's and Sutherland's use of feminist arguments against the women's minimum wage law was disingenuous, since these men opposed all labor standards regulation, sex-based or not.[24]

Coming on the heels of the modestly encouraging *Stettler* ruling, the hostility to minimum wage of the *Adkins v. Children's Hospital* decision created shock waves whose effects resounded into the 1930s and beyond. Kelley

Nation Wide Conference

called by

National Consumers' League

on the

Minimum Wage Decision

of the Supreme Court of the United States

This decision affirms your constitutional right to starve

The NCL expresses its opinion of the *Adkins v. Children's Hospital* ruling (1923). The idea for the cartoon came from the league. (National Consumers' League Collection, LC)

called *Adkins* "a new 'Dred Scott' decision," one that gave unorganized, unskilled women wage earners "the constitutional right to starve." (After the ruling, District of Columbia department stores and hotels promptly cut women's wages by 50 percent.) Test cases in three other states only confirmed the *Adkins* precedent, suspending the drive for new minimum wage laws and making the enforcement of surviving laws problematic.[25] This was exactly what the Woman's Party had hoped for. Its leaders later called the *Adkins* decision the "*Magna Charta* [*sic*] of women's rights."[26] The minimum wage movement would show few signs of life until Franklin Delano Roosevelt became governor of New York in 1928.[27]

Lightning Rod for Conflict: Night Work Restrictions

With hours laws for women upheld and minimum wage laws for women struck down, women's night work laws became the next battleground. In 1924 the same Supreme Court justices who had ruled in *Adkins* that the

Nineteenth Amendment eliminated the rationale for separate treatment of the sexes upheld a New York statute that prohibited women's employment in restaurants between ten at night and six in the morning. The majority opinion in this case, *Radice v. New York*, stated that "night work so seriously affected the health of women, so threatened and impaired their peculiar and natural functions, and so exposed them to the dangers and menaces incident to night life that the State felt impelled" to restrict their night work.[28] To understand the elation of the Consumers' League at this ruling one must consider the context. The new law affected only a small number of women, but with several types of laws recently struck down, the legitimacy of all labor regulation was at stake. According to the NCL, the ruling's real significance was "the reaffirmation by the highest judicial authority of *the power of the State to forbid contracts* under which women of any age are to work long hours, or during work periods *which experience shows to be harmful*."[29] Florence Kelley's determination to salvage some remnant of the *Muller* precedent, and to check the pendulum swing back to legal formalism and "liberty of contract," led her to downplay the costs that night work restrictions imposed on some women.

Laws restricting night work initially developed in response to manufacturers' evasion of maximum hours laws through manipulation of second-shift schedules. Night work laws thus were first intended to prevent excessive hours resulting from working all day and into the evening. Later, as various industries sought to use machinery around the clock, the problem of night work was perceived not only as part of the long hours problem but as a question of whether workers should work an all-night second or third shift. Prevailing scientific wisdom held that daytime sleep was of lower quality than nighttime sleep. Like hours laws, night work laws ostensibly were for women only, but for some industries they curtailed men's night work as well.[30] The first U.S. night work law was passed in Massachusetts in 1890 on the initiative of textile workers who wanted the mills to close from 10 P.M. to 6 A.M. A women's night work law was struck down in New York in 1907, but the New York Court of Appeals sustained a new night work law for women in 1915. The Consumers' League was active in the passage of this law and offered a weighty brief in its court defense. In stressing the special risks of night work to women's health, the NCL emphasized women's "double burden" and greater difficulty than men in securing uninterrupted sleep during the day, rather than their biological weakness. It was a broadened version of this New York law that the Supreme Court upheld in 1924.[31]

Night work laws never passed in as many states or affected nearly as many workers as hours laws, but they became the flashpoint of controversy over sex-based legislation.[32] Night work laws were more likely than other types of law to be advocated in moralistic terms that set a double standard for men and women. Florence Kelley wrote in 1920 that night work left exhausted young women vulnerable to foremen's advances and to attack or seduction on their way home. In this respect, Kelley shared nineteenth-century feminists' emphasis on the dangers, rather than the pleasures, of sexual activity for women. Changing men's behavior probably seemed less feasible to Kelley than preventing women from working at night. But Kelley's argument that night work required women to be on the streets at "unsuitable hours" fit easily with perspectives that were less feminist and more coercive.[33]

More than hours or minimum wage laws, night work laws had the potential to block women's access to higher-paying jobs, such as printing, streetcar conducting, and waitressing during high tip hours. Unionized men sometimes supported women-only night work legislation to reduce competition from women, infuriating working women as well as elite feminists.[34] In 1928 the U.S. Women's Bureau, which supported women's labor laws, reported its finding that night work laws restricted some women's employment options. This study found that sex-specific laws handicapped about 2 percent of women workers affected by them, and that night workers such as waitresses comprised the majority of those adversely affected. The Women's Bureau tried to soften this admission by observing that few after-theater (high tip) restaurants hired women as waiters, and that establishments that did employ women after 10 P.M. rarely paid well. This denied waitresses the opportunity to assess these circumstances themselves. It also ignored the effect that a law could have in reinforcing a preexisting pattern of preferential access for men to desirable jobs.[35] Determined to defend the legal principle of government regulation of labor standards, which it expected eventually would extend to men as well as women, into the 1930s the Consumers' League and its allies viewed the lost opportunities of a small number of night-working women as an unfortunate but unavoidable sacrifice for a greater good.

Working Women and Protective Legislation

The controversy over sex-based labor legislation usually is portrayed as a conflict between affluent women in which the voices of wage-earning women themselves were silent or not heard.[36] Working women never organized en masse for or against protective labor laws, but they did agitate on both sides of the issue, working with the WTUL or NCL on one hand, and with the NWP on the other. Wage-earning women appeared at legislative hearings, circulated petitions, and sent letters to elected officials. They shared personal anecdotes of the workplace at NCL and NWP conferences.[37]

The contest for working women's support of protective legislation did not take place on neutral, even terrain. Most employers opposed hours and wage regulations. The working women who opposed labor standards bills generally were on the same side as their own employers. By contrast, women who agitated for a league bill often were aligning themselves against their employers and risking their jobs. Florence Kelley believed working women's public demonstration of support was inhibited by lack of time and money, as well as by their fear of dismissal. "It is precisely their defenseless poverty that silences them," she observed.[38]

Whether women workers supported or opposed women-only labor laws had less to do with their gender ideology—their views on the proper roles of women and men—than with their assessment of whether they stood to benefit by government regulation of the workplace. Women wage earners who opposed women-only bills were in occupations or personal circumstances that predisposed them to an "anti-regulationist" stance. They usually opposed the very principle of regulation, not just the women-only aspect of it. Often they were women trying to break into male-dominated trades, such as printing and streetcar conducting. Almost all of these women mobilized specifically to oppose night work laws. Others were textile workers in places like Wisconsin and Rhode Island, whose employers were threatening to migrate southward for cheaper labor. Still others were desperate piece workers—paid by the piece rather than by the hour—who needed income so badly that they feared any attempt (women-only or sex-neutral) to reduce hours. They scoffed at the idea that women needed "protection," but they did not think men needed protection either. These workers believed that hours, night work, and wage laws—whether for women only or for both sexes—would put them at a competitive disadvantage with other workers. Mary Murray, head of the NWP Industrial Council in New York, was a transit worker who actually opposed equal wages for men and women, on the ground that women would be dismissed if they earned as much as men.[39]

The women workers who supported protective labor laws seem to have had higher hopes for collective approaches to improving their labor standards than the working women who opposed league bills. Many of them worked in industries that employed large numbers of women in heavily sex-typed occupations, so they felt less direct competition from men. Others worked in service occupations, in which employers could hardly threaten to migrate to another state. Many working women came to the protective legislation cause through YWCA industrial clubs and through the Summer

Schools for Women Workers, which flourished in the 1920s and 1930s as an outgrowth of the labor education movement. In these venues women workers practiced their writing and public speaking skills and studied topics such as labor history and political economy.[40] This background may have made them receptive to the NCL goal of setting limits on the competition that pitted workers against each other, driving them to work longer hours for lower wages. The workers who most enthusiastically supported protective labor laws often were members of the WTUL, the International Ladies' Garment Workers' Union (ILGWU), or the Amalgamated Clothing Workers of America (ACWA). From the Progressive Era into the 1930s, female trade unionists in these groups argued that women's labor laws helped women in the workplace far more than they hurt them, not least by facilitating unionization.[41]

The National Woman's Party claimed that women workers who favored sex-based laws were the dupes of male trade unionists who wanted women out of the workforce. Trade unions did discriminate against women, most egregiously by persuading legislatures to prohibit them from certain occupations.[42] However, unions rarely devoted enough resources to women's labor laws to become a leading force in their enactment. If the chief intent, or effect, of such laws was to block women's access to certain jobs, the AFL's support might have been less tepid, and women trade unionists would not have been so supportive.[43]

Activists for the WTUL and NCL were not uncritical of trade unions, but they believed that working women needed to make common cause with working men against the power of employers.[44] These women's critique of sexism was embedded in, and sometimes overshadowed by, their critique of class domination. In NCL and WTUL anecdotes of female oppression, exploitative employers were the foremost villains, not working men. This was notwithstanding labor reformers' exasperation with the indifference of the American Federation of Labor toward the worst-off workers. Often NCL leaders could barely contain their frustration with leading labor men. Florence Kelley referred to Samuel Gompers as "that aged Dodo." She warned that eliminating women's labor laws would bring a "new subjection of wage-earning women to wage-earning men."[45] Later, in response to an AFL leader's tirade on the ineffectiveness of labor laws, Molly Dewson asked, "But what are you going to do about industries where labor has not been organized, particularly the big women's industries? Haven't we got to do it this way until you organize them?"[46] Despite their annoyance with some union leaders, the NCL and WTUL maintained a united front with the labor movement, soliciting its support for their bills and defending workers' right to organize. By contrast, the National Woman's Party implied that working women's problems were created primarily by their "male competitors," not by employers. After the AFL came out against the Equal Rights Amendment in 1922, the Woman's Party usually characterized the labor movement as a hindrance to working women rather than a help.

Postsuffrage Feminism I: Common Ground

The disagreement between the Consumers' League and the Woman's Party did not stem from competing ideas about gender differences and gender roles. Former suffragists all, they believed not only in women's political equality but also in their right to economic and sexual independence. At the same time, in both organizations there were activists who believed that women tended to be more cooperative and less selfish than men.[47]

During the interwar years NCL activists took an increasingly positive view of women's wage-earning. They defended women's right to pursue whatever educational or employment paths they chose. Lucy Mason, along with a host of younger league women, insisted that both justice and the welfare of society required that educational, economic, and political opportunities be open to all without discrimination by sex. Mason observed that "the human family has never been able to subsist on the labor of men only." Industry needed women workers, she added, and women workers needed their wages. Mason also understood that wage-earning could be liberating for women, and not just an evil necessity: "The work of women in industry must be made truly an opportunity to develop to the fullest of their powers as workers, both for their own happiness and for the service of society. To this end they must have adequate schooling before entrance into industry, and be free to choose their occupations, to secure training for them, to enlarge their opportunities as their experience grows, to receive fair compensation, and to work under safe and wholesome conditions."[48]

The NCL believed hours and wage laws would increase women's independence, not reinforce their dependence on male breadwinners. Shorter hours and higher wages would put a woman in a better position to advance her own interests — whether through joining unions, taking classes, having more leverage with her husband, or simply enjoying a higher standard of living — rather than spending every ounce of energy on the struggle to survive. In the case of minimum wage laws, the league worked to set minima as high as possible and rejected the idea that women could be paid low wages because they were supported in part by men. In the *Adkins* brief and later, NCL writers argued that women supported not only themselves but dependents as well. The NCL also strove to broaden the definition of minimal needs to include recreation and education. Although the NCL did not win minimum wage levels that enabled a woman to support dependents, its efforts did raise wages for the lowest-paid workers covered by the laws.[49]

Thus league thinkers did not disapprove of women's wage-earning, nor did they expect or hope that social policy would eliminate the need for it. NCL attitudes toward working *mothers* were more complicated, however. League activists wanted it to be possible for mothers with young children not to *need* to earn wages. They hoped that one day all mothers with young children would have the option of being supported by well-paid male breadwinners or by generous mothers' pensions. The league's wider program sought to achieve this ideal by promoting union rights, minimum wages for men, and mothers' pensions. In the 1910s Florence Kelley's resentment of the circumstances that forced poor mothers to shoulder a heavy burden of low-paid and unpaid labor led her into some unfortunate positions. She opposed cash maternity benefits and day nurseries because she feared they would cut off political support for mothers' pensions and higher wages for working men.[50] By the 1930s younger NCL activists were less equivocal toward wage-earning by mothers. They favored publicly funded day care, and they tried to win working mothers the best working conditions and highest wages possible. During the Depression, when employment discrimination against married women increased, league leaders were careful to explain that they supported women's "right to work, single or married" but believed women should not be "driven to work by poverty when home and children need care." The NCL did not propose that fathers assume a primary (or equally shared) role in child rearing. But its leaders never suggested that young mothers should be legislated out of the workforce. The Consumers' League was concerned with reforming the conditions under which women were employed, not women's practice of motherhood.[51]

The NCL's failure to criticize the sexual division of labor that exempted men from housework and child care responsibilities was a serious limitation of its feminism. However, in the interwar decades no women's organization sustained a public critique of the presumption that unpaid "reproductive labor" was women's obligation. Women's groups on both sides of the ERA question did defend married women workers from popular portrayals of them as "enemies of society" who were "disrupting the home" and competing with men at work. But, increasingly defensive in the face of a backlash against the perceived influence of feminism, both camps favored justifications of married women's work that skirted the issue of the household division of labor.[52] In the 1920s a few feminists theorized about ways of rewarding or adjusting women's unpaid obligations. However, even the

Woman's Party did not develop any position or proposals on housework. Its journal *Equal Rights* discussed the issue of child care infrequently, and when it did, it stopped short of suggesting fathers could help.[53] The NWP was single-mindedly focused on passing the ERA, which did not in any direct way address the division of labor at home. Indeed, the Woman's Party itself sometimes reinforced assumptions about women's maternal and domestic orientation. One party activist argued that women needed the option of working long hours in order to feed their children. Another NWP leader argued that women "normally" (i.e., in the absence of sex-based labor laws) would be preferred for restaurant jobs because of "their neatness, cleanliness, and general aptitude for that work."[54]

In sum, in their gender ideologies the NCL and the NWP for the most part stood on common ground. On one hand, both groups asserted women's rights to participate in the full range of human experience. On the other hand, both groups hesitated to question the assignment of unpaid labor to women and sometimes suggested that socialization produced distinct gender traits.

Postsuffrage Feminism II: Controversy

The NCL and the NWP both deplored women's inequality with men in the paid workforce. They disagreed on whether women-only labor laws were a step toward gender equality or a step away from it. Assessing the effects of these laws is a complicated task. The immediate impact on female workers varied with the type of law, occupation, and labor market conditions. The broader ideological repercussions of women-only laws are difficult to measure. The NWP emphasized the direct negative effects of such laws on the job opportunities of women. It also insisted that the assertion that women needed state protection more than men insulted all women. On the other side, the Consumers' League emphasized the benefits that shorter hours and higher minimum wages brought to most women protected by such legislation. Its leaders argued against treating women and men as identical at a moment when, for most women, the playing field with men was not level.

The Woman's Party exaggerated the immediate negative effects of women-only labor laws on women workers. It argued that such laws hampered women's ability to compete with men for jobs. If women's hours or wages were regulated, the reasoning went, employers would hire men instead of women, to avoid the regulations. The Woman's Party had to hunt far and wide to find cases of women who lost jobs as a result of sex-based laws. The persistent wage differential, combined with the resilience of occupational sex-typing, meant that men rarely were hired for the sorts of jobs that the laws most affected. This held true to a surprising degree even during the Depression. The Woman's Party predicted men would become desperate enough to take jobs for less than the female minimum wage, but this happened infrequently.[55] The NWP sometimes made the "female displacement" argument in antilabor terms, complaining that the (female) minimum set "such high wages," wages that were "too high" for unskilled labor.[56]

One great risk of the sex-based strategy, however, was that it could reinforce the occupational sex segregation of the paid labor force. Most women worked in a narrow range of "female" occupations. Women earned less than men (sometimes for longer hours) largely because they were in separate, low-paying occupations.[57] This segregation also inhibited women's organization into unions. Although women-only laws restricted the employment opportunities of only a few women already in the workforce — primarily by preventing them from working at night — those women were on the cutting edge of challenges to occupational sex segregation. They were the women trying to break into skilled, male-dominated trades. Protective laws may have deterred an unknown number of women from trying to enter "male" occupations.[58] The NCL was reluctant to concede that this was one cost of the sex-based strategy (although it did quietly phase out its drive for women-only night work laws after 1932). The league suggested weakly that the small minority of women who were hurt by such laws could lobby for exemptions. The league's more convincing answer to the fact that sex-based laws disadvantaged some women was that these laws were to be a stepping stone to sex-neutral ones.

As for the ideological effects of the sex-based strategy, many scholars agree with Woman's Party thinkers that, by classifying women as wards of the state, women-only labor laws sent a message that hurt all women, wage-earning and otherwise. The emphasis on women's greater need for protection than men, which judges interpreted as flowing solely from women's biological potential for motherhood, reinforced restrictive ideas about gender difference, and this was a second pitfall of the sex-based strategy. The Consumers' League marshaled international data to support its claim that there was little correlation between sex-based labor laws and lack of civil liberties for women. Lucy Mason observed that many of the places where women enjoyed the least equality had sex-neutral labor laws (Germany) or none (the U.S. South), and that, by contrast, sex-based labor policies often coexisted with strong protections of women's rights. Economic discrimination against women was not caused by sex-based labor laws, the NCL insisted. Rather, the laws developed in response to sex-specific exploitation.[59] The NCL was correct that women-only laws did not *cause* women's inequality, but it understated the potential of such laws to legitimize and perpetuate gender discrimination. However, the NCL viewed sex-based laws as an interim strategy. The Consumers' League was willing to risk the costs of sex-based treatment because those costs seemed justified by the dire immediate circumstances of many working women, and by the possibility that women's labor laws would be an entering wedge for building a feminist, social democratic state.

The Consumers' League believed the Woman's Party offered working women an abstract "theoretical equality" while obstructing progress toward substantive equality for women who faced disadvantages of class as well as of gender. The NWP program was fitted for an idealized labor market in which women, and workers in general, enjoyed boundless opportunity. While the NWP celebrated the accomplishments of extraordinary individuals like flyer Amelia Earhart and English Channel swimmer Gertrude Ederle, the Consumers' League pictured women stitching in dimly lit sweatshops, breathing lint in textile mills for sixty hours a week, or losing fingers while canning fruit or wringing wet laundry. The Consumers' League fashioned solutions aimed at the labor market as it actually was.[60] But the league was not accepting the workplace status quo as inevitable. It sought more than piecemeal relief for women workers. NCL thinkers believed that protective legislation would do more to make the labor market what it should be than the ERA would. The Consumers' League was willing to restrict the opportunities of some individual workers — women, for the time being — in order to win laws that would lay a national "floor" for labor standards. This floor would, the league hoped, reduce employers' ability to pit workers against workers of different regions, races, ages, or sexes, making unionization easier. The league hoped to use the state not only to set national wage-hour standards but also to curb employer practices such as night work, piecework, and homework, which lowered the labor standards of workers as a group.[61]

The NWP's attitude toward the state was ambivalent, and during the New Deal it became more negative. The Woman's Party program ended with giving individual women free rein to compete with individual men. In advocating the ERA, the party took an older, negative conception of liberty and asked that women be guaranteed the same liberties as men, namely, the freedom to enter employment contracts without state intervention. This meant, in effect, "freeing" women to compete with other workers (men, or women in other regions, for example) by working longer hours or for lower wages. The NWP claimed it did not object to labor laws as long as they were sex-neutral, but it cooperated behind the scenes with conservative judges and lawyers and with antiregulatory employers and workers. In 1923 and repeatedly in the 1930s the party formed alliances that blocked a more positive role for the state. The contrast between the priorities of the Consumers' League and those of the National Woman's Party emerged even more starkly when the sex-based approach became entangled with another state-building strategy, the league's drive to reform labor standards in the South.

chapter 3

A Subtle Program Come Down from the North?

The Consumers' League Develops a Southern Strategy

On March 12, 1929, in a rayon plant in Elizabethton, Tennessee, section leader Margaret Bowen was demoted after she asked for a raise from the $10.64 she received for a fifty-six-hour week. Over five hundred women walked out in support of Bowen. Soon more than 5,000 workers, 70 percent of them women, had left the local mills. The next month, in Gastonia, North Carolina, almost 2,000 employees of the Loray mills went on strike, demanding better pay and working conditions. One woman who had worked in a Gastonia mill since she was fourteen reported, "We worked thirteen hours a day, and we were so stretched out that lots of times we didn't stop for anything. Sometimes we took sandwiches to work, and ate them as we worked. Sometimes we didn't even get to eat them. If we couldn't keep our work up like they wanted us to, they would curse us and threaten to fire us." Hundreds more mill women struck in Marion, North Carolina, in July. They told a similar tale: "I work twelve hours and twenty minutes a day and I am completely worn out at stopping time. Men and women who work in the mill are weak and sallow looking, some of them just dragging along half dead and overworked until they don't know what it is to take a rest and feel good." The strike wave in southern textiles culminated the following year in a massive walkout in Danville, Virginia.[1]

Despite their militance and perseverance, the strikers were defeated everywhere, thanks to brutal resistance from employers and halfhearted support from national unions. Employers reneged on settlements, hired private guns, and brought in National Guardsmen to protect strikebreakers. Vigilante violence led to deaths on both sides. Those who killed workers were acquitted, while strikers received long sentences, often on shaky evidence. Women took places at the front of picket lines and parades, where they were clubbed, bayoneted, and jailed along with the men. Ella May Wiggins, a mother of nine who inspired Gastonia strikers with ballads like "The Mill Mother's Lament," was fatally shot, becoming the best-known martyr of the uprising of 1929. The strikers were keen to organize. Aided in places by Matilda Lindsay, a Virginia-born organizer for the WTUL, union membership swelled. But the United Textile Workers and the AFL hung back. These organizations were reluctant to provide relief support for protracted strikes and remained ambivalent toward the heavily young and female workforce. The AFL undertook a southern organizing drive in 1930, but it was too little, too late. In Gastonia a Communist-led union fared little better, although there the problem was not lack of commitment but rather a visceral reaction against the union's communism and its organization of black workers alongside whites.[2]

The strikers were defeated, but their rebellion shattered the perception — long cultivated by southern chambers of commerce and other boosters — that southern workers were docile and contented.[3] The violence of the strikes, combined with the prominence of girls and women in them, drew international attention and spurred reformers to action. The National Consumers' League board went on record in support of the strikers. Margaret Bowen, the Elizabethton rayon worker, spoke at the league's thirtieth anniversary meeting in November 1929.[4] But the outcome of the strikes suggested that for the moment, unionization was not a promising avenue to improving southern workers' conditions.

The desperate rebellion of the mill workers presented an opening to those who increasingly appreciated the strategic significance of the South to raising labor standards nationwide. Low wages and long hours in the South not only hurt southern workers, they discouraged state legislation elsewhere and national regulation as well. Growing numbers of employers were threatening to move southward toward low-cost labor. In the wake of the strikes, a small group of southern white women undertook a campaign to win uniform state labor laws for women throughout the region. The

Textile workers struggle with a National Guardsman in Gastonia, North Carolina (1929). (Walter P. Reuther Library, Wayne State University)

National Consumers' League sponsored Lucy Randolph Mason of Virginia to lead this group. At the same moment, the national trade association for the cotton textile industry decided to experiment with a policy against employing women at night. To protest this policy and to block the extension of sex-based labor laws to the South, the National Woman's Party sent former labor organizer Josephine Casey to Atlanta.

The ensuing conflict reveals how gender ideology and inequality shaped debates over industrial planning on the eve of the New Deal. The cotton textile industry used widespread assumptions about women's need for protection to justify its tentative experiment in limiting competition, at a moment when the legal climate with respect to antitrust policy was unpredictable. Also, gendered facts and assumptions underpinned the expectation of liberal industrialists and women reformers that the women-only ban would in practice reduce night work for both sexes: the rigid sex-typing of mill tasks, and women's much lower wages, meant that most mills would find it too costly to operate at night with an all-male shift.

This southern manifestation of the conflict among women's groups over sex-based labor laws also yields insights into the priorities and tactics of each side. Anticipating certain strands of New Deal discourse, the Consumers' League favored state economic planning to smooth out peaks and troughs in production levels, along with minimum wage standards and union protection to increase mass purchasing power. League thinkers hoped such planning and redistribution would level out many kinds of inequalities, including regional disparities. The actions and alliances of the Woman's Party in Georgia in 1931, on the other hand, demonstrate that its "equal rights" feminism had become cut off from other visions of social transformation. The party's insistence on sex equality, narrowly defined, aligned it with politically conservative forces and in practice advanced prosperous white women's interests to the exclusion of others.[5]

Neither the textile industry's night work policy nor the women's drive for state labor laws in the South succeeded in 1931. However, the lessons learned during those campaigns guided the making of New Deal policy. The cotton textile industry's experiment paved the way for the attempt at economic planning embodied in the National Recovery Administration (1933–35). Moreover, the battle lines for the struggle over the Fair Labor Standards Act of 1938, which established the first permanent national regulation of adult wages and hours, were sketched during these earlier efforts to raise southern labor standards. The nation's federated political economy was a key factor, along with resistance from the courts and organized labor, in the development of American wage and hour regulation.

The Southern Textile Industry and Labor Reform before 1930

The relocation of the textile industries from northern to southern states was an early example of how the availability of low-cost labor in one state or region could exert downward pressure on wages, hours, and working conditions elsewhere. Between the 1880s and 1920s textile mills sprang up all over the South, particularly in the Piedmont regions of the Carolinas, Georgia, and Alabama. This development accelerated during the 1920s, as stagnation in international demand for cotton pushed the southern economy further toward manufacturing. During hard times for the textile industry as a whole, the South continued to increase its share of the national market. Much of this growth came from new investment as capital went to the South rather than to the North, but some northern operations migrated southward. By 1931 66 percent of the nation's active spindles were in the South.[6]

Reasons for the southern industry's gains at the expense of New England included the subsidies offered by southern communities to attract capital, New England mills' slowness to modernize machinery, and, above all, low labor costs in the South. Wages represented a high percentage of every sales dollar in textiles, and the average southern textile wage in the 1920s was about 25 percent below the nonsouthern wage. Southern employers claimed that services they provided to employees through mill villages offset the regional wage differential, but this was rarely the case. Subsidized rent, utilities, recreation, and other alleged benefits of company-owned mill villages often were substandard and amounted to a tool for labor control. Although southern textile wages were lower than northern ones, they were higher than what southerners could earn in agriculture. Agricultural earnings were depressed by increasing mechanization and by exploitation of black labor. Textile employers enjoyed a growing labor surplus as displaced white farmworkers were attracted to mill villages. This surplus labor pool, as well as the virtual absence of labor unions and labor legislation, kept southern industrial labor standards low relative to those in the North.[7]

In the mid-1920s increasing competition and surplus labor gave a new generation of southern cotton mill owners the incentive and the leverage to restructure the mill workplace. A key aspect of this restructuring was the "stretch-out" system, which raised labor productivity by increasing the number of machines tended by each worker. The stretch-out resulted in backbreaking, eyestraining workdays and took away what vestiges of control over the work process the workers had retained. Gastonia strikers satirized the stretch-out by parading a coffin down the main street from which an effigy of the factory superintendent would rise at intervals to ask, "How many men are carrying this thing?" The workers would shout out, "Eight," to which the response was "Lay off two, six can do the work." The 1929 strikes reflected long-building resentments over wage cuts, long hours, poor workplace and living conditions, and, above all, the hated stretch-out.[8]

Southern textile workers were less protected from long hours than northern ones, which exacerbated the effects of the stretch-out in the South. In 1931 the laws on the books in major southern textile states allowed fifty-five or sixty hours per week and ten hours per day. Because these laws were loosely drafted, and because southern labor departments were weak or nonexistent, southern mills in practice were free to require unlimited hours of their employees. By contrast, six New England states limited women's work weeks to between forty-eight and fifty-six hours. As women constituted a major portion of the textile workforce (46 percent in New England and 37 percent in the South) and performed operations that were interdependent with male-typed tasks, women's work schedules tended to set the hours for the entire mill. Mills in unregulated states thus enjoyed a real advantage over those where women's hours were limited.[9]

The South had fewer labor regulations in large part because southern employers were fiercely determined to protect the advantages they derived from a cheap, unorganized labor force, and they had a range of economic, political, and ideological weapons (as well as actual ones) at their disposal. Southern economies depended on agriculture and a few industries; this lack of diversification enhanced the control of major employers over legislatures. Textile mills were the South's largest industrial employers by far, and they hired whites almost exclusively. After textiles, the region's major industries were lumber and wood products, food products, clothing, and tobacco products. Employing approximately half of all southern workers, agriculture was a larger political force to be reckoned with than in other regions.[10] Agricultural interests concerned about losing control over their labor force and about higher prices of manufactured goods rarely supported wage-hour regulations in any state. Southern impediments to political democracy—restricted primaries, poll taxes, rural-dominated legislatures, and one-party rule—further complicated challenges to the elite. More generally, arguments against state involvement in relations between employers and workers were highly salient in the South.[11] Lucy Mason believed this was because a "slave-holder psychology" persisted in the region. "Domination of the Negro has made it easy to repeat the pattern for organized labor," she bitterly observed.[12]

Textile employers were especially powerful. In the Carolinas and Georgia, mill owners' political allies routinely prevented labor reform bills from reaching the floor of the legislature. Opposition to mill owners was difficult because New South mythology portrayed them as philanthropic public servants whose benevolence created employment for impoverished rural people and nearby markets for cotton farmers. Southern localities strove to lure and keep mills: chambers of commerce advertised cheap and pliable labor, tax rebates, and subsidized utilities, and churches sang the praises of mill owners.[13]

This regional myth of the benevolent mill owner was laden with gender and race meanings. Mill owners historically had been portrayed as protectors of poor white women, providing them with an alternative to field work and thus preserving a crucial marker of white supremacy. In 1891 an investigation of Georgia mills was denounced as an assault on the honor of mill owners, "patriotic Georgians" who had come to the rescue of needy

Confederate widows. In the mid-1920s a call from the North Carolina League of Women Voters for a survey of mill conditions by the U.S. Women's Bureau provoked an uproar. Clergymen, public officials, and the editor of *Southern Textile Bulletin* accused the LWV of everything from communism to carpetbagging (for inviting in a federal labor agency). The LWV's North Carolina membership plummeted.[14] By casting their critics as traitors to the South, mill owners avoided opening their factories and records for inspection.

One might expect the glorification of southern white womanhood to have strengthened southern support for "protective" labor laws for women (white women, at least), but mill women were not ladies, and in any case, mill owners were to protect them, not the state. The lingering ideal of the southern lady actually weakened the cause of women's labor laws in the South because it inhibited the development of a progressive women's movement of the sort that won those laws elsewhere. Chastity and submissiveness, prescriptive norms of true womanhood throughout nineteenth-century America, had taken on special importance in the South, where control of white women's sexuality was vital to upholding white racial purity and dominance. White women were considered the property of white men, and their inaccessibility to black men was jealously enforced. Ostensibly this meant protecting them from black men, but it also presumed ladylike obedience to white men. In the early twentieth century, opposition to woman suffrage was strongest in the South, and it drew its force from the planter and manufacturing elites. More virulently then elsewhere, southern suffragists were attacked as "unwomanly." Even after southern white women's enfranchisement, the idea that public activism was unfeminine remained a potent disincentive to their participation in secular reform movements. When white women's organizations did venture into politics, they were less likely than their northern counterparts to support laws that challenged employer prerogatives.[15]

Despite all these obstacles, progressive southern women won small victories in the 1910s and 1920s in the labor standards field. Lobbying by women's organizations produced what mild restrictions on child labor the South had. More impressively, the Kentucky Consumers' League won a ten-hour law for women in 1914. A women's minimum wage law passed in Texas in 1919 (but was repealed two years later). The Virginia League of Women Voters was gratified to see a slate of its labor bills passed in 1922. Still, as of 1930 the southern states with the largest numbers of women in industry — namely, the textile states — had no effective labor departments, no minimum wage laws, and permissive and unenforceable hours laws.[16]

The Southern Council for Women
and Children in Industry

The interest of national labor reformers in the South had sharpened over the course of the 1920s, as the relationship between the labor standards of southern and northern workers became steadily more obvious. In 1923 Florence Kelley tried unsuccessfully to hire Lucy Mason as the league's secretary for the southern states. In 1926 the WTUL undertook a southern "educational campaign" that culminated in Matilda Lindsay's organization of textile strikers in 1929 and 1930.[17] The unsuccessful strike wave and the continuing downward spiral of national standards spurred longtime advocates of southern labor reform to try again. State hours laws, in particular, were coming under stronger fire around the country from employers who threatened to move to more permissive states. Garment and other manufacturers began to follow the example of textiles in this regard.[18] Accordingly, in March 1930 the NCL board announced its "permanent intent to promote in the South, where the indications are that there is greater interest than ever before, legislation for the short working week and working day."[19]

In October 1930 a group of southern white women met in Atlanta to form the Southern Council for Women and Children in Industry. Agreeing to interpret "industry" broadly, the group planned to work for uniform state laws establishing a maximum nine-hour day / fifty-hour week for women in a range of occupations, as well as laws abolishing child labor and night work for women.[20] The Consumers' League almost certainly had a hand in the Southern Council's formation. The league soon displayed its commitment to the group by arranging to pay Lucy Randolph Mason's salary as its chief executive through February 1931.[21] Mason had declined earlier job offers away from Richmond because of obligations to her ailing father. By 1930 her father had died; she had also lost her beloved partner, Katherine Gerwick, a YWCA reformer, to a sudden and early death. Devastated, Mason was ready to put Richmond behind her and pour her grief into social justice causes.[22]

Mason had inherited a legacy of activism, along with an impeccable Virginia pedigree that helped her get away with controversial stands in the South. Born in 1882 to an Episcopalian minister and a reform-minded mother, Mason was a direct descendant of George Mason, the revolutionary-era statesman and author of the Virginia Declaration of Rights (the model for the federal Bill of Rights). Although a southern aristocrat by blood, she was not one by most other yardsticks. She never attended college or married, and she supported herself as a stenographer before taking a series of paid staff positions with reform associations. From

Lucy Randolph Mason
(ca. 1920s). (National
Consumers' League
Collection, LC)

1914 to 1918 Mason was industrial secretary of the Richmond YWCA; from 1920 to 1931 she held various paid offices with the Richmond YWCA and the League of Women Voters. Profound religious convictions fueled Mason's political activism. She was nineteen and teaching Sunday school to young women who worked in the tobacco fields when she dedicated herself to a reform career. "If I had been a man," she once said, "I would have become a minister."[23]

In Virginia, Mason developed the ideas about the interdependence of gender, class, and racial justice that would guide her leadership of the Southern Council and then the National Consumers' League. In 1927 she summarized her interests for *Who's Who in the South*: "Civic and political development of women; more democratic and just industrial system; interracial good will; international cooperation."[24] Mason had been a passionate woman suffragist. Even more unusual for a white southerner in this period, she promoted labor rights and black civil rights. As YWCA industrial secretary, she lost a large contribution because she organized support for women strikers at a local baking powder company. During World War I, AFL leader Samuel Gompers appointed Mason the Virginia chairman of the Committee on Women in Industry of the National Advisory Commission on Labor. She organized against lynching and tried unsuccessfully to block a segregation statute in the Richmond City Council. She was a key member of a biracial Negro Welfare Survey Committee, whose 1929 report called for increased educational and economic opportunities for Richmond's black men and women. The Richmond Urban League emerged from this report, and Mason chaired its Economic Committee. When Mason left Virginia to head the NCL, her friends from Richmond's black community presented her with a thick scrapbook of tributes.[25]

When Mason began work with the Southern Council in late 1930, the New Deal was not yet on the horizon. With the textile strikes defeated, working conditions were deteriorating further in mills all over the country. The problems of overproduction, falling prices, and irregular operation that had long plagued textiles were spreading to other manufacturing industries as the effects of the stock market crash of 1929 rippled through the economy. President Herbert Hoover resisted direct relief measures and pro-labor policies for the unemployed and the working poor. Hoover also was reluctant to suspend antitrust rules to allow industries to cooperate in limiting production. With unemployment rates rising and underemployment chronic, workers had little leverage to resist declining wages and lengthening hours. Employers who had offered amenities such as recreation and medical services cut them back.[26]

To advocates for working women, the situation seemed especially dire because the Depression increased both parts of wage-earning women's "double burden." In an effort to stretch family budgets, women reversed the earlier trend toward relying on store-bought goods. More women made clothes at home, baked their own bread, and canned their own produce. As women's unpaid labor became more important to family survival, they spent more time at it. At the same time, sex segregation of the workforce meant that some women could find jobs when men could not. The occupations hit hardest by the Depression were in construction and heavy manufacturing, mostly typed as men's jobs. Many "female" service and clerical occupations did not have such high unemployment rates, although wages fell. For most working women, the hours spent in unpaid labor and in doing or searching for remunerative labor lengthened considerably.[27]

This was the context in which the Southern Council formed. Within a few years, its immediate agenda—a uniform system of nine-hour-day/

fifty-hour-week laws across the South — would seem painfully modest. In 1930 it represented a groundbreaking "southern strategy," which progressive southern and northern women hoped would clear the path toward a reformed South and a reformed nation.

The Cotton Textile Industry Proposal to End Women's Night Work

In late 1930 the national trade association for the cotton textile industry unveiled a plan for eliminating the employment of women and minors at night. The intent behind the Cotton Textile Institute's measure was to discourage mills from operating at night, thereby breaking the cycle of overproduction and price-cutting that had beset the industry through the 1920s. Formed in 1926, the Cotton Textile Institute (CTI) reflected a trend away from the ideal of unmodified competition toward a degree of cooperation within a given industry.[28]

The institute anticipated that ending night work for women would reduce night operation because mill tasks historically done by women were interdependent with men's tasks, and replacing women night workers with men would be expensive. CTI expected the ban first to encourage a regular, full-time day shift, and then to discourage production over and above that regular day shift. Targeting women and children, rather than all employees, enabled the institute to publicize the measure as a "humanitarian" effort, rather than as a move to limit production. CTI leaders hoped that this approach would appeal to the public and — especially important — that it would head off antitrust prosecution by the Justice Department. Although this fact was not emphasized in public, the particular target of the proposed night work ban was southern mills, which, unrestrained by unions or state labor laws, comprised a disproportionate share of the industry's night runners. Running mills at night became increasingly common over the course of the 1920s, and by 1930, 64 percent of southern mills reported using night shifts.[29]

Organized women lost no time in commenting on the institute's choice of a sex-based approach. However, their responses differed sharply. The National Woman's Party attacked the proposal as sex discriminatory, arguing that it would cost thousands of women night workers their jobs. In the press and in wires to the nation's governors, the NWP protested CTI's policy, observing that "even if night work were necessarily detrimental to health, nothing is so bad for a woman's health as starvation."[30]

The National Consumers' League applauded CTI's move. NCL leader Florence Kelley maintained that "this is a step forward both social and industrial, the significance of which for American civilization is impossible to overstate." To illustrate what she meant by social progress, Kelley linked women's night work with exhaustion and high death rates for mill village mothers. But her main thrust was that night work had exacerbated the seasonal character of production in the industry, to the detriment of its employers and, especially, its employees. In Kelley's view, the nation was "paying fearful penalties for our past planless conduct of industry." The institute's action was a model for further "planned production on a national scale." By substituting "for cutthroat competition and ruin, enlightened concerted action," the CTI plan would "make daylight employment steady throughout the year."[31] Kelley denied that the institute's policy would cause women night workers to lose their jobs. Men would not take women's places on the night shift, but, rather, both women and men would have steadier work in the daytime. Mills would be forced to run daylight shifts all week long, instead of running around the clock for a few days and then closing until the next orders came in. Characterizing the Woman's Party as ignorant of the legal and political obstacles to sex-neutral measures, Kelley wrote that the NWP proposal "that men, too, be eliminated from night work as a matter of equality, should be bracketed with the French queen's question why people who had no bread did not eat cake."[32]

Kelley's pessimism about the possibility of sex-neutral measures reflected a differing assessment of constitutional precedent from the NWP's. In the 1917 *Bunting v. Oregon* decision, the Supreme Court had declined to overturn a ten-hour law for men and women, but the NCL did not believe that this 5-3 decision not to overrule a lower court was a firm precedent for regulation of men's hours.[33] Also, although some trade unions and state labor federations had endorsed a legislative approach to shorter hours, in 1931 the most powerful national labor leaders still resisted hours laws for men. Not until late 1932 would the American Federation of Labor back such legislation.[34]

Florence Kelley recognized the Cotton Textile Institute's concerns about antitrust prosecution, and also its need to persuade reluctant mills to adopt the plan. She considered these legitimate grounds for the sex-based approach. Kelley rejected the NWP's hard-line stance on the principle of women's equal treatment because she believed the CTI ban, whatever the industry's motivations, could be turned to good effect for all workers.

Lucy Mason's Work for the Southern Council

The efforts of Lucy Mason for the Southern Council and Florence Kelley for the Consumers' League aided the implementation of the CTI policy against night work for women and minors. In order for the plan to take effect, 75 percent of the industry's night running mills had to agree to participate. By December 1930 about 70 percent of night runners had subscribed, but then the CTI hit what historian Louis Galambos calls the "bedrock of nonconformers," a strong minority of southern mills. Assisted by the publicity efforts of women reformers, CTI obtained the requisite number of signatures only one day before the deadline, when some North Carolina mills had a last-minute change of heart. Women reformers were more vocal on this issue than northern or southern labor groups, who supported the policy but were not a major force on its behalf.[35]

Although Southern Council members supported CTI's voluntary agreement, they did so not as an end in itself but because they hoped it represented an opening through which they could breach southern industrialists' opposition to permanent legislation. Mason correctly predicted that the voluntary agreement would be only temporarily effective, even in the unlikely event of 100 percent subscription. One of her chief efforts as head of the Southern Council was to convert employers into supporters of hours laws. This was a delicate project. Although some employers thought of the voluntary agreement as a step toward legislation, more of them saw it as a way to ward off legislation.

In the late 1920s a handful of major employers had begun to support wage-hour regulation and union rights, but very few of them were in the South. Edward Filene of the Boston department store, for example, along with Henry Kendall, a northerner who owned textile mills in New England and the South, had joined with progressive social workers and academics in the Twentieth Century Fund and the Taylor Society to consider the long-term benefits of industrial democracy. Such employers often represented mass-consumption industries, which had an interest in higher purchasing power for the working class.[36] The South's key industries were labor-intensive, and bitter competition with northern states as well as from southern neighbors made the prospect of increased labor costs anathema to most southern manufacturers. A few of the region's larger industrialists had come to favor state labor laws, hoping that such laws would reduce competitive pressure from in-state rivals and forestall national regulation. According to Mason, however, a "much larger number of employers are vigorously opposed to legislative regulation of hours and look upon it as an attack upon industry itself." The South was "still gripped by paternalism," Mason sighed. "We are still living in feudal castles in our socio-economic thinking."[37]

Through interviews and extensive correspondence, Mason tried to lure southern textile manufacturers out of their feudal castles, hoping that the

Depression had alarmed them into considering new ideas. She tried to persuade southern mill men that state hours laws were in their own best interest, citing studies by southern academics to support her contention that such legislation would benefit southern industry, not its northern rivals. Not surprisingly, Mason did not advertise the Southern Council's affiliation with the National Consumers' League, portraying the council as a purely southern initiative.[38] She gathered data, circulated questionnaires, and pressed regional trade associations for support. She solicited statements from big mill owners in neighboring states that they would support hours laws in their own state if similar ones passed in the neighbor state.[39] This reliance on behind-the-scenes influence and superior information was a characteristic of women's political style that dated back to the presuffrage era. Without votes to deliver, female activists had honed their skills in persuasion to a high art.[40]

Some mill owners welcomed women's agitation for hours limits, within certain parameters, but others accused the Southern Council of meddling in men's affairs. One southern mill owner who favored hours laws wrote anonymously to urge women's groups to take the lead, because it was difficult for men in his position to challenge "our wealthiest and most influential manufacturers." CTI representatives proposed a sexual division of political labor under which the Southern Council would argue "the humanitarian point of view" and CTI would stress the overproduction problem. But the council's reformers refused to leave economic analysis to the men. A Georgia mill owner who opposed legislation, W. D. Anderson, angrily told the council it should leave the economic problems of the textile industry to more qualified people, namely mill owners. He recommended that the council instead promote religious training and programs for young married women, "who stand badly in need of enlightenment . . . concerning the problems of motherhood and the raising of babies." Anderson insinuated that the Southern Council was self-promoting and naive or disloyal to the South. Spreading "propaganda" for hours and wage laws was "flashy" and "will rally to your support many of the sinister influences that are now attacking the industrial order in the South," but it would not help women and children engaged in industry.[41]

Ignoring such reactions, Mason continued to argue that uniform state laws limiting hours and raising wages would attack overproduction by reducing output and increasing demand. Such laws would limit price competition from "chiselers" who were able or willing to work employees longer for less. Mason asked southern mill men to envision themselves as part of a new breed of employers. Rejecting the old model of the unregulated, renegade entrepreneur, Mason called for "decent employers" to cooperate to curb the competition that destabilized working shifts, lengthened hours, and reduced wages; she cast noncooperators as antisocial, cutthroat competitors. This language, a legacy of Progressive Era campaigns against sweated labor, would come into wide usage by the Roosevelt administration.

The NCL's emphasis on curbing the competition that led to overproduction represented a shift in its arguments against long hours and night work. During the Progressive Era and both world wars, the league produced abundant evidence that shorter hours increased productivity because workers became less efficient the longer they worked. During the Depression, when the concern was with *over*production, it argued (depending on the industry) that fewer shifts would curb production, or that shorter shifts would spread working time among different workers and reduce unemployment.[42] In the 1920s and early 1930s, the league's opposition to all night work was based on its conviction that it destabilized daytime employment. CTI agreed that night work contributed to irregular daytime operation and also to overproduction. Night work most often occurred in mills that were running on "short time," that is, only a few days per week. These same mills, which in slow seasons operated around the clock only a few days a week, in busy periods operated around the clock every day but Sunday. CTI's ban sought to encourage a shift to regular day production, and then to limit any increase in production above that.[43]

Although Mason chiefly emphasized the economic benefits to employers and all workers of regulated labor standards, on one occasion she resorted to arguments that reinforced assumptions about women's obligations to motherhood, asking an employer to think of "the future citizens of the southern states and of the difference in type that will be produced if women have time to give adequate attention to their homes, and children remain in school long enough to secure an adequate education."[44] Mason deferred to the convention that held women responsible for the unpaid domestic labor of housework and child rearing, but she did not suggest that mothers should not work in the mills. Rather, she used maternalist rhetoric to argue instead for shorter hours and an end to child labor. Another Southern Council leader, Jessie Daniel Ames, celebrated female economic independence and promoted women's rights, not as "mothers of civilization," but on equal terms with men.[45] But the Southern Council, apparently not optimistic about transforming the sexual division of labor at home, advocated policies to alleviate women's crushing "double burden" of paid and unpaid labor. Ideally, these policies would shorten hours and increase daytime employment options for all workers.

In the South, calls for protecting mothers and children often had white supremacist connotations, which may be one reason the Southern Council generally eschewed that approach. Earlier southern labor reformers, particularly advocates of child labor laws, had focused almost exclusively on the whites-only textile industry; some of them warned that mill work was debilitating to white mothers and children and thereby weakened the white race.[46] Unlike many southern white "progressives," the Southern Council sought not to shore up white dominance but to erode it, albeit gradually. The Southern Council hoped to shorten hours for black and white women alike. Mason publicly criticized the fact that occupations in which black women worked tended to have lower wages, longer hours, and harsher working conditions than predominantly white occupations.[47] Like hours bills everywhere, the Southern Council's model bill excluded domestic and agricultural occupations, thereby exempting most black women from protection. However, the council bill pointedly included laundries, restaurants, and other minority-employing services, as well as canneries and tobacco processing. The Southern Council did not directly attack the "color line" in southern employment, but few southern groups, black or white, were making that demand publicly in 1931.[48]

By mid-1931 small Southern Council groups were active in fourteen states. Bills limiting women's hours and establishing a labor department passed in North Carolina; this was a victory because that state had the region's largest and least unionized nonagricultural workforce. Otherwise, legislative progress was slow. Unions, labor departments, and progressive women's organizations were weak in the South, and mobilizing effective coalitions was difficult. In Georgia, the Southern Council encountered an additional obstacle in the form of the Woman's Party.[49]

The Woman's Party in Georgia

In March 1931, after word of the Southern Council's progress filtered back to NWP headquarters, the Woman's Party dispatched Josephine Casey to Atlanta. Lucy Mason's departure at the end of her term in early March had left a local Southern Council group promoting women's hours and night work bills in the Georgia legislature. Casey's assignment was to generate local criticism of the Textile Institute's policy and to block the Southern Council's sex-based bills. The NWP hoped Casey would organize an "Industrial Council" of female textile workers in addition to a permanent Atlanta branch of the Woman's Party.[50]

Casey was uniquely qualified to undertake the NWP's first initiative in the South since the days of the woman suffrage drive.[51] A former labor organizer, she had come to oppose women-only labor laws during World War I.

Equal Rights

VOL. XVII, No. 3 1/4
FIVE CENTS

SATURDAY
APRIL 11, 1931

Josephine Casey

Trade Unionist and member of the Industrial Council of the National Woman's Party, who is leading a campaign for Equal Rights for women in the textile industries in Georgia. Miss Casey was formerly an organizer for the American Federation of Labor.

Josephine Casey on the cover of *Equal Rights* in April 1931. (State Historical Society of Wisconsin)

In the 1920s she became one of the few working-class women to publicly champion the Equal Rights Amendment. Although raised in Chicago, Casey was born in Tennessee, a valuable credential in the South. When the NWP contacted her in 1931, Casey was a single woman in her forties who, after a "series of misfortunes," had taken a housekeeping job at $5 per week.[52]

Years earlier, Casey had worked with some of the trade unionists and reformers whom she now opposed on the issue of women-only labor laws. In 1904, as a ticket agent on Chicago streetcars, Casey persuaded her female coworkers to form a union; two years later the Boston WTUL hired her to organize there. In 1909 Casey quit the WTUL and became an organizer for the ILGWU. Between 1911 and 1914 she helped lead garment strikes in Cleveland, Kalamazoo, and St. Louis. She then became a suffrage activist, working with Harriot Stanton Blatch's Women's Political Union in New York and for the Congressional Union (forerunner of the NWP) in the western states. Blatch already opposed the principle of women-only labor laws, and Casey probably began developing her ideas on the subject at this point.

A confrontation in 1926 between Casey and her former labor movement colleagues embittered her toward supporters of sex-based legislation and solidified her devotion to the Woman's Party. At a U.S. Women's Bureau conference on women in industry, Casey represented the Woman's Party position. She criticized anti-ERA women trade unionists as "old and tired, women . . . who do not believe that women can be made an integral part of the labor movement." WTUL activists harshly rebutted Casey's charges. Former glove worker Agnes Nestor retorted that "the trouble with you, Josephine, is that you have been away from the labor movement so long, you don't know what is happening in it." Millinery organizer Melinda Scott asserted indignantly that she herself was still "on the organizing job," and she would "beat Josephine Casey at it, two to one, any day." A few days after this fiery scene, Women's Bureau head Mary Anderson wrote to WTUL leader Margaret Dreier Robins, "I am sure you would not have recognized Josephine as what she used to be."[53]

Casey's labor background enabled the Woman's Party to counter NCL charges that only professional and "leisure class" women opposed sex-based labor legislation. Now the NWP could retort that Josephine Casey "makes her decisions for those who work while actually performing work," in contrast with "mistaken reformers" who had not "been actual wage-earners in industry in twenty years."[54] This was a dig at leading defenders of sex-based laws such as Rose Schneiderman of the WTUL and Mary Anderson of the Women's Bureau, former laborers who had moved into administrative work. The fuss that was made over Casey suggests how atypical a Woman's Party activist she was. The NWP used Casey's reports for a column, "A Workingwoman in Georgia," that became a regular feature of its weekly bulletin, *Equal Rights*. Casey apparently perceived the NWP as ill-informed about the lives of laboring women, because her letters back to party headquarters explained basic labor slang and terms such as "mill village" as if to someone from another world.[55]

Upon her arrival in Atlanta, Casey ran into a stumbling block when she discovered that the Textile Institute ban had not in fact caused women to lose their jobs: "It does not seem that any [mills] in this place laid off women from night work. I can't seem to find any around Atlanta."[56] The claim that prohibiting women's night work caused female unemployment had been the core of the NWP attack. Muna Lee, the party's director of national activities, told the press that letters from fired mill women were pouring in, "begging the Woman's Party to continue its campaign," but this claim seems to have been fabricated.[57] Casey soon reported that the ban was curtailing men's night work as well as women's, and that night workers were being switched onto day shifts. Some mills were now running two shifts a day all week—rather than three shifts a day, three days a week—just as Florence Kelley had predicted.[58]

Contrary to the hopes of women reformers and CTI, a minority of mills operated at night with all-male shifts, but even in this atypical circumstance, women workers were shifted to daytime work, not fired. The extent to which the Depression eroded the sex-typing of jobs in the textile industry is not clear. The economic crisis heightened two conflicting pressures on the sexual division of labor in the workplace. On the one hand, the idea that men needed or deserved jobs more than women gained new force. On the other hand, the fact of women's lower wages made female substitution for men an attractive step for employers. Sociologist Ruth Milkman finds that both pressures were mitigated during the 1930s by a remarkably inflexible sex-typing of manufacturing occupations. The initial sex-typing of a task depended on many factors, but once an industry's pattern of employment by sex was established, it quickly became perceived as natural and inevitable by workers and employers alike. Ironically, although it helped keep women's wages low, this rigidity protected some women from unemployment.[59] "The women didn't lose their jobs through the Institute's decision," Casey explained to NWP headquarters. "We must make our statements fit the facts."[60]

The discovery that the CTI ban had not caused female unemployment did not soften the NWP stance against the measure. To the contrary, Casey was outraged: "If this is true it all gets back to the degrading thing of using women as smokescreens to their detriment in the name of humanitarianism. . . . [W]hile the law will read women it will actually regulate for the men. . . . [W]hen something happens to cause overproduction in cotton mills we should not let them hand a slam to women in one industry which may cause her to lose her job in another and put every proffesional [sic] woman eternally in the amateur class."[61] This point had validity, but it also illustrates that what was at stake for the NWP in the fight over CTI's policy was not mill women so much as the precedent for professionals and other women trying to break into male-dominated occupations. However, the Woman's Party bulletin, *Equal Rights*, continued to represent the struggle as on the behalf of women mill workers and to issue false warnings about widespread dismissals.

Georgia industrial workers did not flock to the Woman's Party to protest CTI's policy and to lobby against sex-based labor bills. After four months of recruiting, Casey could list approximately twenty women workers who had signed membership cards for the NWP Industrial Council, even though the party waived dues for industrial members.[62] This was not for lack of boldness or initiative on Casey's part. She was an imaginative organizer, of whom it was remarked years earlier that "she knows how to hold the girls — is a wonderful leader in that respect."[63] But few Georgia workers seem to have found the NWP message compelling. Industrial Council members' activity consisted of responding to Casey's occasional requests; in a typical instance, Casey prompted a mill worker to send a telegram to party headquarters, which the NWP then released to news services as if it had been unsolicited. Neither side of the sex-based legislation debate attracted masses of women workers. However, the Woman's Party grossly exaggerated its support from working women. Muna Lee reminded Casey, "We greatly need the force that actual industrial membership gives to our argument for industrial equality."[64] The NWP was more interested in publicizing that some working women opposed sex-based labor laws than in changing conditions for mill women.

Organizing an Atlanta Woman's Party

NWP publications stressed that Casey's mission was to organize textile workers. In fact, organizing a Woman's Party branch that could fund an ongoing battle with the Southern Council was at least as high a priority. Several obstacles initially hindered Casey's efforts to mobilize affluent Atlanta women against women-only labor measures. First, the Southern Council had been there first. "All the women who are well-known here are rather tied up with 'protection' or they are fearful to take a stand," Casey complained. After being invited to join a League of Women Voters speaker in presenting both sides of the problem to a meeting, Casey grumbled, "I'll go but frankly it's like trying to wake up A. Nestor or R. Schneiderman."[65] Casey also encountered profound skepticism of nonsouthern groups. She suggested forming a "Southern League for Women's Equality" to counter the Southern Council for Women and Children in Industry, which she claimed was mainly League of Women Voters people: "That 'Southern' thing was done for effect."[66] Furthermore, Atlanta's rich women were the most likely to be influenced by the southern lady ideal, which constrained elite women's activism on controversial issues. Casey tried sectional appeals by arguing, for example, that the ERA gave "the States' Rights idea perfect expression."[67] But soon she was lamenting, "Seeing club women or popular [society] ladies is a total loss this side of Mason and Dixon in my experience. Working women, their bosses, and business and professional women seem more helpful. I have tried so hard to interest the woman of means here in the South but it is just burning up time."[68]

On the other hand, in its growing number of business and professional women, Atlanta may have had an unusually large pool, for the South, of white women receptive to the NWP's brand of feminism. Atlanta grew rapidly after 1910 as a commercial center, and white women streamed into the new clerical and sales occupations. By 1920, 42 percent of all Atlanta women older than sixteen worked for pay; only Washington, D.C., and Massachusetts textile towns had a higher rate. The state of Georgia now had as many clerical and professional women (who were less likely to back sex-based labor laws) as it had women in manufacturing.[69]

Gradually, Casey's persistence paid off, and an Atlanta Woman's Party (AWP) took shape. Its members had connections to conservative southern interests, although they moved in professional circles rather than the most elite ones. The Atlanta chapter drew on women in journalism, business, medicine, and law. Mildred Seydell, the new chapter's president, wrote a newspaper column for the conservative *Georgian American*; vice chairman Adeline Swagerty had created a professional association called the Doctor's Exchange. At least four AWP officers had ties to the Atlanta Chamber of Commerce, as members of its board of directors or its women's division, but the Woman's Party did not publicize this connection. Its newsletter announced that the new branch was led by members of "the South's inner aristocracy," who "charmingly exemplifie[d] the culture of the Old South and the audacious vigor of the New."[70] This description resembled the Chamber of Commerce's definition of the "Atlanta spirit," and indeed, the Chamber of Commerce became a useful platform for the fledgling AWP. Its women's division held an "aviation dinner" at which nine women were recognized as Woman's Party members. These professional women may have seen embracing the NWP's feminism as one way of rejecting "traditionalism" and "backwardness."[71]

Although perhaps tolerant of some feminist ideas, southern Chambers of Commerce were not known for their sympathy to the labor movement, to the nascent interracial cooperation movement, or to liberal reforms in general. The Chamber of Commerce connection may explain why the Atlanta Woman's Party made its symbolic debut in an event staged by manufacturers: a parade in July 1931 celebrating "Georgia Food Products Week." The contrast with the formative event for the Southern Council, the violent repression of the textile strikes, could hardly have been greater. The Woman's Party parade float was "a silver coach with a Cinderella-load of girls [working women]" bearing Woman's Party placards, followed by a car carrying Casey and the new local officers. The silver bus, "festooned with cotton," had been loaned to the Woman's Party by a mill owner.[72]

The southern women who were drawn to the NWP were those whose position necessitated support for white women's access to the professions but not for any challenge to the existing race or class hierarchy. Black and white women in Atlanta had begun to organize for interracial cooperation, especially against lynching. (Georgia was second only to Mississippi in number of lynchings, and most victims were black men.) These women did not join the Atlanta Woman's Party. Trying not to alienate conservative women, Casey discouraged interest from black groups.[73] When she reported to NWP headquarters that she had accepted an invitation to address the "Colored Atlanta School of Social Workers," Casey was apologetic. "Being of the South and knowing its view I did not seek this. But when Mr. Washington the director asked me, I accepted. There won't be any publicity. I shall stick to the woman's cause and not touch on Race. I hope you understand the situation."[74] Casey had spent weeks seeking publicity of any kind, but she promised to keep this address private, hardly welcoming black participation. The definition of "woman's cause" as separate from issues of "Race" was biased toward white women, because only they could afford to perceive gender as their exclusive concern and as a nonracial construct.

The white women who joined the Southern Council were not all crusaders for full-fledged racial equality, but their goals and backgrounds produced a more liberal collective position on race than that of the Atlanta Woman's Party. Jessie Daniel Ames headed the Women's Committee of the Georgia Commission on Interracial Cooperation, and she founded the Association of Southern Women for the Prevention of Lynching. Ames's racial liberalism had its limits, but where the NWP avoided all discussion of race, Ames took public positions such as denouncing the Ku Klux Klan (which was headquartered in Atlanta).[75] Other Southern Council members were affiliated with the YWCA, Methodist women's groups, or the Atlanta League of Women Voters. These organizations had more liberal records on race questions than the Atlanta Chamber of Commerce and the Business and Professional Women's Clubs, the groups from which the NWP recruited.[76] Mason and Ames believed that the "race issue" blocked virtually all reform in the South. Ames recalled that in the 1920s, labor reform had run aground on white fears of racial equality. One white coalition in Texas had collapsed "when it was suggested that 'nigger wenches' would be getting the same wages as 'pure white girls.' . . . Gradually it came over me that someone . . . was going to have to get out and tell white Texans — the women especially — that until we were ready to stand up and say in public that we would include Negroes in social benefits we might as well quit."[77]

Also in contrast with the Atlanta Woman's Party associations was the cooperation between the Southern Council and Atlanta labor organizations. The Southern Council had multiple connections to Georgia unions, speaking at labor conventions and receiving favorable coverage in labor newspapers. Mrs. Emmett Quinn presented the Southern Council program to the Georgia Federation of Labor's 1931 convention, for example, and she and Steve Nance, president of the Atlanta Federation of Trades, cooperated on a membership drive for the Atlanta LWV. (No doubt this professional cooperation was enhanced by the fact that Quinn's husband was a prominent local labor leader).[78] In short, the women who were drawn to the Southern Council were the same ones who were drawn to Atlanta's fledgling interracial cooperation and union movements. Southern Council leaders had developed a vision for social reform in which progress for women, blacks, and workers were intertwined. By contrast, the Atlanta Woman's Party expressly rejected association with race or labor issues, framing its agenda in terms most appealing to middle-class white women.

Disrupting the Southern Council

The opposition of Georgia's major employers to hours laws set the odds against the Southern Council program; the NWP's opposition helped clinch the council's defeat. After Lucy Mason left Atlanta, the Southern Council lacked an experienced, full-time representative of the NCL point of view. This helped Casey succeed, not in organizing a strong movement for the Equal Rights Amendment, but in dimming local enthusiasm for sex-based laws. Casey discreetly turned two Southern Council women against sex-based laws, and these women provided Casey with inside information on the council's activities. In June Casey reported triumphantly that "the message of Truth" had gotten into the Southern Council, because it had voted to make its bills applicable to "persons" rather than to women. As a result of this internal debate, the Southern Council's own hours bill was not even introduced in 1931, although other women's hours bills were. This was an impressive achievement for the NWP, given the council's reliance on the local LWV and YWCA, whose national organizations opposed the Woman's Party position.[79]

Casey used several different lines of argument to confound the Southern Council. Her portrayal of the NWP as the force of modern feminism, struggling against well-meaning but obsolete traditionalism, may have undermined the Southern Council's appeal to some Atlanta women. Casey explained to Muna Lee that "even in the darkest hour here I could actually feel the correct viewpoint clearing the mist of tradition." She had one of her "plants" tell the council that "they were holding to an attitude that was alright 25 years ago." As a result of this sort of criticism, the Southern Council dropped "for Women and Children" from its name, conceding the antifeminist implications of lumping adult women with children. Casey also appealed to sectional pride, suggesting that it was the northern states with sex-based laws that were "backwards." She frequently remarked that the night work ban was not affecting grandmothers but "modern women." Atlanta women who perceived themselves as thoroughly modern may have been reluctant to identify themselves with an organization that seemed to be using old-fashioned, presuffrage tactics.[80]

Casey confused Southern Council members with a series of arguments that, although ostensibly directed at sex-based policies, in fact fed opposition to all regulation of working hours, wages, and conditions. After it became apparent that CTI's ban was switching night workers to day shifts, rather than resulting in their dismissal, the NWP found it fruitful to stress the issue of women's *choice*. The Woman's Party argued that many women workers preferred to work at night, and that if men were permitted to do it, women should be, too. Women who had found "that night work best suits their arrangements, should exercise their adult privilege of choosing for themselves." More than one Southern Council meeting was thrown into turmoil when someone planted by Casey asked, "Do the workers themselves want the protection?"[81]

The Woman's Party did not agree with the Consumers' League that night work was an "unsound practice" for workers and for employers. NWP writers portrayed night work as pleasant and convenient for women, and party leader Doris Stevens asserted that "opposition to women's working at night had its source, not in any fear for women's health, but in the conjugal bed." Women trade unionists were incensed by this suggestion that their ultimate cause was shoring up husbands' sexual prerogatives, not resisting class exploitation.[82]

Women took night work either because they could get no other employment or because it offered them certain advantages. In Georgia in 1931, the NWP suggested that these advantages were higher wages, shorter hours, better conditions, the opportunity for daytime leisure, and the inability to find daytime care for children or other dependents. Of these, only the last seems to have had basis in fact. The wage premium for night work in textiles had eroded during the 1920s as a labor surplus developed. Even when hourly wages were higher at night, weekly earnings tended to be lower because the work was less regular. In the mid-1920s, night workers' median earnings were lower than day workers' in all branches of the textile industry except woolens. Full-time night workers often did work as many as five fewer hours per week than day workers. However, night workers rarely received any meal break, which almost offset the advantage in terms of time and may have more than offset it in terms of fatigue and liability to injury. Although mill work may have been cooler at night, a factor the NWP made much of in Georgia, night shift supervisors often took away seats to prevent workers from falling asleep. There is no evidence that nighttime conditions were more pleasant overall.[83] The factor that seems to have most affected women's choice of night work was daytime "home responsibilities," particularly caring for children, the elderly, or other dependents. One national survey by the Women's Bureau found that over two-thirds of women night workers were or had been married and that over 90 percent were younger than forty. This suggests that women with young children were the most likely to take night work.[84]

Thus the Woman's Party was correct in claiming that many women wanted night work so they could be with their children and other dependents by day. Ironically, in pursuing this line of argument the NWP turned the debate away from women's equal citizenship rights — their same right to freedom of contract as men — and toward a discussion of which policy better protected motherhood, allowing them to work at night or not. The Southern Council chair reportedly wavered after Casey told her that CTI's ban took food away from children by leaving their mothers unemployed. This was fighting dirty because by this time Casey knew the ban was not costing women jobs.[85] Moreover, this approach ignored the fact that women who preferred night work would lose this option if policies restricting night work were sex-neutral. In other words, the NWP emphasis on women's right to choose night work fed sentiment against all night work regulation, not just women-only measures.

Southern Council and Consumers' League thinkers were sympathetic to the plight of night-working women who cared for dependents by day, but they did not believe leaving night work unchecked would ease these women's circumstances. The NCL hoped to change at least some aspects of the context in which women would choose night work: lack of daytime employment, long shifts, desperately low wages, and low rates of unionization.[86] Individual women's choice of night work was not a free one because they lacked alternatives. From the NCL perspective, individual rights like freedom of contract were a sham when employers held all the cards.

According to Casey, women workers not only did not want labor laws, they did not need them because mill conditions were already good. At the invitation of some mill owners who prided themselves on their modern and humane facilities, Casey visited textile mills in LaGrange, Georgia. She reported that the workers were "nicely dressed girls and not one looked fatigued." Some weeks later, a widely circulated letter from the Atlanta Woman's Party urged Georgians to reject "a subtle program come down from the North recently" to take away night jobs from women. Mill women, the letter claimed, "are working in fine modern mills where every facility for comfort is provided — humidifiers cool the air. They have steady work the year round. Working eight hours, under perfect conditions, they have sixteen hours left for sleep and recreation."[87] This was a highly idealized vision of work in any mill village. The recent textile strikes indicated that most workers — struggling with long hours, underemployment, and the hated stretch-out — would have disagreed with this portrayal.

Casey suggested that if conditions were so bad, mill workers could easily organize and solve the problem. Workers simply needed to "wait until they see an opening to improve conditions . . . and it depends on how well they have prepared and how loyal they are to each other whether they put it over."[88] Coming from a former labor organizer, this placing of responsibility exclusively on workers for the success or failure of organized efforts seems disingenuous. Furthermore, although Casey claimed to prefer unionization to sex-based laws, she avoided public support of workers' right to organize. While the NWP was playing up her labor background in *Equal Rights*, Casey herself was playing it down in Georgia. She wrote that she could not use the bulletins in Georgia because it was "a strong anti-union place and if the employers got mixed up about me it would make it all the harder."[89] After an unsuccessful meeting with the Georgia Federation of Labor, Casey advised Industrial Council members "not to waste their postage [writing to legislators] under instruction from the labor group."[90] Casey's dedication to the Woman's Party program had eclipsed her earlier commitment to the labor movement.

The showdown between the Southern Council and the Woman's Party came in July 1931 at a Georgia House committee hearing on a women's night work bill.[91] Three trade unionists, including one woman, arrived from Augusta to support the bill. Casey brought three night working mill women to oppose it. A former Southern Council member who had defected to Casey's side created general confusion when she denied the claim of Southern Council speakers that the League of Women Voters and the Atlanta Women's Clubs backed the bill. Then, after the Southern Council's Lillian Wade argued that "even European peasants" had an eight-hour day, Casey made a melodramatic appeal to southern pride. "Those who had to cut away trees before they could plant beans and the daughters of the men who rode with Forrest . . . would never submit to being peasants," Casey declared. Here Casey implied that white southern honor would be affronted by "protective" hours legislation. This extension of the values of honor and independence to white women may have appealed to southern women ready to "revolt against chivalry." However, the claim that women mill workers did not need improved conditions fed sentiment against all labor laws, sex-neutral or not.[92]

Textile industrialists were key to the defeat of the women's night work bill, but the NWP downplayed this fact. At the July hearing, top officials of two state manufacturers' associations opposed the bill. Casey already had decided it would be good for NWP morale to call the bill's defeat a victory for feminism. "The cotton manufacturers will fight the bill but I'm not telling anyone because I'd like our women to go to the mat without this knowledge. Licking this unjust measure will give them strength. I don't want to deprive them of it—so I won't ever tell them."[93] The bill was reported favorably out of the House committee, but it was prevented from reaching the floor before the Assembly adjourned on August 22. Jubilant, Casey reported that the "feeling is this one-sided legislation will never come up again in Georgia."[94]

The NWP claimed that defeat of women's hours bills in Georgia and elsewhere made 1931 a year of triumph for female wage earners. *Equal Rights* announced that the fate of the Georgia night work law assured women mill workers "steady work through next winter." Back in New York, Casey claimed that "the carrying out of the great principle of the Woman's Party enabled thousands of women mill workers to be housed, fed, and clothed this winter." Casey implied that by blocking women-only laws, the NWP was guaranteeing women's employment. But women-only policies rarely cost women their jobs, and the absence of women-only laws did not guarantee women's employment at all, much less at wages that would enable them to be "housed, fed, and clothed." Employers' role in defeating such legislation received no mention.[95]

Women-only laws would not have guaranteed jobs for women either, but their proponents did not make this claim. The NCL believed that night work restrictions increased daytime employment options for women (and men) as a group. The league prioritized increasing workers' collective leverage with employers over defending individual workers' right to choose night work. Its leaders believed labor legislation would promote workers' ability to organize by setting a bottom limit to their exploitation. Because formally sex-neutral policies seemed unattainable in 1931, the NCL was willing to trade individual women's right to choose night work for a reduction in all night work that was achieved through a woman-only measure. Although not the optimal solution, sex-based policies seemed better than nothing.

Josephine Casey may have accomplished more for the Woman's Party than she did for mill workers. Within the NWP, Casey created quite a stir. She was congratulated on her "deliciously refreshing and amusing" letters. One member wrote that she found Casey's accounts "so entertaining" because they took her back to the suffrage fight in the Midwest.[96] Casey's work reinvigorated NWP members and stimulated some contributions, but neither the Georgia Industrial Council nor the Atlanta Woman's Party remained active after 1931. The NWP devoted resources to Georgia only long enough to defeat a women's night work bill and get some publicity. When the Georgia legislature adjourned, Casey was sent to fight women-only laws in Rhode Island, Massachusetts, and New York. There her opposition to all labor laws became more apparent as she argued that hours and minimum wage laws had hurt business in the Northeast. Determined to hold on to its token representative of working women, the Woman's Party continued to camouflage Casey's antistatism as feminism.[97]

Unlike the NWP, the National Consumers' League emerged from the confrontation in Georgia determined to make the South an ongoing priority. This was clearly a factor in the choice of Lucy Mason as the NCL general secretary after Florence Kelley died in 1932. During the New Deal, the threat to national "purchasing power" of low-wage competition from southern states became a salient issue in national politics. Changing circumstances also brought sex-neutral regulation into reach. After its extended trial of the voluntary ban on women's night work, the Cotton Textile Institute was on the brink of adopting a male-inclusive ban when Roosevelt's election raised the possibility of national legislation.[98] CTI shifted its attention from expanding the voluntary ban to influencing New Deal legislation. Cotton textiles would be the first industry to have its wage and hour standards regulated under the National Recovery Administration, and those standards would be sex-neutral. Voluntary, women-only policies thus paved the way for mandatory national regulation that included men. In textiles, the "entering wedge" strategy for broadening the authority and obligations of the state succeeded. However, the rationale for women-only laws was not entirely obsolete. The conflict among women's organizations over the sex-based strategy would only intensify over the course of the Great Depression.

A Dilemma for Progressive Feminists in the 1930s

The outcome of the NWP's work in Georgia in 1931 illustrated the limitations of a narrow strategy for gender equality in a setting of pronounced class and race inequality. The party's embrace of conservatives hostile to union rights and racial reform alienated many groups from its women's rights program. The exclusive focus on sex equality under the law, ostensibly an effort to broaden the NWP's appeal by avoiding controversy over labor rights and black rights, in fact discouraged poor women and black women from joining a movement for the Equal Rights Amendment. Moreover, in joining forces with conservatives to defend the liberty of contract doctrine, the Woman's Party earned itself the lasting enmity of progressives and leftists interested in using the state to redistribute wealth to workers. Labor-oriented feminists who were repulsed by the NWP's "equal rights" feminism struggled to find a different language to express their hopes for gender equality.

Before World War I, feminism and the Left had been closely intertwined, but in the 1920s and 1930s a widening chasm divided the leading representatives of those causes. The "radical elitism" of the NWP held that liberating women from male tyranny should be the single goal of "pure" feminism. Meanwhile, the Communist Party maintained that class revolution transcended all other causes.[99] The male-dominated Left was partially responsible for the split. Socialist theory predicted that the demise of capitalism automatically would liberate women (so there was no need to waste energy liberating them now). Left-wing groups were not immune to sexism, although their relatively egalitarian programs attracted many women. Leftist parties and labor unions reserved most leadership positions for men and discouraged women's complaints by labeling them divisive or petty. In the 1930s, despite women's significant presence among radicals and newly organized workers, the iconography of the Left and the labor movement would portray workers as male, casting women in auxiliary roles.[100]

But the Woman's Party, as the standard-bearer for postsuffrage feminism, also contributed to the split between feminism and the Left. The NWP's feminism stood apart from, and took no position on, other social justice movements. The party stated that its goal was "to give the women of each group equality of rights with the men of the same group . . . professional women with professional men; women in industry with men in industry; . . . Japanese women citizens with Japanese men citizens; Negro women with Negro men."[101] The Woman's Party idea of sex equality explicitly avoided challenging the status quo along any axis other than gender relations. The notion of a pure feminism appealed principally to affluent white women who could "gloss over their class, racial, and other status identifications because those [were] culturally dominant and therefore relatively invisible." This strategy narrowed the Woman's Party constituency and linked feminism with reaction in the minds of several generations of reformers and radicals.[102] In 1937 Alma Lutz of the Woman's Party would ask why those "guarding women's hard earned freedom . . . shy away from the designation 'Feminist.'" Lutz might have begun to answer her question by taking a critical look at her own organization.[103]

During the Depression the National Consumers' League tried to navigate a path across the divide between feminism and the Left, identifying gender and labor reform (as well as racial reform) as interdependent. However, the Consumers' League had trouble inventing an alternative language for promoting the interests of laboring women. The NCL began to avoid the phrase "protective legislation" because "the word 'protective' acts as a red flag to the bull, to the Woman's Party type of mind." But finding new words was difficult. Phrases like "equal rights" and "equal opportunity" were linked to the individualistic feminism of the Woman's Party, with all its antiregulatory and antilabor potential.[104]

The muting of progressive feminism in the 1930s was doubly unfortunate because the Depression stimulated new challenges to women's economic independence. The sheer scale of male unemployment triggered intense anxiety about the emasculation of American men. This preoccupation with manhood obscured both female unemployment and the increased importance of women's paid and unpaid labor to family survival. One result was new policies formalizing the sentiment against married women's employment that had been building in the 1920s. In 1932 Section 213 of the National Economy Act effectively prevented wives of federal employees from working for the federal government. A coalition of women's organizations (including both the Woman's Party and Consumers' League) protested against Section 213, stressing women's right to work as well as their need to work.[105] As a result of this united effort, Section 213 was repealed in 1937, but many school boards and private employers continued to dismiss married women.[106] The NCL charged that these restrictions on wives' employment had "the obvious intent to reestablish an ancient discrimination." Measures to "eliminate women from competition with men" by "relegating them to the home and kitchen" were "unsound, futile, and indefensible" violations of women's civil rights. But the NCL did not spell out those "civil rights" issues in terms that explicitly attacked male dominance. This blunted the league's effectiveness in challenging the presumption of female economic dependence on men that underpinned the campaign against wives' employment and that also shaped many New Deal relief and social insurance policies.[107]

Wary of equal rights rhetoric, and perhaps overoptimistic about their own influence on men's views, progressive feminists in the 1930s would try to advance women's equality through their own exemplary achievement and through general social justice arguments more often than through the language of women's rights. As events at home and abroad raised the specter of fascism, the NCL defended its program (including the job rights of married women) by invoking "the essential principles of democracy." The league also advocated higher labor standards for women by arguing that they would stimulate the economy. To Consumers' League ears, these languages of democracy and social Keynesianism had a feminist subtext. Others did not hear this subtext, or they chose to ignore it.[108]

chapter 4

The Acid Test of
the New Deal

*The National
Recovery
Administration,
1933–1935*

In August 1933 representatives of the crushed stone, sand and gravel, and slag industry gathered in Washington for hearings on the industry's proposed code of fair trade and labor practices under the National Recovery Administration (NRA). Among other things, industry leaders proposed a minimum wage of twenty-two cents per hour in the South and thirty cents per hour in the North. Southern employers claimed that the inefficiency of their "negro labor" justified the regional wage differential. Paying black workers more than twenty-two cents per hour allegedly would "upset the whole sociological conditions" in the South. Most of the people present probably were quite startled when a white-haired woman with a soft southern accent took the microphone and denounced the proposed code. She accused southern employers of playing black and white unskilled laborers against each other, "with consequent submerged purchasing power." As for the supposed dangers of paying black workers higher wages, she continued, "That negroes will earn enough to subsist on and then stop work I believe to be a fallacy." Like anyone else, she insisted, African

Americans would use their higher wages to raise their living standard, stimulating the economy in the process. The speaker was Lucy Mason, representing the National Consumers' League.[1]

In 1933 the NCL, like the nation, was under new leadership. Florence Kelley had died in 1932, after recommending Mason as her successor. Mason left her native Virginia for the league's headquarters in New York City, "feeling too small for the work, but impelled to go into it." Her first challenge was to impress Kelley's loyal colleagues, a few of whom seemed skeptical of this southern newcomer.[2] These reservations dissolved in the flurry of activity that followed the election of Franklin Delano Roosevelt to the White House. The league had close ties to the Roosevelts, and its leaders confidently joined the jostling crowd of people who surrounded the new president, seeking to shape his appointments and his policies.

The first New Deal program to address the heart of the NCL program was the National Recovery Administration. One of the most ambitious and controversial programs to emerge from Franklin Roosevelt's "First Hundred Days," this two-year emergency agency aimed to restore economic health by creating a "code of fair competition" for every industry. The labor provisions of each code established minimum wages and maximum hours for that industry. Thus the NRA represented the federal government's first peacetime regulation of adult labor standards. The NRA also granted workers the right to organize and bargain collectively. Some employers welcomed these labor provisions as a way to stabilize production, but most did not. To employers, the NRA's chief appeal was its relaxation of antitrust rules. Its codes allowed competing firms to cooperate in controlling overproduction and downward price spirals. In practice, various interests inside and outside the agency assigned different priorities to labor standards, collective bargaining, and price stabilization. Because the NRA's many drafters had not specified an economic strategy, the agency embodied three conflicting visions for recovery: a "rational, cartelized business order in which the industrialists would plan and direct the economy"; a "cooperative, collectivist democracy" in which organized economic groups (employers, labor, consumers) planned together for the public interest; and a system of enforced competition, under which vigorous anti-monopoly policies would take care of "market riggers." These internal conflicts facilitated the domination of code drafting and enforcement by industry, particularly by the largest firms in each industry. The NRA was under attack from all sides well before it was found unconstitutional in May 1935.[3]

The NCL was in the thick of the fight for the soul of the NRA. League leaders hoped the agency would be a showcase for democratic economic planning. The league had friends among both the planners and the anti-monopolists, but its core activists believed that too much competition, not too little, was the chief threat. Above all, the NCL opposed the "industrial self-government" approach to recovery.[4] The league offered a detailed program for preventing industry domination and making the NRA a successful exercise in democratic planning. It urged NRA officials to listen to labor and consumer voices, to defend union rights aggressively, to set high labor standards, to prohibit race and sex discrimination, and to empower existing state and national labor agencies to enforce code labor provisions. The league also agitated for state wage-hour laws to plug gaps and bolster NRA enforcement. However, the NCL had to fight to share the lessons of its own experience with NRA officials; its broadest recommendations were not taken up.

The NRA failed because its codes were not enforced fairly. Enforcement was poor because industry leaders ran the authorities that were charged with code administration.[5] Some scholars suggest that business domination of the code authorities resulted from a lack of "administrative capacity" on the part of the government. In this view, the federal government's lack of expertise left it little choice but to recruit businessmen to implement the codes.[6] In fact, there was an alternative. A group of women with a quarter-century of expertise in labor standards regulation lobbied hard for authority over the labor provisions of the NRA. Consumers' League activists and their allies in state and federal labor departments had worked for years designing and administering state labor laws for women, implementing minimum wage laws on the same cumbersome industry-by-industry basis used by the NRA. But most government officials, employers, and labor leaders doubted these women were qualified to shape national policies that would affect male as well as female workers. Others may have recognized their expertise but did not like their politics.

The Consumers' League and the Origins of the NRA

During Herbert Hoover's presidency, NCL activists were prominent among those who were searching for fresh approaches to national labor standards policy.[7] In the late 1920s some league thinkers began to argue that high wages and short hours were vital to national economic health as well as to workers' health. Among the NCL officers were such leading proponents of raising consumer purchasing power as Wesley Clair Mitchell and Stuart Chase. Several league women were economists whose own research supported an underconsumptionist analysis of the Depression.[8] In late 1930 and 1931, while promoting the Cotton Textile Institute's effort to reduce night work, Florence Kelley aided a Taylor Society committee in drafting a model industrial code that was similar in concept to the NRA codes. The Taylor Society had emerged as a prominent advocate of industrial democracy; its members included social scientists, labor leaders, consumption-oriented industrialists, and quite a few female labor reformers. Even before the start of the Depression, policy intellectuals in groups like the Taylor Society and the Consumers' League had begun developing the ideas and creating the alignment of political forces that would forge the New Deal.[9]

Immediately after Roosevelt's election, NCL leaders began lobbying for Senate hearings on wages and hours. In December 1932 the league sponsored a national conference that brought together trade unionists, lawyers and economists, labor department officials, and a wide array of activists. After taking stock of the Depression's devastating impact on workers, the conference concluded that "not only are thousands of wage earners being exploited, but legitimate industry is undermined by unfair competitive practices, and the purchasing power of wage earners . . . is dangerously reduced." When FDR took office, the NCL board authorized Molly Dewson, who was close to both the president and his wife, "to explore the possibility of national legislation."[10]

The Consumers' League was quick to move for national regulation, but it also foresaw that federal policy alone would not eliminate low wages and long hours. Unique to the NCL was its fight for an integrated system of state and national labor standards laws. Its leaders were certain that both local and federal rules were necessary to cover all groups of workers and to prevent evasion. The NCL also believed state-level laws helped generate the civic participation that it thought was so important to effective and democratic policy. In late 1932 the league prompted the formation of state labor standards committees in dozens of states around the country. These committees promoted bills for shorter hours and a model minimum wage bill newly drafted by NCL lawyers. These coalitions, which drew on local women's groups, female-employing unions, settlement houses, church groups, and labor departments, were behind the passage of six minimum wage laws for women in 1933, in addition to numerous improvements to hours laws and labor departments.[11] However, promoting state and national laws simultaneously would prove to be an enormous challenge, one that the NCL would wrestle with long after the NRA's demise.

While the NRA was in the gestational stage, Secretary of Labor Frances Perkins proposed a national wage-hour law based directly on the NCL's model state bill. This plan was killed by the ambivalence of the American Federation of Labor to minimum wage regulation and by broad-based hostility to female administrative authority over labor policy. Perkins's plan, which the NCL supported, was an alternative to Senator Hugo Black's thirty-hour-week bill. Black's bill was introduced in December 1932 with AFL approval. The NCL welcomed the AFL's new warmth toward hours laws for men and supported the "share-the-work" principle behind the Black bill. However, like Perkins, league leaders feared the bill would be found unconstitutional. They also believed it would cause severe hardship to the lowest-paid workers (who were disproportionately female). Without any minimum wage provision, the bill's drastic reduction in hours, from the typical forty-eight or more per week to thirty, would worsen poverty. Perkins suggested amending the Black bill to include a minimum wage provision administered by industry boards representing labor, management, and the public. Perkins's proposal created an uproar. Organized labor and business leaders alike declared themselves appalled at her "bid for unlimited power." Perkins stressed that her bill was nothing new, just an extension of the state minimum wage commissions for women. But what organized labor and some businessmen had accepted in the states for women workers they found unacceptable as part of a federal program that included men. Business leaders denounced Perkins's bill as "grossly impractical" and dangerous in its plan to substitute "the judgment of a Federal officer for that of experienced and responsible management" on wages and hours. The AFL's William Green opposed minimum wages for men as well as the "board method" of administration.[12]

NCL leaders lobbied unsuccessfully to close the door to industrial self-government, and then they clashed with the man appointed to head the new agency. Molly Dewson wrote to all the various groups involved in NRA drafting, urging them to mandate a short workday and mandatory minimum wage, and warning against entrusting recovery to trade associations.[13] The final bill remained vague, however, and FDR's selection for the NRA's executive was a poor omen. General Hugh Johnson, who had worked for the War Industries Board during World War I, was a former businessman who envisioned industrialist-led recovery.[14] Johnson suggested skipping the public hearings phase of code drafting. Instead, he proposed setting each industry's code by meeting with the executives of the companies involved. The Consumers' League network was horrified. Public participation in policy making was at the core of the league's faith in a planning-oriented administrative state. The NCL believed public input not only yielded fairer policy, it also legitimized that policy. Grassroots interest enhanced enforcement. Frances Perkins insisted on public hearings at which labor and public representatives could speak: "We're operating a democracy here. You're going to adopt a code which will affect thousands of people's lives. . . . If [the people] don't cooperate, it will be a failure."[15]

Hoping its own vision of the NRA would triumph over Hugh Johnson's, the NCL combined public agitation with what Lucy Mason called "behind-the-scenes" work, which required mastery of the NRA's intricate bureaucratic channels. In the code-drafting process, each industry submitted a proposed code to NRA administrators, who consulted with labor representatives to arrive at a preliminary code, which then was discussed at a public hearing. Each code established fair trade practices, labor standards, and a code authority empowered to administer the code. From the public hearing, the revised code went to the NRA's Industrial, Labor, and Consumers' Advisory Boards for approval and then to Johnson, who submitted it to the president for final authorization. The NCL influenced this process at various stages, mainly through direct lobbying of NRA code administrators. In some circumstances, the league appealed for intervention to Franklin or Eleanor Roosevelt, or to the Department of Labor (DOL).[16] Other channels of NCL influence were through the Consumers' Advisory Board (CAB) and Labor Advisory Board (LAB). The league had good connections on these boards, which, although weak, did exert some pressure against employer demands.

The Consumers' Advisory Board, the Consumer Movement, and the NCL

The existence of the NRA Consumer Advisory Board was an indicator of the extent to which the Great Depression had made policymakers, intellectuals, and ordinary citizens more conscious of the economic and political importance of the consumer. The new consumerism had diverse manifestations with varying political implications. A social democratic strain asserted that a mass consumer movement would be an indispensable complement to a strong labor movement in the fight against corporate domination of the nation's economic and political life. These laborite consumerists included New Dealers like Paul Douglas, Frederic Howe, Leon Henderson, and Caroline Ware, who with others used federal agencies such as the CAB, the Agricultural Adjustment Administration, the Tennessee Valley Authority, and later the Office of Price Administration to organize citizens into grassroots consumer councils and cooperatives. These government-backed initiatives emerged with the approval of new left-leaning voluntary associations such as the Consumers' Union and the League of Women Shoppers. But not all consumer activists were pro-labor. Groups like Consumers' Research complained that higher labor standards translated into higher prices and therefore did little for purchasing power. Moreover, to counter the growth of labor-allied consumer groups, trade associations began funding their own consumer movement, which blamed government spending and unions for high taxes and high prices.[17]

The NCL welcomed the wider recognition of the consumer's importance, but the league's relationship to the consumer movement was ambiguous. The NCL board repeatedly rejected proposals to expand the league program to include consumer protection, worried about losing focus and diminishing the commitment to high labor standards. Time and time again the NCL explained to people confused by its name that its field was labor standards, not product prices and quality. The league also took pains to discourage new groups from taking names too close to its own. Although league officers tried to preserve some distinction between the NCL and the new consumer movement, as individuals many of them were active in consumer cooperatives and the Consumers' Union. Eventually, the emergence of antilabor consumer voices pulled the league into a struggle to keep the consumer movement united with the cause of labor. The NCL joined the Consumers' National Federation, an umbrella group, and league officers helped expose "fake consumers' organizations" that were "falsely attributing price increases to wage increases." High wages and low prices could go together, they explained, if workers and consumers allied to take away employers' power to command unreasonable profits. "We the consumers can have a functioning democracy only as we consciously organize to break the bonds of a monopolistic dictatorship which now can control prices, wages, and production," one league leader proclaimed.[18]

The Consumers' Advisory Board, on which the NCL was represented, became a platform for forceful criticism of NRA policy by dissatisfied liberals.[19] However, the CAB's authority was limited, in part because it was trivialized as a female-dominated group. Hugh Johnson did not take the consumer movement seriously, holding firmly to a producer-centered vision of economic recovery. He created the CAB as a token gesture and then generally ignored it. Johnson selected Mary Harriman Rumsey (who was Frances Perkins's housemate) to head the board. Other members included Molly Dewson of the NCL, Belle Sherwin of the League of Women Voters, and a long list of academic men, several of them NCL officers.[20] Critics often attacked the CAB in latently antiwoman terms, even though men outnumbered women on the board. Frederick Schlink of Consumers' Research grumbled that the CAB was dominated by "dull social worker types," "gutless economics professors," and "society matrons." (Schlink's real gripe was that Consumers' League influence helped keep the CAB committed to high wages. Not incidentally, Schlink's own organization soon would be embroiled in scandal over unfair labor practices.) Johnson's appointment of Rumsey to the CAB may have been a deliberate attempt to marginalize it by "feminizing" it. In any case, the appointment reflected his low opinion of the board's significance.[21]

The NCL sought to influence CAB policy without compromising league autonomy. Both Lucy Mason and Elinore Herrick (Consumers' League of New York) took turns pinch-hitting for Molly Dewson on the CAB, but they declined a permanent seat. Mason declared that being on the board impaired her freedom to criticize proposed codes. Later, when some members argued that the Consumers' League should have greater representation on NRA consumer boards, Mason reiterated her view that "it is necessary to be free of affiliation to effectively represent the consumers' conscience *on labor standards*."[22]

The league took a similarly supportive but aloof attitude toward the Women's Section of the NRA, which amounted to a public relations effort to encourage women to buy only from businesses that displayed the Blue Eagle, the symbol of compliance with the NRA codes. Hugh Johnson announced, "It is women in homes — and not soldiers in uniforms — who will this time save our country."[23] Contemporaries noted the debt of the Blue Eagle campaign to the NCL's older methods of ethical consumption, and many activists in branch leagues led Blue Eagle drives in their states. Kentucky league president Anna Settle organized a Blue Eagle campaign that obtained almost 50,000 signatures in Louisville, for example. The Consumers' League believed that civic involvement by grassroots constituencies resulted in more effective public policy, but national league activists also sought more direct authority over the NRA. They appreciated the benefits of mobilizing shoppers, but they did not accept that it was only as "women in homes" that they could wield influence.[24]

NCL women thus worked primarily through the agency's policy-making divisions, despite repeated NRA efforts to recruit them into public relations work. In New York, state NRA official Averell Harriman asked Elinore Herrick to head the state Women's Division, but she refused. One reason was that she was "not sure what kind of campaign would be put on" and did not want to lend "the prestige of [the Consumers' League] to a campaign of which we might be ashamed." However, Herrick also sought a more powerful role. She persuaded Harriman to let her be his behind-the-scenes adviser on NRA policy, which worked out "very satisfactorily." Herrick reported to the league that Harriman consulted her extensively and that she directed NRA policy throughout the state. She wrote most of Harriman's speeches for him, and she created a Division of Investigation that implemented "the Consumers' League technique of inspection." Eventually, Herrick "allowed" Harriman to appoint her to the state NRA's executive committee.[25]

In April 1934 the NRA tried to hire Lucy Mason to do publicity work among social workers and church groups. Some league board members thought the invitation offered an opportunity to influence the NRA for the better, and that "such an offer could not be turned down lightly." Others argued that the NCL was more effective "from outside" and should not put itself in the position of "whitewashing NRA." By this time quite disillusioned with the agency, Mason declined, explaining that the job "would not give me sufficient opportunity to be critical of the weak places in NRA."[26] Gratified as they were to see the principle of federal labor standards established, league leaders saw that the battle had only begun, and they strove to maximize their leverage over NRA policy.

The Labor Advisory Board and a Changing Labor Movement

The NRA's Labor Advisory Board was closer to the concerns of the Consumers' League than either the CAB or the Women's Section. The LAB was appointed by and reported to Frances Perkins. Its chairman, Leo Wolman, a Columbia labor economist with ties to the ACWA, was on the NCL board.[27] Other LAB members included William Green of the AFL, John Lewis of the United Mine Workers, ACWA president Sidney Hillman, Rose Schneiderman of the WTUL, and Reverend Francis Haas of the National Catholic Welfare Conference. Schneiderman and Haas were regulars at NCL conferences.[28]

The LAB had more influence over NRA policy than the CAB, but it was weak compared to the Industrial Advisory Board and the trade associations. This accurately reflected the relative power of organized employers, unions, and consumers. During the 1920s, welfare capitalism and other, harsher anti-union practices had combined with general prosperity to erode the labor movement's numbers and spirit. When the Depression hit, employers rapidly cut amenities and wages. Many workers in formerly organized industries reconsidered the open shop bargain. Unorganized workers, too, were increasingly militant, most obviously in the southern textile strikes. Section 7a of the NRA emboldened workers by putting the official stamp of approval on the right to organize. Union memberships swelled during the NRA's short lifespan, but even by 1935, unions represented less than 10 percent of the nonagricultural workforce.[29] In industries that were at least partially unionized, the LAB had some success in negotiating better labor provisions and stronger representation on code authorities. But labor's power in Washington remained modest.

The Depression stimulated the emergence of new voices that were transforming the labor movement. The initiatives of people like John Lewis and Sidney Hillman in "industrial unionism" — organizing an industry's workers across boundaries of skill and craft — increased the pressure on the AFL to do more for unskilled workers in mass production industries. Also, insurgents within the AFL were forcing the old guard to modify its antistatism. In 1932 the AFL's annual convention endorsed national hours standards and unemployment insurance. However, unskilled workers, especially those outside the manufacturing sector, continued to be a low priority for most labor leaders.

The NCL directly influenced the leaders who would transform the labor movement's attitude toward wage-hour regulation. John Lewis and Sidney Hillman, who soon would found the CIO, came to believe that the state could play a positive role in setting a floor for labor standards. Lewis's support of an administrative state was more grudging than Hillman's, but both men represented workers in industries plagued by the sorts of problems that the NCL long had railed against. In coal mining and the needle trades, labor surpluses combined with workforce divisions (of race, ethnicity, age, or gender) to inhibit organizing and to enable employers to play workers against each other. Unlike garment factories, coal mines could not migrate toward cheaper labor, which may help explain why Hillman was more eager for national wage-hour regulation than Lewis. Nevertheless, Lewis was receptive to new ideas, in part because he had been impressed by his union's positive experience with a Colorado coal mining company owned by the NCL's Josephine Roche. Roche impressed the miners again during negotiations over the NRA's coal code, when she persuaded a group of coal operators to compromise on the code's labor provisions.[30]

The ACWA's Sidney Hillman owed his rise to power in part to support from female labor reformers. The Chicago WTUL promoted Hillman after he demonstrated his ability during the dramatic garment worker uprisings of 1909. When Hillman moved to New York, he sought out Florence Kelley, who introduced him to Walter Lippmann and Felix Frankfurter. Kelley, Hillman, and Frankfurter were the chief actors in the wartime experiments with labor policy that convinced Hillman and many others of the positive potential of the state. In New York in the 1920s, social scientists in the league's orbit helped shape Hillman's ideas about the importance of consumer demand to a modern mass production economy. During the New Deal, it was Frances Perkins who promoted Hillman, this time to the position on the LAB that greatly advanced his career as a "labor statesman."[31] Other union officials who became key league allies came from the Hosiery Workers and the United Electrical Workers. It was no coincidence

Josephine Roche with John L. Lewis after she addressed the annual convention of the United Mine Workers of America in January 1936. (AP/Wide World Photos, Washington Star Collection, courtesy of District of Columbia Public Library)

that most of the first labor leaders to actively promote government labor standards came from industries with large numbers of female workers.

An Independent Voice for Unorganized Workers

Because most union members already had higher wages and shorter hours than the codes would set, unions' interest in code labor provisions depended on whether they faced unorganized competition within their industry. The interests of unorganized workers were attended to only when they coincided with those of employers or unions, unless a group such as the NCL intervened. The Consumers' League submitted written criticisms and appeared at hearings on "countless" codes, "especially on codes that deal with unorganized labor, as that group most needs help." North Carolina tobacco workers, for example, not organized enough "to feel safe in openly making demands," asked Lucy Mason to testify against their employers at a hearing on the proposed tobacco code.[32]

Mason's work on the NRA codes continued the NCL's long tradition of focusing on the interests of less skilled workers. Mason once observed, "Industry includes both skilled and unskilled tasks. . . . The conditions of those who do the hardest and most unskilled work, which is a necessary part of our whole industrial system, should be our first concern."[33] Throughout her career, Mason implored skilled workers to see that their own interests were intertwined with those of the unskilled groups they often despised. As she put it some years later, "The special bargaining power of the skilled is linked with the mass power of the greater number of semiskilled and unskilled. All workers in the industry must be organized and protected without discrimination because of race, religion, or sex. There must be a fair distribution of wages to each group according to its skills, but the least skilled workers must be adequately paid for the essential labor they perform."[34]

One hallmark of the NCL effort to influence the NRA was its attack on code provisions that perpetuated competition between groups of workers. The league argued that raising purchasing power required the elimination of "underbidders" who pulled all wages down. Beneath this technocratic language of economic recovery lay a genuine commitment to justice for workers who were vulnerable because unions had been unable or unwilling to organize them. As the league emphasized again and again, setting different minimum wage provisions by race, sex, age, or job classification exploited the lower-paid groups. Codes on which the league testified or submitted criticisms included cotton textiles, rayon, retail dry goods, newspapers, paper and pulp, crushed stone, laundries, restaurants, canning, tobacco, knitted outerwear, lace, embroidery, and candy making. Heavily reliant on the labor of women and racial minorities, these industries were prone to the practices the NCL abhorred: sex- and race-based discrimination, homework, child labor, below-subsistence wages, and long hours.

The league outlined its goals at the hearings on the first NRA code, for the cotton textile industry. The code would affect in particular the thousands of impoverished southern women who comprised the lowest paid segment of the industry's labor force. Almost eight hundred people crowded into a hot Washington, D.C., auditorium for the hearings in June 1933. The Cotton Textile Institute, reflecting its experience with the voluntary ban on women's night work, had shaped the NRA code in the drafting stages, seeking a more comprehensive and compulsory measure than the trade association could enforce on its own. But the trade association's proposed labor provisions were hardly generous. CTI offered a forty-hour week and minimum wages of $10 per week in the South and $11 in the North. Moreover, its proposal exempted outdoor help, cleaners, learners, and office workers from all labor provisions. The United Textile Workers' representative responded by demanding shorter hours and a minimum of at least $14 per week. Cotton textile wages were notoriously low, averaging $13 a week for unskilled males in the northern branch. Women in the southern branch received significantly less.[35] After sitting through three days of testimony, those who had requested to appear as "representatives of the public" at last had their turn. Among these were Lucy Mason, along with Margaret Wiesman of the Massachusetts Consumers' League.

Mason's testimony rapidly established her expertise on the textile industry and the latest economic theories. (The presiding administrator introduced her as representing the consumer's concern about price increases resulting from higher labor standards, but Mason politely set him straight.) After a few conciliatory sentences commending CTI for its cooperative spirit, Mason launched into a penetrating indictment of the proposed code. Her chief concern was raising the minimum wage and making sure it covered all workers. She also addressed daily hours, night work, the stretch-out, enforcement, labor representation, and the regional wage differential. Mason sought to define the NRA's first objective as raising wages, rather than stabilizing prices. She held no illusions about the industry's motivations in submitting its code. Mason observed that CTI's proposal would "merely remove the cotton-textile industry from regulation of the anti-trust laws without providing that basis of rising wages and increased purchasing power which it is the purpose of the Industrial Recovery Act to insure." She invoked FDR's definition of a living wage as not just a subsistence wage but a "decent living" to every worker.[36]

Mason's analysis stressed the interdependence of regional and occupational labor markets to suggest that national recovery depended on addressing the interests of the lowest-paid workers. She challenged the idea that cotton textiles were an inherently low-wage industry (because of the alleged sensitivity of demand to price). She argued that the industry's low wages stemmed from overexpansion during the First World War and from the existence in the South of a "large surplus supply of cheap labor constantly recruited from an agricultural population which has an excessively low standard of living." Low wages in the South dragged down northern wages and also compounded the "overproduction" problem by reducing the size of "home markets" in the South. Furthermore, Mason warned, shortening hours without increasing wages would defeat the NRA's goal of spreading employment, because textile workers would seek additional employment in their new free hours to meet the gap between their textile wages and their survival needs.[37]

Scholars of the textile industry and the NRA note that the federal government and the industry lacked experience in setting minimum wages, but they overlook the contributions that the Consumers' League was able to make at the hearings. Organized labor rarely could fill this gap, but the NCL could marshal impressive amounts of data to make specific recommendations. A New Hampshire Federation of Labor representative protested CTI's proposed minimum wage as insufficient, but when questioned he "frankly admitted that he had no figures on the situation."[38] Mason (and Margaret Wiesman after her) presented extensive statistics on earnings in various branches of the industry and from cost-of-living studies to demonstrate that the proposed minimum rates were "dangerously near the substandard rates hitherto in effect." Although they did not stress this, Mason and Wiesman used data gathered in surveys of women workers to estimate the cost of living for men and women alike.[39]

After Mason's and Wiesman's testimony, industry representatives offered to raise the code minimum wage by 20 percent, to $12 a week in the South and $13 in the North. The Consumers' League and the unions had hoped for more, but it was a significant improvement, particularly as the cotton code set a precedent for the hundreds that followed. Confident that the league's participation had been worthwhile, Mason wrote that "we have a very definite point of view to express in connection with the code hearings, and I have made a real dent in the administration on the cotton code." The NCL may not deserve full credit for the increased minimum, but its statistics and vigorous critique of the industry's proposal increased the leverage of labor and liberals within the NRA.[40] The LAB and CAB indicated their appreciation by keeping the league supplied with up-to-the-minute information on proposed codes. Many code hearings later, one LAB employee urged the NCL to keep up the pressure against industry proposals, because it was "perfectly clear that the Administration is uncertain as to what to do."[41]

The Consumers' League and NRA Race Discrimination

The NCL struggled unsuccessfully at the cotton textile hearings to eliminate racially discriminatory occupational exemptions from the code. This defeat triggered a sustained campaign that placed the NCL at the side of outspoken black critics of the NRA and well ahead of most white liberals. This activism by the Consumers' League, and also by the YWCA, illustrates that women were prominent among the few whites to organize against race discrimination in the New Deal, but it also highlights the indifference of other white women's organizations to the problems of black workers. Neither the League of Women Voters, the U.S. Women's Bureau, nor the National Woman's Party lined up behind the NCL to demand racial justice under NRA codes. This failure contrasts sharply with the well-coordinated attack these groups would launch against NRA sex discrimination.

The exclusion of black-dominated occupations from many NRA codes was neither accidental nor unopposed. The cotton textile code's exemption of outside help and cleaners effectively denied blacks any code protection, because these were the only jobs open to blacks in that industry. Many other industry codes discriminated through similar exemptions, or by setting lower labor standards in regions where African Americans dominated the workforce.[42] Black protest of the NRA codes was sparked by John P. Davis and Robert C. Weaver, who met as graduate students at Harvard before returning to their hometown of Washington, D.C., in 1933. Dismayed by black organizations' inattention to NRA policy, Davis and Weaver established themselves as the Negro Industrial League and spoke at code hearings affecting black workers. In late 1933 this group metamorphosed into the Joint Committee for National Recovery (JCNR), a coalition of organizations concerned with the welfare of black workers. These included, in addition to black church and professional associations, the NAACP, the National Association of Colored Women, the Federal Council of Churches, and the national YWCA. (The YWCA in fact provided staff support and much of the funding for the JCNR.) With John Davis as its most prominent spokesperson, the JCNR led the protest against race discrimination in the NRA and other New Deal programs.[43]

Outside of the JCNR, the National Consumers' League was the most forceful and knowledgeable critic of NRA race discrimination. Lucy Mason, who was on the NAACP board at this time, was the league's most energetic opponent of white supremacy, but many league branches protested race discrimination in employment.[44] Like the JCNR, the Consumers' League denounced code exemptions of black-dominated occupations, race differentials in wages and hours, and the lack of black representation in the NRA. At the cotton textile code hearing, Lucy Mason spoke against the exemption of "outside help," agreeing with John Davis that the purchasing power of all workers should be raised. When asked whether paying the same minimum to all employees might result in the replacement of blacks with whites, Mason conceded that there was such a risk. However, she preferred to "see the principle [of equal wages] established" to test whether experience would justify it. She also cautioned against "that tendency to believe that the colored worker needs less than the white worker." The administrator's private notes suggest that Mason's statement, in conjunction with Davis's, convinced him to eliminate the exemptions. However, the exemptions were restored as a last-minute concession to southern mill owners.[45]

After the cotton textile code, Mason followed the code-drafting process especially closely for industries that employed large numbers of black workers. At hearings for the crushed stone, sand and gravel, and slag industries, Mason met employer justifications of regional wage differentials head on. Southern industry leaders explained that because their operations depended on "inefficient" black workers, the southern branch could not afford the higher rate paid in northern states. They claimed that southern blacks were used to receiving a maximum of seventeen cents an hour. (It was hastily added that "of course we work no white man at any such scale as that.") Raising black wages would create havoc, employers warned. They alleged that blacks would quit work until they had burned up all their money on vice.[46] Mason's response was indignant: "If the negro is to live in a little better home and smoke a little better tobacco, and perhaps have a little Ford and buy gasoline for it, it is going to be a blessed good thing for purchasing power." Here Mason used underconsumptionist thought to insist on black workers' rights to equal pay and a higher standard of living.[47]

Mason's exasperation with the code hearings prompted her to file a lengthy memorandum on race discrimination with all 120 NRA deputy administrators as well as General Johnson and President Roosevelt. Mason noted that "in southern states legislative battles have been fought over excluding from women's hours laws occupations in which Negro women were chiefly employed. We do not want to set the stamp of [federal] Government approval on this attitude." As for the efficiency of black workers, Mason insisted that "there is nothing inherent in the Negro which disqualifies him from being a good worker." She dryly observed that "if it did not pay to employ Negroes they would not be employed at all."[48] Mason also challenged the claim that equal minimum wages would worsen "race relations." She argued that "though he himself is unaware of the cause of his antagonism, deep rooted in the southern white unskilled wage earner is fear of [cheaper] Negro competition." Equal wages would reduce white fears, she implied. On the controversial question of black displacement by whites if equal wages were paid, Mason pointed out that it was employers who were invoking the specter of black displacement. Skeptical of this charity, she asked, "Have Negro workers or their representatives been consulted as to whether they wish to be excluded from such protective provisions, or have white wage earners demanded that Negroes be excluded?"[49]

During the 1930s, advocates of black workers and women workers often confronted the argument that if race or sex differentials were eliminated, blacks or women would be displaced by whites or by men, since employers would prefer those groups if all received the same wage. On both race and sex, NCL leaders stuck by the equal pay principle. They worried about displacement of formerly underpaid groups, but they believed that in the long run allowing any group to underbid another was detrimental to that group, and to all workers collectively. On the question of race, the JCNR also embraced this position, overruling a few black spokespersons who argued that blacks should accept a lower wage in order to protect their jobs. An official race differential ultimately would be stigmatizing and disadvantageous to blacks, the JCNR insisted.[50] Lucy Mason made a point of gathering data on blacks' replacement by whites, which was less common than defenders of race differentials claimed. One analyst observed that even without the NRA, the new willingness of whites to work at low-paid, formerly stigmatized jobs would have caused some black displacement. In other words, it may have been the Depression, not the codes, that in a few places was causing whites to replace blacks.[51]

Even more unusual than the NCL's protest against discriminatory code labor provisions was its pressure for the appointment of blacks to prominent NRA positions. Mason early supported black demands for representation. "Would it not be advisable to have well qualified Negroes on each of the advisory boards and in the research divisions of NRA?" she asked Hugh Johnson. When the Research and Planning Division did hire a black woman, Mason wrote other NRA staff urging them to work with her. These efforts to encourage interaction with the NRA's sole black professional apparently were to no avail. A subsequent report found that the woman, Mabel Byrd, had never been allowed to function as an investigator and had not even been invited to the staff meetings of her division. After much delay, the NRA finally appointed a black economist, Dr. Abram Harris of Howard University, to the Consumers' Advisory Board, but he resigned after only a few months.[52]

Despite exhaustive efforts by John Davis and Lucy Mason, regional differentials were encoded for over one hundred industries by late 1934. These usually were nothing but camouflaged race differentials. The North-South border was located differently in different codes, depending on the proportion of black workers in an industry. For example, most codes defined Delaware as northern, but the fertilizer code, which in Delaware affected primarily black workers, defined it as southern. Furthermore, regional differentials were largest in industries where the southern workforce was mostly black; hence the differential was narrow in cotton textiles but wide in fertilizer.[53] However, without JCNR and NCL protests, the outcome would have been even worse. At the crushed stone hearing, for example, Mason was only one who criticized the race-based regional wage differential. In the approved code, the regional differential was narrowed, although not eliminated.[54] As Walter White of the NAACP told a discouraged colleague, "We cannot always measure effectiveness by things gained; we must also measure results by considering evils prevented."[55]

The Consumers' League and NRA Sex Discrimination

The JCNR did not address the question of sex discrimination in NRA codes. John Davis spent most of his time on codes that affected black men's occupations, not black women's. Davis's personal attitudes, as described by women he worked with, suggest that he would not have been a great advocate of gender equality.[56] Although black women's groups mobilized against NRA race discrimination, they did not protest the agency's sex discrimination. This may be explained in part by the structure of the workforce. Most black women worked in occupations untouched by the NRA, such as agriculture and domestic work, and where black women were in industries covered by the NRA, such as laundries, restaurants, and canneries, their higher-paid competitors were not men but white women. Black women probably perceived their low wages as a function primarily of race discrimination between themselves and white women.[57] However, white activists bore some responsibility for defining sex discrimination as a white women's issue, because most white women's groups did not protest against code race discrimination. The historical tendency of white women to define discrimination against black women as a "race issue" may well have alienated black women from the campaign against sex discrimination.[58]

A long list of white women's groups agitated against NRA sex discrimination. The campaign was led by two camps: the anti-ERA coalition, which included the U.S. Women's Bureau, the Consumer's League, the WTUL, the YWCA, and the League of Women Voters, on one hand, and the National Woman's Party and its pro-ERA ally, the Federation of Business and Professional Women's Clubs, on the other. Both camps worked vigorously to eliminate sex-based wage differentials, and both tried to claim exclusive credit for the fact that such differentials were removed from many codes.[59] However, only the NCL group concerned itself with the details and practical effects of each code, and thus only that group was informed enough to protest latent as well as explicit sex discrimination.

The two factions waged their battles for NRA sex equality in different languages. The pro-ERA group drew on general principles about individual citizenship and property rights. Letters to Hugh Johnson from the Business and Professional Women's Clubs emphasized that discrimination against any class was "unAmerican" and that women paid the same taxes and prices as men. By contrast, the labor-oriented feminists took a technical approach, emphasizing labor market factors such as women's skills, occupational sex segregation, and competition between groups of workers, and stressing the need to raise the purchasing power of the poorest workers. The resistance of NCL allies to the individualistic feminism of the ERA camp made them less comfortable arguing from a women's rights position.[60]

The difference between the Woman's Party and the Consumers' League approaches emerged at the first code hearings, for cotton textiles. Both groups adamantly opposed setting a lower minimum wage for women. Margaret Wiesman of the Massachusetts league observed that a woman could not live any less expensively than a man, and that "she has dependents as much as a man has." She also argued that neither sex should work more than eight hours a day, and that six hours would be even better. On the question of night work, Lucy Mason vacillated at first. The textile union had proposed banning women's night work. Mason thought all night work should be banned, but she hinted that if that was impossible, then women's night hours should be restricted. The code administrator asked Mason whether equal protection was "more strongly done by making no . . . attempt to discriminate or set up those two distinct classes" or by sex-specific measures. Mason answered frankly that he asked "a question which is rather unresolved." When pressed to clarify her position, Mason concluded that the textile code should make no sex-specific provisions.[61] The Woman's Party limited its comment on the codes to an insistence that they make no distinctions by sex. The final code did not distinguish between male and female workers. Night work was in effect eliminated for all workers by the code's establishment of an industrywide maximum of two forty-hour shifts per week.[62]

Subsequent industry codes did set lower minimum wages for women than for men, and the Consumers' League coalition stepped up its campaign against sex differentials. Mary Anderson analyzed code approval patterns to identify which NRA administrators were authorizing lower wages for women and organized conferences with the offenders. Joint press releases by the NCL, WTUL, YWCA, and LWV kept the arguments against lower wages for women fresh in the minds of NRA officials and the public. In September 1933 these groups filed a protest with President Roosevelt and NRA administrators: "Wages should be paid for the type of work done and not on the basis of sex. . . . We believe that the codes adopted by the N.R.A. should not perpetuate an economic injustice." Sex differentials undermined the NRA's objectives of spreading employment and increasing purchasing power, they asserted.[63] The NCL coalition pointed out that in certain occupations lower minimum wages for women displaced men. This

was not an argument that women's wage rates should be raised to discourage their employment and restore "natural" sex roles. Rather, these
groups emphasized the injustice and economic folly of allowing exploitation of one group of workers to hold all wages down.[64]

Whereas the Woman's Party limited its attention to the question of
formal sex differentials, the NCL recognized that gender-blind legislation
was no guarantee against sex discrimination. By November 1933, not only
had fourteen of the eighty-one approved codes set sex-based wage differentials, but eight other codes discriminated against women more subtly by
paying less for "light and repetitive work" or to workers who as of July
1929 had made less than a certain wage. The NCL challenged "light and
repetitive work" clauses, asserting that lighter machines often demanded
more accuracy and endurance, and that, in any case, women had proved
themselves to be quite capable on the "so-called heavy machines." The
league also urged NRA administrators to curb the use of "learner" provisions, which were notoriously abused by employers with unorganized female workforces.[65]

Eliminating industrial homework was another high priority for the NCL.
This practice took advantage of the desperation of women with dependents. It was essentially a code-dodging method because it was so difficult
to monitor. In opposing homework, the league emphasized raising purchasing power and protecting workers, not motherhood. Homework was
a "chisel" that undermined factory labor standards and the whole purpose
of the NRA. When the league used family-oriented arguments, it was to
counter those introduced by the opposition. One NCL board member
called for combating "the sentimental point of view of not breaking up the
home and forcing the mother into the factory. We ought to develop some
sort of propaganda . . . meet sob stuff with sob stuff and show how the
homes are actually being broken up by the introduction and continuation
of homework."[66] The league understood women to be a permanent part of
the labor force, entitled to the same benefits from NRA codes as men. It
sought to protect women and men alike from underbidding by particularly
exploitable groups.[67]

Organized women did not eliminate code discrimination against
women, but they significantly reduced it. In May 1934 the Women's Bureau
claimed that at least 224 changes had been made in 119 codes as a result of
pressure it had applied in conjunction with the NCL and WTUL.[68] That one-
quarter of the NRA codes did, in the end, contain sex differentials has been
taken as evidence of the failure of women's organizations during this period.[69] But it was due to the constant vigilance of organized women that
three-quarters of the codes did not incorporate sex differentials. Further-

New York City garment workers declare their determination to enforce NRA codes (ca. 1934). (Amalgamated Clothing Workers of America Records, Kheel Center, Cornell University)

more, the NCL network made substantial headway on other issues that disproportionately affected women, such as industrial homework and lower learner rates. In some respects NRA codes benefited women more than men: in many industries, women's wages almost doubled, hours were sharply reduced, mechanization opened new jobs to women, and unions grudgingly opened their doors. Of course, not all major woman-employing occupations had codes, with domestic service as the most obvious example.[70]

Enforcing the NRA Codes

"Thay are breaking your code in ever way they can," an anonymous cotton textile worker from South Carolina wrote to FDR. "Thay hade to take the Blue Eagle away from the Clinton Mills . . . and we are almost starved." Imploring the president to take action, the worker concluded, "But rember we poor pople are your friend."[71] The Consumers' League had predicted that enforcing code labor provisions would be as difficult as getting good ones approved. Molly Dewson remarked in 1933 that "the NRA is a great pipe dream come true—but pipe dreams are rather nebulous."[72] In some industries, strong unions were effective enforcers of code labor provisions, thereby converting some employers into grudging supporters of union rights. However, the number of codes in which unions were able to play this role was small. Also, unions rarely were able to enforce their codes as effectively in the South as elsewhere. The NCL's multiprong efforts to improve NRA enforcement policy were an important supplement to the efforts of organized labor.[73] The league's detailed proposals for translating statutory protection of workers into real protection illuminate its hopes for a more democratic NRA, which might be achieved by empowering both organized labor and veteran administrators of women's labor laws. The ambivalence of the agency's response convinced the league that it needed to sustain its state-level, sex-based strategies.

The league sought to improve NRA enforcement in several ways. First, it worked to have codes drafted without loopholes and with explicit enforcement mechanisms. Second, the league pushed for more labor and consumer representation on code authorities. Third, it agitated for a national NRA compliance system that would rely less on the code authorities and more on NCL allies in the federal and state departments of labor. Fourth, the league demanded stronger guarantees of collective bargaining. Lastly, the NCL lobbied for new state laws to supplement NRA codes.[74]

Using Worker Input to Draft Enforceable Codes

Employers, NRA administrators, and most unions lacked practical experience with wage and hours laws, and representatives such as the National Woman's Party and the Negro Industrial League made general statements of principle rather than concrete suggestions for improving the NRA codes. NCL research helped fill this gap. The league's close contact with workers enabled it to make specific recommendations on drafting codes that would be harder to evade. Lucy Mason visited seventeen states in 1934, most of them in the South, asking workers whether NRA codes were being enforced and whether the codes benefited them. The NCL located workers (primarily women, although their sex was not emphasized to the NRA) by contacting the Summer Schools for Women Workers, labor unions, branch leagues, and YWCA industrial secretaries. Sometimes workers who feared that NRA compliance boards would not protect them from reprisals reported code violations to the Consumers' League.[75] In 1933 and again in 1934, Mason circulated 2,000 questionnaires on code effectiveness and tabulated the responses for each year's Labor Standards Conference. Mason also compiled a long list of employers' "chiseling" methods, which she aired at code hearings and conferences. In this respect the Consumers' League acted as a liaison between workers and the NRA.[76]

The league believed that informed workers were the starting point for good enforcement. The NCL advised that codes require conspicuous posting of hours, wages, and other regulations in workplaces, a simple step without which employers easily misled workers about code provisions. Mechanisms were needed to prohibit falsifying payroll records, stretching out or speeding up production, paying by check and forcing the employee to return cash, deducting from wages the cost of meals or uniforms, making employees take work home, and other abuses.[77] The enforcement issue also was one more argument against varying minimum wage rates for different occupational groups, such as learners, executives, or outdoor help. Exemptions and differentials "open[ed] the door to evasion" by tempting employers to reclassify employees into the exempted or lower-paid categories. At code hearings, Mason educated audiences on the notorious abuse of learner and apprenticeship clauses, whereby employees were fired as soon as the learning period expired and replaced with new employees at the low learner rate. Unskilled, unorganized workers were most powerless against this type of exploitation.

Offsetting Employer Control of Code Authorities

In addition to getting enforcement techniques written into the codes, the NCL demanded more labor and consumer representation on the code authorities.[78] Each code authority was to have industry, labor, and "administration" (public or consumer) representatives. However, from the first code on, the authorities tended to be made up of the same trade association bodies that had submitted the proposed codes. Labor representatives often were weak and isolated, and they generally were men who assigned low priority to women's interests. The NCL occasionally managed to have its members appointed as labor or administration representatives to the authorities, or to advisory committees. Lucy Mason was on the advisory board to the coat and suit authority, one of the few authorities able and willing to enforce its code. But, as one LAB official observed, "code authority" remained synonymous with "industry leaders" except in the case of about ten codes. This official complained to an NCL conference that the "standard Chamber of Commerce type of executive who is typical on the code authorities is not equipped to enforce labor provisions." He urged the groups represented at the conference to place their accumulated "experience in enforcing labor provisions . . . at the disposal of the Federal Government."[79]

Women's Advisory Committee on the NRA coat and suit code tells Eleanor Roosevelt of the code's successful first year (October 1934). Left to right: Lucy Mason; Mary Rumsey, CAB; Bessie Beatty, National Garment Label Campaign; Eleanor Roosevelt; Mrs. John A. Selby, Junior League; and Mary Anderson, U.S. Women's Bureau. (Corbis/Bettmann-UPI)

The NCL managed to get some members appointed to other NRA administrative positions. Dozens of league members volunteered for NRA compliance and mediation boards around the country, bringing specific league techniques with them. League members such as Arthur Altmeyer, Clara Beyer, and William Davis held staff positions in the Compliance Division, and they solicited NCL suggestions for appointments to regional and local NRA boards. Elinore Herrick, executive secretary of the New York Consumers' League and adviser to NRA officials in New York, attributed the relatively successful enforcement there to the adoption of the league's own method of inspecting payrolls and timecards.[80]

In January 1934 Lucy Mason was still optimistic that placing league expertise "at the disposal of the Federal Government" would constructively influence the NRA. She believed her comprehensive statement, "Proposed Principles for Labor Provisions of NRA Codes," had "undoubtedly led to the reopening of the whole subject of labor provisions and had gotten the LAB to bring undesirable features to General Johnson's attention."[81] Soon thereafter, Johnson held what became known as the "Field Days of Criticism," hearings during which the NRA was attacked from all sides. The league was well represented at the open hearings.[82] But the hope that the hearings would usher in significant reform of code labor policy proved to be unfounded.

"Not Beauty but Guts": Women's Bid for Authority over Labor Standards Administration

Despairing of the code authorities, the NCL suggested taking the task of enforcing labor provisions away from them altogether. At the open hearings in February 1934, Molly Dewson and Elinore Herrick called for enforcement machinery allied with labor departments. Code authorities could continue to administer fair trade provisions, the league suggested, but enforcement of labor provisions should be turned over to a national NRA compliance network headed by the U.S. Department of Labor. The NCL urged that this compliance effort take advantage of state labor departments, where good ones existed, instead of creating new agencies in every state. Here the league anticipated and hoped to avoid jurisdictional conflicts between the NRA and state agencies. To the NCL it seemed logical to merge administration of existing state laws and of NRA codes. This would produce more strict and efficient enforcement, in the league view. Furthermore, it would keep code labor provisions in the hands of people who would not neglect the interests of female workers.[83]

The labor department officials who had been administering state hours and minimum wage laws for women were the people whose experience was most directly relevant to enforcing labor provisions of the NRA codes. The NCL had long struggled to reform state labor departments and staff them with "qualified" personnel; by the 1930s many league trainees held positions in these departments. "Unless you have the right people to do it," Clara Beyer observed, "the laws are not worth a tinker's damn."[84] When NCL activists spoke of "the right people," they thought especially of league members, who had practical knowledge and, they assumed, the right principles. An advocate of civil service reform, the NCL insisted that appointments be based on qualifications rather than political cronyism. The league did not perceive this effort to insulate labor departments from party politics as undemocratic, because in its experience political appointees did not always operate in the interests of all constituents, especially women workers. Mistrust of party appointments had feminist content in another respect as well: reformers' demand for objective criteria for labor department personnel represented an attack on "custom" and "tradition" as barriers to women officials' advancement.[85]

In some states, such as New York and Wisconsin, league allies dominated relatively clean and strong departments. In other places, they found themselves in constant struggle with "pols," political appointees who were incompetent or made sly deals with employers. These conflicts were not generally with trade union–backed appointees; rather, they were with people who had no labor affiliations or loyalties whatsoever. The Kentucky league found that after women factory inspectors were dismissed, the state industrial commission began closing its eyes to violations "if the offender is politically 'right' or contributes to the party."[86] This sort of incident, which often pitted trained women against less knowledgeable or less scrupulous men, reinforced some league leaders' female chauvinist assumption that women made the best labor law administrators. In 1934 the NCL took the lead in developing standardized qualifications for labor inspectors, which in its view served the double purpose of keeping the corrupt out and helping qualified women get in.[87]

Many league allies headed women's or minimum wage divisions within state labor departments. (Because minimum wage laws affected only women, minimum wage divisions were in effect women's divisions.) Since the 1890s the league had recommended that the staff of such divisions include a certain minimum number of women. Although this demand contained antifeminist potential, it had feminist roots. In the absence of women's departments and under all-male administrations, women workers' interests often were ignored. NCL leaders also were asserting the value of middle-class women's training and expertise. However, the league and its allies rarely offered these feminist rationales publicly. They relied on the loose assumption that a woman could best understand another woman's problems.[88] This reasoning could hamper women's opportunities instead of expanding them. In not being clear about the reasons for women inspectors and administrators, the league network invited the argument that if women should administer policies for women, then men should administer policies that affected men. This was not the scenario that the NCL expected or desired.

Recognizing that a transition to sex-neutral labor laws would require some adjustment, Frances Perkins created the Division of Labor Standards (DLS) within the U.S. Department of Labor in 1934. The DLS was to be a "rallying point" on working conditions for labor unions, "welfare organizations" like the NCL, and state labor departments. It fielded inquiries, drafted model bills, held regional conferences, trained inspectors, and disseminated data on laws and working conditions. As such, the DLS represented the institutionalization of functions long performed by the National Consumers' League and its branches in the states. Because women already

Clara Beyer (ca. 1931).
(Harris and Ewing
photograph, New York
World-Telegram and
Sun Collection, LC)

headed the Department of Labor and two of its divisions, Perkins appointed a man, Verne Zimmer, to head the DLS. Perkins feared the perceived feminization of her department was grist for critics' mills. However,
Consumers' League veteran Clara Beyer was named as Zimmer's assistant,
and she was widely recognized as the real executive of the DLS. Lucy Mason
was appointed to the DLS steering committee, as were later NCL general
secretaries. Through the DLS, the female-dominated labor standards network was to retain a strong voice in the field, but under an officially sex-
neutral rubric.[89]

Consumers' League support of the DLS reflected the league's long-
standing commitment to a system of integrated state and national regulations. The DLS was dedicated to improving the quality of state labor departments and state laws, an unusual mission for a federal agency. The NCL
assumed that because of constitutional limits on federal authority, some
occupations would be reached only by state laws. The league also believed

that state-level enforcement, with vigilant oversight by local watchdog groups, had a greater chance of success than enforcement by a centralized agency alone. The hope was that state administrators with standardized qualifications would cooperate with federal authorities to enforce both national and state labor standards. State-level regulation held potential benefits: flexibility to set standards higher than national ones, fuller coverage, and more civic participation. On the other hand, the drawbacks of state-level regulation included the "race to the bottom" tendency produced by interstate competition, as well as discriminatory or corrupt administration as a result of domination by local elites. It was the latter problem that the DLS, by setting uniform standards for personnel and procedures, sought to control. In seeking to empower the DLS and state labor departments, the Consumers' League was not questioning federal authority over labor regulation, or intending to leave some workers at the mercy of weak and discriminatory state bureaucracies. Rather, league thinkers hoped to capture the advantages and avoid the disadvantages of regulation at each level.[90]

The league's advocacy of a decentralized NRA compliance system using the state labor departments was embodied in the November 1934 report of William H. Davis, the recently appointed NRA special adviser on compliance and enforcement.[91] Davis, a New York lawyer, had become friends with Frances Perkins in the 1920s, and he would soon join the NCL board. Although many hailed Davis's involvement as the best hope for saving the NRA, the agency was slow to adopt his proposal. Neither employers nor most labor leaders were enthusiastic about turning administration of code labor provisions over to the national and state labor departments.[92]

This resistance seems to have reflected, in part, a reluctance to entrust such important matters to female-led agencies. Many policymakers, labor leaders, and businessmen assumed that labor relations and national economic recovery were problems for men to handle. Rhetoric about the New Deal as the "analogue of war" may have further masculinized the crisis.[93] AFL leaders had never been happy with the appointment of a female secretary of labor. The outrage of AFL and business leaders at Perkins's "bid for unlimited power" in her pre-NRA wage-hour bill seems to have been intensified by the fact that she was a woman. Molly Dewson briefly dreamed of becoming assistant secretary of labor under Perkins, but she abandoned the idea after testing the political winds. Having two women in charge of the department would be "too much," she decided. Dewson no doubt remembered how the Consumers' Advisory Board was caricatured as run by social workers and "society matrons." Even when women were invited to participate in policy making, they were perceived as women first and experts second. "This hearing needs some beauty," wrote an NRA official in a note asking Josephine Roche to speak on the coal code. "What this hearing needs is not beauty but guts," Roche retorted.[94]

Opponents also disliked the U.S. Department of Labor because they perceived, correctly, that the agency had strong support from progressive women reformers. Union men often were suspicious of reformers, not least because of their emphasis on unorganized workers. Conservatives viewed women reformers as naive advocates of "pink" solutions to aid the downtrodden. In the late 1920s, North Carolina reformers were assailed for asking the DOL to survey the state's mills: they were labeled "radical women," allegedly in cahoots with female bureaucrats who sought jobs for "an army of women friends." Reformers and their agendas were mocked in gendered terms. Advocates of child labor laws were "sentimental people" who would deprive American boys of "manliness" and turn the country into "a vast kindergarten." Those who would reform labor conditions in textile mills were "muckrakers, uplifters, and sob sisters."[95] Such attitudes help explain the resistance to empowering the labor departments to enforce NRA labor provisions.

The "Davis plan" had not been carried out by the time the NRA was found unconstitutional. It is difficult to know whether NCL-allied administrators might have prevailed in their bid for control of national labor standards enforcement. By the time the labor provisions of NRA codes were re-created in the form of the Fair Labor Standards Act of 1938, the political terrain had changed again. League allies would win positions in the FLSA, but not nearly to the extent they would have liked. This was due largely to circumstances beyond the control of the NCL. However, women labor reformers did not help themselves by tolerating the assumption that women's administrative authority was based on an intuitive connection with women workers rather than on acquired expertise.

The NCL Advocates Stronger Union Rights

The Consumers' League steadily lost confidence in the NRA over the course of 1934, particularly as a result of the agency's seeming indifference to union rights. Voicing its frustration with the NRA's failure to "put teeth in Section 7a," the league became more outspoken than ever before in its support for labor's right to organize, strike, and bargain collectively.[96]

Employers' sweeping disregard of Section 7a, especially in the South, prompted Lucy Mason to join several prominent progressives in drafting a searching critique of the early New Deal. After presenting their proposals in person to FDR in April 1934, the group published an open letter in *The Nation*, *Survey Graphic*, and *The New Republic*. Among the two hundred left-liberals who signed the letter were several dozen Consumers' League activists. The letter proclaimed that "the acid test of the New Deal lies in its effect on the actual distribution of wealth which the machine age creates." The authors called for unemployment, old age, and health insurance, and for permanent relief programs, public housing, increased taxes on the wealthy, and public control of banking, natural resources and other industries. The centerpiece of their argument was for labor rights. The authors regretted the "inability of the NRA to check the growth of company-controlled unions which deny the very essence of true collective bargaining." Flagrant code violations were defeating what they argued was "the real objective of the NRA: the increase of purchasing power." Unions were needed to make the NRA codes enforceable. Beyond stimulating consumption, the goal was to promote industrial and political democracy. Unions must be given their share "not only in the profits of their industry, but what is far more important, in the control of their methods of work, their conditions of life, and their own industrial government." At stake was whether "Government or Big Business will dominate America." The letter recommended the creation of a labor relations board, to be located, significantly, within the U.S. Department of Labor. Little of this agenda was enacted. Nonetheless, Mason believed that the open letter bolstered FDR's resolve to resist pressure from the Right.[97]

Hugh Johnson's actions in the summer and fall of 1934 destroyed Mason's hopes that he would ever crack down on code labor violations. In July, Johnson's red-baiting speeches during the general strike begun by the West Coast longshoremen triggered vigilante violence against strikers. In September, after the cotton textile code authority refused to consider United Textile Workers' complaints about earnings lost through curtailed production, the stretch-out, and anti-union practices, almost 400,000 textile workers struck. In five states, strikers ended up in bloody confrontations with the National Guard. At this delicate moment, in a Carnegie Hall speech to code authority heads, Johnson denounced the textile strikers and unions in general. Enraged, Mason wrote FDR demanding Johnson's removal: "Section 7A of the [National Industrial Recovery Act] has been consistently disregarded by the Cotton-Textile Industry, and the whole set-up of enforcement machinery in this industry seems to be designed to prevent labor from organizing and leave complete control with management. . . . [I]t is tragic that General Johnson should use his position and prestige to arouse public opinion against workers who are exercising a right specifically given them by the organization he heads."[98] Mason's letter was part of a flood of protest, and Johnson resigned shortly thereafter.

However, code labor enforcement improved only slightly after the five-person National Industrial Recovery Board replaced Johnson. The league strongly endorsed the Wagner National Labor Relations Act, which Congress passed in 1935.[99]

Back to the States

The NRA's failure to implement NCL recommendations convinced the league that the most vulnerable workers needed state labor laws as well as guarantees of collective bargaining rights and national standards. Lucy Mason's southern travels confirmed that NRA codes were enforced best in places where good state labor laws were in effect. The local staff had experience, employers were accustomed to factory inspectors, and the record-keeping required by state laws facilitated NRA payroll inspections. Moreover, local citizens who had worked to pass the laws took an interest in their implementation. State laws also were crucial to employees of intra-state services, in which code enforcement was notoriously lax. Women and minorities were concentrated in these services, which included laundries, beauty parlors, and hotels and restaurants.[100]

Unfortunately for these workers, a perception that federal regulation made state wage and hour laws unnecessary hampered NCL campaigns for new state laws and bigger state labor agency appropriations. Seven state minimum wage bills passed in 1933, but then progress at the state level halted until after the NRA expired. A New Hampshire league member lamented that the NRA codes made the public think state regulations were superfluous. In Kentucky, the local league president reported, the NRA most definitely had undermined support for state wage and hours bills.[101]

League work for state laws to bolster the NRA was complicated by the attitudes of groups who never had been sympathetic to such laws. William Collins of the AFL placed a low priority on state-level action. He told his audience at an NCL conference that no code was worth its paper without a strong union — state laws or not.[102] The National Woman's Party also discounted the need for state wage and hour laws. Maud Younger wrote that "protective [state] laws for women and children have been swept aside — superseded and rendered obsolete by the higher standards imposed by the NRA codes."[103] In fact, NRA codes did not cover all workers, code standards often were lower than state standards, and, in any case, NRA labor provisions often went unenforced. Furthermore, the NRA was a two-year, emergency measure whose constitutionality had not been ascertained. State laws were necessary to supplement the NRA and also "to fall back on at such time as NRA goes out of effect."[104] During and after the NRA's existence, the NCL commitment to state laws required that the women-only strategy be preserved as an option.

Although the NCL welcomed national, male-inclusive wage-hour regulation and did all it could to make the agency a success, the NRA greatly complicated the league's work. Initially, league officials were delighted by the surge of interest in labor standards and of demand for league services. Elinore Herrick declared in 1933 that "the League has never had such widespread publicity as it has this year." However, many branch leaders came to agree with Margaret Wiesman, who reported that the NRA had dramatically increased the Massachusetts league's workload, "due to the demands of government agencies upon us." At the same time, "the uncertainty of the NRA plans makes a definite program for the Consumers' League difficult."[105] The NRA not only drained momentum from the league's local programs, but it created a false and dangerous impression that the league's work had been done. Membership contributions to the NCL declined after the agency was established. One league official attributed the drop-off to "the widespread public belief that the NRA has wiped out all industrial evils."[106]

Thus the agency's demise was in some ways a relief to the NCL, despite the fact that it erased hard-won progress in many industries. On May 27, 1935, "Black Monday" for New Deal legislation, the Supreme Court found the NRA unconstitutional. The 9-0 decision in favor of the Schechter brothers, Brooklyn poultry jobbers, held that the NRA represented an "excessive delegation" of legislative power to the executive branch, and also that the Schechters' business was intrastate and hence not subject to federal regulation. The NCL shed no tears. "Our prophecy comes true," a league bulletin announced. "The NCL, never having deviated from its chief function of building up a bulwark of state labor laws, stopped long enough to express its regret at losing what was good in NRA and then continued on its way." This was putting a good face on it, because many league leaders had devoted enormous energy to the NRA. But the gap between the agency's promise and its reality entitled the league to a bit of self-righteousness. The NRA "tried to do in a few months what the league had been doing inch by inch for forty years."[107]

The Consumers' League was present at the NRA's birth, and it did not give up the labor standards field when New Deal administrators stepped in. The NCL formulated a distinctive critique of NRA policy that stressed workers' rights and the right of "the public" to participate in code drafting and implementation. League efforts improved the labor provisions of many codes and in some locations strengthened enforcement. However, the league and its allies were unable to offset employer domination of NRA policy. Resistance to empowering labor departments — built in large part by women to administer laws for women and children — and opposition to unions were too strong. This defeat did not dissuade the NCL from its pursuit of a social democratic state, however. The league believed the failure of the NRA demonstrated the futility of industrial self-government, not the futility of national economic planning. Industrial democracy had not been given a fair test.

chapter 5

Bucking the Bourbons

Lucy Mason Organizes for the Consumers' League in the South

Hire someone "with Southern accent and Northern energy," Florence Kelley had advised the NCL board in 1931 with respect to choosing her successor.[1] Kelley astutely anticipated a coming confrontation between the South's dominant forces and the national Keynesian elite who would be an important force within the New Deal. During and after the NRA years, low wages and long hours in the South persisted as a drag on national standards. The South's isolated, low-cost labor market thus hindered the New Deal objective of stimulating mass consumption. Lucy Mason was one of a group of southerners who embraced the Roosevelt administration in hopes that it would redistribute political and economic power within their region. Mason's goals meshed with those of certain national labor leaders, experts, bureaucrats, and liberal employers who sought to raise the living standard of the working class and to loosen the grip of conservative southerners on the Democratic Party. The work of the Consumers' League in the South was part of a wider struggle whose outcome would define the limits of political possibility in the United States for decades to come.[2]

From the day Lucy Mason became NCL

general secretary in September 1932, she devoted every moment she could to southern labor standards. Initially, her southern work was educational and organizational, or, as she put it, "groundwork-laying." She established a Southern Committee of the league and made extensive speaking and data-gathering tours. After the NRA's demise in May 1935 freed her from monitoring the code-drafting process in Washington, Mason worked full-time on specific legislative campaigns in southern states.[3] She tried to organize isolated pockets of southern liberals and radicals into coalitions that would move beyond study groups and intellectual debate and into activism. The regionwide Southern Committee eventually generated state committees in Virginia, the Carolinas, Tennessee, and Texas. Meanwhile, established league branches spearheaded new initiatives in Kentucky and Louisiana. In the view of North Carolina economist Claudius Murchison, the league's work "promised greater industrial liberalism in the South and the drawing together of scattered forces."[4] In addition to mobilizing scattered forces within the South, Mason forged crucial—if fragile—reform networks across the North-South divide.

Organizing for labor reform in the South was quite different from organizing in the North, and not because southerners lacked "northern energy." Southern politicians adamantly resisted measures that would put upward pressure on southern wages. At the national level, southern legislators supported New Deal relief and social insurance proposals—they did want federal money for their impoverished states—but only after they had amended those proposals to ensure local administrative discretion and to exempt agricultural and domestic workers. After this victory, and as the southern economy continued to shift from agriculture toward low-wage industry, opposition to wage-hour regulation and unionization would become the focal point of southern elite efforts to maintain a dependent, low-cost workforce.[5]

Southern hostility to wage and hour laws at the state level was intense as well. Although states' rights convictions ran deep, some southern manufacturers saw that federal labor standards at least would reduce competition from other southern states. Manufacturers who feared being undercut by their neighbors were a major obstacle to state labor laws in the South, just as they were in other regions. In the South, however, opponents of state laws could mobilize political support by casting such measures as northern-backed efforts to destroy the South's competitive advantage—even when nearby rivals were as much a threat as northern producers. Southern opponents of wage-hour regulation thus could play on sentiments that were woven into the identity of most white southerners. Labor reforms were readily discredited as attacks on southern "superiority," and on the white supremacy that underpinned it.[6]

Lucy Mason tried to disarm these tactics by explaining how social and industrial democracy would help the South, not hurt it. She promoted labor laws, union rights, and racial justice as measures that would be good for the region's economy as well as for its soul. These ideas did not win Mason a mass following. The membership of the NCL's southern regional and state committees totaled about eight hundred people, virtually all of them middle-class whites; only a fraction of these became dedicated league activists.[7] However, this small group did make an impact, and its work paved the way for better-known efforts that came later.

The vast majority of the southerners who responded to Mason's program were women. While southern women showed less support for the Consumers' League than northern women did, they were more supportive than southern men. Southern women have not been prominent in histories of southern dissent or in major works on women and the welfare state, but a striking number of them ardently supported the more radical aspects of the New Deal.[8] Although the South's entrenched system of white supremacy discouraged progressive political activism by non-wage-earning white women, the group that elsewhere spearheaded the drive for wage-hour regulation, for some of them the Consumers' League agenda exerted a strong appeal.

Mason's Program for "Building a Better South"

Unlike many northerners who attacked "the southern problem" as an obstacle to progress elsewhere, Lucy Mason's priority was the welfare of southerners. She linked southerners' interests to national welfare as a strategy for bringing outside resources and pressure to bear in the South. Mason believed that the South stood to benefit from industrialization, but only if a vigilant citizenry made sure that the region developed in a "wholesome and sane" way. Mason cited the words of H. C. Nixon of Tulane University: "The value of history is at stake in the South, where the coming of industry is late enough for a political sophistication to avoid many of the evils of the earlier industrial days in England and New England."[9] Strong labor standards laws and enforcement agencies, along with recognition of workers' right to organize, were the core of Mason's prescription. She insisted that to be effective, such measures had to protect all workers. Furthermore, regulating industry would not be enough. The vast pool of "impoverished rural labor play[ed] into the hands of industrialists." An economic program for the South would have to "rehabilitate" the agricultural population, in addition to developing diversified, regulated industries. Crucial to this program was racial reform, to end the exploitation of black workers that kept all labor standards low.[10]

Mason argued that the Depression revealed the connections between political and economic democracy, demonstrating the ill effects of concentrated economic power and low living standards on the nation's political life as well as on the economy. Southern economic inequality was a cause, Mason believed, as much as an effect of the region's voting restrictions and low voter turnout. In her view, these circumstances made the South especially ripe for authoritarian rule. Mason identified "self-conscious and organized labor" as the strongest "bulwark" against fascism. She often applauded the Scandinavian social democracies for their respect of labor unions.[11]

In her analysis of the South's needs and its relationship to the rest of the country, Mason participated in the intellectual development known as southern regionalism. Associated with the new regionalism (although not unique to its proponents) was the concept of the South as a colonial economy. According to this analysis, the South's difficulties stemmed from its role as a producer of raw materials for manufacturers in other regions. "Lacking industries of its own, the south has been forced to trade the richness of its soil, its minerals and forests, and the labor of its people for goods manufactured elsewhere," claimed one important regionalist statement. Absentee ownership of southern businesses, along with discriminatory tariffs and freight rates, further hampered the South.[12] Regionalists purported to offer an alternative to the old, destructive sectionalism. They sought to channel energies away from divisiveness and toward rational planning for the integration of the region into the nation, to the benefit of both.

This emphasis on planning meshed nicely with the long-standing philosophy of the Consumers' League. Through her league work, Mason became an important exponent of southern regionalism, both in the South and within the New Deal. She exchanged ideas with many of the region's foremost intellectuals, often supplying them with insights and data for their publications. Asked by Charles Pipkin of Louisiana State University for her comments on an article draft, Mason urged him, "Do pay your respects to the garment industry in all its branches. It is coming to the southern states to escape trade union activities in the north." Also, she told Pipkin, he needed to place more stress on the poor enforcement of southern labor laws. Mason in turn promoted southern intellectuals' ideas outside academic circles. She reviewed the work of writers like Claudius

Murchison, Howard Odum, and W. J. Cash in women's, church, and social work publications and habitually enclosed recommended reading lists with her letters to reformers, employers, and government officials.[13]

Mason also forged links among southern intellectuals and promoted the NCL program in her capacity as an active member of the Southern Policy Committee (SPC). This group advocated planning and regulatory measures for the region. For an important SPC conference in Chattanooga, Tennessee, in 1936, it was Mason who wrote the resolutions on labor laws, social security, and collective bargaining rights. The SPC never became the force Mason had hoped, but it did stimulate the formation of the more daring and longer-lived Southern Conference for Human Welfare.[14] Indeed, Mason's Southern Committee of the NCL deserves recognition as a forerunner to both these groups.

Mason was able to build some interregional ties by bringing more southern intellectuals into league activity. Howard Odum, whose *Southern Regions of the United States* (1936) would become the "Bible of the new regionalism," joined the NCL council in 1932. Odum's student Harriet Herring, who soon would publish *Southern Industry and Regional Development* (1940), joined the council as well. University of North Carolina president Frank Graham, who was becoming one of the South's most prominent liberals, agreed to serve as NCL honorary vice president. Claudius Murchison of North Carolina State, who wrote the influential *King Cotton Is Dead* (1930), and political scientist Harriet Elliott were active on a league committee in North Carolina.[15]

Among these southern thinkers, Mason occupied a left-of-center position. She was more directly critical of class and race inequality than Howard Odum, or editors Virginius Dabney of the *Richmond Times-Dispatch* and Jonathan Daniels of the *Raleigh News and Observer*. She certainly was more progressive on race questions than many members of the Southern Policy Committee: several white men resigned from that group after a black intellectual joined. Unlike some southern liberals, Mason held southern elites as responsible as northern capital for the region's poverty, and she insisted that labor unions and federal laws were indispensable to saving democracy in the South.[16]

Such views drew fire from defenders of the region's dominant interests. Local officials and clergy often joined employers in linking labor reform with northern conspiracy, radicalism, and betrayal of the white race. Mason was castigated in the local newspapers when she visited New Orleans in 1934, for example. A leading official of the locally powerful Catholic Church chastised the Louisiana Consumers' League for being "inveigled" (by Lucy Mason) into backing the federal child labor amendment.

He charged that the amendment was a plot to expand federal power over southern children, one that threatened southern independence and prosperity. Revealingly, Father Wynhoven used a racial metaphor to warn voters of the danger of federal interference. "There is a dusky gent in the woodpile who should be carefully watched," he warned, linking female reformers, federal authority, and a lurking black threat to white supremacy.[17] In 1937, when Mason criticized the South's "booster element" for recruiting and subsidizing low-wage industries, she received a tongue-lashing from Georgia governor E. D. Rivers. With a delegation of seven men at his side, Governor Rivers lectured Mason on Georgia's accomplishments. He condemned her and others as "muckrakers who defame the southern states." Stung, Mason vowed not to seek another interview with Rivers, "as they get worse each time." After the meeting, Mason hastily cut the NCL letterhead off an outgoing mailing to Georgians, hoping to avoid the appearance of northern influence.[18]

Mason took solace in her belief that most ordinary southerners supported the league agenda and, more generally, the New Deal. Two dramatic developments in 1934 deepened this conviction that the southern "masses" favored labor and political reform. In the fall of that year, approximately 200,000 southern mill workers joined the national uprising in textiles, the largest strike in American history up to that time. They displayed a determination that was astonishing, given the dismal record of southern textile unions. "Flying squadrons" of strikers traveled from mill to mill waving American flags and rallying isolated groups of workers to the cause. Violent clashes between pickets, nonstriking workers, and mill guards produced many deaths and casualties, most dramatically in Honea Path, South Carolina, where six strikers were killed and twenty others wounded on September 6. Four southern governors called out the National Guard. Although the United Textile Workers claimed victory, the strike ended inconclusively. In spite of this outcome, or perhaps because of it, the South's industrial workers seemed for a time to subordinate regional and race-based loyalties to a national identity. FDR's portrait was found on the walls of countless mill village homes, and South Carolina mill workers helped elect a pro–New Deal governor in 1934. That same year, impoverished black and white sharecroppers in Arkansas joined together to form the Southern Tenant Farmers' Union, a socialist-led group that protested large landowners' control of federal relief money provided by the Agricultural Adjustment Act. Repression of this organization was so brutal that its advocates persuaded Senator Robert La Follette to create a congressional committee to investigate civil liberties violations in the South. Although the Roosevelt administration took little substantive action to back up the

Gastonia, North Carolina, textile strikers celebrate Labor Day, 1934. As many as 10,000 workers reportedly participated in this parade, which followed the closing of the mills for the national strike. (International News photograph, New York World-Telegram and Sun Collection, LC)

textile workers or the sharecroppers, the sympathy of some New Deal officials encouraged both groups.[19]

As powerful southerners demonstrated the lengths to which they would go to preserve their grip on laborers, Lucy Mason took a more pessimistic view of the South's ruling interests and the prospects for peaceful reform. She mused grimly about whether fascism would come "through the dominance of the big and little business men who use government and law to uphold their point of view and 'lynch wages and hours,' or through the uprising of the dispossessed masses who turn to a Huey Long for salvation." Long, the flamboyant Louisiana politician, had attracted mass support with his Share the Wealth program. Mason saw Long as a demagogue who was promoting himself by peddling unrealistic solutions to desperate people. But in her view, the more serious threat to southern democracy came from above: "The Bourbons of the South hate Mr. Roosevelt as much as the workers and farmers love him. . . . The South is fascist — its domination of the Negro has made it easy to repeat the pattern for organized labor."[20] Southern politicians' intensifying resistance to New Deal labor and social

Three Gastonia, North Carolina, strikers wear posters demanding enforcement of the textile industry's NRA code (1934). Some of the signs on the posters read "Enforce NRA," "Kill the Stretchout," "Shorter Hours Higher Wages," and "Labor's for the NRA! Where Do the Bosses Stand?" (International News photograph, New York World-Telegram and Sun Collection, LC)

policies confirmed Mason's opinion that outside support—from federal agencies and national unions—would be necessary to help ordinary southerners democratize the region.

To convince other southerners of this point, Mason used her southern heritage to neutralize the laissez-faire, states' rights, and anti-union arguments of the Bourbons. Southern conservatives of varying stripes had for years deployed a mythologized collective memory of the Confederacy's glorious Lost Cause. Consumers' League activists also played on southerners' pride in their history, but they did so by recalling the American Revolution rather than the Civil War. Lucy Mason frequently invoked her ancestor George Mason, drafter of the Virginia Declaration of Rights, but she rarely mentioned the more recent forebears who fought for the Confederacy.[21] The Virginia Consumers' League invoked Thomas Jefferson. Calling for a redefinition of liberalism, the Virginia league claimed that its opponents confused Jefferson's means with his ends: "Because Mr. Jefferson opposed state intervention and advocated self-reliance in an agricultural era . . . it does not at all follow that a policy of state non-intervention is the way of liberalism today. Too many of us Virginians, inheritors of the Jeffersonian tradition, are parading our standpattism under the banner of Jeffersonian liberalism." It was those who opposed change, the "standpatters," who threatened constitutional government, the league claimed, and "true liberals" had to save it.[22]

Even as she tried to dispel the old sectionalism, Mason pitched her arguments to southern ears. One strategy was to depict the South's low-wage employers as "migrant chiselers," outsiders who came to exploit southern workers and funneled profits away from the South. The last thing the South needed, Mason argued, was to recruit industries that came only for cheap labor and left local communities with nothing. The Virginia league warned against politicians who advocated "attracting to Virginia industrial establishments which might come with the hope of profiting from the lower level of life of its Virginia employees." Southern politicians instead should promote diversification into skilled labor industries. Mason deserves credit for many newspaper stories and editorials to this effect, most notably those by Georgia-born journalist Thomas Stokes, whose "Carpetbaggers of Industry" articles would become a weapon in the fight for a national labor standards bill.[23] As Mason well knew, southern workers were exploited by southern-born employers as well as nonsouthern ones, but she made this message more palatable to southern ears by emphasizing that many of the worst "chiselers" were recent arrivals.[24]

Another strategy was to trump the states' rights card by arguing that the national government could divert northern resources toward the South. Rather than viewing the federal government as an enemy, Mason told the South Carolina legislature in early 1935, they should see that it was "the only power that can touch the concentrated wealth of the Northeast and distribute some of it down here."[25] Sometimes Mason expressed this idea less patiently: "No section has benefited more than the South from the recent extension of Federal powers; and yet no section is so vociferously clamorous in proclaiming 'states' rights.' . . . We of the South are making ourselves ridiculous by this inconsistency."[26] She urged southerners to embrace "a new kind of states' rights . . . [whereby] the highest right of a state is to do all in its power to raise the standard of living for all of its people, every class, every person, the farmer and the industrial wage-earner, and both races." Modern states' rights would require an active state government cooperating with the federal government. The Depression was proof that the states alone could not provide the limits on competition and the material assistance needed to ensure that southern industrial development benefited rather than exploited its people. National laws and unions were needed to check the pressures of interstate competition. Mason thus inverted the states' rights convention, and in stressing the need to raise the living standard of "every person" in the region, she challenged white supremacist (and, implicitly, male supremacist) assumptions.[27]

In Mason's view, the best hope for vanquishing the old states' rights idea and democratizing the South lay in an alliance between the middle class and organized labor. Mason thought that many southerners were willing to support unions, labor standards laws, and social security legislation, but a "lack of coordination" among them necessitated a "unifying force." The Consumers' League had been such a force elsewhere, Mason believed, and she sought to extend that function to the South. "It seems a tragic thing that the enlightened public opinion of the state is not being made sufficiently articulate to impress law makers, at a time when social and economic security demand progressive measures," Mason told prospective Virginia members in 1935. Privately, she grumbled that the Virginia legislature "will be the usual state Democratic machine bunch and I do not know how far they will respond to the people back home."[28] Like many southern dissenters, Mason believed that a "silent South" waited to be aroused, through education and persuasion, to unseat the "reactionary forces" that had made a mockery of democracy in the region.[29]

In 1934, after a third extended tour of the South, Mason reported "a pronounced change in attitude" toward labor legislation. She had given sixty-nine talks in twenty-seven towns in eleven states. Eager audiences kept her for hours and exhausted her supplies of literature. Interest levels were so high that she could have given many more talks, Mason told her board pointedly, had she been allocated more time and money.[30] Many individuals who heard Mason speak, or read about her, wrote the league to find out more. A North Carolina YWCA member read of Mason's Virginia activities in the newspapers and wrote Mason for advice on starting a minimum wage movement in her state. Two Tennessee church women made a similar request in early 1936.[31] Responses like this sustained Mason's faith that "scattered throughout the South are liberal and intelligent people keenly aware of the backwardness of that section in labor legislation and its enforcement. We have to rely on this nucleus."[32]

Whether Mason tried to bring black groups into this reform nucleus during her NCL years is unknown, but she certainly directed the bulk of her energies toward whites.[33] Shortly after leaving the league, Mason would write, "For years I have known that the South cannot be saved by its middle class liberals alone, that they must make common cause with labor, the dispossessed on the land and the Negro. . . . Some liberals may find it too shocking to have the other three groups so articulate about their needs.

But this is the basis of progress in democracy, economic justice and social values in the South."[34] Although Mason had extensive contact with black workers and reformers during her Richmond years and later with the CIO, in organizing for the Consumers' League she focused on white academics, women's and church groups, and labor unions. This may have reflected her sense of who would be most interested in the cause of labor standards regulation, but it also was a matter of political tactics. To win state labor laws to raise the standards of white and black workers, she needed the support of white southerners. Although Mason never tolerated racist arguments as a means of increasing white support, she may have hoped to avoid triggering southern white reaction against the New Deal program. When this reaction came anyway—particularly after northern black voters and union members gave President Roosevelt a resounding victory in 1936— Mason seems to have thrown such diplomacy to the winds. If she had stayed with the NCL after mid-1937, she might have undertaken more public interracial work under its auspices.[35]

Only to a small degree did the Consumers' League solicit the participation of southern working women. The league saw its function as persuading middle-class people to make alliances with labor unions, not as organizing workers. Mason did not want to compete with unions for the scarce time and money of southern wage earners. She also worried that employers would retaliate against workers who joined the NCL, whose work required lobbying and publicity. She feared that "the girls who go on [league] committees, particularly in the South, might be in danger of losing their jobs if their names were published. The Consumers' League is not going to be very popular in the South with the manufacturing group."[36] However, Mason did recruit a few union women for the league's Southern Committee, most of them from garment unions. On her speaking tours, Mason often addressed workers in YWCA clubs and local labor councils, and female wage earners joined the league in successful lobbying drives in Virginia and Kentucky.[37]

Although Mason concentrated her recruiting energies for the Consumers' League on the southern middle class, she believed worker activism would be essential to labor reform. A 1933 tour of the South left her "more convinced than ever that we must turn to the workers for industrial and social progress in the South." Local league committees needed to work closely with working women because "the girls can bring first hand information of actual facts to the committees and thereby stimulate them to action." In turn, the working women could "quietly disseminate" information on upcoming bills to other workers, to bring collective pressure on legislators.[38] The Consumers' League looked for ways to cooperate with workers that enabled the workers to remain anonymous. In 1936, for example, Mason circulated 1,500 flyers through YWCA industrial clubs. Entitled "Something You Can Do," the flyers asked workers for stories about their working experiences. "The more facts we have and the more human they are, the better we can support these bills," said the flyer, which also invited workers to write for information about their state's labor laws.[39]

To promote labor standards regulation and build coalitions, Mason developed two effective educational devices: southern labor charts and regional labor conferences. In the charts, Mason generated the first accessible, up-to-date surveys of southern working conditions, laws, and labor departments. This information was invaluable to southern groups and also to national reformers previously oblivious to "that negligible part of the country known as the South."[40] The NCL's role as a factual clearinghouse was critical in the South, where such information was hard to come by because of the lack of labor departments and of laws requiring that companies make data public. These charts were in such demand that they generated a modest amount of income for the league. Clara Beyer of the new U.S. Division of Labor Standards proposed taking over the copyright for the charts, but Mason resisted, explaining that the charts represented "fifteen months of prodigious correspondence" with southern researchers and officials. Distributing the charts was a good organizing tool for the league, more important than the income. The charts helped the NCL become the central source of information on southern labor laws and enforcement for editors, academics, and other "opinion-forming people."[41] Mason's decision to keep the charts under NCL control is one small example of the league's desire to prevent even its favorite government agencies from usurping its own role entirely.

Another tool Mason used to mobilize southern support was labor standards conferences. Such conferences had been a staple of the NCL and the U.S. Women's and Children's Bureaus for years, reflecting the consultative style and the permeable boundary between volunteers and professionals that were distinguishing features of women's political activism. In response to prodding from the NCL, Secretary of Labor Perkins began holding regular labor conferences, one function of which became improving relations between state and federal labor officials.[42] Lucy Mason made sure that southern states were included in these. In late 1934 she suggested to Clara Beyer that the Labor Department hold a southern conference: "It would serve a double purpose—crystalize good intentions about labor legislation that are in the minds of some people I know down there—and introduce to these people the new department of federal government [the DLS]."[43] Mason's idea came to fruition in the Southern Regional Conference on State

Labor Legislation and Economic Security, held in Nashville, Tennessee, in January 1935. Mason supplied lists of invitees, advised on the program, and led a roundtable discussion on labor standards. Mason also reminded her Washington allies to be sensitive to local custom, recommending that the Sunday session include "a couple of ministers for blessing and benediction."[44]

The Nashville conference was the first of a series of southern gatherings that brought reformers, labor representatives, and government officials together in support of state and national labor and social policies. Many women participated in these conferences. The Nashville conference spurred the formation of a Virginia Consumers' League, and it prompted the governor of South Carolina to invite Perkins to hold another regional conference in Columbia the following year. Meanwhile, a productive conference took place in Richmond in March 1935, and, of great symbolic importance, the U.S. Labor Department held its Second Annual Conference on Labor Legislation in Asheville, North Carolina, in October 1935. Mason believed these gatherings were a good way to get concrete action from local people, and she frequently pleaded with Beyer not to be too strict about limiting attendance. "Unless there is liberal support in the communities," she explained, "the state Federations of Labor and the Labor Departments will not be able to buck manufacturers' opposition. We have got to build the liberal group, university people, and social workers into a strong movement for labor legislation. The conferences offer the best method."[45]

In building liberal coalitions in the South, Mason had to avoid the appearance of "foreign interference," or meddling in regional affairs by outsiders, whether federal officials or national organizations. In suggesting an article to journalist Thomas Stokes, Mason asked him to not mention her, as "it doesn't do to prod southern states from this office." She had "excellent newspaper contacts" in the Carolinas, but she always asked for "editorial support without allusion to the CL or me."[46] After Mason persuaded the U.S. Department of Labor to hold southern labor standards conferences, she worried that the department would get carried away and hold too many. Mason's delicate task was to help the federal agency build its presence in southern states, while making this seem like a local initiative. In 1935 Mason told Beyer that the Department of Labor should not call a conference in Louisiana so soon after the Asheville conference because it might be perceived as federal pressure on the South. She craftily suggested that the local Consumers' League could call a Louisiana conference and then invite the DOL in for assistance. Mason did manage to foster some connections between southerners and the Division of Labor Standards, remarking after one field trip that it was "great fun to be a volunteer supporter of the US DOL and its sub-divisions." Sometimes she was able to break through southern localism, reporting, for example, that South Carolinians "all accept me now, even the Governor, as a South Carolina institution." However, finding local people to promote the league legislative program remained politically essential.[47]

Wrapped in Cotton Batting?: Obstacles to Organizing Southern White Women for Labor Reform

That Mason's first task was to organize a Southern Committee for the Consumers' League itself suggests the different approaches needed in the North and South. At the 1932 Conference on the Breakdown of Industrial Standards, the NCL and its allies agreed to form a labor standards committee in every state possible, to work for minimum wage and maximum hours laws using model bills drafted by the league. In 1933 and 1934 these coalitions helped win new or improved state labor laws in many states outside the South. The state committees also became important local advocates for New Deal policies such as social security and labor rights. In New York, Massachusetts, New Jersey, Ohio, and Michigan, league branches and labor standards committees led pro–New Deal coalitions and insurgencies.[48] However, a labor standards committee formed in only one southern state, the border state of Kentucky. With nine member organizations, the Kentucky committee was a significant development by southern standards, but its scale was modest compared to its northern counterparts. The New York Labor Standards Committee, for example, represented over fifty women's, civic, labor, and religious groups.[49] In southern states, however, few groups were willing even to affirm the principle of labor laws, much less lobby for them. Accordingly, Mason began with the regionwide Southern Committee. This group could be publicized and armed with methods and arguments that would produce local groups later.

In the Northeast and Midwest, the NCL could work through a dozen strong branch leagues in addition to a well-defined network of allies, but in the South, Mason began with little more than her contacts from the YWCA and the Southern Council for Women and Children in Industry. She looked for prominent people who would lend respectability to the league's program — academics, clergy, and editors (usually men) — and for people with the time, commitment, and skills to do the practical work of organizing and lobbying (usually women). This strategy yielded noticeable results. Sociologist George S. Mitchell reported in late 1933 that wherever he went in the South, he found evidence of the "leavening influence of the CL."[50]

The southerners who were most responsive to the league's leavening influence were middle-class white women. In the South as in the North, it was women who spearheaded campaigns for protective labor legislation. However, compared to their northern counterparts, southern women's support of the league program was limited. The autonomous women's reform networks that were so influential in northern and midwestern urban politics in the presuffrage era emerged later and on a smaller scale in the South. Many of the factors that stimulated the development of white women's political culture in the North were weaker or absent in the South, with elite women's colleges (and their attendant institution, "the Boston marriage") and the U.S. Sanitary Commission as the most obvious examples. The southern lady ideal and the South's later industrialization delayed white women's access to higher education and their entry into the professions and new clerical occupations. As a result, the South had fewer of the college-educated, economically independent, urban women who had been so prominent in Progressivism in other regions. During the interwar years, however, the number of such women in the South was increasing.[51]

In virtually every southern state, middle-class white women had formed organizations that were active on a wide variety of issues.[52] However, as Lucy Mason observed, southern women's groups "rarely endorse[d] any form of labor legislation." From the turn of the century into the 1930s, most southern women's groups offered only lukewarm support for child labor regulation, and they gave regulation of adult labor standards a wide berth. Women were important in winning what child labor laws the southern states did have, but those were won through intensive activity by a few unusually progressive women, rather than by the large coalitions of mainstream women's groups that were typical in the North.[53]

Reaching out to women's organizations, and to female-dominated church and social work groups, was a key aspect of Mason's strategy for forging links between labor and middle-class liberals. However, Mason often became exasperated with mainstream women's groups in the South. While working for the Southern Council in 1931, she confided, "Never, in all my life, have I seen women with so much potential power and so little conception of how to use it as the women of these states! . . . They have a series of women's clubs and federations with legislative programs about birds and flowers and flags and mottoes." Mason complained that she got "no support of any intelligent kind" from North Carolina women's groups. "They just don't know how to do it, poor lambs, and those that know, haven't time."[54]

Political inexperience was only part of the explanation for southern women's ambivalence to the NCL program, as Mason well knew. Regional pride made many white women loath to criticize the industries on which New South prosperity rested. Many white club women played leading roles in inventing and sustaining the myth of the Lost Cause, which honored the Confederacy and cast Reconstruction as a corrupt era of northern-imposed black supremacy. In the South as in the North, the activism of women broadened the obligations of local and state governments in areas such as public health and education, but southern women displayed less relish for reforms like woman suffrage or labor regulation, which could be construed as threats to white supremacy, states' rights, and New South industry.[55]

For some white women, ideological allegiance to the New South was clearly linked to plain old self-interest. In the South's shallow pool of urban, educated women, many had ties to major employers. This was especially true in the larger textile states, the Carolinas, Georgia, and Alabama. In turn-of-the-century Alabama, AFL organizer Irene Ashby mobilized the state Federation of Women's Clubs (FWC) behind child labor reform, only to be undercut when the FWC president compromised away the heart of the bill. (The president's family held stock in a major Alabama mill.) Even when women were sincerely committed to labor reform, pressure from relatives who were industrialists could hinder their activism, as the Legislative Council of North Carolina Women discovered in the late 1920s.[56]

Southern women's coalitions were constrained by the Federations of Women's Clubs, generally the largest and least progressive women's group in each state. The FWC acted as a drag on the Legislative Council of North Carolina Women, hampering its support of labor regulations for adult women. Even in less industrialized Mississippi, where one might expect labor reform to be less controversial, club women displayed little interest in labor legislation. In private, Mason maintained that "no organization sponsored chiefly by Women's Clubs is going into a strong program of labor legislation."[57]

In South Carolina, even more than in other textile states, most white club women viewed labor reform through the lens of southern nationalism. The shots fired on Fort Sumter reverberated still in South Carolina politics, thanks in no small part to the United Daughters of the Confederacy and the women's clubs.[58] In 1936 the president of the South Carolina Federation of Women's Clubs, Jessie Laurence, angrily protested a statement by Lucy Mason that child labor had increased in South Carolina during the 1920s. Laurence accused Mason of assaulting South Carolina's honor. However, after Mason explained her statistics, Laurence changed her mind and volunteered to work for anti–child labor bills. This was a victory for Mason because Laurence headed not only the state FWC but also the new Council for the Common Good, a coalition of white women's groups similar to the women's legislative councils that existed in many states.[59] Mason brought Laurence together with Mary Frayser, a home economist at Winthrop State College for Women. Frayser, who grumbled that South Carolina club women "knew little about how the other half lives," agreed to head the FWC's Committee on Women in Industry. After attending meetings of 152 women's clubs in one year, Frayser reported that only eleven clubs had programs on women in industry. Most of the club women seemed to "live wrapped in cotton batting," Frayser commented, using a metaphor apt for South Carolina.[60] Mason's and Frayser's work to increase South Carolina women's support for labor laws brought only modest results. Laurence lobbied hard for various labor bills, meeting with numerous legislators, but she did so only in her own name, because her organization had not approved the bills. Similarly, Claudia Lea Phelps, president of the South Carolina Garden Club, was converted to activism for the league program, but she was unable to bring her organization with her.[61]

In trying to explain South Carolina club women's ambivalence toward women's hours laws, Mary Frayser said the group struck her as "NWPish." In fact, after 1931 the National Woman's Party was not a significant presence in the southern legislative battles of the Consumers' League. By the mid-1930s the only active Woman's Party in the South was a small one in Virginia; the Atlanta branch that formed in 1931 had faded away. The NWP perspective was represented in the South by individual members of the national organization, and by sympathetic Federations of Business and Professional Women's Clubs.[62]

Although the Woman's Party mounted no sustained legislative initiatives in the South after 1931, it did advance arguments that resonated with white southern hostility to the New Deal. In scattered articles and appearances, NWP members opposed women-only labor laws by playing to states' rights sentiment and white racism. In 1935 the NWP claimed that member Helen Hunt West had defeated a Florida women's minimum wage bill supported by the U.S. Women's Bureau. "The legislature voted with its Florida women and against the Federal Government's representative," *Equal Rights* announced triumphantly.[63] A 1938 NWP article opposed a Virginia hours law by stirring white racial anxieties. The article quoted a District of Columbia woman worker as saying, "When we had this law before, [white] women were replaced by negro men."[64] While arguments such as these hardly helped Consumers' League bills, the National Woman's Party was more a nuisance than a major political adversary in the South.

More influential over the views of southern club women than the NWP were antilabor church officials. Mason worked to offset this influence by circulating endorsements of labor reform by liberal ministers. She also made sure her southern tours included addresses to religious groups. She wrote articles on labor reform for church publications such as the Methodist *World Outlook*, the Congregational *Adult Bible Class Magazine*, and the Churches of Christ periodical *The Church Woman*.[65] A member of the industrial division of the Federal Council of Churches, Mason distributed reading lists that included works such as Alva Taylor's *Christianity and Industry in America*. Because church activity was so central to southern women's reform activism, and because most southern church groups were less supportive of labor causes than northern ones, educational efforts directed at church groups were a distinctive feature of the NCL's southern organizing.[66]

Some women's church groups were receptive to Mason's ideas, but they still did not lobby wholeheartedly for wage-hour laws and union rights. The Women's Missionary Council of the Methodist Episcopal Church, South, was one of the most progressive white groups in the South on race and labor issues. In 1913 this group endorsed the revised social creed of the Federal Council of Churches, which supported protective labor laws for women, old-age pensions, and collective bargaining. Motivated by beliefs in "women's work for women" and in "work for Christ which only women can do," these women undertook projects including day nurseries, homes for unwed mothers, and schools for young black and Appalachian women. In the 1930s Bertha Newell, superintendent of the Bureau of Social Services within the Women's Missionary Council, became one of Mason's most useful allies in North Carolina. *World Outlook*, this group's publication, declared that the South's lack of labor regulations made it "only too easy for human values to be subordinated to profits." Methodist women's study groups consumed the league's supplies of printed materials, and in 1934 Mason reported with delight that the Women's Missionary Council had endorsed the NCL agenda.[67]

Despite these progressive views, the Methodist women hung back from some controversies because they lacked full autonomy from male church authority. One of Mason's articles for *World Outlook*, "Why Industry Comes South," was published without the section she had written on chronic oversupply of labor, "the crucial point." Newell's own book on southern problems skirted the topic of industrial regulation. Apparently Newell's husband, a Methodist minister, did not wholly approve of her work. Newell remarked that she and her colleagues worked not only against popular opinion but, "hardest of all, in opposition to members of their own households." Methodist women supported Mason's work individually, and they allowed Mason access to their membership, but their organizations did not put significant resources into campaigning for wage and hour laws.[68]

The Gendered Appeal of Social Democracy in the South

There was less space for a progressive women's political culture in the South than in the North, but among southern progressives, women were at the forefront. Women far outnumbered men among the southerners who did join the Consumers' League.[69] These unusual women were among those few southerners willing to openly confront the region's system of racialized class domination. Turning their backs on the sectional rhetoric that long had been used to resist redistributions of power along class, race, and gender lines, they wielded an influence beyond their numbers in promoting labor regulation and other social welfare policies in the South. Their attraction to the New Deal reflected backgrounds and ideas similar to those of northern league women, but in the South these characteristics and views were rarer and more transgressive of prescriptive norms of white womanhood.

Contemporaries noticed women's prominence in white southern liberalism, although few historians have. A Virginia newspaper reported in October 1936 that a "drive to snub [conservative U.S. Senator] Glass at the polls" was gaining among Democratic women, "who are regarded as the most ardent of all New Dealers because of Roosevelt's social welfare program." (This writer did not bother to defend the assumption that women were more likely than men to support social welfare programs — an assumption shared by Consumers' League activists.)[70] A few years later, an official of the Southern Conference for Human Welfare recognized the importance of women in southern dissent when he remarked that Lucy Mason "represents more than labor. She represents the awakened women in the South — the YWCA, welfare workers, church workers — who have the courage to buck the status quo."[71]

The southern women who were willing to buck the status quo by becoming Consumers' League activists had certain characteristics in common. Like their northern counterparts, they were white, urban, and highly educated. Southern league women were less likely than northern ones to have college degrees, but the number of league southerners with college and advanced degrees is noteworthy given that higher education for women was still less common in the South. Significantly, many attended the same schools as northern league members: Vassar, Smith, and, especially, Columbia and the University of Chicago. The influence of brilliant Chicago social scientists like the Abbott sisters and Sophonisba Breckinridge (herself a Kentucky native) and the social work faculty at Columbia radiated widely. Southern women carried their mentors' teachings back to the South and disseminated them there. Mary Frayser of Virginia and South Carolina, Bertha Newell of North Carolina, and Elizabeth Wisner of New Orleans all studied at the University of Chicago. Wisner brought her Ph.D. back to Tulane's School of Social Work, where she established a national reputation in the social work profession while supporting various local reform efforts. Frayser continued her studies at Columbia before obtaining a job in extension work in mill villages under the auspices of Winthrop College in Rock Hill, South Carolina. Illinois native Harriet Elliott took a Columbia degree in political science to the Woman's College of the University of North Carolina in Greensboro, where she mentored future league members such as Gladys Tillett.[72] Many league southerners who did not earn northern degrees nonetheless studied or lived for a time outside the South. Josephine Wilkins of Georgia and Adele Clark of Virginia studied art in New York City, and Ida Weis Friend of New Orleans studied for eighteen months in Europe. Such experiences may have exposed these women to the rebellious ideas about class, race, and gender relations that they would display in their southern reform work.[73]

Again like their northern counterparts, southern league activists were either unmarried or widowed and without young children. Adele Clark and Elizabeth Wisner set up housekeeping with like-minded women, artist Nora Houston in Clark's case and social worker Florence Sytz in Wisner's. Naomi Cohn and Ida Friend each had several children but did not become activists until those children were grown; Anna Settle and Annie Halleck of the Kentucky league never had children. All four became widows before or during the 1930s and thus, like unmarried league activists, had no husbands or children to make demands on their time. (That Ida Friend and Annie Halleck had married Yale-educated northerners illustrates another way in which southern league women were exposed to "outside" influences.)

Unlike the most elite southern women, few Consumers' League activists had ties to major industrial or agricultural interests.[74] Many southern league women were at least partially self-supporting, typically as librarians, teachers, or social workers, but sometimes as artists, government administrators, lawyers, or university professors. Such work experiences may help to explain these women's belief in the virtues of female economic independence.

A significant number of southern league women were Jewish or Catholic, which distinguished them from the vast majority of southerners as well as from the planter and industrial elite. Although she married a Protestant, Anna Settle herself was Catholic. Adele Clark was of Jewish and

Episcopalian parentage (and later would convert to Catholicism). Small Jewish communities in Richmond, New Orleans, and Louisville produced several important league members. Not only were Jewish Americans relatively liberal on labor issues, but Jewish southerners may have been more likely to have ties outside the region that broadened their political perspective. Given their familiarity with persecution and prejudice, it is hardly surprising that these particular southern whites were less susceptible than others to Lost Cause rhetoric. Southern reactionaries often attacked the New Deal with anti-Semitic slurs, as well as antiblack ones, which may have made southern Jews still more sympathetic to the Roosevelts.[75] Nationally, of course, Jews and Catholics were emerging as key constituents of a new Democratic Party coalition. In the South, such religious affiliations were one more way—on top of their unconventional educational and marital profiles—in which Consumers' League women found themselves at odds with the region's restrictive norms of white female respectability.

By the time they became league activists, most of these southern women already had experience in regional and national women's organizations. These affiliations seem to have dissolved localist tendencies, encouraging broader thinking about regional and national planning and development. Many league women had belonged to the short-lived Southern Council for Women and Children in Industry; they also were members of the Association of Southern Women for the Prevention of Lynching. Some NCL activists were mainstays of the local League of Women Voters, although in some places the LWV had become too conservative to back labor laws.

The YWCA was generally bolder than the LWV on labor and race questions, particularly in its industrial departments. YWCA industrial secretaries were among the most progressive people in the South, and they became an important base of support for the NCL. In Richmond, Lucy Mason herself had been the South's first YWCA industrial secretary. She claimed that "in places where there is no Consumers' League, no other organization is so close to the workers or so interested in their welfare as the YWCA." In almost every state, Mason's short list of key contacts included someone in the YWCA industrial department. The conferences held by these departments and by the Southern Summer School for Women Workers brought female reformers and wage earners together with left-wing activists like Howard Kester of the Southern Tenant Farmers' Union and labor journalist Tom Tippett. Indeed, the YWCA and the Southern Summer School offered more support to the region's female workers than labor unions did, until the CIO's southern drive began in 1937.[76]

Organized social workers also offered a receptive audience to Lucy Mason, and occasionally she gleaned a committed league activist from their ranks. Mason was the first speaker ever to address the topic of labor legislation before the South Carolina social work conference, and the 250 people present swamped Mason with applause and questions. But aroused interest did not always lead to concrete action. Mason commented, "The difficulty is in finding a person to take the leadership and go on when I leave." She was delighted when Florida social workers organized the Florida Association for the Promotion of Social Legislation, a predominantly female coalition that backed reforms including wage-hour regulation. This group soon faded away, however.[77]

Southern universities, especially women's colleges, yielded many league sympathizers. Elinor Nims Brink, a professor at Georgia State Women's College, wrote Lucy Mason: "The students here need to know women from the South who have social vision and who are making notable contributions to the solution of the problems of our social order. You are such a woman and could do much to shake some few of them out of their rut of complacency and social introversion."[78] Gladys Boone of Sweet Briar College in Virginia had her undergraduates do research for league projects, and Elizabeth Wisner encouraged her graduate students at Tulane to write theses on the subject of labor legislation.[79] Although they provided critical support to the league in the South, academics rarely were the lead instigators behind legislative drives. Professors had other obligations, and their positions did not always permit them to spearhead controversial campaigns. In South Carolina, social work professor Leila Johnson nominally headed a league committee, but she was unable to make it a high priority. Mason was left circulating letters about upcoming legislative hearings to that state's committee herself.[80]

Mason did receive help in South Carolina from Mary Frayser, the home economist at Winthrop State College for Women. Frayser's life charted a path that was especially remarkable in the South. Born in Richmond in 1868, she became a schoolteacher to support herself after her father died. Not long after she took a summer course at the University of Chicago, Frayser became a founding member of the Virginia Equal Suffrage League. (She probably met Lucy Mason then, if she had not before.) Frayser eventually earned a sociology degree from Columbia and held a series of teaching, extension, and government-funded positions in Georgia, South Carolina, and Virginia. These included a stint as assistant inspector for child labor in Georgia in the employ of the U.S. Children's Bureau, until the national child labor law was struck down in 1918. Frayser finally secured a long-term position at Winthrop, and she proceeded to become a pillar of the South Carolina reform movement. South Carolina club women were impressed with Frayser's "feminine charm" and her reliance on gentle persuasion—"the sun and not the wind"—to effect change, but behind this sweet exterior lay views that in the South were insurrectionary. "Roosevelt veers to the right," Frayser lamented in 1935. She believed that if he had held firm, he could have "accomplished much that remains to be done," particularly for sharecroppers and agricultural laborers. Unlike some South Carolina women who maintained that slavery had benefited "African savages," Frayser declared that she would have been a "rank abolitionist" had she lived before the Civil War. She was active in a succession of interracial civil rights groups. Also committed to women's rights, Frayser pressed the Southern Regional Council to encourage female participation, and in the 1940s she headed the South Carolina Status of Women Conference.[81] As a single, social work–oriented and geographically mobile professional, Frayser was the rare southern counterpart to northern league activists like Margaret Wiesman and Elizabeth Magee.

Virtually every southern woman who became a Consumers' League activist had been, like Mary Frayser, an avid supporter of woman suffrage. Experience in woman suffrage activity seems to have fostered support for labor legislation in several ways. First, after the states' rights cry was used against the Nineteenth Amendment, many southern suffragists came to see the state sovereignty argument as an excuse for blocking reform. (A few southern suffragists themselves opposed the Nineteenth Amendment as an infringement on states' rights, but these were not the women who supported the Consumers' League in the 1930s.)[82] Former suffragists may well have been more likely than other white southerners to embrace federal legislation. This would explain why southern NCL activists backed federal measures that many southern liberals did not, such as the child labor amendment, the Fair Labor Standards Act, and the Wagner Labor Relations Act.

Former suffragists also may have been attracted to the Consumers' League, and to the broader New Deal agenda, because the New Deal offered unprecedented political opportunities to women. One vital impulse behind woman suffrage had been the conviction that men were doing a poor job of governing. In the South as in the North, this conviction fit well with Consumers' League assumptions about women's rights and obligations to political participation. As suffragists, as reformers, and as individuals seeking advancement, southern league activists often had found themselves stymied by local politicians. During the New Deal, women officials of the NCL, the Democratic National Committee Women's Division, and the U.S. Department of Labor offered themselves as allies in these local struggles. North Carolina women forged ties with Molly Dewson's Women's Division as a strategy for reforming the local Democratic Party.[83] In

New Orleans, a Women's Committee that included league members instigated a Senate investigation of Huey Long's administration. "Women Seek Scalp of the Crawfish," New Orleans newspaper headlines announced.[84] In Georgia, Democratic Women's Division officials worked secretly with dissident state Democratic women in an unsuccessful attempt to unseat Senator Walter George in 1938, thus assisting FDR's failed effort to purge his party of conservatives. Indeed, women in many states were prominent in the "party purge" insurgencies of 1938 that exacerbated the southern reaction against the New Deal.[85] In the Carolinas, Virginia, and Kentucky, league activists also formed fruitful alliances with women in various divisions of the U.S. Department of Labor, who provided bills and data and sometimes sent representatives to help lobby state legislators.[86]

Through these alliances, southern league activists came to believe the federal government was willing to use the energies of women like themselves. Although many New Deal programs did not challenge gender inequality, under the Roosevelt administration women obtained a larger share of federal and Democratic Party jobs than they had before, winning as much as a third of the positions in some New Deal agencies. The high profile of women like Frances Perkins, Molly Dewson, and Ellen S. Woodward of Mississippi in the Federal Emergency Relief Administration conveyed a new sense of possibility for female professionals and reformers. Several southern league women took or sought positions in New Deal agencies.[87] They did not call themselves feminists, reflecting their distaste for anything "NWPish." But in their ideas, actions, and ambitions, they were feminists.[88] When Lucy Mason's friend Helen Douglas Mankin became a Georgia congresswoman, Mason rejoiced and looked forward to the day when Mankin might become a U.S. senator. Mason predicted that "labor and liberals — both men and women — will soon hold the balance of power." The prediction was overoptimistic, but telling. For Mason and other southern women of the Consumers' League, the New Deal years were "days of hope," offering new possibilities for women as well as for labor and black southerners.[89]

League women in the South, in sum, were people whose personal backgrounds and political experiences combined to inure them to many of the assumptions that bound most southern white women of the middle and upper classes. Their education, marital status, and religion often distinguished them from their peers. Through study or residence outside the South, suffragism, and alliances with women in national organizations and government agencies, they absorbed new ideas and developed a gendered, national perspective that qualified their local loyalties.[90] These women believed that national social democracy, not laissez-faire and states' rights, would be their region's salvation. This perspective transcended sectionalist thinking and also held that women should share in the making of government policy. In the context of the southern social order, these views were deeply subversive.

The perception that women were key supporters of the New Deal may have been a factor in southern conservatives' growing hostility to the New Deal over the course of the 1930s. Initially, most southern congressmen warmly supported Roosevelt, glad to have a Democrat back in the White House and eager for their states' shares of New Deal spending. However, southern suspicions of the Roosevelt administration mounted over time, particularly after FDR's landslide reelection in 1936. The importance of the new industrial labor unions and of northern African Americans to Roosevelt's win alarmed conservative southern Democrats. Women seem to have been another group in the emerging Democratic coalition. New Deal policies were hardly transformative in their effect on white supremacy, employer power, or male dominance. But the New Deal offered more to blacks, labor unions, and women than previous administrations, and those voters rewarded FDR with their support. This worried those southern conservatives who were accustomed to having significant control over the Democratic Party. In early 1937 the CIO sit-down strikes and Roosevelt's injudicious effort to "reform" the Supreme Court triggered a wave of southern defections from the New Deal. During the 1938 election season, when FDR campaigned against certain Democratic incumbents (with help from the Democratic Women's Division), outraged southern conservatives escalated their anti–New Deal rhetoric. The race- and union-baiting of this southern reaction is well known, but its gender content has not received attention.[91]

When southern conservatives attacked white women associated with the New Deal as "nigger lovers," they were reacting to a perception that white women, as well as black people, were forgetting their "place." The followers of Georgia governor Eugene Talmadge, who in 1936 formed a "Grass Roots" anti-Roosevelt movement, regularly accused Eleanor Roosevelt of having "Negro blood" or a black lover. This group also popularized the refrain in which a fictional FDR said to Eleanor, "You kiss the negroes, I'll kiss the Jews, We'll stay in the White House, As long as we choose." Senators Theodore Bilbo of Mississippi and Carter Glass of Virginia denounced the New Deal for promoting "social equality," which they equated with racial intermarriage. Bilbo charged that pro–civil rights New Dealers wanted "to see white women nursing black babies — their babies!"

Such remarks were extreme, but the "Bilbonic Plague" was not easy to contain.[92] These denunciations of "race-mixing" featured images of white women mixing with black men, not white men with black women. Southern politicians were stirring up antiblack sentiment, of course, but they were appealing to white *men* in particular. White women who broke the rules forswore their right to white men's chivalrous protection.[93]

Attacks on white women's authority were not always racial. Talmadge called Georgia's relief administrator a "crabbed old maid" and accused the Federal Emergency Relief Administration of hiring "about the richest ladies in town."[94] Running a close second to Eleanor Roosevelt in unpopularity with southern conservatives was Secretary of Labor Frances Perkins; not only was she personally denounced, but her agency was bypassed and threatened with budget cuts. Louisiana critics of the child labor amendment warned that it would empower the women of the U.S. Children's Bureau, as if that alone were reason to oppose it.[95] Senator E. D. Smith of South Carolina charged that the federal antilynching bill was drafted by "long-haired men and short-haired women."[96] This complaint conflated female political activism with a collapse of traditional gender hierarchies and distinctions.

Southern conservatives' hostility toward the New Deal in the late 1930s thus seems to have been in part a reaction against challenges to male prerogatives — as well as to employer prerogatives, white supremacy, and states' rights. Southern women of the Consumers' League were in the thick of these struggles. This significant development in southern politics illustrates the impact of progressive southern women's activism and, at the same time, helps explain why and how the program these women supported was blocked.

Lucy Mason was able to harvest only a small crop of southern league activists, but as she put it, "those few are of high quality."[97] Mason advanced southern reform causes through her educational work and network building. She developed local coalitions of female reformers, union members, academics, and state officials, and then linked these coalitions into a fledgling regional labor standards network. Margaret Wiesman of the Massachusetts league told Mason that her "stunning work" was "very definitely a rare contribution which only you could make. . . . I had for years felt embarrassed at our failure to do something about the South and my Consumers' League conscience has been on a much higher plain since you have been stirring the place up . . . , starting Labor Departments, having conferences and the like."[98] Mason shaped southern opinion through addresses and articles in many forums, through the conferences she conceived and helped organize, and through contact with southern journalists. Many newspaper editors frankly acknowledged their debt to her ideas. One of them jokingly urged her to "write a best-seller on how you influenced editorial writers." Francis P. Miller of the National Policy Committee believed that through these activities, Mason made "an absolutely invaluable contribution to the liberal movement in the South."[99] The NCL Southern Committee gathered together many of the people and ideas that would form the Southern Policy Committee and the Southern Conference for Human Welfare. Mason's work also generated support for labor-liberal ventures such as the Southern Summer School for Women Workers and the Highlander Folk School. Mason herself was active in all these groups, and their linkage of race and labor reform probably reflected her influence.[100]

In addition to helping build a progressive network within the South, the Consumers' League linked southern reformers with national groups. Mason believed that diminishing southern liberals' distrust of national measures and agencies was crucial to effecting meaningful change in the South.[101] Her accomplishments in this regard should not be overstated, because Mason herself believed that suspicion of national organizations remained a major reason that more southerners did not join the NCL. However, thanks to Mason, southerners were better represented among league officers than before, and southern activists and bureaucrats formed lasting contacts with their counterparts in other states and in the U.S. Department of Labor.

Mason tried to get northerners to look southward as well, and her work helped bring the South to the forefront of national reformers' agendas. A fitting symbol for the culmination of this effort was the famous *Report on Economic Conditions of the South* (1938). Mason had a hand in writing this report, which FDR backed in a failed attempt to recapture southern support. Although the final report disappointed Mason in certain respects, it represented her belief that national resources and national regulations were necessary to help transform the South from "the Nation's Number One Economic Problem" to "the Nation's Number One Economic Hope." As such, the 1938 report reflected much of the thinking that had guided Mason's work for the Consumers' League.[102]

In the end, the New Deal did not effect revolutionary change in relations between the classes, races, or sexes, but for a time some women perceived new possibilities. Their ranks included a small but striking group of southern white women whose activism on behalf of labor reform transgressed the southern social order by defying the conventions of states' rights and the southern lady. These women won a few legislative victories, as we shall soon see, and they nurtured ideas that would later bear more fruit. That they ultimately failed to achieve their program for the South reflects the power of the reaction they helped stimulate more than flaws in their vision.

chapter 6

Agents of the New Deal

Consumers'
League Women
Campaign
in Virginia,
South Carolina,
and Kentucky

The demise of the National Recovery Administration in mid-1935 left southern workers with a body of state labor laws that had improved little since 1931, when Mason documented their inadequacy in *Standards for Workers in Southern Industry*. NCL surveys indicated that many employers were responding to the termination of NRA codes by cutting wages and lengthening hours. In late 1935 the Consumers' League pledged its meager resources to an all-out southern offensive that included, in addition to Mason's ongoing regionwide work, specific legislative drives in carefully targeted states. The NCL board relieved Mason of all other responsibilities so that she could focus on the South. The board also agreed to fund this activity from the NCL budget, instead of requiring Mason's southern work to pay for itself through lecture fees and fund-raising. With league finances in a more precarious state than ever, this was a major commitment by the NCL board.[1]

Before long Mason was reporting, "How little the members of my own board realize conditions in the South and what one is up against in organizing a group or creating public opinion! I wish some of them could work in this field for a week or two—it would be illuminating to them."[2] Apparently the NCL board did not fully appreciate the obstacles facing the league in the South. Some board members seemed to blame southerners in general for not being more responsible citizens. Beulah Amidon attributed the lack of labor laws to the region's lack of "informed, alert, and effective public opinion."[3] But in the South, of course, employer opposition to labor standards regulation was deeper and less tractable than in other parts of the country. Labor unions in the region were weaker and even less interested in wage-hour laws than unions elsewhere. The split between the AFL and the emerging CIO also complicated cooperation with labor in the South, just as it did in other places. When industrial workers were able to elect friendly representatives, they faced an uphill battle in rural-dominated legislatures. Labor departments were nonexistent or tiny and were often run by political appointees. Few reformers were willing to agitate for labor laws. Looming behind these factors was the region's poverty, and the racial inequality that helped perpetuate it.

The story of labor standards campaigns in the South gives new meaning to V. O. Key's classic insight that "the politics of the South revolves around the position of the Negro."[4] The imperative to maintain white supremacy had deep implications for gender and class relations as well as race relations. Not only were racist arguments used against bills affecting black labor, but advocates of any labor standards bill might find themselves accused of disrupting the South's social order and threatening white dominance. As we have seen, the middle-class white women who elsewhere were instrumental in the development of wage-hour regulation showed less support for such policies in the South. However, those few wage and hours laws that did pass in the southern states — notably in Virginia, North Carolina, Kentucky, and Louisiana — were won largely through the efforts of small groups of progressive white women. Such women also were key activists in failed campaigns in other southern states. The three case studies examined here illustrate how the league's southern drives differed from its northern ones. They also help explain why legislative outcomes varied within the South. Key variables included the salience of racial divisions, the strength and attitude of organized labor, and the culture of state labor departments and party politics. A critical factor in the fate of labor standards bills in a given state was whether a dedicated local activist or group of activists emerged and persevered in the face of intense public criticism.

The Plan of Attack

Mason and the NCL board mapped out a plan for late 1935 and 1936 in which Virginia would be Mason's first priority, followed by South Carolina and Kentucky. In late 1936 Mason interrupted her southern work in order to coordinate the league's response to a major legal setback in the minimum wage movement. In early 1937 she returned to the South, concentrating on the Carolinas and Georgia. Despite intensive efforts by Mason and local leagues, southern employers stymied virtually all league bills from 1935 through mid-1937. But in late 1937 and 1938 the work of the league and allied groups bore fruit. Hours laws of unprecedented scope and stringency passed in North Carolina and Virginia, and Kentucky and Louisiana adopted the South's first minimum wage laws.[5]

NCL goals for the southern states were uniform laws establishing shorter hours and minimum wages (beginning with women-only bills) as well as independent labor departments. The question of men's inclusion in state bills caused much debate in league strategy sessions during the 1930s. The Consumers' League embraced the principle of sex-neutral regulation, as its work on the NRA codes demonstrated, but its long experience with the courts and the AFL led it to proceed cautiously. The league was not reluctant to regulate men's labor, but it did fear jeopardizing laws for women, who needed those laws most urgently, in its view. On hours regulation, the league's policy from 1932 on was to work in principle for men's inclusion but to ensure that opposition to men's coverage did not inhibit regulations for women.[6] The question of including men in minimum wage bills was even more problematic. When the league resurrected its drive for state minimum wage laws in 1933, its new model bill applied to women only. Although some league activists had hoped to try a sex-neutral bill, they deferred to the advice of their legal counsel, Felix Frankfurter. In June 1936 the Supreme Court ruled against the league's New York minimum wage law for women. But in March 1937 the Court unexpectedly reversed itself and sustained a Washington State minimum wage law for women that dated back to 1913. The ruling did not emphasize workers' gender, holding out the possibility that the Court would rule favorably on minimum wage for men.[7] The NCL now was ready to work for state minimum wage bills applying to both men and women, but pockets of AFL resistance forced a continued reliance on women-only laws as a fallback option. The league adopted a policy on men's minimum wage similar to its earlier one on men's hours: its model bill included men, but in a separate section that local groups could decide whether or not to keep.[8] In the South, most groups opted to begin with women-only bills, a choice probably influenced by Lucy Mason. Mason believed that "it is obviously impossible for a southern state to lead the way" in including men in labor standards laws. The positions taken by southern employers, state labor federations, and judges would confirm her fears.[9]

Several factors shaped the NCL's prioritization of particular states. First, the league aimed at states that employed large numbers of women in the occupations established as "regulatable." By the mid-1930s NCL leaders were searching for ways to legislate the labor standards of domestic and agricultural laborers, but they considered it futile to begin with such "advanced" bills in the South. League bills there did cover some nonindustrial occupations, including laundry and restaurant work. Nonetheless, in its targeting of certain states, the league maintained its bias favoring women in manufacturing. This strategy dovetailed with the priorities of national labor leaders, who were concerned primarily with interstate competition in industrial occupations. The South's largest manufacturing industry was textiles, concentrated in the three-hundred-mile-long region stretching from southern Virginia through the Carolinas and Georgia to Alabama. Other major industrial employers of southern women were tobacco processing (especially in North Carolina, Virginia, and Kentucky), garments (in Kentucky and scattered elsewhere), and food processing (especially in Georgia and Virginia).[10]

In terms of numbers of workers directly affected, Virginia, the Carolinas, Georgia, and Kentucky were top targets for the NCL. Within this group, the league concentrated on those states where it could make the greatest impact. League resources were limited, and Lucy Mason could only be in so many places at once, so the league chose its battles carefully. Although North Carolina had more wage earners than any other southern state, a good nucleus of reformers and academics already was promoting labor reform there. Mason did not spend much time in North Carolina, but she corresponded with local activists, shaping their bills and tactics from behind the scenes.[11]

Local political circumstances were another consideration in the league's allocation of resources. Where the opposition to labor legislation was particularly ferocious, without offsetting support from labor or liberals, Mason limited herself to sporadic educational work, reserving her lobbying energies for more fertile ground. Georgia might be classed in this category, along with Alabama and Mississippi.[12] Mason also avoided states where she believed local infighting would make it impossible to get substantial bills passed, such as Louisiana.[13] Her immediate priorities also depended, of course, on which state legislatures were meeting; in 1936 the legislatures of Virginia, South Carolina, Kentucky, Louisiana, and Mississippi were in session. Mason concentrated on Virginia and South Carolina, while the Consumers' League of Kentucky coordinated lobbying efforts in that state.

Campaigns in Virginia, South Carolina, and Kentucky: An Overview

Of all the states in the nation, Virginia was possibly the most hostile to the New Deal. The political machine of Democratic U.S. senators Carter Glass and Harry Byrd was supported by the state's leading industries, tobacco and cotton textiles, and it benefited from consistently low voter turnout. New Deal agricultural and industrial programs were not particularly relevant to Virginia's needs, and the New Deal's promises to African Americans, vague as they were, threatened the South's social order.[14] In 1935, however, the moment seemed ripe for a challenge to the Glass-Byrd faction. A *Richmond Times-Dispatch* poll confirmed Mason's opinion that there was "much New Deal and anti-Byrd sentiment in the rank and file of the people"—especially among women.[15] Mason's goals for the 1936 legislative session were to amend the state's feeble hours law for women and to have a minimum wage bill introduced to "break ground" for its passage in 1938.[16]

The 1936 session was disastrous for league bills but not entirely fruitless, because it spurred the formation of the Virginia Consumers' League (VCL). The minimum wage bill had to be withdrawn after being crippled with amendments. A more bitter disappointment came when the hours bill, after passing in the house, was killed by a senate committee (of "Virginia old men," according to Mason) that refused to release the bill for a floor vote despite an unusual degree of protest by sympathetic senators. On the heels of this narrow defeat, the VCL formed. Women comprised well over half the members of this "'who's who' of good Virginia people," as Mason called it, and a handful of women did the bulk of its work. The branch emerged as a vital force when Naomi Cohn became its secretary. She took over the job from a young man named John Corson, who juggled three professional commitments and gave the VCL low priority. By contrast, Cohn undertook legislative work for the NCL on a full-time, unpaid basis. Other important figures in the VCL included Virginius Dabney, editor of the *Richmond Times-Dispatch*, and artist Adele Clark.[17] The new VCL made an immediate impact with a successful campaign for a special session of the legislature in December 1936. The special session passed state unemployment insurance legislation but refused to consider other VCL issues, including the women's hours bill and poll-tax repeal.[18]

In 1938 Virginia at last amended its women's hours law to make it the South's broadest and most enforceable such law. The new law established a maximum nine-hour day and forty-eight-hour week for women in most occupations outside domestic and agricultural work. VCL secretary Naomi Cohn spent hours each day at the state capitol, becoming so closely identified with the bill that legislators began calling it "the Cohn bill." On one occasion, Cohn addressed the legislature "breathing fire and armed with statistics and accompanied by several mill and factory women in their work clothes." In addition to mobilizing women workers, Cohn brought in a Virginia-born expert from the U.S. Women's Bureau to testify. (This strategy was Mason's idea and illustrates her success in forging ties between local liberals and federal officials. Of course, it still helped if the officials were southerners.) Cohn was named to the annual honor roll of the *Richmond Times-Dispatch* for her efforts on the law's behalf.[19]

In many respects, South Carolina was even less auspicious than Virginia for a labor law campaign. "Dominated by cotton manufacturing, saw-mill and agricultural interests, the legislature usually proves the graveyard of labor bills," sighed Mason. Indeed, the textile industry occupied an even more dominant position in the state's political economy than in other textile states. South Carolina's per capita income was one of the lowest in the country. Its unionization rate was the lowest in the South, and it had no department of labor. South Carolina women's groups were relatively uninterested in changing these statistics. More vigorously than in Virginia or North Carolina, white club women in South Carolina opposed legislative approaches to labor reform as a threat to Old South honor and New South prosperity.[20] Given these circumstances, it is hardly surprising that the state's representatives in Washington were unfriendly to labor causes. Senator E. D. ("Cotton Ed") Smith would become legend for his hostility to the New Deal, especially the Fair Labor Standards Act. Senator James Byrnes was a confidant of FDR's, but his commitment to labor legislation was questionable.[21]

This generally bleak climate for labor reform improved slightly in the mid-1930s. Because the state constitution did not disfranchise poor whites, white wage earners had a louder voice in South Carolina politics than they did in most southern states. One in five South Carolina voters lived in a mill village. In 1934 textile workers rejected the patriarchal antistatism of their former hero Cole Blease and helped elect onetime mill hand Olin D. Johnston to the governor's office. Johnston did not eschew white supremacy, but he ran as a New Dealer and labor ally.[22] Friends of southern labor were encouraged, the NCL among them. In February 1935, just after the inauguration of the "linthead governor," Lucy Mason addressed both houses of the state legislature. With Mrs. Olin Johnston and Mary Frayser at her side, Mason urged South Carolina legislators to act for shorter hours, the child labor amendment, a labor department, workers' compensation, and compulsory education laws.[23] Mason persuaded Governor Johnston to host a Southern Regional Labor Standards Conference in Columbia the following year. This conference stimulated the formation of a South Carolina league committee.

Despite these glimmers of hope, the Consumers' League agenda was stymied in South Carolina in 1936 and thereafter. A labor department was created in the 1936 session, but it had little authority or money. An eight-hour-day/forty-hour-week bill for men and women in textiles passed, with the enormous caveat that it would not take effect unless Georgia and North Carolina (South Carolina's southern rivals in textiles) passed similar legislation. A nine/forty-eight hours bill for women in other occupations languished in committee. In 1938 the eight/forty bill for both sexes in textiles (now without the joint action proviso) and a mild, exemption-ridden twelve/fifty-six bill for both sexes in other occupations passed, but neither law survived for long. Meanwhile, despite the support of mill workers and FDR, Olin Johnston lost his bid for E. D. Smith's U.S. Senate seat in the 1938 elections. Smith used FDR's opposition to paint the New Deal as a second Reconstruction. After Smith's victory, a local league member lamented that "states' rights, white supremacy, Bourbonism, low wages, long hours, and the right to ignorance, prejudice and superstition are no longer in jeopardy in South Carolina." In 1941 and for decades thereafter, the state labor commissioner would still be begging for an hours law to protect those not covered by federal law. The narrow portal of opportunity for state labor legislation in South Carolina had slammed shut.[24]

In Kentucky, the tobacco industry, coal mining operators, and agricultural interests were powerful, but they did not dominate state politics to the extent that employer interests did in most southern states. The influential Senator Alben Barkley led Kentucky's congressional delegation, most of whom remained loyal to Roosevelt after other southern Democrats started defecting from the New Deal in 1937. Kentucky's state politicians were less predictable in their sympathy for New Deal programs. This included the governor until 1935, Ruby Laffoon. Laffoon's ambitious young successor, Albert "Happy" Chandler, took office as a Roosevelt supporter, but in many respects he, too, was a conservative, holding Kentucky's relief spending close to the lowest levels in the country and backing employers in the Harlan County mining conflicts.[25]

The Kentucky Consumers' League (KCL) was so well established and capably led that Mason did not make extended stays in the state. Led by Louisville natives Annie Ainslie Halleck and Anna Hubbuch Settle, the KCL was one of the oldest and most solidly female league branches. Halleck attended Vassar and married a Yale-educated author and school principal.

Women at work in a Louisville, Kentucky, garment factory (1942).
(National Archives)

The Hallecks did not have children, and Annie devoted her prodigious energies and resources to many reform causes. The KCL, which she founded in 1901, was her primary platform.[26] Twenty years younger than Halleck, Anna Settle earned a law degree at the University of Louisville and became a respected lawyer and judge. Like Halleck, Settle held office in a long list of voluntary associations, but the KCL was the focal point of her reform activity.[27] Kentucky league women could claim credit for a 1902 child labor law, a 1912 ten-hour law for women, and the reorganization of the labor department in 1924. KCL minimum wage bills were defeated several times from 1920 on, as were bills to further shorten women's hours. In the 1930s the Kentucky league built an effective coalition of middle-class women's and labor groups, including the predominantly female local of the ACWA. This coalition was behind the passage of the South's first minimum wage law in 1938.[28]

The Kentucky league, more than any other NCL branch, contradicts the claim of historian Alan Brinkley that southern liberals were either too timid to fight or not really very liberal.[29] The KCL shared mailing lists with the Socialist Club and the ILGWU, investigated ACWA complaints about specific

Anna Settle, president, and Annie Halleck, past president, of the Consumers' League of Kentucky, on the fortieth anniversary of the branch in 1941. (*The Courier-Journal*)

employers, and interceded with the Louisville mayor on behalf of strikers arrested by employers' hired guards. The KCL stopped state labor inspectors from waiving child labor laws for black children in tobacco, and later it stopped the state labor commissioner from forcing laundresses (most of whom were black) to settle minimum wage violation claims for the nominal amount of $1. In 1938 it recommended that a black woman be appointed to the advisory board of the new minimum wage board. Annie Halleck attended the first meeting of the Southern Conference for Human Welfare, the interracial group that promoted desegregation, poll-tax repeal, and labor rights, and other KCL members soon joined the group as well. The KCL thrived for over four decades as a progressive women's institution, and it also was able to mobilize other female-dominated local groups on behalf of labor standards regulation.[30]

Consumers' League activists managed to win an hours law for women in Virginia and a minimum wage law for women in Kentucky, but in South Carolina they made little headway, except for the creation of a labor department. A closer look at racial politics, alliances with labor unions, and labor departments in each of these states will illuminate the crucial role of league women and the reasons for their varying degrees of success.

Racial Politics and Labor Standards Regulation

In some states more than others, employers' interest in preserving control over low-paid workers who were occupationally segregated by race undermined NCL campaigns. In general, the smaller a state's black population, the better its labor laws and its labor departments. This was true even though labor standards bills did not apply to domestic and agricultural work, the occupations employing most blacks.[31] Employers dependent on black agricultural and domestic labor opposed any measure — wage-hour legislation, relief, public works — that might put upward pressure on wages or disrupt the paternalistic labor system.[32] Those African Americans who did work in "regulatable" occupations were concentrated in the jobs with the lowest wages, longest hours, and worst conditions, so their employers had the most to lose from laws that raised wages or cut hours. Low-paying industries and agricultural interests everywhere opposed labor laws, but in the South these groups could deploy racist arguments to undercut support for them.[33]

Lucy Mason understood all too well how racial division of the southern labor force hindered labor standards bills. Fuming about the fate of the Virginia minimum wage bill in early 1936, she observed that "of course, back of all this opposition is the low wages of Negro women."[34] In 1937 a Tennessee legislator tried to dodge supporting a league bill by telling Mason that the "large amount of Negro labor" brought "far-reaching complications" to the minimum wage issue. Mason replied tartly that "until we can raise the wages of Negro labor we cannot assure white workers living wages. Any group of workers which can be employed at very low wages threatens the living standards of competing groups." Here she stressed white workers' self-interest in equal wages, rather than black rights.[35]

Opposition from employers of black labor prevented the Virginia league's hours bill from passing in 1936, weakened the bill that passed in 1938, and perennially prevented the passage of a state minimum wage law. In 1936 it was tobacco rehandlers, peanut cleaners, and laundries who killed the women's eight-hour bill. From a list of women's manufacturing occupations in Virginia, tobacco rehandling and peanut cleaning leap out as the occupations that employed large numbers of black women and virtually no white women. Laundries employed many black women and some whites. These were the jobs in which significant numbers of women worked more than fifty-five hours per week and thus would have been most affected by the bill.[36] The peanut and tobacco employers howled about the threat of interstate competition, "saying North Carolina every time they opened their mouths," according to Mason.[37] Fear of competition was a common argument against labor laws, but legislators seem to have been exceptionally sensitive to such concerns when they were voiced by employers of black labor. In 1936 the Virginia league refused to exempt tobacco rehandling and peanut cleaning in exchange for an eight-hour day for other (mostly white) women. In 1938, however, Naomi Cohn finally compromised on the hours bill. After being "flooded with amendments" to the bill and fighting all of them, Cohn accepted an amendment that allowed ten hours per day during the ninety-day peak season in tobacco rehandling, peanut cleaning, canning, and oyster shucking. Most employees in these occupations were black. Otherwise elated at the bill's passage, Cohn was disappointed about this amendment. Still, she stressed, the amendment allowed "only a ten-hour day" even during the peak season, so the bill was an improvement over prevailing conditions. The 1938 law's inclusion of laundries was no small feat; in southern cities, most laundresses were black.[38]

In southern states where many black men worked outside agriculture, the issue of whether to include men in league bills took on extra significance. One U.S. Department of Labor lawyer suggested that men's inclusion might trigger extra opposition from politicians and manufacturers, "particularly in the southern areas where there is a race problem." This remark makes sense only when one understands that more black men than black women worked outside agriculture and domestic service.[39] In South Carolina, the 90,000 textile workers were virtually all white, male and female; the lumber industry employed over 150,000 male workers, roughly three-quarters of them black. A sex-neutral hours law likely would have covered the lumber industry (but not domestic or agricultural work). Whereas the eight/forty textile bill for men and women came close to passing several times and eventually did pass, no general-coverage hours law affecting substantial numbers of black men got very far. Such bills faced tremendous opposition from both industrial and agricultural employers. They also received little support from southern Federations of Labor.[40]

White supremacy inhibited the development of southern wage-hour legislation in another, less direct way. Racial politics in each state influenced how much political space was open for white women's prolabor activism. In South Carolina, supporters of Senator E. D. Smith accused Governor Johnston and FDR of hastening the day when "dirty, evil-smelling negroes will be going to church with you, your sister, your wife, or your mother."[41] White women who supported even modest labor reforms, like those of Johnston and FDR, faced the insinuation that they craved contact with black men. It is difficult to imagine activity like the Kentucky league's occurring in South Carolina, Georgia, or Alabama. Such variation within the South suggests that white supremacy inhibited the development of southern wage-hour laws in part by constraining the activism of the group that elsewhere got these laws passed, namely, progressive middle-class white women.

League Cooperation with Southern Unions

Southern labor groups displayed varying levels of support for labor standards regulation from one state to the next. Although they rarely were the instigating force behind hours and wage bills, unions usually played a critical role in the fate of a given bill.

Certain national unions were as worried about low southern labor standards as the Consumers' League. One ACWA organizer for the shirt industry reported in 1936 that "of late the unorganized sections of the industry, particularly the South, have been becoming more of a menace to the organization. Manufacturers in the East are becoming nervous and . . . they all talk about moving south."[42] Lucy Mason believed that one obstacle to a minimum wage law in Virginia was local hope for a continuation of "the influx of garment, knitting, bleaching and other industries that have been coming here to escape the unions in the last two or three years."[43] These concerns about industry migration to the South led a few key labor leaders to prioritize raising southern labor standards. Of particular importance was the ACWA's Sidney Hillman, who shared the NCL conviction that wage-hour laws would work hand in hand with unionization efforts. Both organizing and legislating were essential to cracking the "solid South" as an obstacle to social and industrial democracy.[44]

The textile strikes of 1934 suggested that federal recognition of union rights would not alone solve the difficulties of organizing southern workers. The ACWA's shirt organizer explained: "People are poor and afraid. And the communities are always anxious to keep the plant in the town. . . . [A]fter you get to the people, in come the police and mayor and tell the girls how hard they worked to get the shop into town, and how much they and their parents depend on it, that they will be traitors to the town if they join the union." As these words suggest, the workers in the "fly-by-night" plants often were young women. Low-wage employers sought out captive pools of female labor, women whose male relatives worked in occupations such as agriculture or mining and who were thus tied to one place.[45] Young women were subject to lower wages, and usually to tighter control by foremen and relatives, than most men. Pushed by women workers themselves, though, some labor leaders were making more serious efforts at organizing female-employing industries. The NCL and ACWA saw hours and wage laws as valuable aids to that effort.

One task of the Consumers' League was to rouse the enthusiasm of southern unions for state hours and wage laws, which was not always easy. Some southern trade unionists shared the regional distrust of outside efforts to discourage industry migration southward. One exasperated northern labor organizer called for getting "Southern labor folk to understand . . . that exploitation is equally bad for the South as for the North."[46] Mason worked her contacts to generate proregulatory publicity in the southern labor press, and regional labor conferences served a similar purpose.[47] Given the AFL's historical stances toward labor laws and women workers, making common cause with AFL groups could be tricky for the league in any state. The problem was particularly delicate in the South, where the league and the unions were weaker and more dependent on each other for support.[48] After 1936, competition with the CIO, which actively promoted wage and hour laws, increased the pressure on state Federations of Labor to broaden their legislative programs. On the other hand, the split made labor's position less predictable and forced southern league activists to proceed with great tact in wooing both sides.

State Federations of Labor had a tendency to ignore the interests of workers in less organized occupations, which infuriated Lucy Mason. This tension was manifested in disagreement over what maximum number of hours should be the goal. By late 1935 the strongest hours laws in the country, in Massachusetts, New York, and Connecticut, established a maximum nine-hour day/forty-eight-hour week for women. Since 1934 the NCL had been working for eight/forty bills wherever possible.[49] But in the South, Mason did not even dream of passing such a bill. Southern states either set no hours limit or mandated between fifty-four and sixty hours per week, and even these laws were unenforceable or had narrow coverage. Mason merely aimed to bring southern states in line with the nine/forty-eight states of New England: "Our only hope is to make a moderate beginning in the South, using New York as our basis."[50]

In both Virginia and South Carolina, the state Federations of Labor proposed bills for shorter hours than nine/forty-eight. Mason disagreed. She thought it was fine to work for a *federal* bill setting a forty-hour or even thirty-hour week, but she believed it pointless to do so in individual states, where fears of interstate competition would almost certainly kill such bills. Mason believed that national gains for labor were making southern labor leaders overconfident. She remarked in April 1936, "The chief trouble in the South just now is that the new growth in the cotton-textile unions makes the workers feel that they can pass almost any labor legislation and they put in bills which are too drastic to be passed anywhere in the United States. We have got to find some way to bring the labor and liberal groups together that will have a chance of passage."[51]

The split between the AFL and CIO further encouraged rival labor groups to submit ambitious bills in an effort to impress their constituencies. The problem for Mason was not that labor was being too militant. Mason admired worker militance and wished AFL leaders were more responsive to it.[52] Her concern was that the federations' insistence on "drastic" bills (which rarely passed) left the unorganized, unskilled workers who worked the longest hours no better off than before. Mason was irritated that the state labor federations, whose constituencies were predominantly skilled, white, and male, were willing to leave other workers behind.

In Virginia, Mason's goal was to replace a porous ten-hour law for women that set no weekly limit with a nine/forty-eight bill that covered more occupations and had stronger enforcement provisions. In November 1935 she met with Federation of Labor men and believed she had their commitment to a nine/forty-eight bill. To Mason's dismay, it soon became apparent that, although the Virginia federation's *legislative* committee had recommended working for the league's bill, its *executive* committee decided it must abide by an earlier resolution to work for the eight-hour day. "So there will be two bills in," a frustrated Lucy Mason explained, "but the Federation men will support our bill as well as theirs because they know theirs cannot pass."[53]

To Mason, it seemed that some labor men were paying more attention to internal and party politics than to reducing hours in long-hour occupations. In early 1936 Mason and Adele Clark of the Virginia league struggled to get "it into [the union men's] heads that we are not so much interested in putting legislators on the spot two years from now as we are in amending the hours law this winter." For union leaders, whose members generally already worked fewer than forty-eight hours per week, testing the position of state legislators may have seemed more important. To the league, whose particular concern was unorganized, long-hour employees, this seemed like so much symbolic posturing. Nonetheless, recognizing that a VCL bill had no chance if the state Federation of Labor opposed it, Mason worked to reconcile the two groups. She organized a meeting of the labor commissioner, union men, and VCL members at which it was agreed that the league would work for the federation's eight-hour bill, but if that bill got killed, they all would back the league's nine/forty-eight measure.[54] The VCL kept its promise and rallied behind the "straight-8" hours bill, which made it through the house but died in a senate committee. It was too late by that point to revive the VCL's nine/forty-eight bill. Mason thought the league's bill, had it been supported from the beginning, would have squeaked through the committee. The VCL would not win passage of the nine/forty-eight bill for another two years.[55]

Mason never publicly criticized organized labor, and she supported its bills once they were introduced. It was at an earlier stage that she sought to moderate southern unionists' demands. An important tactical consideration in a federated political system was the need to convince manufacturers in neighboring states that a given bill might really pass. Accordingly, in 1935 Mason worked to get tightly drafted and "realistic" hours bills introduced in Georgia, North Carolina, and Alabama, mainly to undercut Virginia and South Carolina manufacturers' complaints about interstate competition. In urging George Googe of the Georgia Federation of Labor to support a nine/forty-eight bill, she argued that there was "little point in introducing an ideal bill and never getting it out of committee. . . . Don't you agree with me that it would be better to have such a law on the statute books than to continue to talk about an 8 hour law and not get it?" Googe did not take Mason's suggestion, and no progress on hours was made in Georgia that year or in 1937.[56]

The fate of hours bills in South Carolina was a subtle variation on the Virginia theme. Factional competition within the state Federation of Labor produced an ambitious bill for textile workers that ultimately was defeated. Meanwhile, more modest bills affecting unorganized workers in long-hour occupations were neglected. Ironically, South Carolina mill workers' newly class-conscious flexing of their political muscle hindered the achievement of permanent state hours laws, because state labor leaders underestimated the extent to which the political deck remained stacked against them.

In late 1935 Mason believed she had lined up South Carolina's new Federation of Labor president, John Nates, and Governor Olin Johnston behind the nine/forty-eight plan. Mason urged Nates to join "all the people who *really* want to shorten women's hours" in backing the bill, "the best we can hope for in a Southeastern state."[57] However, the South Carolina leader of the United Textile Workers believed its members would be disgusted if the union pushed for anything less than a forty-hour bill. Most textile workers were already working forty-hour weeks, but this was only because the industry trade association (CTI) was trying to hold its members to the defunct NRA labor standards. The agreement was crumbling, however, and some mills were raising hours and dropping out of CTI. Even those South Carolina industrialists who supported CTI were ambivalent toward permanent state legislation because they feared competition from longer-hour neighbors. When the CTI agreement collapsed, Mason predicted, mill worker hours would rise back up to the legal limit of ten hours per day and fifty-five hours per week. Mason strove to convince the Federation of Labor that winning a nine/forty-eight law was urgent and would represent a meaningful victory of which labor could be proud.[58]

The Consumers' League committee in South Carolina had good intentions but no full-time leader.[59] This situation, combined with the importance of the mill village vote in South Carolina, meant that labor union support was even more critical to hours legislation there than in Virginia. Mason persuaded the state labor federation to invite her and U.S. Division of Labor Standards lawyer Charles Hodges to address the federation's executive council. Mason briefed Hodges in advance on "what a southern state faces when it undertakes a genuine 8-hour day." She added, "The labor groups find it hard to face this reality and go on making gestures to 8 hour laws, which die in committee."[60]

The best Hodges was able to do was to obtain an agreement not unlike Mason's with the Virginia federation. The South Carolina federation leaders promised him, Hodges explained to Mason, that when their forty-hour bill was killed, "they will throw their support to the 48 hour bill which you are going to have introduced, and which they will then accept as a 'compromise.' This will leave them on record publicly for a 40 hour principle in the State and they can let your group assume responsibility for whatever happens — unless of course the 48 bill passes, in which event it will have been their support which put it over."[61] In other words, federation leaders knew the eight/forty bill had little chance but insisted on introducing it anyway, because they did not want to lose face to a rival faction in the eyes of 30,000 textile workers. When Olin Johnston pledged his support for the federation's bill, Mason grumbled that the "sincere young Governor" would get better advice "if only he would take counsel of some of the University people and social workers, as well as the labor leaders."[62]

Mason's misgivings about forty-hour bills were justified. The state legislature passed the eight/forty textile bill in May 1936, but with the proviso that it would not take effect without matching legislation from North Carolina and Georgia.[63] In March 1937 the South Carolina house struck the requirement of identical action from neighboring states, and the senate promptly amended the bill to forty-eight hours. Mason urged the labor federation and John Nates — now commissioner of the state's new labor department — to compromise on forty-four hours, but Nates and the Federation of Labor held out for the eight/forty bill. The 1937 session ended with the bill stuck in conference committee. Meanwhile, a forty-eight-hour bill for women in occupations other than textiles sat ignored on the house calendar, just as it had in 1936. His optimism somewhat deflated, Commissioner Nates reported that "no law was passed controlling hours in any establishment" in 1937. Two hours bills did pass in South Carolina in 1938, but they were short-lived. A temporary forty-hour textile bill expired after one year, and a feeble twelve/fifty-six law for nontextile occupations was found unconstitutional because it applied to men as well as women.[64]

Viewed without attention to context, Mason's efforts to persuade southern labor unions to work for forty-eight-hour bills rather than forty-hour ones might suggest that she and her middle-class allies sought to co-opt worker militance and achieve only the mildest ameliorative reforms. Close scrutiny of developments in South Carolina suggests otherwise. Mason seems to have understood better than South Carolina labor leaders the limits on mill workers' political power, Olin Johnston's win in 1934 notwithstanding. The governor's office had little power in South Carolina. More important, mill villages were greatly underrepresented in the rural-dominated senate. Indeed, cynical house politicians backed labor bills on the safe assumption that the senate would kill them; easy wins in the house further misled mill workers about their political strength.[65] Lucy Mason was all too familiar with these political realities. She also was keenly aware of the dynamic created by the threat of interstate competition, predicting correctly that southern employers would not permit permanent forty-hour bills to pass in their state legislatures.

In South Carolina, the Consumers' League persuaded organized labor and the governor to take greater interest in hours legislation and to establish working relationships with the federal labor department and local reform groups.[66] Once mobilized, however, these labor men did not always value the advice of female reformers, nor did they demonstrate much interest in the circumstances of women workers outside of textiles. These priorities came at a cost, for textile workers and others. Although mill hands' political power was limited, it was not entirely illusory. Had South Carolina unions thrown their weight behind the league's nine/forty-eight bill in 1936, when Johnston's victory and regional union gains were fresh, and before E. D. Smith's 1938 triumph, that bill might have passed. This would have brought South Carolina hours law in line with the best laws in New England and would have facilitated the passage of similar bills in other southern states. Such developments could have had wide reverberations, for workers and for the New Deal.

In Kentucky, the local Consumers' League found the state Federation of Labor a more congenial colobbyist. This happier relationship reflected the local league's long record and its ties with women workers, as well as the federation's desire to undercut the popularity of rival CIO unions. More Kentucky workers belonged to unions than workers elsewhere in the South, which gave organized labor a measure of political leverage.[67]

In the 1938 fight for the women's minimum wage bill, representatives of both the Kentucky Federation of Labor and the ACWA-CIO supported the league bill. The federation's lobbyist, Edward Weyler, did not have the wholehearted backing of his organization, and the minimum wage bill for women was not his highest priority. But, rather to the surprise of the Consumers' League, Weyler made the case for the bill in meetings with legislators. Weyler was one of several federation officials who in the late 1930s regularly criticized their own organization for failing to actively support "desirable social and labor legislation."[68] The CIO was represented in lobbying for the minimum wage bill by Emma Saurer of Louisville's ACWA Local 120. Saurer had worked with the Kentucky Consumers' League since the mid-1920s and held the middle-class women's group in high esteem. Indeed, Saurer seems to have received more support from the local Consumers' League than from ACWA headquarters. Both the Federation of Labor and ACWA gave the Kentucky Consumers' League primary credit for the 1938 law.[69] The KCL took the initiative, but it owed its success in part to the fact that rival labor groups united behind its bill.

The Consumers' League and Southern Labor Departments

Unable to attend a 1935 conference of southern labor department officials, Lucy Mason remarked that it would be no great loss, as she already knew "the southern commissioners of labor so well and [knew] how little can be expected of most of them."[70] In addition to the prominence of race, and the weakness and ambivalence of organized labor, another distinctive feature of southern campaigns for wage-hour regulation was that state labor commissioners were more often a hindrance than a help to the league. Southern labor departments, where they existed, were woefully underfunded, and they usually were staffed by political appointees rather than experienced administrators. Outside the South, many state labor departments drew personnel from the NCL network and were at least somewhat accountable to women reformers. In some southern states, too, women's organizations had helped strengthen labor departments, notably in Virginia, the Carolinas, and Kentucky. However, even in these places reformers generally took less interest in labor departments than their counterparts did in the North.[71]

Mason observed that in the South, "wretched as the provisions of [a] law actually are, the actual enforcement may be infinitely worse." North Carolina's eleven-hour day law, for example, lacked provisions for posting of hours or record keeping, and "detection of violations is almost impossible under those circumstances." Stingy appropriations and poorly drafted laws were one part of the problem; unreliable appointees were another. Mason lamented, "The one factory and child labor inspector for Georgia is an incompetent, ignorant man, who when he finds violations of the unenforceable hours law reports it to the secretary of the Georgia Cotton Manufacturers' Association." Virginia Labor Commissioner John Hall undermined the league's minimum wage campaign in that state by taking a conciliatory approach to manufacturers. Hall told sponsors of the bill that he did not need the right to inspect company records. He would not want to insult employers' honor by doubting their word, he explained.[72]

In southern states even more than elsewhere, female reformers had difficulty preventing labor department jobs from going to industry allies or politicians' campaign supporters. During the drafting of a bill to create a labor department in South Carolina, Mason wrangled with a "disheveled, innocent, green and greedy group of young men" comprising the state's Industrial Commission, who wanted the labor department to be created within the commission. Mason spoke against it, but the men were "hungry for power and more jobs for their friends," so she was pessimistic about the outcome.[73] In designing a labor department bill for Florida, Mason worried about creating a "single-headed" department because she feared "the senile old governor will appoint one of his relatives."[74] In Louisiana, the Bureau of Women and Children was run by the "lady leader" of the Choctaws (the New Orleans machine). When she came to work at all, she assigned the staff to political work. In the rare event that inspections uncovered violations, employers who were "right politically" were not penalized.[75] There were a few exceptions to the region's poor enforcement, in Mason's view. The examples she offered were female-run agencies. She praised the Alabama Child Welfare Department's administration by "a capable and socially minded woman" and her "efficient staff of young women."[76] But this agency was atypical, a beacon in a dim field.

Even where the local league and labor groups were fairly strong, state officials could not always be trusted. In Kentucky, the commissioner of industrial relations, William Burrow, rewrote the league's minimum wage bill at the eleventh hour to eliminate the proposed Division of Minimum Wage, ensuring his own authority over the bill's administration. Then, as the bill was being debated in the last moments of the legislative session, it was stripped of its appropriation, meaning that the law would be on the books but unenforceable. The Consumers' League and labor groups favored returning the bill for reconsideration in the next session, but Commissioner Burrow persuaded them to accept it as a first step. The league suspected that Burrow, who was part of Governor Chandler's faction, did this so the governor could tell labor groups that he deserved credit for this minimum wage bill, while telling antilabor donors that he had staved off real regulation.[77]

In Virginia and South Carolina, the labor commissioners were Federation of Labor men, but this did not ensure receptiveness to advice from the women reformers who had helped create their positions. John Nates, the labor leader who became South Carolina's first labor commissioner, needed to be prodded into cooperating with local women's groups.[78] In Virginia, Lucy Mason was furious to learn that Commissioner Hall was telling legislators that she had withdrawn a labor bill because she was new to legislative work and did not know how to compromise. In fact, she withdrew the bill because Hall and others had piled on so many amendments that the bill was "emasculated and worthless." Mason cast this conflict as a battle of feminine principles against masculine self-interest: "Of course, all the women lined up with me on this."[79] Fifteen years later, women labor reformers would be reporting from Virginia that they got no help on labor bills from the state labor commissioner, because he wanted to be reappointed by "the machine."[80] In the 1930s, despite their faults, Nates and Hall were among the South's best labor commissioners, and Mason respected them for their commitment to the labor movement. Most southern commissioners were even less receptive to league input and more friendly to employers.

The rituals, posturing, and winking that Consumers' League women associated with masculine politics may have been especially characteristic of southern state politics. Southern league activists waxed sarcastic in their descriptions of state legislative work. In Kentucky, the delegation from the Consumers' League coalition waited for several hours outside the governor's office for a meeting, only to discover that their quarry had escaped. "Governor Chandler went out the side door to the House and introduced a guitar player. Congress and the Governor indulged in an hour of song." Only after extended pursuit did the prolabor group get their meeting.[81] In this and other instances, league women found male political behavior ridiculous. They implied that if women were in charge, they would put a stop to such nonsense. This illusion eventually would be dispelled, but in the meantime it inspired Consumers' League activists both North and South.

Assessing the League's Southern Drive

By early 1937 no significant new hours or wage laws had passed in the South, and Mason was getting discouraged. To Louise Stitt of the Women's Bureau she grumbled, "I have been in the closest contact with three legislatures, several Governors and many other people in the last ten days, and my pessimism is somewhat in the ascendancy." She confided to Frank Graham, "Sometimes I wonder if I am fooling myself as to the significance of the work we have done in the South these five years. So much of my time and energy are spent that I may have lost a sense of proportion as to the relation between the effort and the accomplishment."[82]

One reason Mason was discouraged was that the NCL's financial situation was reaching a crisis point. Fund-raising was an uphill battle in the South. Gertrude Weil in North Carolina told Mason flatly that she did not know anyone "of wealth" in the South who would give large sums in support of labor legislation. In May 1937 Mason wrote a Kentucky league officer that "raising our budget has become so difficult and Emily Marconnier is so worn down by it that I have decided I must either raise several thousand dollars each year myself, or leave the League."[83]

Two weeks later, Mason resigned. Although the difficulty of raising money was the overt reason, at the bottom of Mason's decision was a desire to make working in the South her sole priority. The extent of Mason's southern focus perturbed a few NCL veterans who thought she was neglecting the northern branches. One well-informed observer believed some NCL board members did not grasp the fact that "efforts to bring the backward South abreast of the rest of the country in labor legislation are of central national importance."[84] Mason privately expressed impatience with what she saw as tentativeness on the NCL board: "Unless there are several changes on the board I fear the League will sink gently into conservatism."[85] In her letter of resignation, Mason wrote pointedly that she was "glad to have had the opportunity to extend to new areas the principles and ideas to which Mrs. Kelley and the League under her leadership were dedicated. I hope that there will be lasting results in territory once largely untouched."[86] Subsequent NCL executives did keep in touch with southern league members, but the southern states never occupied as prominent a place on the NCL agenda as they had from 1931 through 1937.

Mason's irritation over the board's handling of her resignation, which was submitted simultaneously with that of associate general secretary Emily Marconnier, further suggests simmering tensions. The NCL board accepted Marconnier's resignation but voted "almost unanimously" to ask Mason to reconsider and remain as the only staff member. Mason was offended at the board's assumption that she would "continue right along with an impossible job." Had the board taken her concerns more seriously, Mason confided to Margaret Wiesman, "it is barely possible that I might have suggested a combination with Elizabeth [Magee, of the Ohio League] in this office and me in the South."[87] But the NCL board made no such overtures.

On the very day that the NCL board was deliberating, Mason met John L. Lewis, the charismatic leader of the ascendant CIO, a contact that would lead to a job working full-time in the South. Mason and Lewis met in Washington when they testified at the hearings on the Black-Connery wage-hour bill. Mason offered Lewis her services as a public relations representative in the South for the CIO's Textile Workers Organizing Committee (TWOC). Lewis liked the idea. Formed earlier in 1937 under the leadership of Sidney Hillman, TWOC sought to bring industrial unionism to the nation's textile workers. TWOC was "more than an attempt to extend modern labor relations into the country's largest industry," in the words of historian Steve Fraser. It "threatened [the South's] oligarchy at its weakest point, where rural and small-town potentates enforced a rough-and-ready patrimonial and pietistic order over the dispossessed multitudes from Southern agriculture." Lucy Mason offered a complementary analysis of the contest and the stakes: "The Roosevelts realize that the CIO unions' struggle in the South is part of an economic-political struggle with reactionary forces here. They know that the upper economic group hates Roosevelt as intensely as Republicans hate him in the North. They know that the only hope of a liberal or progressive Democratic party in the South lies in organized labor, chiefly of the CIO variety." TWOC's goals meshed with Mason's long-standing vision for a reformed South. TWOC needed to hire southerners in order to have any chance at all, so Mason's timing was excellent.[88]

Mason had accepted the NCL job in 1932 in order to extend the league's program to the South. In June 1937 the NCL was struggling financially, and the pace of its southern legislative campaign was glacial. Meanwhile, the CIO's promise seemed limitless, especially after the Supreme Court sustained the Wagner Labor Relations Act in April. It is hardly surprising that Mason leapt at the opportunity to join TWOC. Mason wrote one league friend, "When I tell you that my next job is as an interpreter for the labor movement working directly for the CIO and for the present centering on the South, you will realize that I had an overwhelming reason for going."[89] Mason did not want to be part of an exodus of talent from the South. "The cream rises and goes off," she told a group of college students in Kentucky. Southerners should "stay here after some outside experience and help build a better South."[90]

Mason's move to the CIO was not a rejection of the goals or methods of the National Consumers' League. In fact, Mason's CIO work had much in common with her NCL activity. Mason defined her role for TWOC as "an interpreter of the labor movement to the middle classes and to opinion makers." She would "make contacts [between] liberals and labor, greatly intensifying what I have done in this direction for the last five years."[91] Mason still believed wage-hour regulation was essential to reforming the South. But her southern legislative experience had deepened her conviction that middle-class southerners would not win comprehensive labor legislation without a strong labor movement. "Volunteer groups usefully pioneer in showing what is needed and in arousing public opinion," she argued, but "labor laws do not come until labor is strong enough to demand them."[92] With the emergence of the proregulatory and relatively inclusive CIO, labor seemed ready to make this demand.

Mason's journey from the NCL to the CIO is a fitting symbol for how the locus of labor reform initiative had begun to shift from women's organizations toward labor unions. This shift should not be overstated, however. The Consumers' League continued to make essential and distinctive contributions to the development of a wage-hour regulatory system, as Lucy Mason would have been the first to agree. From her CIO job, Mason cooperated often with the NCL, and she served on the league council from 1939 until her retirement in 1954. Under Mary Dublin, Mason's successor at the NCL, ties between the league and the CIO would proliferate. The rise of the labor movement, like the growth of federal agencies, hardly rendered the NCL obsolete. But the league was gradually becoming less a groundbreaker and more a reactive force, and unions rather than women's groups were becoming its primary collaborators.

In mid-1937 Mason chafed at the snail's pace of progress, but in retrospect, southern developments in hours and wage regulation in the 1930s were important, and the Consumers' League had a hand in most of them. The hours laws in Virginia and the Carolinas in 1937 and 1938, the Kentucky and Louisiana minimum wage laws of 1938, and several labor department reorganizations would likely not have passed without league activism. A 1941 study of southern labor laws found that "between 1935 and 1938 noteworthy progress was made" toward closing the gap with nonsouthern states, and that "belief in the inevitability of lower southern standards is losing ground." These were the years that the Consumers' League put its resources into the South.[93]

These gains, which the league hoped were but early ripples of an impending flood of tougher legislation, were the only southern wage and hours laws to pass for many years. After 1938 a conservative reaction forced the NCL and state leagues to abandon new initiatives in order to defend past gains. In Virginia and Kentucky the celebrated 1938 laws came under attack almost as soon as they passed.[94] After 1939 little new state wage-hour legislation passed until the 1960s, least of all in the South.[95] Given the dearth of progress in the region before or after the 1930s, the league's southern legislative achievements during that decade seem less paltry.

In 1937 the slow progress of its southern offensive persuaded the league to shift some of its energies back toward the national regulatory arena. Despite all the efforts of Mason and southern league members, the NCL still was receiving letters such as this one describing the situation at a silk mill in Wilkes-Barre, Pennsylvania: "Because the wages of the mill were cut and the workers protested, the mill has already purchased both ground and a building in the South. This they are holding over the heads of the workers so that it is impossible to [persuade them to] organize or better their conditions."[96] Interstate competition posed a seemingly insurmountable obstacle to the universal passage of rigorous state laws. Even modest efforts to shorten hours or raise wages were thwarted by employer claims that competitors from more permissive states would drive them out of business. The NCL began to insist unequivocally that state laws alone were "no longer sufficient to meet the needs of a complex society."[97] A combination of state and federal action was needed.

chapter 7

Ambiguous Victory

The Fair Labor Standards Act of 1938

When Consumers' League veteran Josephine Goldmark wrote that "New Deal labor legislation did not spring full-blown. Its roots lie in the preceding thirty years or more," she referred especially to the history of the Fair Labor Standards Act of 1938.[1] For adult workers whose occupations were judged to be in the flow of interstate commerce, the FLSA established a nationwide minimum wage rate and maximum hours standard. It also prohibited the employment of minors younger than sixteen. This legislation represented the culmination of four decades of activism by the National Consumers' League. In the years before 1937, when the FLSA was introduced in Congress, the league laid much of the legal and political groundwork for the bill. Then, under the leadership of its new general secretary, Mary Dublin, the NCL coordinated a lobbying campaign in Washington and across the country that helped win the bitter struggle in Congress over the bill in 1938. For this drive, the NCL drew on its traditional constituencies of middle-class women and progressive academics and also cooperated closely with ascendant proregulatory forces in the labor movement.

As enacted, the FLSA was a disappointment to the Consumers' League. The law's standards were low and its coverage was limited. Yet the FLSA held much potential as a tool for increasing the power of wage earners. The league expected that, in addition to the FLSA's direct effects, the measure would facilitate unionization, not least by reducing employers' incentive to migrate across state borders. After the FLSA passed, the league immediately sought to maximize the law's impact by broadening its coverage and tightening its enforcement. Insisting that public participation was essential to effective labor standards regulation, the NCL tried with limited success to keep FLSA administration in the hands of the people it expected would look out for women workers.

Labor Standards and the Courts from *Adkins* to the FLSA

The change from state-level, women-only labor standards laws to the national, male-inclusive policy that passed in 1938 occurred gradually and unevenly.[2] The NCL built the foundation for this transition and shaped its process. Throughout the 1930s, on a shifting legal and political terrain, the league found itself at war with old opponents, especially low-wage employers and the National Woman's Party. The league's work also was complicated by tensions with its allies, including some labor groups and its own legal counsel. An examination of the legal road to the FLSA illuminates the NCL's role in finding a way around court resistance to national, sex-neutral wage-hour policy.

Several of the key promoters and drafters of the FLSA, including Frances Perkins and Benjamin Cohen, were veterans of the NCL minimum wage campaign, which since 1923 had focused on circumventing the unfavorable *Adkins v. Children's Hospital* ruling. In early 1933 New Dealer and NCL lawyer Ben Cohen produced a new model minimum wage bill for women that became law in six states that year. The league then orchestrated the New York case that tested the constitutionality of these state laws. To the astonishment of the NCL and many others, the Supreme Court struck down the new type of minimum wage law on June 1, 1936, in *Morehead v. New York ex rel. Tipaldo*. The ruling had profound repercussions. It prompted the league to campaign to amend the Constitution, and it stimulated Roosevelt's politically disastrous plan to "pack" the Supreme Court. In March 1937, arguably in response to the reaction to the *Morehead* ruling, the Supreme Court reversed itself. Overturning both *Adkins* and *Morehead*, the *West Coast Hotel Company v. Parrish* decision sustained a 1913 Washington state minimum wage law for women. This and other decisions in the spring of 1937 amounted to a constitutional revolution that reopened the path toward a national wage-hour law.[3]

Between 1923 and 1936 the women of the NCL and their lawyers disagreed over minimum wage strategy on two points. After the *Adkins* ruling, Florence Kelley wanted to stick with the police power rationale for labor standards regulation, keeping the focus on the health of workers. Kelley declared herself fed up with "legal tinkering" and proposed a constitutional amendment to clarify the state's police power authority to govern labor standards. Felix Frankfurter and his protégé Ben Cohen had other priorities, only abstractly related to worker welfare. Frankfurter longed to reform the prevailing judicial interpretation of the Constitution by narrowing the scope of the Fourteenth Amendment. To satisfy the complaint in *Adkins* that the league's living wage bill violated employers' Fourteenth Amendment right to due process, Frankfurter proposed to develop a fair wage concept. The lawyers prevailed, and their strategy ultimately shifted the legal emphasis from the health of workers to the health of industry and commerce. One unintended consequence of this shift would be to define some low-paid female occupations out of coverage.[4]

The second point of contention between NCL lawyers and female activists was whether to include men in the new model state bill. When the NCL revived the minimum wage campaign in the late 1920s, Josephine Goldmark and veteran minimum wage administrators Molly Dewson, Elizabeth Brandeis, and Clara Beyer were the league's chief legal strategists. They were ready to include men in the model bill, but Frankfurter overruled them. League activists also anticipated resistance from AFL unions, but it was Frankfurter's adamant refusal to pursue a sex-neutral strategy that was decisive. On the face of it, Frankfurter's position might seem illogical, because one ground on which *Adkins* invalidated the old law was its application to women alone. Chief Justice Sutherland had ruled that the Nineteenth Amendment obviated women's greater need for protection. But a few justices had dissented on this point, and because dissenting opinions often form the basis of overrulings, Frankfurter's decision to stick with a women-only bill was not unreasonable from a legal perspective. NCL lawyers focused on meeting Sutherland's due process objections rather than his objection to the sex basis of the law. Although league leaders believed that the District of Columbia minimum wage law would have been struck down even if it had included men, the question of whether to include men in a redrafted bill remained open. Why not try to meet all of the Court's objections at once?[5]

In 1934, when the male-inclusive NRA codes were in effect, Clara Beyer and Lucy Mason suggested revising the league's model minimum wage bill to include men. Again following Frankfurter's advice, Josephine Goldmark and Molly Dewson vetoed this proposal. Goldmark was "*totally opposed* to including men in any state minimum wage legislation until a statute for women is sustained by the U.S. Supreme Court." Frankfurter said the very suggestion of men's inclusion smacked of "the old women's party type of legislation," and that it was "surely madness to tie up the case for women with that of men." Dewson warned that unless the NCL reined in its Rhode Island branch, which was backing a male-inclusive bill, the league might lose Frankfurter's services.[6] The women's deference to Frankfurter is not surprising, given his national prominence, his long association with the beloved Florence Kelley, and the league's tiny budget, which made it dependent on lawyers willing to work for free. Only later would it become clear just how conservative Frankfurter's gender ideology was.[7]

Had the NCL's model minimum wage bill of 1933 included men, the legal outcome probably would have been the same — an unfavorable ruling in 1936. However, gender equality would not have become the red herring that it did in the *Morehead* case. At the suggestion of lawyers for the employers bringing suit in *Morehead*, the National Woman's Party filed an amicus curiae brief. The employers' counsel did not emphasize employees' sex; rather, it was the NWP that argued that women-only laws violated women's constitutional rights. Furthermore, it was the NWP that asserted that in applying to women only, the New York law was indistinguishable from the District of Columbia law struck down by *Adkins*. The Court majority ruled that minimum wage regulation abridged women's rights, quoting the NWP brief almost verbatim. The majority also concluded that the New York law was not distinguishable from the older type of law.[8]

The Woman's Party claimed that in *Morehead* the Supreme Court spoke "in defense of the rights of American women." But sex discrimination was not the court's fundamental concern.[9] The more important way in which the 1933 bill was not distinguishable from the old law was that it retained a reference to the living wage that had so troubled the majority in *Adkins*. It was the wage principle, not the sex basis, that most concerned the Court majority in *Morehead* as well.[10] In any case, a sex-neutral minimum wage bill probably would not have reached the courts in the early 1930s because state Federations of Labor prevented such bills from passing. In 1933, for example, the New York Federation of Labor defeated a sex-neutral alternative to the league's bill, and in 1937 the federation would also reject a sex-neutral measure proposed by the league.[11] Assuming that such union opposition could have been overcome, however, and that the Supreme Court would have struck down the law anyway (because of the living wage clause), backing a sex-neutral model bill in 1933 still would have had some advantages. Although the NCL's desire to keep a united front with the labor movement is understandable, it was not a happy development for feminism that the Woman's Party was drawn into the attack on the New York minimum wage law. The party's prominent role in the case — a role that seemed decisive, although it probably was not — immeasurably deepened the contempt of labor-liberals and the Left for the NWP. In turn, the NWP may have convinced some people that the Consumers' League held an old-fashioned view of womanhood. The conflict among women's groups over sex-based labor laws certainly was confusing to politicians and to a new generation of younger women. Even though NCL leaders themselves favored sex-neutral laws, they were forced to continue defending the sex-based strategy, the rationales for which had become increasingly complicated.

The NCL responded to the *Morehead* ruling with two campaigns, one aimed at the Woman's Party and the other at the Supreme Court. First, the league joined a coalition of women's groups in drafting the Women's Charter, a document that tried to formulate a progressive feminist alternative to the Equal Rights Amendment. Avoiding the term "equal opportunity," the charter called for "self-determination" for women, who deserved a "full and rightful share in the power to control the conditions affecting human life and happiness" as well as access to "the training which develops fully the individual's abilities for work and for creative leisure." Charter feminists distinguished themselves from ERA advocates by defining women's rights to include the "right to be safeguarded against the physical harm and social injustice to which the machine and the forms of organization of modern industry expose women *to an even greater extent than men*." Such safeguards would be necessary until "special handicaps *imposed by custom or tradition* upon women" were removed or until "the tendency to any form of human exploitation is controlled or eliminated." Women's Charter drafters thus believed social inequality, not biology, necessitated sex-based laws, and they hoped that industrial capitalism would be regulated or even "eliminated." The Women's Charter initiative fizzled in 1937, caught between NWP antagonism and the nervousness of mainstream women's organizations about the charter's sweeping, left-influenced program.[12] Meanwhile, the wave of pro- and anti-ERA propaganda reached a new peak in the press, fanning old antagonisms and new confusions.

The second project the league undertook in the wake of *Morehead* was as short-lived as the Women's Charter campaign, but it may have generated more constructive results. After the Supreme Court invalidated the NRA and the New York minimum wage law, the league's program was blocked at both national and state levels.[13] The board decided that drastic action was in order. After surveying prominent economists and lawyers, the NCL fashioned a plan. It would lead a movement for an amendment to "clarify" the U.S. Constitution. Arguing that reactionary courts were subverting the intentions of the nation's founders and blocking social progress, the league organized national conferences and radio broadcasts to promote an amendment that would explicitly permit federal and state labor legislation — for both women and men.[14]

In turning to a wide array of experts and embracing the constitutional amendment strategy, NCL women were breaking away from Frankfurter, Ben Cohen, and the other Harvard lawyers on whom they had relied for so long. They had tried Frankfurter's approach to getting around *Adkins*, without success. Zealously led by Lucy Mason, the NCL returned to the more radical strategy that Florence Kelley had favored a dozen years earlier. But two developments soon checked the momentum of the clarifying amendment drive. In February 1937 FDR introduced his court reorganization bill, better and more honestly known as the court-packing plan. This bill was similar in objective to the league's proposed amendment but offered a shortcut of questionable legitimacy.[15] Then, in its March 1937 ruling in *West Coast Hotel Company v. Parrish*, the Supreme Court amazed minimum wage advocates and opponents alike by upholding the 1913 Washington state minimum wage law for women, reversing its 1923 and 1936 decisions. Rulings sustaining the Wagner Labor Relations Act and Social Security Act soon followed. The Consumers' League argued that a constitutional amendment was still necessary, not least because these rulings upheld New Deal legislation by the slimmest of majorities.[16] But support for an amendment waned, and the NCL quietly tabled its proposal.

Although truncated, the amendment campaign may nevertheless have served a political purpose by generating pressures on the Supreme Court that led to the unexpected pro–New Deal rulings of spring 1937. Both *Morehead* (against women's minimum wage) and *West Coast Hotel* (for women's minimum wage) were 5-4 decisions. Justice Owen Roberts joined the majority in both cases. It was not the threat of the court-packing plan that accounted for Roberts's switch, which occurred before that plan was unveiled. Legal scholars have concluded that FDR's landslide reelection in November 1936 must have influenced Roberts, but the clamor of the NCL's amendment campaign probably had an effect as well. Both the Consumers' League and the Woman's Party thought this was the case.[17]

The *West Coast Hotel* ruling, in combination with the upholding of the Wagner Act, offered new hope that a constitutional basis for national labor legislation could be found. The Wagner Act decisions pointed toward basing a national labor standards bill on federal authority to regulate interstate commerce.[18] This shift to the commerce clause, and away from invoking the government's police power to protect public health and welfare, provided an opportunity to move away from women-only labor standards toward a sex-neutral policy at the national level. Earlier rulings had found a closer connection between the public welfare and workers' health when those workers were women. Now the shift from the police power to the commerce clause made including men in national regulation more logical for the purposes of constitutional argument than leaving them out.[19] Emphasizing the health of commerce rather than the vulnerability of workers also may have made male-inclusive bills more palatable to men's unions.

Changing the legal focus from the health of workers to the health of interstate commerce had mixed implications for workers, especially women. Women were more likely than men to work in occupations defined as "intrastate" and thus not protected by the national policy.[20] Nonetheless, the Consumers' League ended up encouraging the shift to the commerce clause, notwithstanding Florence Kelley's early reservations. In the context of accelerating industrial migration across state borders and a series of legal roadblocks, NCL leaders embraced whatever constitutional reasoning would allow them to circumnavigate a Supreme Court that they viewed as reactionary and intransigent. The league was not abandoning workers in intrastate industry, however. League activists already knew that an integrated system of state and national regulation would be necessary to raise the labor standards of all workers.

After the Supreme Court's favorable rulings in the spring of 1937, Frances Perkins asked Ben Cohen, now an administration lawyer, to update a federal wage and hour bill she had "locked away in a desk drawer" a few years earlier. This bill had much in common with the state minimum wage bill that Cohen had drafted for the NCL in 1933. Several rival groups worked on the national legislation, but Cohen was the chief drafter, and the bill that was introduced to Congress as the Black-Connery bill on May 24, 1937, owed a good deal to the legal and administrative experience of the National Consumers' League.[21]

The 1937 bill offers a better indication than the act that ultimately passed of what the Consumers' League hoped for from national wage-hour regulation. The Black-Connery bill provided for a statutory minimum hourly rate and maximum standard workweek (not specified, but understood to be at least forty cents and at most forty hours). The final law would set initial standards of twenty-five cents and forty-four hours. The 1937 bill empowered a five-person board to fix higher wages and shorter hours where it deemed appropriate. The 1938 act called for a single, less powerful administrator. The 1937 bill was hardly perfect, as the NCL well knew. It

contained concessions to anticipated court objections and political opponents. Like the final act, the 1937 bill exempted executive, administrative,
supervisory, and professional work, most retailing, and adult agricultural
labor. Retailing, which employed many women, was taken to be intrastate
and thus outside the scope of federal protection under the commerce
clause. The exemption of adult agricultural workers, which the NCL protested, reflected political rather than legal considerations. It was no small
victory that the bill's prohibition of labor by children under sixteen did
apply to agriculture.[22]

The Fight in Congress

Although the legal prospects for a national wage-hour policy now were
more promising than ever, the political obstacles remained daunting. After
testifying for the Black-Connery bill in June 1937, Mason accurately predicted that the measure would have "hard sledding" because of manufac-
turer opposition and lukewarm labor support.[23] The benefits the bill provided to workers were whittled down substantially in the process of getting
it through Congress. The NCL resisted these compromises at every step of
the way. However, the league preferred a limited law to none. "I like
aiming at the moon," Mason once remarked, "and think that perfect bills
have a long time educational value, but on the other hand it is encouraging
sometimes to get a bill thru a legislature."[24] Leaders of the Amalgamated
Clothing Workers, one of the trade unions that actively backed the FLSA,
concurred: "We supported every kind of bill that was turned out . . . on the
theory that an unsatisfactory law is better than no legislative protection of
wages and hours. The unsatisfactory law might later be amended."[25]

Mild as it was, the FLSA passed only after protracted struggles and ma-
neuverings in Congress. The act's long legislative history reveals the diver-
sity and strength of its opposition, and only in this context can the NCL's
contribution be appreciated. A weakened bill passed in the Senate in July
1937 and probably would have passed in the House had it come to the
floor. However, conservatives in the House Rules Committee bottled up
the bill for the rest of the legislative session. FDR called a special session to
convene on November 15, demanding action on the wage and hour bill,
among other measures. A petition drive led by House Labor Committee
chair Mary Norton (D.-N.J.) finally forced the House Rules Committee to
discharge the bill.[26] But at this juncture the AFL-CIO split undermined
support for the bill, and the AFL introduced a substitute. Also, by this time,
a sharp recession had strengthened the conservative coalition in Congress.
In a major defeat for FDR, the House sent the bill back to the Labor

Committee in December. In the spring of 1938, the House Rules Committee again sat on the bill, and the bill once more was forced out to the floor by a discharge petition. From that point on, the question was not whether a federal wage-hour bill would pass, but how strong it would be when it emerged from the joint conference session to reconcile the House and Senate versions.[27]

The NCL's influence over the FLSA's passage and final content cannot be measured precisely, but it was certainly a factor. Most scholars credit the Roosevelt administration with getting the bill through, especially the efforts of Frances Perkins and Tom Corcoran. Some also stress the all-out push by Sidney Hillman's ACWA, David Dubinsky's ILGWU, and their joint offspring, Labor's NonPartisan League.[28] The Consumers' League worked closely behind the scenes with all of these supporters. After Mason's departure in July 1937, the league's work in Washington was curtailed until Mary Dublin took office in March 1938, but the campaign in the states continued with little interruption. Once the new general secretary was in place, the NCL resumed a central coordinating role in local as well as Washington lobbying for the FLSA. The most distinctive feature of the league's campaign may have been its mobilization of middle-class support for the bill. This support was strategically critical in the South, where employer resistance was strongest and where many wage earners could not or did not vote.

Southern employers and their political allies led the opposition to the FLSA. Some employers orchestrated letter-writing campaigns against the bill. Beverly Mills of Fort Worth, Texas, pressured employees to sign variations on an anti-FLSA letter to congressmen. The letters claimed the act would cost workers their jobs and hurt southern industry. Southern textile mills, which employed thousands of white women at wages below the proposed minimum, and lumber mills, whose predominantly black male labor force earned less than the proposed minimum, were particularly vociferous in their opposition.[29] Trying to rally popular support by stirring sectional loyalties, southern politicians portrayed the bill as a northern conspiracy to upend white supremacy and take away the South's "natural" advantages. Congressman Martin Dies of Texas was applauded with rebel yells for his remark that "under this measure what is prescribed for one race must be prescribed for the others, and you cannot prescribe the same wages for the black man as for the white man." South Carolina's "Cotton Ed" Smith complained that the bill's intent was "by human legislation, to overcome the splendid gifts of God to the South."[30] That northern textile industrialists supported the bill, along with ordinarily conservative politicians like Republican senator Henry Cabot Lodge of Massachusetts, added

"Southern solons band to fight wage-hour measure" (June 1938). Southern senators who opposed the FLSA included, from left to right, Tom Connally, Texas; Lister Hill, Alabama; Ellison D. Smith, South Carolina; Charles Andrews, Florida; John Bankhead, Alabama; and Walter F. George, Georgia. (Underwood and Underwood photograph, Washington Star Collection, courtesy of District of Columbia Public Library)

weight to such charges. In fact, not all northern employers backed the bill. The National Association of Manufacturers opposed it on the principle that all government regulation of labor standards was undesirable. Employers' positions on national wage-hour regulation depended not only on sectional allegiance but also on factors such as the competitiveness and labor-intensity of a particular industry, as well as an industry's degree of interest in stimulating consumer demand through higher wages.[31] Southern and antiregulatory employers exercised their influence over the bill in Congress most clearly through the House Rules Committee, where a coalition of five southern Democrats and four Republicans repeatedly blocked the bill's path. Among these, Dies of Texas, Howard Smith of Virginia, and Edward E. Cox of Georgia were the FLSA's bitterest foes.[32]

Southern industrialists and politicians were correct in charging that the FLSA was an attack on the social and economic order of the South. For certain New Dealers, national wage-hour regulation was one prong of an ambitious strategy for breaking up the solid South. The region's low-wage

Lucy Mason testifies at the Black-Connery bill hearings in June 1937. (Corbis/Bettmann-UPI)

economy was impeding unionization and depressing labor standards nationwide. Furthermore, because politicians from the one-party South accumulated more seniority than representatives from regions with more competitive elections, southern Democrats controlled many key congressional committees. They maintained this grip on Congress even as new constituencies diluted the importance of southern voters to the Democratic Party. New Dealers such as Frances Perkins, Tom Corcoran, and Sidney Hillman had come to share the NCL view that the South was blocking national progress, and some New Dealers agreed with Lucy Mason that eradicating race discrimination was an essential part of reforming the South.[33]

In a variety of forums, the NCL rebutted southern arguments that wage-hour regulation was best left to the states and that a national policy would be unconstitutional and would hurt the South. At congressional hearings on the FLSA bill in June 1937, Lucy Mason insisted that state legislation, while still important, could no longer do the job alone because of interstate competition. Mason argued that the South in fact had the most to gain from the FLSA because without it, outside employers took advantage of cheap southern labor and siphoned wealth away from the South. Turning sectionalist sentiment to her own purposes, Mason discussed the damage to southern communities wrought by "gypsy industries." These migratory employers entered the South—enticed by the prospect of a docile, low-waged workforce and substantial tax breaks—drained local resources, and moved on. National regulation would permit states and regions to regard themselves "not as rivals but as they are—producers and markets for each other."[34] Mason's successor, Mary Dublin, told radio listeners that federal legislation was necessary because areas without legislation "act[ed] as a magnet attracting the runaway shop" and paid wages "inadequate to provide a decent living," thereby undercutting the national wage scale. Dublin clearly had the South in mind.[35]

In addition to countering states' rights arguments, the NCL opposed southern-led attempts to lower the minimum wage level or incorporate regional wage differentials into the FLSA. Mason argued that southern employers would benefit from paying higher wages because their employees would have more money to spend. Mary Dublin warned that without a federal wage-hour law, national purchasing power would erode further, sending "us rushing headlong into an even deeper economic abyss. . . . It is not only that these millions of families know the deep meaning of hardship, but their poverty and exploitation is a burden which does and must affect every person in this land."[36] Despite these efforts, the bill's minimum wage rate was lowered from forty cents to an initial rate of twenty-five cents per hour. Southern demands for an even lower regional minimum were staved off, but just barely. Roosevelt had been willing to accept a regional differential if necessary, but protests from the NCL, the garment unions, and the NAACP helped offset the pressure from southern employers.[37]

One distinctive aspect of NCL lobbying was its mobilization of southern voters to apply pressure from home on anti-FLSA politicians. As historian William Leuchtenburg has observed, the FLSA symbolized a contest not only of conservatives against liberals, southern industry against unionized northern industry, and antistatist AFL leaders against labor statesmen like Sidney Hillman, but "perhaps most important[, of] . . . southern conservatives like Cotton Ed Smith against southerners of advanced views like Hugo Black."[38] The Consumers' League rallied southerners of "advanced views"—prominently including women—on behalf of the wage-hour bill. This activity was invaluable because the pro-FLSA unions had few southern members. Delegations of ACWA and ILGWU members journeyed to Washington to back the FLSA, but they came from places like New York and Pennsylvania, not from the South.[39] In early 1938, Mary Dublin targeted the southern Democrats on the House Rules Committee. Dublin sent dozens of wires like this cryptic one to Lucy Mason in Atlanta: "Rules Committee deadlocked 7-7—extremely urgent you wire Rep. Cox [D-GA] now opposing sending wage-hour bill to floor vital persuade others influence do likewise." Although the league had no more than a few hundred southern members, they were active and well connected. The NCL's network of southern white women joined its National Labor Standards Committee, signed resolutions to be read into the congressional record, and generated local editorial support for the act.[40] In the spring of 1938, southerners demonstrated sufficient enthusiasm for the FLSA in surveys and at the polls to trigger a shift in congressional attitudes.[41] This shift made it possible to extract the bill from the Rules Committee and thus was critical to the bill's passage.

Advocates of national wage-hour policy faced opposition from some labor leaders as well as from southern employers. Although CIO leader John Lewis had some reservations about the bill's form in mid-1937, the more potent resistance came from the American Federation of Labor. NCL activists later claimed, with good reason, that the AFL's recalcitrance delayed the act's passage by a year and weakened the measure considerably.[42] At the time, league lobbyists downplayed differences within organized labor and tried to allay AFL fears. One AFL concern was that the minimum wage would become a maximum wage.[43] The league publicized data supporting its contention that historically the minimum wage rate had not become the maximum. Lucy Mason testified that under the NRA codes wage differentials above the minimum had narrowed at first but soon adjusted back up, to higher than before. The fear that the minimum wage would become the maximum, and that wage differentials would disappear, had a gender component: Would raising wages for the unskilled workers reduce wages for the skilled (predominantly men)? Would women and men earn the same amount? The league opposed the practice of paying women lower wages than men for the same work, but it denied that setting minimum wages would eliminate skilled workers' premiums. Mason concluded that under NRA codes "the increases gained by women and the unskilled [were] not at the expense of the skilled." Elinore Herrick of the New York league agreed, citing wage data from New York laundries before and after the state minimum wage law took effect.[44]

Some trade unions were more receptive than others to government regulation of labor standards. For all unions, the chief attraction of a national wage-hour policy was the creation of a wage floor and hours ceiling for unorganized competition. The ACWA and the ILGWU struggled to organize highly competitive, decentralized industries that migrated readily and employed large numbers of women at very low wages. The garment unions agreed with the Consumers' League that wage-hour regulation would complement union organization rather than undermine it. Within these unions, female leaders like Dorothy Jacobs Bellanca and Fannia Cohn had ties to the NCL network. They may have pushed these unions toward a proregulatory stance.[45] Eventually, in 1938, the wider labor movement did close ranks behind the fair labor standards bill, but many unions' support was only nominal. Mary Dublin later recalled, "Labor wasn't supporting [the FLSA] strongly. The people at 25 cents an hour weren't union members."[46]

The most strongly pro-FLSA unions regretted the bill's narrow coverage, but they did not try to force the inclusion of groups who did not compete directly with unionized workers, such as domestic and agricultural workers. ACWA lobbyists argued that the FLSA indirectly would benefit excluded workers because the downward competitive spiral of wages would be halted. Some excluded workers shared this view. In New York, the president of the Building Services Union supported the FLSA because, he argued, the wages of cleaning women in New York would stop declining if more space was rented in the state's factory buildings. But the ACWA and other unions spent little energy arguing to expand FLSA coverage to workers in nonmanufacturing occupations. It was the NCL that would advocate coverage of those workers.[47]

Enter Mary Dublin

In February 1938, between the fierce opposition of southern employers and the resistance of the American Federation of Labor, the outlook for a national wage-hour law was grim. While AFL objections were dividing the bill's supporters, its opponents had united to form a powerful coalition of southern Democrats and anti–New Deal Republicans. Activists who a year earlier had expected a stronger bill to pass easily began to wonder whether any bill would pass at all. The ILGWU's Merle Vincent doubted the bill would get past the House Rules Committee "unless the President steps on the members pretty hard," or unless another petition drive could force the bill out of the committee.[48]

It was at this juncture that the NCL recruited a long list of prominent individuals to form a new group called National Labor Standards Committee (NLSC), a "propaganda committee" to push the FLSA. The NLSC was basically a Consumers' League lobbying device; the NCL was its headquarters, and the league's new general secretary, Mary Dublin, became its coordinator.[49] The NLSC hoped to make it impossible for legislators to hide behind claims of public indifference. In December 1937, when the NCL was without an executive, the House Rules Committee's stalling tactic had provoked little public reaction: "The Rules Committee are not being hanged in effigy or seriously denounced anywhere. . . . Mostly there is a vast, indifferent silence," one reporter had claimed.[50] In March 1938, with Mary Dublin at the helm, the NLSC mounted a multifaceted publicity campaign to generate popular pressure on the House.

Mary Dublin came to the NCL firmly committed to its wider goals of increasing the economic and political power of wage earners, especially women. She brought an array of skills and experiences that was unusually broad for a woman of her age. Dublin was born in New York City in 1910 to Jewish parents who had immigrated from Russia as children. Augusta Salik Dublin was a social worker and settlement house resident. Louis Israel Dublin was a prominent public health expert and statistician who worked for the Metropolitan Life Insurance Company. Dublin followed in her mother's footsteps by attending Barnard, where she studied with cutting-edge economists Wesley Clair Mitchell, Raymond Moley, and Arthur Burns (husband of Columbia's star economist, Eveline Burns, who would become Dublin's good friend). By all accounts a brilliant student, Dublin edited the *Barnard Bulletin* and won a fellowship to the Geneva School for International Studies in the summer of 1929. In Geneva, Mary Dublin drank in lectures by John Maynard Keynes and learned from English students about the Fabian Society and the British labor movement. Dublin's subsequent *Bulletin* editorials demonstrated a growing enthusiasm for labor and feminist causes. Her senior honors thesis, "The Changing Status of Women in New England," analyzed the impact of the industrial revolution on women's economic and educational opportunities. After graduating from Barnard in 1930, Dublin acquired research and lobbying experience working for private groups on health policy.[51]

With her parents' support, Dublin decided to pursue an academic career in economics. In 1931–32 she studied at the London School of Economics. Disappointed to find that those she considered the most innovative economists had taken positions in the Labor government, she branched off into statistics with a project on maternal mortality rates. Returning to New York, Dublin passed the qualifying exams for the Ph.D. program in economics at Columbia in May 1933. She abandoned her dissertation, though, to take a teaching position at Sarah Lawrence College. There Dublin experimented with interdisciplinary and applied methods of teaching privileged young women. Dublin required her students to design family budgets based on various incomes, to survey slum housing conditions, and to simulate the legislative process through mock hearings and debates.[52] Before she came to the Consumers' League, Dublin already was politicizing affluent women in support of reform causes. She commuted to work from Greenwich Village, where her calendar was packed with political and social engagements, and where she became a regular at the Henry Street Settlement. As part of the settlement's worker education project, she spoke with wage earners about the Wagner Labor Relations Act and minimum wage regulation. Helen Hall of Henry Street was sufficiently impressed with Dublin to attempt to "pry her loose from Sarah Lawrence and get her to work for us."[53]

Mary Dublin occupied that part of the political spectrum between radicalism and liberalism that was so fluid in the "red decade." Her later career casts her as a mainstream New Deal Democrat, but in the 1930s she was intrigued by more radical ideas. Capitalism's international crisis increased the vitality and legitimacy of the American Left. Columbia was a center of student radicalism in Dublin's years there, and the London School of Economics exposed her to leftist professors like Harold Laski and to students active in the Independent Labor Party. In the summer of 1932, Dublin joined the stream of American intellectuals who flocked to the Soviet Union to observe the socialist experiment firsthand. At that moment the USSR seemed to be weathering the world depression better than capitalist economies, and Stalin's abuses were not yet widely recognized. After a year of hearing so much about Russia, she yearned to see it for herself.[54]

In these years Dublin was deeply disillusioned with the capitalist system. She wrote in 1932 that the "company town" was the ultimate expression of capitalism, not a fading remnant of feudalism. She observed that company town employers controlled all branches of local government as well as the production of knowledge by media and educational institutions, and thus they dominated all aspects of workers' lives. In the absence of a neutral public or impartial agencies, Dublin claimed, the company town was a "vacuum jar for capitalist institutions," in which one could analyze "the supposed distinction between business and government . . . the extent of capitalist influence on the life of the spirit . . . and the concept of free individual choice, which is commonly assigned a central place in our economic system." She concluded by wondering whether the "forces that work in the company town . . . may soon overspread the cinema screen of industrial civilization. The company town may expand to the company state."[55] These thoughts came at a moment when the Depression was at its worst. As President Hoover clung to economic orthodoxy, the U.S. Army violently repressed the "Bonus Army" of protesting World War I veterans. In Harlan County, Kentucky, coal mine operators hired thugs to brutalize strikers. Such events radicalized many Americans, Mary Dublin among them. She voted for Norman Thomas of the Socialist Party in 1932, rather than Hoover or Roosevelt. Later in the decade she registered with the

American Labor Party. Throughout the 1930s she cooperated with a wide range of leftists and progressives on the burning political questions of the day.[56]

Dublin was extremely attractive to the NCL leadership in 1938. She was known in New York reform circles for her skills in writing, public speaking, and legislative work, as well as for her expertise in economics and statistics. She wrote scathing reviews of works by free-market economists, and she was personally acquainted with many of the era's leading left and liberal economists. Dublin insisted that increasing mass purchasing power was necessary for economic recovery and for a healthy democracy.[57] She also had demonstrated a commitment to gender and race justice. Although Dublin's priorities and style eventually brought her into conflict with a few league members, in the spring of 1938 NCL activists were delighted to have hired this high-powered, outspoken young woman.[58]

The NLSC and the Final Push

Within a few weeks of the formation of the National Labor Standards Committee, Dublin obtained thousands of signed resolutions supporting the wage-hour bill from individuals around the country. She drafted press releases, spoke before consumer, labor, and settlement groups, and made nationally broadcast radio speeches. She called on state labor commissioners around the country, urging them to exert whatever political leverage they could. The NLSC also placed direct pressure on the House Rules Committee. Dublin tracked each committee member's statements and actions on the bill, and she used this record to decide which members to target and what lines of argument to use with each. NLSC members spoke at a House Rules Committee hearing on the bill but were unable to persuade the committee to release it.[59]

NCL activists believed that no worthwhile federal labor standards bill would be passed without support from the middle class. Again, middle-class backing was of particular significance in the South, where voting restrictions and anti-unionism limited workers' political power. Mary Dublin defined her task as communicating "the need for the federal FLSA to the middle-class, intellectuals, churches, women's organizations." Because "labor is making itself so strongly felt," she explained, the NCL could help most by organizing "community opinion" and not working publicly with the unions.[60] The NLSC tried to convince members of Congress that "it is not labor alone which speaks for itself" for the wage-hour bill, but "leaders of the community in every walk of life." Countering the charge that the FLSA was "class legislation," league publicity stressed the need to protect the general welfare against selfish private interests, especially the "chiselers" among employers. Dublin downplayed labor-capital conflict in order to mobilize citizens who would support restrictions on chiselers more enthusiastically than they would embrace structural reform. She cited the opinion of Justice Hughes in the 1937 minimum wage ruling that the community was not bound to provide a "subsidy for the unconscionable employer." In a similar vein, Elinore Herrick told radio listeners that almost 7,000 women wage earners in New York City were on the relief rolls because their earnings were too low to sustain them. (Was it not curious, Herrick added, that the same people who denounced high relief expenditures were leading the opposition to the FLSA?) High labor standards were in the interest of every citizen: "Five-dollar weekly pay envelopes burden not only the underprivileged workers who receive them but lead to the insecurity of . . . employers, workers, and farmers alike."[61]

The need to defend the community welfare from private interests was always a favorite NCL topic. In the 1930s, as the specter of fascism loomed, this theme became intertwined with exhortations about the need to reinvigorate American democracy. Mary Dublin argued that most citizens resented unscrupulous employers' parasitism on the community and that the majority favored a federal wage-hour bill. Unfortunately, she explained, selfish forces were "vigorously organized to press for private interest. . . . All too often, majority demand goes unrecognized only because we tend to take too easily for granted the process of democracy." Writing about the FLSA's holdup by "eight men" on the House Rules Committee, Dublin lamented, "It's incredible how meekly we all take a challenge to the [d]emocratic process." (Here she sounded very much like Lucy Mason.)[62]

The NLSC received varying degrees of support from national civic groups. The YWCA, the National Council of Jewish Women, and the League of Women Shoppers wholeheartedly endorsed the FLSA. The League of Women Voters took no stand on the bill except to support the child labor provisions. The National Urban League supported the FLSA but felt it "unwise" to work publicly for the bill. The Urban League believed a federal wage-hour law would benefit African Americans, but it declined to lobby, so as not to strengthen the hand of racist opposition.[63] The NAACP encouraged its members to write their representatives about the bill, but its only criterion for support was that the bill not include a regional wage differential.[64]

Consistent with its historical practice, the Consumers' League concentrated on mobilizing women's groups, but some of these equivocated. Although the National Woman's Party claimed to support labor legislation as long as it was sex neutral, in May 1938 the NWP declined to take a position on the FLSA. This stand deepened the league's conviction that the

Woman's Party covertly opposed all labor legislation. If ever there was a time for the NWP to convince the Consumers' League and other anti-ERA groups of the sincerity of its professed commitment to wage-earning women, this was it. In 1937 the Woman's Party had mobilized against a short-lived proposal (not the NCL's) to prohibit women's night work under the FLSA, but once this threat had passed, the NWP did nothing to help the bill along its difficult path through Congress.[65] Nor did the General Federation of Women's Clubs take a stand on the Fair Labor Standards Act. The National Association of Women Lawyers declared that it "must be opposed or neutral."[66] These three organizations were loud opponents of women-only state labor laws on the grounds that they hurt working women. The fight for the FLSA exposed these groups' reluctance to endorse even sex-neutral labor laws. Either they opposed all state regulation of labor standards, or they were unwilling to risk internal conflict along regional or ideological lines that such endorsement might create.

For most of the spring of 1938 it appeared that the House Rules Committee's obstinacy would kill the FLSA. But when a petition to force the bill out of that committee was laid on the House Speaker's desk on May 6, legislators almost stampeded in their eagerness to sign the measure. The surprise success of this unprecedented second petition drive was spectacular. The necessary 218 signatures were gathered in only two hours and twenty minutes; other legislators crowded the aisles hoping to get their names on the list.[67] Clearly many representatives had had a change of heart since December, when gathering signatures for the first petition had taken weeks. The display of public support that produced this change of tune had been orchestrated by the NLSC along with certain labor groups and administration officials.

In the first week of May, the National Labor Standards Committee had joined the ACWA, ILGWU, CIO, and Labor's NonPartisan League in pulling out all the stops to get the bill out of the Rules Committee. Each group generated floods of telegrams to legislators. On May 1, an ACWA-CIO rally in support of the bill drew huge numbers of demonstrators.[68] On May 3, the victory of pro-FLSA Claude Pepper in the Florida Senate primary assuaged lingering doubts about the popularity of the bill among southern voters. On May 5, the day before the petition was presented, the *New York Times* published an open letter from the NLSC to Congress with the signatures of hundreds of "leading citizens" from more than three-quarters of the states. News services picked up the story and the names of local signatories appeared in papers around the country.[69]

The NLSC combined these publicity stunts with behind-the-scenes tactics. Mary Dublin persuaded Dean Roscoe Pound of the Harvard Law

School (an honorary vice president of the NCL) and other law school deans to call the legislators who were their former students and urge them to sign the discharge petition. Years later, speaking as a seasoned lobbyist and administrator, Dublin still believed that this particular league effort was "quite a strategic factor in getting the bill out of the Rules Committee." She added that "the Labor Department will take primary credit for getting the bill through, I think, but . . . we in the League know that we had a very strategic and important role."[70] Once the bill was out of the Rules Committee, there was little question that some form of national wage-hour law would be adopted that year. In combination with the Roosevelt administration and the ACWA, ILGWU, and CIO, the middle-class women of the NCL had won the passage of the Fair Labor Standards Act.

"Heartbreaking Gaps"

The FLSA that finally emerged from Congress was, in the words of one observer, "crippled, undersized, and hardly recognizable to its progenitors." The Consumers' League was painfully aware of these limitations. For a radio forum on the bill, the NCL posed the question, "If the bill does so little, why is an organization like the Consumers' League for it?" The league's answer was that establishing the principle of national regulation was a victory, and the bill's coverage and standards would have to be improved later.[71]

The FLSA's direct effects on covered workers were modest indeed. The U.S. Department of Labor estimated that the FLSA of 1938 applied to roughly one-fifth of the labor force, or about 11 million workers in interstate industry.[72] For those workers, the act set an hourly minimum wage of twenty-five cents (to increase to forty cents over seven years) and a weekly hours maximum of forty-four hours (to decrease to forty hours by the third year). Because only about 300,000 of those 11 million workers were earning less than twenty-five cents per hour, the minimum wage provision brought immediate wage increases to a relatively small group. However, that number does not include those whose pay increased as a result of the act's overtime requirement that employers pay time-and-a-half wages for hours in excess of the weekly maximum. Approximately 1.4 million workers immediately were entitled to overtime pay for long working hours. Also increasing the number of workers to see pay raises was the act's mechanism for setting minimum wage rates above the statutory hourly minimum of twenty-five cents. For each industry, the FLSA administrator could appoint a committee (representing employers, labor, and the public) to recommend minimum rates above the statutory minimum, but not to exceed forty cents an hour. These industry committees gradually did issue orders raising the minimum wage rate ahead of the scheduled increases.[73] But there was no denying that the minimum wage standard set by the FLSA was much lower than what the NCL had hoped for in 1937.

Perhaps an even bigger disappointment was the FLSA's narrow coverage. The vast majority of workers who earned below-subsistence wages fell outside the law's scope. Legal considerations and political concessions carved large sectors of the labor force out of the FLSA. The act exempted workers in agricultural, retail, and service occupations, along with professional workers, seamen, and fishermen. NCL leaders believed agricultural labor standards should be regulated. However, they never seriously expected the FLSA to cover agriculture at the outset because of the political clout of growers (and the minimal political power of agricultural workers, who frequently could not vote). Seasonal workers had to work fifty-six hours per week for twelve weeks of the year before they were entitled to overtime pay. Employment of children younger than sixteen was prohibited in most occupations, including, most notably, agriculture, but the act did not touch certain occupations that employed many children, including the notorious "street trades" (newspaper selling, shoeshining, and the like).[74]

The shrunken scope of the FLSA confirmed the insight of economist and league honorary vice president Paul Douglas, who observed "a common tendency for social reform to gather emotional strength from a desire to help the workers who are down at the bottom, but for it to be concentrated in practice upon the middle groups of labor."[75] An act purporting to set a wage floor and hours ceiling for all workers at first benefited primarily non-union workers who competed with unionized groups in other states. Many of the most exploited workers, isolated in marginal sectors, were excluded from direct benefits.[76] Assessing the demographic impact of this legislation is, therefore, a complicated task. On one hand, women, southerners, and African Americans were overrepresented among those workers who were entitled to immediate pay raises and hours reductions under the FLSA, because those groups were concentrated in the occupations with low standards. Many women in the garment, shoe, and textile industries, and many southern men (most of them black) in fertilizers, furniture, and sawmills, for example, were entitled to immediate improvements.

But this achievement should not obscure the fact that women and minority workers were disproportionately penalized by exclusion from the act. The exemption of domestic service and agricultural labor denied FLSA protection to most minority workers. Although the percentage of male workers excluded from FLSA protection was about the same as the percentage of female workers excluded, many of those men were in well-paid professional occupations, while most excluded female workers had sub-minimum labor standards. Women thus suffered more than men from being defined outside of the act's coverage.[77] The FLSA's basis in the federal power to regulate interstate commerce, and the political compromises made to get the bill passed, meant that women workers were at the margin of national wage-hour policy. Rather than simply bringing men in under the umbrella that had covered women, the shift from state to national policy transformed the basis of regulation, and male workers were now the center of attention due to their dominance in interstate occupations (i.e., manufacturing).

None of this was set in stone, however. Women and other low-paid groups stood to gain the most from the FLSA if standards could be raised and coverage could be expanded. Lamenting the "heartbreaking gaps" in the FLSA, the Consumers' League immediately began lobbying to expand federal coverage to protect "all those most needy now excluded," including domestic and agricultural workers. At the same time, the league launched a highly publicized drive for state wage-hour laws for men and women, laws that were to supplement and, if possible, improve upon the national policy.[78] Finally, the league hoped to improve the act's meager standards by influencing its implementation. Good administration was essential to ensuring that workers actually received the protection offered by the FLSA. Proworker administration might also accelerate the increase in minimum wage rates above the statutory twenty-five-cent level.

Administering the Fair Labor Standards Act

The questions of who would administer the FLSA and what method would be used to determine minimum standards had been among the chief sticking points during the bill's tortuous legislative history. Both supporters and opponents of the bill disagreed among themselves on whether Congress should write a single minimum wage rate and maximum hours standard into the act, or whether minimum standards for each industry should be determined by the "board method." Under the latter, a wage and hour board would be empowered to determine standards in consultation with advisory committees for each industry. Those who preferred statutory standards (set by Congress) still disagreed over whether the act should be implemented by a single administrator or a board. Another point of contention was whether FLSA administration would come under the jurisdiction of the U.S. Department of Labor.

These issues were fraught with gendered implications. The NCL argued for the board method of determining standards, which was the method developed and tested by the league in state minimum wage laws for women. The NCL favored a five-person board rather than a single administrator, in part because it hoped one board member would be a league activist. NCL leaders knew it was unlikely that a woman would be appointed as sole administrator. FDR and Frances Perkins were nervous about the political costs of giving women top appointments. A multiple-person board would make it easier to appoint a woman. Preparing for such an eventuality, Clara Beyer wrote Molly Dewson, "You would be grand on the Wage and Hour Board and a saving grace. . . . [T]errific pressure is going to be brought by all groups to control the action of the Board—all the more reason why you should be on to help hold the fort."[79] The NCL also fought to locate FLSA administration in the U.S. Department of Labor, which the league expected would cooperate with state labor departments. In the league view, the people most qualified to administer the FLSA were in the state and federal labor departments, and many of them were women.

On the question of administrative authority, gendered perspectives shaped the disagreement between the NCL and ACWA, on the one hand, and unions with predominantly male constituencies on the other. The AFL and some CIO leaders feared that board-administered wage increases would jeopardize collective bargaining agreements and undercut unions' appeal to workers. Defenders of the board method explained that for unionized industries, standards established by collective bargaining would be taken as fair and left alone by the board. As for the impact on unorganized workers, the NCL, ACWA, and ILGWU argued that board authority to raise wages above the statutory minimum would stimulate union organizing, not hinder it.[80] In these groups' experience with women workers, legislated standards facilitated unionization. Workers had more time, more money for dues, and the threat of industry migration to lower-wage, unorganized states was reduced. Furthermore, enforcing the legal standards became a mobilizing tool for union organizers.[81]

Fighting employer violations of FLSA standards could be an organizing tool whether the standards were set by flat rate or by a board, but in the NCL view, the board method was best at stimulating worker participation. Because industry boards were made up of business, public/consumer, and labor representatives, the NCL believed the board method encouraged worker (and consumer) involvement in the process of "industrial democracy." Florence Kelley had held that one benefit of minimum wage laws was their fostering of political activism by women workers. Frances Perkins similarly argued in 1937 that industry boards would give workers and employers in unorganized industries "education in the technique of collective bargaining."[82] NCL leaders envisioned a labor standards system in which experts, workers, and local citizens combined to challenge employer power. Contrary to the view of some labor leaders, advocates of the board method did not seek to create bureaucratic machinery that would supplant worker activism.[83]

The Consumers' League favored the board method over statutory standards for other reasons as well. One was flexibility. Setting rates by industry would prevent the lowest-paid industry from becoming the common denominator for all. It also would avoid the necessity of returning to Congress for adjustments to the minimum. (Indeed, persuading Congress to authorize increases became an ongoing and often unsuccessful struggle.) Finally, the board's investigative procedures would help prevent the act from being overturned as an unconstitutional violation of employer or employee due process rights. The NCL insisted that the board method would not produce the much-feared "arbitrary standards by fiat." To the contrary, it would prohibit arbitrariness.[84]

Organized labor was joined in the attack on the board method by conservatives, who claimed it would create an expensive, inefficient bureaucracy. Elinore Herrick rebutted such charges by documenting the successful board administration of women's minimum wage laws in eight states. Herrick also rejected the argument that the board method had been tried and found wanting under the NRA. The NRA was a poor model, she observed, because it had not made use of existing state labor agencies. As a result, "business-dominated code authorities" had assessed themselves huge enforcement budgets and passed the cost on to the consumer, often without actually spending the money on enforcement.[85] Lucy Mason testified that federal-state cooperation in labor standards administration had a good track record. One example she cited was the enforcement of the short-lived 1916 federal child labor law by the U.S. Children's Bureau and state labor departments. Mason offered as model state labor administrators Maud Swett in Wisconsin and Ethel Johnson in Massachusetts and New Hampshire.[86]

Lucy Mason's promotion of the U.S. Children's Bureau and female administrators in state labor departments probably had the opposite of her intended effect. The AFL and congressional conservatives united in opposition to Department of Labor authority over the FLSA. Hostile congressmen who warned against giving a board "dictatorial powers" over American industries seemed to resent particularly the prospect of increased authority for Frances Perkins. Senator Pat Harrison grumbled, "If the measure is passed, that Madam is going to have a good deal to say in its administration. And to be perfectly frank . . . that is one among many reasons that I am not for this legislation."[87]

The Consumers' League hoped the FLSA would create the cooperative system of federal-state labor standards enforcement that the NRA for the most part had failed to adopt. In advocating a large role for existing labor departments, the league hoped to prevent authority from going to hastily appointed, inexperienced, often probusiness newcomers to an expensive new agency — as had happened under the NRA. The NCL's faith that the board method of labor standards administration would be fair and efficient was based on its assumption that the people in charge would include its own members, women with decades of experience in regulating the labor standards of women and children.

In its final form, the FLSA did not guarantee the NCL network as much authority as its leaders had hoped for, but the potential for league influence remained alive. Instead of a five-member board, the law provided for a single administrator to head a new Wage and Hour Division of the U.S. Department of Labor. Frances Perkins could not freely choose the administrator, who was to be appointed by the president with the advice and consent of the Senate. The Women's Bureau would have little to do with the act, but the Children's Bureau won jurisdiction over the child labor provisions. As the ILGWU's Merle Vincent observed, much would depend on whether "we are lucky in getting a good administrator," and on "the quality of Board Members he appoints." If he were wise, Vincent continued, the administrator would appoint "public representatives who know what it's all about."[88]

When Elmer F. Andrews was appointed to head the new Wage and Hour Division, NCL activists at first believed their luck had not been too bad. Formerly the industrial commissioner of New York, Andrews seems to have been a compromise candidate on whom Perkins, Sidney Hillman, and FDR could agree. Also, Andrews was willing to do the job, unlike some others Perkins had approached.[89] Many similarly qualified women would have leapt at the job, but they were ruled out by the assumption that political considerations prohibited appointing a woman to head a new agency or division. (This assumption was only occasionally made explicit. In 1939 Roosevelt rejected NCL president Josephine Roche as a candidate to head a proposed Federal Security Administration. NCL and CIO activists argued that Roche was the most qualified for the position, but the word came back through Eleanor Roosevelt that she and FDR believed "it should be a man.")[90] Given the various constraints, NCL leaders initially were happy enough with the selection of Andrews to head up the Wage and

Hour Division. As a consolation to the South, North Carolina labor commissioner Major A. L. Fletcher was appointed as Andrews's assistant. Fletcher had cooperated with Lucy Mason's southern campaign, and NCL leaders hoped he would be an ally from his new position.[91]

A few months later, league activists and their friends in the Department of Labor were utterly exasperated with Elmer Andrews. He immediately challenged Frances Perkins by trying to set up his division so that it would operate independent of and insulated from the DOL. FDR backed Perkins, but Andrews's conduct continued to undermine her and inhibit FLSA enforcement.[92] Andrews also made pro-employer statements and gave employers undue representation on the first industry board, the textile committee. Eveline Burns and Jane Perry Clark, Columbia academics and officers of the Consumers' League of New York, met with Andrews to air league criticisms. Conceding that he had made some mistakes, Andrews promised to be more careful in his public statements and to consult more fully with Clara Beyer and other league allies in the Labor Department. Andrews also invited league suggestions for industry committee appointments. It had been quite worthwhile, Burns and Clark concluded, to remind Andrews "that people like ourselves are watching carefully what he is doing."[93]

The Consumers' League hoped to work as a representative of the public to influence FLSA administration and to guard the interests of unorganized workers in particular. The league followed up the meeting with Andrews by bombarding him with recommendations for public representatives on industry boards. Of the forty people the league initially nominated, twenty-three were women.[94] NCL members sat on the first eight industry committees formed; of these, the first five to issue wage orders established minimum rates from thirty-two and a half to forty cents per hour. These five industries were textiles, apparel, hosiery, millinery, and shoes, all major employers of women. League members thus helped raise FLSA minimum wage rates above the stingy statutory minimum for many women workers.[95]

On the whole, however, the NCL and its labor department allies found that the FLSA's implementation left much to be desired. They seemed to blame in part the large egos and small expertise of the men in charge. Clara Beyer was soon complaining to Molly Dewson that "Wages & Hours is a worse mess than ever. . . . I look back at the hours we spent trying to get a decent bill and then think of the administration and it makes me pretty sick."[96] In mid-1939 Perkins finally fired Elmer Andrews. But the NCL was not much happier with his successor, Colonel Philip Fleming. With war clouds gathering, league leaders feared that an "army man" would prioritize increasing productivity in the name of "preparedness" over raising labor standards. This mistrust of the military may have reflected the historical links between the NCL's reform community and pacifism; General Johnson's tenure at the NRA had done little to dispel league reservations. By December 1939 Mary Dublin was fuming that the Wage and Hour Division had "appointed more old Congressional war horses than probably any other in Washington. The slowness in the handling of complaints has by no means merely been a function of the lack of funds."[97]

The administration of the FLSA by a new division, run by men not steeped in the perspective of the NCL network, threatened the league's efforts to build efficient and harmonious cooperation between federal and state administrators. NCL activists believed that women in voluntary associations and government office had become especially good at this kind of cooperation. In the presuffrage years, political weakness had forced women to build coalitions and develop a dense web of personal associations across professional and jurisdictional lines.[98] The NCL worked with Clara Beyer at the Division of Labor Standards to alleviate the tensions of FLSA administration by holding conferences to "get the federal and state people together."[99] However, the responsiveness of the Wage and Hour Division to the Division of Labor Standards, Women's Bureau, and state labor departments was limited. Clara Beyer complained in 1940, "It has been a job, and still is, to convince the Wage and Hour Division of the importance and necessity of keeping good State relations and utilizing State facilities wherever they are sufficiently good. You know the 'yen' for power that we find among Washington officials and there is plenty of this in the W&H set-up."[100]

The task of promoting federal-state cooperation in labor standards administration involved not only curbing the egos of federal officials but stimulating the commitment of state officials. In states with poor labor departments, the Consumers' League and the Division of Labor Standards redoubled their efforts, displaying in the process some contempt for officials — usually, but not always, men — whose motivations they perceived as self-serving. Beyer recalled wryly that through conferences and training schools, they taught "some of the most impossible people" to be conscious of "the need for doing a good job" in the states. Frances Perkins created an incentive system of awarding ribbons to state labor commissioners at annual conferences to recognize improvements in legislation and administration. One state commissioner — "an insurance executive who didn't give a damn about workers' conditions" — was so distraught not to win a single star or ribbon that he went back to his state and pushed through a variety of reforms in order to win recognition at the next conference. The NCL and the Division of Labor Standards publicly gave state labor commissioners full credit for any improvements. Beyer recalled, "There was no publicity whatsoever on our work because Miss Perkins made that its foundation, that we [were] there to help the states and they would get the publicity." This self-effacing style, whereby women did the work and gave men the credit, remained a trademark of women's political behavior.[101]

Despite its frustrations with the Wage and Hour Division, the NCL defended the division from conservative attacks. "Budget cuts menace enforcement," warned one league article in 1940. Violations were outstripping the division's capabilities, and yet a House committee dominated by FLSA "enemies" was trying to slash the Wage and Hour Division's budget from about $6 million to $5 million. (The division estimated its needs at $8 million.) Appropriation cuts did not affect all workers evenly: the NCL linked inadequate funding to inequalities in enforcement, whereby violations were tolerated when they affected racial and ethnic minorities.[102] The league urged members to write their representatives demanding restoration of the full appropriation, but this effort was only partially and temporarily successful. In 1941 Congress appropriated $5.7 million for the division. In 1942, even as war production expanded employment, the appropriation shrank to $5 million. After a brief initial period of growth, the Wage and Hour Division's budget, number of field staff, and ability to enforce the FLSA entered a long period of decline. Without the NCL, reductions in the division's enforcement capacity probably would have been larger.[103]

The NCL influenced FLSA administration by winning modest increases in the minimum wage for important woman-employing industries, and it fostered cooperation between federal and state officials. The NCL also functioned as a defender of FLSA appropriations. But the FLSA confirmed what the NRA had suggested: as the establishment of national and male-inclusive policy attracted men to the field of labor standards, women experts in and out of government found it ever more difficult to shape wage-hour administration according to their own vision.

The FLSA passed with low standards and with gaps in coverage that especially hurt women and minority workers. However, it represented a significant state intervention in the labor market that had the potential to benefit all wage earners, women and minority men most of all. By setting a national floor beneath wages and ceiling over hours, the act limited the attractiveness of factory relocation across state borders for lower-cost labor. This indirectly helped workers who were not among those employed at the lowest standards. The FLSA bolstered the bargaining power of organized workers and offset some obstacles to unionizing others. As it turned out, the FLSA's passage was not followed by the massive wave of unionization among low-paid women, minorities, and southerners that the Consumers' League and its labor allies had expected. Broad shifts in the national political climate hampered the spread of unionization, and underfunding and questionable appointments at the Wage and Hour Division permitted widespread violations of the FLSA. These outcomes were not caused by the FLSA, however, nor did they prove that the FLSA was not a good strategy for workers.[104]

The Consumers' League was unable to win national wage-hour policy in the form it wanted. Employer opposition, the ambivalence of some labor leaders, and general resistance to a female-dominated labor standards regime were too strong. However, the NCL indisputably made a mark on the FLSA. League activists and lawyers drafted state bills and defended their constitutionality in court, paving a winding path toward court acceptance of wage-hour regulation. NCL educational campaigns converted some labor unions, some southerners, and many middle-class voters, especially women, to the labor standards cause. The league also helped steer the FLSA around the shoals that almost sank it in Congress in the spring of 1938. If the measure had not passed in 1938, it is unlikely that such legislation would have passed for many years. After the FLSA's enactment, the NCL tried to ensure that it was administered by capable people committed to the interests of workers; league activists hoped workers and public-minded experts could use the law's administrative machinery together to challenge employer control. The NCL also tried to increase FLSA appropriations and broaden its coverage. However, instead of expansion, the next years brought a conservative counterattack that kept the league scrambling to salvage even the limited achievements of 1938.

chapter 8

Reaction

The Consumers' League Program under Attack

The ink was scarcely dry on the Fair Labor Standards Act when it came under fire from a conservative blitz against New Deal labor and social policies. A drive to weaken the FLSA proceeded in tandem with a campaign to undermine the National Labor Relations (Wagner) Act of 1935. State wage and hours laws also faced bitter challenges, especially after war mobilization got under way. The Consumers' League had envisioned that the FLSA, state wage-hour laws, and the Wagner Act together would increase the economic security and political power of American wage earners, especially for "submerged groups" within the working class. The league also had expected that its network of middle-class white women would participate in the implementation of these policies. However, these hopes ran aground on the resistance of employers and politicians, whose leverage was increased by impending war and the accompanying surge of superpatriotism, and of male policy experts and bureaucrats, who took new interest in labor standards administration now that it was sanctioned at the national level for men as well as women.

The rightward turn at home coincided with fascist triumphs abroad. Alarmed, left-liberals escalated their rhetoric. NCL general secretary Mary Dublin told a league audience that the moment called for bold action. The league's traditional program of gradual reform had been colored by its "sense of the inevitability of progress," she argued. But right-wing victories were shattering "every assumption of continuity, and continuous social gains." With the nation's fate hanging in the balance between social democracy and fascism, cautious tactics would not suffice: "The disenfranchised cry out . . . the status quo clings to the past, with violence if need be."[1] Despite such passionate sentiments, progressives in and out of the New Deal administration found their strength sapped by the politics of "preparedness." To the dismay of Mary Dublin, the league was forced to spend most of its energy fighting a rear-guard action.

Defending the FLSA

Not surprisingly, employers whose labor costs were most affected by the FLSA led the assault on it that gathered momentum in 1939. Dublin identified the key lobbyists as the "homework interests" and the "so-called farm groups." The NCL spent enormous energy during the 1939 and 1940 legislative sessions fighting amendments that sought to lower minimum wages for rural employees engaged in industrial homework and to broaden the FLSA's definition of "agricultural occupations" to exempt more workers in agricultural processing. These workers long had been among the lowest paid, and most of them were women and minorities.[2]

In 1939 the league and labor department allies blocked an amendment that would have exempted rural homeworkers from the Act. Groups such as the National Knitted Outerwear Association and the National Association of Leather Glove Manufacturers argued that homeworkers were women, often rural women with few wage-earning options, who (they assumed) worked for supplemental rather than necessary earnings. These employers also argued that hours regulations were impractical for homeworkers, whose tasks blended into their daily schedule of meal preparation and tending children. By contrast, the NCL and administrators like Clara Beyer insisted that homework was a way of evading labor laws. Exempting or paying lower wages to rural homeworkers would "deprive a much exploited group of essential protection," and it also would drive down factory labor standards in industries historically reliant on homework.[3] While employer associations played on sympathy for the needs of rural women (especially mothers), the women's labor standards network argued that it was unfair, and economically unsound, to pay such workers lower wages: "The

The Barden bill would have exempted from the FLSA workers such as these Italian women packing asparagus in Pennsylvania in 1941. (Marion Post Wolcott photograph, LC-USF 34 57559-D)

needs of farm women are as great as those of their city sisters. Their labor has the same intrinsic value as that of other workers in the productive process." Building on this 1939 victory, the Department of Labor secured administrative bans on homework in various garment-related industries in 1941 and 1944.[4]

A triumph for which the NCL could claim much credit was the defeat of the Barden bill, which would have drastically weakened the FLSA. An NCL memo described the bill, sponsored by North Carolina congressman Graham Barden, as "written by the canning, packing, slaughterhouse, sugar, lumber, and ice cream and cheese lobbies." The Barden bill would have exempted from the FLSA most workers whose wages the act had raised, with the exception of textile and apparel workers. The bill also proposed to eliminate overtime requirements and hours limits for many other categories of workers. Many of these occupations were dominated by women or, particularly in the South, by minority men.[5]

Rather than challenge head-on the exclusion of agricultural labor from the FLSA, the NCL fought to define such labor as narrowly as possible.

Barden bill proponents invoked the old idea that agricultural work was not labor so much as a way of life, one that was private, family-oriented, and subject to the laws of nature rather than government.[6] The NCL responded by trying to expose the "so-called farm groups" as representing industrial interests. The hundreds of thousands of workers "engaged in industrial operations performed on agricultural, horticultural, and dairy products" should be "protected in the same way as workers in factory, mill, and mine," the league argued. In an appeal to rural voters, the NCL denied that raising wages in agricultural processing harmed farmers by forcing processors to pay less for produce. League figures showed that labor costs in agricultural processing were a tiny factor in prices paid to farmers or charged to the public. The Barden amendments actually would hurt farmers, the league argued, by reducing workers' ability to purchase farm produce. An open NCL letter to Congress signed by 750 citizens pleaded for defeat of the Barden bill, to let "hundreds of thousands of pitifully underpaid workers . . . earn at least the meagre living the Act assures."[7]

It was the Consumers' League that masterminded the anti-Barden bill effort, prodding the CIO to make it a higher priority. "I hope you won't stay too clear of this battle," Dublin told a CIO official. Dublin rejected a CIO suggestion that there was nothing to fear because the House's folly could be undone in the Senate or, failing that, by presidential veto. "This thing should be fought in the House," Dublin insisted, because passage in the House would "give encouragement to all the forces of reaction, particularly in the states."[8] Dublin spent the summer of 1939 in Washington coordinating the opposition to such amendments, and her efforts helped prevent action on four anti-FLSA bills in 1939. However, the bills waited ominously on the congressional calendar for 1940. The NCL organized an FLSA defense campaign that involved another round of meeting with legislators, mass mailings, publications, and local branch activity.[9] Dublin testified against the Barden amendments and entered into the *Congressional Record* the names of about 4,000 people who signed a resolution against them. In a prime-time radio debate in April, league president Josephine Roche so wittily dissected the arguments of Representatives Barden and Coffee that the league circulated a printed transcript of the debate. In May 1940 the House voted 205-175 to recommit the Barden bill. Newspapers called this an impressive victory for "Administration forces." NCL activists were justifiably proud, but they also confessed dismay at the dim prospects ahead. The NCL's moment of triumph had been a very short one, and its leaders' optimism was rudely punctured.[10]

The "Civilizing of Labor Relations"

After the Wagner Act was upheld by the Supreme Court in 1937, its opponents used various tactics for limiting its effects. In 1939 they introduced a range of amendments that originated with anti-union employers as well as with the American Federation of Labor. Under Mary Dublin's leadership, the NCL made defending the Wagner Act from these weakening amendments a top priority.[11] In the process, the NCL reiterated the commitment to public participation in labor policy that had brought it into conflict with the AFL during the battle for the FLSA. The league's willingness to impinge on union prerogatives through public involvement in labor relations and labor standards policy derived from its historical experience with a union movement that scorned the most exploited workers.

The NCL leadership understood collective bargaining and labor standards policy to be mutually reinforcing. "Trade unions . . . are just as important as minimum wage laws in the development of our industrial civilization," claimed Elinore Herrick, league activist and New York regional director of the National Labor Relations Board (NLRB).[12] Wage-hour regulation and collective bargaining were complementary means of increasing economic and political democracy. Labor standards laws would facilitate unionization, and strong unions would promote the passage and enforcement of good labor standards laws. Influential figures like Senator Robert Wagner of New York and CIO secretary-treasurer James Carey shared this view. Indeed, both Carey, then the "boy wonder" from the United Electrical Workers, and Wagner himself joined the NCL board in 1939.[13] Yet most scholars have treated labor standards as a policy issue separate from and subordinate to collective bargaining, replicating the historical wariness of many labor leaders toward wage and hour regulation. This separation has distorted the history of labor relations as well as that of wage-hour policy.[14]

Conservatives shared the NCL view that labor standards and union rights were two sides of a coin. It was southern Democrats who led the attack on the Wagner Act in 1939; their anger at the NLRB was intensified by their resentment of the "intrusion" of Wage and Hour Division inspectors into the workplaces of their states.[15] Conservatives complained that the Wagner Act was "one-sided," giving rights to employees but not to employers, that it gave the NLRB an unprecedented and dangerous amount of authority with no provision for appeal, and that industrial conflict had increased as a result of the act. Meanwhile, key AFL leaders also believed the NLRB had too much authority. They especially disliked its power to determine the bargaining unit in a given workplace; the AFL deplored the board's ability to invalidate a union contract that it found did not represent the free choice of a majority of workers. The AFL leadership also complained that NLRB rulings in jurisdictional disputes between the rival labor organizations favored the CIO.[16]

Thanks to an extensive publicity effort by the NCL and other left-liberal organizations, in 1939 all amendments to the NLRA were blocked. Congressional conservatives then tried a different tactic, one that ultimately worked: they forced the creation of a special House committee to investigate the NLRB. Named for its chairman, Howard Smith (D.-Va.), and dominated by anti–New Dealers, the Smith Committee conducted a sensationalistic and lopsided investigation that was designed to undermine public support for the NLRB and, more broadly, for the New Deal.[17] In June 1940 amendments proposed by the Smith Committee passed by a large margin in the House, due in part to the committee's startling alliance with the AFL's William Green. New Dealers in the Senate managed to delay further action until after the 1940 elections, when the amendments were rejected. However, the Smith Committee achieved its objective. The pressure on FDR from the AFL-conservative alliance resulted in personnel and policy changes on the NLRB that restricted its pursuit of democracy in labor relations.[18]

Although ultimately unsuccessful, the league's defense of the Wagner Act in 1939 and 1940 illuminates the high hopes that advocates of marginalized workers had for the NLRB. Supporters of women and minority workers were prominent among the board's defenders. In addition to the NCL, groups that testified against NLRA amendments included the Washington WTUL, the League of Women Shoppers, the Church League for Industrial Democracy, and the National Negro Congress. For the latter, John P. Davis stated that the NLRB had shown "every disposition to be fair to all parties at interest in disputes" — fair to employers, to AFL members, and to black workers. In 1935 black leaders had been angry that the Wagner bill did not include an antidiscrimination clause, predicting that without it the legislation would increase the AFL's power to discriminate. But by 1939 African American labor activists were impressed with NLRB efforts against exclusionary practices.[19]

The league used its familiar range of tactics in the campaign against NLRA amendments. In July 1939 Mary Dublin and NCL chairman Paul Brissenden, a Columbia labor relations expert, testified before congressional labor committees. The NCL gathered 1,500 signatures from "prominent citizens" who opposed the amendments and had them entered into the *Congressional Record*.[20] Working behind the scenes, Dublin persuaded other witnesses to testify against the amendments. The issue of who "lined up" pro-NLRB witnesses would become front-page news in 1940, when the Smith Committee accused the NLRB of inappropriately "rounding up" friendly witnesses. In fact, the NCL had contacted potential supporters, illustrating the delicate unofficial role the league played on behalf of government agencies with which it sympathized.[21] Dublin wrote a pamphlet analyzing the proposed amendments and distributed 20,000 of them to members of the league's traditional female constituency across the country. These efforts created a ripple effect around the nation. Articles opposing Wagner Act amendments soon appeared in the publications of groups such as the Federal Council of Churches, the YWCA, and the League of Women Voters. From Atlanta, Lucy Mason signed the NCL resolution and also drafted her own letter in defense of the NLRA, which she sent on TWOC-CIO letterhead to southern editors (in typical Mason style, a reading list on labor relations was attached). League branches in ten states and impromptu committees in eleven others mobilized to defend the act.[22]

This groundswell of support for the NLRB suggests an aspect of its appeal that Wagner Act scholars have overlooked. In an influential study, historian Christopher Tomlins argues that the AFL leadership was correct in perceiving by 1938 that the Wagner Act represented "a severe encroachment upon union autonomy." Tomlins challenges the conventional wisdom that New Deal labor policies dramatically increased the power of unions. He argues that from the very birth of the NLRB (and not just after the restrictive 1947 Taft-Hartley Act), the legitimacy of collective bargaining was contingent on its capacity to promote "higher productivity and efficient capital accumulation."[23] It is true that one effect of the NLRA on the labor movement was to increase its dependence on the federal government, subjecting unions, as well as employers, to government interference. But this "system-sustaining function" was not the foreseen objective of the act's drafters or its supporters. The Consumers' League defended the Wagner Act with such passion in 1939 and 1940 because league leaders appreciated the NLRB's support for workers historically ignored, or worse, by the AFL. In its early years, the NLRB emphasized worker self-organization and offered "spirited defenses of workers' rights" that won it the loyalty of labor radicals and their sympathizers. Not until 1940 would the NLRB begin to prioritize stability and seek to curb rank-and-file activity.[24]

The Wagner Act took as its constitutional basis the "tangible public interest in the stabilization of the wages, hours and working conditions of the labor force at large." This was a departure from common law precedent, and also from the AFL view of collective bargaining as a private activity between unions and employers. The NLRB's responsibility was not primarily to protect *union* rights, but the *public interest* in the welfare and purchasing power of *individual* employees. Many AFL leaders were horrified as the implications of this dawned on them.[25] Advocates of unskilled or unorganized workers saw it differently. They welcomed the shift toward the public interest as a means of countering union discrimination. Also, both the CIO and the NCL believed that without federal government support, unions would be unable to overcome massive business opposition. Groups concerned with southern workers were especially likely to believe federal intervention would be more a help than a hindrance to the labor movement.[26]

Long experience with AFL indifference to unskilled workers prevented the NCL from undue sympathy with the AFL over curbs on its jurisdictional claims. Tomlins observes that before the NLRB, "the AFL had claimed for itself the authority to decide, through assignment of jurisdiction, which union represented which workers. It based its assignments on a complex web of considerations; tradition, custom, the 'property rights' accumulated by a particular organization in the course of its development as an organic representation of a particular craft, . . . and the distribution of power within the Federation."[27] Small wonder that advocates of women and minority workers welcomed the NLRB's disruption of that system. Custom and tradition had proven themselves tools of discrimination in the workplace.[28]

The NCL denied that the NLRB had treated the AFL unfairly. The league adopted a position of impartiality between the AFL and the CIO, but its sympathies were with the latter. In fact, by 1940 the tactics and style of the CIO were changing in ways that would marginalize the women whose militance had helped build the organization.[29] But this outcome was hardly discernible as of yet, and alongside the AFL, the CIO still looked like women workers' best bet. "Obviously, if there were evidence of partisanship we should be among the first to object," Dublin told congressional labor committees. She claimed the NLRB had upheld the AFL in twenty-nine cases and the CIO in only twenty-three. She also portrayed the AFL leadership as out of touch with its membership: "Our 18 branches scattered throughout the country are in constant close touch with happenings in local labor situations. They report that local AFL groups do not seem to share the views of AFL leadership on this issue." As for the NLRB's power to invalidate certain union contracts, which the AFL so resented, Dublin argued that unions needed "merely to turn to their own membership to seek democratically the strength which will give their contracts validity before the law." Curbing this NLRB power would "make for collusion between employers and minority representatives and deal a powerful blow to the cause of industrial democracy."[30] Certain workers were especially likely to be victims of such collusion with employers. The AFL's past failures thus created groups who viewed a shift away from AFL autonomy toward public participation in labor relations as a gain rather than a loss.

League officials sometimes spoke in terms calculated to make the labor movement less threatening to its middle-class constituency, but they did so to widen support for union rights, not because they feared working-class militance. NCL leaders emphasized changing the conduct of employers, not workers. Elinore Herrick declared that collective bargaining was "a wholesome movement," which, instead of fearing, "decent" employers should encourage, to protect themselves from the competition of wage cutters.[31] Herrick told radio listeners that collective action by workers represented self-reliance "in the best American tradition." As such, it should be embraced by those who worried that Americans would "look to the government for everything instead of standing on their own two feet." Herrick cast trade unions as an organic product of modern industrialism. In the preindustrial past, she explained, when "every employer knew each of his workers by his first name . . . and when each new baby arrived," workers could negotiate individually with the boss. But now the owners of a given factory were likely to reside far away, and they set labor standards for groups of employees rather than for individuals. Individual employees were powerless. Herrick illustrated this point with a poignant story about black women in Newark fur factories. All that the Wagner Act did, she concluded, was empower the government to protect workers' efforts at self-help.[32]

Although the NCL welcomed state intervention in labor relations, it did not believe collective bargaining rights should be contingent upon industrial stability and productivity. "All of us have an interest in peaceful industrial relations. . . . But our interest is in a peace that is consistent with justice and the principles of the democratic way of life." So began the league's widely circulated pamphlet of April 1939. Dublin expanded on this before the House Labor Committee: "We consumers want peace based on the dignity of working men and women, and recognition of their essential rights, not the shotgun peace that comes from acquiescence in the suppression of those rights." Maximizing production was less important than distributing output more evenly.[33] To conservative complaints that the Wagner Act was "one-sided" in favor of workers, NCL leaders retorted that the act "already is balanced, and more than balanced, by the preexisting laws of the land." Furthermore, "the treatment of employers at the hands of the labor relations boards, Federal and State, is gentle indeed by comparison with the normal way of the cop on the beat and the judge on the bench in dealing with workers."[34] The league was an important supporter of the La Follette Civil Liberties Committee, which documented brutality against strikers in incidents like the 1937 "Memorial Day massacre" of Chicago steelworkers.[35]

NCL leaders believed that the right to strike was essential, although in an ideal world strikes would not be necessary. A national labor board that could enforce labor rights and standards without strikes would represent the "civilizing of labor relations." But sometimes strikes were unavoidable, and for this the NCL blamed employers, not unions. The league doubted that the Wagner Act had stimulated strikes, but even if it had, league chairman Paul Brissenden testified, that was not "an unmixed evil. The extent to which strikes emerge at this stage is perhaps in direct ratio to the obstinacy with which employers continue their interferences."[36] The NCL believed that workers, not employers, suffered the most from strikes, especially the lowest-paid groups, who rarely had savings. The Newark fur workers had been forced to go on public relief during their strike, "thus throwing the burden of the employer's unfair labor practices upon the community."[37] In 1940, as war loomed and no-strike pledges were solicited from unions, Consumers' League leaders continued to defend labor's right to strike, claiming it was unfair to ask workers to make sacrifices (by promising not to strike for higher wages) when capital could threaten to withdraw if not guaranteed an attractive rate of return.[38] The league hoped that stronger guarantees of union rights, like higher labor standards, would reduce the incidence of strikes, but it did not value industrial peace over social justice.

The league's prominence in the defense of the NLRB did not go unnoticed. One syndicated editorial confirmed by its virulence the efficacy of the NCL campaign: "An organization styling itself as the National Consumers' League is flooding the mails with propaganda in opposition to any amendments of the national labor relations act, and in support of its position makes appeals as specious and absurd as ever came from the 'minister of propaganda and enlightenment' in Nazi Germany." This editorial also complained that after the NLRA was upheld came "the period of the sit-down strike and the statement from the Perkins woman that the illegality of such a strike had never been established."[39] The writer seems to have noticed that many women were defending the NLRB. Indeed, Wagner Act critics exaggerated women's role in an effort to undermine New Deal labor policy.

Women were surprisingly well represented on the nation's early labor relations boards, although they were hardly dominant. Several league women served on NRA labor boards, the most prominent example being

Elinore Herrick, New York regional director of the NLRB. The original caption for this April 1937 photograph quotes Herrick as saying that labor organizations were better informed than employers on the procedure and technique of the NLRB. (AP/Wide World Photos, New York World-Telegram and Sun Collection, LC)

Elinore Herrick, who was director of the NLRB's largest regional headquarters, in New York, from the NRA days until 1942. The NLRB in its early years attracted many women lawyers and researchers. "The Labor Board was the place to go if you were concerned about justice in the workplace," recalled one such lawyer, Ida Klaus, whose colleagues included "at least ten women." Eleven percent of the 105 attorneys in the NLRB's allegedly Communist-leaning Review Division were women. The NLRB was no feminist utopia; Ida Klaus reported that "women got the little jobs and on promotions they didn't fare so well." Still, at a time when just over 2 percent of lawyers were female, the demographics at the NLRB suggest that labor policy administration offered unusual opportunities to women and that progressive women were drawn to the field.[40]

In 1940 the Smith Committee hearings highlighted this female presence in an attempt to discredit the NLRB's competence. The first six Review Division attorneys summoned by the committee's general counsel were women (when only 11 of 105 division attorneys were women). NLRB personnel were at a great disadvantage because the Smith Committee had all the board's files. The witnesses did not know which cases they would be questioned on, and they had no opportunity to refresh their memories. Under General Counsel Edmund Toland's aggressive questioning, the witnesses sometimes had trouble remembering details and contradicted themselves.[41] The front page of the *New York Times* daily featured smiling portraits of the women lawyers, who like their male counterparts at the NLRB averaged about thirty years of age. Headlines included "Inexperience Laid to Aides of NLRB" and "Lawyer of NLRB Changed Her Mind." The Smith Committee tried to turn public opinion against the NLRB by portraying it as staffed by young, attractive women who were ignorant of political and economic realities, enamored of idealistic social policies, and malleable enough to be controlled by Communists. The questions asked of these women emphasized their youth and their sex in an obvious attempt to challenge their qualifications. If the women were married, the Smith Committee implied they were earning salaries that should go to men or to women without male breadwinners. If single, they allegedly were subverting American gender roles. The female lawyers had backgrounds in social work and economics, and many of them came to the NLRB from other agencies with left-leaning reputations, such as the Resettlement Administration. None too subtly linking these women to radicalism, the committee asked Margaret Bennett Porter about her "leftism" and Hungarian-born Ann Landy Wolf about her accent and her date of naturalization.[42]

The Smith Committee's tactics were calculated to generate titillating media coverage, but the more fundamental objective was to undermine the credibility of the NLRB. Toland bullied female witnesses differently than male witnesses, shouting at the women to speak up and to give more "responsive" answers. He interspersed personal questions (on marital status, husband's salary, husband's employer) with questions about intricate details of NLRB cases. This not only disrupted the witnesses' concentration on the cases, it revealed that three of the lawyers had husbands who also worked for the federal government. The *New York Times* reported that "members of several women's organizations" began attending the Smith hearings because they were concerned over reports of "sex discrimination by Mr. Toland." These women no doubt worried that the hearings might reignite protests against married women's employment.[43]

The Smith Committee succeeded in making the NLRB the subject of ridicule on the House floor and probably in many circles around the nation. Congressman Clare Hoffman (R.-Mich.) told his colleagues that if they "take a look at the 'reviewing attorneys,' [they] will understand why there has been so much trouble. Those girls who are acting as reviewing attorneys for the Board are fine young ladies. They are good looking; they are intelligent appearing; they are just as wonderful, I imagine, to visit with, to talk with, and to look at as any like number of young ladies anywhere in the country, but the chances are 99 out of 100 that none of them ever changed a diaper, hung out a washing, or baked a loaf of bread."[44] These NLRB lawyers were not successful as women, according to Hoffman's rating system, but their neglect of the domestic arts did not make them competent lawyers either: "None of them has had any judicial or industrial experience to qualify her for the job they are trying to do, and yet here they are . . . good looking, intelligent appearing as they may be, and well groomed all of them, writing opinions upon which the jobs of hundreds of thousands of men depend and upon which the success or failure of an industrial enterprise may depend and we stand for it."[45] The assumption that women were inherently unsuited to work in government labor agencies — and especially, to have authority over *men's* jobs — was utterly at odds with the NCL view of women's role in the "civilizing of labor relations." The Smith Committee's treatment of female NLRB employees no doubt deepened the antagonism that league leaders already felt toward the investigation.[46]

The NCL's historical experience with unions and employers, and its success in creating state and federal labor agencies in which middle-class women held important positions, led it to embrace a larger role for what Christopher Tomlins pejoratively labels the "liberal bureaucratic-administrative state."[47] When labor relations were defined as a private matter between employers and workers, gendered assumptions and facts about both groups hindered women's participation. When labor relations were a matter of the public interest, women had a greater chance of participating (although they still had to contend with the likes of Congressman Hoffman). In other words, from the NCL's female perspective, shifting the basis of labor law to protecting the public or consumer interest represented an opening up of the process rather than a loss of autonomy, a democratization rather than a sacrifice of democracy to stability. Women workers would gain by having the government make sure that unions represented them. NCL members also expected that through government involvement, women like themselves could participate in labor relations. Here the league emphasized not the self-interest of female administrators and consumer representatives but rather their dedication to the interests of all workers, particularly women and other "submerged" groups. But this vision collided with the assumptions and agendas of male politicians and bureaucrats, a conflict which played into the hands of opponents of a more comprehensive welfare state.

State Wage-Hour Law in the Shadow of the FLSA

The anti–New Deal reaction that hampered the FLSA and NLRB also was manifested at the state level, as employers of low-wage workers tried to block new state laws and weaken old ones. Moreover, as the NCL battled conservatives, it had to fight on another front as well. The transition to male-inclusive, national legislation had expanded the profession of labor standards administration and diminished the influence of women in the field, in state labor departments as well as at the national level.

The passage of the FLSA in 1938 and its upholding in 1941 by no means obviated the necessity for state laws.[48] Immediately after the FLSA's passage the NCL mounted a sweeping drive for new and revised state wage and hour laws. State laws were needed most urgently to cover those "exploited groups" who were excluded from the national policy because their occupations were defined as intrastate; as the NCL noted, the majority of these were female or African American, or both. It became apparent that some employers were evading the FLSA by redefining themselves as intrastate businesses. This practice was widespread in the southern lumber industry, for example, which chiefly employed black men.[49] A second NCL objective was to win state laws that set higher standards than the national policy, thereby creating pressure to raise the national standards. Finally, the NCL pushed state laws because they enhanced enforcement of national policy.

Despite the league's efforts, progress on all state wage and hour bills was slow after the passage of the FLSA. Working through advisory committees to the Division of Labor Standards and Women's Bureau, the NCL helped develop a model bill that, like the FLSA, combined wage and hour regulation into one measure and applied to both sexes. The NCL network arranged this bill's introduction in twenty-nine of the forty-four states whose legislatures were in session in 1939. Not a single state passed the bill. It came close in New Jersey, after an all-out drive by the New Jersey and national leagues. In Connecticut, the existing women's wage law was extended to include men. State minimum wage laws for women passed in a few new states and were broadened in others, and several states strengthened their hours laws for women. But overall, the results were discouraging.[50] Even less successful was a push coordinated by Mary Dublin to bring domestic workers under the protection of state wage-hour laws, as well as workers' compensation laws and the Social Security Act. Domestic workers represented three out of ten women gainfully employed. Bills to establish minimum wages for these workers were introduced in seven states, and bills to limit their hours were proposed in five states, but none of these passed. Even an unambitious bill to limit domestic workers to sixty hours per week met defeat.[51] Meanwhile, government labor agencies at all levels were threatened with reduced appropriations.

This antipathy toward labor standards regulation was expressed in the administrative arena as well as in legislatures. Increasingly, changes in staffing undermined the protection workers were supposed to receive from state wage and hour laws. League allies in state labor departments always had competed for positions with people who knew less about labor conditions but more about party loyalty. As labor regulations multiplied in the 1930s, these conflicts intensified, and the NCL more often ended up on the losing side. Another trend was that more of the political appointees with whom league women competed were other women. In 1934 Ohio's new governor replaced Director of Minimum Wage Louise Stitt (of the Ohio Consumers' League) with a "Democratic vote-getter," Elaine Sheffer. Not only did league women refuse to deliver votes, they were considered too pro-labor: Governor Davey complained that Stitt "never gave the poor employer a chance." The Consumers' League of Ohio protested Sheffer's appointment as a violation of civil service laws, but to no avail. By 1935 the division's staff had turned over completely, and the minimum wage law went virtually unenforced. Similarly, in 1935 New Hampshire league member Ethel Johnson was replaced as that state's director of minimum wage by Republican Party activist Elizabeth Elkins. Interestingly, the league persuaded Elkins to take her job seriously, but she was stymied by Labor Commissioner John Davie, "an impossible person who has held on for years because he plays hand and glove with the employers." In Louisiana the reformers butted heads with the leading lady of the New Orleans machine, who closed her eyes to violations if the employer was a political friend. The pro-employer bias of political appointees, male or female, seemed to be deepening.[52]

In the mid-1930s, when a change in state administration cost a bureaucrat her job, she could readily find a new one, but this was not the case just a few years later. Louise Stitt from Ohio was hired as an industrial economist in the U.S. Women's Bureau. Ethel Johnson soon enjoyed a good position with the International Labor Office. Effie Dupuis, secretary of North Dakota's Minimum Wage Department, would not be so lucky. Dupuis was "politically ousted" after the 1936 elections brought in a new administration. Her successor was "purely a political machine woman, a farm club woman who sold subscriptions for the party paper in the S.E. part of state where they need the woman vote. I played NO politics in my office and hence am not valuable to the party machine." The woman who headed the North Dakota Children's Bureau also had been "frozen out." Dupuis made inquiries at minimum wage departments in many states, but she came up empty-handed. Dupuis became desperate: "I am available for any kind of work, any time, any where, any price," she wrote. "My whole heart is in the minimum wage work."[53] But the NCL no longer was able to place its friends readily. The expansion of government labor agencies had slowed, for one thing, but another dynamic was at work as well.[54]

Contrary to NCL expectations, the passage of the FLSA made the position of women wage-hour officials more precarious than before. Although openings for female political appointees remained, as the foregoing examples illustrate, reform-oriented female experts of the NCL mold found their opportunities contracting, and the arguments used against these women often were gendered. The extension of labor regulation to men brought new resistance to female administrators, to women's divisions, and to female reformers. Naomi Cohn, the Virginia league activist, lost the job she had helped create in the state labor department and ended up living with her daughter in Michigan. Connecticut minimum wage director Christine Buck was forced to resign, and her job went to a "pol."[55] In Kentucky, where the local league had been instrumental in creating the labor department and passing the state's labor laws, the industrial commissioner used the FLSA as an excuse to dismiss women factory inspectors. Commissioner William Burrow explained to indignant league members that the extension of regulations to men "greatly expanded" the department's duties; his small appropriation permitted him only six full-time inspectors, and all six needed "to be competent to perform all duties." Women inspectors had been fine for enforcing laws affecting women and children, he claimed, but they were not qualified to administer men's laws: "I cannot agree that it would be proper to send a woman into a machine shop, forging plant, etc., to convince an employer that certain safety devices should be adopted . . . [or] into the coal mining sections which are in many cases far off the main highways; nor do I believe that I could expect a woman representative to climb upon a ten-story building out on steel framework and point out the necessity for better and safer scaffolding." Burrow added that he lacked the resources "to satisfy the wishes of women's groups," who, he implied, did not understand labor law administration.[56]

Anna Settle of the Kentucky league irately reminded Burrow that she herself as well as women in many other states had proven themselves perfectly capable of inspecting machine shops and coal mines. How many of his men had actually climbed out on the scaffolding of a ten-story building, she asked him. With no little sarcasm, Settle reversed the line usually used against women: "We do not object to men inspectors, but we do want men inspectors who are equally as good as women. It is not . . . the sex of the inspector, rather what are the capabilities to see that the laws are enforced."

Settle's rebuttal brought an apologetic letter from Burrow, but in practice little changed. The Kentucky league remained a watchdog over enforcement, but it now did so as an adversarial outsider rather than in support of allies in the department.[57]

Commissioner Burrow's words are a good example of how sexism prevented the league's authority in the arena of female labor regulation from transferring over to the population at large. Consumers' League activists believed themselves qualified to advise on all labor standards policy. They assumed that the jurisdiction of their female allies in administrative positions would be enlarged rather than reduced by the transition to male-inclusive policy. However, the league underestimated the tenacity of the view that women were not competent to administer programs for men. Once labor standards policy affected men, and received federal funding, the field attracted competition for bureaucratic positions from men who earlier would not have been interested. A similar pattern was apparent in the field of child welfare, which was masculinized after the creation of national programs. In 1922 forty-five of forty-eight state children's bureau directors were women, but by 1939 three-quarters of them were men.[58]

At the same time that state officials were firing women from positions affecting male labor, they also were trying to eliminate women's bureaus, usually under the guise of "economy." Sex-neutral national policy raised the question at all levels of whether women's divisions were obsolete, and in several states women's divisions were threatened with extinction. Mary Anderson of the Women's Bureau grumbled that it was "not economy to dismiss seasoned employees and put in new ones that have to learn again. The economy is always effected upon women in industry." Commissioner Burrow of Kentucky complained that he did not have the funds to set up a women's bureau in his department. Burrow apparently intended to give priority to inspecting men's workplaces, and he wanted male staff to do it. For female inspectors and bureaucrats, therefore, the impact of "sex-neutral" laws was not sex-neutral at all. Furthermore, the extension of protection to men rarely came with funds proportionate to the new demands on labor departments. In this context of scarcity, sex-neutral regulation diverted enforcement resources away from female occupations.[59]

The politics of war mobilization further diminished the NCL's influence over labor standards policy in the late 1930s and early 1940s. Because they remembered that businessmen had dominated newly created agencies during World War I, liberals wanted existing agencies to handle the mobilization effort. The NCL hoped the U.S. Department of Labor would manage the labor side of war production. But the combination of congressional hostility to Frances Perkins and FDR's predilection for creating agencies meant that the DOL was bypassed. The director of the Office of Production Management did not even check with Perkins before he telegraphed the nation's governors urging a suspension of state labor laws.[60] By 1942 the War Production Board was holding state labor conferences without consulting the NCL or the Women's Bureau. One league member complained that these were "all in general 'man' conferences, with no women from labor groups on the program." The War Production Board created a Women's Division but did not give it funding, despite protests from the NCL and others.[61] In 1942 Mary Anderson pressed to have a woman appointed to a committee of the War Manpower Commission. When members of this committee threatened to resign if a woman was appointed, Manpower Commission head Paul McNutt instead created the Women's Advisory Committee. The NCL's Warwick Hobart was one of the advisory committee's thirteen members. The committee produced reports that recommended expansion and improvement of day-care centers, and part-time shifts tied to school hours. But its recommendations were almost without exception ignored.[62]

Exclusion of women from policy making seemed to go hand in hand with inattention to women workers and with lowered standards in general. Reports came in from league members and allies in labor departments in one state after another: their power to hold off hours increases and reduced minimum wage rates was waning.[63] War-related production accelerated long before the United States entered the war in December 1941. Even while some workers remained unemployed, employers began pressing to lower labor standards, especially by relaxing overtime regulations. Women with domestic responsibilities reported that being required to work ten hours and more per day was placing them under severe strain. League women cheered when Mary Anderson "put right" some "young upstarts" from the War and Navy Departments who wanted to mandate a sixty-hour work week. However, standards continued to erode. High wartime wages did not preclude employer efforts to avoid a minimum rate or to have that rate set as low as possible. Louise Stitt confided to Margaret Wiesman her frustration at seeing "the work of years gradually crumble." She later added, "I get so discouraged I could scream."[64]

Reformers resisted the spreading assumption that women did not belong in the arena of labor regulation. Mary Dublin accused businessmen of telling reformers to " 'go home to your knitting and leave us free to starve those whom we will.' "[65] But some of the women reformers' own historical strategies, fashioned in the context of gender inequality, contributed to their marginalization once labor regulations covered men. The NCL's early legislative program had been confined to women and children for constitutional and political reasons, not because the league was not interested in men's labor standards. But once the sex-based strategy was adopted, a female-dominated bureaucracy developed to administer those laws, usually in separate women's (or women's and children's) divisions of labor departments. Many state laws required that the enforcement staff include a certain number of women, without offering an explicit rationale for that requirement. The need to enter restrooms and dressing rooms was one practical reason for female staff; it also was often suggested that female workers would be more likely to report violations to female inspectors. This approach made it logical to conclude that if women should regulate female labor, then men should regulate male labor.

The reality was that league women believed that female administrators tended to be better qualified than men to administer all labor standards laws, not just those affecting women. The history of the field meant that there were more experienced women than men in labor standards administration in the late 1930s. Furthermore, older league women still tended to think of women as less partisan and less susceptible than men to corruption by local political machines and employers — despite mounting evidence to the contrary, as opportunities for women in party politics increased. Nonetheless, many league women still believed that women were more eager than men to civilize capitalism, more interested in protecting the interests of the many rather than of the few. Reformers' personal experiences often supported this perception. Lucy Mason was fond of recalling that the president of the Richmond YWCA voted for a child labor amendment on the same day that her husband, who headed the local chamber of commerce, voted against it.[66] Molly Dewson considered the Social Security Act a female achievement: "It's the culmination of what us girls *and some of* you boys have been working for for so long," she told Arthur Altmeyer in 1935. Dewson went to great lengths to ensure that her successor on the Social Security Board would be a woman. (She had to spend much of her political capital with FDR to succeed.)[67] The assumption that women brought a distinctive perspective to the policy arena was not necessarily invalid, but it needed to be explained. Where an ideological "gender gap" existed, it reflected not innate gender difference but different life experiences. The gulf that had divided most women's and men's daily experiences in the late nineteenth century had narrowed by the 1930s and 1940s — in party politics and in the labor force, at least. The league's younger leaders were less likely than the older ones to attribute distinct motives to men and women. By the 1930s even the league's older activists were discreet about their female chauvinism, perhaps sensing that it was built on slippery ground.[68]

Officially, the female reformers of the NCL staked their authority on expertise, not on "women's intuition" or women's alleged sympathetic bond with female and child laborers. The transition to sex-neutral regulation forced NCL women to clarify that it was qualifications, not gender, that mattered in labor department appointments. As Anna Settle told William Burrow, it was not "the sex of the inspector [but] rather what are the capabilities to see that the laws are enforced." When Mary Anderson proposed to demand the "inclusion of women in framing and executing all policies that relate to the utilization of women in war production," the NCL dissented. Elinore Herrick warned that Anderson's course was "extremely dangerous." The league must work to ensure appointments of qualified women *and* men, she stressed. At their annual meeting in 1942, league members resolved that war agencies should recruit not women, necessarily, but "*persons* with accumulated experience and specialized knowledge in dealing with the industrial employment of women."[69]

The NCL tried to defend the niche that existed for women in labor standards administration without confining them to it. Although the league eschewed any demand for female administrators, it insisted that sex-neutral legislation had not obviated the need for women's divisions within labor agencies. NCL activists argued that as long as women bore primary responsibility for child care, and as long as "social attitudes and prejudices" shaped their opportunities, women workers would have "special needs" that could only be addressed by "trained personnel" who were dedicated to raising the "economic, social, and political status of women."[70] In practice, most of those individuals with the training and commitment to staff women's divisions would be female. The league's distinction between qualifications and gender as the hiring criterion was a shrewd one that in theory preserved women's authority to administer programs affecting men. However, the league failed to articulate a specific defense of female bureaucrats' right to employment. Women administrators and their allies stressed the benefits to workers of enforcement by the most experienced staff, but they rarely protested the unfairness of sex bias against female administrators themselves.[71] This omission reflected in part the reluctance of these labor-oriented feminists to use the individualistic language of rights associated with the antilabor National Woman's Party. On the other hand, this failure was a negative legacy of the view that women took administrative positions to serve the cause of social justice, not themselves.

The year 1939 was a discouraging one for advocates of labor standards regulation. As Mary Dublin said at the NCL's annual meeting that year, the league had spent its energies "trying hard not to take steps backward."[72]

The NCL did help prevent the gutting of the FLSA by low-paying, long-hour employers, who otherwise would have succeeded in exempting more unorganized women and minority workers from the law's protection. The league helped forestall curbs on the power of the NLRB as well. Although the Wagner Act ultimately represented a loss of autonomy for the labor movement, initially it was a prerequisite for the movement's growth.[73] But despite these victories for labor, anti–New Dealers won the wider struggle. Rather than achieving minimum wage increases and coverage of agricultural and domestic workers, the NCL had to settle for defending the modest FLSA that passed. Efforts to close the gaps in labor standards regulation were also thwarted by skimpy appropriations and the defeat of new state bills. Under the cover of war, personnel changes at the NLRB reoriented its policy; similar developments were evident in labor standards administration. The Consumers' League had been too optimistic about the ability of progressive unions and experts, both women and men, to maintain control of the state they built. The prospects for American social democracy, which for a tantalizing moment had shone so brightly before league women, were now dimmed. And male supremacism was one weapon in the conservative arsenal.

chapter 9

Always Democracy

The Consumers'
League in the
Post–New Deal
Era

The Great Depression produced changes that aided the NCL program but forced the league itself to operate in a new milieu. By 1939 the Consumers' League found itself in an environment quite different from the one that had given birth to the organization forty years earlier. Tremendous growth in the American government included significant expansion of state and national labor agencies. The Supreme Court's revolution in interpretation of the Constitution had given legal legitimacy to labor unions and to regulation of working conditions and standards. Social movements of ordinary people — workers, the unemployed, women, African Americans — helped produce these changes and also contributed to a realignment of political forces within the major parties. The newly powerful labor movement was more hospitable to female and minority workers than ever before. Although the NCL welcomed these developments (and had contributed to them), the creation of new divisions in the U.S. Department of Labor and the emergence of the CIO meant that the league now shared leadership in the labor standards field. Also, as we have seen, the achievement of national wage-hour regulation for both sexes with the FLSA attracted a new breed of bureaucrats who were not always receptive to NCL policy advice. Moreover, after the federal law passed it was more difficult to mobilize support for state measures. This undercut the strength of league branches, long a source of institutional vitality. The NCL might have fared better in this transition but for World War II. The quest to maximize production not only threatened to gut the fledgling system of wage-hour regulation, it also further eroded the league's influence.

The combination of these changes posed a considerable challenge for the NCL, forcing its leaders to reevaluate their program and tactics. The organization sustained its pursuit of a social democratic vision, resisting the prevailing drift of postwar liberalism. Although the league's ultimate objectives changed little, the process of adapting to new circumstances produced stresses within the organization. Some of these were resolved by a change in leadership. Others were settled when war and, later, the Cold War narrowed the range of political possibility. During and after the war, an escalating frenzy of anticommunism kept the NCL on the defensive and diminished support for the league among the middle-class women who had been its chief constituency. The idea that women brought distinctive values to the task of civilizing capitalism faded gradually, as the prewar league leadership passed from the scene. The league carried on, however, guided by new women with different understandings of their own activism.

A Period of Adjustment

In 1938 and 1939 the NCL seemed rejuvenated, despite the growing strength of its political opposition. Under the forceful leadership of Mary Dublin, the league demonstrated that the Roosevelt administration and the rise of organized labor had not eclipsed its role. The NCL helped to pass the FLSA and then to repel attacks against both that act and the Wagner Act. It played a point position in the uphill battle for state legislation. The league's resistance to anti–New Deal reaction, particularly its defense of the Wagner Act, brought it new admirers and new allies in left-labor circles. Membership levels rebounded modestly, although the league remained in dire financial straits.[1]

Before long, however, internal tensions emerged that would hamper the league's effectiveness in the 1940–42 period. These clashes reflected personality and generational conflicts within the NCL and, more broadly, revealed divergent opinions on what course the league should set in the wake of the FLSA. Meanwhile, the anti-Communist crusade led by the House Un-American Activities Committee (HUAC) posed new challenges for left-liberal groups, the NCL among them.

Mary Dublin (ca. 1938). (National Consumers' League Collection, LC)

Mary Dublin did not tread lightly when she took over as general secretary. Lucy Mason had arrived at the NCL in 1932 from Virginia "feeling too small for the work," awed at the prospect of succeeding the majestic Florence Kelley. If Dublin harbored any such twinges of self-doubt, she did not let them show. In short order she overhauled certain aspects of the organization. The NCL *Bulletin* received a makeover, becoming bolder in design and tone. Dublin developed a new system for membership appeals that tracked response rates from various mailings. She prodded branch secretaries to place higher priority on increasing membership, and she urged them to reach out to younger people. She reviewed the NCL's long roster of council members and vice presidents and replaced inactive officers. When it came to the board of directors, Dublin proceeded with more delicacy, but there too she engineered the removal of people she deemed less useful. By 1941 NCL officers as a group were younger and arguably closer to the Left than in 1933. Dublin told Josephine Roche proudly that these changes were making the league "a real fighting force again."[2]

The response of the league "old guard" to Dublin was mixed. Board member William Davis later claimed that the board had been "extremely well satisfied" with Dublin. "It was not an easy board to work for," he added, as "some of the women were pretty tough. They were experienced women . . . and she didn't have too easy a time always."[3] Indeed, although NCL officers welcomed Dublin's energy, a handful deeply resented her methods. When tension arose between Dublin and her staff at NCL headquarters, Dublin's detractors took the opportunity to challenge her leadership.

Soon after she was hired, Dublin reorganized the NCL office, earning considerable ill will from the staff in the process. She dismissed a full-time bookkeeper, a woman who had been with the league for many years. Long-time employee Mary Ellen Hughes remained on as a secretary. Hughes developed an intense personal dislike of Dublin, and she went out of her way to undermine Dublin's standing with anyone who would listen. One of those who listened was Margaret Wiesman of the Massachusetts league. Others were Helene Gans, executive secretary of the New York branch, and national board member Florence Whitney. Matters came to a head in April 1939, and soon thereafter Hughes was asked to resign (with a "generous salary settlement"). Hughes's dismissal precipitated protests from Wiesman and Gans, but the board stood firmly behind Dublin. Furious, Wiesman lamented to allies throughout the NCL network that the national no longer respected branch secretaries, and Florence Whitney resigned from the board.[4] As an organization dedicated to improving labor standards for women workers, the Consumers' League was sensitive about its treatment of office staff. A few years earlier, NCL members had resigned from Consumers' Research after it treated striking employees unfairly. Dublin's office reorganization does appear to have been impractical and heavy-handed, and Mary Ellen Hughes may have had cause to be angry. On the other hand, independent accounts confirm Dublin's assessment of Hughes as an extremely difficult person whose obstinacy brought office operations almost to a standstill.[5]

At one level, Hughes's dislike of Dublin suggests a generational clash of political styles in women's activism. Hughes was an unmarried woman in her fifties whose prior bosses at the NCL had been older single women. When Mary Dublin became general secretary at the age of twenty-eight, her social life was quite different from that of her predecessors, at least in the eyes of Mary Ellen Hughes. Florence Kelley and Lucy Mason had worked closely with men, but their personal and professional lives centered on like-minded single women. Dublin's social calendar was packed with dance and theater outings with her many "beaux" and a circle of young mixed couples. Like Kelley's and Mason's, Dublin's personal life blended seamlessly into her professional life, because most of her friends were politically active progressives of one stripe or another. But Mary Ellen Hughes did not see this continuity. Complaining that Dublin made personal calls on office time, Hughes insinuated that Dublin's highest goal was to "catch" a powerful man. In 1939 Dublin's work on the Wagner Act led her to Leon Keyserling, who as an aide to Senator Wagner had drafted that legislation. Dublin and Keyserling began a long-distance courtship, apparently under the disapproving eye of Hughes. Dublin's bonds with young CIO men and male social scientists also suggest a step away from the homosocial world of the previous generation of women reformers.[6] Not all of the older NCL women resisted this change; many believed it would be good for the league to become a mixed-sex group. As it turned out, women remained dominant in the league, but among the core activists the balance shifted from single or widowed women toward married women. This affected the league's culture in ways that some may have regretted.[7]

In addition to criticizing Mary Dublin's personal life, Hughes and her sympathizers perceived the new general secretary as excessively ambitious. This was another way in which Dublin departed from the political style of older league activists. Working behind the scenes and refusing to seek personal credit for achievements were hallmarks of the selfless, feminine style of politics of the older generation. These women felt strongly that self-promotion was for men, or perhaps for the individualistic types over at the Woman's Party. To be labeled a "climber" was a harsh insult from the likes of Margaret Wiesman or Molly Dewson. Even league staff members who discounted Mary Ellen Hughes's opinion perceived Dublin as a "high-powered" woman with "her own agenda," one that included associating with people who would "help her get ahead." Dublin's reports to the NCL board were not modest in tone. The ritualistic self-deprecation that many of the older women used was nowhere in evidence with Dublin. Margaret Wiesman spitefully accused Dublin of seeking "Mrs. Kelley's mantle falling around her horrid shoulders."[8] Despite Dublin's evidently abrasive style, most league activists appreciated Dublin's political engagement and her flair as a speaker and writer. But a few believed their organization was being taken over by someone with a high opinion of herself and insufficient appreciation of older activists.

The dust was still settling from the Hughes upheaval when Mary Dublin found herself embroiled in another internal controversy. When she tried to mobilize various New York groups behind a state wage-hour bill, some New York branch officers accused her of trespassing on their turf. The branch had decided to hold off on the bill until political conditions were more opportune. Dublin may have known this and decided to bypass the state branch. On the other hand, some evidence suggests that a New York league official deliberately created a misunderstanding to make trouble for Dublin. This incident precipitated debate over the relative jurisdictions of the national and branch leagues. The outcome was general agreement that "cooperation and good relationships should be set higher than any other value." Cooler heads at the national level and in the New York branch urged Dublin to proceed with greater tact, but they also seemed weary of the backbiting by her detractors.[9]

The tensions that emerged under Dublin's leadership reflected more than these generational and personality clashes, however. Underpinning the dissatisfaction of Margaret Wiesman and a few others was disagreement about the NCL's direction on several fundamental issues facing the organization in the late 1930s. These included the relationship between the NCL, the ascendant CIO, and the Left; the boundaries of the league program now that the FLSA had passed; and the balance between national and state-level initiatives.

League Alliances in the Era of the CIO and the Popular Front

One of the less obvious costs of the rivalry between the AFL and the CIO was its divisive impact among labor allies. The Women's Trade Union League, for example, was crippled by its older leaders' refusal to embrace the CIO. Rose Schneiderman was captive to AFL threats to cut off funds to any WTUL branch that accepted CIO workers as members. At a moment when most of the women streaming into unions were joining the CIO, the WTUL's waffling cost it the support of a new generation of female trade unionists.[10] By contrast, most NCL activists barely concealed their preference for the CIO, despite their official stance of impartiality. Lucy Mason cooperated with the NCL from her position at the CIO, and James Carey of the CIO was on the NCL board. Because the NCL was not financially dependent on unions, it had more autonomy than the WTUL, although the need to rally both AFL and CIO support for league bills required much tact.[11]

AFL leaders routinely charged that the CIO was Communist-dominated, and in this way the labor movement split contributed to a hardening of ideological distinctions among labor sympathizers. The NCL was not immune to the resulting bitterness and name-calling. Over the years, some league women had built good relationships with local Federation of Labor men. It probably was no coincidence that some of these women were the people who clashed with Mary Dublin. Dublin had brought Carey onto the board, and she was friendly with CIO general counsel Lee Pressman. Margaret Wiesman, fuming over Dublin's intrusion into the New York branch's territory, suggested that "Lee Pressman is back of it all and Mary is just a little errand girl." Perhaps Wiesman got wind of the fact that Pressman had joined the Communist Party in 1934, or perhaps it was some other association that led her to speculate snidely that Dublin was one of the "inner circle" of the Communist Party.[12] Board member Florence Whitney later went so far as to allege that Dublin fired the NCL office staff in order to bring in her Communist friends. Other board members dismissed this as the irresponsible accusation of a disgruntled and ill-informed individual.[13] Less far-fetched was Wiesman's claim that Dublin pressured league staffer Mary Ellen Hughes to join the United Office and Professional Workers (UOPWA), a left-led CIO union. Wiesman also resented Dublin's association with the League of Women Shoppers, which, like UOPWA, she disparaged as run by "left wingers." Publicly, Wiesman herself cooperated with both the League of Women Shoppers and UOPWA, and she was no anti-Communist crusader. Her fundamental complaint was that these groups (allegedly) stole credit for Massachusetts Consumers' League achievements. Nonetheless, that Wiesman expressed her resentment in anti-Communist terms hints at some of the rivalries and tensions that were created within progressive organizations by the growth of the Left.[14]

In the 1930s the NCL cooperated with many radical groups, some of which later were labeled "Communist front" organizations. In 1935 the Communist Party abandoned its earlier sectarianism and joined with liberals and with other radicals to form a "Popular Front" against fascism. Many league leaders were among those who, alarmed by developments in Germany, Spain, and Italy, rallied to the antifascist cause. The American Communist Party (CP) also impressed progressives with its success in organizing for certain CIO unions, and especially with its effective unionization of women and African Americans. Actual CP membership remained small, but the number of people working alongside party members in pursuit of shared objectives swelled.[15] Like the NCL, the CP opposed amending the Wagner Act, opposed the Equal Rights Amendment, and called for repealing poll taxes. Left-led CIO unions such as UOPWA and the United Electrical Workers joined the garment and textile unions as important supporters of wage and hour bills. The NCL's cooperation with all who endorsed its program brought it into contact with the League of Women Shoppers, the American Student Union, the American Labor Party, and the Southern Conference for Human Welfare, all organizations with some Communist members.

Mary Dublin actively forged NCL alliances with these Popular Front groups. Almost certainly never a card-carrying Communist, Dublin is best characterized as an independent leftist in the 1930s. A person who thrived on intellectual debate, Dublin cultivated a circle that cut across the spectrum of progressives, socialists (many of whom were highly critical of Communists), and Communists.[16] In addition to working with the moderate socialists of the League for Industrial Democracy, Dublin participated in labor-oriented groups with leading women of the Left. These included the Institute of Labor Studies, a project started by Dorothy Douglas and Katharine Lumpkin,[17] and the New York League of Women Shoppers, of which Dublin was an officer before she came to the NCL. Formed in 1935 to investigate strikes and organize support for strikers, the League of Women Shoppers (LWS) played a role that NCL leaders initially believed was complementary to their own. Prominent radicals like Josephine Herbst, Lillian Hellman, Jessie Lloyd O'Connor, and Mary Van Kleeck sponsored the LWS, along with progressives like Frieda Miller and Irene Osgood Andrews. Dublin was not the only link between the NCL and the LWS, as there was much overlap between the organizations' New York branches, but she was an important bridge between the Consumers' League and such Popular Front groups.[18]

Other contact between Dublin and the Left came through her older sister Elizabeth, who married a Communist sympathizer named George Marshall. An editor of *Soviet Russia Today*, Marshall defended Stalin after many American radicals had been alienated from the Communist Party by the Moscow "show trials" of 1936–38. It may have been a result of Marshall's influence that in early 1937, before the full story of Stalin's purges was known in the United States, Dublin signed what became a well-known document, "An Open Letter to American Liberals." The letter accused John Dewey's Committee for the Defense of Leon Trotsky, formed to investigate the Moscow trials, of trying to discredit the Soviet government. Printed in *Soviet Russia Today*, the letter was signed by many progressives and Communists.[19] Over the next few years, Dublin lent her name to several groups, most of them antifascist coalitions, that the House Un-American Activities Committee later identified as Communist fronts. These associations became the basis for later charges by Senator Joseph McCarthy that Dublin had been a Communist. Dublin was cleared of this accusation, but only after extended proceedings that exacted a heavy personal and professional toll.[20]

Well before McCarthy's ascendancy, a rising tide of anticommunism put pressure on reformers to identify and disassociate themselves from Communists and any who might be sympathetic to Communists. In 1938 Frances Perkins's resistance to the deportation of Harry Bridges, the reportedly Communist organizer of California longshoremen, triggered a congressional campaign to impeach her. Although unsuccessful, the proceedings kept Perkins on the defensive and damaged the DOL.[21] Communist-hunting activity intensified after the Nazi-Soviet pact of August 1939. At about the same time that the Smith Committee was insinuating that female NLRB attorneys were Communists, HUAC became fascinated with consumer groups. In December 1939 HUAC released a report charging that the Consumers' National Federation, of which the NCL was a member, was a "clearinghouse for communist-dominated consumers' organizations." The report accused these groups of using the "'Trojan horse' technique of undermining confidence in capitalism."[22] Despite immediate protests from Eleanor Roosevelt and two dissenting HUAC members, the rumor of association between communism and consumer groups spread quickly. One syndicated column warned against "false face outfits" that were luring in members on the pretense of comparing prices but were actually "communistic outfits" intent on forcing small businesses to hire black workers. The writer alleged that the New York Consumers' League marched on retailers and threatened to slander merchants' goods and prices unless they hired the "correct racial mixture."[23] The well-organized attack on the consumer movement indicates that conservatives felt threatened by its strength and political orientation. Although the NCL brushed the accusations aside as the hot air of reactionaries, the charges had a chilling effect on the wider consumer movement.

The NCL maintained a civil libertarian stance in the face of red-baiting, but in internal discussions league officials began to draw some boundaries in order to resist closer affiliation with Communists. The NCL's once warm relations with the League of Women Shoppers cooled noticeably. In the mid-1930s the New York branches of the LWS and the Consumers' League had shared officers and cosponsored functions. By 1939 some league activists were complaining that the LWS was creating confusion, treading on NCL turf, and using the NCL name without permission. By then, many of the LWS's original officers had departed, increasing the influence of Communists in the organization. In late 1940 the NCL board rejected a proposal to merge the NCL and LWS, concluding that "differences in approach and thinking" made the merger "unfeasible and undesirable."[24] Similarly, in late 1939 the league council rejected a suggestion to recruit members from the American Student Union, concluding that it was "necessary to distinguish between radical democracy and Communism."[25] This wording suggests that the league's resistance to communism reflected the perspective of the growing anti-Stalinist Left as much as the impact of right-wing anticommunism.

Despite their own reservations about the Communist Party, NCL leaders deplored the "smear tactics" used by HUAC, also known as the Dies Committee (for Congressman Martin Dies of Texas). Josephine Roche and Josephine Goldmark observed that "nine-tenths of the charges are utterly without foundation," but "the denials get buried in the fine print and cannot reverse the damage done." At its December 1939 annual meeting, the league passed a resolution against the methods of the Dies Committee. Thereafter the NCL lobbied to ax Dies Committee appropriations.[26] Many league leaders adopted the position that Lucy Mason enunciated in 1942: "I personally happen to dislike Communists['] tactics. But I cannot see myself saying I will never cooperate with a Communist for a good cause and by good, legitimate means." For the most part, the league sustained this posture through the height of the McCarthyite "red scare" in the 1950s. A few league activists became vocal critics of the Communist Party, but most reserved their harshest criticism for the anti-Communist crusade.[27] Furthermore, the NCL refused to dilute its pro-labor agenda.[28]

The upsurge in left-wing activism in the 1930s energized the NCL and stimulated coalitions that were vital to the league's lobbying successes. The entrance of audacious young groups into labor standards politics required some adjustment, as the sniping by a few territorial league veterans demonstrates.[29] At the same time, left-liberal cooperation enabled Communist hunters to paint the entire labor reform agenda in hues of red. Red-baiting forced reform groups to expend precious resources in self-defense, and it no doubt exacerbated the NCL's membership recruiting difficulties. Between communism and anticommunism lay a range of political positions, but the Cold War era would be characterized by dualistic, "either-or" thinking that obliterated such nuances.

Defining the NCL Program in the Wake of the FLSA

The achievement of national wage-hour regulation in the FLSA of 1938 posed questions that were yet another source of disagreement among league leaders. One issue was the extent to which the FLSA and other changes had obviated the need for the league's sex-based strategy. Another question concerned the NCL's programmatic priorities. Should it devote itself to filling in the gaps in wage-hour policy, while continuing to offer secondary support to other social democratic causes? Or should the league set its sights on a new goal?

The NCL welcomed the FLSA's validation of wage-hour regulation for men and was key in developing the new sex-neutral state bill, as we have seen. Nonetheless, how to prevent the transition to sex-neutral policy from lowering hard-won labor standards for women was a recurring theme in league meetings. One worry was that existing state laws for women would be endangered in the process of extending them to men. In the political climate of 1939, this was not an unreasonable concern; once a law was opened to amendment, opponents often seized the opportunity to gut the measure. Moreover, until 1941 the constitutionality of regulating men's labor standards remained in question. Furthermore, some state Federations of Labor remained ambivalent toward men's inclusion in wage-hour laws. Even where they did not oppose such bills, lack of active union support made victory over employer forces difficult. Although the AFL and CIO now supported national wage-hour standards, it took much prodding by the NCL and the Division of Labor Standards to convince them that supplementary state laws remained a high priority.[30]

The grim political outlook for new state wage and hour laws, especially ones that included men, made some members of the NCL network nervous about adopting a sex-neutral strategy at the state level. They favored sex-neutral laws in principle, but they wanted to proceed cautiously. Margaret Wiesman of the Massachusetts league, Jeanette Studley of the Connecticut league, Elisabeth Christman of the WTUL, and the U.S. Women's Bureau were the chief proponents of this defensive posture. Christman spoke most forcefully of all for "staying away from minimum wages for men" so as not to endanger women's laws. Frustrated by years of setbacks in the courts and in legislatures, these activists focused on defending the protections they had worked so hard to get for women.[31] Their view reflected some inflexibility in the face of new circumstances. However, it was rooted in feminist concern for women wage earners, who as a group were still lower paid and less organized than men. In some states that had enacted laws for women before the FLSA, women's labor standards indeed were declining, either de jure or, as enforcement resources contracted, de facto. Also, women in intrastate occupations (unregulated by the FLSA) remained among the most exploited workers, so the temptation was strong to prioritize coverage for them over coverage for men.

Mary Dublin and Clara Beyer spoke for those who saw this question a bit differently. Whereas the first group recommended testing the waters carefully in each state to determine whether to use the new model bill or the older women-only one, Dublin and Beyer argued that the moment called for plunging ahead with the sex-neutral bill in as many states as possible. Dublin told Wiesman she was not "inclined to subscribe to these fears" of AFL opposition and weakening amendments.[32] Dublin requested Beyer to make the case at the league's annual meeting in December 1939. Beyer declared that "lack of unified support," and not just employer opposition, explained why the new model bill had been defeated in thirty states. Beyer reminded league activists that Florence Kelley "never told us to stand still and wait for the Supreme Court to act or to be fearful of this and of that. She would move forward with her program no matter what the odds." Both the labor movement and the courts were coming to favor regulating men's labor standards, Beyer argued. Bills could be drafted in ways that would safeguard women's standards. In sum, the best way to hold onto past gains was to press forward.[33]

Dublin told Beyer gratefully, "You hit every single point . . . with the resounding bang that is so badly needed." Several of the ambivalent branch leaders had been persuaded.[34] The league pressed ahead in the states, while reiterating stern reminders that "every precaution must be taken to safeguard existing, sound state wage and hour legislation." The NCL recommended that instead of amending women's laws to include men, the sex-neutral bill should be passed on top of existing laws. In states without preexisting laws, new bills should be worded with a "separability" clause, so that if the act were invalidated for men it would stand for women. The NCL discouraged separate new bills for men and women, because separate laws facilitated setting lower wage rates for women.[35]

The differences between these two perspectives should not be exaggerated. They were short-lived, and all these activists favored a transition to sex-neutral legislation. The disagreement was over how quickly the NCL should push for that transition. The conflict reflected different readings of the political possibilities of the moment, rather than different views about women workers. As the wall of opposition thickened against new state labor regulation of any kind, the NCL's compromise strategy effectively addressed the concerns of both perspectives.

Even the NCL's most enthusiastic advocates of a sweeping campaign for sex-neutral state bills did not embrace the Equal Rights Amendment. Because passing male-inclusive state legislation proved to be such a slow process, the NCL did not want the existing body of women-only laws to be swept away by an ERA. For women in non-FLSA occupations, existing state laws were the only legal protection against extremely low wages and long hours. To claim that the FLSA should have settled the conflict between the NCL and the Woman's Party is to fail to appreciate the limits of the FLSA.[36] After the Supreme Court sustained the FLSA in 1941, one league activist after another stopped backing new women-only bills. Growing numbers of female trade unionists wondered whether sex-based laws, especially hours laws, now were hurting women more than helping them. In 1951 the Consumers' League of New York would lobby to repeal night work restrictions that applied to women alone — the very restrictions that it had helped pass several decades earlier.[37] But with conservatives blocking the extension of sex-neutral laws, the league saw no reason to rush toward eliminating (with an ERA) what meager protections were on the books.

Furthermore, the Woman's Party history of alliances with antilabor and anti–civil rights forces gave the ERA a reactionary flavor that inhibited support from labor feminists.

The NWP's antilabor tendencies had become more pronounced over the course of the 1930s. The Woman's Party cooperated with employers in Georgia in 1931 and in minimum wage test cases in Ohio and New York.[38] The NWP also failed to deliver on its proclaimed support of sex-neutral laws. Although the NWP has been credited with introducing a sex-neutral minimum wage bill in New York in 1933, one party leader confided that her group "had nothing to do" with the bill and only made a gesture of support because "we were forced into a position . . . where we had to take a stand."[39] In 1938 the Woman's Party declined to back the FLSA, as we have seen. The NCL's exasperation multiplied a thousandfold in 1939 when some ERA supporters opposed *sex-neutral* league bills. They claimed that under equal minimum wage rates, women would be fired and replaced with men. Mary Dublin responded indignantly, "You can't have it both ways." There were three choices: no minimum wage laws, laws for women only, or laws for both sexes. The NCL could not tolerate the first, and it now seemed the NWP opposed both of the latter options, the second because men theoretically could underbid women's minimum rate, and the third because women would no longer be able to underbid men.[40]

In addition to deliberating over the sex-based strategy, league leaders debated the merits of changing the NCL program in the wake of the FLSA. Although Mary Dublin acknowledged the limits of the FLSA and the gaps in state coverage, she believed it was time for the NCL to broaden its agenda. Specifically, she urged the league to spearhead a campaign for national health insurance. Dublin's long-standing interest in health policy was shared by the league's new president, Josephine Roche, who had chaired FDR's Interdepartmental Committee on Health and Welfare Activities from 1936 to 1939. Dublin and Roche argued that health insurance was a natural extension of the NCL's traditional program. As the league already was on record in support of national health insurance, the issue was not the desirability of such a policy but rather the NCL's place in the fight for it. Dublin made a compelling case that leading a national campaign would keep the NCL on the cutting edge of social advocacy, in the tradition of Florence Kelley. But other board members worried about stretching the league too thin. William Davis argued that the league faced a period in which its role would be "digestion" rather than pioneering. The league's vital, if unglamorous, task was to make sure that the new legal standards were translated into reality for workers. Particularly with the prospect of war, which could be expected to threaten labor standards, the league had to be careful not to overdiversify its agenda. Beulah Amidon and Florina Lasker agreed with Davis, reminding the board that it had already agreed to make state work its priority for 1940. Accordingly, the NCL passed up the opportunity to be the lead organization on national health insurance.[41] A disappointed Mary Dublin expressed impatience with what she perceived as narrow vision on the part of the NCL board. Dublin complained to *Survey* editor Paul Kellogg that "so many of those who worked with Mrs. Kelley have understand[ably] enough grown a little weary, and fail to see as you do that the old tradition must each year be renewed in new terms to meet new situations."[42]

Mary Dublin had difficulty understanding the enduring dedication of many league activists to state-level activity. In fact, the league had good reason to be concerned about the FLSA's impact on its program in the states. Historically, league branches counted on the national organization for assistance in everything from formulating policy to coordinating between states to boosting morale. Many league leaders perceived the national office as insufficiently attentive to the state branches under Dublin's leadership. The tension between national and state activities predated Dublin, but it became more pronounced while she was general secretary, reflecting passage of the FLSA as well as Dublin's priorities. In response to the grumbling, Dublin arranged to have more contact with branch secretaries. She addressed local league luncheons, and she assisted the New Jersey league's almost successful fight for a state wage-hour bill in 1939. However, Dublin never made long speaking tours in the states as Kelley and Mason had done. Wiesman uncharitably attributed Dublin's focus on federal policy to her quest for national prominence. Be that as it may, Dublin's national orientation reflected her coming of political age at a time when sweeping changes emanated from Washington. She shared the NCL vision of an integrated national-state system of wage-hour regulation, but she had not participated in the arduous process of building grassroots support that eventually made the FLSA possible. Older leaders' concern for the health of local branches reflected more than institutional self-interest. They worried that without cultivation in the states, the whole regulatory edifice would become an empty shell. Dublin — who had experienced neither the local campaigns that were a feature of earlier women's activism nor the setbacks during the reactionary 1920s — was too quick to see these older leaders as cautious and unimaginative.[43]

The NCL's post–New Deal struggle to balance national and state priorities, and to define its relationship to the government more generally, came to the fore in 1940. In June, Mary Dublin proposed that the league relocate its headquarters from New York City to Washington, D.C. Dublin already spent much time in the capital, and, she claimed, many people had told her the NCL now belonged there. The board was still deliberating on the move several months later when Dublin announced her engagement to Leon Keyserling. As she would now be moving to Washington in any case, the league would lose her services if it did not relocate. The NCL board at first recommended making the move on a one-year trial basis, but some league veterans began to express reservations about basing the NCL in Washington (no doubt colored by annoyance with the way Dublin had proceeded). As it became clear that the headquarters would remain in New York, Dublin resigned.[44]

Those who opposed relocating to Washington feared that it would be "a mistake for the league to get too closely associated with government officials," and that the league "mustn't lose its independent point of view from government." Even those members with strong Democratic Party ties or government offices wanted to protect the NCL's nonpartisan, independent position. Furthermore, they argued, a move to Washington would reinforce an unhealthy trend away from the state level. Elizabeth Brandeis wrote from Wisconsin that there were plenty of organizations in Washington already. In her view — perhaps influenced by her father's belief that the states should serve as "the laboratories of democracy" — the national league's most important function was to help the branches cultivate state laws and improve their administration. Brandeis added that she had been ready to quit the league over its inattention to the state level.[45]

Dublin's resignation, followed by the U.S. entry into the Second World War, disrupted the operations of the national league. The search for a new general secretary was not easy. Finding someone with the requisite stature, expertise, and political perspective had become more difficult, thanks to competition from labor groups, political parties, and government agencies. In the 1940s, although gender barriers remained, talented, educated women had wider career opportunities than they did when Florence Kelley made the Consumers' League her vehicle for activism. After much deliberation and without great enthusiasm, the NCL chose an Ohio woman, Warwick Hobart of the Cincinnati league, as Dublin's successor. When Hobart left after only a year to take a war-related government job, some league officers wondered whether the organization should throw in the towel. This idea was abandoned after letters poured in urging the NCL to carry on.[46]

League activists heaved a collective sigh of relief when the popular Elizabeth Magee, Ohio league mainstay, agreed in late 1942 to take over as general secretary, on the condition that the national office be moved to Cleveland. Those who had been unwilling to have the league's headquarters in Washington were happy enough to see it in the "American Ruhr."

Magee was an unmarried woman in her early fifties whose experience included work as a YWCA industrial secretary in Detroit and New York. She earned a master's degree in economics from Columbia for her thesis, "Class Consciousness among Women in Industry in the United States." An expert on unemployment insurance as well as labor standards, Magee had been the linchpin of the Ohio branch since 1925. She seems to have enjoyed the unqualified admiration of the entire league leadership, and she would preside as general secretary until 1958.[47]

Magee bridged some of the fissures that had appeared during Mary Dublin's years with the league. As a longtime branch leader, Magee placed a high priority on state-level activity, but through her work on unemployment insurance she also had developed national connections and perspective. Unmarried herself, and a product of the female reform culture of the YWCA, Magee nonetheless sought to bring men into the league leadership. Although she did not cultivate the alliances on the Left that Mary Dublin had, Magee eschewed red-baiting. On the sex-based question, Magee embodied the league's flexible, pragmatic approach, preferring sex-neutral laws but backing women-only measures when the alternative was no legislation at all. Finally, although the labor standards of female workers were her first concern, Magee keenly appreciated that wage-hour regulation was but one piece of a larger social democratic program for empowering wage earners.[48]

Beyond the Second World War

Under Magee's leadership, the NCL sustained the critique of gender- and race-based forms of labor exploitation that had become one of its trademarks in the 1930s. The league continued to argue that because of gender inequality, women workers had "special needs" that necessitated women's divisions in labor agencies, as well as sex-based laws where sex-neutral ones did not exist. At the same time, the NCL opposed policies that treated women as a secondary labor force and that assumed female economic dependence on men. For example, league representatives protested the reasoning advanced by conservatives that no minimum wage increase was needed since most workers at the minimum were women who lived at home for "free" (i.e., with parents or husbands). The NCL called for equal pay measures, not just for "equal" work but for "comparable" work. League leaders advocated better child care facilities, as well as better housing and health programs for the millions of migrants to defense plant communities. The league also documented the especially poor conditions for black migrant labor. The controversial Fair Employment Practices

Committee, created in 1941 in response to black pressure, received the NCL's full backing. And, disgusted by the race-based internment of Japanese Americans, the NCL hired a Japanese American woman as its membership secretary in 1943.[49]

The league also worked with other women's groups to make the wartime opportunities for women in the high-paying manufacturing sector permanent, an effort that was ultimately unsuccessful. Anticipating the competition for jobs that peacetime reconversion would bring, the league promoted training programs to give women skills they could use in the postwar economy. In 1944 the NCL crossed the fault line over the ERA issue to support a Business and Professional Women's Club plank against sex discrimination in postwar employment, proclaiming that hiring and promotion decisions should be made on the basis of merit, not sex. But as men returned from their wartime service, women were fired en masse, regardless of skills or seniority. Even after the economy recovered from reconversion, and employment opportunities began to expand again, women who had been recruited aggressively during the war were told that the jobs they wanted were not for women, no matter how skilled. By 1946 the NCL was lamenting women's displacement back into the lowest-paid sectors. "Rosie the riveter" did not "return to the home" as often as she returned to the service, clerical, and other low-paying jobs she had held before the war.[50] This unhappy development meant that as before, wage-hour policy was of special importance to women workers.

And despite the concentrated efforts of reformers and unions, southern workers continued to labor under lower standards than workers in other regions. Lucy Mason's successors lacked her devotion to and entrée into the South, but the Consumers' League did what it could to nurture labor reform there. Lois MacDonald and Louise Leonard McLaren of the Southern Summer School for Workers joined the NCL board. The national league sent delegates to the Southern Conference for Human Welfare, the interracial left-liberal group that tried to generate public support for the CIO in the South. The NCL lobbied for a permanent version of the Fair Employment Practices Committee, a group loathed by conservative southern whites, not least because it employed black and Mexican American administrators.[51] Southern resistance to "outsiders" persisted as an obstacle to NCL work in the region. When Elizabeth Magee offered to back a minimum wage campaign in Virginia in 1950, she was told that "any known help from 'across the Potomac' is a red rag" that would stir the bull of opposition. With its resources stretched thin after the war, and abundant challenges closer to home, the NCL could do little more than supply advice and encouragement to southern activists.[52]

During and after the war, the league continued to insist that broad social programs and regulatory policies were necessary to mitigate basic tendencies of the capitalist system. In addition to advocating higher labor standards, the NCL lobbied to extend wartime price control measures and to establish a full employment policy. The league endorsed a controversial report on postwar planning, *Security, Work, and Relief Policies*, issued by the National Resources Planning Board in 1943. The report proposed a sweeping expansion of the social insurance and social provision systems, in addition to permanent public works programs. This document became a "programmatic bible" for liberals and a lightning rod for the ire of conservatives, who promptly dismantled the agency. Columbia economist Eveline Burns, a leader of the New York Consumers' League, was the research director and "driving force behind" the 1943 report (indeed, NRPB critics directed much of their wrath at her). The league also continued to support the National Labor Relations Board, although without the passion it had shown in 1939 when the NLRB was more supportive of rank-and-file activism. In 1947 the NCL was one of several nonlabor organizations that coordinated an unsuccessful campaign against the Taft-Hartley bill, which weakened union rights.[53] At a juncture when some liberals were muting their critique of capitalism and emphasizing growth through fiscal stimulation, the NCL still advocated a large planning and regulatory role for the government. Because league leaders envisioned that labor and consumer movements would wield real power in policy making and administration, they showed little concern that a larger role for the state might lead to totalitarianism. "I am *agin* the thing that Russia has produced," Lucy Mason mused in a 1951 letter to Molly Dewson from her apartment in Atlanta. "My philosophy is mostly for a mixed economy — room for private enterprise, considerable government action, more in the way of cooperatives — and always Democracy, of, by and for the people."[54]

League women's adherence to this vision was out of step with the times. The postwar decades saw the Consumers' League struggling to replace a dwindling corps of activists. The national office's files of correspondence with branches bulged again during Magee's fifteen-year tenure. However, as aging state leaders died, so did the branches. In 1950 the league was down to eight branches, and by 1962 only the New Jersey and Ohio leagues remained.[55] The waning of league branches and a dearth of progress in state wage-hour legislation were mutually reinforcing. In 1953 twenty-six states, the District of Columbia, and three territories had minimum wage laws — about the same number as in 1940. (In five states — Connecticut, Massachusetts, New Hampshire, Rhode Island, and New York — minimum wage laws had been extended to men. That these were states where

"She Planned for the Future" was the caption of this 1943 photograph of Eveline Burns. Burns first became an activist when she was recruited to the leadership of the Consumers' League of New York in the 1920s, and she remained an active officer for many years, serving as New York league president in the late 1940s and 1950s. (ACME photograph, New York World-Telegram and Sun collection, LC)

the league first had passed laws for women suggests the effectiveness of the "entering wedge" strategy.)[56] Not until the mid-1960s was progress made on a scale that approached the 1930s record. By 1967 forty jurisdictions had minimum wage laws, of which twenty-eight covered both men and women. Southern workers still had less protection under state laws than workers elsewhere.[57]

NCL leaders searched for ways to attract new members. A proposal to merge with the American Association for Social Security fizzled out. A publicity specialist recommended asking famous members to promote the league, people like southern radical Lillian Smith, a new member, and the Hollywood politicos Melvyn and Helen Gahagan Douglas. Through her column "My Day," Eleanor Roosevelt urged women around the country to join their local league or to start one.[58] But the results were discouraging. The intensifying Cold War strangled political dialogue on labor questions, and social justice campaigns were readily tainted with the charge of subversion.[59]

The Cold War furthered a decline in support for the NCL from its largest traditional constituency, women's voluntary associations. The base of middle-class women willing to endorse labor reform had contracted in the interwar decades, and now it shrank away almost to nothing. In 1947 the head of the Connecticut league reported grimly that women's groups were less interested in labor and the problems of working women than at any time in her fifteen years in the state.[60] Similarly bleak news came in from Virginia. The state League of Women Voters had grown "*very* anti-labor." The Council of Jewish Women would not go on record in favor of minimum wage measures, although some members were supportive. Lucy Mason's old friend Adele Clark, together with state YWCA, NAACP, and CIO officials, was still on the job in Virginia, but with little hope for the near future. Around the nation, organizations that relied on support from progressive women were forced to close their doors. In 1950 both the Southern Summer School for Workers and the National Women's Trade Union League disbanded. (The American Association for Labor Legislation had folded in 1944.)[61]

The Consumers' League survived, but it came to depend on substantial grants from organized labor (and, later, from foundations), rather than on many small contributions from women around the nation. In postwar funding pitches to unions, the league stressed the need to close gaps in state legislation, broaden and raise FLSA standards, and expand the social security program. Elizabeth Magee used the example of Michigan, which had poor regulations even though it was home to the United Auto Workers, to persuade labor leaders that they needed allies like the NCL. Dozens of civic and church groups depended on the league for signals about labor laws, she claimed, and if kept advised, "these potentially powerful groups will often initiate considerable grassroots activity." The NCL also solicited union backing for a campaign to extend labor and welfare protections to migrant agricultural workers; this drive became the league's major new initiative in the postwar period. Many labor groups answered the league's call. The best responses came from unions with large numbers of women workers and unions threatened by unorganized competition. Fittingly, in 1961 John Edelman of the Textile Workers became chairman of the NCL board.[62] In the postwar period, the NCL increasingly acted as the nonlabor lobbying adjunct to the labor movement. This was a subtle but definite shift from its earlier role as the labor arm of a women's movement.

Despite the fight that some officers had put up in 1940, the league eventually became more Washington-centered. Operating with a smaller direct constituency, the NCL influenced postwar labor standards policy primarily by lobbying in Washington. Thanks in part to league efforts, Congress gradually strengthened the FLSA, although these gains were neither spectacular nor irreversible. In 1945, at the request of the Textile Workers

Union, the league spearheaded a nonlabor coalition for the Pepper-Hook bill, which proposed an increase in the hourly minimum wage from forty to sixty-five cents, as well as protection for more workers in food processing. The bill was defeated.[63] In 1949 the FLSA minimum wage was raised to seventy-five cents per hour, but employer interests narrowed the law's coverage. A 1955 drive for a $1.25 minimum, a thirty-five-hour week, and broader coverage achieved only a modest increase to a $1 minimum. However, in 1961 the rate increased to $1.25 an hour, and 3.6 million additional workers were covered. In 1966 the FLSA was extended to agricultural workers at last, and the rate was increased again. In every round, the NCL was at the forefront of the legislative struggle. In the 1970s and 1980s the league continued to advocate a stronger FLSA, often represented before Congress by none other than Mary Dublin Keyserling.[64]

In the postwar years the NCL's identification as a female-led organization concerned above all with female workers gradually became less overt, continuing a shift that began in the 1930s. The league never hired a male general secretary, and it kept up the fight against the Equal Rights Amendment. Not until 1969, when the Equal Employment Opportunity Commission (EEOC) ruled that women-only laws violated Title VII of the 1964 Civil Rights Act, was the sex-based strategy for developing wage-hour regulation put to rest.[65] In the interim, NCL leaders argued that the feminist objectives of the ERA could be achieved at lower risk by bringing test cases on specific sex discrimination issues under the Fifth and Fourteenth Amendments.[66] In the 1970s and early 1980s, however, the ERA conflict took on new meanings. After the EEOC ruling, the NCL and most labor unions dropped their opposition to the ERA. Meanwhile, melding economic and social conservatism, Phyllis Schlafly's "Stop ERA" campaign lashed out at the growing women's movement. Ironically, although the Communist and Socialist Parties had opposed the ERA for decades, Schlafly labeled the amendment a step toward communism.[67] As the New Right attacked it, the ERA lost its antilabor connotations and gained support among feminists whose social analysis was more progressive than that of the National Woman's Party. Mary Dublin Keyserling did an about-face in the early 1970s, conceding that the courts were moving too slowly to eliminate specific discriminations. Before long she was leading a coalition *for* the ERA. This did not strike her as inconsistent. The chief factors underpinning the NCL's historical opposition to the ERA—court hostility to regulation of men's labor standards, union voluntarism, and sex discrimination by unions and employers—no longer applied with their earlier force. Workplace discrimination persisted, but equal pay and civil rights legislation had given women some tools for eliminating it.[68]

An ongoing task that took more league energy in the postwar decades was defending appropriations for national and state labor departments. Government labor agencies in many respects represented the institutionalization of services previously provided by female reformers. By transferring their functions to the government, these women expanded state "administrative capacity." Gathering and disseminating data, drafting bills, inspecting workplaces, and training inspectors, tasks once undertaken voluntarily by NCL activists, now were largely the responsibility of various government bureaus. Under Frances Perkins, the U.S. Department of Labor began organizing labor policy conferences that eventually overshadowed the conferences of activists, bureaucrats, and trade unionists that had been a league trademark.[69] More than any other agency, the U.S. Division of Labor Standards overlapped with the NCL. DLS and league officials reassured each other that the field offered sufficient scope for both organizations, and that activism by voluntary associations remained essential to protecting workers. This was true, but the creation of government labor standards agencies changed the NCL's role. This shift was not apparent during the 1930s, when NCL members held positions in the new bureaucracies and the league wielded substantial behind-the-scenes influence. After a time, however, the DLS and other agencies no longer depended on the expertise and contacts of the voluntary associations that had helped create them, which meant that the league necessarily surrendered some initiative. With government bodies doing much of the research, drafting, and enforcement, the NCL spent more time lobbying lawmakers, often in defense of labor department budgets.[70] This form of civic participation was less likely to arouse grassroots enthusiasm than the league's earlier, broader range of activities had. The NCL's state-building success thus compounded its difficulties in sustaining membership, requiring the league to adapt its methods and seek new issues.

Until about 1960, NCL leaders resisted the pressures to redefine their program that had been building since the New Deal. During the Second World War, the NCL voted to call itself the "National Consumers' League for Fair Labor Standards." This was an attempt to end the confusion caused by the league's name and to settle recurring debates over whether to take up the banner of consumer advocacy.[71] However, as public interest in (or willingness to openly endorse) wage-hour regulation dwindled, league leaders reconsidered. One league committee concluded that labor law administration was a "dull subject" that did not attract young people; it was time to envision a program that reflected the pioneering spirit of Florence Kelley. In the early 1960s the NCL began to "investigate, agitate, and legislate" in the field of consumer protection. The league's efforts included publicizing fraudulent services and hazardous products, and protesting poor administration of consumer protection agencies.[72]

The NCL's embrace of consumer rights did not mean that it had abandoned its traditional agenda. To the contrary, the league tackled consumer problems expressly to attract new members who might be won over to labor's cause.[73] In a consumption-oriented, often antilabor climate, this was an inventive way of publicizing labor issues. However, the tactic did not regenerate league membership to the extent the board had hoped. The NCL did not again become the preeminent vehicle for social justice activists that it had been earlier. In 1970 NCL board member Louise Stitt admired the student antiwar movement and wondered "whether those same young people could be sold on the Consumers' League program."[74] But to young activists of that era, workplace exploitation was not the compelling cause it once had been. And where women of Lucy Mason's and Mary Dublin's eras had imagined a just, social democratic state, the radical daughters of the repressive, militaristic Cold War age saw the state as part of the problem.

conclusion

We have seen how, during the crisis of the Great Depression, a small but well-connected group of women labor standards activists applied their expertise and energy in service of a vision of expanded economic and political democracy. National Consumers' League leaders like Lucy Randolph Mason and Mary Dublin believed that raising the labor standards of the worst-off workers would enhance the welfare of those workers as well as the collective ability of the working class to resist exploitation by employers. This concern for the "submerged groups" led the NCL to focus on female workers and, increasingly, on minority men as well. The league argued that ending labor exploitation — and the gender and race inequality that facilitated it — would restore national economic health and revitalize American democracy, over which fascism seemed to be casting its shadow.

As it turned out, the New Deal era afforded the Consumers' League a mixture of success and disappointment. The NCL and its branches helped produce a body of state labor legislation that rivaled league achievements of the Progressive Era. Thanks to Lucy Mason's cultivation of a network of southern labor reformers, a few of these state laws were enacted against high odds in the South. The NCL was an important force behind the first national labor standards policies, the NRA codes and the Fair Labor Standards Act of 1938. Through these efforts, the NCL contributed to seismic shifts in constitutional interpretation and to the expansion of government regulatory capacity.

However, the labor standards regime that emerged from the New Deal was not the comprehensive and generous system that NCL leaders had imagined. Vast groups of workers were excluded, wage standards were low, and administrative appropriations were too small to guarantee enforcement of the regulations that did exist. In this context of underfunding, the transition from women-only to sex-neutral regulation had the unintended effect of diverting enforcement resources away from women workers. In combination with other factors, the shift to federal, male-inclusive policy eventually diminished women experts' control over labor standards administration. The NCL succeeded in translating its proposals into New Deal policy, but only in skeletal form.

The explanation for the frustration of league intentions is complicated. Some recent scholarship argues that female reformers themselves bear the responsibility for women's inequality in the U.S. welfare state, citing the support of "maternalists" for women-only labor laws as a key example. These critics observe correctly that the United States, where women wielded an unusual degree of influence over social policy, ended up with a welfare state that was stingier and less supportive of women as mothers and as wage earners than the programs offered by most other industrial democracies.[1] But to blame this outcome on female reformers in the United States overestimates their power. Many of the same factors that enabled American women to exercise some authority over social policy, such as the absence of a labor party and of a powerful state bureaucracy, also made it difficult to implement comprehensive social policies in the United States. Furthermore, a potent set of peculiarly American constraints inhibited the development of labor standards regulation. These included the U.S. Constitution, labor movement ambivalence toward the state, and, outlasting these other obstacles, regional variations in labor costs that were protected by racial inequality and a federated political system.

This study has argued for a reassessment of the NCL's "entering wedge" strategy. The Consumers' League promoted sex-based labor laws as an interim tactic at a time when ideas about and legal interpretations of the proper role of government were in flux. League activists were willing to risk truncating the employment opportunities of a small portion of the female workforce because they predicted (correctly) that women-only laws would pave the way for sex-neutral policies. They hoped that the achievement of sex-neutral, uniform national labor standards would be followed and complemented by strong unions, generous social insurance and public assistance policies, and permanent public works programs; here they were disappointed. The NCL was not less committed to women's advancement than the National Woman's Party, but the league believed such advancement would come through expanding the economic and political power of the working class, not through securing for individual women the same legal rights as men. The Woman's Party was right that women-only labor laws sometimes hampered women in the workplace and promoted stereotypes that hurt all women. The Consumers' League also preferred sex-neutral policy, for these very reasons. As soon as sex-neutral laws seemed within reach, the league worked hard to win them (while the Woman's Party declined even to endorse them). The National Woman's Party was an important feminist voice in the interwar decades and deserves praise for many achievements. But in fighting women-only laws, the NWP forged alliances with those who opposed all labor legislation and a strong welfare state more generally. The NWP linked its "equal rights" feminism with laissez-faire capitalism, thereby complicating the task of social democratic feminists in numerous ways.

Ultimately, the sex-based strategy may have been a more effective entering wedge for winning state protection of wage earners than for winning feminist control of the state. It has been alleged that women-only labor laws empowered female reformers while restricting wage-earning women. Taking a longer view, my analysis suggests the opposite conclusion. Although sex-based laws did hinder some women workers, for most women these costs were offset by the protection received from the laws and from the sex-neutral policies that were built on top of them. Meanwhile, the female reformers who designed protective labor laws found to their surprise that the authority they enjoyed in the labor standards field when it applied only to women was contested after wage-hour policy became male-inclusive and national in scope.

The association between women-only laws and female administrative authority was not the only reason that the NCL network saw its influence decline. Again it is important not to blame the sex-based strategy for too much. World War II and the Cold War strengthened antilabor forces and at the same time militarized and masculinized the state.[2] Opponents of the social democratic agenda used the prominence of women among its advocates to discredit it. As we have seen, southern conservatives gender-baited (and race-baited) southerners who expressed sympathy with the New Deal. Right-wing congressmen tied up the National Labor Relations Board, the U.S. Department of Labor, and consumer groups with loyalty investigations in which women were the foremost targets.[3] Suspicions that women could not or should not have authority over regulatory agencies resonated across class and ideological lines (and perhaps across race and gender lines as well). This resistance kept the NCL network busy defending not only labor rights and labor standards regulations but also the legitimacy of women's activism on such issues.

The Consumers' League sustained its emphasis on the negative consequences of unregulated capitalism, advocating planning and regulatory measures even as the popularity of these ideas waned after World War II. The war began to reorient American liberalism from the social Keynesianism of the early New Deal toward the fiscal Keynesianism that prevailed in the postwar years. In the 1930s the NCL had used underconsumptionist economic theory as a tool against labor exploitation and inequalities within the workforce. For example, Lucy Mason argued that paying blacks lower wages than whites hurt the economy by reducing national purchasing power. These social Keynesians saw regulatory intervention in the practices of big business as the best means of raising purchasing power. After the war, however, fiscal Keynesianism became the dominant answer to under-consumption. In this view, instead of regulating production, the state's role was to stimulate consumption, primarily through macroeconomic manipulations. As historian Alan Brinkley has argued, this redefinition gave birth to modern liberalism, which, unlike early New Deal liberalism, pursued growth and stability without any desire to restructure the capitalist economy. A labor-consumer alliance that included the NCL resisted this transformation of liberalism well into the postwar period, but without its earlier breadth of support from experts or grassroots constituencies.[4]

The Consumers' League used economic arguments in the 1930s that were typical of left-liberalism in that period, but these arguments did not diminish the league's historical sensitivity to gender inequality or its growing awareness of race inequality. NCL desires for gender and race justice were embedded in, not in competition with, its opposition to class exploitation. Some historians recently have claimed that early New Deal liberalism, in its submersion of race and ethnic differences under economic categories, was distinct from the Progressivism that preceded it and from the "rights liberalism" that followed it. It may be that to the middle-class northern white men who have been the most studied New Dealers, racial and ethnic politics seemed less relevant than class politics in the 1930s.[5] For others in this period, however, economic arguments were familiar, if newly potent, tools for fighting old battles. The NCL story suggests that recent analytical frameworks for the history of reform thought could be strengthened with further attention to the voices of intellectuals representing women, African Americans, and southerners.

The regulatory achievements of the Consumers' League in the 1930s were flawed, but they laid a foundation that subsequent cohorts of activists have stood on in order to demand better. The NCL weathered the changing political climate, its philosophy remarkably constant even as its form and tactics adapted. During one harsh season, the league's Josephine Goldmark expressed part of this philosophy in words that are as apt today as when she wrote them in 1949: "History repeats itself . . . in the prevalent belief volunteer work is no longer necessary in what is sometimes derisively called the 'welfare state.' Whatever protection any state provides for health, safety, and general welfare is fundamentally dependent today, as it always has been, on public opinion. The 'welfare state' does not operate in a vacuum; and without democratic support and understanding it would soon perish."[6] During the 1960s this sentiment meshed well with that era's spirit of "participatory democracy." The protest movements of the 1960s and early 1970s spurred another phase of expansion in federal and state wage-hour regulation, notably by winning coverage for agricultural and domestic workers.

As the NCL celebrated its centennial in 1999, it continued to express the faith of its founders that organized consumers can combine forces with organized labor to eradicate worker exploitation and improve the quality of life for ordinary Americans. Issues on which the NCL agitated in the 1990s included Internet and telephone fraud, health care, and safety hazards in the home and the workplace. Even as it addressed these consumer issues, new and old, the NCL continued to act as nonlabor adjunct to the labor movement, a role it began to assume in the late 1930s. In 1997 the league protested employer attempts to alter a Smithsonian exhibit on the history of American sweatshops.[7] The NCL also played a lead role in the Apparel Industry Partnership label initiative begun in 1996. This campaign for an international labor code for the apparel industry highlighted the league's enduring alliance with garment and textile unions, even as tactical disagreements strained that alliance. The initiative also indicated that international industrial competition and the global movement of capital brought the NCL back to the strategy of ethical consumption. On the one hand, the shift of power from apparel manufacturers to mass retailers may give reform-minded consumers more clout than they had a century ago. On the other hand, the apparel code quickly ran into fundamental difficulties, and even if those can be resolved, it remains to be seen whether consumers will support a "No Sweat" label. It also is hard to predict whether focusing on the most shocking abuses in garment sweatshops will become a catalyst — rather than a substitute — for wider changes that benefit wage earners more generally.[8]

At the close of the twentieth century, policymakers and activists would do well to consider certain principles and practical lessons that the National Consumers' League derived from its experiences during the 1930s. First, labor standards policy should not set lower standards or permit exemptions for some workers (i.e., of a certain region, age, sex, or race) deemed to need or deserve less than others. Not only is this practice unfair, it opens the door to various methods of evasion. Of course, solving this problem in the context of international free trade will be even more complicated than addressing the problem of interstate competition was in the 1930s. Disparities in labor costs are now wider among nations than they were among the American states in the 1930s, and the international regulatory machinery is even weaker than the national machinery was then.[9]

Second, enforcement should be in the hands of independent agencies.

This is one clear lesson of the failure of the National Recovery Administration codes. (In the words of an NCL audience in 1934, "Can industry police itself? No!") Yet retail and manufacturing associations continue to propose various forms of industry self-regulation. The issue of who will verify compliance with the apparel code has been the most divisive and controversial question of that code's short history.[10]

Third, strong unions are invaluable in enforcing wage, hour, and other standards. The 1990s saw promising signs from the labor movement, not least a new determination to organize workers outside of the manufacturing sector. But a centrist president and conservative Congress gave the movement little help against well-organized anti-union campaigns by employer groups.

Fourth, consumer or public interest promotes higher labor standards and better enforcement. This is one reason the NCL favored a truly federal system. Its leaders hoped that joint national-state administration would produce upward pressure on labor standards, prevent local discrimination, and encourage grassroots involvement all at the same time. Centralization and decentralization each had their pitfalls.[11] The NCL's continued use of "white lists" and similar devices, even after their practical limitations became apparent, reflected its conviction that stirring up the "consumers' conscience" would eventually translate into better mandatory policies. Consumerism has the potential to politicize citizens, as well as to depoliticize them. In the next century, new media like the Internet may narrow the odds in the battle for consumer loyalty between voluntary associations and well-funded corporate interests. One way or another, ethical consumption may prove to be a salient strategy for labor reform yet again.

NCL activists from Florence Kelley to Lucy Mason to Mary Dublin believed the task of civilizing capitalism would be a never-ending one. They recognized that the going would be slow at times, that fighting over the administrative details of labor standards policy would not always be inspiring work. But they continued to master these intricacies in order to keep up their end of the struggle. "No easy words can alter [our] situation," Mary Dublin told the Consumers' League of Michigan one wintry afternoon, as the Depression's pall lingered and as fascism gained strength in Europe. Furthermore, "the thousands of essential small jobs for each of us to do" might seem mundane and inadequate means toward the league's lofty objectives. "But it is work like this which is the essence of democracy — in which each of us can *participate* to translate *conviction* into action directed toward the making of a better world."[12] Capturing the league's characteristic blend of idealism and practicality, Dublin offered a prescription for good citizenship that has not lost potency with time.

appendix 1

National Consumers' League Officers, 1933 and 1941

Italicized names indicate those who were officers in both 1933 and 1941. All board members were elected to two-year terms. After Florence Kelley died, the national league was reorganized to create a more active board. One change was to make room for more board members by making branch league presidents ex officio members with the right to vote. The council met annually.

BOARD OF DIRECTORS, 1933
John R. Commons, President
Nicholas Kelley, Chair
Lucy R. Mason, General Secretary
Emily S. Marconnier, Assoc. General
   Secretary
Hyman Schroeder, Treasurer
Beulah Amidon
Myrta Jones Cannon
Mary W. Dewson
Grace Drake
Mary Childs Draper
Pauline Goldmark
Florina Lasker
John H. Lathrop
Mrs. E. V. Mitchell
George S. Mitchell
Lucy P. Pollak
Florence Canfield Whitney
Leo Wolman

BOARD OF DIRECTORS, 1941
Josephine Roche, President
Paul F. Brissenden, Chair
Mary Dublin, General Secretary
Hyman Schroeder, Treasurer
Beulah Amidon
Elizabeth Brown
Arthur R. Burns
Myrta Jones Cannon
James Carey
William H. Davis
Pauline Goldmark
Nicholas Kelley
Florina Lasker
John H. Lathrop
Lois MacDonald
Louise Leonard McLaren
Lucy P. Pollak
Robert F. Wagner Jr.

COUNCIL, 1933
Edith Abbott, University of Chicago
Mrs. A. A. Berle Jr., New York

COUNCIL, 1941
Edith Abbott
Alfred Bettman, Cincinnati

Sophonisba Breckinridge, Chicago
Stuart Chase, New York
William L. Chenery, New York
Edward P. Costigan, Washington, D.C.
John A. Fitch, New York
Harriet L. Herring, N.C.
Alice M. Howland, R.I.
Alvin Johnson, New York
Lois MacDonald, New York
Broadus Mitchell, Baltimore
Wesley Clair Mitchell, New York
Bertha Newell, N.C.
David Niles, Boston
Howard Odum, Chapel Hill, N.C.
Marguerite Owen, Washington, D.C.
L. S. Rowe, Washington, D.C.
Vida D. Scudder, Wellesley, Mass.
Eric Stone, R.I.
Mrs. Gerard Swope, New York
Mary Van Kleeck, New York
Mrs. A. D. Warner, Del.
Eva Whiting White, Boston
William Allen White, Kan.
Eva Whiting White

Clara Beyer, DLS
Sophonisba Breckinridge
Charlotte Carr, Hull House
Stuart Chase
William L. Chenery
John A. Fitch
Harriet L. Herring
Alvin Johnson
Katharine Lenroot, U.S. Children's
    Bureau
Lucy Mason, CIO, Atlanta
James Myers, New York
George S. Mitchell, N.C.
William A. Neilson, New York
Bertha Newell
David Niles
Howard Odum
L. S. Rowe
Eric Stone
Nathan Straus Jr., Washington, D.C.
Mrs. Gerard Swope
Mary Van Kleeck
L. Metcalfe Walling, DOL
William Allen White

VICE PRESIDENTS, 1933
Jane Addams, Chicago
Newton D. Baker, Cleveland
La Rue Brown, Boston
Mrs. Edward Costigan, Washington, D.C.
Mrs. G. W. B. Cushing, N.J.
Mrs. Samuel S. Fels, Philadelphia
Felix Frankfurter, Cambridge, Mass.
Annie Ainslie Halleck, Louisville
Alice Hamilton, Cambridge, Mass.
John Haynes Holmes, New York
Mrs. B. B. Munford, Richmond
Mrs. W. L. Murdoch, Birmingham
Henry B. Mussey, Wellesley, Mass.
Maud Nathan, New York
Theodore B. Pierce, Providence
Josephine Roche, Denver
Mrs. Franklin D. Roosevelt, Washington,
    D.C.
Mrs. J. A. Strathearn, Wis.
Nathan Straus Jr., New York
Mrs. M. R. Trumbull, Portland, Ore.
Mrs. Laura C. Williams, Washington,
    D.C.

VICE PRESIDENTS, 1941
Elizabeth Brandeis, Wis.
Mrs. Edward Costigan
Dorothy Canfield Fisher, Vt.
Mrs. Thomas Fleming Jr., Calif.
Josephine Goldmark, New York
Annie Ainslie Halleck
Alice Hamilton
John Haynes Holmes
Wesley Clair Mitchell, New York
Mrs. Dwight Morrow, N.J.
Mrs. W. L. Murdoch
Mrs. Franklin D. Roosevelt
Robert Szold, New York
Charles Taft, Cincinnati
John Winant, Montreal
Mary Woolley, Conn.

HONORARY VICE PRESIDENTS,
1933
Irving Fisher, Yale
Frank P. Graham, North Carolina
Walton Hamilton, Yale
Jacob Hollander, Johns Hopkins
Frank McVey, Kentucky
Josiah Morse, South Carolina
William A. Neilson, Smith
Jessica Peixotto, California
Roscoe Pound, Harvard Law
John A. Ryan, Catholic
E. R. A. Seligman, Columbia
Sumner Slichter, Harvard Business
Walter Willcox, Cornell
A. B. Wolfe, Ohio State
Mary Woolley, Mt. Holyoke

HONORARY VICE PRESIDENTS,
1941
Barbara Armstrong, California
Charles E. Clark, Yale
John R. Commons, Wisconsin
Grace Coyle, Western Reserve
Paul Douglas, Chicago
C. Emanuel Ekstrom, Brown
Lloyd Garrison, Wisconsin
Frank P. Graham
Walton Hamilton
Jacob Hollander
Josiah Morse
Jessica Peixotto
John A. Ryan
Sumner Slichter
Caroline Ware, American
Colston Warne, Amherst
Walter Willcox

Source: Ballots, December 10, 1933, reel 5, and January 10, 1941, reel 8, NCLP.

appendix 2

Biographical Data on Fifty Consumers' League Activists in the 1930s

These fifty individuals, listed alphabetically, were among the key figures shaping league policy at the national level or in their state. Most were involved with the league for many decades and made it their primary reform platform, but a few were less exclusively and less enduringly associated with the league. (continued on next page)

Name and League Affiliaton	Year of Birth	Home State	Religion	Education
Beulah Amidon, NCL board	ca. 1895	N.Dak.	E	B.A. Barnard, gr. law
Clara Mortenson Beyer, NCL adviser	1892	Calif./D.C.	P	B.A., M.S. Calif. (labor econ.)
Jean L. Bowie (Mrs. W. Russell), CL-N.Y.	ca. 1887		E	
Elizabeth Brandeis (Raushenbush), NCL adviser	1896	Mass./Wis.	J	B.A. Radcliffe, Ph.D. Wis. (econ.)
Paul Brissenden, NCL board, ch.	1885	Mich.		B.A. Denver, Ph.D. Columbia (econ.)
Eveline M. Burns, CL-N.Y.	1900	Eng.	P	B.A., Ph.D. LSE (econ.)
Myrta Cannon (Mrs. Henry W.), NCL board/CL-Ohio	ca. 1862	Ohio	P	
James Carey, NCL board	1911	Pa.	C	Night school
Adele Clark, VCL	1882	Va.	Eᶜ	N.Y. School of Fine Arts
Naomi Cohn (Mrs. Jacob S.), VCL	ca. 1889	Pa.	J	
William H. Davis, NCL board	1879	Maine		LL.B. George Washington
Mary Dewson, NCL board/CL-N.Y.	1874	Mass.	U	B.A. Wellesley
Grace B. Drake, NCL board				
Mary Dublin, NCL g.s.	1910	N.Y.	J	B.A. Barnard, gr. L.S.E., Columbia
John Edelman, NCL board	1893	N.J.	J	
Harriet Elliott, N.C. Committee	1884	Ill.		B.A. Hanover, M.A. Columbia (pol. sci.)
Mary E. Frayser, S.C. Committee	1868 or 1875	Va.	P	B.S., M.A. Columbia
Ida Weis Friend (Mrs. Joseph), CL-La.	1868	La.	J	18 mos. study in Europe
Josephine Goldmark, NCL adviser/CL-N.Y.	1877	N.Y.	J	B.A. Bryn Mawr, gr. Barnard

Marital Status / # of Children	Self-supporting	Paid Occupation	Other Affiliations[a]	Party Affiliation	Race Equality[b]
sep., w 1926/0	y	Journalist (*Survey*)			y
m/3	y	Labor admin. (DLS)	TS	Dem.	y
m 1909/4	n	Husband: theologian			
m/1	p	Wisconsin economist	LWV, AFT		
m 1924/3	y	Columbia labor economist	ACLU, LID, NRA		
m 1922/0	y	Columbia economist	YWCA, NRPB, NCSW		
m 1930, w 1934/0	n	Father: judge; husband: banker	LWS		
	y	Electrical union official (CIO)		Dem.	
s/0, ssp	p	Artist, columnist, state WPA	LWV, CIC, ASWPL	Dem.	y
m 1909/3, w 1938	p	State labor admin.	LWV, NCJW	Dem.	
m 1906/3	y	Patent law, labor mediation	NRA, TCF	Dem.	
s/0, ssp	p	Party politician (DNC-WD head)	SSB	Dem.	
s/0					
m 1940/0	y	Reform staff, economist	HSS, LWS, AFT	SP, ALP	y
m 1920/3	y	Hosiery union official	CIO	SP?	
s/0	y	Political scientist	AAUW, LWV, FWC, DNC-WD	Dem.	y
s/0	y	Extension work (Winthrop)	CCG, FWC, AAUW, CIC	Dem.	y
m 1890/4, w 1938	n	Family in cotton trade	NCJW, FWC, ASWPL	Dem.	y
s/0	p	Writer/reformer	AALL	Dem.	

Name and League Affiliaton	Year of Birth	Home State	Religion	Education
Pauline Goldmark, NCL board/CL-N.Y.	1874	N.Y.	J	B.A. Bryn Mawr, gr. Columbia
Annie Ainslie Halleck (Mrs. R. P.), KCL	1867	Ky.	P	B.A. Vassar
Elinore M. Herrick, NCL adviser/CL-N.Y.	1895	N.Y.	U	B.A. Antioch (econ.)
Warwick Hobart (Mrs. L. F., Jr.), CL-Cincinnati/NCL g.s.	ca. 1898	Ohio	P	B.A. Cincinnati, M.A. Ohio State (hist./pol. sci.)
Alice Hunt, CL-R.I.	ca. 1872	R.I.	Cong.	B.A. Wellesley
Nicholas Kelley, NCL board, ch.	1885	N.Y.	Q	B.A., LL.B. Harvard
Catherine Labouisse, CL-La.	1878	La.	E	
Rosamond Lamb, CL-Mass.	ca. 1870s	Mass.	P	
Florina Lasker, NCL board/CL-N.Y.	ca. 1890	N.Y.	J	B.A. Vassar?
John H. Lathrop, NCL board			U	
Dorothy McAllister (Mrs. Thomas F.), CL-Mich.	1900	Mich.		B.A. Bryn Mawr, M.A. Mich.
Elizabeth Magee, CL-Ohio/NCL g.s.	1889	Iowa	P	B.A. Oberlin, M.A. Columbia (econ.)
Amy Maher, CL-Toledo	1883	Ohio?		B.A. Smith
Emily S. Marconnier, NCL staff/board	ca. 1893	Wis.		B.A. Wis. (econ.)
Lucy Randolph Mason, NCL g.s.	1882	Va.	E	High school
Frances E. Mueller (Mrs. C. R.), CL-Mich.	ca. 1890s			
Bertha Newell, N.C. Committee	1867	Wis.	M	Ph.D. Chicago
Lucy P. Pollak (Mrs. Francis D.), NCL board		N.Y.	J	
Jane Robbins, CL-Conn./NCL board	ca. 1860	Conn.	Cong.	1 yr. Smith, M.D. Women's Med.

Marital Status / # of Children	Self-supporting	Paid Occupation	Other Affiliations[a]	Party Affiliation	Race Equality[b]
s/0	p	Researcher, N.Y. DOL, RSF	HSS, LWV, TS	Dem.	
m 1896/0, w 1936	n	Father: industrialist; husband: author	LWV, SCHW, NCSW	Dem.	y
m 1916/2, d 1921	y	Govt. labor official (NRA, NLRB)	ACLU, LWV, TS, WCC	Dem. ALP	y
m 1922/2	p	Reform staff, govt. expert	LWV, BPW, Labor ed.	Dem.	
s/0	n	Old R.I. family	LWV	Dem.	y
m 1909/3	y	Corporate lawyer (Chrysler)	HSS, LID		
s/0		Artist	Kingsley House	Dem.	
s/0	n	Wealthy CL-MA backer from 1898			
s/0, ssp?	n	Family in advertising	ACLU, NCJW, N.Y. SSW	Dem.	y
		Brooklyn minister			
m/2	p	Dem. official; husband: judge	AAUW, JL	Dem.	y
s/0, ssp	y	Reform staff	YWCA, NCSW, WCC	Dem.	y
s/0, ssp	y	Reform staff, govt. expert	Housing, SSB, AALL		
w 1941/0	y	Reform staff	WTUL, LWV, WCC	Dem.	
s/0, ssp	y	Reform staff; CIO official	YWCA, FCC, NAACP	Dem.	y
m/2	n	Husband: industrial engineer		Dem.	y
m 1909/0?	p	Social scientist, Methodist leader	CIC, YWCA, ASWPL	Dem.	y
m/?			NCJW	Dem.	
s/0	p	Physician, settlement founder	NCSW		

Name and League Affiliaton	Year of Birth	Home State	Religion	Education
Josephine Roche, NCL officer/pr.	1886	Nebr./Colo.		B.A. Vassar, M.A. Columbia (sociol.)
Hyman Schroeder, NCL board, treas.	ca. 1890s	N.Y.	J?	
Anna Hubbuch Settle (Mrs. George T.), KCL	1887	Ky.	C	LL.B. Louisville
Helena Simmons, CL-N.J. Jeanette Studley, CL-Conn.	ca. 1876	N.J.	P	Private tutors
Gertrude Weil, N.C. Committee	1879	N.C.	J	B.A. Smith
Florence Whitney (Mrs. Caspar), NCL board/CL-N.Y.	ca. 1883	Calif.	P	
Margaret Wiesman, CL-Mass.	ca. 1898	Mass.		B.A. Bryn Mawr
Josephine Wilkins, Georgia activist, NCL	1893	Ga.	E	N.Y. art school
John Winant, NCL board, pr.	1889	N.H.	P	Princeton (no B.A., hon. M.A.)
Elizabeth Wisner, CL-La.	1894	La.	U	B.A. Newcomb, M.S. Simmons, Ph.D. Chicago
Leo Wolman, NCL board	1890	N.Y.	J	B.A., Ph.D. Johns Hopkins (econ.)

Sources: Biographical data was gleaned from numerous fragmentary and widely scattered sources, including manuscript collections of the NCL, branch leagues, and individual activists; oral histories and government hearings transcripts; biographical reference works, including but not limited to those in the *Biography and Genealogy Master Index*; obituaries and other newspaper articles; and secondary sources.

Abbreviations: In addition to the abbreviations used in the text, the following abbreviations are found in this table.

AAUW	American Association of University Women
ACLU	American Civil Liberties Union
AFT	American Federation of Teachers
ALP	American Labor Party
ASWPL	Association of Southern Women for the Prevention of Lynching
BPW	Business and Professional Women's Clubs
C	Catholic
CCG	Women's Council for the Common Good (S.C.)

Marital Status/ # of Children	Self-supporting	Paid Occupation	Other Affiliations[a]	Party Affiliation	Race Equality[b]
m 1920/0, d 1922	p	Govt. admin. (social welfare policy)	WTUL, AALL	Dem.[d]	
m/?	y	Real estate operator	HSS		
m 1913/0, w 1930	y	Lawyer, judge	ACLU, SCHW, WCC	Dem.	y
w/3	n		LWV	Dem.	
s/0		Reform staff			
s/0	n	Father: prominent businessman	FWC, LWV, CIC	Dem.	y
m 1909/2, w 1929	n	Father: oil baron; husband: wealthy writer	DNC-WD, LWV	Dem.	
s/0	y	Social work, reform staff			
s/0	n	Family in banking, garment mfg.	LWV, CFFM, ASWPL	Dem.	y
m 1919/3	p	N.H. governor, diplomat	ILO, AALL	Rep.[c]	
s/0, ssp	p	Public welfare admin., social work faculty (Tulane)	NCSW, SSB	Dem.	y
m 1930/ 1+	y	Columbia labor economist	ACWA, AALL		

Abbreviations continued

CFFM	Citizens' Fact-Finding Movement (Ga.)
ch.	chair
CIC	Commission on Interracial Cooperation
Cong.	Congregationalist
d	divorced
DNC-WD	Democratic National Committee, Women's Division
E	Episcopalian
FCC	Federated Council of Churches
gr.	some graduate study
g.s.	general secretary
HSS	Henry Street Settlement
ILO	International Labor Organization
J	Jewish
JL	Junior League

LID	League for Industrial Democracy
LSE	London School of Economics
m	married
M	Methodist
n	no
NCSW	National Conference of Social Work
p	partially
P	Protestant
pr.	president
Q	Quaker
RSF	Russell Sage Foundation
s	single
SCHW	Southern Council for Human Welfare
sep.	separated
SP	Socialist Party
SSB	Social Security Board
ssp	known to have had same-sex partner(s)
SSW	School of Social Work
TCF	Twentieth Century Fund
TS	Taylor Society
U	Unitarian
w	widowed
WCC	Woman's City Club
WPA	Works Progress Administration
y	yes

[a] This category is indicative rather than comprehensive, as most of these individuals belonged to numerous voluntary and professional associations.

[b] Known to have actively fought race discrimination.

[c] Adele Clark's father was Irish Protestant, and her mother was Jewish; she was Episcopalian until 1942, when, after the death of her partner, Nora Houston, she converted to Catholicism.

[d] Josephine Roche switched to the Republican Party in 1940 (like her friend John L. Lewis of the United Mine Workers).

[e] John Winant, although a Republican, endorsed FDR.

appendix 3

Selected Landmarks in the History of Labor Standards Regulation

1905   *Lochner v. New York*, 198 U.S. 45, strikes down maximum hours law for men.

1908   *Muller v. Oregon*, 208 U.S. 412, upholds maximum hours law for women.

1912   Massachusetts enacts first minimum wage law (for women).

1917   *Bunting v. Oregon*, 243 U.S. 426, lets stand maximum hours law for men and women. *Stettler v. O'Hara*, 243 U.S. 629, lets stand minimum wage law for women.

1918   *Hammer v. Dagenhart*, 247 U.S. 251, strikes down federal child labor law.

1923   *Adkins v. Children's Hospital*, 261 U.S. 525, strikes down women's minimum wage law.

1924   *Radice v. New York*, 264 U.S. 292, upholds law restricting women's night work.

1933   National Recovery Administration created; NRA codes establish maximum hours and minimum wages for men and women; seven states enact minimum wage laws for women.

1935   *Schechter Poultry Corp. v. United States*, 295 U.S. 495, invalidates NRA.

1936   *Morehead v. New York ex rel. Tipaldo*, 298 U.S. 587, invalidates women's minimum wage law.

1937   *West Coast Hotel Co. v. Parrish*, 300 U.S. 379, sustains women's minimum wage law.

1938   Congress passes Fair Labor Standards Act; Kentucky and Louisiana enact women's minimum wage laws; Virginia enacts strong women's hours law.

1941   *United States v. Darby Lumber Company*, 312 U.S. 100, upholds FLSA.

1969   Equal Employment Opportunity Commission rules against women-only labor laws.

notes

Abbreviations

The following abbreviations are used throughout the notes.

ACWA Records	Records of the Amalgamated Clothing Workers of America, Labor-Management Documentation Center, Martin P. Catherwood Library of the New York State School of Industrial Labor Relations at Cornell University, Ithaca, N.Y.
Clark Papers	Adele Goodman Clark Papers, Virginia Commonwealth University, Richmond, Va.
CL-NY Papers	Consumers' League of New York Papers, Labor-Management Documentation Center, Martin P. Catherwood Library of the New York State School of Industrial Labor Relations at Cornell University, Ithaca, N.Y.
DLS Records	Records of the U.S. Department of Labor, Division of Labor Standards, RG 100, National Archives, College Park, Md.
DNC-WD Papers	Democratic National Committee Women's Division Papers, Franklin D. Roosevelt Library, Hyde Park, N.Y.
EBR Papers	Elizabeth Brandeis Raushenbush Papers, State Historical Society of Wisconsin, Madison, Wis.
FDRL	Franklin D. Roosevelt Library, Hyde Park, N.Y.
Graham Papers	Frank Porter Graham Papers, Southern Historical Collection, University of North Carolina, Chapel Hill, N.C.
ILGWU Papers	International Ladies' Garment Workers' Union Papers, Labor-Management Documentation Center, Martin P. Catherwood Library of the New York State School of Industrial Labor Relations at Cornell University, Ithaca, N.Y.
KCL Papers	Consumers' League of Kentucky Papers, Sophia Smith Collection, Smith College, Northampton, Mass.
LC	Library of Congress, Washington, D.C.
LMDC	Labor-Management Documentation Center, Martin P. Catherwood Library of the New York State School of Industrial Labor Relations at Cornell University, Ithaca, N.Y.
Mason Papers	Lucy Randolph Mason Papers, in Operation Dixie: The CIO Organizing Committee Papers, Perkins Library, Duke University, Durham, N.C.
MCL Papers	Consumers' League of Massachusetts Papers, Arthur and Elizabeth Schlesinger Library, Radcliffe College, Cambridge, Mass.
MDK	Mary Dublin Keyserling

MDK Papers	Mary Dublin Keyserling Papers, Arthur and Elizabeth Schlesinger Library, Radcliffe College, Cambridge, Mass.
NA	National Archives, College Park, Md.
NCLP	National Consumers' League Papers, Library of Congress, Washington, D.C.
NCLP-SL	National Consumers' League Papers, Arthur and Elizabeth Schlesinger Library, Radcliffe College, Cambridge, Mass.
NRA Records	Records of the National Recovery Administration, RG 9, National Archives, College Park, Md.
NWPP	National Woman's Party Papers, State Historical Society of Wisconsin, Madison, Wis.
OPM Records	Oversize Personnel Security Investigation Case Files, 1928–92, Records of the Office of Personnel Management, RG 478, National Archives, College Park, Md.
SHSW	State Historical Society of Wisconsin, Madison, Wis.
SL	Arthur and Elizabeth Schlesinger Library, Radcliffe College, Cambridge, Mass.
SLP	State Labor Proceedings, George Meany Memorial Archives, Silver Spring, Md.
WB	U.S. Department of Labor, Women's Bureau
WB Records	Records of the U.S. Department of Labor, Women's Bureau, RG 86, National Archives, College Park, Md.

Introduction

1. For overviews of the history of sweating in garment production, see Ross, *No Sweat*, and Boris, *Home to Work*.

2. On the El Monte Thai workers and other 1990s cases, see "Look Who's Sweating Now," *Business Week*, October 16, 1995; "Sweatshop Raids Cast Doubt," *New York Times*, July 18, 1997; "New Sweatshop Allegations," *Houston Chronicle*, December 7, 1997; Ross, *No Sweat*. For editorial and popular responses, see Saigon embassy cartoon, April 13, 1997, and "Don't Buy into Sweatshop Abuses over the Holidays," October 5, 1997, both *Houston Chronicle*; Garry Trudeau's syndicated "Doonesbury" cartoons, week of May 24, 1997, and March 22, 1998; letter to the editor, "Nike in Asia: This is Prosperity?," *Wall Street Journal*, June 4, 1997. In the *New York Times*, see, for 1997, Bob Herbert, "Nike's Boot Camps," March 31, and responding letters, April 4; Bob Herbert, "A Good Start," April 14; editorials, April 16 and August 20; "Duke Demands Anti-Sweatshop Labor Vow," November 19; and also Bob Herbert, "Nike Blinks," May 21, 1998; "Anti-sweatshop Law Proposed," March 2, 1999; "17 Top Colleges Enter Alliance on Sweatshops," March 16, 1999. On the student antisweatshop movement, see "Campus Awakening," *Time*, April 22, 1999, and "No Sweat," *Nation*, June 7, 1999.

3. In the *New York Times*, see "Apparel Industry Group Moves to End Sweatshops," April 9, 1997; "Accord to Combat Sweatshop Faces Obstacles," April 13, 1997; "Anti-Sweatshop Coalition Finds Itself at Odds on Garment Factory Code," July 3, 1998; "Groups Reach Agreement for Curtailing Sweatshops," November 5, 1998. Also see Conclusion, below.

4. NCL president Linda Golodner cochaired the task force. Other members represented UNITE (formed in 1995 through a merger of the International Ladies' Garment Workers' Union and the Amalgamated Clothing and Textile Workers Union), religious and human rights groups, government labor agencies, and apparel manufacturers.

5. Published and unpublished scholarship on the NCL includes, in chronological order, Athey, "Consumers' Leagues"; Allis Wolfe, "Women, Consumerism"; Sklar, "Two Political Cultures"; Dirks, "Righteous Goods"; and Claudia Clark, *Radium Girls*. On an important league branch, see Dennis Harrison, "Consumers' League of Ohio." The league appears in many broader studies of reformers; see subsequent notes.

6. Middle-class and elite women were not the only Americans to mobilize as consumers in the decades after 1890. Several recent studies explore the politicization of consumption by working-class and racial minority groups, including Frank, *Purchasing Power*; Glickman, *Living Wage*; Lizabeth Cohen, *Making a New Deal*; and Hine, "Housewives' League of Detroit."

7. On the historical and contemporary predominance of girls and women among the lowest-paid laborers around the world, see Cowie, *Capital Moves*; Enloe, *Morning After*; Boris, *Home to Work*; and Debbie Nathan, "Death Comes to the Maquilas," *Nation*, January 13/20, 1997. For a survey of obstacles particular to female workers, see Kessler-Harris, *Out to Work*.

8. For a synthesis of the literature on this point, see Scott, *Natural Allies*.

9. Mason, *Shorter Day*, 8, and "I Turned to Social Action," 149. In the latter, written in 1947, Mason still claimed that women had a "special responsibility to humanize politics and legislation."

10. Using gender analysis means not only studying women but also examining how gender ideologies and inequalities influence various policy actors (male or female). Gender analysis does not imply a monocausal explanation of historical change, or that gender "trumps" other analytical categories such as race and class. Some (but not all) political historians increasingly appreciate the fruitful potential of gender analysis, part of a wider trend toward reintegrating social and political history; see, for example, Leff, "Revisioning U.S. Political History."

11. Historians have distinguished between the "first" and "second" New Deals and argued over the dominant impulses of each; some suggest even a third New Deal. See Jeffries, "'Third New Deal?'" The findings of specific works on wage-hour regulation rarely are integrated into broader New Deal studies; see Brinkley, *End of Reform*; Colin Gordon, *New Deals*; and Sullivan, *Days of Hope*.

12. This is true even of historians of labor law. The Fair Labor Standards Act does not appear in the index of Tomlins, *The State and the Unions*; Gross, *Reshaping of the National Labor Relations Board*; or Forbath, *Law and the Shaping of the American Labor Movement*.

13. Muncy, *Creating a Female Dominion*; Linda Gordon, *Pitied But Not Entitled*; Mink, *Wages of Motherhood*. Two recent studies that do link labor standards, gender, and state formation are Boris, *Home to Work*, and Mettler, *Dividing Citizens*.

14. To sample recent debates, see the following *New York Times* articles: "Labor Wants Shorter Hours to Make Up for Job Losses," October 11, 1993; "NAFTA: Friend or Foe?," November 15, 1993; "Minimum Wage, Maximum Debate," March 31, 1996; "Welfare Recipients Taking Jobs Often Held by the Working Poor," April 1, 1997; "Labor Sets Its Sights on a Workfare Union," July 7, 1997; "Nonprofit and Religious Groups to Fight Workfare," July 25, 1997; and "Better Pay vs. Job Stability in Wage Debate," March 20, 1998. On the "living wage" movement for local and state minima higher than the federal minimum, see "Some Cities Pressuring Employers to Pay a Higher Minimum Wage," *New York Times*, April 9, 1996; "States Are Arenas on Minimum Wage," *New York Times*, April 18, 1996; and also Robert Pollin, "Living-Wage Campaign," *Nation*, November 23, 1998.

15. The major exceptions are Boris, *Home to Work*, and Hart, *Bound by Our Constitu-*

tion. Hart analyzes how different legal contexts in Britain and the United States shaped minimum wage policy. Historians interested in the post-1923 conflict over the Equal Rights Amendment have discussed sex-based labor laws, but at a very general level.

16. Hays, *Response to Industrialism*, typifies the modernization school. The New Left's "corporate liberalism" formulation stresses business support for reform measures or, where direct evidence of this is lacking, the ways in which workplace reforms functioned to shore up capitalism — by diminishing the impetus of union organizing drives, for example, or by disciplining marginal competition. See Weinstein, *Corporate Ideal*, and Brandes, *American Welfare Capitalism*. On intracapitalist conflict as a key variable shaping social welfare and labor policy, see Ferguson, "Industrial Conflict," and Colin Gordon, *New Deals*. Gordon rightly stresses the obstacles to state development posed by the nation's federated political system; see also Graebner, "Federalism in the Progressive Era," and Moss, *Socializing Security*.

17. Abramovitz, *Regulating the Lives of Women*; Baer, *Chains of Protection*; Ann Hill, "Protection of Women Workers." A study that went against this grain by documenting and applauding female reformers' role in the Progressive Era is Lieberman, "Their Sisters' Keepers."

18. Sklar, "Two Political Cultures," 41, and see Sklar, "Historical Foundations." For a related view that puts women's labor laws at the center of a contest between conflicting legal philosophies, see Zimmerman, "Jurisprudence of Equality." Also see Lipschultz, "Social Feminism," and Kirkby, "Wage-Earning Woman."

19. Skocpol, *Protecting Soldiers and Mothers*.

20. See Kessler-Harris, "Paradox of Motherhood"; Mink, "Lady and the Tramp" and *Wages of Motherhood*. For earlier versions, see Lehrer, *Origins of Protective Labor Legislation*, and Kessler-Harris, *Out to Work*, chap. 7.

21. Scholars disagree on the definition of "maternalism" and therefore on its relation to "feminism." Skocpol defines a maternalist welfare state as "female-dominated agencies implementing regulations and benefits for the good of women and their children" (*Protecting Soldiers and Mothers*, 2). Koven and Michel call maternalist all ideologies that "exalted women's capacity to mother and applied to society as a whole the values they attached to that role: care, nurturance, and morality" (*Mothers of a New World*, 4). For these and other views, see Linda Gordon, "Gender, State and Society: A Debate with Theda Skocpol"; Weiner et al., "Maternalism as a Paradigm"; Ladd-Taylor, *Mother-Work*. Maternalism could take feminist or antifeminist forms; the NCL used it as a feminist strategy for subverting men's dominance over public policy. After the word "feminism" became associated with the National Woman's Party, Consumers' League leaders rarely identified themselves with it. However, the league's ideology fitted the inclusive definition of feminism offered by Linda Gordon: "A critique of male supremacy, formed and offered in the light of a will to change it, which in turn assumes a conviction that it is changeable" (Gordon, "What's New in Women's History," 29).

22. Quotation from historian Daniel Rodgers, cited in Muncy, *Creating a Female Dominion*, xvi. See Boris, *Home to Work*; Linda Gordon, *Pitied But Not Entitled*; Ware, *Beyond Suffrage*; and Wilkerson-Freeman, "Women and the Transformation of American Politics." To varying degrees, these writers recognize the persistence of women's voluntary associations into the 1930s, but for the New Deal era they see initiatives flowing almost entirely from the government "down." Even scholars who correctly stress the policy impact of social movements during the 1930s discount the importance of civic groups; see Goldfield, "Worker Insurgency."   .

23. Other historians have noted the debt of specific New Deal policies to the leaders trained and models developed by women's organizations in the Progressive Era and

1920s. This was one way the NCL shaped the New Deal, but the league exerted a more direct, contemporaneous influence as well. On women's groups as a bridge between the Progressive Era and the New Deal, see especially Clarke Chambers, *Seedtime of Reform*; Lemons, *Woman Citizen*; and Chafe, "Women's History and Political History."

24. On suffrage as an endpoint, see O'Neill, *Everyone Was Brave*; Freedman, "Separatism as Strategy"; Skocpol, *Protecting Soldiers and Mothers*; and Sklar, "Historical Foundations." Muncy, *Creating a Female Dominion*, finds women's power in government child welfare agencies peaked in the 1920s and dissolved by the mid-1930s. Ware, *Beyond Suffrage*, sees the 1936 election as the peak for the women's network. Freedman has revised herself in "Separatism Revisited," now seeing the Cold War as the death knell. State and local studies that have weighed in on this issue include Wilkerson-Freeman, "Women and the Transformation of American Politics," for North Carolina; Felice Gordon, *After Winning*, for New Jersey; and Tyler, *Silk Stockings*, on New Orleans.

25. See introduction to Fraser and Gerstle, *Rise and Fall*; Brinkley, *End of Reform*; Lichtenstein, "From Corporatism to Collective Bargaining"; Rosenof, *Economics in the Long Run*. "Left-consumerist" is another, more recent label for the social Keynesian perspective; see Jacobs, "Democracy's Third Estate," and Lizabeth Cohen, "New Deal State."

26. Linda Gordon, *Pitied But Not Entitled*; Mink, *Wages of Motherhood*; and Kessler-Harris, "Paradox of Motherhood."

27. Dennis Harrison, "Consumers' League of Ohio," Scharf, "Women's Movement in Cleveland," Felice Gordon, *After Winning*, and Claudia Clark, *Radium Girls*, provide some history of the Ohio and New Jersey branches. Ingalls, *Herbert H. Lehman*, hints at the importance of the New York branch.

28. See John Chambers, "Big Switch"; Vose, *Constitutional Change*; Hart, *Bound by Our Constitution*; Lipschultz, "Social Feminism"; and Zimmerman, "Jurisprudence of Equality."

Chapter One

1. Kelley quoted in Mason, *To Win These Rights*, 12. See also *Survey* 68 (June 15, 1932): 258.

2. Kellogg's tribute at Kelley's memorial service in 1932, quoted in Goldmark, *Impatient Crusader*, 69.

3. Molly Dewson to Grace Abbott, December 4, 1931, quoted in Ware, *Partner and I*, 156.

4. Historians sometimes characterize women reformers as motivated by instinct and sentiment rather than by intellectual commitment. One occasionally hears echoes of Arthur Schlesinger Jr.'s description of the "subtle and persistent saintliness" of women reformers, who overcame the "bluster of business" with the "implacability of gentleness." See Schlesinger, *Age of Roosevelt*, 25.

5. Meeting resolution quoted in Nathan, *Epoch-Making Movement*, 22. Sklar, "Two Political Cultures," contrasts the academic origins of the American Association for Labor Legislation with the "grassroots" origins of the Consumers' League.

6. In states with no league branch, members were affiliated directly with the national league. The largest branches were in New York, Massachusetts, New Jersey, and Ohio. Allied branches sprang up in France, Germany, Holland, Belgium, and Switzerland, but of these only the Swiss league survived the disruption and resurgent nationalism of World War I. NCL, *First Quarter Century*, 4, and Athey, "Consumers' Leagues," chap. 4 and 236–37. Membership figure from NCL, "1916's Record," reel 4, NCLP.

7. For overviews of this well-documented activity, see Scott, *Natural Allies*, Sklar, "Historical Foundations," and Linda Gordon, "Black and White Visions."

8. For a finding that some elite women looked more favorably on labor rights and state regulatory authority than men of their own group, see Flanagan, "Gender and Urban Political Reform." Flanagan attributes these different ideologies to distinct daily experiences, not to innate tendencies.

9. Felix Frankfurter, foreword to Goldmark, *Impatient Crusader*, v.

10. Sklar, *Florence Kelley*, 22, 85. That the NCL's first leader, Josephine Shaw Lowell, also came from a prominent abolitionist family further suggests such a connection.

11. Kelley's children joined the household of wealthy Chicago muckraker Henry Demarest Lloyd. Kelley was the only woman to head a state labor department until Governor Al Smith of New York appointed Frances Perkins to such a position in the 1920s; see Josephine Goldmark, "Fifty Years — The National Consumers' League," *Survey* 85 (December 1949): 674–76.

12. Sklar, *Autobiography of Florence Kelley*, introduction, 12–13, and "Hull House in the 1890s"; Brandeis, "Labor Legislation," 465–66. Commons quoted in Josephine Goldmark, "Fifty Years — The National Consumers' League," *Survey* 85 (December 1949): 675. The Illinois Supreme Court ruling was *Ritchie v. People*, 155 Ill. 98 (1895).

13. Chapter 2 discusses the development of this legislation more fully.

14. Kelley, "The Need of Theoretical Preparation for Philanthropic Work" (1887), reprinted in Sklar, *Autobiography of Florence Kelley*. In 1913 Kelley wrote that "socializing industry consists of two elements, acquiring public possession and making that public possession democratic." Kelley, "Possible Methods of Socializing Industry," quoted in Allis Wolfe, "Women, Consumerism," 382.

15. Florence Kelley to Richard T. Ely, University of Wisconsin, June 21, 1894, quoted in Sklar, *Autobiography of Florence Kelley*, 11.

16. Kelley corresponded extensively between 1884 and 1894 with Friedrich Engels, whose classic investigation, *The Condition of the Working Class in England in 1844*, she translated into English. Kelley and her husband were suspended from the Socialist Labor Party in the late 1880s because she publicly criticized that party's preference for the views of Ferdinand Lassalle over those of Marx and Engels. See Sklar, *Florence Kelley*, 124–35; Blumberg, "'Dear Mr. Engels'"; Allis Wolfe, "Women, Consumerism," 380–83.

17. Dirks, "Righteous Goods," 66, citing a 1914 sampling of 258 league members. The majority of these did not volunteer any party identification, reflecting in part the fact that women did not yet have the national ballot.

18. The 1926 quotation is from Vose, *Constitutional Change*, 418 n. 6. The FBI started a file on Kelley after her denunciation of the *Adkins* ruling in 1923. Sklar, *Autobiography of Florence Kelley*, introduction, notes that Kelley's memoirs were written in response to this red-baiting and were crafted to deemphasize her socialism rather than to offer a principled defense of it. Kelley was red-baited even after her death; see Nicholas Kelley to *Louisville Courier-Journal*, February 28, 1934, reel 27, and James Myers to National Broadcasting Co., January 16, 1935, reel 25, NCLP.

19. In 1931 the Massachusetts league reported that its membership was down to 490 because the Boston Daughters of the American Revolution had blacklisted the NCL as a threat to the national interest. Presumably those 490 members were less easily intimidated. Allis Wolfe, "Women, Consumerism," 391.

20. Quotation from Kloppenberg, *Uncertain Victory*, 6. Marxist doctrine held that class conflict was inevitable and that only revolutionary class consciousness would end capitalism. Social democratic theory suggested that the development of capitalism

would increase the interdependence of classes and create the potential for cooperation between workers and the bourgeoisie.

21. Dirks, "Righteous Goods," chap. 3. This and the following two paragraphs draw on Dirks's analysis.

22. NCL, *First Quarter Century*, 1. The concern with a "respectable existence" for workers revealed typical Progressive Era anxiety about underpaid women turning to prostitution or lacking the leverage to repel sexual advances from workplace supervisors.

23. Lowell quoted in Dirks, "Righteous Goods," 163. On working-class consumer politics, see Lizabeth Cohen, *Making a New Deal*; Frank, *Purchasing Power*; Glickman, *Living Wage*.

24. Dirks, "Righteous Goods," chap. 3; Sklar, "Consumers' White Label Campaign," 25–26. Dirks observes that the NCL borrowed selectively from and blended together many competing economic theories. The league seems to have influenced diverse economic thinkers, including Arthur Hadley, Simon Patten and his student Edward Devine, and later Paul Douglas and Caroline Ware.

25. Allis Wolfe, "Women, Consumerism," 384; Nathan, *Epoch-Making Movement*, 46. Nathan claimed that businesses excluded from the list threatened to withdraw advertising accounts from newspapers that published it. Some local leagues sustained this tactic for much longer than the national organization did; the New York league continued its "Candy White List" until 1933.

26. Interestingly, by 1925 league literature usually dropped the word "white," referring to the "league label" and "league recommended list." See NCL, *First Quarter Century*, 3, and Allis Wolfe, "Women, Consumerism," 388.

27. Allis Wolfe, "Women, Consumerism," 385–90; Athey, "Consumers' Leagues," 245; Sklar, "Two Political Cultures" and "Consumers' White Label Campaign."

28. Josephine Goldmark, "The New Menace in Industry," *Scribner's*, March 1933.

29. See correspondence between labor leader John Edelman and the NCL's Emily Marconnier, November 1936, reel 34, NCLP, arranging support of a hosiery strike in Reading, Pennsylvania. This sort of activity became the specialty of a new group called the League of Women Shoppers, which some NCL members joined. Many NCL officers also continued to participate in the consumer cooperative movement.

30. NCL, "Dining Out," October 1935, box J20, NCLP.

31. On Webb's view, see Kloppenberg, *Uncertain Victory*, 286–88.

32. Edwin Smith, NCL Second Labor Standards Conference, December 12, 1933, proceedings transcript, p. 22, reel 5, NCLP. On Tugwell, see Donohue, "Conceptualizing the 'Good Society,'" chap. 4. Tugwell's analysis negated the value of housewives' unpaid labor.

33. Mary Dublin, July 1940 speech, quoted in Angevine, *History of the National Consumers' League*, 52.

34. Josephine Goldmark, "The New Menace in Industry," *Scribner's*, March 1933. On consumerist activists and policymakers in the 1930s, see Jacobs, "Democracy's Third Estate"; Lizabeth Cohen, "New Deal State"; and Chapter 4, below.

35. NCL, *First Quarter Century*, 1.

36. Quotation from Mrs. Daniel Bartholomew, Joplin, Missouri, excerpted in Adeline Taylor to Mary Dewson, April 23, 1935, reel 54, NCLP. During World War II the government would enlist consumers, but especially housewives, to fight inflation by refusing to pay high prices; see Jacobs, "'How About Some Meat?'"

37. George S. Mitchell, review of Mason, *To Win These Rights*, in *Labor Relations Review* (ca. 1952), copy in private papers of C. S. Taylor Burke Jr.

38. On the influence of Rauschenbusch, see Mason, "I Turned to Social Action"; on Mason, see Salmond, *Miss Lucy of the CIO*.

39. See MDK Papers and MDK interview with J. Cheek, 1982, OH-40, SL. Wehmeyer, "Mary Dublin Keyserling," is a useful but not entirely reliable biography.

40. This data actually understates the continuity in league leadership because many people moved between the board and the league council (see below) in accordance with their other obligations.

41. Later in the 1930s the board met in members' homes in order to save money.

42. Quotation from Kelley (1902) in Goldmark, *Impatient Crusader*, 60.

43. On Roche, see Appendix 2; NCL press release, April 27, 1941, reel 8, NCLP; Ware, *Beyond Suffrage*, 152. Also see Sicherman, *Alice Hamilton*.

44. Pauline and Josephine Goldmark, Molly Dewson, Clara Beyer, Alice Hunt, Annie Halleck, Anna Settle, Margaret Wiesman, Myrta Jones Cannon, and Elizabeth Magee were league activists for over thirty years. Josephine Roche had volunteered for the New York league as a young Vassar graduate, thirty years before she became NCL president. A few men also served the league for many years, including treasurer Hyman Schroeder. The NCL leadership had low turnover: in 1941 at least forty-four of the league's seventy-eight officers (not including branch heads) had been officers in 1932; about half a dozen dated back to 1910. See NCL annual ballots and reports, reels 4–8, NCLP. Lucy Mason was hired at $5,000 per year, and her successor Mary Dublin received $4,000 per year. These were respectable incomes in the 1930s, especially for women, but they were less than what female administrators could earn in federal agencies.

45. By contrast, the National Woman's Party charged a $10 initiation fee plus $10 per year. Cott, *Grounding of Modern Feminism*, 73. Most of the NCL's regular small dues payers were women. In 1933 the average contribution was below $7. It seems that branches stopped paying dues to the national league at some point during the 1930s. See board minutes, reports of treasurer, reel 2; ledgers for 1937–43, reel 47, NCLP.

46. During the 1930s the NCL budget was somewhat larger than that of the Women's Trade Union League and somewhat smaller than those of the American Association for Labor Legislation, the American Association for Social Security, and the National Child Labor Committee. Arluck, *Papers of the American Association for Labor Legislation*, 67; Clarke Chambers, *Seedtime of Reform*, 164–65, 260.

47. The Massachusetts league did receive some money from the Julius Rosenwald Fund during the 1930s, and some other branches may have as well. See board minutes, reports of treasurer, reel 2, and ledgers for 1937–43, reel 47, NCLP. Post-1945 developments are discussed in Chapter 9.

48. League branches in 1932 included Connecticut, Delaware, Kentucky, Louisiana, Massachusetts, Maryland, New Jersey, New York, Ohio (three), and Rhode Island. Additional state committees and branches formed in Michigan, California, the Carolinas, Virginia, Tennessee, and Texas. See memos to branches, reel 16, NCLP. The NCL was active through individuals in other groups in many other states. Sklar, "Two Political Cultures," portrays the NCL as a grassroots organization, while Skocpol, *Protecting Soldiers and Mothers*, characterizes it as a northeastern group of elite policy experts. Skocpol overstates the NCL's centralization.

49. Sklar, "Two Political Cultures," 16–17.

50. Effie Dupuis to Lucy Mason, October 11, 1935, reel 96, NCLP.

51. Board minutes, October 6, 1932, reel 2, NCLP. These tensions had recurred over time. In 1922 the national office's decision to drop the league label triggered a debate over the relationship of the state leagues to the national organization; the Connecti-

cut and Massachusetts secretaries argued that the national league should not adopt new policies without the consent of each branch. The NCL board refused to make its agenda subject to unanimous approval from the branches. Athey, "Consumers' Leagues," 245–46. Other conflicts developed with the Rhode Island branch in 1934 and the New York branch in 1940. Chapter 9 discusses this issue further.

52. Among activists in the national organization this group includes those who over a sustained period attended and spoke up at most meetings and/or served on important committees. A longer list would be generated by including more branch activists and board members who served for fewer years. This group was selected subjectively, but there is little reason to think that those discussed here differed markedly in their views from the wider league membership. For profiles of related but distinct reform circles, see Graham, *Encore for Reform*; Ware, *Beyond Suffrage*; and Linda Gordon, *Pitied But Not Entitled*, chap. 4.

53. William H. Davis, Loyalty Review Board hearing transcript, November 16, 1951, p. 231, box A168, OPM Records. Forty-one of the fifty NCL activists profiled here were women.

54. The number of branch officers for 1917 does not include the all-female officers of the twenty-seven college locals. Of the forty-three people who were NCL board members between 1932 and 1942, twenty were men. Calculated from NCL annual reports and ballots, 1914–16, 1927, 1932–42, 1949, reels 2–10, NCLP.

55. In 1937 Lucy Mason declined to continue serving on a committee to promote the Women's Charter, offering as her excuse to the U.S. Women's Bureau that "ours is not a women's organization." Lucy Mason to Mary Anderson, January 27, 1937, reel 54, NCLP. Also see Mary [Switzer] to Lib [Elizabeth Brandeis], October 27, 1939, file 2, box 9, EBR Papers, and Elinore Herrick to Elizabeth Magee, May 12, 1944, reel 26, NCLP.

56. See Appendix 2.

57. On the changing gender identity of social science, see Linda Gordon, "Social Insurance."

58. Lucy Mason, Molly Dewson, and at least six of the other women profiled here sustained relationships that today probably would be called lesbian; see Appendix 2. For discussion of the impact of these relationships on female activism, see Cook, "Female Support Networks"; Ware, *Partner and I*; Linda Gordon, *Pitied But Not Entitled*, 78–83; and Rupp, *Worlds of Women*.

59. Lucy Mason to Arthur Altmeyer, August 28, 1935, reel 15, NCLP.

60. Reports of the general secretary, annual meeting minutes, December 11, 1934, reel 5, and December 10, 1935, reel 6, NCLP.

61. Emma Zanzinger to Lucy Mason, February 27, 1933, reel 96, NCLP. Husbands' pressure also caused some women to resign from the North Carolina League of Women Voters in the late 1920s; see Chapter 3.

62. This was consistent with national trends; women born after 1890 were increasingly likely to combine career and marriage.

63. See Muncy, *Creating a Female Dominion*, and Linda Gordon, *Pitied But Not Entitled*, chap. 4 (quotation, 71).

64. See Appendix 2. Two scholars of the Consumers' League in Cleveland notice a shift from "elite ladies bountiful" to professional experts of more diverse class and ethnic backgrounds. See Scharf, "Women's Movement in Cleveland," and Dennis Harrison, "Consumers' League of Ohio."

65. Also, Emma Saurer of the ACWA was active in the Consumers' League of Kentucky; see Chapter 6. On Nord, see annual meeting minutes, November 22, 1934,

vol. 5, Consumers' League of Rhode Island Papers, John Hay Library, Brown University, Providence; on Leslie, see board minutes, box 6B, CL-NY Papers.

66. Salmond, *Miss Lucy of the CIO*, 9.

67. U.S. Department of Labor, *Employee Newsletter*, April 1989; thanks to Daniel Lazorchick for this material on Beyer. Also see Beyer Papers, SL.

68. James, *Notable American Women*, 335; obituary, *New York Times*, October 12, 1964; Elinore Herrick Papers, SL.

69. Little evidence of ethnic consciousness could be found in the correspondence of Protestant or Jewish league activists in the 1930s. Mink, *Wages of Motherhood*, and Linda Gordon, *Pitied But Not Entitled*, find that white female social workers in the Progressive Era and 1920s were the racial liberals of their day but still assumed that WASP culture was the norm to which other groups needed to assimilate. The cutoff of immigration in the 1920s, the economic depression, and the rise of Hitler combined to deprioritize assimilation and to delegitimize among liberals the racialist thinking that had been acceptable earlier.

70. See Appendix 2. Liberal religious groups were recruiting bases and lobbying allies for the league, and its nominating committees tried to ensure the representation of the major religious denominations among league officers. Most but not all Jewish league leaders were from affluent German Jewish families who arrived before the influx of impoverished Eastern European Jews. See Glenn, *Daughters of the Shtetl*, and Rogow, *Gone to Another Meeting*. Catholics were a major force against child labor and compulsory school attendance laws, perceiving them as a native-born Protestant effort to disrupt Catholic parental authority. Catholics also were more antisocialist than average. However, some American Catholics were inspired by the papal encyclicals of 1891 and 1931 to become labor reformers and trade unionists; see Schatz, *Electrical Workers*, 96–99.

71. Black women reformers were deeply concerned with domestic workers' labor standards, but they rarely called for government regulation, perhaps reflecting their low expectations of southern legislatures. A review of publications and annual proceedings in the records of the National Association of Colored Women's Clubs at the M. D. Anderson Library, University of Houston, found that labor standards laws were a very low priority within that organization. In 1920 a black women's caucus led by Lugenia Burns Hope of Atlanta proposed an agenda that did not include protective labor legislation. See Hall, *Revolt Against Chivalry*, 85. On black women's activism, begin with Giddings, *When and Where I Enter*; Neverdon-Morton, *Afro-American Women*; Linda Gordon, "Black and White Visions"; and Gilmore, *Gender and Jim Crow*.

72. For example, in 1930 domestic work and agricultural work accounted for about 23 percent and 4 percent, respectively, of the 8.8 million employed white women, and 63 percent and 27 percent, respectively, of the 1.8 million employed black women. U.S. Department of Commerce, Bureau of the Census, *Social and Economic Statistics of the Black Population*, 72; WB, *Negro Woman Worker*, 14.

73. On the legal and ideological constructions of agricultural and domestic labor, see Hart, "Minimum-Wage Policy," and Palmer, *Domesticity and Dirt*.

74. Palmer, *Domesticity and Dirt*, 125, finds that the NCL was an exception to the rule that white women's groups were more interested in education than regulation for domestic workers. At an NCL conference in 1932, some spoke for a more inclusive bill. The conference group agreed that, ideally, domestic and agricultural work should be covered, but that the political problems of winning such regulation and the practical problems of enforcing it precluded attempting it at that time. For this debate and Ames's comment, see NCL Conference on the Breakdown of Industrial Standards,

December 12, 1932, pp. 32–33, reel 117, NCLP. A few years later, lawyer Ben Cohen discouraged Clara Beyer from including farm labor and domestics as "inexpedient" because it would be difficult to enforce and would arouse opposition from farmers and housewives. See Ben Cohen to Clara Beyer, September 6, 1935, reel 94, NCLP. In 1932 Wisconsin did extend minimum wage legislation to domestic workers, but no state followed suit for many years.

75. See Cott, *Grounding of Modern Feminism*, 71. Du Bois spoke warmly of Kelley at her memorial service. See "Florence Kelley Memorial Service," March 16, 1932, reel 5, NCLP; also Sklar, "Historical Foundations," 50 n. 1. On her threat to resign from the NAACP, see Lewis, *W. E. B. DuBois*, 478.

76. Laundries and other employers of minority women were often the first targeted by new minimum wage laws. The Kentucky, Ohio, and New York leagues worked against race discrimination, and others may have as well. In New York, a league lobbying coalition that formed in 1933 included the Urban League, Harlem House, and a labor union of black beauticians; see file 5, box 29B, CL-NY Papers.

77. Such was the prosuffrage background of NCL women that a rumor that FDR had appointed a former antisuffragist caused consternation; see Mary Dublin to Mrs. Caspar Whitney, March 7, 1939, reel 1, NCLP. In one 1914 sample of 258 league women, 188 identified themselves as suffragists and 19 opposed woman suffrage. Only 45 of these 258 named a party affiliation, and most of these 45 backed the Progressive or Socialist Party rather than the mainstream ones. This was not a scientifically derived sample, so its patterns are only suggestive. See Dirks, "Righteous Goods," 66.

78. Margaret Wiesman, NCL Third Labor Standards Conference, December 10, 1934, proceedings transcript, p. 127, reel 6, NCLP; this exchange was omitted from the printed version.

79. Molly Dewson to Mary Norton, June 13, 1933, reel 96, NCLP. In 1937, as if to prove that the NCL considered individual qualifications more important than party affiliation, league members defended New Hampshire's minimum wage director, Elizabeth Elkins, who was a Republican national committeewoman; see Clara Beyer to Molly Dewson, July 27, 1937, Beyer Papers, SL.

80. Molly Dewson to Eleanor Roosevelt, June 22, 1937, cited in Ware, *Beyond Suffrage*, 21; Beyer interview with Vivien Hart, 1983, p. 12, SL. On the nonpartisan, altruistic, education-oriented style of white women's political culture in the Progressive Era and 1920s, see Perry, *Belle Moskowitz*; Sklar, "Historical Foundations"; Skocpol, *Protecting Soldiers and Mothers*, chap. 6; Felice Gordon, *After Winning*. Rebecca Edwards argues that nonpartisanship was actually a new strategy adopted by politically active women at the turn of the century and that some nineteenth-century women were very active in party politics; see Edwards, *Angels in the Machinery*.

81. Florence Whitney of the NCL board, Helena Simmons of the New Jersey league, Dorothy McAllister of the Michigan league, and Gladys Tillett of the Southern Committee were Democratic Party workers. Many league women had supported Democrat Al Smith's presidential nomination in 1928, contrary to the general impression that women reformers opposed him because he was an urban Catholic "wet." The NCL board chairman through the 1920s, Daisy Harriman, was a cofounder of the Women's National Democratic Club in Washington, D.C. See Martin, *Madam Secretary*; Ware, *Partner and I* and *Beyond Suffrage*; Perry, *Belle Moskowitz*.

82. House Labor Committee, *Proposed Amendments to the National Labor Relations Act*, 5:1606.

83. Herrick, who stayed with the American Labor Party until 1940, hoped it would be more than "a tail on the Democratic donkey"; see "American Labor Party," in Buhle

et al., *Encyclopedia of the American Left*, 24. Also see Fraser, *Labor Will Rule*, 364. After the war, Herrick drifted to the right, perhaps reflecting her negative experiences with Communists in the American Labor Party and the National Labor Relations Board.

84. "Industrial democracy" came to mean different things to different people. For some, the emphasis was on giving workers a measure of control over production; others emphasized its potential to contain worker militance and raise productivity. NCL activists stressed the former, as subsequent chapters demonstrate. See Lichtenstein and Harris, *Industrial Democracy*.

85. This planning orientation in the 1930s distinguishes the NCL leadership from the U.S. Children's Bureau leaders, who "did not do economic planning," according to Linda Gordon, *Pitied But Not Entitled*, 260. Lucy Mason was active in the Social Policy Committee, the Southern Policy Association, and the National Policy Committee. Mary Van Kleeck, Clara Beyer, and Elinore Herrick were in the Taylor Society; Mary Van Kleeck supported the Communist Party. NCL board member Beulah Amidon promoted the work of the National Resources Planning Board; see her "Blueprinting the Machine Age," *Survey Graphic* (September 1937): 474–75, and "The NRPB and Beveridge Reports," *Survey Mid-Monthly* (May 1943): 141–43. New York league officer Eveline Burns was a key figure on the NRPB; see Warken, *History of the NRPB*, 216, and Reminiscences of Eveline Burns (1965), 102–14, Oral History Collection, Columbia University.

86. Florence Kelley, "Ending Women's Night Work in Cotton," *Survey* 67 (October 15, 1931): 84.

87. One ideological indicator is an open letter from two hundred liberals to FDR, "The Acid Test of the New Deal," in *Survey Graphic* 23 (June 1934) and other progressive magazines. Lucy Mason helped draft this Social Policy Committee document, and at least a quarter of the signers had league ties. Eveline Burns's *Security, Work, and Relief Policies* (Washington: National Resources Planning Board, 1943) also lays out this program. For emphasis on women's benefits from such social policy, see Elinore Herrick, "The Fight for Minimum Wage Legislation," address for ILGWU radio program, WEVD, n.d. [late 1937 or early 1938], file 7B, box 81, ILGWU Papers.

88. MDK interview with Kathryn Kish Sklar, 1983, and MDK Papers, SL.

89. Kelley became frustrated with the NCLC's conservatism in the 1920s; see Clarke Chambers, *Seedtime of Reform*, 34–35. For an example of Kelley's mentoring of Paul Douglas, University of Chicago economist and later an important league ally as U.S. senator from Illinois, see Paul Douglas to Florence Kelley on the subject of the NCLC, November 26, 1929, reel 25, NCLP. In 1935 over half of the AALL officers also were, or had been at one time, on the NCL letterhead. The NCL and NCLC, along with the social work journals that publicized their work, *Survey* and *Outlook*, all occupied the Charities Building in New York. In 1933 the AAOAS changed its name to the American Association for Social Security.

90. On the AALL, see Sklar, "Two Political Cultures"; Moss, *Socializing Security*; Skocpol, *Protecting Soldiers and Mothers*.

91. John A. Fitch, in *John B. Andrews Memorial Symposium*, 84. Also see John Andrews to Lucy Mason, December 12, 1935, reel 23, NCLP. By contrast, there was competition between the AALL and the AAOAS; see Arluck, *Papers of the American Association of Labor Legislation*, 59.

92. Lucy Mason referred most requests for assistance on child labor issues to the NCLC and the U.S. Children's Bureau. The NCL passed annual resolutions on behalf of the child labor amendment in the 1930s, and some branches continued to make its ratification a high priority. But see Molly Dewson, NCL Conference on the Breakdown

of Industrial Standards, December 12, 1932, p. 5, reel 117, and Lucy Mason to Jessie Laurence, South Carolina, August 14, 1936, reel 96, NCLP.

93. Frankfurter was a Brandeis protégé, and Cohen was Frankfurter's student. On legal formalism, see Chapter 2. On the different visions of male lawyers and female activists, see Chapter 7 and Hart, *Bound by Our Constitution*, chap. 7.

94. The Women's Christian Temperance Union claimed half a million members at the turn of the century; the GFWC had nearly a million members in 1910; the National Congress of Mothers (later the Parent-Teachers' Association) had about 100,000 members in 1917; the YWCA had about 500,000 members in 1920. Epstein, *Politics of Domesticity*; Cott, *Grounding of Modern Feminism*, 87–88.

95. I disagree with Theda Skocpol's claim that the league was not "the weightiest feminine influence" behind Progressive Era labor laws (*Protecting Soldiers and Mothers*, 391). Skocpol underestimates the league's influence in states where it did not have branches, and she overstates the independent activism of mainstream women's clubs. When women's clubs did pass resolutions in support of certain bills, they often did so on the initiative of a Consumers' League member. In the early 1900s Florence Kelley chaired the GFWC committee on women and children in industry, as well as the child labor committees of the National Congress of Mothers and the National American Woman Suffrage Association. See Sklar, "Two Political Cultures," 18–19. For similar findings from the South in the 1930s, see Chapters 5 and 6. One NCL leader later recalled of the 1938 battle for the Fair Labor Standards Act that mainstream women's organizations were "terrified" to act on minimum wage, but they dove right in once the bill was amended to include child labor provisions; see *John B. Andrews Memorial Symposium*, 74. One exception was the YWCA, which was more progressive on labor issues than the other large women's groups.

96. The Sheppard-Towner Act provided federal funds to the states for maternal and infant health programs; another victory, the Cable Act, began to establish independent U.S. citizenship for American women who married foreigners. Kelley quoted from the "Spider-Web Chart," reprinted in Cott, *Grounding of Modern Feminism*, 242. The chart attacked organizations that belonged to the Women's Joint Congressional Committee (WJCC), some of which were pacifist groups. Kelley headed the WJCC committee on Sheppard-Towner. On red-baiting of female labor reformers by employers in the states, see Lehrer, *Origins of Protective Labor Legislation*, 126, and Dennis Harrison, "Consumers' League of Ohio," chaps. 4–5. More generally, see Cott, *Grounding of Modern Feminism*, 97–99, 317 n. 21, and Neilsen, "Security of the Nation."

97. On these wider changes in the 1910s and 1920s, see Cott, *Grounding of Modern Feminism*.

98. In some states, settlement houses also were important allies. There was such overlap between the major settlement houses, the NCL, and the WTUL that I do not offer a separate discussion of the settlements here.

99. In New York, Frances Perkins and Eleanor Roosevelt (in the 1920s), Nelle Swartz, Mabel Leslie, and Frieda Miller were prominent in both groups. Roosevelt was closer to the WTUL, and Perkins identified herself more strongly with the Consumers' League. See Ware, *Beyond Suffrage*, 36. The two groups also cooperated closely in Illinois.

100. Until the publication of Orleck, *Common Sense*, the WTUL was, like the NCL, neglected for the postsuffrage period. Orleck's study and Kirkby's "Wage-Earning Woman" revise studies by Nancy Schrom Dye and Elizabeth Payne, who in my view misinterpret the WTUL's legislative strategy. Orleck's book, a fascinating study of the personal and political ties among selected working-class WTUL members, overstates

WTUL influence on New Deal labor standards policy, most obviously in discussing Schneiderman's work with the NRA. See also Kessler-Harris, "Rose Schneiderman."

101. On the NCL's lead role in creating the U.S. Children's Bureau, see Josephine Goldmark, "Fifty Years—The National Consumers' League," *Survey* 85 (December 1949): 674–76, and Muncy, *Creating a Female Dominion*. Clara Beyer (Division of Labor Standards, 1934–58) and Mary Anderson (Women's Bureau chief, 1920–44) were the NCL's day-to-day contacts at the Department of Labor in the 1930s. Anderson was a Swedish-born boot and shoe worker who came into the labor standards network through the WTUL; see Anderson and Winslow, *Woman at Work*, and Sealander, *As Minority Becomes Majority*. Grace Abbott and Katharine Lenroot, the Children's Bureau chiefs, were on the outer edges of the NCL's circle in the 1930s, due to the league's decreased emphasis on child labor.

102. Historians have described women's reform work as a progression from voluntary association to state government to federal government, but for most league activists the pattern was not so clear-cut or unidirectional. They moved in and out of government office, and while in office they usually remained active in the league. Some were government workers before they joined the league, drawn in by its national conferences.

103. See Elinore Herrick to Paul Kellogg, May 11, 1934, reel 92, NCLP. Chapters 4 and 9 offer additional examples.

Chapter Two

1. Rose Schneiderman of the WTUL, quoted in Orleck, *Common Sense*, 141. In 1939, after the ERA was introduced for the sixteenth year, members of the Consumers' League board gnashed their teeth at "the endless time wasted on this futile effort." Board minutes, February 27, 1939, reel 2, NCLP. For the NWP side, see its journal *Equal Rights*, which lambasted sex-based labor laws and their advocates in virtually every issue.

2. Most writers on women's interwar politics discuss the ERA–protective labor law controversy. Clarke Chambers, *Seedtime of Reform*, 78, called the debate an "irrelevant wrangle," and many have followed his and similar assessments. An early tendency to criticize the Woman's Party for its "strident" and "hard-core" feminism has given way to criticism of anti-ERA activists for holding a backward-looking view of gender roles. Kessler-Harris, "Paradox of Motherhood," 339, writes that the NCL camp "possessed a vision of family as traditional as that of trade union men" and that protecting a middle-class ideal of family life was the reformers' chief motivation. Also see Sealander, "Feminist against Feminist"; Becker, *Origins of the Equal Rights Amendment*; Scharf, *To Work and To Wed*; and Moss, *Socializing Security*. Even the most evenhanded treatments characterize the split in terms of competing assumptions about gender; see, for example, Cott, *Grounding of Modern Feminism*, chap. 4. The latest trend has been to ignore the split altogether, evaluating interwar women reformers ("maternalists") without scrutinizing the NWP; see Skocpol, *Protecting Soldiers and Mothers*, and Mink, *Wages of Motherhood*. For a valuable critique of the terms of the debate, see Cott, "What's in a Name?" For an argument that the two camps had similar objectives in the 1920s, see Sarvasy, "Beyond the Difference vs. Equality Debate."

3. Many historians have noted the lack of a women's movement in the 1930s, but they have not analyzed how the NWP itself contributed to the demise of public feminism in those years. More commonly, they portray the Woman's Party as the last principled standard-bearer of feminism. Sarvasy, "Beyond the Difference vs. Equality

Debate," calls for greater attention to a postsuffrage "NWP left." By contrast, I would suggest that the full extent and impact of the NWP's conservatism has not been appreciated, especially for the New Deal period.

4. The Massachusetts Supreme Court sustained this law in *Commonwealth v. Hamilton Manufacturing Company*, 120 Mass. 383 (1876). In both the United States and England, contemporaries accused men of improving their hours from "behind the women's petticoats." In other respects, the history of the sex-based strategy was different in England, because reformers there did not face constitutional obstacles. See Brandeis, "Labor Legislation," 462–63; Sklar, "'The Greater Part.'"

5. *Lochner v. New York*, 198 U.S. 45 (1905); *Muller v. Oregon*, 208 U.S. 412 (1908). The Utah decision was *Holden v. Hardy*, 169 U.S. 366 (1898). See Vose, *Constitutional Change*, chap. 7; Zimmerman, "Jurisprudence of Equality," 198–99; Sklar, "'The Greater Part.'"

6. The courts shaped Gompers's strategy as well as the NCL's. Gompers came to believe that securing legislation was a waste of energy because the courts could undo legislative gains. The AFL nonetheless continued to support laws protecting union rights, notably anti-injunction laws. On AFL voluntarism, see Brandeis, "Labor Legislation," 556–57; Forbath, *Law and the Shaping of the American Labor Movement*; Sklar, "Historical Foundations," 56–57; and Tomlins, *The State and the Unions*.

7. The assumption that women were temporary workers benefited men at home, where women cared for them, and at work, where men enjoyed higher wages and status than women. Kessler-Harris, *Out to Work*, 201–5; Lehrer, *Origins of Protective Labor Legislation*, chap. 7.

8. Mason, *Standards for Workers*, 29. On real and perceived obstacles to women's organization, see Kessler-Harris, "Where Are the Organized Women Workers?," and Tentler, *Wage-Earning Women*.

9. Florence Kelley, "The New Woman's Party," *Survey* 45 (March 21, 1922): 827. The first minimum wage legislation was passed in Australia. England established a minimum wage board for all workers in certain low-paid occupations in 1909. According to Vose, *Constitutional Change*, 183, it was Beatrice Webb who sparked Kelley's enthusiasm for a minimum wage in 1908. Also see Hart, *Bound by Our Constitution*; Sklar, "Two Political Cultures," 38–42.

10. Molly Dewson to Reva Beck Bosone, Utah, February 19, 1934, reel 23, NCLP.

11. Thereafter Molly Dewson and Felix Frankfurter formed a similar partnership. The literature on *Muller v. Oregon* is large; this description draws especially on Vose, *Constitutional Change*, 171–72, and Sklar, "Two Political Cultures" and "'The Greater Part.'"

12. On the contest between sociological jurisprudence and legal formalism, see Zimmerman, "Jurisprudence of Equality" (quotation, 194).

13. *Muller v. Oregon*, 208 U.S. 412 (1908), 420–22. On the difference between Goldmark's brief and Justice Brewer's opinion, see Lehrer, *Origins of Protective Labor Legislation*, 34, and Sklar, "'The Greater Part,'" 123–24.

14. *Stettler v. O'Hara*, 243 U.S. 629 (1917). Brandeis, "Labor Legislation," chaps. 5 and 6, notes that employers were much better organized after the war, forming associations that hired "young men who could use statistics and surveys" and "marshal 'contented workers' to appear at legislative hearings." Brandeis, a league activist, portrays the conflict between the trade associations and the Consumers' League as one between pro-business men and pro-worker women, each wielding social science and publicity tools developed by the reformers. See also Kessler-Harris, *Woman's Wage*, chap. 2.

15. *Bunting v. Oregon*, 243 U.S. 426 (1917), upheld a mild law with many loopholes

that permitted ten hours a day. Reformers wondered whether the courts would look favorably upon a more stringent law for men. I disagree with Kessler-Harris, "Paradox of Motherhood," 345, 351, that the NCL "hesitated to infringe on the citizenship rights of men." However, in these cases the courts did base women's and men's rights to protection on different obligations to the state: *Muller* in effect said that women needed protection to be good mothers, and *Bunting* suggested men needed protection to be good soldiers (at a moment of national concern about the unfitness of U.S. servicemen). See Ann Hill, "Protection of Women Workers," 272 n. 14, and Sklar, "'The Greater Part,'" 124. By 1933 Josephine Goldmark was calling for labor laws that protected "the great body of unorganized men . . . by constitutional amendment if necessary." Goldmark, "The New Menace in Industry," *Scribner's*, March 1933.

16. *Hammer v. Dagenhart*, 247 U.S. 251 (1918); *Bailey v. Drexel Furniture Co.*, 259 U.S. 20 (1922); and see Brandeis, "Labor Legislation," 440–42. Limits on men's hours in nonhazardous occupations and federal regulation of child labor would not be firmly upheld until 1941.

17. *Adkins v. Children's Hospital* 261 U.S. 525 (1923). See Brandeis, "Labor Legislation," 517; Zimmerman, "Jurisprudence of Equality," 201; and Hart, "Feminism and Bureaucracy." Hart points out that the Washington, D.C., location and efficient operation made that board the focal point of oppositional attack.

18. Brief for Appellants, *Adkins v. Children's Hospital*, 1023–24, quoted in Lipschultz, "Social Feminism." Although she argues that the NCL's *Adkins* brief expressed a feminist vision of industrial equality, Lipschultz suggests that the NCL's dependence on male legal culture ultimately channeled it away from arguments based on radical visions of women's independence. Her article does not examine the 1930s.

19. Amidon quotation from Cott, *Grounding of Modern Feminism*, 73; see also Becker, *Origins of the Equal Rights Amendment*, 38. The NWP claimed a mailing list of 9,000 in 1930, but only a few hundred paid dues.

20. Quotations from Goldmark, *Impatient Crusader*, 187, 144, and Zimmerman, "Jurisprudence of Equality," 202, 224. Also see Cott, *Grounding of Modern Feminism*, 127.

21. Zimmerman, "Jurisprudence of Equality"; Cott, *Grounding of Modern Feminism*, 120–29.

22. Kelley wrote of the ERA: "It is cunningly framed to attract women voters unacquainted alike with the intricacies of constitutional law and the daily experience of their wage earning sisters. It appears to the uninitiated to carry forward the process begun in the Nineteenth Amendment, and to contribute towards establishing a more perfect equality between men and women. How misleading this appearance is." Florence Kelley to Senator Charles Curtis, October 21, 1921, quoted by Zimmerman, "Jurisprudence of Equality," 215. Also see Florence Kelley to Victor Berger, December 19, 1923, file 1, box 14, Victor Berger Papers, SHSW (thanks to Suzy Wirka and Linda Gordon for this document). Socialist Party leader Norman Thomas told the NWP that he wanted a federal labor code that applied to both sexes, but "until we can get it I do not want to jeopardize such protection as is now given to women." Thomas to NWP, April 12, 1931, reel 45, NWPP.

23. Ellis took care to distinguish between the wage law and hours laws, so that the Court would not need to overrule the *Muller* precedent. Justice Holmes's dissent in *Adkins* found the distinction spurious. Zimmerman, "Jurisprudence of Equality," 212, 216, 221; Vose, *Constitutional Change*, 192, 194, 212–13.

24. Zimmerman, "Jurisprudence of Equality." Again Louis Brandeis could not vote, this time because his daughter was on the staff of the District of Columbia's minimum wage board.

25. Kelley quoted by Zimmerman, "Jurisprudence of Equality," 221. On wage cuts, see Orleck, *Common Sense*, 140. The three subsequent cases were in Arizona, Arkansas, and Kansas; see Cheyney, "Course of Minimum Wage Legislation," 28. Dewson prepared an amicus curiae brief to defend the California minimum wage law, but the case was dismissed when it was discovered that an employer association had bribed the employee to file suit against the law. Ware, *Partner and I*, 102.

26. Brief as Amici Curiae for the National Woman's Party, *Morehead v. New York ex rel. Tipaldo*, 298 U.S. 587 (1936), 34. Alice Paul did not publicly acknowledge her cooperation with Challen Ellis until 1935, but the NCL had its suspicions; see Kelley to Victor Berger, December 19, 1923, file 1, box 14, Victor Berger Papers, SHSW.

27. Wisconsin's passage of a minimum wage law in 1925 was an aberration. The law was based on John Commons's alternative to the NCL's early bill. League member and Commons colleague Elizabeth Brandeis thought his bill flawed, but it was not tested in court. Hart, *Bound by Our Constitution*, 140.

28. Justice Sutherland's opinion in *Radice v. New York*, 264 U.S. 292 (1924), quoted by Kessler-Harris, *Out to Work*, 194–95. Kessler-Harris points out that this concern for women's morals did not prevent the exemption of singers, actors, and cloakroom attendants, suggesting that concerns for female morality were not to interfere with male entertainment.

29. NCL, *First Quarter Century*, 10–11 (emphasis added).

30. WB, *Night Work for Women*, 2–3, 5. The consensus that daytime sleep was intrinsically inferior began to change in the late 1930s.

31. See NCL, *First Quarter Century*, list of briefs prepared, 17, and discussion of night work, 10–11. The 1924 ruling sustained extending the law to waitresses. The roots of the intrafeminist conflict over sex-based laws go back to the 1915 New York night work case.

32. After 1924 only one additional state (New Jersey) adopted a women's night work law, bringing the number of states with such legislation to eighteen. Brandeis, "Labor Legislation," 471–73; Steinberg, *Wages and Hours*.

33. Florence Kelley, ed., "An Honest Cloth Law, Pt. 3: The Work of Women at Night in Rhode Island," typescript study, 1920, reel 101, NCLP. On changing feminist attitudes on sexuality, see DuBois and Gordon, "Seeking Ecstasy on the Battlefield."

34. After World War I the Amalgamated Association of Street and Electric Railway Employees backed a New York bill against women's night work, a law that critics blamed for 800 of 1,500 female union members' losing their jobs to returning soldiers. Kessler-Harris, *Out to Work*, 194, citing Woman's Party sources. The WTUL claimed that a company policy of replacing women with men, and not the law, caused these dismissals; see *Life and Labor Bulletin*, February 1926. In 1921 women ticket agents won an exemption to the law.

35. See WB, *Summary: The Effects of Labor Legislation*, 15, *Women in the Economy*, and *Night Work for Women*, 8.

36. Most discussions of the women-only labor law–ERA controversy comment on the absence of working women. Kessler-Harris, "Paradox of Motherhood," 339, asserts that the NCL strategy did not reflect "the agenda of poor working women."

37. It is difficult to quantify this participation. For the 1930s, I have evidence of support by female workers (not counting WTUL activists) for sex-based labor laws in ten states and of their opposition in four states. I know of only a few dozen individual workers who were activists on either side (more were on the NCL side), but these claimed to represent many others. See Storrs, "Working Women's Participation."

38. Kelley and Marsh, "Labor Legislation for Women." League officials on several

occasions discussed the need to avoid jeopardizing the jobs of cooperating workers. One result was that the Consumers' League usually deployed working women in less public ways than the Woman's Party did. This difference skews the evidence on working women's participation in the debate; see Storrs, "Working Women's Participation."

39. Murray led a predominantly female company union that defeated the Transit Workers' Union in 1937; see Freeman, *In Transit*, 107. On NWP industrial councils, see Chapter 3. On conflicts among waitresses, see Cobble, "Drawing the Line," 226–27, and Mead, "Trade Union Women."

40. See Kornbluh and Frederickson, *Sisterhood and Solidarity*.

41. See the reports on the 1926 Women's Bureau conference in *Life and Labor Bulletin*, February 1926, and *American Federationist*, March 1926. On the ILGWU, see Lehrer, *Origins of Protective Labor Legislation*, 168–81, and ILGWU official Fannia Cohn's remarks at the NCL Conference on the Breakdown of Industrial Standards, December 12, 1932, p. 25, reel 117, NCLP. Cohn had reservations about women-only laws, but she too supported them as an interim strategy.

42. In the 1930s the number of occupations excluding women by law was small: selling liquor, grinding and polishing metal, taxicab driving, and electric-meter reading were prohibited for women in some states. These prohibitive laws aroused little controversy because they "merely confirmed custom," according to Kessler-Harris, *Out to Work*, 186.

43. On the limited role of unions, see Brandeis, "Organized Labor," and Skocpol, *Protecting Soldiers and Mothers*, 379–82, 412–13. Skocpol finds that state labor federations were important in campaigns for women's hours laws but not wage laws.

44. Some labor historians have drawn a distinction between WTUL and NCL motivations for backing protective legislation, portraying the former as "industrial feminists" and the NCL's middle-class activists as maternalists who sought to shore up the traditional roles of male breadwinning and female domesticity. See Orleck, *Common Sense*, 124–25, and Kessler-Harris, *Out to Work*, 205, 213–14, and "Paradox of Motherhood," 399. In fact the groups' arguments and objectives were very similar.

45. Clarke Chambers, *Seedtime of Reform*, 232; Goldmark, *Impatient Crusader*, 185.

46. NCL Third Labor Standards Conference, December 10, 1934, proceedings transcript, p. 97, reel 6, NCLP.

47. On NWP beliefs in women's pacifist and selfless tendencies, see Fry, "Alice Paul and the ERA," 17, and Becker, *Origins of the Equal Rights Amendment*, 49–51. In the 1930s neither group officially worked for birth control, but individual members of both groups did.

48. First quotation from Mason, *Shorter Day*, 8; second from Mason, resolution proposed at the U.S. Women's Bureau's first Women's Industrial Conference, reprinted in *Life and Labor Bulletin*, February 1923.

49. In Washington, D.C., Clara Beyer and Elizabeth Brandeis were able to define a living wage that was higher than what 70 percent of women were earning at the time; see Hart, "Feminism and Bureaucracy." I am not convinced by Alice Kessler-Harris's argument that minimum wage laws for women produced a "stingy budget discourse" that sent women a prescriptive warning against trying to get by without a male breadwinner. Kessler-Harris, *Woman's Wage*, chaps. 1–2.

50. Moss, *Socializing Security*; Hoffman, "Insuring Maternity"; Boris, *Home to Work*, 111–15. Linda Gordon suggests that Kelley supported the family wage ideal only because to her "no alternatives seemed practicable for the poor," and not because she believed women's dependence on men was natural or desirable (*Pitied But Not Entitled*, 55).

51. Quotation from Mason, notes for lectures at Agnes Scott College, May 1938, reel 64, Mason Papers. Also see Orleck, *Common Sense*, 124–25, and Boris, *Home to Work*, 84, 111–15. Some erroneously have claimed that Frances Perkins, and by association the NCL, urged married women to stay home. This claim is traceable to a misreading of an example in George Martin, *Madam Secretary*, 210; see Foner, *Women and the American Labor Movement*, 278, followed by Strom, "Challenging 'Woman's Place,'" 361. I believe Mink is incorrect to assert that these reformers "treated a woman's labor rights as contingent and ephemeral," that they tried to discourage working-class mothers from wage-earning, and that they were horrified by the increase in mothers' wage-earning during World War II (Mink, *Wages of Motherhood*, 129, 153–54).

52. Although by 1930 only 12 percent of married women worked for pay, that percentage represented a significant increase from a generation earlier, and it also represented a third of the women in the workforce. Cott, *Grounding of Modern Feminism*, 182, and chap. 4.

53. On feminist analyses of women's domestic obligations and their rights to reward, see Sarvasy, "Beyond the Difference vs. Equality Debate"; Cott, *Grounding of Modern Feminism*, chap. 6; and Becker, *Origins of the Equal Rights Amendment*, chap. 7. Becker (248, 258) concludes that the NWP as an organization devoted little attention to this question.

54. Alma Lutz, "Women and the New Deal," November 1933 typescript, p. 5, file 56, box 3, Alma Lutz Papers, collection A-34, SL. On another occasion the NWP printed a member's letter that attacked Frances Perkins for earning a salary when she had an able-bodied husband and children; see Mary Murray, "Answering Miss Perkins," *Equal Rights*, April 26, 1930.

55. See file 50, box 3, Alma Lutz Papers, A-34, SL, and the case study in Chapter 3. The same fragment of evidence from North Dakota in the early 1930s was recycled in many NWP speeches, articles, and briefs. Women's wages were so much lower than men's to begin with that the minimum wage levels set for women only partially closed the gap. Men did enter some "female" occupations during the Depression, notably social work and teaching, but these fields were not covered by labor laws. Few men became chambermaids or laundresses, and the sex-typing of tasks in manufacturing held quite firm. See Scharf, *To Work and To Wed*; Kessler-Harris, *Out to Work*; and Milkman, *Gender at Work*.

56. See *Equal Rights*, December 1, 1936, and May 1, 1938, for complaints about high minimum wages. Elsewhere, the NWP blamed women's *low* wages on women-only laws; see *Equal Rights*, June 1, 1936.

57. Before the Equal Pay Act of 1963, some women also received lower pay than men even when they did exactly the same jobs.

58. See Kessler-Harris, *Out to Work*, chap. 7, and Cott, *Grounding of Modern Feminism*, 153, for cogent summaries of these restrictive effects. Economist Claudia Goldin, *Understanding the Gender Gap*, 198–99, concludes that in the short run protective legislation for women had little adverse effect on female employment and indeed raised labor standards for both women and men. Goldin believes that women-only laws did harm women in the long run by delaying antidiscrimination laws.

59. Mason noted that Germany, "which has recently relegated women to the home and kitchen, includes *both* men and women in its regulation of hours and wages." Lucy Mason to Harold Butler, International Labor Office, May 18, 1935, box 169, Winant Papers, FDRL.

60. Cott, *Grounding of Modern Feminism*, 136–37.

61. For samples of league thinking on these points, see Kelley and Marsh, "Labor

Legislation for Women"; Lucy Mason to Harold Butler, International Labor Office, May 18, 1935, box 169, Winant Papers, FDRL; "Equal Rights" files, reels 51–53, NCLP; and Chapter 3.

Chapter Three

1. Margaret Bowen address to the NCL Thirtieth Annual Meeting, November 16, 1929, proceedings transcript, pp. 25–48, reel 5, NCLP; Gastonia worker Bertha Hendrix quoted in Miller, *Workers' Lives*, 169; Marion worker quoted in Foner, *Women and the American Labor Movement*, 240. See also Marshall, *Labor in the South*, chaps. 7–8; Tippett, *When Southern Labor Stirs*; Frederickson, "'I Know Which Side I'm On'"; Hall et al., *Like a Family*; and Salmond, *Gastonia 1929*.

2. See sources cited in preceding note.

3. Southern employers and their supporters created various myths to explain southern workers' low unionization rates: they were native-born individualists, less amenable than "foreigners" to following union orders; they enjoyed the slow pace of southern life and had little ambition for upward mobility; mill village paternalism made them loyal to their employers, whom they perceived to be taking good care of them. In addition to sources previously cited, see Hodges, *New Deal Labor Policy*; Flamming, *Creating the Modern South*; and Simon, *Fabric of Defeat*.

4. Board minutes, May 27, October 29, 1931, reel 2, and annual meeting proceedings, November 16, 1929, reel 5, NCLP.

5. Almost none of the literature on the conflict between sex-based laws and the ERA examines the South.

6. Fifty-one mills had relocated from the Northeast to the Piedmont by 1929; see Hall et al., *Like a Family*, 197. Spindle data from Mason, *Standards for Workers*, 45. Also see Wright, *Old South, New South*, 10; Galambos, *Competition and Cooperation*; Hodges, *New Deal Labor Policy*; and Vittoz, *New Deal Labor Policy*.

7. In addition to sources cited in preceding notes, see Quadagno, "From Old Age Assistance."

8. Hall et al., *Like a Family*, 197–99, 295–98; on the Gastonia parade, Tindall, *Emergence of the New South*, 344.

9. Hodges, *New Deal Labor Policy*, 11–13, 31; Mason, *Standards for Workers*; Wright, *Old South, New South*, 139. The largest northern textile state, Massachusetts, limited women's hours to forty-eight; Vermont had a fifty-six-hour law. Female labor force percentages are as of 1920. For more on the interdependence of male and female tasks, see below.

10. Mason, *Standards for Workers*, 8–9; Marshall, *Labor in the South*, 346, 349. In 1940 agriculture employed 49 percent of southern workers but only 16 percent of other American workers.

11. Tindall, *Emergence of the New South*; Quadagno, "From Old Age Assistance"; Alston and Ferrie, *Southern Paternalism*. Alston and Ferrie argue that southern planters opposed even policies that did not affect them if those policies had potential to disturb the region's paternalistic labor system.

12. Quotations from Mason, notes for an address to University of Kentucky Forum, early 1938, reel 64, and Lucy Mason to Molly Dewson, September 6, 1937, reel 62; also see Mason's notes for an address at Georgia Tech YMCA, November 10, 1937, reel 64, all in Mason Papers.

13. In Georgia in 1922, a women's hours bill backed by the League of Women Voters had gathered support but was defeated when mill owners kept the bill from coming to

the floor; see Scott, "After Suffrage." For good descriptions of New South boosterism, see Hodges, *New Deal Labor Policy*, 10, and Tippett, *When Southern Labor Stirs*, 1–6.

14. Whites, "De Graffenreid Controversy"; Nasstrom, "'More Was Expected of Us'"; Wilkerson-Freeman, "Women and the Transformation of American Politics," 422–27, 469.

15. Hall, *Revolt Against Chivalry*; Bland, "Fighting the Odds"; Wheeler, *New Women of the New South*; Elna Green, *Southern Strategies*. On conservative activism by white women in South Carolina, see Joan Johnson, "'This Wonderful Dream Nation.'" Within the relatively safe and respectable confines of the church, southern black and white women in the 1910s and 1920s did begin to develop autonomous organizations and demand greater authority over their programs and finances; see Hall (above), and Higginbotham, *Righteous Discontent*. The literature on southern women's activism is developing rapidly; see Chapters 5 and 6.

16. For overviews of child labor reform in the South, see Davidson, *Child Labor Legislation*, and Link, *Paradox of Southern Progressivism*; on Texas, Hall, *Revolt Against Chivalry*; on the Virginia campaign (in which Lucy Mason was active), Scott, *Southern Lady*, 199. For a survey of southern laws and labor departments as of 1930, see Mason, *Standards for Workers*.

17. Lucy Mason to Florence Kelley, May 6, 1922, reel 51, NCLP; Kelley to Mason, September 5, 1923, reel 62, Mason Papers; Mason, *To Win These Rights*, 7, 10; Boone, *Women's Trade Union Leagues*; Clarke Chambers, *Seedtime of Reform*, 237–40. From 1913 to 1915 the league had a New Orleans–based secretary for the southern states, but for reasons that are unclear, this initiative fizzled out.

18. Rhode Island employers had used this threat against a forty-eight-hour-week law in 1922, and in 1929 Pennsylvania textile mills threatened to move South if a forty-four-hour bill passed; see Kessler-Harris, *Out to Work*, 199. For cases from Illinois and Wisconsin in the early 1930s, see night work files, boxes 53–54, Industrial Commission of Wisconsin Papers, SHSW, and box 14, EBR Papers.

19. Board minutes, March 27, 1930, reel 2, NCLP.

20. The Southern Council's history has been reconstructed from the Mason Papers, the Clark Papers, and numerous scattered sources.

21. In 1929 Kentucky league member Marguerite Marsh went to Georgia to investigate working conditions; Florence Kelley claimed that Marsh's work contributed to the formation of the Southern Council. Marion Roydhouse suggests the Southern Council was conceived at a YWCA conference in July 1930, following a meeting in North Carolina of southern liberals upset by the 1929 strikes. Many of the people at that meeting also had been at the NCL's November 1929 annual meeting (at which the Elizabethton strikers spoke). Lucy Mason was among the fourteen women at the council's formative gathering in Atlanta on October 3, 1930. NCL minutes, March 27, 1930, February 11, 1931, reel 2, NCLP; Roydhouse, "'Universal Sisterhood,'" 325, 355; Southern Council minutes, October 3, 1930, box 34, Clark Papers.

22. Mason, *To Win These Rights*; Salmond, *Miss Lucy of the CIO*.

23. Mason quoted in Lawrence Lader, "The Lady and the Sheriff," *New Republic*, January 5, 1948, 17. The measure of prominence Mason achieved with the CIO has diverted scholarly attention from her earlier career, including her five busy years with the NCL. One useful source on Mason's Virginia years is Brinson, "'Helping Others to Help Themselves.'" Also see Mason, *To Win These Rights*, and Salmond, *Miss Lucy of the CIO*.

24. *Who's Who in the South, 1927*, 473.

25. See Hall, *Revolt Against Chivalry*; Scott, *Southern Lady*; Brinson, "'Helping Oth-

ers to Help Themselves'"; Salmond, *Miss Lucy of the CIO*. In 1912 Mason wrote a suffrage pamphlet, *The Divine Discontent*, and in 1919 she was president of the Richmond Equal Suffrage League. In 1922 she published *The Shorter Day and Women Workers*, which helped win modest improvements in Virginia labor laws that year. She also joined the International Ladies' Garment Workers' Union Label League. On the black welfare survey, Mason chaired the Subcommittee on Economic Status and Dependency Problems, whose report asserted black women's right to mothers' pensions and criticized race discrimination by unions. See Richmond Council of Social Agencies, *The Negro in Richmond*. The scrapbook presented by the black community is on reel 65, Mason Papers.

26. See Hodges, *New Deal Labor Policy*, and James Green, *World of the Worker*.

27. Domestic workers fared worse than other female service workers. Many families dismissed their servants, causing great hardship for minority women in particular. For the Depression's impact on women, see Milkman, "Women's Work and the Economic Crisis"; Ware, *Holding Their Own*; Jones, *Labor of Love*; Kessler-Harris, *Out to Work*; and Foner, *Women and the American Labor Movement*.

28. Given the industry's troubles in the 1920s, it is hardly surprising that cotton textiles manifested the associational impulse early. See Fifth Annual Report of the Cotton Textile Institute, October 21, 1931, file 6, box 6, George Sloan Papers, SHSW; Galambos, *Competition and Cooperation*, 116–18, 143–67; Wright, *Old South, New South*, 207–13; and Hodges, *New Deal Labor Policy*, 17–19. On the long-standing tension between cooperation and competition in U.S. political economy, see Hawley, *New Deal*.

29. H. P. Kendall to President Hoover, November 30, 1929, and Helen W. Gifford interview with Mr. Halsted, Textile Institute, February 6, 1931, reel 62, Mason Papers; notes on address by Walker Hines, CTI, to the Consumers' League of New York, in *Women's Bureau Newsletter*, no. 74, May 1931. Gavin Wright argues that those who blamed night work for overproduction had it backwards, because night work in southern textiles was more a symptom than a cause of the industry's depression. He mentions women reformers' support of CTI's ban and implies that they were motivated by moral fervor rather than a clear analysis of the industry's problems. In fact, Lucy Mason argued along much the same lines Wright does, that a chronic labor surplus was at the heart of the overproduction problem, although she stressed agricultural workers' impoverishment rather than the "stickiness" of mill wages. Wright finds it ironic that "national policies to raise the wages of Southern labor ensured the failure of the crusade to abolish Southern night work" (because high wages attracted willing night workers). From the NCL's perspective, this was not ironic; once national policies raised southern labor standards, reducing night work was not so imperative. See Wright, *Old South, New South*, 207–12; Shiells and Wright, "Night Work as a Labor Market Phenomenon."

30. Muna Lee, "Fight Ouster of Women from Night Textile Jobs as Sex Discrimination," *New York World-Telegram*, March 14, 1931, 18, and NWP minutes, September 30 and October 17, 1930, reel 115, NWPP.

31. Florence Kelley, "Ending Women's Night Work in Cotton," *Survey* 67 (October 15, 1931): 84.

32. Florence Kelley to Ludwell Denny, editor, March 19, 1931, *New York World-Telegram*, March 21, 1931, draft on reel 32, NCLP.

33. Felix Frankfurter opined in 1922 that *Bunting* left the constitutionality of men's hours laws unresolved; see Mason, *Standards for Workers*, 27–28. The NWP, on the other hand, assumed that *Bunting* clearly reversed the 1905 *Lochner* ruling; see Jane Norman Smith to Muna Lee, April 1, 1931, reel 45, NWPP. A few states did have on

their books hours laws that applied to both men and women, but these permitted long hours and were so loosely enforced that they were unlikely to provoke a challenge in the courts.

34. Hunnicutt, *Work without End*, 150; Brandeis, "Labor Legislation," 558–59. In December 1932 Senator Hugo Black introduced the AFL-backed thirty-hour-week bill.

35. Galambos, *Competition and Cooperation*, 151. Unions may have feared that their active support would deepen the opposition of the hard-core nonconforming mills. Labor editors did favor the measure, however; significantly, they applauded it as a step toward eliminating all night work, not as a way to discourage women's wage-earning. See *Journal of Labor* (Atlanta) editorials on October 3 and 24, 1930, February 27 and March 27, 1931.

36. Fraser, "'Labor Question'"; Pabon, "Regulating Capitalism."

37. Mason, *Standards for Workers*, 9; Lucy Mason to H. P. Kendall, February 17, 1931, reel 62, Mason Papers. See also Lucy Mason to W. D. Anderson and his reply, February 13 and 14, 1931; Mason to W. M. McLauren, February 17, 1931; Mason to B. E. Geer, February 21, 1931, all reel 62, Mason Papers. Also see Galambos, *Competition and Cooperation*.

38. For claims that the Southern Council was homegrown, see Mason, *Standards for Workers*, and Lucy Mason to Donald Comer, January 23, 1931, reel 62, Mason Papers; on the need for discretion, Lucy Mason to Henry P. Kendall, February 17 and April 4, 1931, ibid. Initially the Southern Council succeeded in representing itself as 100 percent southern, but in mid-1931 the Woman's Party discovered that the Consumers' League financed it, and by mid-1932 the connection was public. See Josephine Casey to Muna Lee, July 12, 1931, reel 45, NWPP, and NCL press release on Mason's appointment, June 1932, reel 62, Mason Papers.

39. Lucy Mason correspondence with southern textile manufacturers, January and February 1931, reel 62, Mason Papers.

40. Baker, "Domestication of Politics"; Fitzpatrick, *Endless Crusade*; Skocpol, *Protecting Soldiers and Mothers*, chap. 6.

41. Anonymous to Mary Anderson, January 27, 1931; Helen W. Gifford interview with Mr. Halsted, February 6, 1931; W. D. Anderson to Lillian Wade, May 7, 1931, all reel 62, Mason Papers.

42. Goldmark, *Fatigue and Efficiency*. During World War II, as manufacturers pressed for a relaxation of hours laws to expand production, the league would again argue for a connection between short hours and high productivity. In all periods the league emphasized increasing demand (by raising wages and spreading employment) more than restricting output, but in the 1930s the NCL did try to appeal to employers worried about overproduction.

43. Fifth Annual Report of the Cotton Textile Institute, October 21, 1931, file 6, box 6, George Sloan Papers, SHSW; Galambos, *Competition and Cooperation*, 116–18, 143–67; WB, *Employment of Women at Night*. The textile industry was the largest employer of women night workers.

44. Lucy Mason to Robert Arnold, January 28, 1931, reel 62, Mason Papers.

45. Mason, *Shorter Day*; Hall, *Revolt Against Chivalry*, esp. 27–28.

46. Kirby, *Darkness at the Dawning*; Link, *Paradox of Southern Progressivism*. One white supremacist child labor reformer, Jean Gordon of New Orleans, was associated with the Consumers' League in the 1910s. Her racial views were atypical of southern league activists, as we shall see; this may be why she apparently drifted from the league after World War I.

47. Mason, *Standards for Workers*, 22, 35, for example. In some states, Urban League

branches joined Councils on Women and Children in Industry. See Clarke Chambers, *Seedtime of Reform*, 67.

48. Ninety-eight percent of textile workers were white; the few blacks were men in custodial jobs. Tobacco processing, the second largest manufacturing occupation for southern women, employed about 30,000 women, black and white in about equal numbers, but under very unequal conditions. Mason, *Standards for Workers*; Janiewski, "Southern Honor," 96. Black groups in some cities began developing "Don't Buy Where You Can't Work" campaigns in the 1930s, but not in the Deep South; see Moreno, "Racial Proportionalism."

49. North Carolina legislators narrowed the coverage of the Southern Council's bill so that the 1931 law covered fewer black-dominated occupations than the model bill did; see Roydhouse, "'Universal Sisterhood.'" On Southern Councils in other states, see box 105, Clark Papers.

50. The NWP's offer to Casey went out the day that the party received a batch of clippings about Lucy Mason's efforts with the Southern Council; see Muna Lee to Josephine Casey, February 21, 1931, and Marion Read to Muna Lee, same date, reel 45, NWPP. The NWP assumed from the outset that working-class women and professional or upper-class women would have separate organizations. This plan drew on the party's experience in New York, where it had organized an industrial council in the early 1920s. This structure perhaps offered working women a way of participating that was tailored to their circumstances: no dues and little time commitment. However, it also preserved the gulf between the groups and denied working women access to the inner circle of party leadership.

51. In 1922 a nationwide NWP campaign resulted in the formation of chapters in a few southern states, but not in Georgia. By 1930 NWP minutes and newsletters contained little reference to activities in any southern state.

52. Muna Lee to Jane Norman Smith, February 26, 1931, reel 45, NWPP. Biographical data on Casey has been culled from scattered references in many manuscript collections and secondary sources on woman suffrage, garment workers, the WTUL, and the NWP. The best starting points are the chronologically organized correspondence files for 1931, reel 45, NWPP, the biographies file, reel 113, ibid., and *Equal Rights*.

53. Quotations from *Life and Labor Bulletin*, February 1926, and Mary Anderson to Margaret Dreier Robins, February 4, 1926, reel 3, Papers of the WTUL and Its Principal Leaders, SHSW. Anderson added that "after it was all over Josephine was on the verge of collapse but I do not think she will soon forget what she got." Casey did not forget; her letters to the NWP from Georgia in 1931 are full of gibes at the Women's Bureau and the WTUL. Nestor claimed that Casey had left the labor movement in 1913 to join the NWP; Nestor also believed Casey's Chicago streetcar union only won an eight-hour day after the WTUL won a ten-hour law for women in Illinois. See *Equal Rights*, January 30, 1926, and Agnes Nestor, "The Women's Industrial Conference," *American Federationist* 33 (March 1926): 296–304.

54. *Equal Rights*, April 11, 1931.

55. Josephine Casey to Muna Lee, n.d. [June 1931, #10], reel 45, NWPP, for example. The Woman's Party had had difficulty meeting workers in New York and counted on Casey to bridge this gulf. See Jane Norman Smith to Muna Lee, March 27, 1931, reel 45, NWPP.

56. Josephine Casey to Muna Lee, April 9, 1931, reel 45, NWPP.

57. Muna Lee, "Fight Ouster," *New York World-Telegram*, March 14, 1931; also see *Equal Rights*, April 11, 1931. No letters from workers are in the NWP's otherwise comprehensive correspondence files for February or March.

58. "When women are sent home, men are sent home also because those operating spindles are women and it would be a loss to run without the spindles. I asked [the manufacturers' association] if men might be trained to handle the spindles and they said Georgia men would not fit in to that work. . . . They said it can't be done. If there is a 40-hour law for women the mills will work on a 40-hour schedule." Casey to Lee, n.d. [April 1931], reel 45, NWPP.

59. Sixth Annual Report of CTI, October 19, 1932, file 6, box 6, George Sloan Papers, SHSW; for a report that one mill had shifted women to days and put men on at night in their places, see Casey to Lee, April 16, 1931, reel 45, NWPP; Milkman, *Gender at Work*. By 1932 a minority of mills were running all night without women. Men may have been doing "women's" jobs (if so, it is unclear whether they did so at women's wages), or perhaps only some mill functions occurred at night. Galambos, *Competition and Cooperation*, 165, assumes that during the Depression plenty of men were willing to work at women's wages; Wright, *Old South, New South*, 213, and Hall et al., *Like a Family*, 235, follow Galambos. Even if one could show that men took over female tasks at female wages, however, one would need to prove it was sex-based policy that caused such displacement, and not the Depression-induced willingness of white men to work at jobs they previously would not consider.

60. Casey to Lee, n.d. [April 1931], and June 6, 1931, reel 45, NWPP.

61. Casey to Lee, n.d. [April 1931], ibid.

62. *Equal Rights*, August 22 and 29, 1931, on the Georgia Industrial Council. Only three of the women Casey signed up were textile workers; others were shopkeepers and sales clerks. One of the mill women worked three hours a day, from 9 P.M. to midnight, not a typical circumstance.

63. "Report of an Investigation of the present strike situation at the Kalamazoo Corset Co. Factory" [unsigned, probably by Pauline Newman of the ILGWU], April 17, 1912, reel 4, Papers of the WTUL and Its Principal Leaders, SHSW. The report also remarked that Casey was "ever ready to talk for all" and had "made many enemies by her hysterical and exaggerated manner of talking."

64. Quotation from Lee to Casey, n.d. [June 1931]; also see Lee telegram to Casey, August 14, 1931; Casey to Lee, August 15, 1931; Mrs. Pearl Henry telegram and letter to Lee, August 17 and 18, 1931, all reel 45, NWPP.

65. Casey to Lee, April 16, 1931, reel 45, NWPP.

66. Ibid.; Casey's suggestion was not taken up.

67. Casey to Lee, August 8, 1931, reel 45, NWPP. Casey apparently meant that states had the right not to ratify the ERA. Casey's animosity toward the U.S. Women's Bureau also fitted well with conservative southerners' resentment of that federal and labor-oriented agency; see Casey to Lee, May 14 and 20, 1931, reel 45, NWPP, and *Equal Rights*, August 1, 1931.

68. Casey to Lee, April 20, May 2, 1931, reel 45, NWPP. Casey's working-class background also may have alienated the "leisure-class" women. However, working for the Southern Council, the blue-blooded Lucy Mason made similar observations about the difficulty of rallying affluent women. These women's indifference to both the NCL and the NWP is consistent with findings that southern women of the established elite were the most resistant to woman suffrage; see Elna Green, *Southern Strategies*.

69. The change in black women's employment was less dramatic. Until World War II, over 90 percent of black women employed in Atlanta were domestic servants; see Blackwelder, "Mop and Typewriter," 24. See also Lyson, "Industrial Change."

70. *Equal Rights*, August 15 and August 22, 1931; Casey to Lee, June 26 and July 28, 1931, and undated letter [late June 1931, misidentified as July 1931], all reel 45, NWPP.

AWP officers included Miss Laurence Thompson (whose father was an official with the Georgia Bureau of Markets), Mrs. Winnie Colvin (household economist and Women's Division, Chamber of Commerce), Mrs. Clara Bovard (lawyer), and Miss Elma Burnette (Chamber of Commerce). For Seydell's Chamber of Commerce affiliation, see *Who's Who in America, 1938–39*, 2238, and Mildred Seydell Papers, Robert Woodruff Library, Emory University, Atlanta.

71. Casey to Lee, June 18, July 20, 1931, reel 45, NWPP. On the Chamber of Commerce and the "Atlanta spirit," see Blackwelder, "Mop and Typewriter"; Bartley, *Creation of Modern Georgia*, 124; Roth, *Matronage*; and Marshall, *Labor in the South*, 45.

72. Casey to Lee, July 28 and 31, 1931, reel 45, NWPP. The Woman's Party had a history of funding its pageantry with Chamber of Commerce money. After the *Adkins* ruling in 1923, the Rochester, New York, chamber subsidized the NWP's Seneca Falls gathering, and the Denver chamber did the same for a convention there. See Florence Kelley (citing *Equal Rights*) to Victor Berger, December 19, 1923, file 1, box 14, Victor Berger Papers, SHSW.

73. This policy was not without precedent. In 1922, when white southern members asked for a national policy excluding blacks, NWP leader Alice Paul compromised by promising not to *recruit* black women. Paul curried southern white favor by comparing suffragists to Confederate soldiers and claiming that white women's vote would "great[ly] simplify the Negro question." See Bland, "Fighting the Odds." Not all NWP members were hostile to racial reform; at a memorial tribute to Inez Millholland in 1924, the omission of her civil rights activities from the program triggered several resignations. See Pardo, *National Woman's Party Papers*, 20. On women's interracial organizing, see Hall, *Revolt Against Chivalry*.

74. The Atlanta School of Social Work evolved at the initiative of Lugenia Burns Hope, who had founded the Neighborhood Union settlement house in 1906 and the Social Service Institute at Morehouse College in 1919. It was Forrester B. Washington, director of the training program for black social workers, who approached Casey. This group was affiliated with the National Conference of Social Work, which opposed the ERA. The invitation to Casey probably reflected the spirit of hearing both sides. In fairness to Casey, she did tell Lee, "I could not have refused without forfeiting something in character." See Casey to Lee, May 23 and 27, 1931, reel 45, NWPP; Rouse, *Lugenia Burns Hope*, 83–85.

75. Like many white interracialists, Ames assumed whites would direct the movement. Unlike Lucy Mason, Ames would oppose federal action against lynching, favoring state-level laws. See Hall, *Revolt Against Chivalry*.

76. Hall, *Revolt Against Chivalry*, finds that few Business and Professional Women's Club members joined the antilynching fight. YWCA industrial secretaries and Methodist women were on the leading edge of race and labor reform in the South. See Roydhouse, "'Universal Sisterhood,'" and Frederickson, "Citizens for Democracy" and "Shaping a New Society." Nobody on the Southern Council was associated with the Chamber of Commerce. Members included Ames (Commission for Interracial Cooperation, LWV), Mrs. Marvin Underwood, Miss Lillian Wade, Miss Risley (YWCA), Mrs. Sam Boykin, Mrs. Emmett Quinn (LWV, YWCA), Mrs. J. N. McEachern (Methodist), Adeline Swagerty, and Eleonore Raoul (LWV). Some were affluent (Underwood was married to a federal judge; McEachern was very wealthy), and others were not (Wade struggled to support dependents). Affiliations were gleaned from sources including Casey's letters to Muna Lee, reel 45, NWPP; boxes 34 and 105, Clark Papers; and Papers of Eleonore Raoul and Josephine Wilkins, Robert W. Woodruff Library, Emory University, Atlanta.

77. Hall, *Revolt Against Chivalry*, 53, citing Ames to Lillian Smith, December 31, 1941.

78. Although some southern unions were white supremacist, this Atlanta group seems to have been less so, perhaps because of the influence of the racially liberal Nance. A widely respected figure who was receptive to women's groups, Nance was chairman of the Georgia Federation of Labor's legislative committee in the early 1930s. He would become president of the Georgia federation before leaving for the CIO (where he and Lucy Mason would become close friends). Emmett Quinn was president of the Atlanta Machinists' Union and a pallbearer at the funeral of Mrs. Jerome Jones, wife of the editor of the *Journal of Labor* (the South's major labor newspaper). For union support of the Southern Council, see *Georgia Federation of Labor Proceedings*, April 15– 17, 1931, Brunswick, Ga., in SLP; *Journal of Labor*, January 30, 1931, 4, March 13, 1931, 4, and May 14, 1931, 1, 13.

79. Casey to Lee, n.d. [March 1931], April 30, 1931, and n.d. [May 1931]. Adeline Swagerty and Eleonore Raoul reported to Casey on the council's internal conflict; see Casey to Lee, June 18, 26, and n.d. [July] 1931, all reel 45, NWPP.

80. Casey to Lee, June 12, 1931, reel 45, NWPP; Southern Council minutes, January 4, 1932, box 105, Clark Papers; Casey to Lee, April 30, 1931, reel 45, NWPP. On southern women's modernity, see Hall, "Disorderly Women."

81. Muna Lee to Roy Howard, *New York World-Telegram*, March 23, 1931, reel 45, NWPP.

82. Stevens quoted in *Life and Labor Bulletin*, February 1926, 4. The WTUL reported sarcastically on Stevens's delivery of this speech "in sparkling evening gown and jewels, rich furs, and silver slippers" (ibid.). One article by Muna Lee began, "Even if night-work were necessarily detrimental to health . . . " (*New York World-Telegram*, March 14, 1931). Casey's columns in *Equal Rights* portrayed night work as attractive. Sometimes NWP writers called for eliminating all night work, but without acknowledging the obstacles to doing so.

83. See WB, *Employment of Women at Night*, a collation of data from other Women's Bureau studies made from 1919 to 1925. As late as 1949, good statistics on the extent of night work were not available. On erosion of the night work premium, see Wright, *Old South, New South*, 211.

84. WB, *Employment of Women at Night*, 10–12. This study lumped together married, separated, widowed, and divorced women, making it difficult to determine how many of the married women night workers had husbands present. Presumably, young mothers without male breadwinners were especially likely to prefer night work so that they could care for the children by day. (On the other hand, Wright, *Old South, New South*, 211, notes that some mills required families to provide a night worker, so it may have been that while men were present, women more often ended up on the night shift, reflecting the sexual division of unpaid labor.) An earlier survey of Georgia working women found that about 20 percent of them were widowed, separated, or divorced; see WB, *Women in Georgia Industries*. Almost half of fifty-seven women night workers interviewed by the Women's Bureau in 1928 said that daytime "home responsibilities" were the reason they preferred night work; see WB, *Effects of Labor Legislation*, 172–73.

85. Casey to Lee, n.d. [August 1931], reel 45, NWPP.

86. Florence Kelley, letter to editor, *New York World-Telegram*, March 21, 1931, reel 32, NCLP; Mason, *Standards for Workers*. The Consumers' League did not tackle the sexual division of domestic labor, but, as discussed in Chapter 2, neither did the NWP.

87. Casey to Lee, n.d. [June 1931, #12], reel 45, NWPP; Miss Laurence L. Thompson, AWP, to Georgians, July 18, 1931, reel 45, NWPP, circulated through AWP net-

works. Thompson's letter reached a female professor from Shorter College, who wrote Casey to protest its inaccuracy; Casey stood by the letter (Casey to Lee, August 8, 1931, reel 45, NWPP). LaGrange mill conditions were well above average; see Whitley, *Fuller E. Callaway*. Also see the column "A Workingwoman in Georgia," in *Equal Rights*, May 30, June 13 and 27, 1931, for rosy portraits of life in the mills.

88. Casey to Lee, n.d. [late June 1931, mistakenly identified as July 1931], reel 45, NWPP. According to Casey, the reason that women were not unionized was that women labor organizers had always been selected as "rubber stamps of rich women." Presumably this was a jab at the WTUL.

89. Casey to Lee, April 20 and June 6, 1931, reel 45, NWPP. Georgia was indeed strongly anti-union. In 1926 the Georgia Federation of Labor started a public education campaign to counter the Chamber of Commerce's open-shop drive; the federation also revived some dormant unions and central labor organizations in the late 1920s. Still, as late as 1939 (after both the AFL and CIO had enjoyed significant growth), only 7 percent of Georgia's nonagricultural workforce belonged to a union. This compared to 11 percent on average in the South and 22 percent outside the South. See Marshall, *Labor in the South*, 299, 102.

90. Casey to Lee, August 3, 1931, reel 45, NWPP. When Casey discussed the sex-based question with the Georgia Federation of Labor's Steve Nance, he tellingly replied, "It isn't anything about women. It is industry." Casey to Lee, June 26, 1931, reel 45, NWPP.

91. H.B. 120 was a bill to prohibit employment of women and minors between 7 P.M. and 6 A.M. in manufacturing. *Georgia House Journal, 1931*, 298, 612. Introduced July 1 by three Richmond representatives, H.B. 120 was not the Southern Council's own bill, but it had the group's support.

92. Casey to Lee, July 16, 1931, reel 45, NWPP; *Journal of Labor*, July 16, 1931, on Miss Allie Ware and two other Augusta unionists. The *Atlanta Constitution*, July 17, 1931, 9, reported on the hearing but did not record the presence of working women on either side. "Revolt against chivalry" is from the title of J. D. Hall's classic work.

93. Casey to Lee, July 12 and 16, 1931, reel 45, NWPP. At the hearing, T. M. Forbes of the Georgia Cotton Manufacturers and J. P. McGrath of the Georgia Manufacturers Association opposed H.B. 120; see *Atlanta Constitution*, July 17, 1931, 9. An NWP chart on 1931 legislative activity similarly obfuscated the employers' role in defeating women-only labor laws. The chart listed unions, the NCL, and the WTUL as supporters of sex-based bills and under "opponents" listed only the NWP, the Zonta Club, and the Business and Professional Women's Clubs. The chart shows that women's hours bills in thirteen states were defeated in 1931, but it does not point out that no sex-neutral bills passed. *Equal Rights*, March 26, 1932.

94. Casey to Lee, n.d. [August and September 1931], reel 45, NWPP; *Georgia House Journal, 1931*, 612.

95. *Equal Rights*, August 15 and November 7, 1931.

96. *Equal Rights*, April 25, 1931; member comment reported by Lee to Casey, April 21, 1931, reel 45, NWPP.

97. Lee to Casey, September 26, 1931, reel 45, NWPP; *Equal Rights*, October 31, 1931. On Casey's work in the Northeast, see *Equal Rights*; file 89, box 6, and file 58, box 4, Alma Lutz Papers, collection MC-182, SL; and Storrs, "Working Women's Participation." When Casey first arrived in Georgia, Eleonore Raoul of the LWV (with whom Casey had done suffrage work in West Virginia years earlier) told her that "the NWP jumped in and then out and all they did was to mess things up." Casey warned the NWP

against perpetuating this impression; she herself wanted to continue organizing for the ERA in the South. See Casey to Lee, May 18, 1931, reel 45, NWPP.

98. Sixth Annual Report of the Cotton Textile Institute, October 19, 1932, file 6, box 6, George Sloan Papers, SHSW; Hodges, *New Deal Labor Policy*.

99. Cott, *Grounding of Modern Feminism*, 73–77.

100. Buhle, *Women and American Socialism*; Strom, "Challenging 'Woman's Place' "; Gluck, "Socialist Feminism"; Faue, *Community of Suffering*, chap. 3; Shaffer, "Women and the Communist Party." Women represented one-sixth of Communist Party members in the early 1930s and almost half its membership a decade later.

101. Quoted by Florence Kelley to Victor Berger, December 19, 1923, file 1, box 14, Victor Berger Papers, SHSW. Kelley penciled in, "What do you think the Negroes think of this kind of South Carolina equality?" See also Florence Kelley, "The New Woman's Party," *Survey* 45 (March 21, 1922), 827.

102. Quotation from Cott, *Grounding of Modern Feminism*, 9, 76. On working-class women's rejection of the label "feminist" because they associated it with elite women, see Gluck, "Socialist Feminism," 285, and Orleck, *Common Sense*, 6. For Communist women's criticism of the NWP, see Ware, *Holding Their Own*, 133. Ladd-Taylor, *Mother-Work*, chap. 4, offers a similar reading of the schism between feminism and the Left in the 1920s.

103. Alma Lutz, "A Feminist Thinks It Over," *Equal Rights*, December 15, 1937.

104. "Red flag to the bull" quotation from Lucy Mason to Ruth Hanna, Texas, May 12, 1937, reel 54, NCLP. Many league activists no doubt remembered Florence Kelley's scathing comments on the pursuit of "equal opportunity." She wrote in 1921 that "many young women, who are not in daily touch with the wage earners, are easily captivated by empty phrases about equality of opportunity. . . . This year's grist of bills shows an alarming capacity on the part of women for serving as tools (consciously or unconsciously) of the worst exploiters." Quoted in Zimmerman, "Jurisprudence of Equality," 203.

105. When the University of Wyoming dismissed league member Caroline Ware in 1935 because she was married, Ware protested the damage to "the status of American women." Scharf, *To Work and To Wed*, 54. Ware was married to Gardiner Means, an important New Deal economist. Occasionally a feminist voice suggested that if need were to be the basis of the right to a job, then men too should be subject to a needs test; see Mary Robinson (WB) to Elisabeth Christman (WTUL), September 1939, cited by Kessler-Harris, *Out to Work*, 258.

106. By the end of the decade, three-quarters of American cities surveyed refused to hire married women as teachers; 84 percent of insurance companies and 65 percent of banks restricted married women's employment. Cott, *Grounding of Modern Feminism*, 209–10; Scharf, *To Work and To Wed*.

107. *NCL Bulletin*, June 1939; Lucy Mason to Harold Butler, International Labor Office, May 18, 1935, box 169, Winant Papers, FDRL. Scharf, *To Work and To Wed*, Faue, *Community of Suffering*, and Linda Gordon, *Pitied But Not Entitled*, may underestimate the extent to which the NCL and other women's groups protested sex discrimination in both temporary and permanent New Deal programs. The point here is that the protests of the anti-ERA side were less potent because they were afraid of sounding like the NWP.

108. *NCL Bulletin*, June 1939; Lucy Mason to Harold Butler, International Labor Office, May 18, 1935, box 169, Winant Papers, FDRL; Scharf, *To Work and To Wed*, 63–64.

1. Hearings, crushed stone, sand and gravel, and slag code, August 28, 1933, pp. 72–74, 81–82, 89–92, Entry 44, and Code Histories: Code 109, NRA Records.

2. Mason, *To Win These Rights*, 12. Molly Dewson confided to Grace Abbott that Mason seemed "pretty pale beside FK and you, but she has personality, devotion to industrial women, experience, prestige in her state and the South where I believe we should do a lot of work, and is, I understand, a good speaker and well respected by conservative men although they consider her 'advanced.'" Dewson to Abbott, October 4, 1931, quoted in Ware, *Partner and I*, 157. Dewson's Yankee bias also appears in her initial skepticism of Ellen Woodward, who she feared would be a "bit of southern fluff." Swain, *Ellen S. Woodward*, 41.

3. Quotations from Hawley, *New Deal*, 35. Signed by FDR on June 16, 1933, the National Industrial Recovery Act had three titles, the first of which created the NRA; the other two created a $3.3 billion public works program. Among the many studies of the NRA, see especially Hawley, *New Deal*; Bellush, *Failure of the National Recovery Administration*; and Colin Gordon, *New Deals*. For an overview of the New Deal, begin with Leuchtenburg, *Franklin D. Roosevelt*.

4. Mrs. Gerard Swope, whose husband headed General Electric and favored the cartelization approach, was on the NCL council, so one might argue that the league had ties to all three groups. However, Mrs. Swope's own views are unknown, and in any case she was not an active force in the league.

5. Had the NRA been better enforced and thus popular with at least some groups, it might have been renewed in June 1935 in a form revised to meet court objections. There is wide agreement that poor enforcement was a major stumbling block for the NRA, and that business domination of the process was to blame. See Hawley, *New Deal*, 33–34, 20–21; Fine, *Automobile under the Blue Eagle*; Galambos, *Competition and Cooperation*; Bellush, *Failure of the National Recovery Administration*; and Hodges, *New Deal Labor Policy*.

6. Theda Skocpol argues that the NRA "had to be created from scratch and through the emergency recruitment of administrators from business backgrounds. There was no pre-existing federal bureaucracy with the manpower and expertise needed to supervise a sudden, massive effort to draw up hundreds of codes to regulate wages, working hours, prices, and production practices in every U.S. industry" ("Political Response," 175). Also see Finegold and Skocpol, *State and Party*, and Hodges, *New Deal Labor Policy*.

7. The precedents for national wage and hour regulation were two child labor laws, found unconstitutional in 1918 and 1922, and the Board of Control of Labor Standards for Army Clothing, created during World War I at the NCL's initiative to prohibit government purchase of uniforms made under "substandard" conditions. On the latter, see Boris, *Home to Work*, chap. 4.

8. Mitchell and Chase were on the NCL council. Elizabeth Brandeis, Eveline Burns, Jessica Peixotto, Mary Van Kleeck, and later Mary Dublin and Caroline Ware were economists and league officers who promoted the underconsumptionist view. On underconsumptionist thought, see Fraser, *Labor Will Rule*, chap. 10; Brinkley, *End of Reform*, chap. 4; Rosenof, *Economics in the Long Run*; and Donohue, "Conceptualizing the 'Good Society.'"

9. See Taylor Society draft of an industrial code, October 1930, reel 54, and Florence Kelley to Alice Hamilton, November 10, 1932, reel 26, NCLP. Pabon, "Regulating Capitalism," discusses this code but does not note Kelley's participation. Other NCL

members who were active in the Taylor Society include Mary Van Kleeck, Clara Beyer, and Elinore Herrick. Guy Alchon posits a connection between women's expanding public activism and "efforts to equip managerial society with a planning capacity." See Alchon, "Mary Van Kleeck," 5–7. Besides the Taylor Society, other important cradles of industrial democracy were the Russell Sage Foundation and the Twentieth Century Fund; these groups overlapped substantially. See Fraser, "The 'Labor Question.'"

10. Board minutes, November 10, 1932, February 28 and April 28, 1933, reel 2; NCL Conference on the Breakdown in Industrial Standards, December 12, 1932, p. 1, reel 117, NCLP. Dewson believed her input "helped crystallize" FDR's commitment to an industrial recovery program that included national wage-hour standards (for both sexes). See Molly Dewson to "Franklin," n.d. [penciled "February 1933"], box 7, Mary Dewson Papers, FDRL.

11. In 1933 New York, Ohio, New Jersey, Connecticut, New Hampshire, Illinois, and Utah passed women's wage laws, the first six based on the NCL's new bill, and Massachusetts converted its law to a mandatory one. In 1936 Rhode Island enacted the NCL bill. NCL Conference on the Breakdown in Industrial Standards, December 12, 1932, and NCL Second Labor Standards Conference, December 12, 1933, reel 117, NCLP; Brandeis, "Organized Labor"; Cheyney, "Course of Minimum Wage Legislation."

12. Quotations from Martin, *Madam Secretary*, 262, and Hawley, *New Deal*, 22. Martin's account is more precise than that offered by Hunnicutt, *Work without End*, 157–61. Green soon relaxed his opposition to the minimum wage provision in exchange for recognition of labor's right to organize. On Perkins's use of the NCL bill as a model, see board minutes, April 28, 1933, reel 2, and Molly Dewson draft letters to FDR, Robert Wagner, and other legislators, May 11, 1933, reel 54, NCLP. On the Black bill, see board minutes, November 10, 1932, February 28, 1933, reel 2, NCLP.

13. Dewson wrote to the under secretary of commerce that strong minimum wage and maximum hours provisions would do more to aid industry and employees than "the best that could be worked out by trade associations." Molly Dewson to John Dickinson, May 17, 1933, reel 54, NCLP. Also see Dewson to Ruben Wood, House Labor Committee, and to Robert Wagner, Hugh Johnson, and others, May 11, 1933, reel 54, NCLP. On similar efforts by other progressives, see Bellush, *Failure of the National Recovery Administration*, chap. 1.

14. Roosevelt believed he owed Johnson an appointment, and neither FDR nor Perkins wanted him in charge of the public works program that was the other half of the National Industrial Recovery Act. Martin, *Madam Secretary*, 269.

15. Ibid., 271.

16. Ware, *Beyond Suffrage*, 91, briefly examines the channels of influence between the "women's network" and the NRA. In December 1933 Eleanor Roosevelt sent Hugh Johnson a stack of NCL material that would be "worth your reading"; a few months later, she wrote him, "I wish you would have a representative of the Consumers' League on the Committee which is reviewing the codes for inconsistencies. I'm sure it would be most helpful."

17. See Lizabeth Cohen, "New Deal State"; McGovern, "Consumption and Citizenship"; Jacobs, "Democracy's Third Estate"; Silber, *Test and Protest*; National Consumers Committee, *Consumer Activists*; and Mary Dublin, "The Consumer and Organization," address to Consumers' Union, May 16, 1938, reel 101, NCLP.

18. Quotations are from Mary Dublin's annual report, December 8, 1938, reel 2; Mary Dublin to Margaret Wiesman, April 30, 1938, reel 16; and Mary Dublin, "The Consumer and Organization," address to Consumers' Union, May 16, 1938, reel 101, all NCLP. Observing that wages were growing more slowly than prices and profits,

league activists called for tying NRA minimum wage rates to cost-of-living indices; see "The Acid Test of the New Deal," printed in *The Nation*, May 31, 1934 (Lucy Mason helped draft this open letter to FDR, and many league members signed it). Later the NCL supported a call for a permanent U.S. Consumers Division. Also see Lucy Mason to Mrs. [Marvin] Underwood, April 8, 1936, reel 94; Lucy Mason to Anna Settle, June 8, 1936, reel 15; Molly Dewson to Reva Beck Bosone, February 19, 1934, reel 23; board minutes, October 9, 1933, January 26, 1934, reel 2, all NCLP; policy committee minutes, March 22, 1934, file 18, box 5B, CL-NY Papers; Mary Dublin to Dorothy Bellanca, June 2, 1938, reel 34, NCLP; board minutes, June 14, 1938, reel 2, NCLP.

19. Bellush, *Failure of the National Recovery Administration*, 40; Hawley, *New Deal*, 75–81. The CAB's pressure resulted in February 1934 hearings at which dozens of small businesses, reformers, and representatives of black, female, and other workers ventilated complaints about the NRA.

20. NCL officers Paul Douglas, Frank Graham, Walton Hamilton, and William Ogburn were on the CAB. Other important figures on the CAB included Robert Lynd, Gardiner Means (married to Caroline Ware, a league member), and Frederic Howe. For a full account of the CAB, see Campbell, *Consumer Representation*.

21. Donohue, "Conceptualizing the 'Good Society,'" chap. 4, suggests Johnson deliberately feminized the CAB. On Schlink and the strike at Consumers' Research, see Silber, *Test and Protest*, and Donohue (Schlink quotations from 193, 195). Some historians inadvertently echo Schlink's gendered condescension toward the CAB. Ellis Hawley concludes that "the advocacy of the consumer's cause was left largely to eccentrics, nonconformists, misfits, dilettanti, and amateur enthusiasts; to such groups as college professors, club women, social workers, recent immigrants, and a few professional agitators, none of whom could wield much political power or speak for any well-organized constituency." Hawley, *New Deal*, 199.

22. Mason filled in for Dewson at the CAB for six days in October 1933. Board minutes, October 9, 1933, reel 2; annual meeting minutes, December 13, 1933 (emphasis added), reel 5, NCLP. It was Pauline Goldmark and Margaret Wiesman who suggested closer cooperation with NRA consumer agencies. Also see Elinore Herrick, "Summer of 1933 in the Consumers' League of New York," file 18, box 5B, CL-NY Papers.

23. Leuchtenburg, "New Deal," 121.

24. On the Blue Eagle's debt to the NCL, see *Survey* 69 (August 1933): 292. On the Women's Section of the NRA, see Ware, *Beyond Suffrage*, 88. On Settle's work, see executive board minutes, October 20, 1933, reel 2, KCL Papers. During World War II the Office of Price Administration would successfully combine technocratic expertise with grassroots participation in enforcement, for a time representing a model of the NCL's vision of a democratic administrative state. See Jacobs, "'How About Some Meat?'"

25. Herrick, "Summer of 1933," file 18, box 5B, CL-NY Papers. The NRA codes were enforced better in New York than in most states, and Herrick's competence did not go unnoticed. She eventually did take a government job, as New York regional director of the National Labor Relations Board. In this period she also was an adviser to Senator Robert Wagner, and she would head the New York campaign of the American Labor Party later in the 1930s.

26. Mason worried that if she accepted, "it might be impossible to maintain that friendly, but impartial and critical judgement" that had animated league criticism of various codes. Board minutes, April 4 and May 17, 1934, reel 2, NCLP. Also see Lucy Mason to Molly Dewson, April 11, 1934, box 15, DNC-WD Records.

27. During the 1930s "Wolman surprised and disappointed his former labor associates by becoming increasingly critical of the growing power of unions and of governmental policies regulating labor relations," according to Broadus Mitchell, *Dictionary of American Biography*, Supp. 7, 800. In 1937 Wolman proposed weakening the National Labor Relations Act; he was dropped from the NCL board in 1938.

28. Bellush, *Failure of the National Recovery Administration*, 41. Orleck, *Common Sense*, 151–54, erroneously suggests that Rose Schneiderman single-handedly wrote the labor codes for most industries employing large numbers of women. Schneiderman was influential on the LAB, but not to that degree, and in any case, the LAB lacked that kind of power.

29. Zieger, *The CIO*, chap. 1 (statistic from 18).

30. On Lewis's admiration of Roche, see Fraser, "The 'Labor Question,'" 79 n. 11, and Ware, *Beyond Suffrage*, 89.

31. Fraser, *Labor Will Rule*, 64, 116, 126, 163–70, 293–94; Boris, "Tenement Homework."

32. Lucy Mason to Martha Adamson, Missouri YWCA, September 4, 1933, reel 54, NCLP; on Winston-Salem tobacco workers' request, see Lucy Mason to Frances Perkins, May 15, 1934, reel 32, ibid.

33. See the resolution Mason proposed at the U.S. Women's Bureau's first Women's Industrial Conference, in *Life and Labor Bulletin*, February 1923.

34. Mason, "I Turned to Social Action," 149. For a less succinct statement of the same principles, see Mason, "Objection to exception of janitors . . . and other classes of unskilled labor in codes," August 1933, Item 542, Entry 23, NRA Records.

35. At the time of the hearings, the northern-born United Textile Workers could only claim to represent 3 percent of the textile workers. This weakness contrasted sharply with CTI's strength. See Hodges, *New Deal Labor Policy*, 35–37, 5; Galambos, *Competition and Cooperation*; and Lucy Mason testimony from Hearings, cotton textile code, vol. 3, June 27–30, 1933, pp. 34–48, Entry 44, NRA Records. Average wages in industries like steel and autos ranged from $20 to $30 a week. In heavily female-employing industries, the range was more like $16 to $20; see Kessler-Harris, *Out to Work*, 262–65.

36. Hearings, cotton textile code, vol. 3, June 27–30, 1933, pp. 34–48 (quotations, 35), Entry 44, NRA Records. Mason skipped over her prepared comments on child labor because CTI earlier in the hearing had volunteered to end child labor. Hodges, *New Deal Labor Policy*, points out that this was a CTI publicity stunt; child labor already had been virtually eliminated as a result of surplus adult labor.

37. Hearings, cotton textile code, vol. 3, June 27–30, 1933, pp. 34–48 (quotations at 37, 46, 47), Entry 44, NRA Records.

38. Hodges, *New Deal Labor Policy*, 53, asserts that "the consumer groups expressed strong disapproval of the code but offered no solution to the problems at hand." The league offered solutions, but few of them were adopted. Also see Skocpol, "Political Response." Quotation from notes of Deputy Administrator William L. Allen on testimony of June 29, 1933, Allen's vol. A/B, Entry 44, NRA Records. Ware, *Beyond Suffrage*, 90, notes that the U.S. Children's and Women's Bureaus often had the best data available on which to base code labor provisions. On the LAB's urgent need for data, see Frances Williams to Miss Roelofs, September 25, 1933, box I-C314, NAACP Papers, LC.

39. Hearings, cotton textile code, vol. 3, June 27–30, 1933, pp. 34–51 (quotation, 36), Entry 44, NRA Records. Kessler-Harris, *Woman's Wage*, 7–18, argues that minimum wage advocates who calculated women's subsistence budgets in the Progressive Era reinforced ideas about women's economic dependence by defining women's wages

in terms of needs rather than the value of the job performed. The NCL was willing to define men's wages in terms of need as well. The NCL believed that cost-of-living data gave workers a definite figure to fight for, and that the alternative approach, basing wages on "industry health," was more subject to employer manipulation. See Hart, *Bound by Our Constitution*, chap. 7. The NCL also made the unusual suggestion that every code should require a 10 percent bonus above the hourly minimum when a full week's work was not provided. NCL, "Proposed Principles for Labor Provisions of NRA Codes," December 1, 1933, reel 54, NCLP.

40. Lucy Mason to Josephine Goldmark, July 24, 1933, reel 92, NCLP. On the final code, see Code Histories: Code 1; "Statement of the CAB on the Code of the Cotton Textile Industry"; and confidential wire from Leo Wolman, LAB, to Hugh Johnson, July 8, 1933, Entry 21, Microfilm 213, reels 40–41, all NRA Records. The code set a maximum work week of forty hours, so the increase in hourly wages was more dramatic than the weekly increase. Bellush, *Failure of the National Recovery Administration*, claims the cotton textile code nonetheless increased both wages and real purchasing power.

41. See correspondence with Lucy Mason scattered in LAB and CAB correspondence files, Entry 353 and Item 532, Entry 23, NRA Records. Quotation from Gustav Peck to the NCL's Second Labor Standards Conference, December 12, 1933, proceedings transcript, p. 12, reel 5, NCLP.

42. Textile industry scholars have paid little attention to the exclusion of certain groups from NRA labor provisions, dismissing the issue as "quibbling" over "administrative minutiae." See Galambos, *Competition and Cooperation*, 214–15, and Hodges, *New Deal Labor Policy*, chap. 4. Fuller treatment is offered by Wolters, *Negroes and the Great Depression*, chap. 6; Sitkoff, *New Deal for Blacks*, 54–55; and Sullivan, *Days of Hope*, 44–52.

43. Historians have overlooked the YWCA's contribution to the JCNR. See correspondence of Frances Williams, a black woman who worked for the national YWCA as well as the JCNR, boxes I-C311 and I-C314, NAACP Papers, LC. Henrietta Roeloffs and Elisabeth Eastman (white YWCA leaders) also worked closely with John Davis. A Harvard Law School graduate, Davis was associated with the Communist Party. His radicalism and his tactics would cause tension within the JCNR, particularly when he tried to force it to support the National Negro Congress.

44. On Mason's NAACP affiliation, see Lucy Mason to George Haynes, April 8, 1935, reel 25, NCLP. For branch activities, see memos to branches, reel 16, NCLP, and Herrick, "Summer of 1933," file 18, box 5B, CL-NY Papers. In Ohio, Elizabeth Magee's branch was working to unionize laundry workers and to raise their minimum wage. For efforts by the New York WTUL to help black and Hispanic workers in the 1920s and 1930s, see Orleck, *Common Sense*, 160–66.

45. Hearings, cotton textile code, vol. 3, June 27–30, 1933, pp. 19–28 (Davis), 34–48 (Mason, quotations at 43–44), Entry 44, NRA Records. On the NRA administrator's reaction, see notes of William L. Allen on testimony of June 29, 1933, and Allen to Hugh Johnson, June 30, 1933, both in Allen's vol. A, ibid.; on retaining the exemptions in exchange for a narrow regional wage differential, see Hugh Johnson to FDR, July 9, 1933, Entry 21, Microfilm 213, reel 40, NRA Records.

46. Hearings, crushed stone, sand and gravel, and slag code, August 28, 1933, pp. 72–74, 81–82, Entry 44, NRA Records.

47. Ibid., 89–92; Mason, *To Win These Rights*, 15.

48. L. R. Mason, "Objection to Minimum Wage Discriminations against Negro Workers," August 29, 1933, reel 101, NCLP. Many copies of this memorandum are in NRA files.

49. Ibid.

50. T. Arnold Hill of the Urban League was one black activist who repeatedly defended wage differentials as serving black workers' interest; Walter White, Bill Hastie, Frances Williams, and John Davis all opposed him. See Walter White to Bill Hastie and White to Rose Coe, December 9, 1933, box I-C311, NAACP Papers, LC.

51. Wolters, *Negroes and the Great Depression*, 113–24, 127, 140, and 164 n. 63, cites Arthur Raper, "The Southern Negro and NRA." Will Alexander's reports to Mason on the subject expressed similar ideas. As noted in an earlier chapter, Mary Murray of the NWP Industrial Council opposed equal wages for women and men because she feared it would cost women their jobs. NRA codes and women-only state hours laws were easily blamed — by workers and by those hostile to all labor regulation — for costing blacks and women jobs, but the chief factors in displacement of blacks and women were underlying economic conditions and the fact that employers preferred white males if they could get them at the same rate.

52. Lucy Mason to Hugh Johnson, August 30, 1933, "Negroes" file; Mason to Solomon Barkin, September 16, 1933, and Clark Foreman to Harold Ickes, December 13, 1933, in "Differentials: Negroes and Whites" file; all Entry 23, NRA Records; George Haynes to JCNR members, October 4, 1933, box I-C311, NAACP Papers, LC. Harris resigned out of frustration with NRA officials, according to John Davis to Elmer Andrews, July 18, 1938, file 23, box 80, ACWA Papers. Harris was one of the young Marxists then challenging the NAACP "old guard." See Bates, "New Crowd," 352.

53. Wolters, *Negroes and the Great Depression*, 127–31. Eventually 176 NRA codes provided for a simple North-South differential, and forty-five codes defined other regional differentials; see WB, *Employed Women under NRA Codes*, 16.

54. Hearings, crushed stone, sand and gravel, and slag code, August 28, 1933, pp. 72–74, 81–82, 89–92, Entry 44, and Code Histories: Code 109, NRA Records.

55. Walter White to Frances Williams, June 2, 1934, box I-C311, NAACP Papers, LC. For a suggestion of cooperation between Mason and the JCNR, see Frances Williams to Miss Roeloffs, September 25, 1933, box I-C314, ibid.

56. Mabel Byrd's situation as a black employee at the NRA was complicated by the fact that Davis did not think she was competent, so she received no support from the JCNR or the NAACP. After observing Davis's behavior toward herself and other women, Frances Williams concluded that anyone hired by the JCNR would have to be a man, to get along with Davis. See Frances Williams to Walter White, September 25, 1933, Bill Hastie to Walter White, December 7, 1933, and Frances Williams to Elizabeth Eastman, March 22, 1935, box I-C311, NAACP Papers, LC. Codes on which Davis focused included cotton textiles, shipbuilding, lumber, iron and steel, and coal, all employers of black men; a report on the lack of progress in domestic service came last in Davis's "Summary of Work," September 15, 1933, ibid.

57. Only 12 percent of the 1.8 million black women wage earners in 1930 worked in occupations covered by NRA codes. See WB, *Employed Women under NRA Codes*, 17. That 12 percent, or 216,000, was still a significant number — more than all the women employed in the U.S. textile industry in 1930, for example. See letters in "Differentials: Negroes and Whites" and "Differentials: Men and Women" files, Item 542, and "Negroes" file, Item 581, both Entry 23, NRA Records. Nannie H. Burroughs and Hallie Q. Brown of the National Association of Colored Women registered their organization's opposition to race differentials; Burroughs was the treasurer of the JCNR.

58. The minutes of a September 5, 1933, strategy session called by the U.S. Women's Bureau, and attended by the NCL, YWCA, WTUL, and LWV, make no mention of race discrimination. This was despite Mason's comprehensive memo on the subject the

previous week. The group agreed to work for the elimination of child labor, home-work, lower rates for learners, exemptions for aged and handicapped workers, and sex-based wage differentials. See Unpublished Studies, 1936: "Cooperation with NRA," box 25, WB Records.

59. Taking NWP literature at face value, Pardo, *National Woman's Party Papers*, 3, gives full credit to the NWP for eliminating many sex differentials in NRA codes. Mary Anderson of the Women's Bureau meticulously documented the extensive activities of the bureau and its allies in shaping the codes; see her monthly reports in "Cooperation with NRA," box 25, WB Records. For the league's early advocacy of sex-neutral codes, see Molly Dewson to "Franklin," [February 1933], box 7, Dewson Papers, FDRL.

60. Based on a survey of letters in "Differentials: Men and Women" file, Item 542, Entry 23, NRA Records.

61. Mason's prepared testimony stated: "We believe in the basic principle that night work is unsound economically and socially and should be allowed only in those certain processes [that make] a continuous operation necessary, and that in such operations a higher hourly rate should be required for the 'grave yard' shift—a grave yard shift in more senses than one." If night work had to be permitted, and if night shifts were to be long, Mason at first said she would distinguish by sex: "If we are going back to the 8 or 10 hour night I would like to see women excluded, let us say, between 10 P.M. and 6 A.M." Hearings, cotton textile code, vol. 3, June 27–30, 1933, pp. 54 (Wiesman), 44 (Allen, Mason), Entry 44, NRA Records.

62. Ibid.; Code Histories: Code 1, NRA Records. Only nineteen NRA codes ex-plicitly prohibited night work; fourteen of these affected women only. A few other codes regulated night work by specifying plant closing and opening times, and the Women's Bureau urged that these be set in order to preserve women's access to both daytime shifts. WB, *Employed Women under NRA Codes*, 37.

63. Joint statement signed by Lucy Mason, Louise Baldwin of the LWV, Elisabeth Christman of the WTUL, and Theresa Paist of the YWCA, to NRA officials and FDR, September 15, 1933. Copies are scattered through NRA files, including "Differentials: Men and Women" file, Item 542, Entry 23, NRA Records. See also joint statement by Elisabeth Christman on behalf of ten women's organizations (including the NCL) at the February 28, 1934, NRA open hearings, *New York Times*, March 1, 1934, 1, 13, and protests against code sex discrimination by NCL, WTUL, and WB women, "Coopera-tion with NRA," box 24, WB Records.

64. See preceding note. Kessler-Harris has argued that "equal pay for equal work" campaigns had a double meaning, attracting the support of both the individualistic NWP and the "family-oriented" Women's Bureau. She believes the latter stressed keep-ing women from undercutting men's wages in order to preserve the traditional family. See *A Woman's Wage*, esp. 83–92. I find little emphasis on preserving the "family wage" in NCL sources for this period.

65. Maud Younger stated bluntly that the content of code labor provisions did not concern the Woman's Party, as long as the worker's sex was not mentioned. Hearings, cotton textile code, vol. 3, June 27–30, 1933, p. 32, Entry 44, NRA Records. On the number of code discriminations, see Mary Anderson to Frances Perkins, November 8, 1933, "Cooperation with NRA," box 24, WB Records. For NCL positions, see joint statement of women's organizations, September 15, 1933, "Differentials: Men and Women" file, Item 542, Entry 23, NRA Records (source for "so-called heavy ma-chines"); NCL, "Proposed Principles for Labor Provisions of NRA Codes," Decem-ber 1, 1933, reel 54; resolutions at NCL Second Labor Standards Conference, Decem-

ber 12, 1933, reel 5; and NCL recommendations for NRA renewal, in board minutes, March 1 and April 23, 1935, reel 2, all NCLP.

66. Florina Lasker, NCL Third Labor Standards Conference, December 10, 1934, proceedings transcript, p. 46, reel 6, NCLP. For attacks on homework, see Lucy Mason testimony at the hearings on lace and knitted outerwear industries, Entry 44, NRA Records. For more on homework regulation under the NRA, see Boris, *Home to Work*, chap. 7. The latter represents a shift from Boris's earlier work, which argued that the NCL camp primarily sought to protect "sacred motherhood" and to "save the home from the factory."

67. For an argument that working women, like working men, needed protection from undercutting by "their daughters" and other child laborers, see Kelley and Marsh, "Labor Legislation for Women."

68. Mary Anderson to Frances Perkins, May 31, 1934, "Cooperation with NRA," box 31, WB Records. An August 29, 1933, WB memo claimed learner provisions had been corrected in seven female-employing industries. In October 1934 Anderson claimed homework had been eliminated or tightly controlled in 104 of 121 code industries in which it occurred.

69. Scharf, *To Work and To Wed*, 111–14; Dawley, *Struggles for Justice*, 364–66.

70. For a useful assessment of the NRA's mixed impact on women workers, see Kessler-Harris, *Out to Work*, 262–72.

71. "A mill worker at Clinton, South Carolina," to Mr. Roosevelt, May 16, 1935, referred to Clara Beyer, box 22, entry 1A, DLS Records.

72. NCL Second Labor Standards Conference, December 12, 1933, reel 5, p. 5, NCLP.

73. Colin Gordon, *New Deals*, chap. 5, may overstate the extent to which labor was able to "organize capitalists," although he is correct that employers in certain labor-intensive industries came to appreciate unions' role in stabilizing labor standards and raising purchasing power. Significantly, many of these industries were large employers of female labor (coat and suit, hosiery, boot and shoe); NCL activists worked with these unions.

74. In addition to its recommendations at hearings and in policy statements, the league made NRA enforcement a focus of its annual conferences in 1933 and 1934. See NCL Second Labor Standards Conference, December 12, 1933, reel 5, and "Can Industry Police Itself?" session, NCL Third Labor Standards Conference, December 10, 1934, reel 6, NCLP.

75. Mason received many such letters, as did the Kentucky and Massachusetts branches. For example, North Carolina worker Helen Gregory asked Mason to send an inspector because the state NRA board had done nothing and the workers were afraid to complain. Gregory to Mason, May 19, 1935, reel 96, NCLP.

76. The NCL provided violations data from eighty-six sources in twenty-five states for Molly Dewson's testimony at the NRA open hearings on February 28, 1934. See "Code Evasions and Violations," February 28, 1934; Lucy Mason to Arthur Altmeyer, February 21, 1934; and Rosilla Hornblower to Hugh Johnson, March 19, 1934, all NCL file, box 15, DNC-WD Records. For questionnaires and correspondence, see NRA file, reel 92, NCLP. Also see *New York Times*, March 1, 1934, 13, and Mason, "Report on Southern Trip," March 1934, reel 6, NCLP.

77. See preceding note. NCL, "Proposed Principles for Labor Provisions of NRA Codes," December 1, 1933, reel 54, NCLP, also urged that codes require payment of the minimum wage in cash, without deductions for equipment, uniforms, lodging, or

meals. Deductions and payment in scrip were a particular problem for southern mill town workers and for women restaurant workers.

78. See remarks of Elinore Herrick, NCL Second Labor Standards Conference, December 12, 1933, pp. 7–9, reel 5; NCL, "Proposed Principles for Labor Provisions of NRA Codes," December 1, 1933, reel 54; suggestions for NRA renewal, board minutes, April 23, 1935, reel 2, all NCLP.

79. Gustav Peck, NCL Second Labor Standards Conference, December 12, 1933, proceedings transcript, pp. 38–39, reel 5, NCLP. Because the codes were so uneven in fairness to labor, a "white list" of NRA codes was organized. Dewson and Mason were on the advisory committee to the Approved Codes Label Council, as discussed by Miss Beatty at the NCL's Third Labor Standards Conference, December 10, 1934, proceedings transcript, pp. 177–79, reel 6, NCLP. Beatty cited Florence Kelley as the council's inspiration.

80. Kentucky league officer Mrs. Lawrence Leopold was on her state's NRA compliance board; Massachusetts league executive Margaret Wiesman was on the executive committee of the Massachusetts Recovery Board; and Mason recommended two men who were named to Virginia NRA boards. See board minutes, May 17, 1934, reel 2, NCLP; on Beyer's work evaluating local and state compliance boards in 1933, see file 213, Beyer Papers, SL. Herrick, NCL Second Labor Standards Conference, December 12, 1933, pp. 7–9, reel 5, NCLP. Anna Settle of the Kentucky branch later recalled that women "sat on compliance boards all over the country during NRA," and that their opinions were "unusually helpful." Settle to W. C. Burrow, February 4, 1941, reel 1, KCL Papers.

81. Board minutes, January 26, 1934, reel 2, NCLP.

82. On these hearings, which produced the National Recovery Review (Darrow) Board, see Bellush, *Failure of the National Recovery Administration*, 74, and *New York Times*, March 1, 1934, 1, 13. The NCL was represented by Elinore Herrick and Molly Dewson, and by Elisabeth Christman's joint statement for women's organizations.

83. NCL Second Labor Standards Conference, December 12, 1933, reel 5, NCLP; statements of Herrick and Dewson at the open hearings, *New York Times*, March 1, 1934, 13.

84. Beyer interview with Vivien Hart, 1983, p. 12, SL. A partial list of league members in state labor departments in the 1930s includes Frieda Miller and Emily Sims Marconnier in New York; Ethel Johnson in Massachusetts and then New Hampshire; Margaret Ackroyd, Louise Blodgett, and Metcalfe Walling in Rhode Island; Edna Purtell in Connecticut; Louise Stitt, Grace Meyette, and Margaret McFarland in Ohio; Beatrice McConnell in Pennsylvania; Naomi Cohn in Virginia; Maud Swett and Arthur Altmeyer in Wisconsin; and Effie Dupuis in North Dakota. Some of these moved to the U.S. Department of Labor. For league influence on minimum wage appointments in New Jersey, the District of Columbia, and Kentucky, see Emily Marconnier to Helena Simmons, July 31, 1936, reel 96, NCLP; Clara Beyer to Molly Dewson, July 27, 1937, Beyer Papers, SL; KCL minutes, May 18 and October 10, 1938, and "Annual Report of the President for Year 1938–9," reel 2, KCL Papers.

85. The elitist bias of the anti–machine politics movement is well known, but its feminist basis is not. On the feminist use of objectivity, see Fitzpatrick, *Endless Crusade*; on a "feminine version" of civil service reform in the Progressive Era, see Skocpol, *Protecting Soldiers and Mothers*, 155–61.

86. KCL board minutes, October 2, October 30, December 18, 1940, reel 2, KCL Papers. Women in labor departments in Massachusetts, Ohio, New Hampshire, and North Dakota made similar complaints. In states that had industrial commissions

rather than separate labor departments, appointees seem to have been especially likely to be friends of employers. The league lobbied for separate, independent labor departments, which were notably lacking in the South (see Chapters 5 and 6).

87. Molly Dewson proposed to "draw up a standard man and woman" labor department official in 1934. In 1938 Mary Dublin in effect drafted the U.S. Labor Department's guide to "the qualifications essential to the man or woman" wage-hour inspector. (In a typical behind-the-scenes initiative, Dewson had asked Arthur Altmeyer to have this statement drafted so the NCL could lobby for it.) See NCL Third Labor Standards Conference, December 10, 1934, reel 6; board minutes, March 1, 1935, reel 2; *NCL Bulletin*, April 1935; NCL correspondence with Division of Labor Standards, 1938, reel 36, all NCLP.

88. The 1893 Illinois hours law drafted by Florence Kelley required that a certain number of inspectors be female, as did many women's labor laws thereafter. In 1924 Kelley wrote that the best hope for laws favorable to working women would be "women judges and a responsible court" (quoted by Zimmerman, "Jurisprudence of Equality," 225). Elizabeth Brandeis recalled that on early minimum wage boards, union men "were apt to know and care little" about women workers' problems; see Brandeis, "Organized Labor," 231–32. Although Brandeis believed labor unions should be represented in labor law administration, she noted that union participation did not guarantee attention to the interests of female workers.

89. See "The Division of Labor Standards: Its Functions and Organization" [Clara Beyer, 1934], box 24, entry 1, DLS Records; Clara Beyer to Lucy Mason, October 30, 1935, reel 36, NCLP; NCL Third Labor Standards Conference, December 10, 1934, reel 6, NCLP; Martin, *Madam Secretary*, chap. 32; Murray, "The Work Got Done." Women headed the Children's and Women's Bureaus. A raft of mid-level employees (mainly female industrial economists) in the U.S. Department of Labor also were league members.

90. There is tension in the welfare state scholarship between critiques of decentralization and centralization. On the one hand, the New Deal is criticized for allowing states to administer many programs, which exacerbated sex and race discrimination in the distribution of benefits; see Quadagno, "From Old Age Assistance," and Mettler, *Dividing Citizens*. Suzanne Mettler argues that New Deal policy incorporated white men into a national polity but left women workers and welfare recipients under the inferior protection of the states (and she claims this was the result of political priorities rather than legal constraints). But other scholars emphasize the negative effects of bureaucratic centralization on community activism; see Faue, *Community of Suffering*, on the 1930s, and literature on the 1960s War on Poverty. For a suggestion that national policies could be conducive to grassroots activism, see Jacobs, "'How About Some Meat?'"

91. For earlier NCL versions of the Davis proposal, see NCL Second Labor Standards Conference, December 12, 1933, reel 5, NCLP, and statements of Herrick and Dewson at the NRA open hearings, *New York Times*, March 1, 1934, 13. For official approval of the Davis proposal, see NCL Third Labor Standards Conference, December 10, 1934, reel 6, NCLP.

92. See "NRA Needs an Overhauling: William H. Davis Only Outstanding Man on Johnson's Staff," *Washington Post*, February 15, 1934. During the Second World War, Davis would head the National War Labor Board. Like Sidney Hillman, Davis rose to prominence in New Deal labor circles in part because he had the support of progressive women of the NCL network. An oral history of Davis reveals both his professional cooperation with women and his gendered perception of their work (for example,

Mabel Leslie's outstanding work in labor mediation is described in the metaphor of "efficient housekeeping"). See interview with Donald Shaughnessy, 1958, box 5, unprocessed addition to William H. Davis Papers, SHSW.

93. Leuchtenburg, "New Deal." Muncy, *Creating a Female Dominion*, and Linda Gordon, *Pitied But Not Entitled*, offer parallel findings for the welfare policy arena.

94. This was the hearing at which Roche so impressed the coal miners; quotation from *Current Biography, 1941*, 724. On gendered hostility to Perkins, see Martin, *Madam Secretary*; Wandersee, "'I'd Rather Pass a Law'"; Sealander, *As Minority Becomes Majority*, 136. On Dewson's aspirations in late 1936, see Ware, *Partner and I*, 233.

95. Quotations from David Clark, cited in Wilkerson-Freeman, "Women and the Transformation of American Politics," 469; a New York employer in 1924, in Clarke Chambers, *Seedtime of Reform*, 38; and a textile industrialist in 1935, in Hodges, *New Deal Labor Policy*, 131. This last quotation echoes the 1916 condemnation by a South Carolina mill owner of reformers as "tender-hearted women living on incomes" (Davidson, *Child Labor Legislation*, 152–53). For the perception that women reformers were radical, see also Jensen, "All Pink Sisters."

96. Even in the Progressive Era many NCL members were pro-union, but in the 1930s promoting workers' right to organize became a central part of the NCL program. Scholars generally portray advocates of protective labor laws as ambivalent toward union rights. This reflects their focus on an earlier period and also the tendency to flatten out political differences among middle-class women.

97. *Survey Graphic* 23 (June 1934): 283–84. Editors Oswald Garrison Villard, Paul Kellogg, and Bruce Bliven, along with Mason, Helen Hall, John Dewey, and a few others, initiated the open letter to FDR. The group reconvened in 1935 as the Social Policy Committee. Mason's name was omitted from the published list of original drafters, with the result that historians have overlooked her involvement. See apology to Mason from Villard, May 23, 1934, reel 92, NCLP; Graham, *Encore for Reform*.

98. Lucy Mason to FDR, September 18, 1934, and September 17 draft, reel 92, NCLP.

99. On Johnson and the strikes, see Bellush, *Failure of the National Recovery Administration*, 126–33, and Hodges, *New Deal Labor Policy*, chap. 7. Noting that Perkins would not always head the department, Elinore Herrick and William Davis dissented from the 1934 proposal of the "Acid Test" letter to locate the national labor board in the U.S. Department of Labor. In light of this argument, in the recommendations for NRA renewal that the league sent to senators in early 1935, the NCL requested that an independent agency be created to guarantee workers' rights to organize and strike. See board minutes, March 1 and April 23, 1935, reel 2, NCLP. On this jurisdictional dispute between Frances Perkins and her friend Robert Wagner, see Wandersee, "'I'd Rather Pass a Law.'"

100. Mason, "Report on Southern Trip," March 1934, reel 6, NCLP. Cooperation with state labor departments and passage of new state laws were chief themes of the NCL's Third Labor Standards Conference, December 10, 1934, reel 6, NCLP. On intrastate services, see NCL, *Thirty-Five Years of Crusading*, and board minutes, April 23, 1935, reel 2, NCLP.

101. New Hampshire member comment from NCL Second Labor Standards Conference, December 12, 1933, proceedings transcript, p. 60, reel 5, NCLP. The Kentucky league dropped its own bills for the "bait" of a state NRA bill, only to have that bill fail to pass. The NRA also undermined the Kentucky league's enforcement activities. The lack of a state minimum wage law or a local NRA enforcement statute "created an impossible situation for the League." See Reports of the President, April 24, 1934, and

April 24, 1935, reel 2, KCL Papers. Also see Rosilla Hornblower to branch leagues, February 1934, in "Wages and Hours: Texas" file, reel 97, NCLP.

102. NCL Third Labor Standards Conference, December 10, 1934, proceedings transcript, p. 94, reel 6, NCLP.

103. Maud Younger, "The NRA and Protective Laws for Women," *Literary Digest* 117 (June 2, 1934): 27.

104. Board minutes, January 26, 1934, reel 2, NCLP.

105. Herrick, "Summer of 1933," file 18, box 5B, CL-NY Papers; board minutes, January 25, 1934, box 2, MCL Papers.

106. Board minutes, October 9, 1933, reel 2, NCLP.

107. On *Schechter Poultry Corp. v. United States*, 295 U.S. 495 (1935), see Leuchtenburg, *Franklin D. Roosevelt*, 145. On the NCL reaction, see *NCL Bulletin*, October 1935, and NCL, *Thirty-Five Years of Crusading*, September 1936 supplement.

Chapter Five

1. Board minutes, February 11, 1931, reel 2, NCLP.

2. On the emergent Keynesian elite and the southern strategy developed by Sidney Hillman and others, see Fraser, *Labor Will Rule*, 378, 391–92. On southerners who hoped the New Deal would democratize their region, see Sullivan, *Days of Hope*. Also see Wright, *Old South, New South*, chap. 7; Quadagno, "From Old Age Assistance"; Katznelson, Geiger, and Kryder, "Limiting Liberalism."

3. The next chapter reconstructs several of these campaigns.

4. Board minutes, February 28, 1933, reel 2, NCLP.

5. Not only was the southern industrial sector expanding, but continued mechanization between the 1930s and the 1950s diminished the importance to planters of labor relations in the agricultural sector. See Alston and Ferrie, *Southern Paternalism*.

6. For recent examinations of the shifting politics of memory and identity among southern whites, see Simon, *Fabric of Defeat*, and Joan Johnson, "'This Wonderful Dream Nation.'"

7. This estimate is based on Mason's state correspondence files and mailing lists. According to Mason's later recollection, only about sixty of those eight hundred became permanent NCL members. Mason's southern mailing list as of April 1937 is in box 316, DNC-WD Records; also see Mason to Elizabeth Magee, November 15, 1944, reel 29, NCLP. The early Southern Committee had about two hundred members from ten states; see annual meeting minutes, December 13, 1933, reel 5, NCLP. These figures do not include the memberships of the Kentucky and Louisiana leagues, which totaled approximately two hundred.

8. Recent studies demonstrating the vitality of southern dissent in this period include Reed, *Simple Decency*; Egerton, *Speak Now Against the Day*; and Sullivan, *Days of Hope*. These authors build on Sosna, *In Search of the Silent South*; Sitkoff, *New Deal for Blacks*; Dunbar, *Against the Grain*; Singal, *The War Within*; and Matthews, "Dissenters and Reformers." Some of these note women's participation, but none tries to explain it. Broad analyses of women's political activism, such as Sklar, "Historical Foundations," usually focus on the Northeast after a cursory exemption of the South. One exception is Scott, *Natural Allies*, which implies basic similarities in northern and southern women's reform activity. The literature on southern women's politics is developing rapidly (see subsequent notes), but little of it examines the years between 1930 and 1955.

9. First quotation from "A Southern Woman Succeeds Mrs. Florence Kelley," *World Outlook*, December 1932, reel 101, NCLP; second quotation from Mason, *Standards for*

Workers, 8, citing H. C. Nixon. Once a member of the Nashville Agrarians, Nixon had moved away from that group's antigovernment, anti–"Yankee capital" analysis; see Egerton, *Speak Now Against the Day*, 176.

10. Mason, "The Industrial South," address to the conference of the National Federation of Settlements, Norris, Tenn., June 4, 1936, reel 101, NCLP. This widely publicized address brought Mason attention from admirers and critics alike. Also see Mason, "Industrial Social Security in the South," address to the Southern Policy Committee conference, Chattanooga, Tenn., May 4, 1936, reel 64, Mason Papers, and Mason's addresses to the South Carolina senate and house, as reported in *Columbia (S.C.) State*, February 8, 1935, and *Anderson (S.C.) Independent Tribune*, February 11, 1935, reel 101, NCLP.

11. "Reverse old slogan that political democracy [must precede] industrial democracy. Political democracy is dependent on industrial democracy. Circular response theory works here too, [the] two grow together." Mason, notes for an address to Georgia Tech YMCA, November 10, 1937, reel 64, Mason Papers. Deploring "the nightmare in Europe," Mason hoped that "the Scandinavian countries may show the others the way." Mason to George Fort Milton, *Chattanooga News*, November 4, 1936, reel 97, NCLP. Mason, who favored universal suffrage and direct primaries, agitated to repeal poll taxes, which inhibited voting by people without ready cash (affecting the poor more than the affluent, and, arguably, women more than men).

12. National Emergency Council, *Report on Economic Conditions of the South*, 8; Mason helped write this report (see n. 102, below). On southern regionalism, see Tindall, *Emergence of the New South*, 584–85, 594–99, 626; Singal, *The War Within*; and Dorman, *Revolt of the Provinces*.

13. Lucy Mason to Dean Pipkin, January 26, 1936, reel 95, NCLP. Mason was helping Pipkin with his *Social Legislation in the South*, which would become, along with her *Standards for Workers*, the standard source on the subject. Mason also commented on articles for W. T. Couch and H. D. Wolf of the University of North Carolina, and H. C. Nixon of Tulane. Mason's correspondence with southern academics and editors is in files organized by state, reels 94–97, NCLP; also see Mason, "Report on Southern Trip," March 1934, reel 6, NCLP.

14. For Mason's work with the SPC, see "Industrial Social Security in the South," address to the Chattanooga conference, May 4, 1936, reel 64, Mason Papers; Mason's invitations to five female academics, reel 96, NCLP; Mason to J. Charles Poe, June 3, 1936, reel 29, NCLP; and Mason's report at the annual meeting, December 14, 1936, reel 6, NCLP. On the Southern Policy Committee (also Association), see Singal, *The War Within*, 290–91; Sullivan, *Days of Hope*, 63; and Egerton, *Speak Now Against the Day*, 175–77 (only Egerton notes that Mason was involved).

15. These intellectuals joined other southern academics who had been NCL officers when Mason was hired, including Josiah Morse of the University of South Carolina and Frank McVey of the University of Kentucky. See League annual ballots, reels 5–8, NCLP. Quotation about Odum's book from Tindall, *Emergence of the New South*, 584. On Elliott, see Appendix 2.

16. On the resignations from the SPC, see Egerton, *Speak Now Against the Day*, 175. For an effort by Mason to persuade an editor to support unions and wage-hour laws, see Mason to Jonathan Daniels, September 17, 1938, reel 62, Mason Papers. On the tentativeness of most southern liberals on labor and black rights, see Sosna, *In Search of the Silent South*, and Brinkley, "New Deal and Southern Politics."

17. "Father Wynhoven Opposes Federal Child Labor Plan," *New Orleans Times-Picayune*, March 7, 1934. Wynhoven directly criticized Mason and Florence Kelley.

18. Lucy Mason to George Googe and Steve Nance, May 15, 1937, reel 94, NCLP. In 1936, newspapers distorted Mason's speeches on "The Industrial South"; see Paul Kellogg to Sidney Hillman, June 14, 1937, reel 62, Mason Papers. David Clark, editor of the *Southern Textile Bulletin*, like others linked labor reform to Florence Kelley and northern radicalism. Another 1930s manifestation of southern fears of carbetbagging northern radicals was the famous "Scottsboro boys" case; see Dan Carter, *Scottsboro*.

19. See Tindall, *Emergence of the New South*; Hodges, *New Deal Labor Policy*; Simon, *Fabric of Defeat*; Sitkoff, *New Deal for Blacks*. On the textile strike, see also the award-winning film, *Uprising of '34*.

20. Quotations from Lucy Mason to Jonathan Daniels, September 17, 1938, and Mason to Molly Dewson, September 6, 1937, reel 62, Mason Papers. These letters were written in the context of southern violations of CIO organizers' civil liberties in 1937, but the substance of Mason's analysis was in place by the early 1930s.

21. Lucy's father, Landon Randolph Mason, a minister, rode with the legendary Mosby's Rangers for the Confederacy.

22. Virginia Consumers' League, *The General Assembly of Virginia and Social Legislation, 1936*, reel 97, NCLP. The Virginia league also called for protecting human persons before legal persons, lamenting that the Fourteenth Amendment had been used to protect corporations more than individual citizens.

23. Stokes's articles appeared in the *New York World-Telegram* and throughout the Scripps-Howard chain; ACWA reprinted them in 1937 in a pamphlet entitled *Carpet-baggers of Industry*. For Mason's contributions, see Mason-Stokes correspondence, reel 32, NCLP. On the significance of these articles in the national wage-hour bill fight, see Fraser, *Labor Will Rule*, 394.

24. Some southerners gave this argument a gendered twist. Virginia's labor commissioner demanded a women's eight-hour law to protect "country girls" from exploitation by "fly-by-night" industries, which came and went, recruiting and then "stranding" female labor forces and forcing them to turn to prostitution and relief. See *Richmond Times-Dispatch*, December 6, 1936. Since girls and women were the first to be sent out for wages by struggling farm families, and since women's wages were lower than men's, the "fly-by-night" industries tended to employ female labor. Particularly when this was white female labor, these circumstances were ripe for regulationist arguments that stressed protecting southern womanhood from profit-obsessed northerners.

25. *Columbia (S.C.) State*, February 8, 1935, clipping on Mason's address to South Carolina house, reel 101, NCLP.

26. Quoted in H. C. Nixon and Charles Pipkin, eds., *Southern Symposium in Advocacy of the Child Labor Amendment* (Louisiana Committee for Ratification, 1934). A copy of this flyer is in Appendix B of McNeill, "History of Child Labor Legislation in Louisiana."

27. "Consumers' League Official Thinks S.C. to Progress under Johnston," *Anderson (S.C.) Independent Tribune*, February 11, 1935. Mason told the South Carolina senate that "today, states' rights consists in using every bit of machinery the state has in order to raise the level of the people." *Sumter (S.C.) Item*, February 6, 1935; see also Mason address to National Federation of Settlements conference, June 4, 1936, all reel 101, NCLP.

28. Lucy Mason to Virginia prospects, April 12, 1935, reel 110; Mason to James Sidel, Alabama, August 31, 1935, reel 94, NCLP.

29. Sosna, *In Search of the Silent South*, 102, quotes Mason as saying, "We have democracy with a great big 'D' in the South, but we do not have democracy for the people." Also see Mason to Molly Dewson, September 6, 1937, reel 62, NCLP.

30. Mason, "Report on Southern Trip," March 1934, reel 6, NCLP.

31. Nettie Keever to Mason, February 16, 1936, reel 96; Robbie Trent, Southern Baptist Convention, to Mason, and Beth Cunningham, Director of Religious Education, Centenary Church, to Mason, both January 24, 1936, reel 97; also see Howard Emerson, TVA administrator, to Mason, June 17, 1936, reel 97, all NCLP.

32. Mason, "Report on Southern Trip," March 1934, reel 6, NCLP.

33. Mason rarely identified the race of her contacts, although some were African American, such as Charles Johnson of the Southern Policy Committee. Later, reporting on a seminar at Talladega College in Alabama, Mason did not indicate that this was an African American institution (although she did remark that Talladega's women faculty seemed better informed and more pro-union than the men). See Mason to Augusta Roberts, April 14, 1941, reel 62, Mason Papers.

34. Mason to Frank Graham, December 6, 1938, quoted by Salmond, *Miss Lucy of the CIO*, 155.

35. Even in later years, Mason soft-pedaled her own views when trying to penetrate white southern racism. In her 1945 article, "The CIO and the Negro in the South," she deliberately took a middle-of-the-road tone to avoid "scaring off new white members with all their racial prejudices still unremoved or mitigated." Mason to Molly Dewson, March 1, 1946, box 3, Dewson Papers, FDRL. On Mason's interracial activities in Richmond and later for the CIO, see Salmond, *Miss Lucy of the CIO*. For an analogous reading of white woman suffragists in Virginia, see Lebsock, "Woman Suffrage and White Supremacy."

36. Mason to Louise Leonard McLaren, Southern Summer School, March 6, 1933, reel 34, NCLP.

37. At Mason's request, Louise McLaren provided names of former Southern Summer School students who were union members and in a position to join the league safely; see McLaren to Mason, November 3, 1932, reel 34, NCLP. For reports on Mason's address to the Miami Central Labor Council, see Mason to Zoe Manning, April 3, 1937, and Mason to James Chace, March 29, 1937, reel 94, NCLP. On Virginia and Kentucky, see Chapter 6. In North Carolina, three women testified against their employers to support an hours bill for women; see *Raleigh News and Observer*, September 9, 1936, clipping on reel 96, NCLP.

38. Mason to Louise McLaren, March 6, 1933, reel 34, NCLP.

39. Mason, "Something You Can Do," October 1936, reel 110, NCLP. Some responses are enclosed in Charlotte Califf, Atlanta YWCA, to Mason, November 30, 1936, reel 94, NCLP.

40. Mason to Margaret Wiesman, March 25, 1936, reel 16, NCLP. Until the charts were made, the best source was Mason's 1931 pamphlet, *Standards for Workers in Southern Industry*.

41. Mason to Clara Beyer, January 10, 1934, reel 35, NCLP; minutes of annual meeting, December 14, 1936, reel 6, NCLP. Gladys Boone, an economist at Sweet Briar College for Women in Virginia and a former WTUL leader, helped Mason compile the charts.

42. On the conference method as a hallmark of women's political style, see Linda Gordon, *Pitied But Not Entitled*, 93, and Sealander, *As Minority Becomes Majority*. Martin, *Madam Secretary*, chap. 32, suggests that the labor conferences ranked among Perkins's most important achievements.

43. Mason to Clara Beyer, November 18, 1934, reel 35, NCLP; also see Mason to Frances Perkins, December 16, 1933, reel 32, NCLP.

44. See Mason-Beyer correspondence (quotation from Mason to Beyer, January 8,

1935), reel 36, NCLP; report on Nashville conference, reel 68, NCLP; list of participants, folder 196, Beyer Papers, SL; and *Proceedings of the Southern Regional Conference
on Labor Standards and Economic Security*, Nashville, Tenn., January 20–21, 1935, file 71,
Graham Papers.

45. Mason to Clara Beyer, December 20, 1935, reel 36, NCLP. On Mason aid to Labor
Department conferences, see Beyer to Mason, February 2 and December 2, 1935, reel
36; board minutes, February 28, 1936, reel 2; Report of Committee on Minimum Wage
(including Mason) at Asheville, N.C., conference, October 1935, reel 68, all NCLP.
Wilkerson-Freeman, "Women and the Transformation of American Politics," 546, incorrectly claims that the March 1935 conference in Richmond was the first of its kind.

46. Mason to Thomas Stokes, January 27, 1937, reel 32, NCLP; Mason to Clara
Beyer, January 26, 1937, reel 36, NCLP; and see William Shands Meacham to Mason,
June 3, 1937, box 3, Dewson Papers, FDRL. Mason's tactic rendered the Consumers'
League less visible to historians as well as to contemporaries.

47. Mason to Clara Beyer, February 13, October 26, and November 18, 1935, reel 36;
Mason to Charles Pipkin, January 26, 1936, reel 95, all NCLP. U.S. Division of Labor
Standards files document Mason's effectiveness at persuading local southern officials to
work with the agency; for example, see T. E. Whitaker, Georgia Commissioner of
Labor, to Clara Beyer, May 12, 1937, file 6-1(12), entry 1A, DLS Records.

48. In 1933 these coalitions were behind the passage of the NCL's minimum wage
bill for women in New York, Connecticut, New Jersey, Ohio, Illinois, and Massachusetts (where the new law replaced an older nonmandatory minimum wage law).
The league's bill became law in New Hampshire as well, apparently without the aid of a
labor standards committee. See NCL Conference on the Breakdown of Industrial Standards, December 12, 1932, pp. 21–22, and minutes of annual meeting, December 13,
1933, both reel 5, NCLP, and Cheyney, "Course of Minimum Wage Legislation." On
local leagues' promotion of the New Deal, see Trout, *Boston, the Great Depression, and
the New Deal*; Ingalls, *Herbert H. Lehman*; Felice Gordon, *After Winning*; Dennis
Harrison, "Consumers' League of Ohio"; and Dorothy Smith McAllister Papers,
Michigan Historical Collection, Bentley Historical Library, University of Michigan,
Ann Arbor. On the usually prickly state-federal relations in the New Deal, see Patterson, *New Deal and the States*, and Brody, Braeman, and Bremner, *The New Deal*, vol. 2.

49. "Digest: Kentucky Minimum Wage Bill," n.d. [probably late 1933], reel 1, KCL
Papers. On the New York committee and its victories, see NCL Second Labor Standards Conference, December 12, 1933, p. 13, reel 5, NCLP; "Minimum Wage, 1921–
1946," file 5, box 29B, CL-NY Papers; and Ingalls, *Herbert H. Lehman*, 182.

50. Minutes of annual meeting, December 13, 1933, reel 5; see also board minutes,
February 28, 1933, reel 2, NCLP. Mitchell was on the NCL board until he took a
position with the Resettlement Administration.

51. On the origins of women's political culture in the Northeast, see Sklar, "Historical Foundations." The gap between southern and northern women in education, occupation, and birthrate was narrowing but would not close until after World War II;
see Hall, *Revolt Against Chivalry*, 170, and Blackwelder, "Mop and Typewriter."

52. The growing list of state and local studies of southern women's reform work
includes Roth, *Matronage*, on Atlanta; Wedell, *Elite Women and the Reform Impulse*, on
Memphis; Thomas, *New Woman in Alabama*; Gilmore, *Gender and Jim Crow*, Sims,
Power of Femininity, and Wilkerson-Freeman, "Women and the Transformation of
American Politics," on North Carolina; Tyler, *Silk Stockings*, on New Orleans; Turner,
Women, Culture, and Community, on Galveston, Texas; McArthur, *Creating the New
Woman*, on Texas; and Joan Johnson, "'This Wonderful Dream Nation,'" on South

Carolina. See also Swain, *Ellen S. Woodward*, and valuable data on women in six southern states in Elna Green, *Southern Strategies*.

53. Mason quoted from minutes of annual meeting, December 13, 1933, reel 5, NCLP. Many of the studies cited in the preceding note discuss southern women's groups and child labor reform; for an early overview, see Davidson, *Child Labor Legislation*.

54. Mason to Eleanor Copenhaver, February 13, 1931, quoted by Roydhouse, "'Universal Sisterhood,'" 356. Mason's comment was to an old friend from Richmond, so she may have been comparing women of the Carolinas and Georgia unfavorably with Virginians. On league work in North Carolina, see reel 96, NCLP, and correspondence with Mason in Graham Papers. In public, Mason carefully praised southern women; see Mason, *Standards for Workers*, 39.

55. On southern white women's cultivation of the Lost Cause myth, see Sims, *Power of Femininity*, and Joan Johnson, "'This Wonderful Dream Nation.'" On club women and suffrage, see also Elna Green, *Southern Strategies*, 175. Johnson's study of South Carolina women questions the emphasis of Anne Scott, Mary Thomas, and others on the similarity between southern and northern female reformers. Johnson finds that South Carolina white women's reform work had distinctively southern meaning and served conservative ends. She does not examine Mary Frayser or the handful of other progressive white women who worked with the NCL in South Carolina. Still, Johnson's and my work together underscore my point that historians must pay more attention to variations in political ideology among white middle-class women in all regions.

56. See Thomas, *New Woman in Alabama*, 101, and Davidson, *Child Labor Legislation*, on the work of English-born Ashby. According to Roydhouse, "'Universal Sisterhood,'" husbands and brothers pressured many members of the Legislative Council of North Carolina Women after the group proposed a survey of mill conditions. On South Carolina, see Joan Johnson, "'This Wonderful Dream Nation,'" chap. 8.

57. Roydhouse, "'Universal Sisterhood,'" 355–56; Swain, *Ellen S. Woodward*, 36; quotation from Mason to Mary Frayser, May 4, 1936, reel 96, NCLP. Mason's view was seconded by consumer activist F. J. Schlink, who claimed that getting the GFWC to support antimanufacturer legislation was like asking the American Legion to support pacifism. Donohue, "Conceptualizing the 'Good Society,'" 224. Skocpol, *Protecting Soldiers and Mothers*, incorrectly casts club women as major backers of labor laws in the Progressive Era.

58. Joan Johnson, "'This Wonderful Dream Nation.'"

59. Mason correspondence with Jessie Laurence, April–May 1936, reel 96, NCLP. In 1935 Laurence founded the South Carolina Women's Council for the Common Good, which claimed a membership of "60,000 women with real weight with legislators." Claudia Phelps to Mason, January 31, 1937, reel 97, NCLP.

60. Mary Frayser to Mason, October 22 and April 23, 1936, reel 96, NCLP. Frayser was legislative chairman of the Council for the Common Good until 1943.

61. Jessie Laurence to Mason, February 16, 1937, reel 97, NCLP. Laurence worked on child labor, shorter hours for men and women, social security, and compulsory school attendance. Mary Frayser to Mason, August 20, 1936, reel 96; Claudia Lea Phelps to Mason, December 16, 1935, reel 96, and January 31, 1937, reel 97, all NCLP.

62. Southern NWP members included Anita Pollitzer of South Carolina, Burnita Shelton Matthews of Mississippi, and Helen Hunt West of Florida. At its 1937 convention, the National Federation of Business and Professional Women's Clubs resolved to oppose all sex-based legislation; see *Equal Rights*, February 1, 1938.

63. *Equal Rights*, August 1, 1935. It is unlikely that West's objections were the primary cause of the bill's defeat. For NWP hostility to federal programs and the

Roosevelts, see Helena Hill Weed, "The New Deal that Women Want," *Current History* 41 (November 1934): 179–83.

64. "Virginia Working Women Threatened," *Equal Rights*, February 1, 1938.

65. For examples, see Mason, "Work, Wages and Security," *Adult Bible Class Magazine*, November 1933, reel 101, NCLP; Mason, "Industrial Democracy," *The Church Woman* (1937), reel 65, Mason Papers; articles listed in Mason, "Report on Southern Trip," March 1934, reel 6, NCLP.

66. On this issue, see Mason to Clara Beyer, January 8, 1935, reel 35, NCLP, and Mason to Margaret Wiesman, August 4, 1937, MCL Papers. For Mason's work with the Federal Council of Churches, see reel 25, NCLP.

67. First two quotations from Frederickson, "Shaping a New Society," 352; third quotation from "A Southern Woman Succeeds Mrs. Florence Kelley," *World Outlook*, December 1932, reel 101, NCLP. Also see Mason, "Report on Southern Trip," March 1934, reel 6, ibid. A member of the NCL Council, Bertha Newell was a founder of the Southern Council on Women and Children in Industry in 1931. Mrs. A. M. Tunstall of the Alabama Child Welfare Department was another Mason ally in the Methodist women's network. See Tatum, *A Crown of Service*.

68. Mason to Estelle Haskins, March 24, 1936, reel 101, NCLP. Bertha Newell quoted in Frederickson, "Shaping a New Society," 351. Newell initially was ambivalent to national reform organizations, but male church officials' hostility pushed the Methodist women into alliances with groups like the NCL.

69. See "Wages and Hours" files by state, reels 94–97, NCLP.

70. *Richmond Times-Dispatch*, October 29, 1936, p. 1.

71. George C. Stoney to Frank Graham, April 29, 1940, quoted by Salmond, *Miss Lucy of the CIO*, 201.

72. Appendix 2 provides biographical data on some of these southerners. Wisner was inspired by Eleanor McMain, head resident of Kingsley House in New Orleans; McMain in turn was influenced by Jane Addams. See Wisner, *Social Welfare Legislation*, 122. On Newell, see Frederickson, "Shaping a New Society"; on Elliott's relationship with Tillett, see Wilkerson-Freeman, "Women and the Transformation of American Politics." Eleonore Raoul of the Southern Council for Women and Children in Atlanta earned her B.A. from Chicago in 1912; see her papers at Emory University, Atlanta.

73. See Appendix 2. Virginia Durr of Alabama, who does not seem to have been active in the league but worked with Lucy Mason in the Southern Conference for Human Welfare, claimed that studying at Wellesley transformed her racial attitudes. See Margaret Wolfe, *Daughters of Canaan*, 160. A few southern league women were not actually native southerners. In addition to Harriet Elliott, these included Pennsylvania-born Naomi Cohn and Louise Leonard McLaren and Wisconsin-born Bertha Newell.

74. Some were the daughters of merchants and bankers, but none came from major textile or landowning families. Anna Hubbuch Settle's father was a Louisville merchant, and Ida Weis Friend's father was a cotton merchant in New Orleans; Josephine Wilkins came from a prominent Athens, Georgia, family with interests in banking and garment manufacture.

75. See Appendix 2. The Kentucky Consumers' League had several Jewish officers and used the membership lists of the Council of Jewish Women for recruiting purposes. Naomi Cohn of Virginia and Ida Weis Friend of the New Orleans league were officers of the National Council of Jewish Women (NCJW). Rogow, *Gone to Another Meeting*, does not discuss the South, but see Wilkerson-Freeman, "Two Generations of Jewish Women"; Wenger, "Jewish Women of the Club"; and Berman, *Richmond's Jewry*.

76. Mason quoted from "Report on Southern Trip," March 1934, reel 6, NCLP, and

see correspondence files by state, reels 94–97, NCLP. Mason's successors at the Richmond YWCA, Brownie Lee Jones and Eleanor Copenhaver, had long careers as activists for class and race justice; so did Louise Leonard McLaren, who was a YWCA industrial secretary before she founded the Southern Summer School for Women Workers in 1927. All these women were NCL allies in the 1930s and later. On southern YWCAs and the Southern Summer School, see Brinson, "'Helping Others to Help Themselves'"; Roydhouse, "Bridging Chasms"; Salmond, *Miss Lucy of the CIO*, chap. 3; Margaret Wolfe, *Daughters of Canaan*, 162–68; and Frederickson, "'I Know Which Side I'm On.'" On Katharine Lumpkin, another radical southerner with roots in the YWCA, see Hall, "Open Secrets." For an argument that YWCAs were more pro-labor and pro–race reform than YMCAs, see Ken Fones-Wolf, "Gender, Class Relations."

77. Mason to Clara Beyer, November 17, 1935, reel 36, NCLP. Mason addressed the Georgia and Florida social work conferences in early 1937; see Florida file, reel 94, NCLP.

78. Elinor Nims Brink to Lucy Mason, October 29, 1936, reel 94, NCLP. Brink, a social scientist, previously worked for the Florida Works Projects Administration. Mildred Mell, dean of Shorter College, corresponded with Mason about Georgia politics, lamenting Governor Rivers's betrayal of labor bills; see Mell to Mason, October 1936, reel 94, NCLP. In 1937 Mason lectured to the classes of Beulah Bailey, head of the Economics and Commerce Department of Florida State College for Women; see Florida file, reel 94, NCLP.

79. Master of social work theses supervised by Wisner include McNeill, "History of Child Labor Legislation in Louisiana," and Edler, "Administration of the Child Labor Law in New Orleans."

80. Mason to Miss Mel, U.S. Division of Labor Standards, October 8, 1936, reel 36, NCLP. Mason sympathized with Leila Johnson's heavy teaching load, small salary, and lack of secretarial support.

81. Club woman Eunice Ford Stackhouse quoted from the club-sponsored biography she authored in 1944, *Mary Elizabeth Frayser*. First Frayser quotation from Frayser to Lucy Mason, October 7, 1935, reel 96, NCLP; second from Madden, "In the Thick of the Fray," 119. On other South Carolina women's positive view of slavery, see Joan Johnson, "'This Wonderful Dream Nation,'" 258.

82. On southern suffragists' disillusionment with states' rights, see Wheeler, *New Women of the New South*, chap. 5. Elna Green, *Southern Strategies*, and Lebsock, "Woman Suffrage and White Supremacy," suggest a correlation in the 1910s between southern suffragism and other democratic movements. Not all white suffragists were progressive on labor and race questions, but virtually all women who were progressive on race and labor had been suffragists. Green finds that the racist, states' rights suffragism of Kate Gordon of New Orleans was atypical. In the 1910s Kate Gordon's sister Jean led a league drive against child labor, but she died in 1931; no other states' rights suffragists are known to have been NCL members.

83. Wilkerson-Freeman, "Women and the Transformation of American Politics," chaps. 8–9.

84. The elitist bias of the anti-Long campaign is well established, but Tyler, *Silk Stockings*, finds a gender component to that campaign as well. Tyler may overstate these women's concern with Long's vulgarity and sexual infidelity at the expense of discussing their political ideologies. Members of the Women's Committee actively supported the National Recovery Administration and were outraged at Long's attacks on it. See "Long's Attack on NRA Is Condemned: Women of U.S. Are Urged to Insist on Ouster from Senate," unidentified clipping, and "Women Seek Scalp of the Crawfish," *New*

Orleans States, September 2, 1933, both in box 18, Ida Weis Friend Papers, Tulane University Library.

85. The Democratic National Committee Women's Division tried to get Georgia Democratic women to back Lawrence Camp, a liberal rival to Senator George. The state's leading female party regulars apologetically resisted, but others organized for Camp. See May Thompson Evans–Lucy Mason correspondence, NCL file, box 316, and Georgia file, box 204, DNC-WD Records. My evidence indicates similar alliances between the Women's Division and progressive women in Virginia. On the importance of these "purge" attempts, see Patterson, *Congressional Conservatism*. For more on Dewson and southern women Democrats, see Ware, *Beyond Suffrage*; Swain, *Ellen S. Woodward*; and Wilkerson-Freeman, "Women and the Transformation of American Politics."

86. See the case studies in Chapter 6.

87. Anna Settle of the Kentucky league unsuccessfully sought an appointment to the Social Security Board in 1935; Adele Clark worked for the Works Projects Administration in Richmond; Leila Johnson was the assistant state relief administrator for South Carolina; and Elizabeth Wisner of New Orleans was named to the Advisory Committee on Social Security of the Senate Finance Committee. Correspondence in the DNC-WD Records illuminates the struggle of women in southern as well as other states for fifty-fifty gender representation in party politics.

88. The recently noted link between feminist labor reformers of the interwar years and liberal feminists of the 1960s seems to hold true for the South. In the 1960s Mary Frayser would be the "moving spirit" behind the South Carolina Commission on the Status of Women, according to Chepesiuk, Evans, and Morgan, *Women Leaders in South Carolina*, 147. Gladys Tillett, a league ally and Democratic Party activist from North Carolina who succeeded Molly Dewson as head of the party's Women's Division, would emerge in the 1970s to lead the state campaign for the ERA; see Wilkerson-Freeman, "Women and the Transformation of American Politics," 593. For a similar connection in New Orleans, see Tyler, *Silk Stockings*. For this link outside the South, see Lerner, "Midwestern Leaders"; Peterson, "You Can't Giddyup by Saying Whoa"; and Horowitz, *Betty Friedan*.

89. Mason to Helen Mankin, October 22, 1936, reel 94, NCLP. Mason would not be so optimistic about the strength of progressive forces a year later. Sullivan, *Days of Hope*, argues that the New Deal created new possibilities for class and race reform by raising the expectations of certain southerners; I extend that argument to include gender relations and women.

90. For a somewhat analogous argument about the shifting political identity of South Carolina mill workers in the 1930s, see Simon, *Fabric of Defeat*.

91. See Sitkoff, *New Deal for Blacks*, esp. 110–11; Sullivan, *Days of Hope*, chaps. 2–3; Brinkley, "New Deal and Southern Politics"; and Patterson, *Congressional Conservatism*. Political scientist Kristi Andersen suggests that an electoral "gender gap" emerged in the 1930s; see Andersen, *Creation of a Democratic Majority* and *After Suffrage*. Molly Dewson and Mary Dublin frequently claimed that women were more supportive of Roosevelt than men.

92. Quotations from Sitkoff, *New Deal for Blacks*, 106, 118. Talmadge supporters circulated a picture of Eleanor Roosevelt with ROTC cadets at Howard University that bore the caption, "A picture of Mrs. Roosevelt going to some nigger meeting, with two escorts, niggers, on each arm." They also attacked her for hosting a garden party for students of the National Industrial Training School for Girls, calling the guests "nigger whores." Bilbo castigated white Americans for lacking the race-consciousness of Hitler's Germany.

93. On the relationship between gender inequality and white supremacy in southern politics, see Hall, *Revolt Against Chivalry*; MacLean, *Behind the Mask of Chivalry*; and Gilmore, *Gender and Jim Crow*.

94. Patterson, *New Deal and the States*, 138. Here Talmadge was stirring class as well as gender resentment.

95. "Father Wynhoven Opposes Federal Child Labor Plan," *New Orleans Times-Picayune*, March 7, 1934.

96. Simon, *Fabric of Defeat*, 195.

97. Mason to Olivia Fuller, Houston YWCA, August 14, 1936, reel 97, NCLP.

98. Margaret Wiesman to Mason, June 15, 1937, MCL Papers.

99. William Shands Meacham, associate editor, *Richmond-Times Dispatch*, to Mason, June 3, 1937, box 3, Dewson Papers, FDRL; also see "Press and Periodicals" files, reel 32, and wage-hour files for specific states, NCLP. Francis P. Miller, letter of reference for Mason, May 18, 1937, reel 62, Mason Papers.

100. The Southern Conference for Human Welfare, best known for its black civil rights work, in late 1938 passed a resolution urging the southern states to enact wage and hour laws to supplement the new FLSA standards. A copy of the resolution, almost certainly sponsored by Lucy Mason, is in box 8, International Division, WB Records. In response to postwar red-baiting, the Southern Conference would drop its labor agenda and emphasize race reform; see Dunbar, *Against the Grain*. On Mason's role in these groups, see Salmond, *Miss Lucy of the CIO*, and Mason Papers.

101. For an argument that outside assistance indeed was indispensable to local labor activists in the South, see Draper, "New Southern Labor History."

102. Mason tried unsuccessfully to make the section on labor "more emphatic"; see Lucy Mason to Ralph Hertzel Jr., May 30, 1939, reel 62, Mason Papers. Accounts vary on the origins and authorship of the "anonymous" report by the National Emergency Council. Writing in Lillian Smith's controversial *North Georgia Review*, Mason claimed that the report took its inspiration from the Georgia Citizens' Fact-Finding Movement, of which her old friend Josephine Wilkins was the guiding spirit. By advertising the report's southern origins, Mason sought to alleviate southern defensiveness about the report's unflattering portrait of the region. She also was suggesting that white southern women played a key role in instigating social reform. See Mason, "Southerners Look at the South," and Mason, "Citizens' Fact-Finding Movement of Georgia," n.d., reel 65, Mason Papers; also see box 12, Josephine Wilkins Papers, Robert Woodruff Library, Emory University, Atlanta. Most scholars rely on Clark Foreman's account and credit him with writing the report (see Tindall, *Emergence of the New South*, 598, and Sullivan, *Days of Hope*, 63–65), but Sitkoff, *New Deal for Blacks*, 130, recognizes that Mason (and H. L. Mitchell of the Southern Tenant Farmers' Union) also were important. Mason was the one woman on the advisory committee of twenty-four southerners that reviewed the report. In an unsuccessful effort to make the report more palatable to southern conservatives, blacks were excluded from its preparation. Brinkley, "New Deal and Southern Politics," 107, is incorrect to claim that virtually all southern liberals reacted defensively and angrily to the report, because some of them conceived, wrote, and promoted it.

Chapter Six

1. Board minutes, October 28, 1935, reel 2, NCLP. Associate general secretary Emily Sims Marconnier took responsibility for the New York office, for fund-raising, and for NCL activities outside the South. Formerly a student of John Commons's in her native

Wisconsin, Marconnier was active in the league for years before and after she joined the New York Department of Labor in 1940. Profile, "ESM," November 3, 1949, reel 10, NCLP.

2. Mason to Clara Beyer, November 17, 1935, reel 36, NCLP. Mason similarly would tell Sidney Hillman, "You in New York don't know what it means to have the politicians, the local and state administrators, the press and the public lined up with the employers and against the workers." Mason to Hillman, September 11, 1937, quoted by Salmond, *Miss Lucy of the CIO*, 79.

3. See NCL Conference on the Breakdown in Industrial Standards, December 12, 1932, pp. 22–23 (Amidon quotation), reel 117, NCLP. Echoing Amidon, Molly Dewson complained that "the south has not seemed to gather itself together to feel that they could do something" (ibid.).

4. Key, *Southern Politics*, 5.

5. The histories of the Virginia and Kentucky laws are analyzed closely below; information on the North Carolina and Louisiana laws appears in the notes. For an overview, see Virginius Dabney, "Wage and Hour Beginnings in Dixie," *The South Today*, May 1938, and Cutler, "Labor Legislation."

6. Night work laws were no longer an NCL priority, reflecting the decrease in the practice as a result of the NRA codes, and perhaps also a recognition that some women resented night work restrictions. The NCL's 1932 conference agreed that state labor standards committees should work for the eight-hour day, forty-eight-hour week for men, "when practicable," as well as for women. Union men's attitude was a key factor in the decision of whether to make bills sex-specific. A proposal by Rose Schneiderman carried: "I should leave it to [each] state committee as to whether the bill limiting men's hours of work should be separate from the women's bill. But there should be this understanding, that no committee should hold up legislation for women if the men were not ready to come in on it." See Conference on the Breakdown of Industrial Standards, December 12, 1932, p. 37, reel 117, NCLP. For a similar statement of policy, see Mason to George Googe, Georgia Federation of Labor, November 4, 1935, reel 94, NCLP. In 1936 the second U.S. Department of Labor–sponsored Southern Regional Labor Conference resolved that men's and women's hours should be regulated on an equal basis, but that bills should be drafted so that the law could be saved for women if opposition blocked it for men. This resolution passed over the objection of an NWP representative; see Helen Hunt West, "The Southern Labor Conference," *Equal Rights*, February 1, 1936.

7. *Morehead v. New York ex rel. Tipaldo*, 298 U.S. 587 (1936); *West Coast Hotel Company v. Parrish*, 300 U.S. 379 (1937). On the drafting of the new model bill, see Vose, *Constitutional Change*, 199–205; Lash, *Dealers and Dreamers*, chaps. 4, 23; Hart, *Bound by Our Constitution*, chap. 7. Also see Chapter 7, below.

8. This policy also was adopted by the U.S. Department of Labor's minimum wage advisory committee, of which Lucy Mason was a member. On Federation of Labor resistance to including men in New York and Michigan, see Emily Marconnier to Mabel Pitts, April 17, 1937, reel 95, and, more generally, Lucy Mason to W. A. Pat Murphy, Oklahoma, May 20, 1937, reel 96, NCLP.

9. Mason, "Proposed Amendment to South Carolina Hours Law," December 11, 1935, reel 96; also see Clara Beyer to Mason, November 12, 1935, reel 36, both NCLP. NCL leaders may have weighed the relative political strength of state Federations of Labor and ERA supporters in deciding whether to push a women-only or sex-neutral bill; see Mason to Clara Beyer, November 1, 1935, reel 36, and Marconnier to Pitts, April 17, 1937, reel 95, NCLP. State court rulings on labor laws were very unpredictable

in this period. After several appeals, the Oklahoma Supreme Court upheld the principle of men's minimum wage but blocked its application in Oklahoma on a technicality; see Brandeis, "Organized Labor." In 1938 the Pennsylvania Supreme Court struck down an eight-hour day/forty-four-hour week law for men but left intact the parallel law for women. Either the employers who brought suit challenged only the minimum wage principle for men, or the women's bill was drafted more carefully. See U.S. Department of Labor, Bureau of Labor Statistics, *Monthly Labor Review*, September 1938, 548–51. In 1939 the South Carolina Supreme Court struck down a twelve-hour day/fifty-six-hour week law in part because it applied to men; see below. On the other hand, the 1937 North Carolina law regulated both men's and women's hours (interestingly, at different maxima), but it went untested in the courts. In January 1938 Montana judges upheld an hours law affecting women and men in retail stores in large towns.

10. North Carolina had the South's largest manufacturing base, with about 200,000 wage earners in 1929, and Georgia was next with about 150,000. Tennessee, Alabama, Virginia, and South Carolina each had between 100,000 and 130,000 workers in manufacturing. The major employers of women in southern manufacturing were textiles (130,000), tobacco (30,000), clothing (25,000), and food processing (15,000). Mason, *Standards for Workers*, 8; Marshall, *Labor in the South*, 349.

11. The key groups in North Carolina were the League of Women Voters, the Legislative Council of North Carolina Women, and liberal academics in Chapel Hill. Mason's cooperation with North Carolina forces was covert in part because local activists feared that association with the NCL (particularly with Florence Kelley) would damage their cause; see Gertrude Weil to Mason, May 3, 1932, quoted by Wilkerson-Freeman, "Women and the Transformation of American Politics," 513, and board minutes, October 28, 1935, reel 2, NCLP. For Mason's assistance to these forces, which won improved hours laws in 1931 and 1937, see North Carolina file, reel 96, NCLP, and Graham Papers.

12. Mason found Mississippi hopeless. She noted the legislature's relish for "slaying all labor bills" and the fact that "no one can get names [of progressive contacts] out of Mississippi." See Mason, "Report of Southern Trip," March 1934, reel 6, and Mason to Clara Beyer, December 14, 1935, reel 36, NCLP. Alabama had a significant union presence, but this was among men in mining and steel. On the bleak political outlook in Georgia, which, unlike Mississippi, employed many women in industry, see Josephine Wilkins to Mason, October 1936, reel 94, NCLP. Mason also corresponded with Texas YWCA women who led some "hot fights" for minimum wage there, but she did not travel to Texas.

13. After Mason's visit to New Orleans in 1934 precipitated attacks by Catholic clergymen on the local league, Mason kept her distance. Just as problematic as Catholic influence, she believed, was the "Long dictatorship." See Mason to Margaret Wiesman, September 16, 1935, reel 16, NCLP. The Consumers' League of Louisiana included prominent settlement and social workers who battled both the Long machine and the rival New Orleans machine of "Old Regulars." Similarly, although Mason had good contacts in Tennessee through the YWCA, Scarritt College, and the *Chattanooga News*, she never made that state a high priority because she believed Boss Crump's machine made progress unlikely.

14. Hunter, "Virginia and the New Deal."

15. Mason to James Sidel, August 31, 1935, reel 94, NCLP; *Richmond Times-Dispatch*, October 29, 1936, p. 1; Koeniger, "The New Deal and the States."

16. Board minutes, October 28, 1935, reel 2, NCLP.

17. Mason to Margaret Wiesman, March 25, 1936, reel 16, NCLP; Mason to Jo-

sephine Goldmark, January 23, 1936, "Hours—Virginia" file, box 48, entry 1A, DLS Records. About seventeen of twenty-eight Virginia league directors were female. See Virginia league letterhead, April 1938, reel 97, and "Virginia" file, reel 23, NCLP. Cohn also held office in the National Council of Jewish Women and was president of the Virginia Women's Council of Legislative Chairmen of State Organizations; see Appendix 2. On Corson, see Mason to Clara Beyer, November 17, 1935, reel 36, NCLP.

18. Hunter, "Virginia and the New Deal."

19. Reconstructed from "Wages and Hours: Virginia" file, reel 97, "Virginia" file, reel 23, and Mason to Margaret Wiesman, March 25, 1936, reel 16, NCLP; Naomi Cohn to Louise Stitt, October 12, 1937, "Consumers' League-Virginia" file, box 66, A1 entry E8, WB Records; "Hours-Virginia" file, box 48, entry 1A, DLS Records; "Consumers' League" file, box 31, Clark Papers; Virginia Consumers' League, *General Assembly of Virginia*; *Virginia Senate Journal and Documents*, 1936, 1938; Hunter, "Virginia and the New Deal"; articles in the *Richmond Times-Dispatch*: "Virginia Blazes the Way," March 12, 1938, "1938 Honor Roll," January 1, 1939, and "What Happened to Mrs. Jacob S. Cohn?" July 26, 1971; and Virginius Dabney, "Wage and Hour Beginnings in Dixie," *The South Today*, May 1938.

20. Quotation from Mason, "Report on Southern Trip," March 1934, reel 6, NCLP. In 1939, 4 percent of nonagricultural wage earners in South Carolina were union members, compared to 10.7 percent for the South and 21.5 percent nationwide; see Marshall, *Labor in the South*, 299. On club women, see Johnson, "'This Wonderful Dream Nation,'" chap. 8.

21. Tindall, *Emergence of the New South*, 533, 610, 629; Brinkley, "New Deal and Southern Politics"; Leuchtenburg, *Franklin D. Roosevelt*, 268.

22. Simon, *Fabric of Defeat*. Under the 1895 South Carolina constitution, all white males could vote in the Democratic Party primary.

23. "Consumers' League Official Thinks S.C. to Progress under Johnston," *Anderson (S.C.) Independent Tribune*, February 11, 1935, reel 101, NCLP. Mason addressed the state senate on February 6 and the house the next day.

24. "Wages and Hours: South Carolina" file, reels 96–97, NCLP; South Carolina Department of Labor, *Annual Report*, 1937–40. On the 1938 Senate race, see Simon, *Fabric of Defeat*; surprisingly, Simon does not discuss the textile hours bills. Josiah Morse of the University of South Carolina, an honorary vice president of the NCL, quoted by Tindall, *Emergence of the New South*, 629. In 1966 South Carolina still had no general hours law or minimum wage law; see WB, *Summary of State Labor Laws for Women, 1967*, 4.

25. Blakey, *Hard Times and New Deal in Kentucky*, chap. 7.

26. Halleck was one of three Louisville women honored by the National Association of Social Workers in 1933. In the 1940s she led a drive to establish a school of social work at the University of Louisville. Perhaps she inherited some of the ideas of her grandfather, Hew Ainslie, a Scottish poet who participated in Robert Owen's utopian community at New Harmony, Indiana. See Appendix 2 and Kleber et al., *Encyclopedia of Louisville*; thanks to Kathie Johnson of the University of Louisville Library for a draft copy of this entry.

27. When Halleck stepped down as KCL president in 1930, Settle took over, holding that position until about 1944. Settle's husband, twenty-five years her senior, died in 1930; they had no children. In the 1920s Settle was national president of the Altrusa Club for professional women, an affiliation that was more typical of Woman's Party memers than NCL members. Her parents were German Catholic immigrants to Louisille. See Appendix 2; Bessie A. Ray, *A Dictionary of Prominent Women of Louisville and Ken-*

tucky (Kentucky Work Projects Administration, Louisville Free Public Library, 1940); and Laura Miller Derry, ed., *Digest of Women Lawyers and Judges* (n.p., 1949). Thanks to Claire McCann, Special Collections and Archives, University of Kentucky Library, and Kathie Johnson, University of Louisville Library, for locating these documents.

28. See especially Ethel duPont, "Report of Consumers' League Lobbyist for the Minimum Wage Bill," n.d. [March 1938], and Kentucky Labor Standards Committee, "Digest: Kentucky Minimum Wage Bill," n.d. [probably late 1933], both reel 1, KCL Papers. The members of the Kentucky Labor Standards Committee included the KCL, ACWA, LWV, FWC, Girls' Friendly Society, Congress of Parents and Teachers, and Kentucky Children's Bureau and Labor Department. Consumers' League women headed the FWC industry committee. Despite a 1937 suggestion by the board "to get some men in our community to join with us," in 1940 all of the KCL's fourteen directors and twenty-four vice presidents were women. On the KCL's lead role on labor standard bills, see *Proceedings of the Southern Regional Conference on Labor Standards and Economic Security*, Nashville, Tenn., January 20–21, 1935, remarks of Mr. Cavedo, p. 24, file 71, Graham Papers, and union sources cited below.

29. Brinkley, "New Deal and Southern Politics," 111.

30. Files 5 and 7, reel 1, KCL Papers.

31. In 1930 the black population in North Carolina, Virginia, and Kentucky constituted 29 percent, 27 percent, and 9 percent, respectively, of the total population. Those states had the region's best labor departments and, by 1938, the strongest labor standards laws. South Carolina (46 percent black), Georgia (37 percent), Alabama (36 percent), and Mississippi (50 percent) had terrible labor laws and departments; Arkansas (26 percent), Oklahoma (7 percent), and Tennessee (18 percent) had better labor departments. See Mason, *Standards for Workers*, and U.S. Department of Commerce, Bureau of the Census, *Statistical Abstract of the United States, 1943*, 16–19. An exception to this pattern was Louisiana (37 percent black), which passed a minimum wage law in 1938. This law affected only New Orleans, however, and no wage orders were issued until 1941. Louisiana was atypical of the Deep South in that the battle between the Long machine and New Orleans–based Old Regulars (Choctaws) gave the state something approximating a two-party system. The state senators who introduced the minimum wage bill in Louisiana were Longites, and their motivation remains obscure. They may have been trying to co-opt the Old Regulars (who controlled the labor department) or local women reformers, or they may have been responding to federal wage-hour legislation that passed in the same year. Lucy Mason may have been wrong to assume that factional rivalry would hinder the cause of labor laws in Louisiana. See *Woman Worker*, September 1938, 9, and November 1941, 5; U.S. Department of Labor, Bureau of Labor Statistics, *Monthly Labor Review*, October 1946, 539; WB, *Summary of State Labor Laws for Women, 1967*, 4.

32. Wright, *Old South, New South*; Quadagno, "From Old Age Assistance"; Alston and Ferrie, *Southern Paternalism*.

33. As noted in Chapter 3, when bills targeted whites exclusively, as many Progressive Era child labor bills did, racist ideology could be deployed *in favor* of the laws.

34. Mason to Josephine Goldmark, January 23, 1936, "Hours-Virginia" file, box 48, entry 1A, DLS Records.

35. Harry Phillips to Mason, April 30, 1937, and Mason to Phillips, May 14, 1937, reel 97, NCLP. No response from Phillips is on file.

36. The largest employers of black women outside agriculture and domestic service were tobacco rehandling, fruit and vegetable canning, laundries, and peanut cleaning, in that order. White women worked in other tobacco processing occupations, but

rehandling, the dirtiest and most grueling occupation, employed only black women. In 1937 tobacco rehandling employed 5,801 black and no white women, and peanut cleaning, shelling, and grading employed 1,166 black and 27 white women. Two other occupations worked women over fifty-five hours per week: bags and burlaps (blacks and whites) and veneers (blacks and a very few whites). *Forty-first Annual Report of the Virginia State Department of Labor and Industry, for the Year Ended September 30, 1938*, 16–19.

37. Mason to Harriet Herring, April 14, 1936, reel 96; see also board minutes, February 18, 1936, reel 2, both NCLP.

38. Naomi Cohn to Mary Elizabeth Pidgeon, February 10, 1938, box 66, A1 entry 8, WB Records. In Virginia, laundries employed 1,797 black and 1,289 white women in 1937. Oyster shucking primarily employed black women (832 blacks and 26 whites), and canneries employed 2,907 black and 3,610 white women. *Forty-first Annual Report of the Virginia State Department of Labor and Industry*, 16–19; also see WB, *Survey of Laundries and Their Women Workers*. On the 1938 law (S.B. 56/H.B. 58), see *Virginia Senate Journal and Documents, 1938*; *NCL Bulletin*, March 1938; and Virginius Dabney, "Wage and Hour Beginnings in Dixie," *The South Today*, May 1938.

39. Charles Wyzanski to Mason, January 23, 1934, reel 94, NCLP. In 1930, 36 percent of the 3.7 million black men gainfully employed were in manufacturing, mechanical, transportation, and communication occupations, which were within the established scope of labor laws; only 5 percent of 1.8 million wage-earning black women were in such occupations. U.S. Department of Commerce, Bureau of the Census, *Social and Economic Statistics of the Black Population*, 72.

40. South Carolina Department of Labor, *Annual Report*, 1937, 1940. The twelve/fifty-six hours bill that passed in 1938 for both sexes exempted sawmills and logging, among other black-employing occupations. In any event, the South Carolina courts soon declared the law unconstitutional because it applied to men. See U.S. Department of Labor, Bureau of Labor Statistics, *Monthly Labor Review*, May 1939, 1106. Commissioner Nates may have neglected to cite pertinent precedents in support of regulating men's hours; see Clara Beyer correspondence with John Nates, file 12(44)-8, entry 1B, DLS Records.

41. Simon, *Fabric of Defeat*, 211.

42. Alex Colser, minutes of general executive board, April 16–18, 1936, file 20, box 165, ACWA Records. Colser added that only a few actually had moved so far.

43. Mason to Josephine Goldmark, January 23, 1936, box 48, entry 1A, DLS Records.

44. Fraser, *Labor Will Rule*, 378, 391.

45. Alex Colser, minutes of general executive board, April 16–18, 1936, file 20, box 165, ACWA Records.

46. Quotation from *Proceedings of the Southern Regional Conference on Labor Standards and Economic Security*, Nashville, Tenn., January 20–21, 1935, p. 24, file 71, Graham Papers. The speaker was John Edelman of the Full-Fashioned Hosiery Workers, an NCL board member. See also Mason to Josephine Goldmark, January 23, 1936, box 48, entry 1A, DLS Records. For general evidence of the lack of commitment to labor standards laws on the part of southern Federations of Labor, see discussions in SLP.

47. For example, Mason prompted a labor column by H. Monahan in the *Richmond News Leader*, February 4, 1936, that criticized states' rights arguments and migrant industry. Copy annotated by Mason in box 48, entry 1A, DLS Records.

48. In 1939, even after substantial increases in union membership stimulated by the Wagner Act and the rise of the CIO, only 10.7 percent of southern nonagricultural workers were union members, compared to 21.5 percent outside the South. Kentucky

was the anomaly, with 22.5 percent organized, and Alabama was next with 16.1 percent—but mining and other male-employing occupations provided most of these members. In women's chief manufacturing occupations—textiles, tobacco, food processing, and clothing—unions were very weak, although garment and tobacco unions did make substantial gains in the late 1930s. Marshall, *Labor in the South*, 299, 267–68, 214–18, 175–81.

49. NCL Third Labor Standards Conference, December 10, 1934, proceedings transcript, p. 165, reel 6, NCLP.

50. Mason to Charles Hodges, U.S. Division of Labor Standards, December 27, 1935, South Carolina file, reel 96, NCLP. Massachusetts and New York strengthened their forty-eight-hour bills in spring 1935. In summer 1935 Connecticut shortened its fifty-five-hour law for women in factories to forty-eight hours; in early 1936 Rhode Island passed a forty-eight-hour law for women. *NCL Bulletin*, 1935–36.

51. Mason to Effie Dupuis, North Dakota, April 15, 1936, reel 96, NCLP.

52. See Mason to Sidney Hillman, August 19, 1938, file 16, box 79, ACWA Records.

53. Mason to John Nates, South Carolina Federation of Labor, December 27, 1935, reel 96, NCLP. See also Mason to Adele Clark, January 22, 1935, box 31, Clark Papers, and Mason to Clara Beyer, February 7, 1936, box 48, entry 1A, DLS Records. The annual proceedings of the Virginia Federation of Labor for the 1934–39 period have not survived.

54. Quotation from Mason to Clara Beyer, January 11, 1936; see also Mason to Beyer, November 17, 1935, and January 17, 1936, and Beyer to Mason, January 8, 1936, all reel 36; Mason to Nates, December 27, 1935, reel 96, NCLP. The Virginia Federation of Labor did subsidize the printing of a 1936 pamphlet on hours by Mason; see Virginia file, reel 23, NCLP.

55. Mason to Margaret Wiesman, March 25, 1936, reel 16, NCLP.

56. Mason to George Googe, November 4, 1935, reel 94, NCLP.

57. See November and December 1935 correspondence among Mason, Earl Britton (outgoing president of the state Federation of Labor), Clara Beyer, Nates, and Johnston; quotation from Mason to Nates, November 28, 1935, reel 96, NCLP.

58. See Mason to Beyer, November 17, 1935, reel 36; James Johnson, United Textile Workers, to Mason, December 18, Mason to Nates, December 27, Mason to Charles Hodges, December 27, and Hodges to Mason, December 28, all 1935, reel 96, NCLP. South Carolina had two hours laws from the 1890s, one limiting hours in textiles to ten per day and fifty-five per week for men and women, and one limiting women in mercantile establishments to twelve hours per day and sixty hours per week.

59. Mason circular to S.C. Committee, December 11, 1935, reel 96; Mason to Clara Beyer, December 20, 1935, and Mason to Miss Mel, October 8, 1936, reel 36, NCLP.

60. Mason to Charles Hodges, December 27, 1935, reel 96, NCLP. To persuade Frances Perkins to send Hodges, Mason warned, "Unguided [the S.C. Federation of Labor] will put in freak bills[;] with guidance they can back a strategic program." Mason to Clara Beyer, December 20, 1935, reel 36, NCLP. According to Mason, John Nates was "an honest young man with excellent intentions, but he is going to need a lot of good advice." Nates belonged to the labor faction that would join the CIO. See Mason to Harry Brainard, June 11, 1936, reel 96, NCLP, and Simon, *Fabric of Defeat*, 301 n. 98.

61. Hodges to Mason, December 28, 1935, reel 96, NCLP. Illness prevented Mason from attending the meeting as planned.

62. Mason to Beyer, November 17, 1935, reel 36; Mason to Hodges, January 6, 1936, reel 96, NCLP.

63. Brandeis, "Organized Labor," 214. Mason threw her weight behind joint action on hours from North Carolina and Georgia, along the lines of the "regional compact" approach being tried in New England; see Mason to Columbia law professor and AALL president J. P. Chamberlain, September 24, 1936, and her correspondence with governors and league members in the Carolinas and Georgia, January and February 1937, reels 96–97, NCLP.

64. Nates quoted from South Carolina Department of Labor bulletin, May 20, 1937, reel 97, NCLP. The twelve/fifty-six bill exempted saw mills, logging, turpentine, agriculture, canning, cotton gins, and other significant employers of black workers; even so, the Federation of Labor did not bother to support it. See DLS, *Digest of State and Federal Labor Legislation, 1938*, 14; South Carolina Department of Labor, *Annual Report*, 1941, 12; U.S. Department of Labor, Bureau of Labor Statistics, *Monthly Labor Review*, May 1939, 1106; *Proceedings of the Twenty-fourth Annual Convention of the South Carolina Federation of Labor*, Columbia, S.C., June 24–25, 1938, p. 41, SLP.

65. Simon, *Fabric of Defeat*, 69–71 (he does not examine the case of hours legislation).

66. Additional examples of such relationships are in *Proceedings of the Annual Convention of the South Carolina Federation of Labor* for 1935 (Greenville), and for 1936 (Columbia), esp. 15–16, 38, SLP.

67. In 1939, 22.5 percent of Kentucky's nonagricultural workers belonged to unions, compared to the average of 10.7 percent for southern workers and 21.5 percent outside the South; see Marshall, *Labor in the South*, 299. Most Kentucky union members were men in mining.

68. Ethel duPont, "Report of Consumers' League Lobbyist," n.d. [March 1938], file 5, reel 1, KCL Papers; *Proceedings of the Thirty-fourth Annual Convention of the Kentucky State Federation of Labor*, Paducah, Ky., November 21–23, 1938, pp. 18–19, 49–50, SLP.

69. Ethel duPont, "Report of Consumers' League Lobbyist," n.d. [March 1938], file 5, reel 1, KCL Papers; Emma Saurer correspondence with Dorothy Jacobs Bellanca, file 10, box 32, ACWA Records; ACWA, *Report and Proceedings, Thirteenth Biennial Convention*, p. 151; *Proceedings of the Thirty-fourth Annual Convention of the Kentucky State Federation of Labor*, Paducah, Ky., November 21–23, 1938, pp. 18–19, 49–50, SLP. Saurer was single, Catholic, and a pillar of her local from the early 1920s until at least 1940. The KCL Papers contain frequent references to cooperation with Saurer's local. In 1939 Annie Halleck attended a dance held in Saurer's honor, which suggests that KCL and working women met socially as well as politically; see Halleck to Lucy Mason, May 26, 1939, reel 62, Mason Papers.

70. Mason to Clara Beyer, September 14, 1935, reel 36, NCLP.

71. In 1934 Molly Dewson proposed creating advisory committees of "unpaid leading citizens" in each state to meet with the labor department every few months and give it constructive criticism. Lucy Mason, always thinking of the South, and wondering who would appoint these committees, complained that the advisory committees "would have to develop in some states by spontaneous combustion." See NCL Third Labor Standards Conference, December 10, 1934, reel 6, NCLP. Virginia's Department of Labor and Industry, with sixteen employees in 1931 and a $54,000 budget, was one of the South's most effective and best financed labor departments; the local YWCA and LWV were behind the 1922 bill that strengthened it. In 1931 the Legislative Council of North Carolina Women won a law that reorganized that state's department, creating a Division of Standards and Inspection to administer hours laws for women and minors. In 1915 and 1924 the Kentucky league won improvements to their Department of Agriculture, Labor, and Statistics that required permanent record keeping and exams and higher salaries for inspectors (some of whom were women). Kentucky's depart-

ment employed seven people with $15,000 in 1931. South Carolina (until 1936) and Alabama had no labor departments at all, and the departments in Georgia, Florida, Mississippi, and Louisiana had tiny budgets and staffs; see Mason, *Standards for Workers*. On Kentucky, see also *Life and Labor Bulletin*, April 1925, and historical materials, file 5, reel 1, KCL Papers.

72. Quotations from Mason to Charles Pipkin, Louisiana, January 26, 1936, reel 95, and see Mason to Clara Beyer, January 23, 1936, reel 36, NCLP.

73. Mason to Beyer, November 17, 1935, reel 36, NCLP. The South Carolina legislature created an independent but weak labor department the following May.

74. Mason to Beyer, March 29, 1937, reel 36, NCLP.

75. Quotations from Martha Gilmore Robinson to Mrs. Preston, January 25, 1941, file 7, and "A Victim" to Martha Robinson, September 14, 1940, file 6, box 1, New Orleans League of Women Voters Papers, Special Collections, Tulane University Library. In 1941, after a campaign of at least a decade, the Consumers' League of Louisiana and the Women's Citizens' Union ousted this administrator, Mary Ellen Pilsbury. See also McNeill, "History of Child Labor Legislation in Louisiana."

76. Mason, *Standards for Workers*, 14.

77. Ethel duPont, "Report of Consumers' League Lobbyist," n.d. [March 1938], file 5, reel 1, KCL Papers. Chandler was hoping for Republican antilabor money for an upcoming campaign against Senator Barkley. Burrow's subsequent actions confirmed league suspicions that he was more a Chandler machine man than a labor ally. This conflict with Burrow was part of an ongoing disagreement over who would have jurisdiction over labor law administration. The Kentucky league lobbied for a labor department separate from agriculture; instead, to KCL dismay, a labor relations division was created in the Department of Industrial Relations. See KCL president's 1935 annual report and regular league minutes, reel 2, KCL Papers.

78. Mary Frayser wrote Nates that the women's organizations were ready to help on the hours bills, pointedly adding, "I have not been sure that you thought we could help." Frayser to Nates, March 12, 1937, and see Charles Hodges to Mason, January 3, 1936, reels 96–97, NCLP.

79. Mason to Josephine Goldmark, January 23, 1936, and see also Mason to Beyer, February 7, 1936, box 48, entry 1A, DLS Records.

80. Brownie Lee Jones, Southern School for Workers, to Elizabeth Magee, April 24, 1950, reel 34, NCLP.

81. Ethel duPont, "Report of Consumers' League Lobbyist," n.d. [March 1938], file 5, reel 1, KCL Papers.

82. Mason to Louise Stitt, February 19, 1937, reel 36, NCLP; Mason to Frank Graham, May 15, 1937, Graham Papers.

83. Gertrude Weil to Mason, January 16, 1936, reel 96, and Mason to Annie Halleck, May 14, 1937, reel 15, NCLP.

84. Paul Kellogg letter of reference for Mason to Sidney Hillman, June 14, 1937, reel 62, Mason Papers. Kellogg wrote that Mason had centered on the South, "so much so as to cause disquietude on the part of certain members of her board." Kellogg backed Mason fully, commending the "drive and vitality of her leadership" and expressing "every confidence in her integrity, ability, and effectiveness."

85. Mason to Margaret Wiesman, June 16 and August 4, 1937, MCL Papers. Mason begged Wiesman to keep this negative remark confidential, because she never made such comments outside "the immediate family." Mason almost certainly referred to Florence Whitney, a wealthy woman who volunteered for the Democratic National Committee Women's Division in the mid-1930s but then became disenchanted with

the New Deal. Other board members recalled that Whitney was wary of national minimum wage legislation and became "a discordant note" on the board. She resigned in 1939 (see Chapter 9); quotation from William H. Davis, Loyalty Review Board hearing transcript, November 16, 1951, p. 235, box A168, OPM Records. Mason also may have been thinking of Leo Wolman, who by 1937 had disappointed his former friends in the labor movement. In 1938 Wolman was dropped from the board.

86. Mason to Nicholas Kelley, May 28, 1937, reel 1, NCLP.

87. Mason to Wiesman, June 16 and August 4, 1937, MCL Papers; Mason to Clara Beyer, confidential, June 18, 1937, Beyer Papers, SL.

88. On the origins of Mason's CIO job, see her *To Win These Rights*, 16–17; Salmond, *Miss Lucy of the CIO*, 73–74; and Fraser, *Labor Will Rule*, 387–88, quotation 377. Mason quotation from Mason to Sidney Hillman, January 13, 1939, file 16, box 79, ACWA Records. Months earlier Hillman had urged Lewis to hire southerners with "genteel connections" for the TWOC drive; see Mason to Clara Beyer, June 18, 1937, reel 36, NCLP.

89. Mason to Jeanette Studley, June 29, 1937, reel 15; also see Mason to Josephine Wilkins, June 26, 1937, reel 94, and Mason to Anna Settle, June 26, 1937, reel 95, all NCLP.

90. Mason notes for lecture to University of Kentucky political science class, March 10, 1938, reel 64, Mason Papers.

91. Mason to Frank Graham, June 10, 1937, Graham Papers.

92. Mason to H. M. Douty, June 28, 1937, reel 96, NCLP; Mason notes for lecture to Georgia Tech YMCA, November 10, 1937, reel 64, Mason Papers.

93. Cutler, "Labor Legislation." It is also significant that, of the fifteen states that created or strengthened labor departments between 1933 and 1941, nine were in the South. See DLS, *Recent Progress in State Labor Legislation*, 25.

94. On Virginia, see board minutes, February 17, 1942, reel 2; "Virginia Consumers' League," n.d. [probably 1943], reel 23; Brownie Lee Jones correspondence with Elizabeth Magee, 1950, reel 34, all NCLP. Also see Virginia file, box 36, A1 entry 10, WB Records. On Kentucky, see board minutes, January 12 and March 14, 1939, reel 2, NCLP, and minutes, reel 2, KCL Papers. See Chapter 8 on this reaction more generally.

95. U.S. Department of Labor, Bureau of Labor Statistics, *Monthly Labor Review*, October 1946, 535–54; WB, *Summary of State Labor Laws for Women*, 1953, 1958, 1967.

96. H. W. Ransom, settlement worker, to Lucy Mason, January 28, 1937, reel 54, NCLP.

97. NCL press release, n.d. [March 1937], reel 93; also see board minutes, June 11, 1936, reel 2, NCLP.

Chapter Seven

1. Goldmark, *Impatient Crusader*, 205.

2. Even after the FLSA's passage in 1938, workers in some occupations were protected only by state laws. Until 1969 many of these applied to women only; see Chapter 9.

3. *Adkins v. Children's Hospital*, 261 U.S. 525 (1923); *Morehead v. New York ex rel. Tipaldo*, 298 U.S. 587 (1936); *West Coast Hotel Company v. Parrish*, 300 U.S. 379 (1937). This legal history is covered well by John Chambers, "The Big Switch"; Vose, *Constitutional Change*, chap. 9; Paulsen, *Living Wage*; and Hart, *Bound by Our Constitution*, chap. 7. Noting that the league deliberately obscured its own role from the courts, Vose reconstructs the leading part of the NCL in the *Morehead* case. Much of the league's

contribution was in writing briefs and coordinating among the states, but it also operated in less formal ways. At one critical juncture, when all else had failed, Elinore Herrick called on several Supreme Court justices and, playing the part of the "innocent, anguished lady," persuaded them to allow league counsel Dean Acheson to file its amicus curiae brief (Vose, *Constitutional Change*, 209–11).

4. See Hart, *Bound by Our Constitution*, chaps. 7–8; for an account that emphasizes political rather than legal considerations, see Mettler, *Dividing Citizens*, chap. 7.

5. On the drafting of the new model minimum wage bill, see Hart, *Bound by Our Constitution*, chap. 7; Lash, *Dealers and Dreamers*, chaps. 4 and 23; Vose, *Constitutional Change*, 199–205; and correspondence between Elizabeth Brandeis and Josephine Goldmark, files 4 and 6, box 8, EBR Papers. Elizabeth Brandeis often disagreed with Frankfurter and Cohen, but she yielded to the former because he would have to argue the case in court. Brandeis's minimum wage work had to be anonymous because her father was on the Supreme Court.

6. Josephine Goldmark to Lucy Mason, January 24, 1934 (emphasis in original); Felix Frankfurter to Ben Cohen, February 1934, reel 93; board minutes, January 26, 1934, reel 2, all NCLP. See correspondence between U.S. Department of Labor solicitor Charles Wyzanski, Mason, Beyer, Cohen, Goldmark, Dewson, and Frankfurter, January and February 1934, reel 93, NCLP.

7. The league broke with Frankfurter during World War II (his protégés Tom Corcoran and Ben Cohen parted ways with him in 1939). Frankfurter would outrage the NCL in 1948 by writing the opinion in *Goesaert v. Cleary* (335 U.S. 464), which perversely used the words of *Muller* and *West Coast Hotel* to uphold a Michigan law prohibiting women from bartending; see Ann Hill, "Protection of Women Workers," 259. Josephine Goldmark wrote in 1949 that she was "out of sympathy" with his judicial opinions and that she had not spoken to him in five years. Clara Beyer later disparaged Frankfurter in an unfavorable comparison to Louis Brandeis. In 1960 Frankfurter would decline to hire Ruth Bader Ginsburg as his clerk because she was a woman. Frankfurter thus disagreed with Florence Kelley that "women need votes, and wage statutes, *and* unions, *and* women judges." Brinkley, *End of Reform*, 54; Goldmark to John Lathrop, October 8, 1949, reel 25, and Molly Dewson to Elizabeth Magee, November 18, 1949, reel 25, NCLP; Beyer interview with Vivien Hart, 1983, SL; "Clinton Names Ruth Ginsburg, Advocate for Women, to Supreme Court," *New York Times*, June 15, 1993, 1; Kelley quoted by Hart, *Bound by Our Constitution*, 132. See also Lipschultz, "Social Feminism." Despite this conflict, Hart's assertion that "lawyers hijacked the minimum wage movement after 1923" (*Bound by Our Constitution*, 137) seems overstated.

8. National Woman's Party, *Brief as Amici Curiae on Behalf of the National Woman's Party . . .* , file 51, box 3, Alma Lutz Papers, collection A-34, SL; *Morehead v. New York ex rel. Tipaldo*. Historians of the ERA conflict among women's groups are incorrect in dismissing NCL charges that the NWP cooperated with employers. Lawyers for the restaurant industry approached the NWP. The suit was brought by laundryman Joseph Tipaldo, but the restaurants supported his case. Vose, *Constitutional Change*, 212.

9. National Woman's Party, "The Ruling of the Supreme Court," n.d. [1936], flyer in file 38, box 2, Alma Lutz Papers, collection A-34, SL. Indeed, the judicial majority sounded more concerned with men's jobs than women's opportunities: "More and more [women] are getting and holding jobs that otherwise would belong to men." Hart, *Bound by Our Constitution*, 143, quoting *Morehead* decision, 615.

10. Frankfurter erred in asking the Court to *distinguish* the new law from the earlier one; he should have asked it to *overturn* its 1923 ruling. The new model bill incorpo-

rated a hodge-podge of wage-determination theories, blending "fair" and "oppressive" wage concepts with the old "living" wage. According to Vose, Frankfurter also was wrong to insist on bringing the test case in New York State; see *Constitutional Change*, chap. 9.

11. Ingalls, *Herbert H. Lehman*, chap. 5. George Meany of the Federation of Labor rejected minimum wage for men in 1937, and Governor Lehman backed him. Discussing Federation of Labor resistance to including men in New York and Michigan, Emily Marconnier concluded, "In principle, of course, we believe that men should be included, but as a matter of strategy and constitutionality, it seems safer and wiser to exclude men at present." See Marconnier to Mabel Pitts, Michigan, April 17, 1937, reel 95, NCLP. Lucy Mason regretted the negative attitude of state Federations of Labor "toward the inclusion of men in state hours and wage legislation"; see Mason to Oklahoma labor commissioner W. A. Pat Murphy, May 20, 1937, reel 96, NCLP.

12. Quotations from the charter and accompanying primer, reel 54, NCLP (emphasis added). Lucy Mason represented the NCL in the drafting and promotion of the charter. Probably because Communist sympathizer (and NCL officer) Mary Van Kleeck was a prime instigator of the charter, it became associated with the Popular Front. See Storrs, "National Consumers' League, 1932–1937"; Sealander, "Feminist against Feminist"; Alchon, "Mary Van Kleeck"; and Weigand, "Vanguards of Women's Liberation," 41–42.

13. Of small consolation was the passage in June 1936 of the Public Contracts (Walsh-Healey) Act, which required most government contractors to abide by an eight-hour day and forty-hour week and to pay a prevailing minimum wage determined by the secretary of labor. Drafted at Frances Perkins's initiative, the Walsh-Healey bill drew upon a World War I precedent of regulating the labor standards under which army clothing was produced. However, it was weakened by amendment before passage and ended up as a largely symbolic gesture. For Lucy Mason's testimony, see House Committee on the Judiciary, *Conditions of Government Contracts*, 188–92, 493–96.

14. Board minutes, June 11 and December 10, 1936, reel 2; annual meeting proceedings, December 15, 1936, reel 7, and printed version, *Clarify the Constitution by Amendment*, reel 117; "FLSA Correspondence, 1930–1938," reel 54, all NCLP. Also see *New York Herald-Tribune*, December 16, 1936, and Nichols and Bacchus, *Selected Articles on Minimum Wages*.

15. This disingenuous plan was a gaffe by FDR that played into the hands of opponents of the New Deal. See Leuchtenburg, *Franklin D. Roosevelt*, 231–38. The NCL offered only lukewarm support for the bill, which proposed to "reorganize" the Supreme Court by enlarging it, allegedly to lighten the caseload of an aging bench.

16. On April 12 the Supreme Court voted 5-4 to uphold the Wagner Act in a ruling on five cases. The most important was *National Labor Relations Board v. Jones and Laughlin Steel Corporation* (301 U.S. 1–148). On May 24 the Court upheld the unemployment insurance provisions of the Social Security Act with 5-4 decisions in *Steward Machine Company v. Davis* (301 U.S. 548) and *Helvering v. Davis* (301 U.S. 619). See Leuchtenburg, *Franklin D. Roosevelt*, 236–37.

17. Ironically, the Washington state law upheld in *West Coast Hotel* was more similar to the law struck down in *Adkins* than the New York law had been. John Chambers concludes that "th'election returns" were the biggest factor in Roberts's switch; see Chambers, "The Big Switch." Also see Vose, *Constitutional Change*, and Leuchtenburg, "The Case of the Chambermaid." For NCL and NWP interpretations, see Clara Beyer, address to NCL annual meeting, December 8, 1939, reel 7, NCLP, and *Equal Rights*, April 1937.

18. In *National Labor Relations Board v. Jones and Laughlin Steel Corporation*, the Labor Relations Act was held to be constitutional "in so far as it used the powers of the federal government over interstate commerce to attempt to reduce labor disputes at points which were in the 'flow' of interstate commerce." This suggested that the Court had changed its position since the 1918 ruling against a federal child labor law in *Hammer v. Dagenhart* (247 U.S. 251). Douglas and Hackman, "Fair Labor Standards Act of 1938," pt. 1, 493.

19. Hart, *Bound by Our Constitution*, chap. 8.

20. Hart notes that the boundary between interstate and intrastate occupations ran through much gray area, and that gendered assumptions shaped how the line was drawn (ibid.).

21. Grossman, "Fair Labor Standards Act of 1938," 24; Lash, *Dealers and Dreamers*, chaps. 4, 23. The standard accounts of the FLSA's origins credit Perkins, Ben Cohen, or Sidney Hillman, without appreciating the NCL's role or the ties between these three people and the NCL network. One account that does note the NCL is Paulsen, *Living Wage*.

22. For summaries of the initial and final bills, see Douglas and Hackman, "Fair Labor Standards Act of 1938," pts. 1 and 2. Originally covered in a separate bill, child labor provisions were rolled into the adult bill in 1937 in an attempt to make it politically awkward to oppose the latter. These child labor provisions carried over to the 1938 law. Child labor provisions were incorporated into the adult bill on the initiative of Grace Abbott of the Children's Bureau, according to Martin, *Madam Secretary*, Muncy, *Creating a Female Dominion*, and Perkins, *The Roosevelt I Knew*, 257. For a contradicting claim that the combination of child and adult labor standards met with the bureau's resistance, see Grossman, "Fair Labor Standards Act of 1938," 25.

23. Mason to Jeanette Studley, Connecticut, June 10, 1937, reel 15, NCLP.

24. Mason to Louise Stitt, U.S. Women's Bureau, February 19, 1937, reel 36, NCLP.

25. ACWA, *Report and Proceedings, Twelfth Biennial Convention*, 71.

26. Mary Norton actually opposed the wage-hour bill and only supported it under heavy pressure from FDR. In July 1937 Norton was "proving even worse than anticipated . . . and has done all that she could to obstruct [the bill] in the Committee," by approving bad amendments to it. Beyer to Molly Dewson, July 27 and August 7, 1937, Beyer Papers, SL. Norton, who succeeded William Connery as House Labor Committee chair, was too close to New Jersey boss Mayor Hague's machine for the comfort of many league people. See also Merle Vincent correspondence with David Dubinsky, files 7A and 7B, box 81, ILGWU Papers.

27. FDR signed the final bill on June 25. On the FLSA's legislative history see Douglas and Hackman, "Fair Labor Standards Act of 1938"; Grossman, "Fair Labor Standards Act of 1938"; Burns, *Congress on Trial*, chap. 5; Hart, "Minimum Wage Policy"; Paulsen, *Living Wage*; and Mettler, *Dividing Citizens*, chap. 7. Additional insight can be gleaned from the detailed accounts of lobbyists; see Merle Vincent correspondence with David Dubinsky, files 7A and 7B, box 81, ILGWU Papers, and FLSA files, reel 63, NCLP.

28. These groups got support in the Senate from Elbert Thomas (D.-Utah), Robert Wagner (D.-N.Y.), Robert La Follette Jr.(Prog.-Wis.), and, in 1938, Claude Pepper (D.-Fla.); in the House, Maury Maverick of Texas and Arthur Healy of Massachusetts headed a group of pro-FLSA Democrats. The Democratic National Committee Women's Division, which demonstrated its promotional effectiveness in the 1936 election campaign, also worked to stir support for the FLSA. See Ware, *Beyond Suffrage*, 104. Most scholars follow Douglas and Hackman, "Fair Labor Standards Act of 1938," and

Burns, *Congress on Trial*, in emphasizing the Corcoran-assisted primary win of Claude Pepper. Fraser, *Labor Will Rule*, emphasizes the role of the ACWA and Labor's NonPartisan League. See also Voorhis, *Confessions of a Congressman*, and Patterson, *Congressional Conservatism*.

29. After the FLSA passed, it was southern lumber and textile employers who challenged it in the courts. On Beverly Mills, see Thomas Mahan of Southern Auto Supply to Mrs. Franklin D. Roosevelt, December 1937, box 62, entry 1B, DLS Records, and other letters in the same file.

30. Patterson, *Congressional Conservatism*, 195; Leuchtenburg, *Franklin D. Roosevelt*, 261.

31. For employer attitudes toward the act, see box 62, entry 1B, DLS Records; Douglas and Hackman, "Fair Labor Standards Act of 1938," pt. 1, 501–2; Hart, "Minimum-Wage Policy," 326–27; and Fraser, *Labor Will Rule*, 391–94.

32. For other Rules Committee members whom the NCL accused of "choking the legislative process," see Mary Dublin, "Publicity on the Rules Committee," a summary of statements by each member from November 1937 to April 1938, reel 63, NCLP.

33. Other prongs of the southern strategy were the work of the Textile Workers Organizing Committee and an electoral purge of conservative southern Democrats. According to Fraser, the Keynesian elite within the administration hoped the FLSA would work with other New Deal legislation such as the Public Utilities Holding Companies Act and the Securities Act to weaken FDR's enemies within his party. Fraser, *Labor Will Rule*, 392, 378, 391.

34. Senate and House Labor Committees, *Fair Labor Standards Act of 1937*, 403–10.

35. Mary Dublin radio speech, WNYC, March 30, 1938, reel 101, NCLP. Also see Dublin's draft memorandum on the constitutionality of the proposed bill, April 26, 1938, reel 63, NCLP.

36. Senate and House Labor Committees, *Fair Labor Standards Act of 1937*, 403–10; Dublin memo to league branches, April 1, 1938, reel 16, and Dublin radio speech, WNYC, March 30, 1938, reel 101, NCLP.

37. A year earlier, many thought that forty cents and forty hours represented the worst-case outcome for the bill; see Merle Vincent to David Dubinsky, July 8, 1937, file 7B, box 81, ILGWU Papers. While the joint conference committee was combining the Senate and House versions of the bill, the NCL and CIO lobbied hard against further concessions to southern industry, with the limited victory that no rate was to be "fixed solely on a regional basis." The final act authorized industry committees to consider lower costs of living and higher freight rates in the South before recommending wages above the minimum. See Brandeis, "Organized Labor," 228; *NCL Bulletin*, June 1938; Grossman, "Fair Labor Standards Act of 1938," 28; FLSA file, box C-256, NAACP Papers, LC. For FDR's position, see Burns, *Congress on Trial*, 78.

38. Leuchtenburg, *Franklin D. Roosevelt*, 262.

39. See ACWA, *Report and Proceedings, Twelfth Biennial Convention* and, especially, *Report and Proceedings, Thirteenth Biennial Convention*, 42–44. For details on the New York ACWA delegation, see untitled memorandum, April 30, 1938, file B702, box 546, ACWA Records.

40. Mary Dublin to Lucy Mason, April 28, 1938, reel 63, and see "FLSA correspondence, 1938: Congressmen," reel 54, NCLP. League activists Naomi Cohn of Virginia, Anna Settle of Kentucky, Catherine Labouisse of Louisiana, and Bertha Newell of North Carolina joined the NLSC, for example, as did the labor commissioners of the Carolinas and Virginia; see list of NLSC members, reel 63, NCLP. These individuals sometimes were able to persuade local Leagues of Women Voters and other women's

groups to lobby for the bill. On Kentucky league activities in support of the FLSA, see board minutes, May 18, 1938, reel 2, KCL Papers.

41. Southerners favored the FLSA in a February 1938 opinion poll, and they voted for pro-FLSA candidates Claude Pepper and Lister Hill. See Douglas and Hackman, "Fair Labor Standards Act of 1938," pt. 1, 511.

42. The AFL nevertheless was quick to claim credit for the bill that did pass, to the irritation of NCL and CIO activists. Initial standards likely would have been higher had the bill passed in 1937. The AFL position on specific provisions of the act shifted several times in 1937–38, reflecting disagreement within the organization among William Green, state federations, and powerful leaders such as "Big Bill" Hutcheson of the carpenters union and John Frey of metal trades. Many observers believed the AFL's objections and counterproposals were camouflaged attempts to kill the bill. Brandeis, "Organized Labor," 220–28; Grossman, "Fair Labor Standards Act of 1938," 26.

43. The AFL also argued that the 1937 bill gave too much authority to an administrative board; see discussion of FLSA administration below.

44. Senate and House Labor Committees, *Fair Labor Standards Act of 1937*, 403–10 (Mason) and 363–70 (Herrick).

45. ACWA and ILGWU women did not hold leadership positions in proportion to their union membership numbers, but these unions had better records on women's issues than most. Female leaders included Bellanca, Bessie Hillman, Katherine Ellickson, and Esther Peterson at the ACWA, and Cohn and Pauline Newman at the ILGWU. The literature on women in garment unions is large; see Jensen and Davidson, *A Needle, a Bobbin, and a Strike*, and Orleck, *Common Sense*.

46. MDK interview with J. Cheek, 1982, OH-40, p. 93, SL.

47. Untitled memorandum on a New York ACWA delegation to Washington, April 30, 1938, p. 4, file B702, box 546, and Research Department (Gladys Dickason) memo, "The Wages & Hours Law," June 25, 1938, p. 3, file 12, box 263, ACWA Records. Union lawyer Merle Vincent regretted the bill's narrow definition of interstate commerce; see Vincent to David Dubinsky, May 22, 1937, file 7B, box 81, ILGWU Papers.

48. Merle Vincent to David Dubinsky, February 17, 1938, file 7B, box 81, ILGWU Papers. In early 1937 FDR advisers had hoped the FLSA would unify the party after the divisive court-reform bill; see Burns, *Congress on Trial*, 69.

49. With this tactic the NCL was building on the early New Deal successes of the state Labor Standards Committees. For NLSC sponsors, see board minutes, February 8, 1938, reel 2, NCLP.

50. Patterson, *Congressional Conservatism*, 193, citing *New York Times*, December 1, 1937.

51. After college, Dublin unsuccessfully sought work with the New York Department of Labor. Her father helped her obtain a research position with the Committee on the Cost of Medical Care, where she came to side with the minority who favored national health insurance. See MDK Papers and MDK interview with J. Cheek, 1982, OH-40, SL; MDK interview with Katie Louchheim, June 18, 1981, Oral History Collection, Columbia University; and Wehmeyer, "Mary Dublin Keyserling." My 1991 interview with Keyserling was of limited value because by then she was in very poor health.

52. Wehmeyer, "Mary Dublin Keyserling," chaps. 2–3; Dublin lecture notes for June 6, 1934, folder 61, carton 2, MDK Papers.

53. MDK interview with J. Cheek, 1982, OH-40, SL; MDK appointment books, carton 2, unprocessed accession 96-M106, MDK Papers; Wehmeyer, "Mary Dublin Keyserling" (quotation, 92).

54. Dublin's first biographer turned up little on the Russia trip; see Wehmeyer, "Mary Dublin Keyserling," 67. Dublin's interviews and the papers she donated to the Schlesinger Library are silent on the trip, but in 1999 the library acquired letters from Dublin to her parents that offer some insight. It is conceivable that Dublin destroyed records pertaining to the trip in response to allegations of communism that she faced later in her career. For a thoughtful analysis of the erasures created by the Cold War, see Horowitz, *Betty Friedan*. On American and British intellectuals' admiration of the Soviet Union, see Eugene Lyons's vitriolic *Red Decade* and Hobsbawm, *Age of Extremes*; on radicalism at Columbia, see Robert Cohen, *When the Old Left Was Young*.

55. Mary Dublin, "The Company Town," 1932 typescript, marked "Industrial Research Group, New York City" (this may have been a misidentification of the Industrial Relations Institute associated with Mary Van Kleeck, whom Dublin knew and admired), speeches and articles file, MDK Papers. The article specifically cited the Kentucky coal strikes; for the radicalizing effect of these strikes on New York college students, see Robert Cohen, *When the Old Left was Young*.

56. For Dublin's voter registration history, see report of FBI Agent E. M. Holroyd, May 22, 1941, p. 13, box A168, OPM Records.

57. Dublin later claimed to have been friends with John Maynard Keynes. In Geneva in 1929 Keynes included her in a small clique of his top students. See Mary Dublin to Mother and Father, July 25, 1929, unprocessed 1999 accession, MDK Papers.

58. Economist Eveline Burns of the New York league nominated Dublin for the NCL job. MDK interview with J. Cheek, 1982, OH-40, p. 89, SL. Margaret Wiesman was "thrilled at the thought of someone as young and keen as Mary Dublin being our national secretary"; later she would be less enthusiastic. See Wiesman to Emily Marconnier, May 10, 1938, file 189, MCL Papers. Dublin's racial liberalism is indicated by her rejection of eugenicism, her great admiration for Paul Robeson, and her alliances with James Dombrowski of the Southern Conference for Human Welfare and farmworker advocate Carey McWilliams.

59. Dublin to George Burke, April 30, 1938, and Dublin telegrams to NLSC steering committee, April 26, 1938, reel 63, NCLP. On NLSC activities, see board minutes, February–June 1938, reel 2; FLSA correspondence files, reel 54; and NLSC files, reel 63, all NCLP; *New York Times*, March 28 and May 5, 1938. George Burke, an Ann Arbor lawyer, was the NLSC's nominal head, but Dublin did most of the work.

60. MDK interview with J. Cheek, 1982, OH-40, p. 93, SL; Dublin to John Edelman, March 30, 1938, reel 34, NCLP.

61. Dublin, "Outline for Speech at New Jersey CL Annual Luncheon," July 1938, reel 101, and Dublin memo to league branches, April 1, 1938, reel 16, NCLP. Herrick, "The Fight for Minimum Wage Legislation," address for ILGWU radio program, WEVD, n.d. [late 1937 or early 1938], file 7B, box 81, ILGWU Papers; Dublin radio speech, WNYC, March 30, 1938, reel 101, NCLP.

62. Dublin, "Outline for Speech at New Jersey CL Annual Luncheon," July 1938, reel 101, and Dublin to Margaret Wiesman, Massachusetts, April 30, 1938, reel 16, NCLP.

63. Dublin memo, "Organizations that were approached on their stand on wage-hour bill," May 5, 1938, reel 63, NCLP; Dorothy K. Brown, LWV, in Senate and House Labor Committees, *Fair Labor Standards Act of 1937*, 389.

64. "Wages and hours" file, box C-256, NAACP Papers, LC.

65. The editor of the NWP papers mistakenly claims that the passage of the FLSA was an NWP achievement (Pardo, *National Woman's Party Papers*, 90). On the NWP's opposition to the House Labor Committee's sex-based night work amendment, see correspondence, August 1937, reel 59, NWPP.

66. Dublin memo, "Organizations that were approached on their stand on wage-hour bill," May 5, 1938, reel 63, NCLP.

67. Douglas and Hackman, "Fair Labor Standards Act of 1938"; Burns, *Congress on Trial*.

68. Fraser, *Labor Will Rule*, 411; files 7A and 7B, box 81, ILGWU Papers; *New York Times*, May 2, 1938, 1.

69. MDK interview with J. Cheek, 1982, OH-40, p. 93, SL; *New York Times*, May 5, 1938, 4. For records of this publicity blitz, see NLSC files, reel 63, NCLP.

70. MDK interview with J. Cheek, 1982, OH-40, p. 94, SL. Other participants in the FLSA battle also credited the NCL; see Jerry Voorhis to George Burke, June 2, 1938, reel 54, Frances Perkins to Mary Dublin, December 9, 1938, and board minutes, December 8, 1938, annual meeting, reel 6, NCLP.

71. Burns, *Congress on Trial*, 69; "Question and Answer Forum on the Federal Wage-Hour Bill," June 12, 1938, station WVFW, transcript on reel 54, NCLP.

72. Most scholars have relied on these U.S. Department of Labor figures. Mettler, *Dividing Citizens*, 199, uses census data to argue convincingly that over 15 million workers initially were covered by the FLSA, not 11 million.

73. The analysis of the FLSA's impact on wages by Mettler, *Dividing Citizens*, 198–205, considers only coverage under the statutory minimum wage provision and hence does not take into account the other ways in which the FLSA raised wages.

74. Hart, "Minimum-Wage Policy," 328; Douglas and Hackman, "Fair Labor Standards Act of 1938," pt. 2; *NCL Bulletin*, June 1938 and October 1939. See also Boris, *Home to Work*, chap. 9; Palmer, "Outside the Law"; and Mettler, *Dividing Citizens*, chap. 7. For the league's commitment to regulating agricultural labor, see Dublin radio speech, WNYC, March 30, 1938, reel 101, NCLP, and also her statement that "only as the rights and securities of the millions who labor in industry and agriculture are safeguarded and advanced can our society as a whole progress" (House Labor Committee, *Proposed Amendments to the National Labor Relations Act*, 5:1596).

75. Paul H. Douglas to Charles O. Gregory, December 31, 1936, cited by Hart, "Minimum-Wage Policy," 337.

76. Mettler, *Dividing Citizens*, 184–87, suggests that the FLSA benefited textile and garment workers more than others because the former had more political power, but this seems backwards. The ACWA and ILGWU supported the FLSA strongly because they had the most to gain from it as drafted by Constitution-conscious lawyers. Although the political weakness of agricultural workers facilitated their exclusion, workers in intrastate services were excluded more for legal reasons than political ones (although legal distinctions between intra- and interstate labor did reflect gendered and racialized assumptions).

77. Mettler, *Dividing Citizens*, 203–4, finds that in the early 1940s 62 percent of women excluded from the FLSA earned subminimum wages, but only 36 percent of excluded men earned less than the minimum. Fraser, *Labor Will Rule*, 411, and Hart, "Minimum-Wage Policy," 337, claim that male workers were covered much more fully than female workers, but Mettler demonstrates that the act covered about 32 percent of female workers and 35 percent of male workers.

78. Quotations from *NCL Bulletin*, March and January 1939.

79. Clara Beyer to Molly Dewson, August 5, 1937, Beyer Papers, SL. Some southerners favored a multiple-person board for a similar reason, hoping for regional representation.

80. Grossman, "Fair Labor Standards Act of 1938," 25–26; Douglas and Hackman, "Fair Labor Standards Act of 1938," 494, 501–2; testimony of John L. Lewis (p. 271),

Sidney Hillman (p. 943), Merle Vincent (p. 262), Lucy Mason (p. 403), and Elinore Herrick (p. 363), in Senate and House Labor Committees, *Fair Labor Standards Act of 1937*.

81. On the NRA codes as an organizing tool, see Faue, "Paths of Unionization," 302. After the FLSA took effect, reporting violations became a form of union participation. The ACWA set up a Wage-Hour Bureau, to which workers wrote to report violations; see file 13, box 263, ACWA Records.

82. Senate and House Labor Committees, *Fair Labor Standards Act of 1937*, 180. For a league assertion that the board method was democratic, see *NCL Bulletin*, Fall 1946. Hart argues that the FLSA in the long run empowered excluded groups by mobilizing them to claim their right to the same protection as other workers. See *Bound by Our Constitution*, 139–40 (on Kelley's view), 169–77.

83. During World War II, NCL friends in the Office of Price Administration would implement a similar vision of technocratic expertise operating in tandem with grassroots (female) activism. See Jacobs, "'How About Some Meat?'" For a more pessimistic assessment of the impact of bureaucratic methods on working-class women's activism, see Faue, "Paths of Unionization."

84. Testimony of Lucy Mason (p. 403), and see also testimony of Assistant Attorney General Robert Jackson (p. 1), in Senate and House Labor Committees, *Fair Labor Standards Act of 1937*.

85. Ibid., 363–71, and see Perkins testimony, 180. In fact, league activists recognized that the industry board method was slow and cumbersome, but in 1937–38 this disadvantage was outweighed by legal and other considerations; see Mason to Josephine Wilkins, Georgia, June 2, 1936, reel 94, NCLP, and Elinore Herrick statement to the New York legislature, December 4, 1946, file 5, box 29B, CL-NY Papers.

86. Senate and House Labor Committees, *Fair Labor Standards Act of 1937*, 403–10. Also see NCL recommendations on fair labor standards bill, December 9, 1937, reel 54, NCLP. Other examples of successful national-state administration were the Walsh-Healey Act of 1936, which regulated labor standards for goods produced under government contracts, and the Sheppard-Towner Maternity and Infancy Act of 1921.

87. Martin, *Madam Secretary*, 390. For the position of various groups, see Merle Vincent to David Dubinsky, December 18, 1937, February 12 and 17, March 22, April 15, May 19, and June 3, 1938, files 7A and 7B, box 81, ILGWU Papers. The ILGWU favored the board method, but Vincent also believed the Department of Labor was being territorial in insisting on jurisdiction over the FLSA.

88. Merle Vincent to David Dubinsky, June 11, 1938, file 7A, box 81, ILGWU Papers.

89. Roosevelt reportedly hoped to find a businessman for the position. Andrews was Perkins's third choice to head the division, after Leon Henderson (who had been a league ally within the NRA) and Isidor Lubin of the Bureau of Labor Statistics. See Martin, *Madam Secretary*, 542 n. 43. Donald Nelson of Sears declined the job (but he did become chairman of Textile Committee No. 1). See Vincent to Dubinsky, July 13, 1938, file 7A, box 81, ILGWU Papers, and Fraser, *Labor Will Rule*, 412.

90. Lucy Mason and Lee Pressman of the CIO backed Roche. Mason chided Eleanor Roosevelt for suggesting that a woman could not get the job. See Mason to Roosevelt, May 11 and June 1, and Roosevelt to Mason, May 15 and July 7 (quotation), all 1939, reel 62, Mason Papers; Lee Pressman to Sidney Hillman, May 22, 1939, file 28, box 82, ACWA Records; Ware, *Beyond Suffrage*, 120.

91. The support of some southern Democratic women for the FLSA, and for Major Fletcher, is indicated by May Thompson Evans to Clara Beyer, July 27, 1938, "Appli-

cants for positions in wage-hour division" file, entry 1B, box 62, DLS Records. This file suggests that Clara Beyer wielded some influence over Wage and Hour Division appointments.

92. Andrews tried to make an "empire" of the Wage and Hour Division, planning separate personnel, publicity, and legal offices, and proposing to submit his budget directly to the budget director rather than to Perkins. Martin, *Madam Secretary*, 392–93. Gender conflict within the DOL was not new; "cigar-chomping" male bureaucrats had resisted Perkins when she arrived in 1933. See Sealander, *As Minority Becomes Majority*, 134.

93. Board minutes, November 18, 1938, file 1, box 6B, CL-NY Papers.

94. NCL board minutes, October 17 and November 21, 1938, reel 2, and Mary Dublin to Elmer F. Andrews, February 17, 1939, reel 54, NCLP.

95. Textiles was the first FLSA industry committee to form (as under NRA), but employer recalcitrance so delayed the committee that wage gains were tiny and slow in coming. Hodges, *New Deal Labor Policy*, 180, calls the FLSA a "hollow victory" for southern textile workers. He neglects to observe that those who did benefit were women workers, who probably did not perceive the improvements as hollow. Elizabeth Magee, Rosamond Lamb, Charlotte Carr, Elizabeth Brandeis, Amy Hewes, Paul Brissenden, Sumner Slichter, and Philip Taft were league officers appointed to the first eight boards; see *NCL Bulletin*, October/November 1939, reel 6, NCLP. For Brandeis's influence on the millinery and textile committees, see file 5, box 8, EBR Papers.

96. Clara Beyer to Molly Dewson, April 27, 1939, Beyer Papers, SL.

97. Mary Dublin to George Soule, *The New Republic*, December 11, 1939, reel 7, and see minutes of meeting with branch secretaries, November 9, 1939, reel 2, NCLP. Lucy Mason had regretted the NRA's appointment of "industrialists and army men." Mason to Clara Beyer, December 28, 1934, reel 35, NCLP. On women's pacifism and conflict with the War Department, see Jensen, "All Pink Sisters." Frances Perkins disagreed with the NCL about Fleming, at least initially. One reason she favored a military man was that he could not refuse the job as had several civilians. See Martin, *Madam Secretary*, 393. This underscores how limiting was the refusal to consider a woman for the job.

98. See Muncy, *Creating a Female Dominion*, on Children's Bureau methods of federal-state cooperation and, more broadly, on the consultative, cooperative values that female reform professionals developed in contrast to those of male bureaucrats. Jane Perry Clark's optimism about federal-state administration of social policies probably derived from her experience with the New York Consumers' League; see Clark, *Rise of a New Federalism*. Citing Clark, Patterson, *New Deal and the States*, offers wage-hour administration as an exception to the norm of poor relations between federal and state agencies during the New Deal.

99. Clara Beyer to Molly Dewson, April 2, 1940, Beyer Papers, SL.

100. Ibid. For a discussion of different forms of federal-state coordination, see "Memorandum to the Secretary," December 22, 1938, box 1, historical files, Records of the U.S. Wage and Hour and Public Contracts Division, RG 155, NA.

101. Beyer interview with Vivien Hart, 1983, p. 35, SL. More generally, see Perry, *Belle Moskowitz*.

102. *NCL Bulletin*, Spring 1940; Summary report, Committee on the Extension of Labor Law Protection to All Workers, October 31, 1938, Beyer Papers, SL. On FLSA violations in the southern hosiery and lumber industries, see Seltzer, "Effects of the Fair Labor Standards Act."

103. In 1942 the division made 67.6 million inspections; in 1948 it made fewer than 30 million. In 1953 budget cuts forced a reduction from fifty-nine to thirty-four field

offices. U.S. Department of Labor, Wage and Hour Division, *Annual Report, 1939*, 124; U.S. Department of Labor, Wage and Hour and Public Contracts Division, *Annual Report, 1948*, 32, and *Annual Report, 1953*, viii. For appropriations, see U.S. Office of Management and Budget, *Budget of the U.S. Government* (annual).

104. Steinberg, *Wages and Hours*, concludes that union members benefited most from wage-hour regulation, and she suggests this was counter to the hopes of reformers concerned about the unorganized. But Steinberg's data also show that wage-hour legislation expanded more quickly than unionization (201–2). Thus, some of those who benefited from wage-hour laws became union members *after* they were covered by these laws. This was what the NCL predicted — that workers would be easier to organize once minimum labor standards were in effect.

Chapter Eight

1. Mary Dublin, handwritten notes for address to Consumers' League of New Jersey, November 30, 1938, carton 5, MDK Papers.

2. NCL, "Analysis of the Barden Bill, H.R. 7133," reel 56, NCLP. Simultaneous battles were waged over Social Security Act coverage; see Finegold, "Agriculture and Politics." On family wage assumptions and the 1939 Social Security Act amendments, see Kessler-Harris, "Designing Women and Old Fools." Some conclusions of the latter might be qualified with further research on the thinking of NCL activists Elizabeth Wisner, Josephine Roche, Eveline Burns, and Mary Dublin Keyserling.

3. NCL, "Analysis of the Barden Bill, H.R. 7133," reel 56, NCLP.

4. Kate Papert, New York Labor Department, to Robert Ramspeck, June 12, 1939, cited by Boris, "Regulation of Homework," 268. My discussion of homework regulation relies on Boris's analysis, although I do not agree with her that the women's reform network was as concerned with "saving the home from the factory" as with protecting the factory from the home (ibid., 265).

5. The bill sought to exempt additional workers in the dairy industry (250,000), canneries (160,000), fresh fruits and vegetables (120,000), meatpackers (128,000), cotton (125,000), lumber (100,000), sugar and molasses (70,000), tobacco stemming and handling (68,000), and many others, right down to pecan shellers (13,000). Other workers the bill would exempt were in storage and warehousing (30,000), livestock handling and driving (75,000), poultry (30,000), stockyards (30,000), grain elevators (55,000), wholesale distribution of fruits and vegetables (42,000), and nurseries (6,000). The bill also proposed a six-month time limit on bringing suits for back wages, which would have crippled enforcement, given the inadequate appropriations for the Wage and Hour Division. NCL, "Analysis of the Barden Bill, H.R. 7133," reel 56, NCLP.

6. Hart points out that "the image of agricultural production as anti-industrial" had severe consequences for agricultural workers. In 1939 the median annual wage for farm workers was $309; for all black workers it was $460, and for all white workers, $1,112. Hart, "Minimum-Wage Policy," 327.

7. NCL, "Analysis of the Barden Bill, H.R. 7133," and NCL letter to House of Representatives, April 24, 1940, both reel 56, NCLP.

8. Mary Dublin to Joseph Kovner, June 8, and Kovner reply, June 10, 1939, reel 34, NCLP. Kovner replied that he could not promise anything. Lee Pressman of the CIO had told Dublin he was not too concerned about the amendments.

9. Board minutes, May 9, September 9, 1939, and January 11, 1940, reel 2, NCLP; *NCL Bulletin*, October/November 1939.

10. Board minutes, May 24, 1940, reel 2; "American Forum of the Air," April 14, 1940, and clippings and correspondence on Barden bill, reel 56, NCLP. The fate of another bill suggested the dangers of attempting any revisions to the FLSA in this period: a bill that sought "administrative improvements" to the FLSA was loaded with twenty-three weakening amendments. See *NCL Bulletin*, Spring 1940; National Consumers Committee, *Consumer Activists*, 357.

11. The NCL also registered dismay at attacks on the "little Wagner Acts" — in New York, Pennsylvania, Wisconsin, and Massachusetts, for example — and denounced a 1939 petition initiative in Oregon against collective bargaining. See NCL memo, "NLRB 1939 campaign" file, reel 83, NCLP; on the state Wagner acts, see Patterson, *New Deal and the States*, 123.

12. Herrick, "The Fight for Minimum Wage Legislation," address for ILGWU radio program, WEVD, n.d. [late 1937 or early 1938], file 7B, box 81, ILGWU Papers. Herrick was executive secretary of the New York league from 1929 to 1933 and again after 1942, when she also joined the NCL board. On Herrick's influence with Senator Robert Wagner, Frances Perkins, and Eleanor Roosevelt and her importance at the NLRB, see Gross, *Reshaping of the National Labor Relations Board*, 117–21, 181–82.

13. On Wagner's view, see Boris, "Regulation of Homework." Carey, an Irish American organizer in a female-employing industry, attended NCL meetings regularly in 1940 and 1941; Wagner attended only a few meetings. On Carey, see Appendix 2; Schatz, *Electrical Workers*, 95–99; and Rosswurm, *CIO's Left-Led Unions*, which criticizes Carey's role in expelling Communist unions from the CIO after the war.

14. For example, two major studies of the NLRB make virtually no mention of the Fair Labor Standards Act: Tomlins, *The State and the Unions*, and Gross, *Reshaping of the National Labor Relations Board*.

15. Patterson, *Congressional Conservatism*, 317, attributes the origin of the Smith Committee's hostile 1939 investigation of the NLRB to Representative Cox of Georgia, who was angry about inspections in his state's hosiery mills.

16. Tomlins, *The State and the Unions*.

17. Many on the Left believed the Smith Committee was a continuation by new means of the American Liberty League campaign against the Wagner Act; see Merle Vincent, "Meet Mr. Smith's Committee," *Equality* 2, no. 5 (May 1940), copy in entry 23, box 17, Records of the National Labor Relations Board, RG 25, NA. As Auerbach, *Labor and Liberty*, observes, the New Deal was the heyday of special congressional committees whose aim was swaying public opinion for political purposes; the Smith Committee was a prime example.

18. This is the argument of Gross, *Reshaping of the National Labor Relations Board*. Tomlins, *The State and the Unions*, offers a different analysis; see below.

19. Davis claimed that since the Wagner Act had taken effect, the number of blacks in trade unions had grown from roughly 125,000 to 400,000. He also argued the NLRB treated blacks better than most federal agencies did. See House Labor Committee, *Proposed Amendments to the National Labor Relations Act*, 4:1441–45, 1458–67. Herbert Hill, *Black Labor*, documents the efforts of the NAACP and Urban League for an antidiscrimination provision in the Wagner Act. Wagner aide Leon Keyserling claimed that the bill originally prohibited discrimination but that the AFL "fought bitterly to eliminate this clause and much against his will Senator Wagner had to consent to the elimination in order to prevent scuttling of the entire bill" (Hill, *Black Labor*, 106). Hill's criticism of NLRB acquiescence in race discrimination is based on the post-1944 period; he concedes that "in the New Deal period there was a short-lived attempt to use the NLRB's powers on behalf of nonwhite workers" (97n).

20. Dublin told the NCL board she had sent out 12,000 resolutions, but when questioned by the Senate Committee on Education and Labor, she said she had sent out 5,000. Apparently her commitment to social scientific methodology did not prevent her from trying to beef up the response rate to her mailing, which she represented to the congressional committees as a random sample of "unbiased" public opinion. The resolution affirmed the principles of the NLRA and urged that all amendments be rejected until there had been more time to evaluate the act's functioning. See Senate Committee on Education and Labor, *National Labor Relations Act*, 2951; board minutes, September 12, 1939, reel 2, NCLP. For returned resolutions, press releases, testimony, and other records of this drive, see reels 83–84, NCLP.

21. *New York Times*, February 21, 1940, 1. The league cooperated in these publicity efforts with the CIO, the ILGWU, and Senator Wagner's office; see testimony folder, reel 84, NCLP.

22. NCL, *Should the National Labor Relations Act Be Amended?* In addition to women's groups, Dublin cooperated with a group of social scientists who formed the Committee for the Defense of NLRA. See Dublin to Philip Levy (secretary to Senator Wagner), March 20, 1940, reel 84; "Wagner Act, 1939 Campaign, Publicity" file, reel 83; Mason, "Letter to Southern Editors," April 27, 1939, reel 83; board minutes, April 18, May 9, September 12, 1939, May 24, 1940, reel 2, all NCLP; *NCL Bulletin*, April and June 1939, Spring 1940. Also see Mason to Clara Beyer, January 17, 1939, Beyer Papers, SL.

23. Tomlins, *The State and the Unions*, 101, xiii. For the traditional view, see Brody, "Emergence of Mass-Production Unionism," and Bernstein, *Turbulent Years*.

24. "System-sustaining function" from Harris, "Snares of Liberalism," 184. Second quotation from Tomlins, *The State and the Unions*, 102. Goldfield, "Worker Insurgency," interprets the Wagner Act as a corporate-liberal response to an upsurge in radical labor activism. His emphasis on social movements as an influence on policymakers is valuable, but he incorrectly discounts voluntary associations.

25. Tomlins, *The State and the Unions*, 122, 102.

26. On the CIO attitude toward the state, see ibid., 188, and Fraser, *Labor Will Rule*. Recent scholarship emphasizing the strength of employer opposition includes Harris, "Snares of Liberalism"; Plotke, *Building a Democratic Political Order*; and Draper, "New Southern Labor History." These offer a corrective to Tomlins's valuable but legalistic account, which downplays the political context of the fight to amend the NLRA.

27. Tomlins, *The State and the Unions*, 118.

28. On AFL discrimination, see Kessler-Harris, *Out to Work*; Wolters, *Negroes and the Great Depression*; and Herbert Hill, *Black Labor*.

29. On these changes, see Faue, "Paths of Unionization." On the NCL position, see council minutes, December 7, 1939, reel 7, NCLP.

30. House Labor Committee, *Proposed Amendments to the National Labor Relations Act*, 5:1602–3. Also see *NCL Bulletin*, January 1939; board minutes, February 14 and 29, 1939, reel 2, NCLP; NCL, *Should the National Labor Relations Act Be Amended?*, 6.

31. NCL Second Labor Standards Conference, December 12, 1933, pp. 8–9, reel 5, NCLP.

32. Herrick, "The Fight for Minimum Wage Legislation," address for ILGWU radio program, WEVD, n.d. [late 1937 or early 1938], file 7B, box 81, ILGWU Papers.

33. NCL, *Should the National Labor Relations Act Be Amended?*, 3; House Labor Committee, *Proposed Amendments to the National Labor Relations Act*, 5:1598; Dublin review of Harry Scherman, *The Promises Men Live By* (1937), file 61, carton 2, MDK Papers.

34. Paul Brissenden in House Labor Committee, *Proposed Amendments to the National Labor Relations Act*, 5:1594. On this point the NCL parted ways with Frances Perkins, who believed the "one-sidedness" of the Wagner Act triggered the reactionary labor laws of 1943 and 1947; see Martin, *Madam Secretary*, 386.

35. On the NCL campaign for La Follette Committee appropriations, see board minutes, January 12, May 9, September 26, 1939, reel 2, NCLP, and *NCL Bulletin*, March, May, and June 1939.

36. "Civilizing of labor relations" is Herrick's phrase, from NCL Second Labor Standards Conference, December 12, 1933, p. 8, reel 5, NCLP; Brissenden, in House Labor Committee, *Proposed Amendments to the National Labor Relations Act*, 5:1595; NCL, *Should the National Labor Relations Act Be Amended?*, 4.

37. Herrick, "The Fight for Minimum Wage Legislation," address for ILGWU radio program, WEVD, n.d. [late 1937 or early 1938], file 7B, box 81, ILGWU Papers.

38. For Florina Lasker's complaint that capital demanded a risk-free 12 percent return, see board minutes, June 20, 1940, reel 2, NCLP; also see Dublin's address to the Kentucky Consumers' League, reported in the *Louisville Courier-Journal*, April 30, 1941. To persuade manufacturers to convert to war production, government officials offered cost-plus contracts and other risk-reducing incentives.

39. *Daily Republican* (Phoenixville, Penn.), April 24, 1939, and other papers of same syndicate, reel 83, NCLP; in some papers the reference was changed from "the Perkins woman" to "Mrs. Perkins." In fact the NLRA was not upheld until April 1937, months after the sit-down strikes began. Ironically, as noted above, Perkins herself had reservations about the Wagner Act; see Martin, *Madam Secretary*, 328, 381–86.

40. Ida Klaus quoted in Lash, *Dealers and Dreamers*, 432. On Herrick and the female Review Division attorneys, see Gross, *Reshaping of the National Labor Relations Board*, 117–21, 181–82. The reportedly Communist-influenced Review Division was in conflict with socialists in the Economics Division. At least three of twenty-two NLRB regional directors were women, and many attorneys and other professionals in all divisions were female; see 1939 list of NLRB employees, reel 84, NCLP. On women as a percent of all lawyers, see Cott, *Grounding of Modern Feminism*, 219.

41. Gross, *Reshaping of the National Labor Relations Board*, 181–83.

42. *New York Times*, January 8–12, 1940; House Special Committee, *Hearings to Investigate the National Labor Relations Board*, 1061, 1222, 1587, 1594; Gross, *Reshaping of the National Labor Relations Board*, 181–83. Additional information on Review Division attorneys can be found in file A-10, entry 23, and box 4, entry 25, Records of the National Labor Relations Board, RG 25, NA.

43. House Special Committee, *Hearings to Investigate the National Labor Relations Board*, 1061, 1222, 1587, 1594; *New York Times*, January 12, 1940, 1. It is unclear which women's groups went to the hearings. Neither NCL nor National Woman's Party sources mention this particular protest.

44. *Congressional Record*, 76th Cong., 2d sess., 1940, 86, pt. 1:302.

45. Ibid.

46. Mary Dublin had faced similarly offensive questions when she testified before the House Labor Committee. Blacks also were insulted. See House Labor Committee, *Proposed Amendments to the National Labor Relations Act*, 5:1604–5 (Mary Dublin) and 4:1466 (John P. Davis).

47. Tomlins, *The State and the Unions*, 102.

48. The Supreme Court sustained the FLSA in *United States v. F. W. Darby Lumber Company*, 312 U.S. 100 (1941), which overruled the 1918 *Hammer v. Dagenhart* decision (247 U.S. 251). The Court also upheld the FLSA's administrative procedure, in a

case brought by a southern textile employer, *Opp Cotton Mills v. Administrator of Wage and Hour Division of the Department of Labor*, 61 Sup. Ct. 524 (1941). See U.S. Department of Labor, Bureau of Labor Statistics, *Monthly Labor Review*, February 1941, 423.

49. Lucy Mason, board minutes, April 26, 1937, reel 2, NCLP. Seltzer, "Effects of the FLSA," 412, finds that southern lumber companies began claiming they only sold to in-state customers.

50. Alaska, Maine, and Utah passed new minimum wage legislation for women (these were not states with a league presence); six league bills affecting women's hours passed in Massachusetts. Dublin rebutted opponents of New Jersey bill S. 40/A.B. 40 in an open debate before the state assembly; see her address, January 21, 1940, reel 96, and board minutes, May 24, 1940, reel 2, NCLP. On this drive in the states, see NCL minutes, reel 2, NCLP, and *NCL Bulletin* for late 1938 through 1940; Mary Dublin to Clara Beyer, October 31, 1938, reel 36, NCLP, for specific NCL impact on bill drafting; and "Consumers' League Backing Campaign," *New York Times*, October 30, 1938.

51. The NCL organized a Conference on Household Employees attended by the Domestic Workers' Union as well as the WTUL, YWCA, and LWV. *NCL Bulletin*, June 1938, March and October/November 1939; board minutes, May 10, June 14, 1938, January 12, 1939, reel 2, NCLP. For Kentucky league efforts on behalf of black domestic workers, see Anna Settle to Mary Anderson, February 1, 1943, box 64, A1 entry 8, WB Records. In 1945 New York finally passed a compensation law for domestic workers.

52. On Ohio, see Dennis Harrison, "Consumers' League of Ohio," 278–94. On New Hampshire, see exchanges between Margaret Wiesman and Lucy Mason, June 1935, reel 16, NCLP, and Clara Beyer to Molly Dewson, July 27, 1937, Beyer Papers, SL. On Louisiana, see Martha Gilmore Robinson to Mrs. Preston, January 25, 1941, file 7, box 1, New Orleans League of Women Voters Papers, Special Collections, Tulane University Library.

53. Effie Dupuis to Lucy Mason, October 11, 1935, January 14 and 26, 1937; see also Mason to Dupuis, January 21, 1937, reel 96, NCLP.

54. Ware, *Beyond Suffrage*, chap. 6, and Sealander, *As Minority Becomes Majority*, chap. 7.

55. Irene James to Elizabeth Magee, December 5, 1942, and Margaret Wiesman to Elizabeth Magee, n.d. [mid-1943], both reel 16, NCLP.

56. William C. Burrow to Anna Settle, December 18, 1940, reel 1, KCL Papers.

57. Anna Settle to William C. Burrow, February 4, 1941, and Burrow response, reel 1, KCL Papers. Despite his conciliatory letter, it does not appear that Burrow rehired the women inspectors. From 1941 to 1944 the KCL battled Burrow over his poor administration of the minimum wage and child labor laws. This included a confrontation over his coercing of (predominantly black) women laundry workers into settling wage violation claims for the sum of $1. The KCL also led the legal defense of the minimum wage law after the state attorney general declared he was too busy to do it.

58. Ladd-Taylor, *Raising a Baby*, 32. Julia Lathrop, the head of the U.S. Children's Bureau, assumed wrongly that the Children's Bureau would become a Department of Public Welfare, with her as its head. Robyn Muncy argues that politicians' real objection to the Sheppard-Towner Act was not its legitimation of federal social spending but its administration by the female reform professionals of the Children's Bureau; see *Creating a Female Dominion*, 144, 148.

59. Quotation from Mary Anderson to Annie Halleck, October 10, 1940, box 64, A1 entry 8, WB Records. See also William C. Burrow to Anna Settle, December 18, 1940, reel 1, KCL Papers. In 1939 Rhode Island almost abolished its Division of Women and Children, but the local league staved this off and reportedly selected the new division

head; see Louise Stitt to Margaret Wiesman, March 23, 1939, box 64, A1 entry 8, WB Records. In 1944 the New York Division of Women in Industry, headed by league officer Emily Marconnier, was under attack; see board minutes, January 14, 1944, reel 2, NCLP.

60. Brinkley, *End of Reform*, chap. 8; Martin, *Madam Secretary*, 448. Jeffries, "'Third New Deal,'" 408 n. 44, astutely notes that women experts were displaced during the later New Deal, but his suggestion that this occurred as economists displaced social workers is not strictly accurate, since many of the marginalized women were economists themselves.

61. Board minutes, March 10, April 11, 1942, reel 2, NCLP.

62. Sealander, "Moving Painfully and Uncertainly." Anna Settle of the Kentucky league chaired the women's committee of the War Manpower Commission for Louisville. *NCL Bulletin*, February 1944.

63. See correspondence of Annie Halleck of Kentucky and Margaret Wiesman of Massachusetts with Women's Bureau officials, discussing these and other states, 1939–44, box 64, A1 entry 8, WB Records, and board minutes, 1939–45, reel 2, NCLP.

64. *NCL Bulletin*, late 1939–42; annual meeting proceedings, December 8, 1939, January 11, 1941 ("young upstarts"), reels 7–8, NCLP; Louise Stitt to Margaret Wiesman, January 3, 1942, March 23, 1943, box 64, A1 entry 8, WB Records. For testimony about the worsening of the "double burden" during the war, see the classic documentary film, *The Life and Times of Rosie the Riveter*.

65. Mary Dublin, address to state assembly in support of New Jersey wage-hour bill, January 21, 1940, reel 96, NCLP.

66. This event transpired in 1922; see Mason, *To Win These Rights*, 8.

67. Ware, *Partner and I*, 233 (emphasis added), 238. Ellen Woodward replaced Dewson on the Social Security Board. Woodward, too, perceived men and women to have distinct priorities. Appointed to the United Nations Relief and Rehabilitation Administration, Woodward wanted a committee on social welfare, but she found the men were focused on industrial recovery and economic development. She lamented that "there was so little social thinking among the men on the USA delegation." Swain, *Ellen S. Woodward*, 170. An ideological divide along gender lines also may have existed on the National Resources Planning Board; see Jeffries, "'Third New Deal,'" 408 n. 44.

68. Flanagan, "Gender and Urban Political Reform," argues that the gender division of labor produced ideological differences between elite women and men in the Progressive Era. I do not mean to suggest that the potential for a "gender gap" disappeared by the 1930s; as noted in Chapter 5, some research suggests that women were more likely than men to back FDR. See Andersen, *Creation of a Democratic Majority* and *After Suffrage*. Andersen supports the contemporary impressions of Molly Dewson and Mary Dublin; see Ware, *Partner and I*, and MDK interview with Katie Louchheim, June 18, 1981, p. 16, Oral History Collection, Columbia University.

69. Board minutes, February 17, 1942, and annual meeting resolutions, March 21, 1942, reel 2, NCLP. Emphasis added.

70. Elizabeth Magee et al. to Secretary of Labor James Mitchell, June 30, 1954, reel 98, NCLP. The NCL mobilized to save the U.S. Women's Bureau in 1945 and again in 1954; battles to save women's divisions in the states also persisted into the 1950s.

71. See sources cited in preceding notes, and, for a later example, see correspondence of Florence Burton, Division of Women and Children, Industrial Commission of Minnesota, with U.S. Women's Bureau officials, 1950–52, box 36, A1 entry 10, WB Records.

72. Annual meeting minutes, December 7, 1939, reel 7, NCLP.

73. Harris, "Snares of Liberalism"; Draper, "New Southern Labor History."

1. More than 230 new members joined the NCL in 1938–39. The national league's total membership rose by 10 percent, but it still had fewer than 2,000 members, down from about 3,000 at the beginning of the decade. Board minutes, September 12 and 26, 1939, reel 2, NCLP.

2. Mason, *To Win These Rights*, 12; council minutes, December 7, 1939, and Dublin to Roche, November 13, 1939, reel 7, NCLP. Appendix 1 lists NCL officers in 1933 and 1941. Leo Wolman was dropped from the board in 1938, ostensibly for poor attendance but probably because his views were becoming more conservative. Veteran Emily Marconnier left the board, and Margaret Wiesman attributed this to maneuvering by Dublin; see Wiesman to Jennie Mohr, June 26, 1941, file 52, MCL Papers. Years earlier, Dublin made a similar splash when she took over as editor of the Barnard student newspaper; see Wehmeyer, "Mary Dublin Keyserling," 45.

3. Loyalty Review Board hearing transcript, November 16, 1951, p. 239, box A168, OPM Records.

4. Also in the office was a Mrs. Charlotte Williams, whom Hughes turned against Dublin. The board requested both Hughes and Williams to resign. See memo on Dublin's threat to resign, April 4, 1939, file 2, NCLP-SL; Florence Whitney to Josephine Roche, November 8, 1939, reel 1, NCLP; and, in the MCL Papers, Wiesman correspondence with NCL staff and board members, file 230; Gans-Wiesman correspondence, file 52; Marconnier-Wiesman correspondence, file 189. Also see Wiesman to Louise Stitt, June 22, 1939, box 64, A1 entry 8, WB Records.

5. Memo on Dublin's threat to resign, April 4, 1939, file 2, NCLP-SL; Florence Whitney to Josephine Roche, November 8, 1939, reel 1, NCLP; MDK interview with Kathryn Kish Sklar, 1983, p. 21, SL. Dublin hired a Bennington graduate named Asho Ingersoll (later Craine) to handle both bookkeeping and membership work. Although she herself had little affection for Dublin, Craine remembers Hughes as an "impossible person" who would have disliked Dublin no matter what she did. Asho Ingersoll Craine telephone interview with author, May 19, 1997. On the strike at Consumers' Research, see Silber, *Test and Protest*.

6. For her social life, see MDK appointment books, carton 2, unprocessed addition 96-M106, MDK Papers, and MDK interview with J. Cheek, 1982, OH-40, p. 87, SL. Hughes's disapproval is from Asho Ingersoll Craine telephone interview with author. Many historians have discussed this female-centered reform community, including Cook, "Female Support Networks"; Freedman, "Separatism as Strategy"; Sklar, "Hull House"; Muncy, *Creating a Female Dominion*; and Orleck, *Common Sense*. Leon Keyserling was general counsel to the U.S. Housing Authority in 1939; later he would be chairman of President Truman's Council of Economic Advisors. See *Current Biography, 1947*, 352.

7. Josephine Roche reportedly valued the league because it "was about the only organization of its kind where women and men can meet together. Most of the other organizations, she says, segregate the sexes." See Mary [Switzer] to Lib [Elizabeth Brandeis], October 27, 1939, file 2, box 9, EBR Papers. Roche may have been commenting as much on the exclusion of women from men's groups as on the older female generation's separatism. Margaret Wiesman's ambivalence is suggested in the fact that although she recruited men to the league, she believed it would be "pretty much a tragedy" for the league to choose a male general secretary. See Wiesman to John Lathrop, June 16, 1941, file 230, MCL Papers. For tensions in this era between older single feminists and younger married ones within a different circle of activists, see Rupp, *Worlds of Women*.

8. First quotations from Asho Ingersoll Craine interview with author; "Kelley's mantle" from Margaret Wiesman to Emily Marconnier, November 2, 1939, file 189, and also see Wiesman to Helene Gans, December 27, 1939, file 52, both MCL Papers. Women like Dewson engineered to promote themselves and their friends, but they did so more discreetly and self-effacingly. I could find no evidence to support the hypothesis that this negative reaction to Dublin was tinged by anti-Semitism. During her long career, Dublin alienated many people, some of them more forgiving than Wiesman.

9. Quotation from Beulah Amidon, board minutes, February 20, 1940, and also see January 14, 1940, minutes, both reel 2, NCLP. See Wiesman to Gans, December 27, 1939, and Helene Gans to Wiesman, December 20, 1939, January 10, 1940, file 52, MCL Papers. Wiesman knew she had lost the battle, complaining that Dublin had convinced many that she was "the victim of harsh and unfair treatment at the hands of the old guard" (Wiesman to Gans, December 27, 1939).

10. Orleck, *Common Sense*, chap. 7; Kessler-Harris, "Rose Schneiderman."

11. After some debate, league leaders decided that because AFL members were on the league council, it would not be impolitic to have a CIO representative on the board. Council minutes, December 7, 1939, reel 7, NCLP. Annie Halleck of the Kentucky league struggled to keep her admiration for the CIO from offending her AFL contacts. See Halleck to Lucy Mason, May 26, 1939, reel 62, Mason Papers.

12. Wiesman to Gans, December 27, 1939, file 52; Wiesman to Charlotte Williams, April 27, 1939, file 230, both MCL Papers. In fact, James Carey was an anti-Communist (and after the war would aid in purging CIO unions of Communists). Pressman by this time was leaving the Communist Party; see Gross, *Reshaping of the National Labor Relations Board*, 144, and *Current Biography, 1947*, 528. Wiesman and Gans were friends with Federation of Labor officers in their states; Dublin claimed to be a member of both the AFL and CIO.

13. Whitney's accusation nonetheless caused untold trouble for Dublin later. See FBI reports and Loyalty Review Board hearing testimony of NCL board members, boxes A168–A171, OPM Records.

14. Margaret Wiesman to Louise Stitt, February 24, 1939, box 64, A1 entry 8, WB Records; Wiesman-Marconnier correspondence, February 1939, reel 16, NCLP; Wiesman to Nancy Green, August 22, 1939, file 52, and Wiesman to Clara Beyer, August 15, 1939, file 492, MCL Papers.

15. Communist Party membership in the United States rose to about 50,000 in 1938. See Rosswurm, *CIO's Left-Led Unions*; Isserman, *Which Side Were You On?*; Shaffer, "Women and the Communist Party"; Robin Kelley, *Hammer and Hoe*; Zahavi, "Passionate Commitments." On the Popular Front, see also Kutulas, *Long War*, and Denning, *Cultural Front*.

16. This assessment is based on analysis of Dublin's appointment books for the 1930s, cited above, and of materials in boxes A168–A171, OPM Records. On how to label activists who sometimes worked with CP members but were not Communists themselves, and on the disadvantage of the pejorative term "fellow traveler," see Rosswurm, *CIO's Left-Led Unions*, 7, and David Roediger, foreword to O'Connor, O'Connor, and Bowler, *Harvey and Jessie*.

17. Dublin was a trustee of the Institute of Labor Studies, which existed from 1940 to 1953; see Mary Dublin–Dorothy Douglas correspondence, December 1939, reel 7, NCLP, and Katharine Lumpkin to Olive Matthews Stone, [1940], box 1, Olive Matthews Stone Papers, Southern Historical Collection, University of North Carolina at Chapel Hill. On Douglas and Lumpkin, see Hall, "Open Secrets," and Horowitz, *Betty Friedan*.

18. New York Consumers' League leaders who also were in the LWS include Dublin, Helene Gans, Lois MacDonald, Eveline Burns, Myrta Cannon, and Dorothy Kenyon. See Helen Kay to Dorothy J. Bellanca, September 10, 1935, file 3, box 31, and Kathleen McInerney to Friends, December 12, 1938, file 14, box 81, ACWA Records; Emily Marconnier to John Edelman, November 10, 1936, reel 34, and Lucy Mason to Helen Simmons, January 21, 1937, reel 18, NCLP; minutes of New York LWS board meeting, November 1, 1937, Jessie Lloyd O'Connor Papers, Sophia Smith Collection, Smith College; Mary Dublin to Nashville correspondent, March 21, 1939, reel 97, NCLP. In 1939 the LWS claimed 25,000 members in thirteen cities (this probably was an inflated number); see Senate Committee on Education and Labor, *National Labor Relations Act*, 3190.

19. Anti-Communists soon ridiculed signers of this letter as willfully deluded apologists for Stalin or hopeless innocents; see Lyons, *Red Decade*, 255 (the letter is reprinted there). Dublin later said she regretted signing the letter but did so because she thought the Dewey Committee was the pawn of Trotskyites, not the impartial group it claimed to be; see Loyalty Review Board hearing transcript, August 24, 1948, pp. 136–40, box A170, OPM Records. For substantiation of Dublin's view of the Dewey Committee, see Kutulas, *Long War*, 116–21. On Marshall, see Klehr, *Heyday of American Communism*, 477; *New York Times*, August 2, 1946, and May 10 and 23, 1947.

20. *New York Times*, February 10, 1952, 34; April 22, 1952, 14; October 2, 1952, 25; January 10, 1953, 4; and February 4, 1953, 22; boxes A168–A171, OPM Records; *Congressional Record*, 88th Cong., 2d sess., 1964, 110, pt. 6:7522–52; Senate Committee on Labor and Public Welfare, *Nomination of Mary Dublin Keyserling*, April 3, 1964, copy in carton 1, MDK Papers.

21. The Department of Labor continued to suffer from budget cuts even after the impeachment efforts ceased. Martin, *Madam Secretary*, 409–19.

22. *Omaha World Herald*, December 11, 1939, clipping on reel 50, NCLP; board minutes, December 8, 1938, reel 2, NLCP; and *New York Times*, December 11, 1939, 1; December 12, 1939, 22; December 13, 1939, 19. The report named the Consumers' Union, League of Women Shoppers, and Milk Consumers' Protective League, among others. Lucy Mason and Emily Marconnier had joined the collectively run, pro-labor Consumers' Union in early 1936 after it split off from Consumers' Research; see Mason to Mrs. [Marvin] Underwood, April 8, 1936, reel 94, NCLP. Consumers' Union head Colston Warne, an Amherst professor, was honorary vice president of the NCL.

23. "In Washington with George Morris," clipped from the *Memphis Commercial Appeal*, December 13, 1939, reel 50, NCLP. This representation of the league's methods, although inaccurate, illustrates how widely the Consumers' League was associated with race reform as well as labor reform.

24. The conclusion that Communist influence in the LWS increased in the late 1930s is based on analysis of the group's letterheads over time and inferences drawn from scattered sources. Mary Dublin was among the officers who left the LWS; see Dublin to Margaret Wiesman, February 9, 1939, reel 16, NCLP. On the proposed merger, see NCL board minutes, June 20 and September 24, 1940, reel 2, NCLP. Also see sources cited in note 18.

25. Annual meeting minutes, December 7, 1939, reel 7, NCLP.

26. Ibid.; Dies Committee file, reel 50, NCLP. Mary Dublin, Josephine Roche, and Josephine Goldmark argued for the strongest possible denunciation of the Dies Committee, but Paul Brissenden and Elizabeth Magee wanted to be more cautious and condemn only its methods, not its objectives. Brissenden believed it had been "helpful" to have Communist influence in certain unions exposed. The final resolution

demanded the discontinuation of the Dies Committee, but the committee's methods were denounced, rather than its existence.

27. Mason to Roger Baldwin, American Civil Liberties Union, July 4, 1942, quoted by Tindall, *Emergence of the New South*, 635. League members who became strongly anti-Communist include Elinore Herrick, James Carey, and Josephine Roche. But in 1947 the NCL recruited Walter Gellhorn, a Columbia law professor who publicly attacked HUAC's campaign, to its board; see *Current Biography, 1967*. The NCL defended New York league activist Dorothy Kenyon when she was brought before Senator McCarthy's subcommittee in 1950. In 1954 the NCL came to the defense of Mary Heaton Vorse; see Elizabeth Magee memo, April 8, 1954, Massachusetts file, reel 16, NCLP. The NCL did not sever associations with Communist sympathizer Mary Van Kleeck, who remained on the NCL council. Mary Dublin Keyserling still spoke highly of Van Kleeck in a 1989 interview; see Alchon, "Mary Van Kleeck."

28. Other groups, such as the Consumers' Union, adopted less controversial programs; see Donohue, "Conceptualizing the 'Good Society,'" chap. 7.

29. For other analyses of generational conflict within the Left in the 1930s, see Faue, "Women, Family, and Politics," and Kutulas, *Long War*.

30. Clara Beyer to Boris Shishkin, AFL, and Ralph Hertzel, CIO, January 17, 1940, box 6, entry 1, DLS Records; Beyer address to NCL annual meeting, December 8, 1939, reel 7, NCLP. For Federation of Labor indifference in Virginia and Kentucky, see Brownie Lee Jones to Elizabeth Magee, January 13, 1950, reel 34, NCLP, and Annie Halleck–Louise Stitt correspondence, December 1938, box 64, A1 entry 8, WB Records. Also see Brandeis, "Organized Labor," 232–34.

31. Quotation from meeting minutes of advisory committee to U.S. Women's Bureau, October 27, 1938, reel 98, and see minutes and addresses of annual meeting, December 7–8, 1939, reel 7, NCLP. Christman changed her mind after the war; see Orleck, *Common Sense*, 261.

32. Dublin to Wiesman, October 18, 1938, reel 16, NCLP.

33. Beyer address, annual meeting, December 8, 1939, reel 7, NCLP. This tactical disagreement was mirrored in the distinct preferences of the U.S. Women's Bureau and the Division of Labor Standards; see Sealander, *As Minority Becomes Majority*, 100. The Dublin-Wiesman split fits the pattern identified in Faue's case study of Farmer-Labor women in Minnesota. Faue finds that younger, Popular Front–influenced women made broader demands on the state than older Progressive women, and that younger women were less likely to use gender-based approaches because they proceeded from an assumption of gender equality. As Faue notes, the younger women's approach could in fact be conducive to theoretical blindness on gender. Faue, "Women, Family, and Politics."

34. Dublin to Beyer, December 16, 1939, and see Miss Mel to Beyer, December 11, 1939, both box 6, entry 1, DLS Records. For those few with lingering reservations, Beyer made a similar address at the next annual meeting; see NCL annual meeting, January 11, 1941, reel 8, NCLP.

35. NCL resolutions, December 1938 annual meeting, reel 6; Beyer address, NCL annual meeting, December 8, 1939, reel 7; board minutes, January 14, 1940, reel 2, all NCLP.

36. Some scholars have implied that the sex-based strategy only survived after passage of the FLSA because groups like the NCL were inflexible; see Hart, "Minimum-Wage Policy," 319, and Sealander, *As Minority Becomes Majority*, 158–59.

37. Press release, Fall 1951, file 1, box 4, CL-NY Papers. On differences within the WTUL, see Orleck, *Common Sense*, 261, and within the United Auto Workers, Gabin,

Feminism in the Labor Movement, 200–208. Clara Beyer later claimed that she had been ready to support the ERA after the FLSA was upheld but kept quiet to avoid an open rupture with Mary Anderson of the Women's Bureau. Beyer interview with Vivien Hart, 1983, pp. 16–19, SL.

38. For evidence of NWP collusion with employers in Ohio, see Dennis Harrison, "Consumers' League of Ohio." For a critique of the New Deal that expressed hostility to federal programs, the International Labor Office, and organized labor, see Helena Hill Weed, "The New Deal That Women Want," *Current History* 41 (November 1934): 179–83. It seems noteworthy here that the Du Pont family (backers of the right-wing American Liberty League) gave substantial sums to the NWP in the 1930s; see Becker, *Origins of the Equal Rights Amendment*, 38.

39. Jane Norman Smith to Alma Lutz, April 2, 1933, and Lutz to Josephine Casey, March 21, 1933, file 58, box 4, Alma Lutz Papers, collection MC-182, SL. Lutz tried to soothe Casey: "I know that you do not approve of a minimum-wage law in any case [for any workers]. Personally, I do not know whether it is the solution for low wages or not, but I do think we often have to choose the lesser of two evils" (ibid.). Ingalls, *Herbert H. Lehman*, chap. 4, inaccurately credits the NWP with the sex-neutral bill.

40. Board minutes, February 14 and 27, 1939, reel 2, NCLP; *NCL Bulletin*, March 1939. This opposition to sex-neutral bills seems to have come from individual ERA backers, most likely organized by Josephine Casey and Mary Murray, rather than an official NWP plank; however, the NWP continued to back these working women who opposed all labor-standards regulation. As noted in Chapter 2, Mary Murray opposed equal pay for the sexes because she believed women would lose their jobs.

41. Board minutes, June 14, 1938, May 9 and September 12, 1939, reel 2, and fortieth anniversary dinner program, December 8, 1939, reel 7, NCLP. Alice Hamilton and Josephine Goldmark hoped the NCL would play a larger role on health policy, so this disagreement did not follow generational lines. On Roche's effort to make the NCL a platform for health policy, see Mary [Switzer] to Lib [Elizabeth Brandeis], October 27, 1939, file 2, box 9, EBR Papers. Although the NCL did not spearhead the campaign, it did back national health bills in Congress. In 1939 Dublin testified in support of Senator Wagner's S. 1620 (with reservations about the bill's bypassing of state labor departments). Also see Hamilton testimony for the Wagner-Dingell-Murray bill, April 22, 1946, reel 9, and NCL activities on the Committee for the Nation's Health (founded in 1946), reels 24, 89, NCLP.

42. Mary Dublin to Paul Kellogg, December 16, 1939, reel 7, NCLP.

43. In addition to Margaret Wiesman, those who thought the NCL should focus more on the states included Jane Robbins, Beulah Amidon, Florina Lasker, William Davis, Pauline Goldmark, Elizabeth Magee, and Elizabeth Brandeis. See board minutes, September 12, 1939, September 24, 1940, reel 2, NCLP; Wiesman to Louise Stitt, June 22, 1939, box 64, A1 entry 8, WB Records; Wiesman to Warwick Hobart, January 5, 1942, file 5, NCLP-SL.

44. Board minutes, June 20, September 24, November 7, December 13, 1940, and Dublin letter of resignation, December 5, 1940, reel 2, NCLP. Dublin continued as general secretary until early 1941. The search for her successor illuminates views of Dublin's leadership. Several veterans stressed that above all the NCL needed someone who "understood the program and problems of a local league"; this was to be valued over finding a "brilliant speaker." Elizabeth Magee to Hyman Schroeder, May 31, 1941, and see Pauline Goldmark to John Lathrop, December 1, 1941, and Alice Gannett to John Lathrop, December 2, 1941, all reel 1, NCLP.

45. Board minutes, June 20, September 24, 1940, reel 2, and Brandeis to Elizabeth

Magee, December 24, 1942, reel 24, NCLP (Brandeis was reflecting on earlier events). The Woman's Party, too, experienced internal conflict in this period over state versus national priorities. See Becker, *Origins of the Equal Rights Amendment*, 80.

46. Board minutes, 1941 and 1942, reel 2, and board correspondence, 1941, reel 1, NCLP; *New York Times*, December 21, 1941. Hobart's mother-in-law was a prominent right-winger, past president of the American Legion Auxiliary and Daughters of the American Republic, which may have been why some NCL leaders hesitated to appoint Hobart. Hobart had sought a job in Washington in 1938, so it is not surprising that she took a War Department job supervising women's work in arsenals when it was offered to her in late 1942. See Warwick Hobart to Clara Beyer, July 22, 1938, box 62, entry 1B, DLS Records; Hobart to Margaret Wiesman, November 25, 1942, file 5, NCLP-SL; Hyman Schroeder to Mr. Papier, February 8, 1943, reel 1, NCLP. On the senior Mrs. Hobart, see *Who's Who in America*, 5:338.

47. See Appendix 2; *Current Biography, 1950*, 375; and Elizabeth Magee Papers, Western Reserve Historical Society, Cleveland, Ohio. "American Ruhr" from unsigned letter, frame 12, reel 1, NCLP. In 1932 Magee had been a finalist for the position of general secretary.

48. Scharf, "Women's Movement in Cleveland," and Dennis Harrison, "Consumers' League of Ohio," discuss Magee's style and program.

49. Elizabeth Magee to congressmen on increasing the FLSA minimum wage, March 18, 1946, reel 9; resolutions, NCL annual meeting, March 20–21, 1942, reel 8; board minutes, July 21, 1943, October 9, 1944, reel 2, all NCLP.

50. Resolutions, NCL annual meeting, March 20–21, 1942, reel 8, and board minutes, June 9, 1944 (Nicholas Kelley alone voted against the anti-sex-discrimination plank), reel 2, NCLP; Elinore Herrick statement to New York legislature, December 4, 1946, file 5, box 29B, CL-NY Papers. The now-familiar story of the recruitment and then displacement of women in wartime manufacturing is illuminated by case studies in Milkman, *Gender at Work*, and Gabin, *Feminism in the Labor Movement*.

51. Board minutes, April 11, 1942, June 9, September 20, October 10, 1944, reel 2, NCLP.

52. Brownie Lee Jones to Magee, January 13, 1950, reel 34; wage and hour files by state, reels 94–97, NCLP.

53. On support for the Office of Price Administration, see memos to branches, December 1, 1943, June 1, 1944, reel 16; board minutes, March 23, 1946, reel 2; Mary Anderson testimony for NCL, 1945, reel 9, NCLP. Anna Settle and Ida Friend led local defenses of the agency. On full employment, see board minutes, May 22, 1945, reel 2, NCLP, and *NCL Bulletin*, 1945–47. On the NRPB report, see Brinkley, *End of Reform*, 251–64 (quotation, 251); Warken, *History of the National Resources Planning Board*, 216 ("driving force"); "Dr. Burns, Student of Nazis, Works on Post-War Dictatorship," *Knoxville Journal*, March 14, 1943; and Reminiscences of Eveline Burns (1965), 113, Oral History Collection, Columbia University. On Taft-Hartley, see telegram from Senators Pepper, Thomas, and Magnuson to Magee, May 8, 1947; Magee to Dorothy McAllister, May 15, 1947; Magee to Harry S Truman, June 2, 1947, all reel 84, NCLP.

54. Lucy Mason to Molly Dewson, April 12, 1951, box 3, Dewson Papers, FDRL.

55. The league had sixty-four branches in 1916, a dozen in 1932, and eighteen in 1939. The Ohio and New Jersey branches still exist.

56. The territories of Hawaii and Puerto Rico also included men in their wage laws. From 1941 through 1954 no state enacted a minimum wage law, although various amendments to existing laws passed. DLS, *Recent Progress in State Labor Legislation*; WB, *Summary of State Labor Laws for Women* (1953, 1958, 1967).

57. Most of this burst of legislation occurred between 1964 and 1967. Seven of the ten states without any minimum wage laws in 1967 were in the Southeast. Only two southern states, Kentucky and North Carolina, regulated both men's and women's wages; these were states with strong women's labor reform networks in the 1930s, and they first had passed good laws for women. See DLS, *Report on the Bureau of Labor Standards' Thirtieth Anniversary*; WB, *Summary of State Labor Laws for Women* (1967). By 1974 only three state minimum-wage laws were women-only. By then, after significant broadening of occupational coverage, state laws gave minimum wage protection to 5 million workers not covered by the FLSA. There remained 4.8 million nonsupervisory workers who were not covered by either the FLSA or state laws; see WB, *State Labor Laws in Transition*, 3.

58. Board minutes, October 27, 1942, January 14 and September 20, 1944, reel 2, and Eleanor Roosevelt, "My Day: The Joads in New York," February 1–2, 1945, clipping, reel 9, NCLP.

59. On the organized corporate publicity campaign against labor, see Elizabeth Fones-Wolf, *Selling Free Enterprise*.

60. Jeanette Studley to Louise Stitt, January 16, 1947, box 64, A1 entry 8, WB Records.

61. Brownie Lee Jones, Southern Summer School, to Elizabeth Magee, January 13, 1950, reel 34, NCLP.

62. Funds came from the Textile Workers, the United Hatters, the Amalgamated Clothing Workers, and the International Ladies' Garment Workers, among others; the United Automobile Workers also provided support. See board minutes, May 22, 1945, reel 2; and Dorothy McAllister to Jacob Potofsky, ACWA, September 28, 1949, Elizabeth Magee to Walter Reuther, CIO, May 6, 1953, Magee to Joseph Beirne, Communications Workers, June 21, 1957, and other correspondence with unions, reel 34, all NCLP. Edelman (who had been on the league board in the 1930s) believed unions now saw the need for nonlabor allies. See John Edelman to Emily Taft Douglas, May 23, 1962, reel 2, NCLP.

63. This coalition, the National Committee for a Fair Minimum Wage, was formed by Elizabeth Magee, Mary Anderson, and Frank Graham. It included women's, church, and black organizations. Board minutes, September 18, 1945, reel 2, and NCL pamphlet on the Pepper-Hook bill (S. 1349/H.R. 3914), reel 117, NLCP.

64. John Edelman to Emily Taft Douglas, May 23, 1962, reel 2, NCLP; National Consumers Committee, *Consumer Activists*, 362. On FLSA amendments, see Grossman, "Fair Labor Standards Act of 1938," 29, and Brandeis, "Organized Labor," 232–33. Mary Dublin Keyserling testified for the NCL on the FLSA at least half a dozen times between 1971 and 1987; see speech binders and "NCL, 1938–1987" file, MDK Papers.

65. The Equal Employment Opportunity Commission initially held that sex-based labor laws did not conflict with Title VII, but in 1969 the commission reversed itself. Hartmann, *From Margin to Mainstream*, 57, 68, and WB, *State Labor Laws in Transition*.

66. NCL officers Mary Dublin Keyserling and Esther Peterson were on the Presidential Commission on the Status of Women, which formally recommended this approach in the 1960s. See Mary Dublin Keyserling, "Why I Am a Strong Advocate of the ERA," *Barnard Alumnae Magazine*, January 1981, carton 1, MDK Papers; Cynthia Harrison, *On Account of Sex*; Rupp and Taylor, *Survival in the Doldrums*.

67. See Norman Thomas to NWP, April 12, 1931, reel 45, and Communist Party of New York City to Senate Judiciary Committee, August 12, 1937, reel 59, NWPP; *The Phyllis Schlafly Report* 5, no. 7 (February 1972); and more generally, Mathews and De

Hart, *Sex, Gender, and the ERA*. Schlafly asserted that both communism and the ERA sought to erase gender distinctions.

68. MDK interview with J. Cheek, 1982, OH-40, p. 264, SL; Keyserling, "Why I Am a Strong Advocate of the ERA," *Barnard Alumnae Magazine*, January 1981, carton 1, MDK Papers; Hartmann, *From Margin to Mainstream*; Gabin, *Feminism in the Labor Movement*; Goldmark, *Impatient Crusader*.

69. On the concept of administrative capacity, see Skowroneck, *Building a New American State*. On the novelty and importance of Perkins's labor conferences, see Martin, *Madam Secretary*, chap. 32.

70. On the effectiveness of this lobbying, see Sealander, *As Minority Becomes Majority*, 137, and Brandeis, "Organized Labor," 234.

71. The league added the phrase to its letterhead but did not legally change its name. The longer name was in use on occasion into the 1950s. Board minutes, June 9, October 9, 1944, reel 2, NCLP.

72. Board minutes, September 2, 1947, November 16, 1960, and John Edelman to Emily Taft Douglas, May 23, 1962, reel 2, NCLP; also see *NCL Bulletin* after 1960.

73. Board minutes, November 16, 1960, reel 2, NCLP.

74. Quoted in Scharf, "Women's Movement in Cleveland," 89.

Conclusion

1. Many countries with weaker women's movements than the United States implemented policies such as public day care and maternity leaves to help reconcile wage-earning and motherhood; see Koven and Michel, *Mothers of a New World*, and Wikander, Kessler-Harris, and Lewis, *Protecting Women*, introduction. For negative assessments of the "maternalist" legacy, see Mink, *Wages of Motherhood*, and Kessler-Harris, "Paradox of Motherhood." For a contrasting view that emphasizes chronic underfunding of programs won by female reformers, see Orloff, "Gender in Early U.S. Social Policy."

2. For examples of the latter, see Molly Dewson to "Dear Boss" [FDR], Spring 1940, and FDR to Molly Dewson, November 7, 1940, box 7, Dewson Papers, FDRL. Over Dewson's protests, FDR resisted appointing female ambassadors to countries likely to be at war and excluded women from Selective Service appeal boards.

3. Similarly, wartime attacks on the Office of Civilian Defense focused on Eleanor Roosevelt and other women, including Helen Gahagan Douglas.

4. For varying opinions on the timing of the triumph of fiscal Keynesianism over more redistributive, interventionist versions of liberalism, see Brinkley, *End of Reform*; Lichtenstein, "From Corporatism to Collective Bargaining"; and Jacobs, "Democracy's Third Estate."

5. Gerstle, "Protean Nature of American Liberalism"; Brinkley, *End of Reform*. The category of gender is not included in these schematics of the evolving liberal agenda.

6. Josephine Goldmark, "Fifty Years — The National Consumers' League," *Survey* 85 (December 1949): 676.

7. The exhibit, "Between a Rock and a Hard Place: A Dialogue on American Sweatshops, 1820–Present," opened at the National Museum of American History in April 1998. *NCL Bulletin*, November/December 1997.

8. "Apparel Panel Badly Divided on Policing of Sweatshops," November 21, 1997; "Nike Pledges to End Child Labor and Apply U.S. Rules Abroad," May 13, 1998; "Anti-Sweatshop Coalition Finds Itself at Odds on Garment Factory Code," July 3, 1998; "Groups Reach Agreement for Curtailing Sweatshops," November 5, 1998; "Two More Unions Reject Agreement," November 6, 1998, all *New York Times*. For

critiques of the Apparel Industry Partnership from labor perspectives, see Alan Howard, "Partners in Sweat," *Nation*, December 28, 1998; Medea Benjamin, "What's Fair about the Fair Labor Association," February 1999, www.globalexchange.org; and Eyal Press, "A Nike Sneak," *Nation*, April 5/12, 1999.

9. One of the many counts on which the 1998 agreement disappointed trade unionists was its failure to mandate payment of a "living wage" to foreign workers. The agreement called for the U.S. Department of Labor to undertake a study of minimum, prevailing, and living wages in the relevant countries, which supporters argued would be a valuable first step. See "Groups Reach Agreement for Curtailing Sweatshops," *New York Times*, November 5, 1998, and other sources cited in note 8. For a fascinating study of one company's migration toward cheaper labor, see Cowie, *Capital Moves*.

10. Quotation from "Can Industry Police Itself" session, NCL Third Labor Standards Conference, December 10, 1934, reel 6, NCLP; "Groups Reach Agreement for Curtailing Sweatshops," *New York Times*, November 5, 1998.

11. Clara Beyer's work with the Division of Labor Standards epitomized the effort to offer uniform national standards and high quality administration while encouraging initiatives in the states. In 1982 Beyer denounced the idea of eliminating federal programs in favor of block grants to the states (in 1996 this idea became reality in welfare policy with the abolition of the Aid to Families with Dependent Children program). See "The Stupendous Mrs. Beyer," *Second Century Radcliffe News*, January 1982.

12. Mary Dublin, handwritten notes for address to Consumers' League of Michigan, December 30, 1938, carton 5, MDK Papers (emphasis in original).

bibliography

Manuscript Collections

Alexandria, Virginia
  Personal Papers of Lucy Mason (private collection of C. S. Taylor Burke Jr.)
Ann Arbor, Michigan
  Michigan Historical Collections, Bentley Historical Library, University of Michigan
    Dorothy Smith McAllister Papers (microfilm)
Atlanta, Georgia
  Robert W. Woodruff Library, Emory University
    Eleonore Raoul Papers
    Mildred Seydell Papers
    Josephine Wilkins Papers
Cambridge, Massachusetts
  Arthur and Elizabeth Schlesinger Library, Radcliffe College
    Clara Mortenson Beyer Papers
    Clara M. Beyer interview with Vivien Hart, 1983
    Consumers' League of Connecticut Papers
    Consumers' League of Massachusetts Papers
    Elinore Morehouse Herrick Papers
    Lucy Somerville Howorth Papers
    Mary Dublin Keyserling interview with J. Cheek, 1982 (OH-40, Oral Histories of
      Women in Federal Government)
    Mary Dublin Keyserling interview with Kathryn Kish Sklar, 1983
    Mary Dublin Keyserling Papers
    Alma Lutz Papers, collections A-34 and MC-182
    National Consumers' League Papers
Chapel Hill, North Carolina
  Southern Historical Collection, University of North Carolina
    Frank Porter Graham Papers
    Olive Matthews Stone Papers
  Southern Oral History Program Collection, University of North Carolina
    Eleanor Copenhaver Anderson interview with M. Frederickson, November 5,
      1974
    Adele Clark interviews with W. Bradford, February 24 and July 12, 1964
    Harriet Herring interview with M. Frederickson and N. Brown, February 5,
      1976
    Myles Horton interview with M. Frederickson, July 24, 1975
    Brownie Lee Jones interview with M. Frederickson, April 20, 1976
    Eula McGill interview with J. Hall, February 3, 1976

Olive Matthews Stone interviews with S. Gluck, 1975
Jennie Pedigo interview with B. Finger, April 2, 1975
Josephine Wilkins interview with J. Hall, 1972
Louise Young interview with J. Hall, February 14, 1972
Cleveland, Ohio
  Western Reserve Historical Society
    Elizabeth Magee Papers
College Park, Maryland
  National Archives
    Records of the National Labor Relations Board (RG 25)
    Records of the National Recovery Administration (RG 9)
    Records of the Office of Personnel Management (RG 478)
    Records of the U.S. Department of Labor, Division of Labor Standards (RG 100)
    Records of the U.S. Department of Labor, Wage and Hour and Public Contracts Division (RG 155)
    Records of the U.S. Department of Labor, Women's Bureau (RG 86)
Durham, North Carolina
  Perkins Library, Duke University
    Lucy Randolph Mason Papers, in Operation Dixie: The CIO Organizing Committee Papers, 1946–53 (microfilm)
Houston, Texas
  M. D. Anderson Library, University of Houston
    Records of the National Association of Colored Women's Clubs, 1895–1992 (microfilm)
Hyde Park, New York
  Franklin D. Roosevelt Library
    Democratic National Committee Women's Division Papers
    Mary W. Dewson Papers
    Personal Files of President Franklin D. Roosevelt
    John G. Winant Papers
Ithaca, New York
  Labor-Management Documentation Center, Martin P. Catherwood Library of the New York State School of Industrial Labor Relations at Cornell University
    American Association for Labor Legislation Pamphlet Collection
    Mabel Leslie Papers
    Records of the Amalgamated Clothing Workers of America
    Records of the Consumers' League of New York
    Records of the International Ladies' Garment Workers' Union
Madison, Wisconsin
  State Historical Society of Wisconsin
    American Association for Labor Legislation Papers (microfilm)
    Victor Berger Papers
    William H. Davis Papers
    Industrial Commission of Wisconsin Papers
    National Woman's Party Papers, 1913–72 (microfilm)
    Papers of the Women's Trade Union League and Its Principal Leaders (microfilm)
    Elizabeth Brandeis Raushenbush Papers
    George A. Sloan Papers

New Orleans, Louisiana
  Special Collections, Tulane University Library
    Ida Weis Friend Papers
    Kingsley House Papers
    New Orleans League of Women Voters Papers
    New Orleans YWCA Papers
New York, New York
  Oral History Collection, Columbia University
    Mary Dublin Keyserling interview with K. Louchheim, June 18, 1981
    Reminiscences of Eveline M. Burns (1965)
Northampton, Massachusetts
  Sophia Smith Collection, Smith College
    Consumers' League of Kentucky Papers (microfilm)
    Dorothy Kenyon Papers
    League of Women Shoppers Papers
    Jessie Lloyd O'Connor Papers
Providence, Rhode Island
  John Hay Library, Brown University
    Consumers' League of Rhode Island Papers
Richmond, Virginia
  James Branch Cabell Library, Virginia Commonwealth University
    Adele Goodman Clark Papers
Rock Hill, South Carolina
  Winthrop University Archives
    Mary Elizabeth Frayser Papers
Silver Spring, Maryland
  George Meany Memorial Archives
    State Labor Proceedings (microfiche)
Washington, D.C.
  Manuscript Division, Library of Congress
    League of Women Voters Papers
    National Association for the Advancement of Colored People Papers
    National Consumers' League Papers (microfilm and unfilmed additions)
    National Policy Committee Papers

Interviews by Author

Asho Ingersoll Craine, May 19, 1997, by telephone.
Linda Golodner, August 13, 1998, Washington, D.C.
Mary Dublin Keyserling, March 22, 1991, Washington, D.C.

Government Publications

Georgia House of Representatives. *House Journal*, 1931.
National Emergency Council. *Report to the President on the Economic Conditions of the South*. Washington: Government Printing Office, 1938.
South Carolina Department of Labor. *Annual Report*, 1937–40.
U.S. Congress. House. Committee on the Judiciary. *Conditions of Government Contracts: Hearings before the Committee on the Judiciary, Part 2*. 74th Cong., 2d sess., March 16, 18, 20, 21, 23, 1936.

———. Committee on Labor. *Proposed Amendments to the National Labor Relations Act.* Vols. 4–5, *Hearings before the House Committee on Labor.* 76th Cong., 1st sess., July 6, 7, 11, 1939.

———. Special Committee to Investigate the National Labor Relations Board. *Hearings before the House Special Committee to Investigate the National Labor Relations Board.* Vols. 5–8. 76th Cong., 3d sess., January 5, 8–12, 15, 16, 1940.

———. Senate. Committee on Education and Labor. *National Labor Relations Act and Proposed Amendments: Hearings before the Senate Committee on Education and Labor, Parts 16 and 17.* 76th Cong., 1st sess., July 11–14, 1939.

———. Senate Committee on Education and Labor and House Committee on Labor. *Fair Labor Standards Act of 1937: Joint Hearings before the Senate Committee on Education and Labor and the House Committee on Labor, Parts 1 and 2.* 75th Cong., 1st sess., June 2–5, 7–9, 11, 14, 15, 1937.

U.S. Department of Commerce. Bureau of the Census. *The Social and Economic Statistics of the Black Population of the United States: An Historical View, 1790–1978.* Washington: Government Printing Office, n.d.

———. *Statistical Abstract of the United States, 1943.* Washington: Government Printing Office, 1943.

U.S. Department of Labor. Bureau of Labor Statistics. *Monthly Labor Review,* 1932–44.

———. Division of Labor Standards. *Digest of State and Federal Labor Legislation.* Washington: Government Printing Office, annual.

———. *Labor Standards,* vols. 1–5 (April 1938–April 1942).

———. *Recent Progress in State Labor Legislation.* Bulletin 42. Washington: Government Printing Office, 1940.

———. *Report on the Bureau of Labor Standards' Thirtieth Anniversary.* Bulletin 272. Washington: Government Printing Office, 1964.

———. Wage and Hour and Public Contracts Division. *Annual Report,* 1948, 1953.

———. Wage and Hour Division. *Annual Report, 1939.*

———. Women's Bureau. *The Effects of Labor Legislation on the Employment Opportunities of Women.* Bulletin 65. Washington: Government Printing Office, 1928.

———. *Employed Women under NRA Codes.* Bulletin 130. Washington: Government Printing Office, 1935.

———. *Employment Conditions in Beauty Shops.* Bulletin 133. Washington: Government Printing Office, 1935.

———. *The Employment of Women at Night.* Bulletin 64. Washington: Government Printing Office, 1928.

———. *The Negro Woman Worker.* Bulletin 165. Washington: Government Printing Office, 1938.

———. *Newsletter* (May 1931).

———. *Night Work for Women.* Bulletin 233. Washington: Government Printing Office, 1949.

———. *State Labor Laws in Transition: From Protection to Equal Status for Women.* Washington: Government Printing Office, 1976.

———. *Summary: The Effects of Labor Legislation on the Employment Opportunities of Women.* Bulletin 68. Washington: Government Printing Office, 1928.

———. *Summary of State Labor Laws for Women.* Washington: Government Printing Office, 1953, 1958, 1967.

———. *A Survey of Laundries and Their Women Workers in Twenty-three Cities.* Bulletin 78. Washington: Government Printing Office, 1930.

———. *The Woman Worker,* vols. 18–22 (January 1938–May 1942).

———. *Women in the Economy of the United States of America*. Bulletin 155. Washington: Government Printing Office, 1937.
———. *Women in Georgia Industries*. Bulletin 22. Washington: Government Printing Office, 1922.
———. *Women in Kentucky Industries*. Bulletin 162. Washington: Government Printing Office, 1937.
Virginia General Assembly. *Senate Journal and Documents*, 1936, 1938.
Virginia State Department of Labor and Industry. *Annual Report*, 1936–42.

Newspapers and Periodicals

American Federationist (American Federation of Labor)
American Labor Legislation Review (American Association for Labor Legislation)
Atlanta Constitution
Current Biography
Current History
Dictionary of American Biography
Equal Rights (National Woman's Party)
Independent Woman (Federation of Business and Professional Women's Clubs)
Journal of Labor (Atlanta)
Knoxville Journal
Life and Labor Bulletin (National Women's Trade Union League)
Literary Digest
Louisville Courier-Journal
Nation
NCL Bulletin (National Consumers' League)
New Orleans Times-Picayune
New Republic
New York Times
New York World-Telegram
Richmond Times-Dispatch
Scribner's
South Today
Survey
Survey Graphic
Survey Mid-Monthly
Washington Post
Who's Who in America
Who's Who in the South

Books and Articles

Abramovitz, Mimi. *Regulating the Lives of Women: Social Policy from Colonial Times to the Present*. Boston: South End Press, 1988.
Alchon, Guy. "Mary Van Kleeck and Social-Economic Planning." *Journal of Policy History* 3, no. 1 (1991): 1–23.
Alston, Lee, and Joseph Ferrie. *Southern Paternalism and the American Welfare State: Economics, Politics, and Institutions in the South, 1865–1965*. New York: Cambridge University Press, 1999.
Amalgamated Clothing Workers of America. *Report of General Executive Board and*

Proceedings of the Twelfth Biennial Convention, May 9–17, 1938, Atlantic City, New Jersey.
New York: Amalgamated Clothing Workers of America, 1938.

———. *Report of General Executive Board and Proceedings of the Thirteenth Biennial Convention, May 13–24, 1940, New York City.* New York: Amalgamated Clothing Workers of America, 1940.

Andersen, Kristi. *After Suffrage: Women in Partisan and Electoral Politics before the New Deal.* Chicago: University of Chicago Press, 1996.

———. *The Creation of a Democratic Majority, 1928–1936.* Chicago: University of Chicago Press, 1979.

Anderson, Mary, and Mary N. Winslow. *Woman at Work: The Autobiography of Mary Anderson.* Minneapolis: University of Minnesota Press, 1951.

Angevine, Erma. *History of the National Consumers' League, 1899–1979.* Washington, D.C.: National Consumers' League, 1979.

Arluck, Mary S. *Guide to the Microfilm Edition of the Papers of the American Association of Labor Legislation, 1905–1943.* Glen Rock, N.J.: Microfilming Corporation of America, 1974.

Auerbach, Jerold S. *Labor and Liberty: The La Follette Committee and the New Deal.* Indianapolis: Bobbs-Merrill, 1966.

Baer, Judith A. *The Chains of Protection: The Judicial Response to Women's Labor Legislation.* Westport, Conn.: Greenwood, 1978.

Baker, Paula. "The Domestication of Politics: Women and American Political Society, 1780–1920." *American Historical Review* 89, no. 3 (June 1984): 620–47.

Barnard, Hollinger F., ed. *Outside the Magic Circle: The Autobiography of Virginia Foster Durr.* University: University of Alabama Press, 1985.

Bartley, Numan F. *The Creation of Modern Georgia.* 2d ed. Athens: University of Georgia Press, 1990.

Bates, Beth T. "A New Crowd Challenges the Agenda of the Old Guard at the NAACP, 1933–1941." *American Historical Review* 102, no. 2 (April 1997): 340–77.

Becker, Susan D. "International Feminism between the Wars: The National Woman's Party versus the League of Women Voters." In *Decades of Discontent: The Women's Movement, 1920–1940*, edited by Lois Scharf and Joan M. Jensen. Boston: Northeastern University Press, 1983.

———. *The Origins of the Equal Rights Amendment: American Feminism between the Wars.* Westport, Conn.: Greenwood, 1981.

Bell, Daniel. *Marxian Socialism in the United States.* Princeton: Princeton University Press, 1952.

Bellush, Bernard. *The Failure of the National Recovery Administration.* New York: Norton, 1975.

Berman, Myron. *Richmond's Jewry, 1769–1976: Shabbat in Shockoe.* Charlottesville: University of Virginia Press for the Richmond Jewish Community Council, 1978.

Bernstein, Irving. *A Caring Society: The New Deal, the Worker and the Great Depression.* Boston: Houghton Mifflin, 1985.

———. *Turbulent Years.* Boston: Houghton Mifflin, 1970.

Biles, Roger. *The South and the New Deal.* Lexington: University Press of Kentucky, 1994.

Blackwelder, Julia Kirk. "Mop and Typewriter: Women's Work in Early Twentieth Century Atlanta." *Atlanta Historical Journal* 27 (Fall 1983): 21–30.

Blakey, George T. *Hard Times and New Deal in Kentucky, 1929–1939.* Lexington: University Press of Kentucky, 1986.

Bland, Sidney R. "Fighting the Odds: Militant Suffragists in South Carolina." *South Carolina Historical Magazine* 82, no. 1 (January 1981): 32–43.

Blatch, Harriot Stanton, and Alma Lutz. *Challenging Years: The Memoirs of Harriot Stanton Blatch*. New York: Putnam, 1940.

Blumberg, Dorothy Rose. "'Dear Mr. Engels': Unpublished Letters, 1884–1894, of Florence Kelley to Friedrich Engels." *Labor History* 5, no. 2 (Spring 1964): 103–32.

Boone, Gladys. *The Women's Trade Union Leagues in Great Britain and the U.S.A.* New York: Columbia University Press, 1942.

Boris, Eileen. *Home to Work: Motherhood and the Politics of Industrial Homework in the United States*. New York: Cambridge University Press, 1994.

———. "Homework and Women's Rights: The Case of the Vermont Knitters, 1980–1985." In *Homework: Historical and Contemporary Perspectives on Paid Labor at Home*, edited by Eileen Boris and Cynthia R. Daniels. Chicago: University of Illinois Press, 1989.

———. "The Power of Motherhood: Black and White Women Redefine the 'Political.'" *Yale Journal of Law and Feminism* 2 (1989): 25–49.

———. "The Racialized Gendered State: Constructions of Citizenship in the United States." *Social Politics* 2, no. 2 (Summer 1995): 160–80.

———. "Regulating Industrial Homework: The Triumph of 'Sacred Motherhood.'" *Journal of American History* 71, no. 4 (March 1985): 745–63.

———. "The Regulation of Homework and the Devolution of the Postwar Labor Standards Regime: Beyond Dichotomy." In *Labor Law in America*, edited by Christopher L. Tomlins and Andrew J. King. Baltimore: Johns Hopkins University Press, 1992.

———. "Tenement Homework on Army Uniforms: The Gendering of Industrial Democracy during World War I." *Labor History* 32 (Spring 1991): 231–52.

Brandeis, Elizabeth. "Labor Legislation." In *History of Labor in the United States*, vol. 3, *1896–1932*, edited by John R. Commons et al. New York: Macmillan, 1935.

———. "Organized Labor and Protective Labor Legislation." In *Labor and the New Deal*, edited by Milton Derber and Edwin Young. Madison: University of Wisconsin Press, 1957.

Brandes, Stuart. *American Welfare Capitalism, 1880–1940*. Chicago: University of Chicago Press, 1976.

Brinkley, Alan. *The End of Reform: New Deal Liberalism in Recession and War*. New York: Knopf, 1995.

———. "The New Deal and Southern Politics." In *The New Deal and the South*, edited by James C. Cobb and Michael V. Namorato. Jackson: University Press of Mississippi, 1984.

———. *Voices of Protest: Huey Long, Father Coughlin and the Great Depression*. New York: Knopf, 1983.

Brito, Patricia. "Protective Legislation in Ohio: The Interwar Years." *Ohio History* 88, no. 2 (Spring 1979): 173–97.

Brody, David. "The Emergence of Mass-Production Unionism." In *Change and Continuity in Twentieth-Century America*, edited by John Braeman, Robert H. Bremner, and Everett Walters. Columbus: Ohio State University Press, 1964.

Brody, David, John Braeman, and Robert Bremner, eds. *The New Deal*. Vol. 2, *The State and Local Levels*. Columbus: Ohio State University Press, 1975.

Brown, Elsa Barkely. "Womanist Consciousness: Maggie Lena Walker and the Independent Order of Saint Luke." *Signs* 14, no. 3 (Spring 1989): 610–33.

Buhle, Mari Jo. *Women and American Socialism, 1870–1920*. Urbana: University of
Illinois Press, 1981.

Buhle, Mari Jo, et al. *Encyclopedia of the American Left*. New York: Garland, 1990.

Burns, James MacGregor. *Congress on Trial*. New York: Harper and Brothers, 1949.

Campbell, Persia. *Consumer Representation in the New Deal*. New York: Columbia
University Press, 1940.

Carrasco, Rebecca S. "The Gift House: Jean M. Gordon and the Making of Milne
Home, 1904–1931." *Louisiana History* 34, no. 3 (Summer 1993): 309–25.

Carter, Dan. *Scottsboro: A Tragedy of the American South*. Baton Rouge: Louisiana State
University Press, 1969.

Carter, Joseph, ed. *Labor Lobbyist: The Autobiography of John Edelman*. Indianapolis:
Bobbs-Merrill, 1974.

Chafe, William H. *The American Woman: Her Changing Social, Economic, and Political
Roles, 1920–1970*. New York: Oxford University Press, 1972.

———. "Women's History and Political History: Some Thoughts on Progressivism
and the New Deal." In *Visible Women: New Essays on American Activism*, edited by
Nancy A. Hewitt and Suzanne Lebsock. Urbana: University of Illinois Press, 1993.

Chambers, Clarke A. *Seedtime of Reform: American Social Service and Social Action, 1918–
1933*. Minneapolis: University of Minnesota Press, 1963.

Chambers, John W. "The Big Switch: Justice Roberts and the Minimum Wage Cases."
Labor History 10, no. 1 (Winter 1969): 44–73.

Chepesiuk, Ronald, Ann Evans, and Thomas Morgan, eds. *Women Leaders in South
Carolina: An Oral History*. Rock Hill, S.C.: Winthrop College Archives and Special
Collections, 1984.

Cheyney, Alice S. "The Course of Minimum Wage Legislation in the United States."
International Labour Review 38 (July 1938): 26–43.

Clark, Claudia. *Radium Girls: Women and Industrial Health Reform, 1910–1935*. Chapel
Hill: University of North Carolina Press, 1997.

Clark, Jane Perry. *The Rise of a New Federalism: Federal-State Cooperation in the United
States*. New York: Columbia University Press, 1938.

Cobb, James C. "Does *Mind* No Longer Matter? The South, the Nation, and *The
Mind of the South*, 1941–1991." *Journal of Southern History* 57, no. 4 (November
1991): 681–718.

Cobble, Dorothy Sue. *Dishing It Out: Waitresses and Their Unions in the Twentieth
Century*. Urbana: University of Illinois Press, 1991.

———. "Drawing the Line: The Construction of a Gendered Work Force in the Food
Service Industry." In *Work Engendered: Toward a New History of American Labor*,
edited by Ava Baron. Ithaca: Cornell University Press, 1991.

Cohen, Lizabeth. *Making a New Deal: Industrial Workers in Chicago, 1919–1939*. New
York: Cambridge University Press, 1990.

———. "The New Deal State and the Making of Citizen Consumers." In *Getting and
Spending: European and American Consumer Societies in the Twentieth Century*, edited
by Susan Strasser, Charles McGovern, and Matthias Judt. Washington, D.C.:
Cambridge University Press for the German Historical Institute, 1998.

Cohen, Miriam, and Michael Hanagan. "The Politics of Gender and the Making of
the Welfare State, 1900–1940: A Comparative Perspective." *Journal of Social History*
24 (Spring 1991): 469–84.

Cohen, Robert. *When the Old Left Was Young: Student Radicals and America's First
Mass Student Movement, 1929–1941*. New York: Oxford University Press, 1993.

Coleman, Kenneth, et al. *A History of Georgia*. 2d ed. Athens: University of Georgia Press, 1991.

Cook, Blanche Wiesen. "Female Support Networks and Political Activism: Lillian Wald, Crystal Eastman, and Emma Goldman." *Chrysalis* 3 (1977): 43–61.

Cott, Nancy F. *The Grounding of Modern Feminism*. New Haven: Yale University Press, 1987.

——. "What's in a Name? The Limits of 'Social Feminism': Or, Expanding the Vocabulary of Women's History." *Journal of American History* 76, no. 3 (December 1989): 809–29.

Cowie, Jefferson. *Capital Moves: RCA's Seventy-Year Quest for Cheap Labor*. Ithaca: Cornell University Press, 1999.

Cutler, Addison T. "Labor Legislation in Thirteen Southern States." *Southern Economic Journal* 7, no. 3 (January 1941): 297–316.

Davidson, Elizabeth H. *Child Labor Legislation in the Southern Textile States*. Chapel Hill: University of North Carolina Press, 1939.

Davis, Allen F. "The Women's Trade Union League: Origins and Organization." *Labor History* 5, no. 1 (Winter 1964): 3–17.

Dawley, Alan. *Struggles for Justice: Social Responsibility and the Liberal State*. Cambridge: Harvard University Press, 1991.

Denning, Michael. *The Cultural Front: The Laboring of American Culture in the Twentieth Century*. New York: Verso, 1996.

Deutsch, Sarah. "Learning to Talk More Like a Man: Boston Women's Class-Bridging Organizations, 1870–1940." *American Historical Review* 97, no. 2 (April 1992): 379–404.

Dorman, Robert L. *Revolt of the Provinces: The Regionalist Movement in America, 1920–1945*. Chapel Hill: University of North Carolina Press, 1993.

Douglas, Paul H. *In the Fullness of Time*. New York: Harcourt Brace Jovanovich, 1971.

Douglas, Paul H., and Joseph Hackman. "The Fair Labor Standards Act of 1938." Parts 1 and 2. *Political Science Quarterly* 53 (December 1938): 491–515; 54 (March 1939): 29–55.

Draper, Alan. "The New Southern Labor History Revisited: The Success of the Mine, Mill and Smelter Workers' Union in Birmingham, 1934–38." *Journal of Southern History* 62, no. 1 (February 1996): 87–108.

Dublin, Thomas. *Women at Work*. New York: Columbia University Press, 1979.

DuBois, Ellen Carol, and Linda Gordon. "Seeking Ecstasy on the Battlefield: Danger and Pleasure in Nineteenth-Century Feminist Sexual Thought." *Feminist Studies* 9, no. 1 (Spring 1983): 7–25.

Dunbar, Anthony P. *Against the Grain: Southern Radicals and Prophets, 1929–1959*. Charlottesville: University Press of Virginia, 1981.

Dye, Nancy Schrom. *As Equals and as Sisters: Feminism, the Labor Movement and the Women's Trade Union League of New York*. Columbia: University of Missouri Press, 1980.

Edwards, Rebecca. *Angels in the Machinery*. New York: Oxford University Press, 1997.

Egerton, John. *Speak Now Against the Day: The Generation Before the Civil Rights Movement in the South*. Chapel Hill: University of North Carolina Press, 1994.

Enloe, Cynthia. *The Morning After: Sexual Politics at the End of the Cold War*. Berkeley: University of California Press, 1993.

Epstein, Barbara Leslie. *The Politics of Domesticity: Women, Evangelism, and Temperance in Nineteenth-Century America*. Middletown, Conn.: Wesleyan University Press, 1981.

Evans, Sara M., and Harry C. Boyte. *Free Spaces: The Sources of Democratic Change in America*. New York: Harper and Row, 1986.

Faue, Elizabeth. *Community of Suffering and Struggle: Women, Men and the Labor Movement in Minneapolis, 1915–1945*. Chapel Hill: University of North Carolina Press, 1991.

———. "Paths of Unionization: Community, Bureaucracy, and Gender in the Minneapolis Labor Movement of the 1930s." In *Work Engendered: Toward a New History of American Labor*, edited by Ava Baron. Ithaca: Cornell University Press, 1991.

———. "Women, Family, and Politics: Farmer-Labor Women and Social Policy in the Great Depression." In *Women, Politics, and Change*, edited by Louise A. Tilly and Patricia Gurin. New York: Russell Sage Foundation, 1990.

Felt, Jeremy P. *Hostages of Fortune: Child Labor Reform in New York State*. Syracuse, N.Y.: Syracuse University Press, 1965.

Ferguson, Thomas. "Industrial Conflict and the Coming of the New Deal: The Triumph of Multinational Liberalism in America." In *The Rise and Fall of the New Deal Order, 1930–1980*, edited by Steve Fraser and Gary Gerstle. Princeton: Princeton University Press, 1989.

Fine, Sidney. *The Automobile under the Blue Eagle*. Ann Arbor: University of Michigan Press, 1963.

Finegold, Kenneth. "Agriculture and the Politics of U.S. Social Provision: Social Insurance and Food Stamps." In *The Politics of Social Policy in the United States*, edited by Margaret Weir, Ann Shola Orloff, and Theda Skocpol. Princeton: Princeton University Press, 1988.

Finegold, Kenneth, and Theda Skocpol. *State and Party in America's New Deal*. Madison: University of Wisconsin Press, 1995.

Fitzpatrick, Ellen. *Endless Crusade: Women Social Scientists and Progressive Reform*. New York: Oxford University Press, 1990.

Flamming, Douglas. *Creating the Modern South: Millhands and Managers in Dalton, Georgia, 1884–1984*. Chapel Hill: University of North Carolina Press, 1992.

Flanagan, Maureen A. "Gender and Urban Political Reform: The City Club and the Woman's City Club of Chicago in the Progressive Era." *American Historical Review* 95, no. 4 (October 1990): 1032–50.

Flint, J. Wayne. "The New Deal and Southern Labor." In *The New Deal and the South*, edited by James C. Cobb and Michael V. Namorato. Jackson: University Press of Mississippi, 1984.

Foner, Philip S. *Women and the American Labor Movement*. Vol. 2. New York: Free Press, 1980.

Fones-Wolf, Elizabeth. *Selling Free Enterprise: The Business Assault on Labor and Liberalism, 1945–1960*. Urbana: University of Illinois Press, 1994.

Forbath, William E. *Law and the Shaping of the American Labor Movement*. Cambridge: Harvard University Press, 1991.

Frank, Dana. *Purchasing Power: Consumer Organizing, Gender, and the Seattle Labor Movement, 1919–1929*. New York: Cambridge University Press, 1994.

Frankel, Noralee, and Nancy S. Dye, eds. *Gender, Class, Race and Reform in the Progressive Era*. Lexington: University Press of Kentucky, 1991.

Fraser, Steve. "The 'Labor Question.'" In *The Rise and Fall of the New Deal Order, 1930–1980*, edited by Steve Fraser and Gary Gerstle. Princeton: Princeton University Press, 1989.

———. *Labor Will Rule: Sidney Hillman and the Rise of American Labor*. New York: Free Press, 1991.

Fraser, Steve, and Gary Gerstle, eds. *The Rise and Fall of the New Deal Order, 1930–1980*. Princeton: Princeton University Press, 1989.

Frederickson, Mary. "Citizens for Democracy." In *Sisterhood and Solidarity: Workers' Education for Women, 1914–1984*, edited by Joyce L. Kornbluh and Mary Frederickson. Philadelphia: Temple University Press, 1984.

———. "Heroines and Girl Strikers: Gender Issues and Organized Labor in the Twentieth-Century American South." In *Organized Labor in the Twentieth-Century American South*, edited by Robert H. Zieger. Knoxville: University of Tennessee Press, 1991.

———. "'I Know Which Side I'm On': Southern Women in the Labor Movement in the Twentieth Century." In *Women, Work and Protest: A Century of U.S. Women's Labor History*, edited by Ruth Milkman. New York: Routledge, 1985.

———. "Shaping a New Society: Methodist Women and Industrial Reform in the South, 1880–1940." In *Women in New Worlds: Historical Perspectives on the Wesleyan Tradition*, edited by Hilah F. Thomas and Rosemary Skinner Keller. Nashville, Tenn.: Abingdon, 1981.

Freedman, Estelle. "Separatism as Strategy: Female Institution-Building and American Feminism, 1870–1930." *Feminist Studies* 5, no. 33 (Fall 1979): 512–29.

———. "Separatism Revisited: Women's Institutions, Social Reform, and the Career of Miriam Van Waters." In *U.S. History as Women's History: New Feminist Essays*, edited by Linda K. Kerber, Alice Kessler-Harris, and Kathryn Kish Sklar. Chapel Hill: University of North Carolina Press, 1995.

Freeman, Joshua B. *In Transit: The Transport Workers Union in New York City, 1933–1966*. New York: Oxford University Press, 1989.

Fry, Amelia R. "Alice Paul and the ERA." In *Rights of Passage: The Past and Future of the ERA*, edited by Joan Hoff-Wilson. Bloomington: Indiana University Press, 1986.

Gabin, Nancy. *Feminism in the Labor Movement: Women and the United Auto Workers, 1935–1975*. Ithaca: Cornell University Press, 1990.

Galambos, Louis. *Competition and Cooperation: The Emergence of a National Trade Association*. Baltimore: Johns Hopkins University Press, 1966.

Gerstle, Gary. "The Protean Nature of American Liberalism." *American Historical Review* 99, no. 4 (October 1990): 1043–73.

———. *Working-Class Americanism: The Politics of Labor in a Textile City, 1914–1960*. New York: Cambridge University Press, 1989.

Giddings, Paula. *When and Where I Enter: The Impact of Black Women on Race and Sex in America*. New York: Bantam, 1984.

Gilmore, Glenda E. *Gender and Jim Crow: Women and the Politics of White Supremacy in North Carolina, 1896–1920*. Chapel Hill: University of North Carolina Press, 1996.

Glen, John M. *Highlander: No Ordinary School, 1932–1962*. Lexington: University Press of Kentucky, 1988.

Glenn, Susan. *Daughters of the Shtetl*. Ithaca: Cornell University Press, 1990.

Glickman, Lawrence. *A Living Wage: American Workers and the Making of Consumer Society*. Ithaca: Cornell University Press, 1997.

Gluck, Sherna. "Socialist Feminism between the Two World Wars." In *Decades of Discontent: The Women's Movement, 1920–1940*, edited by Lois Scharf and Joan M. Jensen. Boston: Northeastern University Press, 1983.

Goldfield, Michael. "Worker Insurgency, Radical Organization, and New Deal Labor Legislation." *American Political Science Review* 83, no. 4 (December 1989): 1257–82.

Goldin, Claudia. *Understanding the Gender Gap*. New York: Oxford University Press, 1990.

Goldmark, Josephine. *Fatigue and Efficiency*. New York: Charities Publication Committee, 1912.

——. *Impatient Crusader: Florence Kelley's Life Story*. Urbana: University of Illinois Press, 1953.

Gordon, Colin. *New Deals: Business, Labor, and Politics in America, 1920–1935*. New York: Cambridge University Press, 1994.

Gordon, Felice. *After Winning: The Legacy of the New Jersey Suffragists, 1920–1947*. New Brunswick, N.J.: Rutgers University Press, 1986.

Gordon, Linda. "Black and White Visions of Welfare: Women's Welfare Activism, 1890–1945." *Journal of American History* 78, no. 2 (September 1991): 559–90.

——. "Gender, State and Society: A Debate with Theda Skocpol." *Contention* 2, no. 3 (Spring 1993): 139–83.

——. "The New Feminist Scholarship on the Welfare State." In *Women, the State and Welfare*, edited by Linda Gordon. Madison: University of Wisconsin Press, 1990.

——. *Pitied But Not Entitled: Single Mothers and the History of Welfare*. New York: Free Press, 1994.

——. "Social Insurance and Public Assistance: The Influence of Gender on Welfare Thought in the United States." *American Historical Review* 97, no. 1 (February 1992): 19–54.

——. "What's New in Women's History." In *Feminist Studies/Critical Studies*, edited by Teresa de Lauretis. Bloomington: Indiana University Press, 1986.

Graebner, William. "Federalism in the Progressive Era: A Structural Interpretation of Reform." *Journal of American History* 64, no. 2 (September 1977): 331–57.

Graham, Otis. *An Encore for Reform: The Old Progressives and the New Deal*. New York: Oxford University Press, 1967.

Grantham, Dewey W. *Southern Progressivism: The Reconciliation of Progress and Tradition*. Knoxville: University of Tennessee Press, 1983.

Green, Elna C. *Southern Strategies: Southern Women and the Woman Suffrage Question*. Chapel Hill: University of North Carolina Press, 1997.

Green, James. *The World of the Worker*. New York: Hill and Wang, 1980.

Greenberg, Jaclyn. "The Limits of Legislation: Katherine Philips Edson, Practical Politics and the Minimum-Wage Law in California, 1913–1922." *Journal of Policy History* 5, no. 2 (1993): 207–30.

Griffith, Barbara. *The Crisis of American Labor: Operation Dixie and the Defeat of the CIO*. Philadelphia: Temple University Press, 1988.

Gross, James A. *The Reshaping of the National Labor Relations Board*. Vol. 2, *National Labor Policy in Transition, 1937–1947*. Albany: State University of New York Press, 1981.

Grossman, Jonathan. "The Fair Labor Standards Act of 1938: Maximum Struggle for Minimum Wage." *Monthly Labor Review* 19 (June 1978): 22–30.

Hahamovitch, Cindy. *The Fruits of Their Labor: Atlantic Coast Farmworkers and the Making of Migrant Poverty, 1870–1945*. Chapel Hill: University of North Carolina Press, 1997.

Haiken, Elizabeth. "'The Lord Helps Those Who Help Themselves': Black Laundresses in Little Rock, Arkansas, 1917–1921." *Arkansas Historical Quarterly* 49 (Spring 1990): 20–50.

Hall, Jacquelyn Dowd. "Disorderly Women: Gender and Labor Militancy in the Appalachian South." *Journal of American History* 73, no. 2 (September 1986): 354–82.

———. "Open Secrets: Memory, Imagination, and the Refashioning of Southern Identity." *American Quarterly* 50, no. 1 (March 1998): 109–24.

———. "Private Eyes, Public Women: Images of Class and Sex in the Urban South, Atlanta, Georgia, 1913–1915." In *Work Engendered: Toward a New History of American Labor*, edited by Ava Baron. Ithaca: Cornell University Press, 1991.

———. *Revolt Against Chivalry: Jessie Daniel Ames and the Women's Campaign Against Lynching*. New York: Columbia University Press, 1979.

Hall, Jacquelyn Dowd, and Anne Firor Scott, "Women in the South." In *Interpreting Southern History: Essays in Honor of Sanford W. Higginbotham*, edited by John B. Boles and Evelyn Thomas Nolen. Baton Rouge: Louisiana State University Press, 1987.

Hall, Jacquelyn Dowd, James Leloudis, Robert Korstad, Mary Murphy, Lu Ann Jones, and Christopher B. Daly. *Like a Family: The Making of a Southern Cotton Mill World*. Chapel Hill: University of North Carolina Press, 1987.

Harris, Howell. "The Snares of Liberalism? Politicians, Bureaucrats and the Shaping of Federal Labour Relations Policy in the United States, ca. 1915–47." In *Shop Floor Bargaining and the State: Historical and Comparative Perspectives*, edited by Steven Tolliday and Jonathan Zeitlin. New York: Cambridge University Press, 1985.

Harrison, Cynthia. *On Account of Sex: The Politics of Women's Issues, 1945–1968*. Berkeley: University of California Press, 1988.

Hart, Vivien. *Bound by Our Constitution: Women, Workers, and the Minimum Wage*. Princeton: Princeton University Press, 1994.

———. "Feminism and Bureaucracy: The Minimum Wage Experiment in the District of Columbia." *Journal of American Studies* 26, no. 1 (1992): 1–22.

———. "Minimum-Wage Policy and Constitutional Inequality: The Paradox of the Fair Labor Standards Act of 1938." *Journal of Policy History* 1, no. 3 (1989): 319–43.

Hartmann, Susan. *From Margin to Mainstream: American Women and Politics Since 1960*. New York: Knopf, 1989.

Hawley, Ellis W. *The New Deal and the Problem of Monopoly*. Princeton: Princeton University Press, 1966.

Hays, Samuel. *The Response to Industrialism, 1885–1914*. Chicago: University of Chicago Press, 1957.

Hewitt, Nancy A., and Suzanne Lebsock, eds. *Visible Women: New Essays on American Activism*. Urbana: University of Illinois Press, 1993.

Higginbotham, Evelyn Brooks. *Righteous Discontent: The Women's Movement in the Black Baptist Church, 1880–1920*. New York: Cambridge University Press, 1993.

Hill, Ann Corinne. "Protection of Women Workers: A Legal Case History." *Feminist Studies* 5, no. 2 (Summer 1979): 247–73.

Hill, Herbert. *Black Labor and the American Legal System: Race, Work and the Law*. Madison: University of Wisconsin Press, 1985.

Hine, Darlene Clark. "The Housewives' League of Detroit: Black Women and Economic Nationalism." In *Visible Women: New Essays on American Activism*, edited by Nancy A. Hewitt and Suzanne Lebsock. Urbana: University of Illinois Press, 1993.

Hobsbawm, Eric J. *The Age of Extremes: A History of the World, 1914–1991*. New York: Pantheon, 1994.

Hodges, James A. *New Deal Labor Policy and the Southern Cotton Textile Industry, 1933–1941*. Knoxville: University of Tennessee Press, 1986.

Holmes, Michael S. *The New Deal in Georgia: An Administrative History*. Westport, Conn.: Greenwood, 1975.

Horowitz, Daniel. *Betty Friedan and the Making of the Feminine Mystique: The American Left, the Cold War, and Modern Feminism*. Amherst: University of Massachusetts Press, 1998.

Hunnicutt, Benjamin K. *Work without End: Abandoning Shorter Hours for the Right to Work*. Philadelphia: Temple University Press, 1988.

Hunter, Robert F. "Virginia and the New Deal." In *The New Deal*. Vol. 2, *The State and Local Levels*, edited by David Brody, John Braeman, and Robert Bremner. Columbus: Ohio State University Press, 1975.

Ingalls, Robert P. *Herbert H. Lehman and New York's Little New Deal*. New York: New York University Press, 1975.

Irons, Peter H. *The New Deal Lawyers*. Princeton: Princeton University Press, 1982.

Isserman, Maurice. *Which Side Were You On? The American Communist Party during the Second World War*. Middletown, Conn.: Wesleyan University Press, 1982.

Jackson, Kenneth T. *The Ku Klux Klan in the City, 1915–1930*. New York: Oxford University Press, 1967.

Jacobs, Meg. "Democracy's Third Estate: New Deal Politics and the Construction of a 'Consuming Public.'" *International Labor and Working-Class History* 55 (Spring 1999): 27–51.

———. "'How About Some Meat?': The Office of Price Administration, Consumption Politics, and State Building from the Bottom Up, 1941–1946." *Journal of American History* 84, no. 3 (December 1997): 410–41.

Jacoby, Sanford M. "Employers and the Welfare State: The Role of Marion B. Folsom." *Journal of American History* 80, no. 2 (September 1993): 525–56.

James, Edward T., ed. *Notable American Women, 1607–1950*. Cambridge: Belknap Press of Harvard University Press, 1971.

Janiewski, Dolores. "Seeking 'A New Day and a New Way': Black Women and Unions in the Southern Tobacco Industry." In *"To Toil the Livelong Day": America's Women at Work, 1780–1980*, edited by Carol Groneman and Mary Beth Norton. Ithaca: Cornell University Press, 1987.

———. "Southern Honor, Southern Dishonor: Managerial Ideology and the Construction of Gender, Race and Class Relations in Southern Industry." In *Work Engendered: Toward a New History of American Labor*, edited by Ava Baron. Ithaca: Cornell University Press, 1991.

Jeffries, John W. "A 'Third New Deal'? Liberal Policy and the American State." *Journal of Policy History* 8, no. 4 (1996): 387–419.

Jensen, Joan M. "All Pink Sisters: The War Department and the Feminist Movement in the 1920s." In *Decades of Discontent: The Women's Movement, 1920–1940*, edited by Lois Scharf and Joan M. Jensen. Boston: Northeastern University Press, 1983.

Jensen, Joan M., and Sue Davidson, eds. *A Needle, a Bobbin, and a Strike*. Philadelphia: Temple University Press, 1984.

John B. Andrews Memorial Symposium on Labor Legislation and Social Security. Madison: University of Wisconsin Department of Economics, 1949.

Jones, Jacqueline. *Labor of Love, Labor of Sorrow: Black Women, Work and the Family, From Slavery to the Present*. New York: Basic Books, 1985.

Katznelson, Ira, Kim Geiger, and Daniel Kryder. "Limiting Liberalism: The Southern Veto in Congress, 1933–1950." *Political Science Quarterly* 108 (Summer 1993): 283–306.

Kazin, Michael. "The Agony and Romance of the American Left." *American Historical Review* 100, no. 5 (December 1995): 1488–1512.

Kelley, Florence, and Marguerite Marsh. "Labor Legislation for Women and Its Effects on Earnings and Conditions of Labor." *Annals of the American Academy of Political and Social Science*, May 1929, 1–15.

Kelley, Robin D. G. *Hammer and Hoe: Alabama Communists during the Great Depression*. Chapel Hill: University of North Carolina Press, 1990.

Kemp, Kathryn W. "Jean and Kate Gordon: New Orleans Social Reformers, 1898–1933." *Louisiana History* 24, no. 4 (Fall 1983): 389–401.

Kenneally, James. *Women and American Trade Unions*. St. Albans, Vt.: Eden, 1978.

Kerber, Linda. "A Constitutional Right to Be Treated Like American Ladies: Women and the Obligations of Citizenship." In *U.S. History as Women's History: New Feminist Essays*, edited by Linda Kerber, Alice Kessler-Harris, and Kathryn Kish Sklar. Chapel Hill: University of North Carolina Press, 1995.

Kerr, Thomas. "The New York Factory Investigating Commission and the Minimum Wage Movement." *Labor History* 12 (1971): 373–91.

Kessler-Harris, Alice. "Designing Women and Old Fools: The Construction of the Social Security Amendments of 1939." In *U.S. History as Women's History: New Feminist Essays*, edited by Linda K. Kerber, Alice Kessler-Harris, and Kathryn Kish Sklar. Chapel Hill: University of North Carolina Press, 1995.

———. *Out to Work: A History of Wage-Earning Women in the United States*. New York: Oxford University Press, 1982.

———. "The Paradox of Motherhood: Night Work Restrictions in the United States." In *Protecting Women: Labor Legislation in Europe, the United States and Australia, 1880–1920*, edited by Ulla Wikander, Alice Kessler-Harris, and Jane Lewis. Urbana: University of Illinois Press, 1995.

———. "Rose Schneiderman and the Limits of Women's Trade Unionism." In *Labor Leaders in America*, edited by Melvyn Dubofsky and Warren Van Tine. Urbana: University of Illinois Press, 1987.

———. "Where Are the Organized Women Workers?" *Feminist Studies* 3, no. 1 (Fall 1975): 92–110.

———. *A Woman's Wage: Historical Meanings and Social Consequences*. Lexington: University Press of Kentucky, 1990.

Key, V. O., Jr. *Southern Politics in State and Nation*. New York: Knopf, 1949.

Kirby, Jack Temple. *Darkness at the Dawning: Race and Reform in the Progressive South*. Philadelphia: Lippincott, 1972.

Kirkby, Diane. "The Wage-Earning Woman and the State: The National Women's Trade Union League and Protective Labor Legislation, 1903–1923." *Labor History* 28, no. 1 (1987): 54–74.

Kleber, John E., et al., eds. *Encyclopedia of Louisville*. Lexington: University Press of Kentucky, 2000.

Klehr, Harvey. *The Heyday of American Communism: The Depression Decade*. New York: Basic Books, 1984.

Kloppenberg, James T. *Uncertain Victory: Social Democracy and Progressivism in European and American Thought, 1870–1920*. New York: Oxford University Press, 1986.

Koeniger, A. Cash. "The New Deal and the States: Roosevelt vs. the Byrd Organization in Virginia." *Journal of American History* 68, no. 4 (March 1982): 876–96.

Kornbluh, Joyce L., and Mary Frederickson. *Sisterhood and Solidarity: Workers' Education for Women, 1914–1984*. Philadelphia: Temple University Press, 1984.

Korstad, Robert, and Nelson Lichtenstein. "Opportunities Found and Lost: Labor, Radicals, and the Early Civil Rights Movement." *Journal of American History* 75, no. 3 (December 1988): 786–811.

Koven, Seth, and Sonya Michel. "Womanly Duties: Maternalist Policies and the Origins of Welfare States in France, Germany, Great Britain and the United States, 1880–1920." *American Historical Review* 95, no. 4 (October 1990): 1076–1108.

———, eds. *Mothers of a New World: Maternalist Politics and the Origins of Welfare States*. New York: Routledge, 1993.

Krueger, Thomas A. *And Promises to Keep: The Southern Conference for Human Welfare, 1938–1948*. Nashville, Tenn.: Vanderbilt University Press, 1967.

Kutulas, Judy. *The Long War: The Intellectual People's Front and Anti-Stalinism, 1930–1940*. Durham, N.C.: Duke University Press, 1995.

Ladd-Taylor, Molly. *Mother-Work: Women, Child Welfare, and the State, 1890–1930*. Urbana: University of Illinois Press, 1994.

———, ed. *Raising a Baby the Government Way*. New Brunswick, N.J.: Rutgers University Press, 1986.

Lash, Joseph P. *Dealers and Dreamers: A New Look at the New Deal*. New York: Doubleday, 1988.

Lebsock, Suzanne. "Woman Suffrage and White Supremacy: A Virginia Case Study." In *Visible Women: New Essays on American Activism*, edited by Nancy A. Hewitt and Suzanne Lebsock. Urbana: University of Illinois Press, 1993.

Leff, Mark H. "Revisioning U.S. Political History." *American Historical Review* 100, no. 3 (June 1995): 829–53.

Lehrer, Susan. *Origins of Protective Labor Legislation for Women, 1905–1925*. Albany: State University of New York Press, 1987.

Lemons, J. Stanley. *The Woman Citizen: Social Feminism in the 1920s*. Urbana: University of Illinois Press, 1973.

Lerner, Gerda. "Midwestern Leaders of the Modern Women's Movement." *Wisconsin Academy Review* (Winter 1994–95): 11–15.

Leuchtenburg, William E. "The Case of the Chambermaid and the Nine Old Men," *American Heritage* 38, no. 1 (1986): 34–41.

———. *Franklin D. Roosevelt and the New Deal, 1932–1940*. New York: Harper and Row, 1963.

———. "The New Deal and the Analogue of War." In *Change and Continuity in Twentieth-Century America*, edited by John Braeman, Robert H. Bremner, and Everett Walters. Columbus: Ohio State University Press, 1964.

Levine, Louis. *The Women's Garment Workers*. New York: B. W. Huebsch, 1924.

Levitan, Sar, and Richard Belous. *More than Subsistence: Minimum Wages for the Working Poor*. Baltimore: Johns Hopkins University Press, 1979.

Lewis, David Levering. *W. E. B. DuBois — A Biography of a Race, 1868–1919*. New York: H. Holt, 1993.

Lichtenstein, Nelson. "From Corporatism to Collective Bargaining: Organized Labor and the Eclipse of Social Democracy in the Postwar Era." In *The Rise and Fall of the New Deal Order, 1930–1980*, edited by Steve Fraser and Gary Gerstle. Princeton: Princeton University Press, 1989.

Lichtenstein, Nelson, and Howell Harris, eds. *Industrial Democracy in America: The Ambiguous Promise*. New York: Cambridge University Press, 1993.

Link, William A. *The Paradox of Southern Progressivism, 1880–1930*. Chapel Hill: University of North Carolina Press, 1992.

Lipschultz, Sybil. "Social Feminism and Legal Discourse, 1908–1923." *Yale Journal of Law and Feminism* 2 (1989): 131–60.

Lubin, Carol, and Anne Winslow, *Social Justice and Women: The International Labor Organization and Women*. Durham, N.C.: Duke University Press, 1990.

Lyons, Eugene. *The Red Decade*. New York: Arlington House, 1941.

Lyson, Thomas. "Industrial Change and the Sexual Division of Labor in New York and Georgia, 1910–1930." *Social Science Quarterly* 70, no. 2 (June 1989): 356–76.

McArthur, Judith N. *Creating the New Woman: The Rise of Southern Women's Political Culture in Texas, 1893–1918*. Urbana: University of Illinois Press, 1996.

McCreesh, Carolyn. *Women in the Campaign to Organize Garment Workers, 1880–1917*. New York: Garland, 1985.

McFeely, Mary Drake. *Lady Inspectors: The Campaign for a Better Workplace, 1893–1921*. New York: Blackwell, 1988.

McGerr, Michael. "Political Style and Women's Power, 1830–1930." *Journal of American History* 77, no. 3 (December 1990): 864–85.

McGovern, Charles. "Consumption and Citizenship in the United States, 1900–1940." In *Getting and Spending: European and American Consumer Societies in the Twentieth Century*, edited by Susan Strasser, Charles McGovern, and Matthias Judt. Washington, D.C.: Cambridge University Press for the German Historical Institute, 1998.

MacLean, Nancy. *Behind the Mask of Chivalry: The Making of the Second Ku Klux Klan*. New York: Oxford University Press, 1994.

Mansbridge, Jane. *Why We Lost the ERA*. Chicago: University of Chicago Press, 1986.

Marshall , F. Ray. *Labor in the South*. Cambridge: Harvard University Press, 1967.

Martin, George. *Madam Secretary, Frances Perkins*. Boston: Houghton Mifflin, 1976.

Martin, Robert F. *Howard Kester and the Struggle for Social Justice in the South, 1904–1977*. Charlottesville: University Press of Virginia, 1991.

Mason, Karen. "Feeling the Pinch: The Kalamazoo Corsetmakers' Strike of 1912." In *"To Toil the Livelong Day": America's Women at Work, 1780–1980*, edited by Carol Groneman and Mary Beth Norton. Ithaca: Cornell University Press, 1987.

Mason, Lucy Randolph. "The CIO and the Negro in the South." *Journal of Negro Education* 14 (Fall 1945): 552–61.

———. *The Divine Discontent*. Richmond: Equal Suffrage League of Virginia, 1912.

———. "I Turned to Social Action Right at Home." In *Labor's Relation to Church and Community*, edited by Liston Pope. New York: Harper and Row, 1947.

———. *The Shorter Day and Women Workers*. Richmond: Virginia League of Women Voters, 1922.

———. "Southerners Look at the South." *North Georgia Review* (Fall–Winter 1938–39): 17–18, 40.

———. *Standards for Workers in Southern Industry*. New York: National Consumers' League, 1931.

———. *To Win These Rights: A Personal Story of the CIO in the South*. New York: Harper and Row, 1952.

Mathews, Donald G., and Jane Sherron De Hart, *Sex, Gender, and the ERA*. New York: Oxford University Press, 1990.

Matthews, John M. "Dissenters and Reformers: Some Southern Liberals between the World Wars." In *Developing Dixie: Modernization in a Traditional Society*, edited by

Winfred B. Moore Jr., Joseph F. Tripp, and Lyon G. Tyler Jr. Westport, Conn.: Greenwood, 1988.

May, Martha. "Bread before Roses: American Workingmen, Labor Unions and the Family Wage." In *Women, Work and Protest: A Century of U.S. Women's Labor History*, edited by Ruth Milkman. New York: Routledge, 1985.

Mettler, Suzanne B. *Dividing Citizens: Gender and Federalism in New Deal Public Policy*. Ithaca: Cornell University Press, 1998.

Milkman, Ruth. *Gender at Work: The Dynamics of Job Segregation by Sex during World War II*. Urbana: University of Illinois Press, 1987.

———. "Women's Work and the Economic Crisis: Some Lessons from the Great Depression." *Review of Radical Political Economics* 8 (Spring 1976): 73–97.

Miller, Marc S., ed. *Workers' Lives: The Southern Exposure History of Labor in the South*. New York: Pantheon, 1980.

Mink, Gwendolyn. "The Lady and the Tramp: Gender, Race and the Origins of the American Welfare State." In *Women, the State and Welfare*, edited by Linda Gordon. Madison: University of Wisconsin Press, 1990.

———. *The Wages of Motherhood: Inequality in the Welfare State, 1917–1942*. Ithaca: Cornell University Press, 1995.

Moreno, Paul. "Racial Proportionalism and the Origins of Employment Discrimination Policy, 1933–1950." *Journal of Policy History* 8, no. 4 (1996): 410–39.

Moss, David. *Socializing Security: Progressive Era Economists and the Origins of American Social Policy*. Cambridge: Harvard University Press, 1996.

Muncy, Robyn. *Creating a Female Dominion in American Reform, 1890–1935*. New York: Oxford University Press, 1991.

Murray, Meg McGavrin. "The Work Got Done: An Interview with Clara Mortenson Beyer." In *Face to Face: Fathers, Mothers, Masters, Monsters — Essays for a Nonsexist Future*, edited by Meg McGavrin Murray. Westport, Conn.: Greenwood, 1983.

Nasstrom, Kathryn L. "'More Was Expected of Us': The North Carolina League of Women Voters and the Feminist Movement in the 1920s." *North Carolina Historical Review* 68, no. 3 (July 1991): 307–19.

Nathan, Maud. *The Story of an Epoch-Making Movement*. New York: Doubleday, 1926.

National Consumers Committee for Research and Education. *Consumer Activists, They Made a Difference: A History of Consumer Action Related by Leaders in the Consumer Movement*. Mount Vernon, N.Y.: Consumers Union Foundation, 1982.

National Consumers' League. *The First Quarter Century, 1899–1924*. New York: National Consumers' League, 1925.

———. *Should the National Labor Relations Act Be Amended?* New York: National Consumers' League, 1939.

———. *Thirty-Five Years of Crusading*. New York: National Consumers' League, 1935.

Neverdon-Morton, Cynthia. *Afro-American Women of the South and the Advancement of the Race, 1895–1925*. Knoxville: University of Tennessee Press, 1989.

Nichols, Carole. "Votes and More for Women: Suffrage and After in Connecticut." *Women and History* 5 (Spring 1983): 1–87.

Nichols, Egbert, and Joseph H. Bacchus, eds. *Selected Articles on Minimum Wages and Maximum Hours*. New York: H. W. Wilson, 1937.

O'Connor, Jessie Lloyd, Harvey O'Connor, and Susan Bowler. *Harvey and Jessie: A Couple of Radicals*. Philadelphia: Temple University Press, 1988.

O'Farrell, Brigid, and Joyce L. Kornbluh. *Rocking the Boat: Union Women's Voices, 1915–1975*. New Brunswick, N.J.: Rutgers University Press, 1996.

Offen, Karen. "Defining Feminism: A Comparative Historical Approach." *Signs* 14, no. 1 (1988): 119–57.

O'Neill, William L. *Everyone Was Brave: The Rise and Fall of Feminism in America*. Chicago: Quadrangle Books, 1969.

Orleck, Annelise. *Common Sense and a Little Fire: Women and Working-Class Politics in the United States, 1900–1965*. Chapel Hill: University of North Carolina Press, 1995.

Orloff, Ann Shola. "Gender in Early U.S. Social Policy." *Journal of Policy History* 3, no. 3 (1991): 249–81.

Palmer, Phyllis. *Domesticity and Dirt: Housewives and Domestic Servants in the United States, 1920–1945*. Philadelphia: Temple University Press, 1989.

———. "Outside the Law: Agricultural and Domestic Workers under the Fair Labor Standards Act." *Journal of Policy History* 7, no. 4 (1995): 416–40.

Pardo, Thomas. *The National Woman's Party Papers: A Guide to the Microfilm Edition*. Sanford, N.C.: Microfilming Corporation of America, 1979.

Patterson, James T. *Congressional Conservatism and the New Deal: The Growth of the Conservative Coalition in Congress, 1933–1939*. Lexington: University Press of Kentucky, 1967.

———. "Mary Dewson and the American Minimum Wage Movement." *Labor History* 5, no. 3 (Spring 1964): 134–52.

———. *The New Deal and the States: Federalism in Transition*. Princeton: Princeton University Press, 1969.

Patton, Randall L. "The CIO and the Search for a 'Silent South.'" *Maryland Historian* 19, no. 2 (1988): 1–14.

Paulsen, George E. *A Living Wage for the Forgotten Man: The Quest for Fair Labor Standards, 1933–1941*. Selinsgrove: Susquehanna University Press, 1996.

Payne, Elizabeth. *Reform, Labor and Feminism: Margaret Dreier Robins and the Women's Trade Union League*. Urbana: University of Illinois Press, 1988.

Perkins, Frances. *The Roosevelt I Knew*. New York: Viking, 1946.

Perry, Elizabeth Israels. *Belle Moskowitz: Feminine Politics and the Exercise of Power in the Era of Alfred E. Smith*. New York: Oxford University Press, 1987.

Peterson, Esther. "You Can't Giddyup by Saying Whoa." *Labor's Heritage* 5, no. 4 (Spring 1994): 38–59.

Pipkin, Charles. *Social Legislation in the South*. Southern Policy Paper No. 3. Chapel Hill: University of North Carolina Press, 1936.

Piven, Frances Fox. "Ideology and the State: Women, Power and the Welfare State." In *Women, the State and Welfare*, edited by Linda Gordon. Madison: University of Wisconsin Press, 1990.

Plotke, David. *Building a Democratic Political Order: Reshaping American Liberalism in the 1930s and 1940s*. New York: Cambridge University Press, 1996.

Quadagno, Jill. "From Old Age Assistance to Supplemental Security Income: The Political Economy of Relief in the South, 1935–1972." In *The Politics of Social Policy in the United States*, edited by Margaret Weir, Ann Shola Orloff and Theda Skocpol. Princeton: Princeton University Press, 1988.

Rawalt, Marguerite. "The Equal Rights Amendment." In *Women in Washington: Advocates for Public Policy*, edited by Irene Tinker. Beverly Hills, Calif.: Sage Publications, 1983.

Reed, Linda. *Simple Decency and Common Sense: The Southern Conference Movement, 1938–1963*. Bloomington: Indiana University Press, 1991.

Renshaw, Patrick. "Organised Labour and the Keynesian Revolution." In *Nothing Else* to Fear: New Perspectives on America in the 1930s, edited by Stephen W. Baskerville and Ralph Willet. Manchester, Eng.: Manchester University Press, 1985.

Richmond Council of Social Agencies. *The Negro in Richmond, Virginia: The Report of the Negro Welfare Survey Committee*. Richmond: Council of Social Agencies, 1929.

Rogow, Faith. *Gone to Another Meeting: The National Council of Jewish Women, 1893–1993*. Tuscaloosa: University of Alabama Press, 1993.

Rosenof, Theodore. *Economics in the Long Run: New Deal Theorists and Their Legacies, 1933–1993*. Chapel Hill: University of North Carolina Press, 1997.

Ross, Andrew, ed. *No Sweat: Fashion, Free Trade, and the Rights of Garment Workers*. New York: Verso, 1997.

Rosswurm, Steve, ed. *The CIO's Left-Led Unions*. New Brunswick, N.J.: Rutgers University Press, 1992.

Roth, Darlene Rebecca. *Matronage: Patterns in Women's Organizations in Atlanta, Georgia, 1890–1940*. Brooklyn, N.Y.: Carlson, 1994.

Rothman, Sheila. *A Woman's Proper Place: A History of Changing Ideals and Practices, 1870 to the Present*. New York: Basic Books, 1978.

Rouse, Jacqueline Anne. *Lugenia Burns Hope: Black Southern Reformer*. Athens: University of Georgia Press, 1989.

Roydhouse, Marion W. "Bridging Chasms: Community and the Southern YWCA." In *Visible Women: New Essays on American Activism*, edited by Nancy A. Hewitt and Suzanne Lebsock. Urbana: University of Illinois, 1993.

Rupp, Leila J. *Worlds of Women: The Making of an International Women's Movement*. Princeton: Princeton University Press, 1997.

Rupp, Leila J., and Verta Taylor. *Survival in the Doldrums: The American Women's Rights Movement, 1945 to the 1960s*. Columbus: Ohio State University Press, 1990.

Salmond, John A. *Gastonia 1929: The Story of the Loray Mill Strike*. Chapel Hill: University of North Carolina Press, 1995.

———. *Miss Lucy of the CIO: The Life and Times of Lucy Randolph Mason, 1882–1959*. Athens: University of Georgia Press, 1988.

Sarvasy, Wendy. "Beyond the Difference vs. Equality Policy Debate: Postsuffrage Feminism, Citizenship, and the Quest for a Feminist Welfare State." *Signs* 17, no. 2 (Winter 1992): 329–62.

———. "From Man and Philanthropic Service to Feminist Social Citizenship." *Social Politics* 1, no. 3 (Fall 1994): 306–25.

Scharf, Lois. *To Work and to Wed: Female Employment, Feminism and the Great Depression*. Westport, Conn.: Greenwood, 1980.

———. "The Women's Movement in Cleveland from 1850." In *Cleveland: A Tradition of Reform*, edited by David Van Tassel and John Grabowski. Kent, Ohio: Kent State University Press, 1986.

Schatz, Ronald W. *The Electrical Workers*. Urbana: University of Illinois Press, 1983.

Schlesinger, Arthur M., Jr. *The Age of Roosevelt*. Vol. 1, *Crisis of the Old Order, 1919–1930*. Boston: Houghton Mifflin, 1957.

Schneiderman, Rose, with Lucy Goldthwaite. *All for One*. New York: Paul S. Eriksson, 1967.

Scott, Anne Firor. "After Suffrage: Southern Women in the Twenties." *Journal of Southern History* 30 (August 1964): 298–318.

———. *Natural Allies: Women's Associations in American History*. Urbana: University of Illinois Press, 1991.

———. *The Southern Lady: From Pedestal to Politics*. Chicago: University of Chicago Press, 1970.

Sealander, Judith. *As Minority Becomes Majority: Federal Reaction to the Phenomenon of Women in the Workforce, 1920–1963*. Westport, Conn.: Greenwood, 1983.

——. "Feminist against Feminist: The First Phase of the Equal Rights Amendment Debate, 1923–1963." *South Atlantic Quarterly* 81, no. 2 (Spring 1982): 147–61.

——. "Moving Painfully and Uncertainly: Policy Formation and 'Women's Issues,' 1940–1980." In *Federal Social Policy: The Historical Dimension*, edited by Donald T. Critchlow and Ellis W. Hawley. University Park: Pennsylvania State University Press, 1988.

Seltzer, Andrew J. "The Effects of the Fair Labor Standards Act of 1938 on the Southern Seamless Hosiery and Lumber Industries." *Journal of Economic History* 57, no. 2 (June 1997): 396–415.

Shaffer, Robert. "Women and the Communist Party, USA, 1930–1940." *Socialist Review* 9 (May–June 1979): 73–118.

Shanley, Mary Lyndon. "Suffrage, Protective Labor Legislation, and Married Women's Property Laws in England." *Signs* 12, no. 1 (1986): 62–77.

Shiells, Martha, and Gavin Wright. "Night Work as a Labor Market Phenomenon: Southern Textiles in the Interwar Period." *Explorations in Economic History* 20 (1983): 331–50.

Sicherman, Barbara. *Alice Hamilton: A Life in Letters*. Cambridge: Harvard University Press, 1984.

Silber, Norman. *Test and Protest: The Influence of Consumers' Union*. New York: Holmes and Meier, 1983.

Simon, Bryant. *A Fabric of Defeat: The Politics of South Carolina Millhands, 1910–1948*. Chapel Hill: University of North Carolina Press, 1998.

Sims, Anastatia. *The Power of Femininity in the New South: Women's Organizations and Politics in North Carolina, 1880–1930*. Columbia: University of South Carolina Press, 1997.

Singal, Daniel. *The War Within: From Victorian to Modernist Thought in the South, 1919–1945*. Chapel Hill: University of North Carolina Press, 1982.

Sitkoff, Harvard. *A New Deal for Blacks: The Emergence of Civil Rights as a National Issue*. New York: Oxford University Press, 1978.

Sklar, Kathryn Kish. "The Consumers' White Label Campaign of the National Consumers' League, 1898–1918." In *Getting and Spending: European and American Consumer Societies in the Twentieth Century*, edited by Susan Strasser, Charles McGovern, and Matthias Judt. Washington, D.C.: Cambridge University Press for the German Historical Institute, 1998.

——. *Florence Kelley and the Nation's Work: The Rise of Women's Political Culture, 1830–1900*. New Haven: Yale University Press, 1995.

——. " 'The Greater Part of the Petitioners Are Female': The Reduction of Women's Working Hours in the Paid Labor Force, 1840–1917." In *Worktime and Industrialization: An International History*, edited by Gary Cross. Philadelphia: Temple University Press, 1988.

——. "The Historical Foundations of Women's Power in the Creation of the American Welfare State, 1830–1930." In *Mothers of a New World: Maternalistic Politics and the Origins of Welfare States*, edited by Seth Koven and Sonya Michel. New York: Routledge, 1993.

——. "Hull House in the 1890s: A Community of Women Reformers." *Signs* 10, no. 4 (1985): 657–77.

——. "Two Political Cultures in the Progressive Era: The National Consumers' League and the American Association for Labor Legislation." In *U.S. History as*

Women's History: New Feminist Essays, edited by Linda Kerber, Alice Kessler-Harris, and Kathryn Kish Sklar. Chapel Hill: University of North Carolina Press, 1995.

——. "Why Were Most Politically Active Women Opposed to the ERA in the 1920s?" In *Rights of Passage: The Past and Future of the ERA*, edited by Joan Hoff-Wilson. Bloomington: Indiana University Press, 1986.

——, ed. *The Autobiography of Florence Kelley: Notes of Sixty Years*. Chicago: Charles H. Kerr, 1986.

Skocpol, Theda. "Political Response to Capitalist Crisis: Neo-Marxist Theories of the State and the Case of the New Deal." *Politics and Society* 10, no. 2 (1980): 155–201.

——. *Protecting Soldiers and Mothers: The Political Origins of Social Policy in the United States*. Cambridge: Belknap Press of Harvard University Press, 1992.

Skowroneck, Stephen. *Building a New American State: The Expansion of National Administrative Capacity, 1877–1920*. New York: Cambridge University Press, 1982.

Smith, Douglas L. *The New Deal in the Urban South*. Baton Rouge: Louisiana State University Press, 1988.

Sosna, Morton. *In Search of the Silent South: Southern Liberals and the Race Issue*. New York: Columbia University Press, 1977.

Stackhouse, Eunice Ford. *Mary Elizabeth Frayser: Pioneer Social and Research Worker in the South and Leader in Women's Organizations in South Carolina*. N.p., 1944.

Steinberg, Ronnie. *Wages and Hours: Labor and Reform in Twentieth-Century America*. New Brunswick, N.J.: Rutgers University Press, 1982.

Storrs, Landon R. Y. "Gender and the Development of the Regulatory State: The Controversy over Restricting Women's Night Work in the Depression-Era South." *Journal of Policy History* 10, no. 2 (1998): 179–206.

——. "An Independent Voice for Unorganized Workers: The National Consumers' League Speaks to the Blue Eagle." *Labor's Heritage* 6, no. 3 (Winter 1995): 21–39.

Strom, Sharon Hartman. "Challenging 'Woman's Place': Feminism, the Left, and Industrial Unionism in the 1930s." *Feminist Studies* 9, no. 2 (Summer 1983): 359–86.

Sullivan, Patricia. *Days of Hope: Race and Democracy in the New Deal Era*. Chapel Hill: University of North Carolina Press, 1996.

Swain, Martha H. *Ellen S. Woodward: New Deal Advocate for Women*. Jackson: University Press of Mississippi, 1995.

——. "Organized Women in Mississippi: The Clash over Legal Disabilities in the 1920s." *Southern Studies* 13, no. 1 (1984): 91–102.

Tarrow, Sidney. "*Lochner v. New York*: A Political Analysis." *Labor History* 5 (Fall 1964): 277–312.

Tatum, Noreen Dunn. *A Crown of Service: A Story of Women's Work in the Methodist Episcopal Church, South, from 1878–1940*. Nashville, Tenn.: Parthenon Press for Board of Missions, Women's Division of Christian Service, 1960.

Tax, Meredith. *The Rising of the Women: Feminist Solidarity and Class Conflict, 1880–1917*. New York: Monthly Review Press, 1980.

Tentler, Leslie. *Wage-Earning Women: Industrial Work and Family Life in the United States, 1900–1914*. New York: Oxford University Press, 1979.

Thomas, Mary Martha. *The New Woman in Alabama: Social Reforms and Suffrage, 1890–1920*. Tuscaloosa: University of Alabama Press, 1992.

Tindall, George B. *The Emergence of the New South, 1914–1945*. Vol. 10 of *A History of the South*, edited by Wendell Holmes Stephenson and E. Merton Coulter. Baton Rouge: Louisiana State University Press and the Littlefield Fund for Southern History of the University of Texas, 1967.

Tippett, Tom. *When Southern Labor Stirs*. New York: J. Cape and H. Smith, 1931.

Tomlins, Christopher L. *The State and the Unions: Labor Relations, Law, and the Organized Labor Movement in America, 1880–1960*. New York: Cambridge University Press, 1985.

Trout, Charles H. *Boston, the Great Depression, and the New Deal*. New York: Oxford University Press, 1977.

Turner, Elizabeth. *Women, Culture, and Community: Religion and Reform in Galveston, 1880–1923*. New York: Oxford University Press, 1997.

Tyler, Pamela. *Silk Stockings and Ballot Boxes: Women and Politics in New Orleans, 1920–1963*. Athens: University of Georgia Press, 1996.

Varon, Elizabeth R. "Tippecanoe and the Ladies, Too: White Women and Party Politics in Antebellum Virginia." *Journal of American History* 82, no. 2 (September 1995): 494–521.

Virginia Consumers' League. *The General Assembly of Virginia and Social Legislation, 1936*. Richmond: Virginia Consumers' League, 1936.

Vittoz, Stanley. *New Deal Labor Policy and the American Industrial Economy*. Chapel Hill: University of North Carolina Press, 1987.

Voorhis, Jerry. *Confessions of a Congressman*. Garden City, N.J.: Country Life Press, 1947.

Vose, Clement E. *Constitutional Change: Amendment Politics and Supreme Court Litigation Since 1900*. Lexington, Mass.: Twentieth Century Fund, 1972.

Wandersee, Winifred D. " 'I'd Rather Pass a Law than Organize a Union': Frances Perkins and the Reformist Approach to Organized Labor." *Labor History* 34, no. 1 (Winter 1993): 5–32.

Ware, Susan. *Beyond Suffrage: Women in the New Deal*. Cambridge: Harvard University Press, 1981.

———. *Holding Their Own: American Women in the 1930s*. Boston: Twayne, 1982.

———. *Partner and I: Molly Dewson, Feminism, and New Deal Politics*. New Haven: Yale University Press, 1987.

Warken, Philip. *A History of the National Resources Planning Board*. New York: Garland, 1979.

Wedell, Marsha. *Elite Women and the Reform Impulse in Memphis, 1875–1915*. Knoxville: University of Tennessee Press, 1991.

Weiner, Lynn, Ann Taylor Allen, Eileen Boris, Molly Ladd-Taylor, Adele Lindenmeyr, and Kathleen Uno. "Maternalism as a Paradigm: Roundtable." *Journal of Women's History* 5, no. 2 (Fall 1993): 96–130.

Weinstein, James. *The Corporate Ideal in the Liberal State, 1900–1918*. Boston: Beacon, 1968.

Welter, Barbara. "The Cult of True Womanhood, 1820–1860." *American Quarterly* 18, no. 2 (Summer 1966): 151–74.

Wenger, Beth. "Jewish Women of the Club: The Changing Public Role of Atlanta's Jewish Women, 1870–1930." *American Jewish History* 76, no. 3 (March 1987): 311–33.

Wheeler, Marjorie Spruill. *New Women of the New South: The Leaders of the Woman Suffrage Movement in the Southern States*. New York: Oxford University Press, 1993.

Whites, LeeAnn. "The De Graffenried Controversy: Class, Race and Gender in the New South." *Journal of Southern History* 54, no. 3 (August 1988): 449–78.

Whitley, Donna Jean. *Fuller E. Callaway and Textile Mill Development in LaGrange, 1895–1920*. New York: Garland, 1989.

Wikander, Ulla, Alice Kessler-Harris, and Jane Lewis, eds. *Protecting Women: Labor*

Legislation in Europe, the United States and Australia, 1880–1920. Urbana: University of Illinois Press, 1995.

Wilkerson-Freeman, Sarah. "Two Generations of Jewish Women: A Heritage of Activism in North Carolina, 1880–1970." *Southern Jewish Historical Society Newsletter* (July 1989).

Wisner, Elizabeth. *Social Welfare Legislation in the South from Colonial Times to the Present*. Baton Rouge: Louisiana State University Press, 1970.

Wolfe, Allis Rosenberg. "Women, Consumerism, and the National Consumers' League in the Progressive Era, 1900–1923." *Labor History* 16, no. 3 (1975): 378–92.

Wolfe, Margaret Ripley. *Daughters of Canaan*. Lexington: University Press of Kentucky, 1995.

Woloch, Nancy. *Muller v. Oregon: A Brief History with Documents*. Boston: Bedford Books, 1996.

Wolters, Raymond. *Negroes and the Great Depression: The Problem of Economic Recovery*. Westport, Conn.: Greenwood, 1970.

Wright, Gavin. *Old South, New South: Revolutions in the Southern Economy Since the Civil War*. New York: Basic Books, 1986.

Zahavi, Gerald. "Passionate Commitments: Race, Sex, and Communism at Schenectady General Electric, 1932–1954." *Journal of American History* 83, no. 2 (September 1996): 514–48.

Zieger, Robert H. *The CIO, 1935–1955*. Chapel Hill: University of North Carolina Press, 1995.

———, ed. *Organized Labor in the Twentieth-Century South*. Knoxville: University of Tennessee Press, 1991.

Zimmerman, Joan G. "The Jurisprudence of Equality: The Women's Minimum Wage, the First ERA, and *Adkins v. Children's Hospital*, 1905–1923." *Journal of American History* 78, no. 1 (June 1991): 188–225.

Dissertations, Theses, and Unpublished Papers

Athey, Louis Lee. "The Consumers' Leagues and Social Reform, 1890–1923." Ph.D. diss., University of Delaware, 1965.

Baron, Ava. "Chivalry, Paternalism, Protection: Equality Discourses, Protective Night Work Laws, and the Politics of Labor in the U.S. Printing Industry, 1850s–1920s." Paper presented at the Gendering of Labor Law Conference, University of Paris, June 1993.

Brinson, Betsy. "'Helping Others to Help Themselves': Social Advocacy and Wage-Earning Women in Richmond, Virginia, 1910–1932." Ph.D. diss., Union Graduate School of the Union for Experimental Colleges and Universities, 1984.

Dirks, Jacqueline K. "Righteous Goods: Women's Production, Reform Publicity, and the National Consumers' League, 1891–1919." Ph.D. diss., Yale University, 1996.

Donohue, Kathleen G. "Conceptualizing the 'Good Society': The Idea of the Consumer and Modern American Political Thought." Ph.D. diss., University of Virginia, 1994.

Edler, Dorothy. "Administration of the Child Labor Law in New Orleans." M.S.W. thesis, Tulane University, 1945.

Fones-Wolf, Ken. "Gender, Class Relations and the Transformation of Voluntary Organizations: Labor Reform in the Philadelphia YM and YWCAs, 1890–1930" [ca. 1991]. Paper in author's possession.

Harrison, Dennis. "The Consumers' League of Ohio: Women and Reform, 1909–1937." Ph.D. diss., Case Western Reserve University, 1975.

Hoffman, Beatrix. "Insuring Maternity: The Campaign for Health Insurance." Paper presented at the Berkshire Conference on Women's History, Vassar College, Poughkeepsie, N.Y., June 1993.

Johnson, Dorothy Elizabeth. "Organized Women and National Legislation, 1920–1941." Ph.D. diss., Case Western Reserve University, 1960.

Johnson, Joan. "'This Wonderful Dream Nation': Black and White South Carolina Women and the Creation of the New South." Ph.D. diss., University of California at Los Angeles, 1997.

Lieberman, Jacob A. "Their Sisters' Keepers: The Women's Hours and Wages Movement in the United States, 1890–1925." Ph.D. diss., Columbia University, 1971.

McNeill, Garnett. "The History of Child Labor Legislation in Louisiana." M.S.W. thesis, Tulane University, 1935.

Madden, Bianca. "In the Thick of the Fray: The Professional Life of Mary Elizabeth Frayser." Master's thesis, Winthrop University, 1995.

Mason, Karen. "Testing the Boundaries: Women, Politics and Gender Roles in Chicago, 1890–1930." Ph.D. diss., University of Michigan, 1991.

Mead, Rebecca J. "Trade Union Women and Legislated Minimum Wage in California, 1913–1939." Adapted from paper presented at the Berkshire Conference on Women's History, Vassar College, Poughkeepsie, N.Y., June 1993.

Neilsen, Kim. "The Security of the Nation: Anti-Radicalism and Gender in the Red Scare of 1919–28." Ph.D. diss., University of Iowa, 1996.

Pabon, Carlos E. "Regulating Capitalism: The Taylor Society and Political Economy in the Inter-war Period." Ph.D. diss., University of Massachusetts–Amherst, 1992.

Roydhouse, Marion W. "The 'Universal Sisterhood of Women': Women and Labor Reform in North Carolina, 1900–1932." Ph.D. diss., Duke University, 1980.

Schuchat, Betsy A. "Child Labor Legislation in Louisiana, 1935–1942." M.S.W. thesis, Tulane University, 1944.

Storrs, Landon R. Y. "The National Consumers' League, 1932–1937." Master's thesis, University of Wisconsin–Madison, 1989.

———. "Working Women's Participation in the Politics of New Deal Wage-Hour Policy." Paper presented at the annual meeting of the Organization of American Historians, San Francisco, Calif., April 1997.

Wehmeyer, Willadee. "Mary Dublin Keyserling: Economist and Social Activist." Ph.D. diss., University of Missouri–Kansas City, 1995.

Weigand, Kathleen A. "Vanguards of Women's Liberation: The Old Left and the Continuity of the Women's Movement in the United States, 1945–1970." Ph.D. diss., Ohio State University, 1995.

Wilkerson-Freeman, Sarah. "Women and the Transformation of American Politics: North Carolina, 1898–1940." Ph.D. diss., University of North Carolina at Chapel Hill, 1995.

index

Brandeis, Louis, 2, 23, 37, 44–46
Breckinridge, Sophonisba, 143
Bridges, Harry, 236
Brink, Elinor Nims, 146
Brissenden, Paul, 24, 212, 216, 264, 349
  (n. 26)
Brooks, John Graham, 25
Buck, Christine, 222
Building Services Union, 190
Bunting v. Oregon, 46, 72
Burns, Eveline, 191, 202, 246–47, 264,
  337 (n. 58)
Burrow, William, 171–72, 222–23
Business and Professional Women's
  Clubs, 82, 108, 141, 245
Byrd, Harry, 157
Byrd, Mabel, 107, 307 (n. 56)
Byrnes, James, 158

Cable Act, 285 (n. 96)
Cannon, Myrta Jones, 30, 264
Carey, James, 30, 211, 234, 264
Casey, Josephine, 63, 76–88, 351 (n. 40)
Cash, W. J., 129
Catholics: and labor standards activism,
  31, 130, 144–45
Chandler, Albert, 159, 172
Chase, Stuart, 93
Child labor restrictions, 10, 18, 46, 67,
  150, 197, 305 (n. 36), 334 (n. 22)
Christman, Elisabeth, 239
Civil Rights Act of 1964: Title VII, 249
Civil service laws, 115, 221
Clark, Adele, 144, 157, 166, 248, 264, 321
  (n. 87)
Clark, Jane Perry, 202, 340 (n. 98)
Clinton, William, 2
Cohen, Benjamin, 37, 178, 179, 182, 183
Cohn, Fannia, 190
Cohn, Naomi, 2, 144, 157–58, 163, 222,
  264
Cold War, 7, 10, 230, 247, 251, 255. *See also*
  Anticommunism
Collins, William, 121
Commerce clause, 183, 198
Commission on Interracial Cooperation,
  33, 82
Committee for the Defense of Leon
  Trotsky, 236
Commons, John, 16, 25, 289 (n. 27)

Communist Party, 89, 235–38, 249
Confederacy, 132, 140
Conferences on labor standards: importance of, 94, 136–37, 165, 250
Congress of Industrial Organizations
  (CIO), 9, 39, 145, 149, 174, 175; split
  with AFL, 154, 165, 166, 234; and
  FLSA, 196, 199; NCL prods, 210,
  239; and NLRA amendments, 211–15;
  impact on NCL, 229; ties to NCL,
  234–35
Constitution: clarifying amendment
  drive, 181–82
Constitutionality of labor laws, 44–50,
  72, 121, 122, 155, 178–83, 229, 239, 254,
  327 (n. 40)
Consumer: role in social democracy, 18,
  21, 257, 258; class and gender construc-
  tions of, 19, 21–23; representation on
  labor boards, 23, 199, 202, 219. *See also*
  Keynesianism; National Recovery
  Administration: enforcement; Pur-
  chasing power; Underconsumption
Consumer groups: red-baiting of, 237,
  255
Consumers' League of Kentucky. *See*
  Kentucky Consumers' League
Consumers' League of Louisiana, 129,
  137, 148, 324 (n. 13), 330 (n. 75)
Consumers' League of Massachusetts,
  14, 122, 235. *See also* Wiesman,
  Margaret
Consumers' League of Michigan, 258
Consumers' League of New Jersey, 220,
  242
Consumers' League of New York, 14, 30,
  114, 202, 232–34, 237, 240, 246
Consumers' League of Ohio, 221, 243
Consumers' League of Rhode Island, 30,
  180
Consumers' League of Virginia. *See* Vir-
  ginia Consumers' League
Consumers' National Federation, 97,
  237
Consumers' Research, 96, 97, 232
Consumers' Union, 96, 97
Consumption, ethical, 2, 18–23, 98, 257,
  258
Corcoran, Tom, 185, 187
Corson, John, 157

Cotton Textile Institute (CTI), 71–76, 78–79, 88, 102, 103, 167–68
Cox, Edward E., 186

Dabney, Virginius, 129, 157
Daniels, Jonathan, 129
Davie, John, 221
Davis, John P., 105, 107, 108, 212
Davis, William H., 114, 118, 232, 241, 264
Debs, Eugene V., 17
Democratic Party, 10, 33–35, 134, 145; Women's Division, 34, 35, 147–48, 149, 334 (n. 28); conflicts in, 125, 143, 147–48, 149, 174, 187
Dewey, John, 236
Dewson, Molly, 44, 53, 118, 199, 264; on women in politics, 13, 34, 225; and Democratic Party, 34, 35, 147, 148; and minimum wage strategy, 47, 179, 180; and NRA, 94, 95, 97, 111, 115
Dies, Martin, 185, 186, 238
Dies Committee. See House Un-American Activities Committee
Domestic service workers, 32, 111, 156, 197–98, 220, 257, 294 (n. 26)
Douglas, Dorothy, 235
Douglas, Melvyn and Helen Gahagan, 247
Douglas, Paul, 22, 96, 197, 284 (n. 89)
Drake, Grace, 264
Dubinsky, David, 185
Dublin, Augusta Salik, 191
Dublin, Louis Israel, 191
Dublin, Mary, 9, 33, 177, 220, 224, 226, 251, 253, 258; background, 24, 191–93, 264; and passage of FLSA, 185, 188, 190–91, 193–96, 203; defends FLSA, 208–10, 249; defends Wagner Act, 211–19; and internal conflict at NCL, 230–44; supports ERA, 249
Du Bois, W. E. B., 32
Dupuis, Effie, 26, 221–22

Edelman, John, 30, 248, 264, 327 (n. 46)
Elkins, Elizabeth, 221
Elliott, Harriet, 129, 144, 264
Ellis, Challen, 48
Employer relocation. See Industry migration

Entering wedge strategy, 42, 58, 88, 247, 249, 254. See also Sex-based labor laws
Equal Employment Opportunity Commission, 249
Equal Rights Amendment (ERA), 3, 8, 41, 48, 54, 56, 58, 80, 88, 181, 240–41, 249

Fabian Society, 191
Fair Employment Practices Committee, 244, 245
Fair Labor Standards Act of 1938 (FLSA), 4, 6, 9, 10, 64, 119, 147, 177–78, 204–5; NCL and legal origins of, 178–84; provisions, 183–84, 196–98; NCL and passage of, 184–90, 192–96; southern resistance to, 185–89; labor movement ambivalence toward, 189–90, 199–200; benefits for different groups, 197–98; battle over administration, 198–204; efforts to weaken, 207–10, 227; evasion of, 220; impact on female administrators, 222–23, 229; impact on NCL program, 238–44; postwar amendments, 249
Fascism, 18, 131, 194, 208, 253, 258
Federal Council of Churches, 105, 142, 213
Federal Emergency Relief Administration, 148, 150
Federation of Women's Clubs (FWC), 140, 141. See also General Federation of Women's Clubs
Federations of Labor, state, 180; in South, 163, 165–70
Feminism: of NCL, 6, 8; after woman suffrage, 7, 89; NCL and NWP versions compared, 54–59, 88–90, 109–10, 226, 254. See also National Consumers' League: gender ideology
Filene, Edward, 73
Fleming, Colonel Philip, 202
Fletcher, Major A. L., 202
Florida Association for the Promotion of Social Legislation, 146
Fourteenth Amendment, 48, 179, 249, 315 (n. 22)
Frankfurter, Felix, 15, 37, 48, 100, 155, 179, 180, 182, 332 (n. 7)

121–22, 133, 176, 183, 198–204, 258; and consumer movement, 96–98, 237, 250–51, 257; as liaison with workers, 101, 112–13; code drafting and NRA, 101–11; and NRA enforcement, 111–21, 258; impact of NRA on, 121–23; Southern Committee, 126, 127, 129, 135, 151; and legal road to FLSA, 178–84; and passage of FLSA, 184–90, 192–96; and administration of FLSA, 198–204; and labor department appropriations, 204, 244, 341 (n. 5); defends FLSA against weakening amendments, 208–10; defends Wagner Act, 211–19; and state labor laws after 1938, 220–24, 238–41; program during World War II, 224, 244–46; branch decline, 230, 242, 246; internal tensions (1939–42), 230–44; postwar institutional changes, 246–51; postwar lobbying to raise FLSA standards, 249

National Economy Act: Section 213, 90

National health insurance, 120, 241–42

National Knitted Outerwear Association, 208

National Labor Relations Act (NLRA), 10, 121, 147, 174, 182, 192, 207, 246; NCL opposes amendments to, 211–19, 227, 230

National Labor Relations Board (NLRB): and female employees, 216–19, 255. *See also* National Labor Relations Act

National Labor Standards Committee, 189, 190–91, 193–96

National Negro Congress, 212

National Policy Committee, 36, 151

National Recovery Administration (NRA), 9, 64, 92–93, 153, 200, 201, 204, 258; race and regional differentials, 91, 102–8; Consumers' Advisory Board, 96–98, 107, 118; Women's Section, 98; Section 7a, 99, 119–21; Labor Advisory Board, 99–101; cotton textile code, 102–3, 105, 109; sex differentials, 108–11; enforcement, 111–19; effect on state labor laws, 121–22

National Resources Planning Board, 36, 246

National Woman's Party (NWP), 3, 8,

33, 178, 240; conservative alliances, 42, 47–49, 81–88, 141, 180, 241, 254; and minimum wage test cases, 46–49, 180–81, 182; Industrial Councils, 52, 76, 79–80, 87; and labor movement, 53–54, 86; campaign against sex-based measures in South, 71–72, 76–88, 141; and NRA, 104, 108–10, 112, 121; and FLSA, 194–95. *See also* Equal Rights Amendment; Feminism

Nazi-Soviet pact, 237

Negro Industrial League, 105, 112

Negro Welfare Survey Committee, 70

Nestor, Agnes, 78, 80

Newell, Bertha, 142, 144, 266

New England: labor laws in, 65, 165

New Orleans Women's Committee against Huey Long, 148

Night work, 71–76, 78–79, 84–87, 294 (n. 29)

Night work regulation, 10, 49–51, 52, 109, 240, 323 (n. 6). *See also* Cotton Textile Institute; Southern Council for Women and Children in Industry

Nike, 1

Nineteenth Amendment, 7, 38, 50, 147, 179

Nixon, H. C., 127

Nord, Elizabeth, 30

North American Free Trade Agreement, 4

North Carolina, 61, 62, 126, 129, 139, 142, 149; 1931 hours law, 76; 1937 hours law, 154, 155, 156

Norton, Mary, 34, 184

Odum, Howard, 129

Office of Price Administration, 96, 304 (n. 24), 352 (n. 53)

O'Reilly, Leonora, 14

Organized labor. *See* Labor movement

Paul, Alice, 48

Pepper, Claude, 195

Perkins, Frances, 34, 35, 94, 100, 136, 148, 285 (n. 99), 291 (n. 51); hostility to, 95, 118, 150, 200, 202, 212, 223, 236–37; and FLSA, 178, 183, 185, 187, 199, 203; and female appointments, 116–17, 199, 201; and NLRA, 216, 344 (n. 34)